*f*P

Scapegoat

The Jews, Israel,
and Women's Liberation

ANDREA DWORKIN

THE FREE PRESS

New York   London   Toronto   Sydney   Singapore

THE FREE PRESS
A Division of Simon & Schuster Inc.
1230 Avenue of the Americas
New York, NY 10020

THE FREE PRESS and colophon are trademarks
of Simon & Schuster Inc.

This volume includes quotations from: Victoria Schweitzer, Tsvetaeva, Farrar, Straus & Giroux, 1993. "Tenebrae" from Poems of Paul Celan, trans. Michael Hamburger, copyright ©1988 by Michael Hamburger, reprinted by permission of Persea Books, Inc. "Daddy" from "Ariel" from Sylvia Plath, The Collected Poems, copyright ©1963 by Ted Hughes, reprinted by permission of HarperCollins Publishers. "Requiem" by Anna Akhmatova in Selected Poems, trans. D. M. Thomas, Penguin Books, 1988. Hannah Senesh: Her Life and Diary, trans. Nigel Marsh, copyright ©1977 by Schocken Books.

Book design by Ellen R. Sasahara

Manufactured in the United States of America

10 9 8 7 6 5 4 3 2 1

Library of Congress Cataloging-in-Publication Data
Dworkin, Andrea.
Scapegoat: the Jews, Israel, and women's liberation / Andrea Dworkin.
p.   cm.
Includes bibliographical references and index.
1. Jewish women.   2. Feminist theory.   3. Women—Israel.
4. Feminism.   5. Sexism.   I. Title.
HQ1172.D85   2000
305.42'01—dc21   99-053819

ISBN 0-684-83612-2

For my beloved father, Harry Dworkin,
who died during the production of this book:
"Well, I won't be able to read this one, Andrea."

For Leah Kalina, the bravest woman I have ever known.

And for my godson, Isaac Dorfman Silverglate.

All poets are Yids.

—Marina Tsvetaeva, "The Poem of the End"

We cannot die, because we are the question.

—Elie Wiesel, in the novel *A Beggar in Jerusalem*

Contents

Preface

I am an enemy of nationalism and male domination. This means that I repudiate all nationalism except my own and reject the dominance of all men except those I love. In this I am like every other woman, a pretender to rebellion because to break with patriarchy I would need to betray my own: the ones with whom I share a group identity, in this case Jewish, and a presumed history, in this case Jewish men. They have not hesitated to betray me through assertions of superiority intended to hurt my human rights and my human dignity. In this, too, I am like every other woman. Feminists try hard to fight for women at the same time maintaining special loyalties to subgroups of men. How could we not?

I have grown sick of those loyalties, which protect brutal acts as if they were heroic. The line between self-defense and aggression has been breached by my particular ethnic group represented by the Israeli government; the line itself is often not self-evident in that violent acts sometimes serve to head off enemy attack and are arguably a form of self-defense. I believe that threatened peoples and individuals have a right to self-defense. This goes against the pacifism that has been instrumental in my political life.

My pacifism was first challenged when, working on my book on pornography in the late 1970s, *Pornography: Men Possessing Women,* I read a half dozen biographies of the Marquis de Sade. A life of rape and sexual violence, including kidnapping and possibly murder, would have been stopped short if his first (known) victim, Jeanne Testard, had killed him.

I will say here what I have never said before: my pacifism was not challenged by the beating and torture I experienced in marriage some thirty years ago; I finally got away not because I knew that he would kill me but because I thought I would kill him. Understand: this is true generally of women—his life meant more to me than my own; but also I was not willing to kill, even to escape beating and his own promise, which I believed, that he would kill me.

Once having had the serious and true thought that one of his victims should have offed the good Marquis, it was impossible not to apply that insight to the widespread, contemporary beatings and rapes that women sustain. Especially, I have seen a legal system designed to protect male privilege work to do just that. I have seen a generation of antirape activists and antibattery activists sit through trials of guilty men who almost always walk. Like those advocates, I have seen rapists acquitted, batterers put back in the home, child-rapers given custody of the incested child. The legal system is so genuinely perverse that women rarely report crimes involving either rape or battery.

I am, as a result, a lapsed pacifist. I truly abhor violence and I believe that both nationalism and male dominance are systems that promote and produce violence. With extreme difficulty and reluctance I have come to believe that women have to be literate in both strategic violence and the violence of self-defense. It is one thing to choose not to kill; it is quite another to be defenseless by virtue of ignorance and socialization. Women have mastered the articulation of violence in behalf of national liberation movements, including the Jewish liberation movement called Zionism, the claim of a material right to land and sovereignty in the ancient territory of Palestine.

For a couple of thousand years—after the destruction of the second Temple in 70 C.E.—Jews, including Jewish men, were seen as inherently pacifistic, genetically pacifistic, as are women; the existence of the twentieth-century Jewish state and its defense suggest that this pacifism was socially constructed and had no relationship at all to any particle of DNA or to testosterone or any other inevitable hormone or biological fact. The perceived gentleness of Jewish men before the establishment of the state never suggested to anyone that men as a whole could live the way that Jewish men had lived: which is to say, without publicly committed violence. Rather, this perception encouraged group violence against Jews in pogroms and in the Holocaust. Is it the same with women?

I have been trying to grasp the Holocaust since I was ten years old and had Auschwitz-Birkenau told to me by a survivor who was having unbearable flashbacks: I have dedicated this book to her; and to my father, who has stood in his life for the old Jewish gentleness (even with a stint in the World War II U.S. armed forces). In 1988 I went to Israel. I had the honor (as had happened in Northern Ireland in 1983) of meeting a great number of women activists (in Israel both Jewish and Arab) in a very short time. There was no small talk. I was able to meet women all over Israel but especially in Jerusalem, Haifa, and Tel Aviv. I was distressed by what I found, including Holocaust-themed pornography and battered and raped women. Why would I expect it to be different? The answer is simple: because the Israelis are my guys, a miracle of self-determination and courage. Well, they took the land; but they had to. I continue to believe that they (we) had to; but brutality has become institutionalized in Israel as expressions of male dominance and state sovereignty—over Jewish/Israeli women as well as over Palestinian men and women. Would I be so troubled if Jewish women were not among the conquered? Yes, but: I think that women are the internal enemy regardless of the ethnic or racial or nationalist status of the group's men; and that Israel is a perfect example of how male dominance grows in a new state—it needs the subordination of one's own women *and* the subordination of a racial or ethnic other: it needs internal and external scapegoats. The internal, intraethnic contempt for women is apparent in victors and losers. Nevertheless, it is the creation of a hated ethnic marginal and menial class that sustains success in creating a dominant sovereignty.

Israel both embodies and protects male Jews; but the Jewish women inside the state have been disarmed—the pattern for women in liberation struggles that succeed. Yet across the ethnic conflict Israeli and Palestinian women, often motivated by feminist ambitions and feminist ideas, have found ways to work together. This is a fact more hopeful than the outcome of any election or provisional dictatorship. Cooperation is the female equivalent of male conflict, a way of operating in a world filled with injury and hate. This is a social, not a biological, point.

I tell many stories in this book: the story of Nazis, of Jews, of Israelis, of Palestinians, and of women: Jewish, Israeli, and Palestinian women, Indian and Pakistani women, Argentinean and U.S. women, concentration-camp women, resistance women, raped and prostituted women. In the nine-year course of writing this book, I have become certain of one thing: that women cannot be free of male dominance without challenging the men of one's own ethnic group and destroying their authority. This is a willed betrayal, as any assault on male dominance must be.

Brooklyn, New York
June 1999

1

HOMELAND/HOME

In *Memory Fields* Holocaust survivor Shlomo Breznitz goes to *The Oxford English Dictionary* to look up the word *hope*. He finds, he says, "the wisdom of language, as a symbolic product of lengthy cumulative experience"[1]: hope is "a piece of enclosed land, e.g., in the midst of marshes or wasteland"; or "a small enclosed valley"; or "an inlet, small bay, haven."[2] The unabridged *Webster's Third New International Dictionary* still recognizes this old meaning: hope is "a piece of arable land surrounded by waste, especially: one surrounded by a swamp or marsh"; "a broad upland valley sometimes rounded and often with a stream running through it"; "a small bay or inlet."[3] In Hebrew, too, writes Breznitz, "the words for hope and for a small enclosure derived from the same root. . . ."[4] (his ellipses). For Italo Calvino in *The Road to San Giovanni* the first principle of reality began in his home, which was synonymous with his homeland: "A general explanation of the world and of history must first of all take into account the way our house was situated, in an area once known as 'French Point,' on the last slopes at the foot of San Pietro hill, as though at the border between two continents."[5] One might conclude that it is hard to have hope without land.

But even urban refuse can recognize its own. In *A Stained White Radiance,* mystery writer James Lee Burke has his narrator-hero say: "We all have an extended family, people whom we recognize as our own as soon as we see them. The people closest to me have always been marked by a peculiar difference in their makeup. They're the walking wounded, the ones to whom a psychological injury was done that they will never be able to define . . ."[6] These weary, wounded, marginal souls "save us from ourselves. Whenever I hear and see a politician or a military leader, a bank of American flags at his back, trying to convince us of the rightness of a policy or a deed that will cause harm to others; when I am almost convinced myself that setting a humanitarian concern in abeyance can be justified in the interest of the greater good, I pause and ask myself what my brain-smoked friends would have to say. Then I realize that the rhetoric would have no effect on them, because for those who were most deeply injured as children, words of moral purposes too often masked acts of cruelty."[7] One might conclude that hope requires the end of cruelty. The urban dispossessed, the grown children with hollow eyes and scars, the ten-year-old prostitutes and the players who rape and use them, do recognize one another; but have no hope and arguably no homeland either. A sewer replaces the arable land, the bay, the inlet, the haven. The sense of place attaches to a barstool, a street corner, a crack house, a brothel. This is a tribe, not ethnic, not connected by blood but by the experiences of exploitation, violence, and abandonment. Cosmopolitan even if illiterate, rootless, parasitic and self-destructive, this is a ghostly tribe, brutal, fragile, plague-ridden, devastated by "words of moral purposes too often masked as acts of cruelty." The stable middle class romanticizes the despair and wants a taste of the life, after which the tourists go home and wash. The tourists have a home and a homeland; those they rubbed up against are in a perpetual exile from hope.

In *Bury Me Standing: The Gypsies and Their Journey,* Isabel Fonseca describes a Gypsy song: "Nostalgia is the essence of Gypsy song, and seems always to have been. But nostalgia for what? *Nostos* is the Greek for 'a return home'; the Gypsies have no home, and, perhaps uniquely among peoples, they have no dream of a homeland. Utopia—*ou topos*—means 'no place.' Nostalgia for utopia: a return home to no place. *O lungo drom.* The long road."[8] Considered outsiders wherever they have lived, they are thrown out. Fonseca says that the Gypsies "adapted, often by living in abandoned and inaccessible forests and wastelands, the countries within countries, and the borderlands."[9] Stateless, they congregate especially on borders. That means, according to a Gypsy activist, that in international law Gypsies "have the status of trade unions, environmental lobbies, or professional associations [and women]."[10] One Gypsy politician "promoted an alternative—and to many sacrilegious—identity in which people could be seen and discussed independent of property."[11]

The Gypsies,* like the Jews, were nearly exterminated by the Nazis;

---

*Gypsies include Romani, Sinti, and Lalleri subgroups. Himmler considered German Sinti and Lalleri pure and romantic but Hitler disagreed. In English, "Gypsy" is not pejorative but "gypped," derived from "Gypsy," is.

medical experiments were done on Gypsy children in Auschwitz and all of those children died. Living without written language, Gypsies have no written history and no written memory. The past—Auschwitz, for instance—comes into songs; but facts and the landscape of experience get lost. Without writing, memory becomes narrowed, smaller; isolation puts the Gypsies far outside the great conversation, ongoing through centuries, about meaning, hope, and homeland. Wanderers, vagrants throughout Europe—the cohesiveness and integrity of the Gypsy way of life destroyed by the Nazis—the children operate in gangs to rob tourists or anyone vulnerable, circling an individual to get the money, sometimes beating or killing the victim. The Gypsy women beg on the streets of Paris, Vienna, Rome, Berlin. Can a people survive without memory; or without writing; or without history; or without recognition under international law, these survivors of genocide? Can a people survive stateless, with no homeland—*ou topos,* Utopia, no place?

After Hitler's war, the Jewish survivors also had no place. "I thought about all that could be said regarding these two words: return, repatriation," writes Jorge Semprun in *Literature or Life?* "The second one made no sense when applied to me, of course. First of all, I hadn't returned to my homeland, in coming back to France. And then, if you thought about it, it was clear that I would never again be able to return to any homeland. I had no native country anymore. I would never have one again. Or else I'd have several, which would amount to the same thing. Can you die— think about it—for several countries at once?"[12]

The Jews had not known, before the war, that they were stateless, with no meaningful citizenship, with no country. As Benjamin Beit-Hallahmi writes in *Original Sins: Reflections on the History of Zionism and Israel,* "A Jewish community existed in Germany without interruption for 1,700 years before World War II. Jews settled in the fortified cities built by the Romans on the west bank of the Rhine. In Cologne there was a well-organized Jewish community in 321 C.E. and the Rhine Valley was the center of a glorious cultural tradition."[13] Arguing for the maintenance of a convent for Polish Catholic nuns at Auschwitz (against Jewish opposition), Wladyslaw T. Bartoszewski writes about the long history of Jews in Poland: "The Jews lived in Poland side by side, rather than together with the Poles, and therefore many Poles could and did regard them as a nation within a nation. The description of the Jewish community, which had lived in Poland continuously for 800 years, as 'alien' can be understood only in such a context."[14] Nevertheless, Jews and Poles had a lot in common. As Eva Hoffman writes in *Shtetl: The Life and Death of a Small Town and the World of Polish Jews,* "Ironically, as far as nationhood went, Poles and Jews had been in a similar position for a whole century: neither had an actually existing nation to go with their strong sense of collective identity, and both substituted a notional idea for the real thing. It can be fairly said that for both, the substitution of fantasized ideas for solid realities strengthened, with rare exceptions, the drive to separatism."[15] One might conclude that both Poles and Jews were delusional: both groups lived there but where was the "there"? Poland was invaded, occupied, partitioned, cut up repeatedly throughout its history: so what exactly made Poles Polish except for their conviction that there was a Polish people and a Polish nation that were one and the same; and neither aggressors nor Jews were Polish? Is national identity a matter of borders, geographical boundaries; or is it a belief, informed by shared experience, validated or challenged by history, distorted by self-interest? The Poles were Catholic; Poland was Catholic. Polish Jews were not Catholic, therefore not Polish. Can national identity be configured by religious difference or religious prejudice or religious imperialism? History's answer is an unequivocal yes.

Jews, of course, knew about being unwelcome: expelled from England; expelled from Spain, where Jews had a thousand-year history; in Venice in 1516 forced to live in the first state-mandated ghetto. As Nora Levin says in *The Holocaust: The Destruction of European Jewry 1933–1945:* "Between the thirteenth and sixteenth centuries, Jews were expelled from England, France, Italy, Bohemia, and the Germanic states. The unconverted Jew polluted Christian society; the 'racial' Jew polluted German society."[16] The sense of belonging, should it have existed subjectively or socially, could be aborted abruptly, cruelly.

Yet maybe belonging is more ambiguous than the convulsive history of any oppressed people; maybe some in the oppressor group, pressed by conscience, are unable to belong at all. Maybe South African novelist Nadine Gordimer in *Writing and Being* talks about a dislocation not unique to her: "The whites were not my people because everything they lived by—their claimed racial superiority and the methods they were satisfied to use to maintain it as if it were truth—was the stuff of my refusal. . . . The blacks were not 'my people' because all through my childhood and adolescence they had scarcely entered my consciousness. *I had been absent.* Absent from them. Could one, in fact, make the claim, 'my country' if one could not also say 'my people'?"[17] Gordimer's opposite might be Thomas Carlyle, the great (and anti-Semitic) English historian of the

French Revolution, ostracized as a Jacobin. "Deeply a man of place," writes a biographer, "he hated wanderers and wandering, the nomadic obsession. In his mind and in his words he strained always to reproduce the movement of the rooks whose great circles gave form to mystery and established boundaries to the place he called home."[18] Standing against the English hatred of the French revolutionaries, he stood against his people, but he made for himself a place in England nevertheless; he created a territory in which he was the sovereign, very much at the cost of his wife Jane Carlyle. Gordimer did not want power; Carlyle did, small, mean, and petty as it was. Each experienced a subjective exile while living in the country of birth. Belonging is not simple.

Carlyle's beloved French Revolution emancipated Jews for the first time in European history. Jews were recognized as French citizens. Laws discriminating against Jews were struck down. (Male Jews, of course; the French Revolution betrayed women, all women. See Mary Wollstonecraft, *A Vindication of the Rights of Women*.) It was the emancipation itself, according to Sara Bershtel and Allen Graubard in *Saving Remnants: Feeling Jewish in America,* that gave rise to the "'Jewish question,' which asked whether the Jews could truly be integrated into the larger nation." This question, they say, became "the central issue in European Jewish life."[19] A pariah group, the Jews were seen as nomadic and separatist.

It is too easy to say that Jews accepted this characterization because they were a people who did not belong to the nations in which they lived. Beit-Hallahmi describes a version of the Jewish reality prior to the establishment of the state of Israel: "For most of history the Jewish condition has been one of Diaspora or dispersion. The Hebrew term used to describe this means exile, and the term has been used for 2,000 years, as if Jews had just recently moved from their homeland. In their synagogues, Jews mourned over their exile and the desolation of the ancient homeland every day, every week, and every holiday."[20] But the reality is more schizophrenic. Jews developed affection for the countries in which they lived; also loyalty. Devotion to the promised land was a religious devotion contingent on the coming of the Messiah; it was not a mandate for conquest. Cursed by the Catholic Church, then Calvinists and Lutherans, for having killed Christ, Jews were always vulnerable to instant, organized, and sanctioned assault. But in everyday life, one lived in Italy or Austria or Hungary or Russia (or, for example, earlier incarnations of the Austro-Hungarian Empire, Prussia, the Balkans). In daily life it is hard not to love where one lives, where one's life is. Even now, dislocation is a whisper away. "Our neighborhood," writes Cristina Garcia in *Dreaming in Cuban,* "was mostly Jewish then and my mother was always saying, 'They killed Christ! They pushed in the crown of thorns!' I felt sorry for the Jews getting thrown out of Egypt and having to drag themselves across the desert to find a home. Even though I've been living in Brooklyn all my life, it doesn't feel like home to me. I'm not sure Cuba is, but I want to find out."[21] Neither the anti-Semitism nor the sense of dislocation is anomalous. It is not only Jews who long for a country they have not seen; nor is exile the central meaning of a Jewish life. There is the exile that changes the settled into nomads; then there is the mythology of that exile, stronger, bigger, denser, as time passes without return, without justice, without fairness. There is loyalty to one's immediate home and the sense or conviction of exile simultaneously: a geographic and moral schizophrenia. There are questions of assimilation and identity, citizenship and grief.

The myth of exile can be subjectively felt by every member of a group; and generation after generation it will become a bigger wound, but more important—the original wound, the first brokenness, the origin of injury. Over time the sadness of exile is lost and in its place there is a sea of enemies, evil. The exiles are wronged but heroic. Heroism is the carrier of hope: arable land, a haven.

Zionism became the hope of the Jews. Zionism meant lifting a return to the holy land out of the prayer book and putting it into real time. Freud was one of many who believed that Zionism had no future. As he wrote in a 1930 letter to Dr. Chaim Koffler, who was soliciting Freud to oppose British policy in curbing Jewish immigration into Palestine: "Whoever wants to influence the masses must give them something rousing and inflammatory and my sober judgment of Zionism does not permit this. I certainly sympathize with its goals . . . But on the other hand, I do not think that Palestine could ever become a Jewish state, nor that the Christian and Islamic worlds would ever be prepared to have their holy places under Jewish care. It would have seemed more sensible to me to establish a Jewish homeland on a less historically burdened land."[22] In 1932, writing to Arnold Zweig, Freud was contemplative: "How strange this tragically mad land . . . must have seemed to you. Just think, this strip of our mother earth is connected with no other progress, no discovery or invention. . . . Palestine has never produced anything but religions, sacred frenzies, presumptuous attempts to overcome the outward world of appearance by means of the inner world of wishful thinking."[23]

Although there were many patches of land in jungles of various sorts suggested as possible "homelands" for the Jews, the idea seemed to be to bunch Jews all together so that they would be neither seen nor heard, thus ending anti-Semitism, which was almost universally (even among Jews) taken to be a response to Jewishness, to a racial strain abhorrent to the authentic French, the real Germans, the Italianate Italians. Anti-Semitism was generally construed to be a reaction to whatever was distinctive in Jews, something repellent. By January 1939, Robert de Rothschild, a French Rothschild, was "forwarding a proposal to his London cousins concerning the purchase of land in Brazil's still-wild Mato Grosso 'for colonization purposes.' Later that year, Paris transmitted a recommendation that the London Rothschilds look into a plan to settle Jews on a plain in the Sudan's Upper Nile valley between Malakhal and Bor—in deepest Africa."[24]

Max Warburg, also part of an international banking family of Jews, deeply loyal to the Jewish community and the German nation, could not bear the Jewish exodus from Germany as the Nazis rose to power. "In April 1936," writes Ron Chernow in his biography of the Warburg family, "[Max] made a sadly revealing speech to the Aid Society in which he told how Jews were conservative and clung to their soil. He noted that, for sentimental reasons, some departing Jews packed tiny bags of German soil in their suitcases."[25] His advice to emigrating Jews was chilling: "The more quietly the Jewish immigrant lives in his new homeland, the easier it will be for him to establish a foundation for himself."[26] As Chernow notes, "It was a weary prescription for eternal, second-class citizenship."[27]

Hitler's war made Freud's wry detachment and Warburg's tragic despair and the Rothschilds' resourceful efforts to buy a homeland irrelevant. Among Jews, there was no more resistance to Zionism. As Raul Hilberg writes in *Perpetrators/Victims/Bystanders: The Jewish Catastrophe 1933–1945,* "The survivors made their greatest impact on the Jewish community . . . by their presence as 'irrepatriable displaced persons' in camps on German and Austrian soil between 1945 and 1948. Anti-Zionism in the Jewish community collapsed, and a consensus that Jewry, abandoned during the war, had to have a home of its own crystallized overnight."[28] Was Poland home? Was Austria home? Was France home? Displaced Jews were "living under guard behind barbed-wire fences, in camps of several descriptions (built by the Germans for slave-laborers and Jews), including some of the most notorious concentration camps, amidst crowded, frequently unsanitary and generally grim conditions . . ."[29]

In *A Beggar in Jerusalem,* Elie Wiesel describes this same displacement from the inside: "Survivors we were, but we were allowed no victory. Fear followed us everywhere, fear preceded us. Fear of speaking up, fear of keeping quiet. Fear of opening our eyes, fear of shutting them. Fear of loving and being rejected or loved for the wrong reasons, or for no reason at all. Marked, possessed, we were neither fully alive nor fully dead. People didn't know how to handle us. We rejected charity. Pity filled us with disgust. We were beggars, unwanted everywhere, condemned to exile and reminding strangers everywhere of what they had done to us and to themselves."[30] Strategically, writes Tad Szulc in *The Secret Alliance: The Extraordinary Story of the Rescue of the Jews Since World War II,* "the only solution was to make the DP camps so overcrowded as to render them humanely, politically and financially intolerable to the Allies in Germany and Austria, and to set up illegal immigration to Palestine."[31] And they did, "these dark, ubiquitous people who trespassed uninvited upon other people's native soil."[32]

Having come to Zionism as a schoolboy in Russia, Isaiah Berlin "realized quite early in my life that Jews were a minority everywhere. It seemed to me that there was no Jew in the world who was not, in some degree, socially uneasy. . . . I do not think that there is a country where Jews feel totally secure, where they do not ask themselves: '*How do I look to others?*' '*What do they think of me?*' Persians are not interested in the way Turks look on them. Chinese are not worried about how Indians think of them."[33]

After Hitler's war, the Jews could not afford to be a minority everywhere on earth. After the camps, "How do I look to others?" and "What do they think of me?" became unbearable questions because the answers were beyond the reach of language; so the flesh crawled and the mind was a wasteland. Being a majority became an ontological necessity; and the place where that majority would live had to have Jewish meaning—otherwise it would be a void. Only Palestine, the ancient homeland, the biblical homeland, had that Jewish meaning.

In that split second of history after the Nazi defeat, Palestine became both home and homeland to the dispossessed before they ever saw it and no matter what would happen to them there; and also to well-fed North American Jews, who could barely begin to comprehend Auschwitz and Bergen-Belsen. No thought was given to democracy or governance, except that it be Jewish. Israel's purpose was "to be the Jewish nation-state, a state in which the Jews would exercise sovereignty in exactly the same way as other nations did theirs."[34] And so it became.

Jonathan Jay Pollard, the U.S. citizen who used his government job to spy for Israel by handing over U.S. satellite intelligence, traced his infatuation with Israel back to a summer spent there in his junior year of high school. He felt "normal," he said. "I saw a Jewish prostitute. . . . I saw things I had never seen before."[35] Now Palestinian Arabs are in DP camps, in filth and squalor; and, as one Israeli Jew wrote, "The Israeli authorities seem to have discovered Palestinians' most sensitive nerve in their struggle to hold on to their land and homes, for the two harshest punishments meted out to the Arabs in the territories are deportation and the demolition of houses."[36]

Women live in a country called *home.* They are its indigenous population. Sentimentalized by bad observers and romantic propagandists, home exists in contradistinction to the wider world: warm against cold; kind against cruel. Home is a refuge, a place of solace, safety, and comfort (emotional if not material). There is no point in consulting the statistics. They show that violence against women in their home(s) is commonplace, in sociological terms normal as opposed to deviant. No one could say how many women are beaten, raped, or killed in home any more than count the numbers of beaten dogs, mules, horses, camels in the world. Home may be the equivalent of a women's prison: women may be locked inside or not permitted egress or too injured to be able to leave; women may be tortured or burned alive there; women may be menial, brutalized servants; legal chattel; sexual chattel; reproductive chattel. An anonymous Saudi princess asked the hardest question: "How could a mother protect the young of her own sex from the laws of the land?"[37] Urgent and unanswerable, it is a global question, because all nations have laws that hurt women and girls. Recognizing that women are surprised by the momentary experience of freedom, a sudden joy that ends as a dream ends, with memory rare and partial, the Russian poet Marina Tsvetaeva used these words to pay homage to the freedom, fractured and irrecoverable: "And this is how the smiling young girl who does not want a stranger in her body, who does not want a him or a his, but only a *mine,* meets at a turning in the road another *me,* a *she,* in whom there is nothing to fear, against whom she does not need to defend herself. . . . For the moment, she is happy and free, free to love with the heart, not the body, to love without being afraid, to love without doing harm . . ."[38]

One can hear the freedom, even in a translation (from the French in which the exiled poet wrote this piece). Freedom has never been a value for women in home(s). Freedom is not a constituent part of the beating, the rape, the murder, not for her; violence separates women from freedom, the male, man, husband, father, even brother, in the home being the usual agent of violence. Home has more to do with fascism than with freedom: "Fascism is the first thing in the relationship between a man and a woman," says Austrian novelist Ingeborg Bachmann, "I have tried to say that here, that in this society it's always war. Not that there is war and peace, there is only war."[39]

Medea, in Bernard Knox's translation, expresses a more passionate contempt: "*They* say . . . *they* say we live a life free from danger in the house, while they fight, spear in hand. What fools! I'd be ready to take my stand in the shield line three times rather than give birth just once."[40] Calling Clytemnestra "both queen and prisoner," Knox thinks that "in many cases the result of confining a wife to the house, the slaves, and the children was to create a potentially dangerous, explosive force."[41] Alas, no. Confinement creates vulnerability to attack from the jailer and a domesticated Stockholm syndrome.

Jewish homes were no less confining: "For much of Jewish history women were denied access to the intellectual life of the community, which centered around the study of sacred texts . . . The rabbis assumed that, as a practical matter, the vast majority of women would be absorbed in domestic responsibilities for most of their adult lives. . . . One of the rationales for the exclusion of women from study and public worship was that women's physical attractions were perceived as a sexual snare for men."[42] In *The Creation of a Feminist Consciousness: From the Middle Ages to Eighteen-Seventy*, Gerda Lerner underlines the meaning of this exclusion, which is, at the same time, a confinement: "Women, because of educational deprivation and the absence of a usable past, tended to rely more heavily on their own experience in developing their ideas than did men."[43] But there were learned women in many traditions, often schooled by their fathers. Still, more women were pregnant than learned. In *A Breath of Life: Feminism in the American Jewish Community*, Sylvia Barack Fishman is no doubt right—and not only about Judaism—when she writes: "The desire for a life undemarcated by hierarchies may well be feminist, but it is antithetical to historic Judaism as a religion and a culture."[44]

Women were confined, with little or no education, living in a country

with no guarantee of freedom; violence against women was so easy, so ordinary, that it could be used strategically, for instance, by the FBI in Mississippi against the Klan in the civil rights years. "Klansmen were notorious
for 'beating hell out of their wives,'" writes reporter Jack Nelson in *Terror
in the Night: The Klan's Campaign Against the Jews,* "and their wives would
complain to the FBI and request that their husbands be arrested. Instead
the agents would inform the Klansmen of their wives' complaints, generating pressure within the families that the FBI could exploit."[45] To say that
no one cared would be a bit of an understatement. At the same time, retaliation against black civil rights workers was generally more violent and
more intense against the women. In a biography of pioneer civil rights
worker Fannie Lou Hamer, Kay Mills reports that ". . . Charles Payne of
Northwestern University found that some of the most violent reprisals
were against women. 'Women who were even rumored to be part of the
movement lost their jobs. Every adult woman I interviewed got fired, except for those who quit because they expected to get fired. Women were
regularly clubbed at demonstrations or beaten in jail. The homes of
women activists were regularly shot into. Any woman in the Delta who
contemplated joining the early movement had to be aware of all this.'"[46]
Any crime committed in the context of a racial or sexual double standard,
socially sanctioned, legally invisible, is committed with impunity. When
home is your native habitat, there are duties, responsibilities, obligations,
rules; but no rights-based freedom inalienable and inviolable. Any example
in any nation-state given at one time can be found somewhere any time; it
is unlikely to be an anomaly.

In Pakistan, for instance, rape is used as an instrument of personal revenge, male-to-male. As Jan Goodwin reported in *Price of Honor: Muslim
Women Lift the Veil of Silence on the Islamic World:* "In August 1991,
twenty-six men raped Allah Wasai, a woman who was eight months pregnant, to settle a score with her father-in-law. After the attack, she was paraded naked through her community. In November of that same year, two
young women were subject to nearly identical barbaric assaults. In each
case the young woman was gang-raped by eight men, and then had her
nose amputated. . . . The attacks in both cases were reprisals aimed at the
women's brothers. In neither incident did the police conduct an investigation."[47] (Hoover's FBI would understand that.) Pakistani police, like other
police in other countries, will often charge a rape victim as a prostitute or
rape her themselves. For those who think this is at best a third-world
problem: in 1997 ABC's news program *20/20* did a report on police in

Florida who kidnapped lone women motorists, raped, and often murdered them.

There is a consciousness that comes from home-based women, derived from paying attention to others. In *Blood Sisters: The French Revolution in Women's Memory*, Marilyn Yalom noticed that "[d]eath is never faceless in women's memoirs. As caretakers of children and the elderly, nurses of the sick and dying, women were enmeshed in a network of human connections, and their most wrenching memories are of friends and family members loved and lost. Their anxious efforts to ward off death and to sustain life constitute a subtext to their narratives."[48] This fact, that death is never faceless, is particularly remarkable because most of the memoirs Yalom studied were from aristocrats, women consistently stereotyped as vain, lazy, spoiled, unable to love (except adulterously), incapable of work.

Even in Nazi concentration camps, the home-based consciousness of women had material consequences. In particular, men and women had different responses to "hunger and malnutrition. In medical reports from the Warsaw Ghetto during 1941, in Gurs and in Theresienstadt, 1941–43, memoirs and other administrative reports on women prisoners reveal that women tolerated hunger better than men and survived starvation for longer periods than male inmates. Apparently, women had better strategies for sharing and extending the limited supplies of food; in the pre-war years, women had served as cooks, preparing the family meals and as a result learned ways of extending food in times of need. Previous patterns of behavior, housekeeping skills and habits clearly affected and improved women's chance of survival."[49]

Sentimental appreciation of home-based skills is perhaps inappropriate, and not only with respect to Nazi terror. In the face of modern famine, the most egregious of which may have been in China under Mao Tse-tung, women cooked roots, the bark of trees, grass, and cannibalized children. In China the practice was called *Yi zi er shi*—"Swop child, make food." In *Hungry Ghosts: Mao's Secret Famine*, Jasper Becker described a slippery slope of which U.S. civil libertarians never dreamed: "The worst thing that happened during the famine was this: parents would decide to allow the old and the young to die first. They thought they could not afford to let their sons die but a mother would say to her daughter, 'You have to go and see your granny in heaven.' They stopped giving the girl children food. They just gave them water. Then they swopped the body of their daughter with that of a neighbour's. About five to seven women would agree to do this amongst themselves. Then they boiled the corpses into a kind of soup."[50] In an earlier China (Song dynasty A.D. 20–79), "Often a daughter-in-law would cut flesh from her leg or thigh to make soup to feed a sick mother-in-law and this practice became so common that the state issued an edict forbidding it."[51] The daughter-in-law would be the most disenfranchised female in a multigenerational family.

The lower value of girls in the home, their only native place, is transcultural: "Female infanticide has been documented among peoples as diverse as the Eskimo of the Canadian Arctic and the hunter-gatherers of the Australian bush. On the South Sea island of Tikopia, live baby girls have been buried in the earth and covered with stones. In India, they have been held to their mother's poisoned nipples. In rural China, they have been drowned. Even societies that forbid outright infanticide have long managed to manipulate their sex ratios through neglect."[52] The neglect includes too-early weaning, underfeeding, or selling the female infant to the sex industry, a common practice in contemporary Thailand.

In colonial America, underfed and overworked, "girls sometimes died at twice the rate of boys from ages one through nine. In Ireland, this pattern continued well into the twentieth century, and throughout much of Asia and the Middle East it remains a fact of modern life."[53] Even in nineteenth-century England there was "a marked excess of female deaths in the age group 5–15."[54]

Referring to ancient Islamic practices, Fatima Mernissi writes: "We do know one thing: . . . it was the mother who buried the little girl alive, although the decision to do it fell to the father."[55] The story in the Hebrew Bible of Abraham's willingness to sacrifice his son Isaac—a sacrifice that God called off at the last minute—is sometimes used to show the divine will in human progress: the movement from human to animal sacrifice. Girls, being neither human nor animal, continue not to matter very much: from outright infanticide, to hard labor with not enough food, to being prostituted, to incest, to incestuous or pedophilic rape. Those who value children most, especially girls, are those who want to commit genocide. They recognize girls as the future of a people. "Nits make lice,"[56] said a U.S. colonel (in language that Himmler would replicate) bent on exterminating the indigenous tribes of North America; or, in the words of a U.S. Klansman whose agenda was the destruction of a synagogue: "Little Jew bastards grow up to be big Jew devils. Kill 'em while they're young."[57] Dr. Josef Mengele, known as "the angel of death" in Auschwitz, where he selected who would live and who would die and conducted torturing experiments on children who were twins, was described by one survivor as taking "a perverse pleasure in exterminating women who were pregnant. . . . At times, Mengele permitted a woman to deliver her baby, but then he promptly dispatched mother and infant to the gas chambers."[58] According to Lucette Lagnado and Sheila Cohn Dekel, authors of *Children of the Flames: Dr. Josef Mengele and the Untold Story of the Twins of Auschwitz*, ". . . Israeli and Polish scholars learned that a total of three thousand twins had passed through Mengele's experimental laboratories. Their survival rate had been less than 10 percent."[59]

The children left behind sometimes just disappeared. As Susanne Zuccotti describes in *The Holocaust, the French, and the Jews*: "By the evening of August 7 [1942] . . . nine efficiently operated trains had transported more than 9,000 mostly foreign Jews from French soil to Auschwitz. Left behind, however, were about 3,500 of the weakest and most helpless victims of the round-up—the children under fourteen. Their story can only be told by the adults who saw them leave, for not one child returned from deportation."[60]

But the violence did not end when Hitler's war ended. As a male survivor says, "There are times I get so angry. I beat up my son. I get in such a rage. . . . I beat anyone who is near me. Anything can trigger my rages— even a little thing, like a messy room in the house. My second wife, Miriam, knew nothing about my past when she married me. She might not have married me if she had. I used to beat her a lot. She was very frightened when I hit her or the children. But she knew I was not to blame."[61] There are female survivors married to male survivors who beat them. Imagine the horror of that.

Cruelty inside the home, where women and children live, of course has no ethnicity, race, or class. Judith Herman in *Trauma and Recovery* gives an example of what she calls a "scapegoat role" for a girl child: "I was named after my mother. She had to get married because she got pregnant with me. She ran away when I was two. My father's parents raised me. I never saw a picture of her, but they told me I looked just like her. When my dad started raping me, he said, 'You've been asking for this for a long time and now you're going to get it.'"[62] (See also Kathryn Harrison, *The Kiss*.)

Home can be a desperate and devastating place. One might fight for home, as one might fight for a country, if it promised freedom, if it owed its native population rights, if it were safe. Orlando Patterson in *Freedom: Freedom in the Making of Western Culture* holds that "[f]reedom began its long journey in the Western consciousness as a woman's value."[63] He asks, "What could be more personal than the fear of rape and captivity? And what could more forcefully impress upon the individual consciousness the value of freedom than to be released from this condition?"[64]

So where is freedom now? Is freedom where there are women? Is the home freedom? Women escape to find freedom. As Judith Herman writes, "In order to gain their freedom, survivors [of male violence] may have to give up almost everything else. Battered women may lose their homes, their friends, and their livelihood. Survivors of childhood abuse may lose their families. Political refugees may lose their homes and their homeland. Rarely are the dimensions of this sacrifice fully recognized."[65] Escape is a compromised freedom with a very heavy price.

2

JEW-HATE / WOMAN-HATE

On Yom Kippur, the Jews of antiquity would sacrifice two goats: one would be killed as an offering to a harsh and judging God; one would be taken to the wilderness and turned loose, a carrier of the sins of the group. (See Leviticus 16:7–10, 21–24.) Murder and exile are the two paradigmatic fates of scapegoats. Murder can be intimate; exile can be internal, being separated from the common life, one's human dignity and social legitimacy denied. Often attributed to "unconscious projection,"[1] taken as the mechanism that defines a metaphysical other— "'barbarian' meaning not Greek, 'gentile' meaning not Jewish"[2]—the murder and exile are literal, not figurative.

Hating Jews might be described as racism without color, and as such it is a testimony to the will of people to hate, to create social alienation and antagonism—it is xenophobic and includes a mix of envy, contempt, and greed (e.g., the Jews are rich and we're not; the Jews are too smart for their own good; the Jews have all the power). This is a collective hatred, often buttressed by legal and social institutions; individuals are contaminated with it, an emotional toxin. The Jews of the Hebrew Bible are militarist, separatist; strong and fearsome children of a wrathful and abusive father; and yet already in Alexandria three centuries before the start of Christ worship, Jewish culture "is depicted," says Robert S. Wistrich in *Antisemitism: The Longest Hatred,* "as sterile, having produced nothing useful or great"; and further, "the Jews are a superstitious, 'godless' people who worship an ass's head in their Temple in Jerusalem; once a year they kidnap a Gentile Greek, who is fattened in order to be eaten by their deity in his Holy of Holies . . ."[3] This, says Wistrich, is "the first ritual murder charge against Jews known to history."[4]

The Jews, forging monotheism in a multigod world, first separated themselves; this was the chosenness, having a destiny that precluded

16

blending in. Dietary laws, eventual descent through the mother, the ethical framework of the Ten Commandments, devotion to a written word, materially differentiated Jews from others; even in the martial world of the Hebrews, scholarship and fidelity to written law were distinguishing marks. This separateness—with its claims to both dominance and superiority—was turned on its head by pagan and animistic cultures into a stigma, a reason for conquest or persecution. As the militarist Hebrews disappear from legendary history, the scholarly, then the effete, then the effeminate Jew becomes visible. The practices of Jewish devotion become the reason for Jewish identity, the raison d'être for Jewish survival, and an unbending form of resistance to the profane, lawless society of non-Jews. The Nazis destroyed European and East European communities of orthodox practice through genocide; and assimilationist strategies of Jews, developed after and as a result of the French Enlightenment, were proved useless against planned murder and organized hate. "What are your endless sacrifices to me?/says Yahweh./I am sick of holocausts of rams and the fat of calves . . ./who asked you to trample over my courts?"[5] Post-Nazi, these lines from Isaiah (1:11–12) are hard to read.

Christian hatred of Jews is implicit in the origins of the religion; as the Chief Rabbi of Vienna said in 1907: "The Christian kneels before the image of the Jew, wrings his hands before the image of a Jewess; his Apostles, Festivals, and Psalms are Jewish. Only a few are able to come to terms with this contradiction—most free themselves by antisemitism."[6] In the beginning, Jesus was the Jewish Messiah who came to fulfill a Jewish prophecy of redemption and salvation. "Always and everywhere that proposition led swiftly to a division of the worshiping community," writes Roland Oliver about the development of Christianity in Africa, "the 'new way' of attracting a minority of ethnic Jews, but a majority of the gentile fellow travelers, who thereafter tended to be strongly anti-Semitic in their outlook."[7] Jews were taken to be the agents of Christ's crucifixion, a sadistic drama against a resurrected, living deity, all hope being in the acceptance of his divinity. In rejecting Christ as the Jewish Messiah, Jews were responsible for Jesus' failure to fulfill a scriptural promise that was Jewish and prophetic. Jews became the long past against which Christians defined their present and an apocalyptic future. The burden of worshiping a Jew but despising Jews forced the reification of Jew-hate. In time it became not only religion but blood that separated Jews from what became the Christian majority—and not a populous Christian majority but an institutionalized one, part of the apparatus of the state. When the cultural became biological, even conversion to Christianity could not clean the blood; Jewishness became a handed-down trait, inevitable and inescapable.

This new ideology of Jew-hate was an animating dynamic, killing women as witches being the other, of the Inquisition, introduced into Spain in 1480. Those Jews who had converted were called *conversos,* the pejorative of which was *marranos* (pigs). Called "the descendants of the Jews" by the legal authority of the Inquisition, *conversos* were tainted by Jewish blood. "The day was to come in Spain when any taint of Jewish blood was sufficient to affect the 'purity' of any person . . .,"[8] writes Israeli scholar B. Netanyahu in *The Origins of the Inquisition in Fifteenth Century Spain.* The *conversos* had *mala sangre* (bad blood). For the inquisitors, a Jewish past was "not merely a factor that establishes contact between generations through certain attitudes, beliefs and customs," but rather "the very *root* of the common attitudes, etc., and their related forms of behavior."[9] This new anti-Semitism, a racial construct, had at its core a compulsive need to establish *limpieza de sangre* (blood purity). This, according to Wistrich, "was the origin of Spanish racism, the first of its kind in Europe."[10] This belief, says Peter Gay in *The Cultivation of Hatred,* "launched the fiction of blood as the carrier of racial qualities."[11] The Inquisition in Spain, in the words of Frederick Cople Jaher, "was conducted with unsurpassed savagery. . . . Many apostates and their descendants died by *auto-da-fé* or mob violence. Survivors were barred from guilds and government posts and some dioceses and religious orders."[12] Syphilis was called "the Peste of the Marranos," and "Spanish physicians . . . claimed that Jewish men had tails and menstruated."[13] Unreconstructed Jews were expelled from Spain and not let back in until 1869.

The Inquisition was Catholic, but Martin Luther's Protestant rebellion did not help the Jews. It is not wrong to see Luther as an ideological precursor of Hitler, as Nora Levin does in *The Holocaust: The Destruction of European Jewry 1933–1945:* "Where Hitler depicts the Jew as the moral enemy, blocking the road 'to salvation for a struggling Aryan mankind,' Luther charged that Jews 'hold us captive in our own country.' In most of his imagery about the Jew, Hitler is simply reechoing the medieval Christian stereotype of the Jew as criminal, parasite, evil incarnate, aiming at world conquest—an image powerfully reinforced by Luther . . ."[14] Luther's heritage is unambiguously borne out in the structure of the church he preached in. "[Y]ou can just make out a curious sculpture jutting out from the church wall, like a gargoyle, about thirty feet from the ground," says Ian Buruma in *The Wages of Guilt: Memories of War in Germany and Japan*. "It is of a sow suckling three little piglets. Her hind leg is lifted by a little man wearing a pointed hat. The hat identifies the man as a Jew of the fifteenth century. Above this scene of Jew and pigs—the sow, I was told, representing 'Satan's synagogue'—is the Hebrew name for God. The ornament is called a *Judensau*, Jew's [female] pig. Many of these used to adorn German churches, as tokens of Jewish humiliation."[15]

The term *anti-Semitism* was coined in 1879 by Wilhelm Marr, an anarchist journalist who started an anti-Jewish group called the Anti-Semitic League and wrote about the toxic existence of Jews. Jew-hate mutated once again, this time claiming to be race-based sociology; its modus operandi was to insist that race-based Jewishness had unpardonable social, economic, and political consequences. The new anti-Semites claimed no religious animus and their target was emancipated, assimilating Jews: anti-Semitism began as an abreaction to the integration of Jews into the body politic. "What disturbed German Christians," says Ron Chernow in his biography of the Warburg banking family, "was the Jew as alter ego, not the Jew as other."[16] Hitler's hatred of religious Jews, his rabid disgust with their dress and foreignness, has obscured this earlier moment in Jew-hate when Jews were—in civic terms—more alike than different.

Anti-Semitism also claimed to be scientific, based especially on arguments by French philologist Ernest Renan: he considered both Jews and Arabs inferior and degraded; he believed that their languages were primitive. The anti-Semitism of intellectuals spread from Germany to France, where Renan gave it respectability, and also to Austria and Russia. This was a race-based anti-Semitism that was created by producers of culture, the journalist and the philologist being obvious examples. Because this was a hate whose boundaries were defined by the cultured and civilized— and because this was a hate of Jews who were more alike than different— it had to be buttressed by principles that resembled science or partook in the social exercises of Darwinism or were part of a material historicism.

Anti-Semitism became an organizing principle both political and cognitive: it was open, not hidden; mainstream, not marginal; with apparent intellectual heft because it was created by the literate, the wielders of pens, not guns; a lobby with influence on political parties, social and economic initiatives, literature, journalism, and psychology. Its articulacy helps to explain the incorporation of anti-Semitism into highly sophisticated political and social beliefs, including communism (Marxism-Leninism).

In France Captain Alfred Dreyfus was convicted of treason because he

was a Jew; popular anti-Semitism was spawned through anti-Semitic writers and political figures. The Vichy government anticipated the Nazis and
began deporting Jews before there was any Nazi requirement to do so. In
Russia many of the Bolshevik leaders were Jewish, as was Marx himself,
no doubt because "communist universalism presented itself as a paradisi-
cal ideal for persecuted, alienated Jews . . ."[17] Throughout Europe, the
embracing of communism by many, many Jews was seen as proof that
Jews were subversives and destroyers.

But inside the Soviet principality, Jews were treated with violent contempt. Isaac Babel, a Soviet-Jewish writer who rode with the Cossacks on
search-and-destroy missions, noted in his *1920 Diary:* "My first requisi-
tion—a notebook. The synagogue caretaker Menashe accompanies me. I
eat at Murdrik's, same old story, the Jews have been plundered, their be-
wilderment, they expected the Soviet regime to liberate them, and suddenly there were shrieks, whips cracking, shouts of 'dirty Yid.'"[18]
Contemporaneously in Ireland the Irish Republican Army was targeting
Jews: "A touch of anti-Semitism also showed in a series of armed raids on
money lenders in Dublin, Limerick and other centres . . . The parties concerned, who were mainly Jewish, were threatened and all their books and
records seized . . ."[19] The radical politics of liberation did not follow in the
footsteps of the French Revolution or the Enlightenment: the Jews were
outside the domain of radical civility or concern.

The next change in Jew-hate was the genocidal one, called "eliminationist antisemitism" by Daniel Goldhagen and "redemptive anti-Semitism" by Saul Friedländer. This was a racial anti-Semitism that looked
toward the "solving" of "the Jewish problem"—a solution that increasingly promoted the extirpation of the Jews from society. Jews were a race,
parasitic, contaminating, vile; Jews had to be conquered in a war, first economic and social, against them. Friedländer's redemptive anti-Semitism
focuses on the fusion of race-hate and devotional passion: this anti-Semitism was "born from the fear of racial degeneration and the religious belief in redemption. . . . Redemption would come as liberation from the
Jews. . . ."[20] This is not Christian redemption as such; rather it pretends to
articulate a basic human condition in which good and evil take the form
of German and Jew. Goldhagen's eliminationist anti-Semitism centers on
the ordinariness of this same intense hatred; in *Hitler's Willing Executioners: Ordinary Germans and the Holocaust,* Goldhagen posits that "anti-
semitism moved many thousands of 'ordinary' Germans—and would
have moved millions more, had they been appropriately positioned—to

slaughter Jews."[21] Attacking (perhaps unknowingly) the ontological abyss between words and action that now predominates in thought and common understanding in the United States, Goldhagen roused anger when he claimed that "[n]ot economic hardship, not coercive means of a totalitarian state, not social psychological pressure, not invariable psychological propensities, but ideas about Jews that were pervasive in Germany and had been for decades, induced ordinary Germans to kill unarmed, defenseless Jewish men, women, and children by the thousands, systematically and without pity."[22] "Decades" is perhaps judicious understatement: genocidal Jew-hate was slow-cooked in rhetoric, propaganda, and the sorcery of wordsmiths for closer to centuries. (See John Weiss, *Ideology of Death: Why the Holocaust Happened in Germany.*)

In current reckoning, the vileness and normalness of anti-Semitism in Austria and Germany before the Nazi genocide is often minimized, since this real history conflicts with the absurdities of free-speech and libertarian absolutes. Even if premillennial U.S. citizens live in a Panglossian world in which speech cannot cause harm, the Jews of sixteenth-, seventeenth-, eighteenth-, nineteenth-, and pre-1933 twentieth-century Germany (in its various configurations) did not. What distinguished genocidal anti-Semitism from what had gone before it was precisely how rabid *and* how commonplace it was. It became an ordinary truth, an unexamined premise of ordinary as well as intellectual, cultural, militarist, and political-party life; it was a familiar truth to the man in the street; its barely challenged legitimacy was ubiquitous; it was mean; it was cruel; it dehumanized; it threatened; it was meant to intimidate; it established "the Jew" in the popular mind as vicious and depraved; it lowered "the Jew" so low that eventually "[t]here were many bodies found along the river in the mornings, because to kill a Jew was no crime . . ."[23] There were many rivers, many mornings.

The key to the potency and staggering half-life of anti-Semitism is in its irrationality. Despite efforts to make it scientific and intellectually substantive, it was inherently paranoid, a persecution anxiety; fouling perception, it lived in the mind's shadows. Dynamic, sadistic, envious, characterized by greed and sexualized fear, anti-Semitism was the anti-imagination, cognition ruined by hate, a kind of fecal fantasy. "It is a way of imagining Jews," writes Anthony Julius in *T.S. Eliot, Anti-Semitism,*

and Literary Form, "a pernicious, elaborate fiction, and not just a series of theorems about the Jewish people."[24] It cannot be argued down or proven away, says Julius, because it is "bulky with descriptions."[25] These descriptions range from malicious to deranged.

In South Africa's apartheid state, for instance, a police textbook described Jews as "sly and cunning, inclined toward 'fraud, embezzlement and swindling.' "[26] The astonishing belief that Jewish men menstruate did not die with the Inquisition. In the cultural prologue to Shakespeare's time, this menstruation was symbiotically tied to the blood libel—that Jews kidnapped Christian children and ate them: "In the twisted pathology of this argument, these Jewish men are caught in a terrible cycle of bleeding and replacing that lost blood by crucifying children for supplementary blood, blood that then leaks out of them."[27] Jews also "feasted on Christians when they could, literally ate them."[28] The blood-libel scenario for Jews conjures up nothing so much as the Christian Eucharist, in which the carnage is symbolic. But regardless, this commonplace prejudice-narrative may have led to the pound-of-flesh story exploited in *The Merchant of Venice;* "[i]n the later Middle Ages and the Renaissance the pound of flesh story gained in popularity . . . Versions with Jewish villains can be found in Italy . . ., France, Germany, as far afield as Serbia . . ."[29] Here the Jew was a predator. Responsible, too, for cholera epidemics and the bubonic plague, Jews were seen as deadly, infecting, dirty, dangerous, "an impure, unholy, alien element corrupting the body politic."[30]

In *The Protocols of the Meetings of the Learned Elders of Zion,* which purported to document a Jewish conspiracy to control the world (but was in fact a forgery by the Czarist secret police), Jews were set up as an evil cabal; directly as a consequence, Jews were seen to be bankers who manipulated world governments and Bolsheviks who were engineering global communism. In 1804, a study of Jews under Austrian rule found that Jews had "weak feet," which were "the reason that the majority of Jews called into military service were released, because the majority of Jewish soldiers spent more time in the military hospitals than in military service."[31] There was a pro-Jew position that was social, not biological: the feet of Jews are weak because of environmental factors; the Jews live in cities and walk on city streets rather than on the real ground, *echt* earth. There was an anti-Jewish position that was biological, not social: Jews are born with this incapacity; the weakness of Jewish feet symbolizes the weakness of the Jewish body. (See Sander Gilman, *The Jew's Body.*) This suggests that Beit-Hallahmi is right when he says that "[e]ven philo-Semitism is a way of keeping Jews separate: they are different and need special treatment."[32] The special treatment would have been to cultivate stronger feet in Jews. The great German-Jewish poet Heinrich Heine, paraphrased, considered anti-Semitism "a misdirected hatred of the rich";[33] historian Eric Hobsbawn notes that "Jews were almost universally present, and could readily symbolize all that was most hateful about an unfair world, not least its commitment to the ideas of the Enlightenment and the French Revolution which had emancipated them . . . They could serve as symbols of the hated capitalist financier; of the revolutionary agitator; of the corroding influence of 'rootless intellectuals' and the new mass media; . . ."[34] This is, as U.S. writer Stanley Crouch says, "a protean xenophobia" that has the deepest implications for both individual and cultural identity—"[b]ecause the Jew is both Moses and Jesus, we might be talking about a remarkable tale of the Oedipus impulse."[35]

That anti-Semitism provides a canvas for an ominous rendering of a faux world without personal responsibility, empathy, or generosity seems obvious; so does the social utility of anti-Semitism. But why? Julia Kristeva asks, "Is anti-Semitism a fear of circumcision transformed into a fear of castration?"[36] Martin Luther provided at least a provisional answer long before she asked the question: "I hope I shall never be so stupid as to be circumcized. I would rather cut off the left breast of my Catherine and of all women."[37] And yet both Moses and Jesus were circumcized. Their God—the God of the Jews—wanted a piece of penile flesh to mark his covenant with them, not a left breast. Is the hatred of Jews a form of living terror, an internal deicide of both the father and the son, an aggression coded to protect an uncut penis? In the anti-Semitic imagination, are Jewish men always slashed and bleeding, the menstruating male? Does the eminence of Moses and Jesus cause a self-protective, hysterical shielding of the penis to protect it from mutilation? Does the hygienic spread of circumcision to non-Jewish populations subdue the panic, or reinforce it—the dread cutting accomplished, and who is the Jew now?

The transmutation of the Jewish penis into a weapon of cutting and predatory death shows itself in the conviction, in London's East End in the 1880s, that Jack the Ripper was a Jew. There had been an influx of Eastern European Jews into the East End; "there were occasional riots against them, and anti-Semitism generated fears that Jack the Ripper was himself a Jew."[38] A local newspaper dated October 15, 1888, described crowds threatening "the Hebrew population of the District. It was repeatedly asserted that no Englishman could have perpetrated such a horrible

crime . . . and that it must have been done by a JEW . . ."[39] According to
Sander Gilman, "the image of 'Jack' . . . is the caricature of the Eastern
Jew[,] . . . a man 'age 37, rather dark beard and moustache, dark jacket
and trousers, black felt hat, [who] spoke with a foreign accent.'"[40] Graffiti
blamed "the Juwes." The conflation of Jack the Ripper's surgical sadism
with the sexual abuse of his victims, mostly prostitutes, the conflation of
his lowness with their lowness, marked him as a Jew; as Gilman says, "the
Other even in the killing of the Other . . ."[41] Despite the feminization of
the Jew through circumcision, his penis was a deadly weapon, enhanced
by a knife, bathed in blood from the evisceration of women who were
synonymous with the servicing of the male genitalia.

"Beware of the Jew in Thyself," commanded German nativists. If Judaism
was racial, it was inherited, and the intermixing of Jews and Germans
meant that some Germans had inherited characteristics that were Jewish.
"In 1913," says John Weiss, "volkists, under the sign of the swastika, published a guide to the alleged semi-Jewish racial origins of the aristocracy."[42] One needed to be vigilant, because the Jewish taint could make
one act Jewish or think Jewish; one's hopes, desires, or character could be
Jewish.

   This is a little different from the Moses/Jesus problem—they were unambiguously Jewish. This was about inherited pollution, a corruption of
the soul through bad heritage, a poison that could make a German inau-
thentic; alien in his own universe, a foreigner in his own body. Jewishness
could be, or was, parasitic, and later an S.S. handbook would say literally
that the Jews themselves were parasites: "The Jews did not go to the East
as colonizers, but as parasites. . . . Europe's East became a reservoir and
launching pad of Jewry. New hordes of Jews repeatedly descended from
the East on the world."[43] Even the guerrilla resisters who fought the Nazis
were frightened of being infected or contaminated by Jews: "Starting in
the summer of 1943, devilish rumors began to circulate about the Jews. It
was said that the Germans were sending Jews into the woods for the specific purpose of poisoning Russian partisans. Another rumor was that
Germans were dispatching Jewish women infected with venereal disease
into the forests."[44] It is terrifying to think, as W. H. Auden did, that "Jung
hardly went far enough when he said, 'Hitler is the unconscious of every
German'; he comes uncomfortably near being the unconscious of most of

us."[45] What, then, must Jews have thought about being Jewish? Did "Beware of the Jew in Thyself" become an intra-Jewish dynamic? Is this a nearly sentimental rendering of the famous self-hate of Jews?

In the late 1940s at the University of Chicago Jewish Center, psychologist Bruno Bettelheim, a refugee from Vienna, then Dachau, asked: "Anti-Semitism, whose fault is it?" His answer was unequivocal: "Yours! . . . Because you don't assimilate, it is your fault. If you assimilated, there would be no anti-Semitism. Why don't you assimilate?"[46] He himself had been assimilated in Vienna until, as a married adult, he was shipped off to Dachau. Bettelheim was not alone in seeing Jewishness as the cause of anti-Semitism, a causal relationship widely accepted but devastating in its implications. If this causality were real, then the Jew had better rid himself of Jewishness, divest himself of every Jewish trait, interest, propensity, loyalty, ethic, historical attachment. Still, conversion had not mitigated the murderous consequences of being "of Jewish descent" during the Spanish Inquisition; and the perception of assimilated Jews in German and Austrian cities was that they (the assimilated Jews) were valued as citizens, hated by some as Jews had always been hated, but more than tolerated by the polity—counted on, prominent, useful, educated, professional, respected—a community of intellect and skills that took care of its own and also contributed talent and money to the larger Christian society. However seriously anti-Semitism was taken by Jews—whatever its strengths as a political movement or its effectiveness in stigmatizing Jewishness for Jews themselves—ultimately anti-Semitism was ludicrous, especially in its construction of a Nazi-Aryan ideal; as Julius Huxley and a coauthor described this ideal, it was "as blond as Hitler, as dolichocephalic [longheaded] as Rosenberg, as tall as Goebbels, as slender as Goering, and as manly as Streicher."[47] Nazi anti-Semitism was a genocidal absurdity, but it was an absurdity nonetheless.

Yet who would stand up and say so? Who did stand up and say so? In fact, the premises of the anti-Semitic worldview were too widely accepted by both Jews and Christians, artists and politicians, bankers and economists, philosophers and psychologists, to be repudiated; and they were not. Some, Jews and non-Jews, thought that Jews wanted suffering: "they are tempted to desire suffering," said Auden, ". . . hence the tenacity with which the neurotic clings to his neurosis and the Jew to his race consciousness."[48] This easily turns into blaming the victim: the Jews brought it (anything, including genocide) on themselves. In particular, Christians believed that in not accepting Christ after thousands of years of persecution, Jews were a purposeful provocation with the inevitable consequences of humiliation, contempt, and murder. The so-called Jewish problem was unsolvable because Jews themselves refused to solve it.

Instead, Jews drew lines that they thought were both self-protective and warranted; especially, assimilated Jews distanced themselves from observant, separatist Jews, the dreaded Jews of Eastern Europe. As Walter Laqueur writes in his memoir of the pre-Hitler years in Germany: "The assimilated Jews had a dim view of the Ostjuden. When my mother was really angry, she said I talked like an Ostjude—loud, gesticulating, making an exhibition of myself. The Jews from Eastern Europe talked an unlovely language and had no manners, at least as we understood it."[49] On the obnoxious flamboyance of Eastern European Jews, both anti-Semites and assimilated Jews agreed; as expressed by anti-Semitic novelist Wyndham Lewis, "the anti-Semitism that does exist is sustained solely by the extremely bad manners and barbaric aggressiveness of the eastern/slum-Jew immigrant"[50]—a view not modified by Hitler's persecution, even in 1935 when the Nuremberg Laws were passed. Every anti-Semite was a mirror for Jews; every anti-Semitic argument compromised the self-respect of the Jews; every anti-Semitic act created self-blame rather than equal-and-opposite aggression back.

Even in Israel, Holocaust survivor Aharon Appelfeld continues to dissect "this anti-Semitism directed at oneself, an ancient Jewish ailment, which, in modern times, has taken on various guises."[51] Coming from a background not unlike Laqueur's, in Appelfeld's home "German was treasured. German was considered not only a language but also a culture . . ."[52] Yiddish was stigmatized, "absolutely forbidden . . . [A]nything Jewish was blemished."[53] In the aftermath of the Holocaust, this hatred for oneself metastasized: "The inability to make a reckoning for oneself and the desire to forget joined together in secret and became malice, not the malice of a murderer who commits a crime, but malice directed against ourselves. . . . Everything that was Jewish or that seemed Jewish, looked weak, ugly, and damaging to us. What didn't we do to root out every link that still bound us to the world from which we had come?"[54]

This is real, the anti-Semitism planted deep in the Jewish soul, history's curse, a cost of Jewish identity and Jewish survival, part of the heritage of persecution and genocide, a self-blame magnified and enhanced after the Holocaust by the accusations of Jews who had not been there— "harsh comments were made by prominent Jews against the victims, for not protecting themselves and fighting back."[55] Used now as political epithet and insult, "self-hating Jew" is not faced as part of Jewish reality; this is a self-contempt that triumphant pride does not erase. What might?

Woman-hate is a radical antagonism to existence itself; like it or not, some women, and not some men, give birth. Like it or not, the egg, not the sperm, is precious, each egg a potential life: there is no extravagant surplus of eggs. In terms of human descent, eggs are the scarce resource. Like it or not, women bleed every month for three, four, or five decades and live; no man loses blood without losing some measure of life. In childbirth the bleeding can be massive and sexual murders of women often mimic the bloodletting of birth. No woman has to want pregnancy or experience childbirth to symbolize life, although antinatalism on the part of a woman will antagonize, repudiating as it does the inevitability of anatomical meaning. Sexual access to women is access to life present and future; destroying women destroys the present and future—replaces life with death; when men hurt women, they champion death against life. If, as Elie Wiesel says, Jews "are the question,"[56] women precede the question and embody existence itself, without sentimentality or consolation; whatever existence is, women are. What does it mean, to be life itself? "She was demure, attentive, modest, passive, intuitive, all the crap qualities that are ascribed to cipher women," writes novelist Will Self, "the way rhythm is drummed into blacks and miserliness deposited with the Jews."[57] Tamed, made docile, far from the demands of existence as such, the woman is forbidden to use her vitality; her body is stigmatized as filth—"If her bowels and flesh were cut open, you would see what filth is covered by her white skin. If a fine crimson cloth covered a pile of foul dung, would anyone be foolish enough to love the dung because of it?";[58] her qualities of mind— imagination, emotion, intellect—are traduced, as if existence itself blighted them. She is kept from dominating her home, her tribe, two obvious loci of what should be her secular power; she is denied learning to stunt the mind and also to eclipse it from her own self-consciousness; her body is constrained and often captive; battery is commonplace and shows the unity of mind and body—both are trashed, betrayed, insulted, demeaned, injured by physical brutality. Existence is killed in her: energy, ambition, self-rule. Oppression replaces existence, overcomes it, subsumes it. Her body is the first target: control it, use it, make her will dead so that her body is accepting; or use force, cruelty, deprivation, violence.

Take it, conquer it, enslave it, overwhelm it. Trick it, manipulate it, seduce it, drug it. Buy it, sell it, consume it, lend it around. Then get another one and enjoy beginning again. If she resists, break her down. Use
violence or the threat of violence in the right way and she will beg, cringe,
cry; she will help you hurt her so that you will hurt her less—this is the
arithmetic of female oppression. When she is ready to kill you in order to
free herself, she will begin with a defense of her body: "Victim groups
must respond to oppression first at the site where it most threatens their
ability to respond," says Elisabeth Young-Bruehl in *The Anatomy of Prejudices*. To her this means that "a group attacked for its appearance responds
with *négritude* or 'Black is beautiful,' and a group attacked for its mind-
lessness, which means body-onlyness, responds with consciousness raising."[59] That "body-onlyness" requires the assertion of self-consciousness
to examine the meaning of the body; otherwise, the dominant definition
remains in place: her reproductive organs are significant, alive; she, the being with consciousness, is neither. Her reproductive potential or its real-
ization demonstrates her animalism, primitivism, a bloody sensuousness;
as Leonard Woolf noted, women "naked when alive are extraordinarily
ugly; but dead they are repulsive."[60] The particular woman who provoked
this rumination was African and had just been kicked to death for not
bringing her husband dinner. Body functions are animal; thoughts are
human, elevated.

Swimming in the blood of her own body, in labor and in pain, the
woman is a half-human who achieves her half-human fate in pregnancy
and childbearing. The canal through which the infant is extruded is the
man's place of sex; he enters, not wanting blood to drown him or conta-
minate him or pollute him; the blood makes her dirty and threatens his
pristine penis; this makes her an abomination. In *Three Steps on the Ladder of Writing*, Hélène Cixous quotes Tsvetaeva—"All poets are Yids."
Cixous understands that "[t]he word is extremely insulting . . . Poets are
unclean, abominable. When Tsvetaeva used this word in the context of
Russian society, the most abominable of the abominable at that time, poets, she felt, were *Yids*. In another text she suggests that . . . the abominable with whom she identified was the nigger. So in the same line of
substitutions you find: Jews, women, niggers, . . . poets, etc., all of them
excluded and exiled."[61] This was not a Russian barbarity. Thomas Jefferson, who owned slaves and considered blacks inferior despite his children
by Sally Hemings, wanted women outside the parameters of citizenship
and law: "Were our state a pure democracy there would still be excluded

from our deliberations women, who, to prevent deprivation of morals and ambiguity of issues, should not mix promiscuously in gatherings of men."[62] The sex of women became the stigma of women; the sex of women made women base, lower as lower races were inferior; the sex of women—overwhelming to the male the way female blood overwhelmed him, frightened him—was not only the excuse for her internal exile from human status but also the reason. Sex inhered in her; one had to go into her to get sex, get life, get children; she became either chattel property or prey, and her life was as worthless as any life degraded by race-hate. "What care I," wrote George Moore in *Confessions of a Young Man* in 1888, "that some millions of wretched Israelites died under Pharaoh's lash or Egypt's sun? It was well that they died that I might have the pyramids to look on. . . . What care I that the virtue of some sixteen-year-old maiden was the price paid for Ingres' *La Source?* . . . Nay more, the knowledge that a wrong was done—that millions of Israelites died in torments, that a girl, or a thousand girls, died in hospital for that one virginal thing, is an added pleasure which I could not afford to spare."[63]

Women are sacrificed to male desire—including aesthetic desire, art for art's sake—with less concern than the early Hebrews had for their Yom Kippur goats. Art as scapegoating—by race, for instance, in Robert Mapplethorpe's photographs of a pornographized black man; by sex, for instance, by Balthus and David Hamilton in their use of girls—is sophisticated hating and produces sophisticated defenses of hate, as long as the hate is pretty, formally pretty. As such, art becomes the equivalent of anti-Semitism, the principled, intellectually legitimate assertion of Jews' lesser value, a degraded value. Approaching the great paintings of Europe, aghast at Germaine Greer's charge that misogyny is at the heart of Western art, Edwin Mullins is forced to conclude in *The Painted Witch: How Western Artists Have Viewed the Sexuality of Women,* that male painters, including "some of the greatest of them," are "hostile" to women; and further, "[t]he sensibility of artists is not singular, just a personal vision, any more than a judgment of law is personal justice. It is rooted in what society believes and what society wants. There can only be one origin of so pervasive a desire to control woman, abuse woman, set her up in order to tear her down, enclose her in a labyrinth of moral strictures with so many blind exits she will never be free; and that is—fear."[64] In fact, every marked exit from the circus, the cell, off the pedestal, is a dead end because men hunt women—for sex, for children, for rape, for battery, for prostitution, for murder. The children already know. As Deborah Rhode describes, "When 1,100 Michigan elementary students were asked to describe what life would be like if they were the opposite sex, over 40 percent of the girls saw advantages to being male; they would have better jobs, higher incomes, and more respect. Ninety-five percent of the boys saw no advantage to being female, and a substantial number thought suicide would be preferable."[65]

Not too many women live without a suicidal impulse, in sex especially. In Michael Ryan's memoir about his own molestation as a child and its later effects, he articulates a common sexual dynamic: "I was certainly a magnet for some women, as some women were for me—suicidal women for whom sex was both validation and self-annihilation . . . Many of them had also been sexually molested, some of them by their fathers. I could pick them out the minute I walked into a room. Their hunger is what made them sexy to me . . . We always at least half-hated each other, the half that was a mirror."[66] Repeated molestation, with its cyclical seduction and betrayal, accounted for this shared self-regard or lack of it; but Ryan's body stayed male—there was no blood, then more blood, to weary, mark, or shame him—his own male body was not stigmatized or culturally repellent. Ryan acted out some of his sexual confusion on the family dog, who began to hate him. If the dog could not bear it, how do women bear it? Says Greer, "It is almost as if women's rage is, like women's sexuality, too vast and bottomless to be allowed any expression, for fear it would swamp and capsize the male equivalent. Despite the best efforts of feminists to awaken women's anger and to turn their hostility outward so that it becomes a force for social change rather than a procreator of symptoms, we have failed."[67] And this was not the first failure. H. G. Wells wondered why "[t]here has been no perceptible woman's movement to resist the practical obliteration of their freedom by Fascists or Nazis."[68] The abrogation of women's emancipation by both fascists and Nazis was essential to the totalitarian and genocidal program. How else to turn death into the dominant social principle? How else to turn death into the politics of a brutal vanguard, an elite of thugs? How else to make life a servant of death, worthless, meaningless, and contemptible? How else to pollute and destroy creativity, empathy, and simple kindness?

Mussolini, the handsome, womanizing fascist, of course had his own view of feminism, especially the kind Wells knew in England: "In a country where animals are adored to the point of making cemeteries and hospitals and houses for them, and legacies are bequeathed to parrots, you can be sure that decadence has set in. Besides, other reasons apart, it is also a consequence of the composition of the English people. Four million surplus women. Four million women sexually unsatisfied, artificially creating a host of problems in order to excite or appease their senses. Not being able to embrace one man, they embrace humanity."[69]

In the German far-right tradition, anti-Semites and political conservatives "saw women's liberation as a Jewish-socialist attempt to cut the patriarchal roots that made Christian Germanic *Kultur* and society great."[70] The fact that, then as now, "many leading feminists were socialists of Jewish origin, educated, secular . . ."[71] suggested that feminism was a Jewish subversion. As racist Eugen Duehring concluded, "This deformed ephemeral phase of thought may be put down in the main to the discredit of Hebrew women."[72] The assassination of Rosa Luxemburg marked the violent expression of a synthesized hate: feminist, socialist, and Jew, her political leadership, her agitation, her organizing were an intolerable provocation.

When on September 15, 1935, "the Nuremberg Laws repealed the entire history of Jewish emancipation and transported the community back to the Middle Ages,"[73] this legal end of Jewish citizenship was also a set of sexual proscriptions; Germans and Jews could neither marry each other nor have sexual intercourse. The Jewish contagion was fundamentally sexual; and German blood had to be protected from Jewish blood, the circumcized penis being the blood instrument of the rapist Jew and the Jewish female's blood inhering in her sexual organs and when she passed blood. The Jewish woman was now revealed as base, provocative, sensual, foreign, evil, the enticer of innocent German men. Despite all this punishment and legal terror, "[i]n Hamburg, a Jewish brothel was set up to service clients without running afoul of the law."[74] Male Jews, however disenfranchised as citizens, were not to be denied sexual access at will to prostituted Jewish women: lower, poorer, more displaced than they themselves were.

Hitler's social policy was unambiguous and unequivocal. He wanted "'Aryan' victory over the Jew and male triumph over the emancipated woman."[75] As Nazi theorist Gottfried Feder argued, "The insane dogma of equality led as surely to the emancipation of the Jews as to the emancipation of women. The Jew stole the woman from us . . . We must kill the dragon to restore her to her holy position as servant and maid."[76]

In 1933 the Nazis had outlawed birth control, further criminalized the aborting of "Aryan" fetuses, and forced "unfit Aryans" to be sterilized. As Claudia Koonz writes in *Mothers in the Fatherland: Women, the Family*

and Nazi Politics, "It fell to women to put all of these edicts into practice.
. . . [S]ocial workers, teachers, and nurses turned over the names of the
mentally retarded, schizophrenics, alcoholics, and misfits to Nazi sterilization agencies. Brides left the labor market in order to receive state loans
and bear many children; housewives boycotted Jewish businesses and cut
lifelong Jewish friends out of their social lives; women professionals
founded eugenic motherhood schools . . . It fell to women to report 'suspicious' strangers . . . , send their own children to the Hitler Youth, and finally to close the door firmly if anyone who looked 'dangerous' begged for
mercy."[77] Ugly but familiar, this is how women accommodate to danger:
take her, not me; do it to her, not me; she deserves it, I don't. Race-hate
makes it easier to draw that line: I don't have her bad qualities; I could
never be her. Race-hate also makes it possible to deny sameness: woman is
woman is woman; but German is not Jew.

At the same time that German women were hardening their hearts
and cooperating with the policies of National Socialism, Hitler knew to
approach the masses as if they were female; he believed that a crowd, like
a woman, was emotional and wanted to be dominated; Hitler thought the
masses were "feminine in . . . character and outlook."[78] In his oratory, the
small, dark, ugly man with the silly moustache seduced first hundreds,
then thousands, then millions; he fucked them, they swooned, a fairly accurate rendering of a traditional male-female paradigm.

In the concentration and killing camps, the purpose was not to make
masses of Jews swoon; the brutality against male and female betokened a
deeper rage, a cold brutality, organized torture and death; but still, the hatred of women was blatant, brazen, explicit, and sexualized. On arriving
at Auschwitz, "[the women] smelled burning flesh and singed hair. They
were pushed and shoved into the shower rooms, ordered to strip naked
and line up to have all their hair shaved from their heads, underarms and
pubic regions. . . . [T]heir modesty was further violated by the SS men,
who arrived for their bonus show. They made lewd remarks, pointed at
them, commented on their shapes, made obscene suggestions, poked into
their breasts with their riding crops and sicked their dogs on them. . . .
[T]hose newly arrived to these jaws of hell were crushed under the deluge
of foul language, obscene gestures and the fact that they were paraded like
cattle on the market in front of men. To many women it meant an unfor-
givable and never to be forgotten humiliation."[79]

The sadism of labor could be gendered, too: "I saw women shoveling.
I found that so sadistic. The shovel blades were two or three times the size

of the ones the men had."[80] The policy, it seemed, was that "strong women without children were kept alive to work, and the rest were exterminated by gas."[81] Attracting the sexual interest of a Nazi could mean a slower death as he worked on the body to destroy it over time: "When Ibi removed her uniform in the course of an 'inspection,' Mengele found himself staring at her, transfixed. . . . Any other SS officer would have simply made her his mistress. But Mengele evidently could not and would not concede feeling an attraction toward a Jew. In a loud voice, he dispatched Ibi to the infamous Block Ten, where the Nazis were performing sinister gynecological experiments. Few women survived Block Ten. . . . A few weeks later . . . [t]he beautiful young girl looked like a shriveled old woman. Her slender limbs were swollen and disfigured, while her stomach was bloated from the numerous surgeries that had been performed on her."[82] And still, there were brothels filled with Jewish women, for instance, at a German labor camp at Adampol: "Spared the gas chamber, they were kept alive solely for the pleasure of the Ukrainian and Latvian guards and for German soldiers."[83]

Even among the partisans, survival had a sexual price for Jewish women; "the possibility of rape and murder was real"; "if a partisan, any partisan, helped a woman, he expected to be paid with sexual favors"; partisans considered the women to be whores—"The very women they desired as sex partners, they viewed with contempt. In male conversations, for example, whore was often substituted for the word woman."[84] Few Jewish women survived. And for all Jewish women who did survive, "[i]t was common to suggest that [they] had served in brothels . . ."[85] Survivors from inside the camps were seen as whores and so were non-Jewish women who survived outside the camps; for instance, in the aftermath in Paris, "the women were made the scapegoats for the sins of the whole community";[86] moral outrage at collaboration was targeted against women, again as whores, for having had sexual congress with Nazis or French fascists. No amount of force or suffering erased the belief that women in every circumstance whored, were base, were debased not by Nazi cruelty but by their own female nature, which was sluttish and depraved.

Austrian novelist Elfriede Jelinek writes in *Wonderful Wonderful Times* that the war went on, even after the cease-fire: "Apparently the beatings began on the very day the War was lost. Up till then, Father had been beating sundry foreigners. Now only Mother and the children were at his disposal."[87] And those German women who said take her, not me, discovered the utility of having had one Jewish friend: the Hausjude. "I was un-aware," says Alison Owings in *Frauen: German Women Recall the Third Reich*, "how many Hausjude ghosts exist—in the face of a shopkeeper, in a teacher's visit to a child's sickbed, in memories of a neighbor. The leap to salvation is not just in knowing one had a Hausjude, but in knowing that the Hausjude left in time. . . . The Hausjude who escaped and prospered in America became the first patron saint of postwar Germany."[88] Thus, women claim women in a sisterhood corrupted by genocide. Women who hate women, like men who hate women, hate existence, compromise it, betray it, are dishonored and dishonorable, commit treason for death against life. The imperative is to create honor woman-to-woman; to de-stroy the bad but useful ethic of take-her-not-me; the question is how?

3

POGROM / RAPE

Children of Russian Jewish descent are prodigals whose first words were "mommy," "daddy," and "pogrom." Adults, of course, were stingy with information but extravagant with emotion. One learned to feel the men on horses chasing down Jews as if the attackers were wind itself changing the earth's geography through a natural violence; and the Jews, like weak saplings, were bent and broken, uprooted and scattered—some lived, some died. In the abridged version, there were a few Jews, lots of wild, bad men on horses; and some families would have shelters in which to hide as if from tornadoes in the U.S. Midwest—but a Jewish Dorothy never would have reached Oz. *Pogrom* means "devastation" in Russian; the Russian verb *pogromi* means "to destroy"; and the devastation destroyed Jews.

Long before the Jews were burdened and nearly annihilated by Nazi genocide, the pogrom was the paradigmatic expression of violence against Jews. A pogrom could include assault, battery, robbery, rape, murder; it was often described as a riot or a massacre or mass murder. The role of the Jew was to run, to hide, to beg for mercy, to be beaten or raped or killed; also plundered and looted.

There were three periods of epic pogrom against Jews in Russia: 1881–1884; 1903–1906; 1918–1920. In 1881, "more than half of world Jewry lived under Russian rule."[1] So, inevitably, what happened to Russian Jews happened to Jews as Jews; a part stood in for the whole. The 1881 and 1882 pogroms created a multitude of emigrants from Russia, primarily to the United States but also to Palestine. Leaving Russia was a response not only to violent, grass-roots Jew-hate but also to the Russian government's institutional support of that violence. The government agitated for the violence; according to Rabbi Joseph Telushkin in *Jewish Literacy: The Most Important Things to Know About the Jewish Religion, Its*

People, and Its History, there were "six hundred pogroms that took place between 1903 and 1906 [and] the pamphlets calling for the attacks had been printed on the press of the czar's secret police."[2] Even the Cossacks—the wild, bad men on the horses—were basically instruments of the czar. As John Keegan in *A History of Warfare* describes, the early Cossacks "were Christian fugitives from servitude under the rulers of Poland, Lithuania, and Russia, who preferred to take their chance—to 'go Cossacking'—on the rich but lawless surface of the great Central Asian steppe."[3] The word *cossack* means "freeman" or "adventurer." Before the czar reined them in, "they had founded genuinely egalitarian [*sic*] societies—lordless, womanless, propertyless, embodiments of the free and free-ranging warrior band . . ."[4] The czars needed the Cossacks at first for "help in liberating Russian prisoners from Muslim enslavement," but by the sixteenth century Ivan the Terrible "had begun to use force to bring them within the tsarist system."[5]

The problem in understanding the reach and destruction of the pogrom is that the Holocaust dwarfed any other organized anti-Semitic violence. And yet, the pogrom in all its power and horror was the background against which Jews in civilized Germany and throughout Europe, especially after the Enlightenment, measured all other violence. The pogrom became small; bad but tiny; nasty but not genocidal. Yet eyewitness accounts of pogroms show a shocking and purposeful sadism that is more than a precursor of the Nazi genocide: "Some of [the Jews] had their skins flayed off them and their flesh was flung to the dogs. The hands and feet of others were cut off and they were flung onto the roadway where carts ran over them and they were trodden underfoot by horse. . . . And many were buried alive. Children were slaughtered in their mothers' bosoms and many children were torn apart like fish. They ripped up the bellies of pregnant women, took out the unborn children, and flung them in their faces. They tore open the bellies of some of them and placed a living cat within the belly and left them alive thus, first cutting off their hands so that they should not be able to take the living cat out of the belly . . ."[6] Jews who survived "were sold as slaves, usually to Constantinople's slave markets. For many years, Jewish communities throughout Europe raised money to redeem these slaves and free them . . ."[7] It was this kind of savage violence against which German Jews measured German civility: and thought the Germans too civilized for skinning people alive and ripping bellies open. Live and learn.

Regardless of the malign consequences to Jews, the pogrom was sentimental, as Hitler recognized: "Anti-Semitism on purely emotional grounds will find its ultimate expression in the form of pogroms. The anti-Semitism of reason, however, must lead to the planned judicial opposition to and elimination of the privileges of the Jews. . . . Its ultimate goal, however, must absolutely be the removal of the Jews altogether."[8] With sociopathic lucidity, Hitler found the critical flaws in the pogrom as an expression of race-hate: it was ruthless but not systematic; local, not global; it destroyed Jewish communities but not Jewish civilization; it killed some Jews but not all Jews.

Still, the Jewish (or anti-Jewish) twentieth century began with the violence of the pogrom: 1903–1906 and 1918–1920; and Jews were defined as victims and targets. On April 6 and 7, 1903, a pogrom in Kishinev "horrified both the entire Jewish world and large numbers of civilized non-Jews."[9] This pogrom, instigated by the czar and his lackeys, was "notorious," "the most widely publicized and denounced act of anti-Semitic violence before 1914," "the first of ever-rising waves of pogroms in Russia . . . from 1903 to 1906."[10] The Kishinev pogrom became a symbol of Jew-hating violence: "Forty-five Jews were reported killed, over five hundred injured (apparently including rapes), and approximately fifteen hundred homes and shops were pillaged or vandalized. The Kishinev pogrom was thus responsible for many more deaths and injuries in a few days than the hundreds of riots in early 1881."[11] Jews fled Russia; and before 1914 "ninety thousand Russian Jews arrived in Germany . . ."[12] Max Warburg became involved in trying to get Russian Jewish refugees into the U.S.; and Jewish philanthropists made emigration from Russia a priority in fighting Jew-hate.

The Kishinev pogrom raised issues for Jews usually credited to the murderous aggression of the Nazis: "The issue of fighting back was now posed in a most direct and brutal form."[13] Jews accused themselves of cowardice; of course, the Kishinev Jews were accused by Jews who had not been there, a pattern that would be repeated after the Nazi genocide, especially in Israel. *The* question was asked: "How could it happen that tens of thousands of adult Jewish males, of a total Jewish population of fifty thousand, were unable or unwilling to fend off several hundred rioters?"[14] A journalist reported that "ninety percent of [Jewish males] hid themselves, or fled to safer parts of the city for refuge."[15] There were gangs of Jews who defeated rioters in some parts of Kishinev; and there were rich Jews who "bribed the police with substantial sums of money to gain protection."[16] There were Christians who risked their lives to fight the pogromists. And "the entire Jewish world and large numbers of civilized non-Jews" denounced the pogrom with moralistic fervor. The Jewish denunciation of Jewish cowardice was as if written in blood, in flesh, in time, inevitable and unbearable; the Jews of Kishinev, wrote the Jewish poet Chaim Nachman Bialyk, faced the pogroms "with trembling knees, concealed and cowering. . . . It was the flight of mice they fled, the scurrying of roaches was their flight; they died like dogs, and they were dead!"[17] The poet's words had the force of Isaiah. Epitaph for a people: "they died like dogs, and they were dead!"

The argument for both self-defense and retaliatory violence goes back not to the Israelis or the Zionists or the Warsaw Ghetto resisters but to 1903 and the Kishinev pogrom: "Jews must fight back; Jews must learn to rely on their own resources; Jews must stop being physical cowards."[18] And, in the immediate aftermath of the Kishinev pogrom, "[i]n everybody, and before all else, there emerged the thirst for revenge."[19] Still, the Kishinev pogrom was the first of over six hundred pogroms in the next three years. And there were still trials of Jews for the blood libel: "Mendel Beilis was charged with murdering a Christian boy for ritual purposes, as late as 1911. Many ritual murder or 'blood libel' trials were held in the nineteenth and early twentieth centuries, particularly in Russia . . ."[20]

It is heartening to note that Dmitri Nabokov, grandfather of the famous novelist, successfully defeated Jew-hating legislation proposed in 1881, the first year of the first cycle of epic pogrom. The novelist's father, V. D. Nabokov, "became the most outspoken defender of Jewish rights among all Russian gentiles trained in law."[21] He was shot for his efforts; but his son "would marry a Russian Jew, would denounce anti-Semitism in his own works, and would escape Hitler with his wife and son only with the help of Russian Jewish emigres still grateful for his father's sterling defense of their people."[22] In March 1933 in Nazi Germany, Jews were being assaulted, their businesses both boycotted and looted. Nabokov "walked the streets, deliberately entering all the Jewish shops that still remained open."[23] Thomas Mann didn't; Brecht didn't; Auden and Isherwood didn't.

Currently it is common wisdom to draw a straight line from Nazi Germany to the establishment of the Jewish state; but it was the history of Jews in Russia, especially the experience of pogrom, that pushed more than half the world's Jews out: into Palestine; into the United States; into the heart of Europe, especially France, Germany, Hungary, and Austria. It was, according to Beit-Hallahmi, "the immigration wave between 1904 and 1914 [that] made the creation of Israel possible."[24] He points to David Ben-Gurion, Yitzhak Ben-Zvi, Levi Eshkol, and Bert Katznalson, all of whom "were determined revolutionaries who imported ideas about communal living from nineteenth century Russia, together with a commitment to the secular asceticism of Russian revolutionaries."[25] They wanted an ethnically distinct communism, a Jewish socialism, radical and secular.

With the civil unrest that preceded the Russian Revolution, more Jews came to Palestine; and this wave, too, was radical, secular, and shaped the premises of the Israeli state; "[t]hey started building a military force, patiently and consistently."[26] Israel's first three heads-of-state came to Palestine before 1914; the fourth, Golda Meir, came in 1921. In Russia, the czar was deposed, his family murdered; and the red Russians established the Soviet Union. Nearly three million Jews were facing death from famine and armed conflict in the new Soviet state; and "[t]ens of thousands of Jews were being murdered by marauding bandits. Entire villages were wiped out in fierce fighting between [the] Soviets and the Poles."[27] This was the practice, not the theory.

Given czarist support for the pogroms—in fact, making them state policy—Jewish tears were not shed when the Romanovs met their maker; and Soviet communism promised Jews inclusion, dignity, and a repudiation of classic (class-based) anti-Semitism. Lenin's first cabinet was in fact "dominated by men of Jewish origins: Trotsky, the leader of the Petrograd coup and founder of the Red Army; Kamenev, and Zinoviev, Lenin's righthand man . . . Sverdlov was now president of the Party's Central Committee, and Karl Radek, Maxim Litvinov, A. A. Yoffe, and others all held prominent positions. With the exception of Litvinov, they all registered their nationalities as Great Russian, not Jewish."[28] Marxists of Jewish descent "transposed their loyalties to the global proletariat."[29] They wanted to be in the vanguard and just plain folks, too. They wanted power *and* equality. They had a luminous idea that would cannibalize them.

In those early, formative years, it was the unimportant Stalin, later a mass killer and virulent anti-Semite, who wrote the position paper on what Soviets called "nationalities," which included, but was not limited to, Jews. Socialism, he said, must resist nationalism; he meant ethnic bonding, subcultural loyalties; for the Jews the dynamic was clear and widely welcomed—if Jews were Soviets, there would be no basis for anti-Semitism. The defining of nationalities was not seen as an ominous contradiction in the communist idea; nor was anti-Semitism seen as intractable.

During the years of the Stalin-Hitler pact, Soviet Jewish writer Ilya Ehrenburg reported from Berlin "recalling the sign on his Berlin hotel— 'Pure Aryan Establishment. No Jews allowed'—and an editorial from a French newspaper that echoed Nazi racism: 'There is a bit of the Jew in every one of us,' the collaborators proclaimed. 'What we need is an internal, intimate pogrom.'"[30] Essentially, that eloquent French fascism defined perfectly early Soviet ideology as applied to Jews: "What we need is an internal, intimate pogrom."

Ilya Ehrenburg survived even under Stalin; this means he saw writers, friends, colleagues imprisoned, terrorized, killed. It was only on January 27, 1953, when accepting the Stalin prize, that he finally spoke out to support Jews, in this case a number of doctors, primarily Jewish, who were accused of trying to poison Stalin. He was, even then, elliptical: "No matter what his national origin, a Soviet citizen is first and foremost a patriot of his country, and he is a true internationalist, an opponent of racial and national discrimination, a fervent believer in the brotherhood of man, a fearless defender of peace. On this solemn and festive occasion in the white hall of the Kremlin I want to pay tribute to those fighters for peace who are being persecuted, tortured and hounded; I want to call to mind the dark night of prisons, of interrogations, of trials, and the courage of so many."[31] One might say that the Soviet Union restructured the pogrom by using the language of universal brotherhood; Jews did experience the personal violence of an internal, intimate pogrom; but the erasure of Jewish identity no more satisfied the Soviet state, especially under Stalin, than conversion to Christianity had satisfied the Spanish Inquisitors. History taunts: even when Judaism is invisible, anti-Semitism finds it.

Winston Churchill, discussing Stalin's defeat of Trotsky, was right about not only Trotsky but perhaps a whole generation of Russian, then Soviet, Jews. "He was still a Jew," said Churchill. "Nothing could get over that. Hard fortune when you have deserted your family, repudiated your race, spat upon the religion of your father . . ."[32] Churchill had described a tragedy beyond the ken of the Greeks. The Jew becomes someone when he betrays, erases, disowns his origin; but the someone he becomes—in Trotsky's case, the leader of the victorious Red Army—is Jew, as if Jew were an indelible stain, repugnant and vile, on the soul, the body, the humanness of a person. The Jew has accomplished the "internal, intimate pogrom," which is never enough; Bronstein can become Trotsky (he took the name of a Russian prison guard he met when jailed for seditious activity under the czarist government); he can feel "total revulsion for the Jewish past"[33]: but still, the devastation will destroy the Jew, even though he has already disappeared. How does a Jew by birth if not by conviction, not a messiah, get off the cross?

As Andrei Sinyavsky, a Soviet dissident, writes in *The Russian Intelligentsia*, "From my point of view, Russian anti-Semitism represents a kind of alienation of evil. It is a popular, mythic, almost fairy-tale notion that the people cannot be bad. Our people are good. They are *our* people. But some outsiders have wormed their way into the government, and they are to blame for everything."[34] Cold-war antagonism allows the western democracies to infer that the Soviets, regardless of their form of government, are primitive, savage, mentally and morally simple; whereas in November 1969, enraged over growing public hostility to the U.S. massacre at My Lai, Richard Nixon said over and over again to an aide, "It's those dirty rotten Jews from New York who are behind it."[35] He meant the outrage, not the massacre. One concerned him; the other did not.

In the U.S. some fifty years earlier, the exclusion of Jews from colleges was, said a spokesman from Yale University, because Jews were "a foreign body in the class organism."[36] So, foreign or nativist, in government or in media or in the academy, Soviet or U.S., there are ideas of good people and bad people—and the Jews are among the bad people, sometimes so bad that they are likened to parasites and crawling things. In England in 1190 Jews, "besieged by a fanatical Christian mob,"[37] committed mass suicide, and a century later were expelled from the country. In Seville in 1391 four thousand Jews were murdered in a riot; within a few months another fifty thousand were killed throughout Spain. In 1941–1942, 185,000 Jews were deported to a wilderness in Romania, and "in this obscure and remote theater of the war, the [Romanian] army murdered every one of these people, stripping them naked, and shooting them in subzero temperatures. On a few occasions, when soldiers were low on bullets, they shot only the adults and buried the children live."[38] Seville in 1391, a remote patch of Romania 1941–1942: why? Really: why?

Even after the genocide of World War II, Jews were still pogrommed, the best-known event being in Kielce, Poland, where, after the war, there were two hundred living Jews out of what had been a population of thirty thousand: "Violence erupted when a nine-year-old shoemaker's son reported to the militia that Christian children were being murdered in cellars for ritual purposes. Almost instantly, a bloodthirsty mob surrounded the headquarters of the local Jewish committee. Forty-two Jews were killed and scores were injured."[39] Throughout Poland there were individual murders of Jews and small riots. Some say the anti-Semitic post-Holocaust violence, especially in Poland, was because Jewish property had been appropriated, stolen, as Jews disappeared; some postulate an innate Polish anti-Semitism, cousin to and variation on both Russian and German anti-Semitism. Were the forty-two Jews killed in Kielce surprised? Did they think, "I've seen the worst, survived the worst; now I will go home"? Did they think, "I'm alone, the only one left" forty-two times? Did they know each other and the neighbors who killed them? Did they think of "home" and "peace" as synonyms; or did they know that both "home" and "peace" would be more lies and aggression—assault, beatings, murder, plundering?

And the Nazis had used the pogrom: called *Kristallnacht* most commonly. The sustained mass riots against the Jews began on November 9, 1938, and lasted several days: "Approximately a hundred Jews were killed, and thirty thousand Jews were seized and sent to concentration camps. In spite of official attempts to call a halt to the violence on November 10, sporadic incidents continued in some areas until November 13. It was a pogrom the likes of which Central Europe had not seen for five centuries. The destruction of windows in shops owned by Jews gave the event its name—Night of Broken Glass. The shopwindow glass was all imported from Belgium, and replacement would require half the annual production of the Belgian glass industry, as Göring would soon complain."[40] Damage to Jews and Jewish property "was estimated at several million marks."[41] And in the diaries of Jewish women, the emotional anti-Semitism of the Russians was repeated in the reasoned violence of the Germans; as Marion A. Kaplan writes in *Between Dignity and Despair: Jewish Life in Nazi Germany:* "As in Russian pogroms at the turn of the century, the mobs tore up feather blankets and pillows, shaking them into the rooms, out the windows, and down the stairways. Jews were deprived of their bedding and the physical and psychological sense of well-being it represented. Broken glass in public," says Kaplan, "and strewn feathers in private spelled the end of Jewish security in Germany."[42] The public and the private spheres were both targets of the organized violence; writers on *Kristallnacht* have acknowledged the economic loss, the public terror, the savage public violence against Jews, men in particular; it was the pogromists themselves who did not forget the private sphere, the home, where the women and the children were; a night of broken glass, shiny, glimmering, sharp and dangerous; who could care about the feathers—the night of broken feathers?

Understanding that *Kristallnacht* was a pogrom clarifies how the targets reacted: with horror, with fear, with familiarity. Given the patterns of expulsion and murder that were the history of the Jewish people, how could anyone foresee worse? More of the same was not worse. But why was more of the same okay, especially with the "civilized non-Jews"? And why was more of the same all right in the middle of the twentieth century in the middle of Europe? Why was another pogrom okay with the United States and Great Britain, Norway or Sweden, France or Italy? Was Freud right when he said in a letter, "[M]y opinion is that we must as Jews, if we want to cooperate with other people, develop a little masochism and be prepared to endure a little injustice."[43] Empirically speaking, Freud's strategy had been discredited in massacre after massacre. Or was the Polish dissident Adam Mitchnik right when he eloquently proposed, "When they are beating the Poles I will be a Pole. And when they are beating the Jews I will be a Jew. Today they are beating the Jews, and I want to be on the side of those being beaten."[44] Courageous, honest, with authentic conscience, Mitchnik's words provide a counterpoint to the words of Bialyk: "they died like dogs, and they were dead!"

Or was Holocaust survivor and novelist George Konrád right when he wrote, "It is my duty to resist any logic, any line of thought that leads to mass murder."[45] Sounds right, sounds noble; but it is all in the mind. Still, it is true that a head can stop a bullet. Or were radical, secular Jews who emigrated to Palestine before 1914 right when "[t]hey started building a military force, patiently and consistently"? Probably; almost certainly yes; except for Deir Yassin, an Arab village, where the Irgun, a Jewish militia group, slaughtered 250 people, this time Jews committing a pogrom against unarmed civilians; except for the destruction of 450 Arab settlements in 1948 in the new state of Israel; except for this testimony from an Israeli soldier: "I saw many things while stationed in the occupied territories. I was there when demonstrators were beaten, I was there when a family was given ten minutes to clear out of their house because it was going to be blown up. Suddenly you don't feel any hatred anymore. All I saw was women crying, and children—a family standing in front of a house containing most of their belongings, and within seconds it would all be gone. I was filled with self-loathing."[46] There is no record of Cossack introspection; but Jewish conscience existed even in the militarist Israeli modality, hard, smart, tough, one who had benefited from the turn-around: the Jews were "us/the good," the Arabs were "them/the bad." Hate and violence had not yet destroyed him; he knew that he was "one of us" and that he had done bad, not good.

Women, writes feminist historian Gerda Lerner, "have lived in a world in which they apparently had no history."[47] The history would have had to be a history of rape: the pogrom against the female body, the punishment for being her, not him. There was myth, which glorified rape; there was art, which celebrated rape. But until Susan Brownmiller published *Against Our Will: Men, Women, and Rape* in 1976, there were no facts of history that documented rape: no times, places, frequencies, categories, numbers, names; there was no historical record of loss and grief, invasion and violation; there was no conception of either scale or individuality, the mass or the meaning. Brownmiller rescued the reality of rape from the worship of those, primarily men, who made culture. A common strategy among the myth makers was to use irony to endorse rape and also to exert a claim of superiority to the rapist. Perhaps the most famous such witti-cism is from Herodotus, recently cited to enthusiastic reception by Roberto Calasso in his vile but celebrated *The Marriage of Cadmus and Harmony:* "To abduct women is considered the action of scoundrels, but to worry about abducted women is the reaction of fools. The wise man," Herodotus continues, "does not give a moment's thought to the women who have been abducted, because it is clear that, had they not wanted to be abducted, they would not have been."[48] The word *rape* comes from the Latin, *rapere,* abduction. Or as Calasso puts it in his own words: "And the conflict begins with the abduction of a girl, or with the sacrifice of a girl. And the one is continually becoming the other."[49] Women were raped by gods and bulls, demons and one, arguably, by the Holy Ghost; royalty raped or tried to rape women who, in resisting, became saints. (See *Inter-course.*) What the makers of myth have obfuscated by their hyperbole, painters in the Western tradition rescued into visual cogency. The emo-tional legitimacy and secular sacredness of art protected the act of rape from scrutiny: "As with Titian's love objects, and Reubens' rapes, the rep-utation of an artist can sanctify the unacceptable to such an extent that it can feel philistine even to question it."[50]

There is not only the so-called representation of the female body; there is a language that circles it, bounds it, characterizes it. Edward Mullins became "aware that the museums of the world could be hung exclusively with pictures of women being tortured and raped, and the language of scholarship would remain the same."[51] For women rape is the paradigmatic act of contempt and violence. Like the pogrom, the reach of rape goes far beyond any literal rendering of the act. Rape can include assault, battery, robbery, torture, kidnapping, mutilation, stalking, being prostituted, being pornographized, being sold as a sex slave, murder, and cannibalism (particularly in vogue among serial killers). And rape is very lonely. Should she survive, rape can make a woman lonely for the rest of her life. Who is one of them, and who is one of us? Is there an us?

Both Gerda Lerner and Eva Hoffman point out a congruence between women and Jews. For Lerner, these are "the two groups which have for the longest time in human history been marginalized and oppressed."[52] Hoffman notes that "[i]n the last decades of the seventeenth century and the beginning of the eighteenth, several hundred Jews were accused of blood libel and executed. During the same years, more than a thousand women were accused of witchcraft and burned at the stake."[53] After the Holocaust, women poets, in particular Sylvia Plath and Muriel Rukeyser, made connections in their poems between women and Jews and, more offensively to many, men and Nazis. Repeatedly denounced as immoral, cheap, cheapening the Holocaust, disrespectful, ignorant, the insight was not facile. Rape has been both a strategy of war and of genocide over centuries; in national, religious, ethnic, and political wars women are raped the way that Jews are pogrommed. The missing link here is that Jews are generally not massacred by other communities of like-minded Jews; whereas women endure enemy rape and intrafamilial rape, a sort of inescapable friendly fire. Rape is an act of hate committed by both friend and enemy. Rape is an act of revenge committed by strangers and by intimates. Rape has been—and continues to be in most parts of the world— a right of marriage protected by law; the husband owns legal access to the woman's body—he owns it, he decides when to use it. "Must one revolt against God," asks Evelyne Accad in her novel *L'Excisée*, "in order to break these chains which even women attribute to God? Must one revolt against the Man and the Father, against all the fathers . . . What must now be done? Must one revolt continuously, indefinitely?"[54] Ethicist James Q. Wilson in *The Moral Sense* blames, as so many conservatives do, the Enlightenment, not God or the father: the Enlightenment, he suggests, taught hatred of the oppressor; while "Good Samaritans rush to the aid of a rapist's victim instinctively, enraged by the rapist's actions."[55] In other words, the nice, instinctively antirape people, who would help the rape victim in any circumstance, were initiated into hate (of the rapist) by political ideologues who used rage to mobilize the oppressed but "[t]he Enlightenment and its disciples did not tell us how to handle rage."[56] Where is that Good Samaritan; who is he; what is the instinct that put him on the side of the raped; is the rage of the Good Samaritan, as opposed to the rage of the rapist or the rage of the raped, a hidden problem, unarticulated because anomalous?

Still, the Enlightenment was rape-friendly. Diderot was an advocate of incest, because he saw no natural (in nature) argument against it; prohibition of incest was irrational, he thought—and he was an advocate for reason, he thought. Well, that was then and this is now. There are rapists, the raped, and bystanders who watch: for instance, the gang rape in New Bedford, Massachusetts, of a lone woman on a pool table in a bar filled with men who cheered the rapist on; or, for the fainter of heart, real rapes on video. But no one—no one—has been or is now aiding rape victims "instinctively"; such aid is a learned behavior and humans are slow learners.

The only question about rape and rage that deserves any scrutiny is how and why women bear both, endure both, rarely turning violent even in self-defense; rarely committing mass murders even in the face of mass rapes; there is no underground of committed assassins to get the raper: she died like a dog, and she was dead! She has been kept captive (abducted, kidnapped) by husband, friend, or stranger—"the victim cannot express her humiliated rage at the perpetrator, for to do so would jeopardize her survival."[57] She needs a bullet to stop him, but does not have one or will not use it. When he is gone, "the former prisoner may continue to fear retribution and may be slow to express rage against her captor."[58] "Slow" takes on a whole new meaning here; this is the kind of "slow" so slow that galaxies are born and die in the duration. The woman raped "is left with a burden of unexpressed rage against all those who remained indifferent to her fate and who failed to help her."[59] This is a rage too big for any little girl of whatever age; this is a rage from which rapists and their accomplices should die. Therapy is a poor excuse for justice.

Babel, in his *1920 Diary*, documented Cossack rape as well as pogrom: "Terrible business, soldiers' love, two lusty Cossacks made a deal with the same woman. Can you take it, I can take it, one of them had three goes, the other moves in, she spins around the room, makes a mess all over the floor, they throw her out, don't pay her, she'd tried too hard."[60] A whore, she consented; and she was raped. She tried to control it, the violence that would come at her and in her; and she was robbed and raped. She thought, if I give it, they won't take it; if I do what they want, they will stop short of destroying me—money will be recognition that I set the terms; and she was invaded and raped. Or, from Babel, this one-line entry: "The nurse—26 men and a girl."[61]

Babel considered all military rape the same: "The hatred is the same, the Cossacks just the same, the cruelty the same, it's nonsense to think one army is different from another."[62] And he described the aftermath: "The girls and women, all of them, can scarcely walk."[63] He indicted the Poles, the Cossacks, and the Soviets.

Even nakedness can be used to shame, to torture, to destroy: in Castro's Cuba, "they took the women in naked for interrogations by groups of officers . . . and many of the suicides among women are triggered precisely by that humiliation. Even today the government still employs this practice with women political prisoners. When they are confined to solitary, they are completely undressed and then officers from the jail, Prison Headquarters, and the Political Police stop by to see them."[64] Nakedness and the vulnerability it emphasizes were used by the Nazis to destroy what the body should affirm: humanness.

In contemporary Russia, half the murders reported are murders of wives by intimates—not half of the women murdered are wives murdered by intimates, but half of all murders in the new Russian gangland are murders of wives by intimates. Wife-beating is ubiquitous. Women are "kidnapped, then taken to a brothel where they [are] raped and beaten."[65] And, as a consequence of *perestroika,* the years between Babel's diary and the end of the twentieth century are filled in: "A woman recollects the practice of mass rape when guards let the other non-prisoners rape imprisoned women for bottles of vodka."[66]

In Belgrade, women conclude "after two years of war . . .: Violence against women and war against women exists at all times and everywhere; during war it intensifies and increases. The war has indeed proved that most women calling the hotlines already know most forms of war-violence. One woman recently said to us: 'I am not afraid of war, living with my husband. I am already 20 years in war.'"[67] In Croatia women live "as victims of sexual violence, as refugees, as targets of political harassment . . .

and as victims of intensified domestic violence as the consequence of war and militarism (men are returning home from the battle fields armed and every day newspapers are full with 'tragic events' in which women were killed and the killing justified by war and 'his trauma')."[68]

In Nanking during the Sino-Japanese War, "an estimated 20,000–80,000 Chinese women were raped. Many soldiers went beyond rape to disembowel women, slice off their breasts, nail them alive to walls."[69] Because of international criticism, the Japanese decided to build underground prisons that functioned as brothels in which kidnapped women from Korea, China, Taiwan, the Philippines, and Indonesia were used. The first official brothel opened near Nanking in 1938. The women were referred to as "public toilets."[70] There were Japanese soldiers who believed that "raping virgins would make them more powerful in battle. Soldiers were even known to wear amulets made from the pubic hair of such victims . . . The military police forbidding rape only encouraged soldiers to kill their victims afterwards."[71]

The Turks, at the beginning of the twentieth century, "reportedly raped 150 women and girls in Krushovo. Wild dogs and pigs devoured the naked corpses. Throughout Macedonia it was the same. . . . Estimates put the total number of women and girls raped by the Turks at over 3,000."[72] The Turkish genocide against the Armenians set the tone: Hitler found it instructive—no one stopped the Turks, no one would stop him. This genocide "was particularly cruel to Armenian women and girls, who became the objects of a pervasive, tacitly sanctioned campaign of rape. Turkish police encouraged gangs of thugs to prey upon the deportees as a means of humiliating and destroying these women."[73] The females who did survive largely changed their religion to Islam and became concubines and slaves.

It has been easiest to see rape as hostile and hating when the rape is nationalistic or racist or colonial: the aggressors take the women and use them; women are booty; the males of the defeated group are humiliated, proven impotent and inferior; feminized and disgraced. The point has usually been made that the men are hurt; the injury consisting in lost property, including land, animals, and women. Freedom and property are virtual synonyms in war-barter; he who has the most land, women, and animals has the most freedom.

Indians and European whites did war-barter on the newly found continent of the Americas. This is the first record of white-man rape of an indigenous woman: "And she being naked as is their custom, I conceived the desire to take my pleasure. I wanted to put my desire into execution, but she was unwilling for me to do so, and treated me with her nails in such wise that I would have preferred never to have begun. But seeing this . . . I took a rope-end and thrashed her well, following which she produced such a screaming and wailing as would cause you not to believe your ears. Finally we reached an agreement, such that, I can tell you, she seemed to have been raised in a veritable school of harlots."[74] Columbus personally blessed the rape.

The Spanish had the reputation of not forcing women but accepting them as gifts. This is, perhaps, a distinction without a difference. But the tribes of North America also used war-barter; for instance, the Cheyenne, in one circumstance, "gave up the two older German girls, aged fifteen and seventeen, who, for half a year had, as the journals of the period would put it, 'suffered all the unspeakable horrors of Indian captivity.'"[75] These horrors were not modified by a utopian primitivism or a natural savage approach to women: "A woman could usually expect to find herself traded from brave to brave, and her lot was not at all mitigated by the jealousy of the wives whose beds she temporarily usurped and who took every opportunity to cuff the captive about and load her down with onerous tasks."[76] Men of the Modoc nation actually pimped, having organized a traffic in women: " . . . they made themselves brokers in female flesh because they had nothing to offer in the way of handiwork, pelts, feathers, or the other ordinary commodities. They brought girls and young women to annual trade meetings, where the Northern tribes eagerly purchased the unhappy slaves for concubines. So, when they turned their women over to the miners, it was sanctioned by old custom and was not a depravity forced on them by white men."[77] And still, it was the North American Indians who were slaughtered: 100,000 in California in 1848; a decade later there were 30,000 survivors; at the end of the nineteenth century, there were 15,000. In the genocide, which is the right word to describe the fairly systematic killing of Indians in the seventeenth, eighteenth, and nineteenth centuries, "women were brutalized by gang rapes; men were captured like animals and forced to do field labor, kidnapped children were treated as slaves."[78]

In India women can be murdered with impunity any time in life: female fetuses are aborted; female infants are killed; a husband can kill his wife by burning her if he finds her dowry insufficient; and when he dies, she is still supposed to enter a fire live and be ritually burned to death. Widows are disgraced, essentially exiled into a barbarous social death. In a society in which a woman's life never has civil significance, in which her life is worthless at any moment, how does one count rapes? In 1986, "the number of rape cases registered in the country was 7,321; this is believed to be just a fraction of the total number of rapes that take place but do not get reported."[79] Given the low status of females in India and the massive population, the statistical equivocation—a form of female modesty—is almost funny: a heartbreaking, bitter funny. Child marriages were outlawed in India in 1929, but "statistics for Bengal in the early nineteenth century list twelve- and thirteen-year-old widows burning on the pyres of their deceased husbands. At the last census of the nineteenth century, there were 10,000 widows under the age of four, and over 50,000 between the ages of five and nine in and around Calcutta alone."[80]

In Pakistan, "rape is also employed as a weapon by political opponents. In April 1992, twenty female polling agents, including a former woman politician, were raped . . . in an organized effort to disrupt voting."[81] *Zina*, which is sex out of wedlock, is the woman's crime when she has been raped: "[T]he victim is prosecuted. Her legal complaint of rape is considered a confession of illicit sexual intercourse."[82] At the same time, rape is part of torture in Algeria and Sudan; and high school students have experienced mass rape in Kenya. According to documentation presented by at least one Iraqi dissident, Iraqi civil servants are "paid a salary to rape Iraqi women."[83] The dissident asks "what a document like this tells us about how widespread the practice of rape must have become in order for such paperwork to be routinely generated."[84] It is not only in Iraq that prisons for women can be described this way: "Every major prison seems to have had its own specially equipped rape room (replete in one case with soft-porn pictures stuck on the wall opposite the surface being used)."[85]

Any of these rapes or strategies of rape are Kishinev and the six hundred pogroms that followed in the next few years, or the feathers flying from Germany's November pogrom of 1938. Every one of these rapists is a Nazi; and every one of the raped is a Jew: which is to say that rape is a manifestation of sexual fascism, the woman the scapegoated victim.

The Nazis have managed to foster a good reputation as not-rapists. With the Nuremberg Laws passed in 1935, sexual intercourse between so-called Aryans and Jews was forbidden. The rules, of course, were not quite that simple: Jewishness was calibrated according to a statistical scheme invented by the Nazis. For several decades, Hitler's associate Julius Streicher had been publishing *Der Stürmer* (according to one translator: slang for "lady killers"), a purposefully pornographic attack on Jewish men as rapacious assaulters of pure German women, a tabloid in which Jewish women, too, were characterized as provocative, manipulative, seductive whores: "In one case the Jewish woman was accused of being a 'sex-craved, morally degenerate Jew-woman, who with her unrestrained sexual desire and ruthless determination had the defendant under her strong influence.'"[86] "Jew-whore" was favored by the Gestapo as a form of address. The fascist laws against what anti-Semites took to be miscegenation and their deep fear of contamination, a sexually communicated filth, have led to the belief that though the Nazis were sadists on a scale heretofore unknown, they did not rape "Jew-whores." But the system they built was permeated with sexual sadism: from assault and intimidation to physical attack and rape to forced nakedness and torture. The world of women, even under the Nazis, had the written rules, the unwritten rules, and the real rules. Under the real rules, German Nazis (not their Ukrainian or Lithuanian or Polish enforcers) sexually harassed women in the streets of the ghetto: "In daylight they reviled me as a Jewish woman and at night they wanted to kiss me,"[87] said one woman. "During the Hitler era I had the immense burden of rejecting brazen advances from SS and SA men. Each time I answered: 'I'm sorry . . . I'm married. . . .' If I had said I was Jewish, they would have insisted that I had approached them."[88] A political woman, tortured by the SA, "had to undress completely. A howling pack goaded on by alcohol surrounded her. They stuck pens in her vagina and paper flags which they burned so that they could gloat over [her] screams of pain."[89] In Auschwitz, one kapo was "a twenty-two-year-old deranged sadist. . . . He . . . had his own room where girls, including Jewish girls, entertained him."[90] In his last will and testament, dated December 1942, Avraham Tory, who kept a diary in the Kovno ghetto, wrote: "I heard the weeping of women who were raped in public and humiliated despicably . . ."[91] Vera Laska, who extensively documented the day-to-day hell of women in the concentration and killing camps, said: "I know from others that some women were gang raped but that was not routine."[92] Her judgment had much to do with the physical disgust, so antagonistic to being attractive for men, that she and others felt for themselves: "Why should the SS risk their necks for intercourse with dirty, unattractive females, without hair, dirty, smelly."[93] Still, she acknowledged, "the SS could—and did—do as they pleased with any female inmate . . ."[94] Laska considered the possibility of punishment under the Nuremberg Laws a bar to Nazi sexual fraternization with Jewish women; as a result, she talks about intercourse, attractiveness, and desire more easily than she discusses rape, gang rape, and other sexual abuse. She also makes the statistical point, probably correct, that given "the tens of thousands of women incarcerated in the camps, rape by the SS was relatively rare."[95] Still, she laments, as she must, "[t]he crude abuses of the bodies and the subtle torments of the soul; the degradations of human dignity and the humiliation of womanhood, with or without rape!"[96] She describes the SS coming to the showers "to jeer, tease and taunt the defenseless [naked] women. Stripping the women naked was also practiced at times of camp selections, or on long and boring Sunday afternoons, when the SS had nothing better to do than . . . expose the powerless women to a cruel parade."[97] In Warsaw Germany's most important industrialist, Walther Caspar Többens, would give parties "at which he forced young Jewish girls to dance in the nude."[98] Also in Warsaw, SS men Heinrich Klaustermeyer and Josef Blösche—"the latter known to the Jews as Frankenstein— . . . would fire at strollers or people standing in windows, rape and then slay young women, and force some victims to drink poison."[99] Hitler's German biographer Joachim G. Fest describes what he considers a credible story of an attempt by Hitler to rape a half-Jewish woman. In a Nazi labor camp, the senior authority "was an utter beast of a man who derived great pleasure from his bestiality, especially towards defenceless Jewish women and girls."[100] In Auschwitz, a group of male Jewish inmates saw "a group of women, naked and with their heads shaved, [they] ran out, behind them [were] a number of SS men, herding them along with whips. . . . We simply had to stand there and watch as the SS men whipped and beat the women and screamed at them like pigs."[101] There had been 90,000 Jews in Slovakia; 20,000 of them had been "sent to Poland," where it was reported "that a large number of girls between the ages of sixteen and twenty-six 'have been sent to the military brothels created at the Polish frontier.'"[102] In Auschwitz, the angel of death, Josef Mengele, did medical experiments on twins: "Under controlled conditions, the twins were forced into intercourse to see whether their offspring would also be twins,"[103] says Laska; but those who were experimented on and survived (a tiny number) are not certain. "Several twins believe that Mengele had pairs of twins mate," say Lucette Matalon Lagnado and Sheila Cohn Dekel in *Children of the Flames: Dr. Josef Mengele and the Untold Story of the Twins of Auschwitz.* "There are hushed testimonies to that effect. . . .

No twin will elaborate on what he or she knew: Even in the nightmare world of Auschwitz, there were taboos, and this was the ultimate one. That Mengele breached it is not unlikely, given the awful scope of his experiments."[104]

Rape, including Nazi rape, rarely stands alone; it is murder's heartbeat, prostitution's first cause, sadism's undergirding. It is not surprising, then, that Arek Hersh remembers this sight, encountered on a death march: "Before my eyes was a whole wagon full of dead bodies, all women, all unclothed, just skeletons. I was sickened by the sight."[105]

But the story of rape in Hitler's war does not stop there. As the Russians advanced from the east into Germany itself, they raped German women: "Earliest medical estimates placed the number of rapes at a minimum of 20,000. There may have been as many as 100,000. No wonder," says Peter Wyden, that "6,000 Berliners committed suicide at that time."[106] The Russians seemed to see it as payback time, "a collective punishment both personal to the utmost extreme and impersonal"; there was "a wave of rapes . . . that would eventually ravage nearly every female, from children to grandmothers"; "[t]he target had to be female and German . . ."[107] Not too long after in Paris women were being punished for *collaboration horizontale;* "there are photographs of women stripped naked, tarred with swastikas, forced to give Nazi salutes, then paraded in the streets to be abused . . . There are also reports in some areas of women tortured, even killed . . . In the 18th arrondissement, a working-class area, a prostitute who had served German clients was kicked to death."[108]

There is no doubt that there was more Nazi rape of Jewish women than anyone has been willing to acknowledge; and also that more Jewish women were prostituted to Nazis, by Nazis, for Nazis than any one account can comprehend. Rape, gang rape, forced prostitution, forced sibling incest, torture, mass murder and also slow, sadistic murder: the Nazis were number one. No one did it better. So does it matter that German/Nazi women were raped by the Russian liberators of concentration camps; and that French sexual collaborators were sexually debased? Yes.

In Israel, an antirape group began disseminating this slogan in December 1996: "They cannot force [double entendre: rape] you to keep silent."[109] But that forced silence (double entendre) is as old as the heritage of Judaism itself: "For the rabbis, the dominant male role in sexuality and study of Torah were intimately, indeed inseparably, linked."[110] Guns need not be used to exclude women from rights of safety and citizenship; keeping the most holy dimension of a culture out-of-bounds for women pushes women to the margins; and those in the margins get raped—by learned men, by fools, with guns or without. The murder rate in Israel has soared 30 percent in 1997 compared with 1996. Because of the increasing number of fatal attacks on women by their intimates, Israeli women are demanding some kind of gun control; "[c]urrently more than 250,000 Israelis—out of a total population of 5.75 million—have gun permits."[111] Indeed, the men are armed; the women appear not to be. In the promised land, Israeli Jewish men rape Israeli Jewish women; was this the "light among nations" promise or the "normal country" one? Two cases show the malice and the power: the gang rape of a fourteen-year-old girl by a group of older adolescent boys, fellow communards in her kibbutz; and the Supreme Court decision that held rape by an intimate to be a lesser crime than stranger rape (*Binyamin* v. *The State of Israel*).

But beyond malice and power, there is an abyss of absurdity and cruelty that few tourists see, for instance, the situation of a sixty-two-year-old woman who was jailed for two weeks, not allowed to consult a lawyer, because she had left a battering husband and refused to accept no alimony as part of the divorce settlement. As Israeli activist Ofra Friedman said, "Almost every day we hear of men who beat their wives to death and don't even get arrested, or are released immediately by the courts. . . . But an elderly, sick, unemployed woman, with no income, is thrown into prison for two weeks, because she didn't want to be forced into a penniless state?"[112] Is it that men who beat or rape or murder their own commit the same acts against a racial or ethnic other with a certain ease, a certain familiarity, a certain arrogance, a certain conviction of righteousness and self-righteousness? Or, conversely, does the enemy woman (meaning the woman of the enemy) ignite a misogynist anger that is used against her and then taken home to make present what has been an absent manhood? As Simona Sharoni notes in *Gender and the Israeli-Palestinian Conflict: The Politics of Women's Resistance:* "The Gulf War challenged for the first time the clear division of roles between men warriors and women caretakers. This time, unlike in all previous wars and emergency situations, Israeli men were not drafted into service. Men remained on the homefront . . . with the vulnerability and helplessness of being locked in sealed rooms to protect themselves from the threat of gas attacks. . . . Unable to express themselves violently against Arabs, as they were socialized to do, many Israeli men 'cured' their feelings of impotence and longings for the excitement of the battlefield by projecting their aggression onto women and children."[113]

In Israel, masculinity and aggression are expressed in the simple straightforwardness of modern Hebrew, a language stripped of biblical eloquence or lyrical artifice. This denuding of linguistic floweriness or glossy nuance makes the language itself ruder, more brazen, an easy brutality. As Yaron Ezrahi writes in *Rubber Bullets: Power and Conscience in Modern Israel,* "The Hebrew expression for arms (*klei zayin*) is also used as slang for the male organ, and this linguistic connection seems to reinforce the notion that by carrying a gun a boy becomes a potent male."[114] This is a common association, newly invented in modern Hebrew. Not surprisingly and not uniquely, "soldiers who are afraid to fight are often reprimanded for behaving 'like women'; linking shooting and potency fosters the fighting spirit."[115] During the intifada Palestinian boys shouted insults aimed at the genitalia of the Israeli soldiers: "Thus provoked, a few of the soldiers ordered not to shoot were unable to hold their fire."[116] Israeli payback, excluding the shooting, does have a certain *je ne sais quoi,* expressed best by Jan Goodwin in her book on Muslim women: "The Israeli army . . . may be the only one in the world routinely to sexually expose themselves and begin to masturbate as a means to disperse Arab women demonstrators or groups of women."[117] Given the vulnerability of the male sexual organ, the women may be running in the wrong direction.

Inside Israel, the artists keep pushing male violence against women as an indisputable premise of eroticism: "A woman needs strength, too," writes Amos Oz in the novel *Elsewhere Perhaps.* "And violence. Not completely. Right to the end. There's always something that holds back, that doesn't take part. And that's terribly humiliating for a woman."[118] These musings, of course, are put into the mouth of a female character. Peace Now with the Palestinians; but let's heat up the war a little at home. "He thinks about women," writes Oz. "He has read somewhere recently that a woman's heart is a riddle that no man can solve. Women really do live in a different world. A more colorful world. Even when they are with you, they are not really with you. But the fault is yours. You let her fix the rules of the game. There is an expression 'to conquer a woman.' Like an enemy stronghold. Like fortifications. If you are like a woman, no woman will ever surrender to you."[119] It is clear: make her into a Palestinian, conquered; or—another variation on an old theme—you be the Israeli and let her be the Jew.

Michael Ryan's memoir concretized Oz's fictional eroticism: "She was my student during the week, and my lover on weekends. She said she felt invaded. She said she didn't know where I ended and she began. I just wanted more and more of her, to take her further sexually than she had ever gone and then some—further than she ever would go again. This fantasy was the way I could stay inside sex with her, and why she thought I was like another person when we went into sex. I *was* another person: I was her molester. To be invaded, to be confused about where the other person ends and you begin: this is what it feels like to be molested."[120] The "different world" (to use Oz's locution) in which women live is created by hostile sexuality, brutal sexuality, abusive sexuality, domineering and dominating sexuality; the consequences are as Sally Cline describes them in her biography of Radclyffe Hall: "extreme nervousness, outbursts of wild temper, feelings of restriction, fears of being out of control, a sense of dread, usually a fear or belief that the self has been lost, and often the need to recapture an authentic identity by an ambitious drive to greater and greater efforts accompanied by a feeling of wonder or disbelief at the achievement attained."[121] And, says Cline of the sexually brutalized female: "[S]he may abandon her belief in the possibility of her own personal safety and re-create dangerous situations for herself and her intimates."[122]

Women have increasingly understood that the brutalization of enemy women and the brutalization of love in the country of home are more the same than different; in Israel and the West Bank and Gaza, Israeli and Palestinian women have "documented cases of sexual abuse of Palestinian women by the Israeli police (strip searches in public, constant sexual innuendo, threat of rape, use of photographs of Palestinian women being fondled by Israeli security officers as a means of pressuring confessions . . .)."[123] Sharoni discusses "the sexual harassment and sexual violence inflicted upon Palestinian women prisoners . . . not only during interrogation but also in the context of street patrols and the suppression of demonstrations."[124] Threat of rape, unwanted touching, masturbation onto a woman, and threat of publicizing pornography made of her in Israeli captivity (her head on another woman's body) are used to extort confessions. Just as Hoover's FBI used wife-beating by Klan men to manipulate those same men, the Israeli security forces use the Arab honor system, which demands that girls be virgins or be killed, to inflame the anger, intrafamilial and public, of Palestinians. In the Arab code, a brother (or father) is supposed to kill a sister (daughter) for defaming the family's honor by having sex outside of a sanctified marriage. So, when Israeli security agents threaten a woman with the publication of a pornographic picture of her, they are threatening her life; and if she is raped, she can be killed. This, too, has happened: an Arab woman is bludgeoned to death by her brother because she has had forbidden sex, and the murder is made to "look as though she had been killed by a Jew."[125] In the recent past, there have been violent acts by Palestinian women against Israeli targets, the subtext being that the women had been defiled (by Arab or Israeli, an intimate or a stranger) and wanted deaths as political martyrs rather than as not-virgin-enough sacrifices. (See Kanan Makiya, *Cruelty and Silence: War, Tyranny, Uprising and the Arab World.*)

How many rapes would it take to intimidate a population, Israeli or Palestinian? How many pogroms did it take to intimidate Jews? The prototypical violent act directed against a subordinate class of people has astonishing power. Think of the lynching of blacks in the United States South. From 1907 to 1917, "'white Mississippians lynched an estimated eighty-three black men, two white men, and one black woman. . . . [In 1920] thirteen lynchings took place in Mississippi.' Only Georgia, with fourteen, had more."[126] Lynching was the paradigmatic act of violence by white supremacists against blacks; a whole host of insult and injury went with it. How many rapes before women learn their place? How many pogroms? How many wives are beaten in thirty-six seconds or in a ten-by-twelve-foot room? These questions miss nearly every point that matters: these acts of violence are emblematic acts of terror; they are acts of hatred and hostility; they are murderous in intent; and what's the name of the guy and his address? The rest is diversion, except for noting that women have the singular good luck to be raped by men who hate them and by men who love them, by men who know them and by men who do not, by husbands, lovers, friends, and invading armies—as well as by serial rapists, serial killers, and any woman-hater who has had a really bad day. "As a lonely woman," says Susanna Ronconi, a former member of Italy's Red Brigade, "I had a particular relationship with weapons; for me to carry a gun was a defensive action and a protective one as well. I spent seven years going around armed, yet for me the chief importance of my gun was that it defended me. It was an exception when I used it offensively."[127] Ronconi's statement has nearly the same meaning as these words from sex-crimes prosecutor Alice Vachss: "It took me almost all the time I was at the Queens DA's office to understand that doing things right was a direction, not a destination. But I think I understood early on that there were no neutral corners to rest in, and that any power I might have to fight came from being prepared, always, to go the distance."[128]

Inside the law or outside it, the rapist lives in one world with many places to hide, corners that are not so much neutral as unequivocally his. In the U.S. "[o]nly 1 percent of rapes are ultimately resolved by arrest and conviction of the offender. Thus, the most common trauma of women remains confined to the sphere of private life. There is no public monument for rape survivors."[129] But there may be some day, because Israeli men get raped; and Israel has a lot of public monuments. Another part of the Arab code, coexisting with the obligation of the father or brother to kill the sister for sexual impurity, is the rape of a defeated foe, soldier, male. Israeli prisoners of war in Arab custody will be familiar with this form of Arab revenge, practiced, for instance, against an earlier generation of Israeli soldiers: "Some of my friends were raped next to my eyes." Then, later, in a Jordanian prison camp, "We had groups coming in the middle of the night, captured, and most of them suffered the trauma of being raped, not by one or two but by companies. It's a way of disgracing your enemy."[130] This revenge vendetta through male-male rape finally creates an injury that demands blood, murder, a viscous hate. Nothing in Madrid or Oslo or in the Rose Garden of the White House will repair a male-on-male military rape. Nor will raped men join with raped women of any description—wife, mother, sister, Jew, feminist. The revenge rape of male Israeli soldiers in captivity is part of the fear, part of the hate, that drives the Israeli fear of annihilation. Rape takes everything away.

4

THE STATE / THE FAMILY

Without romanticization: there have been sophisticated social groups that were not states or monarchies or feudal hierarchies or colonies or empires. Some indigenous peoples pioneered governance based on association, not hierarchy: for instance, the Iroquois League was formed to stop warfare among its constituent members—the Mohawks, the Oneidas, the Onandagas, the Cayugas, the Senecas, and later the Tuscaroras. Known as the Six Nations, its emblem was "the Tree of Peace, a great white pine whose living roots extended to the four extremities of the world, and whose crown was watched over by a fierce eagle alert for threats."[1] Using the strategy of armed deterrence centuries before it became Cold War Pentagon-speak and foreshadowing the League of Nations by centuries, the Iroquois doctrine "was that power was only the means to the end, and the end was peace."[2] The goal was: "'the land shall be beautiful, the river shall have no more waves, one may go everywhere without fear.'"[3] Clan identity, which traversed tribal lines, came from the mother; in these tribes (unlike in Jewish law), matrilineal descent meant that the status of women was high. A clan mother could replace a male leader (with another male) if she chose. Women could even stop war, because it was their right to withhold provisions. The civilized invaders from England and Europe apparently never grasped the fact that the Iroquois were not a tribe "but a league of tribes that had devised an advanced form of government . . ."[4]

Even now, after centuries of genocide in the Americas, indigenous people continue to pioneer governance based on association, not hierarchy and sectarian separation. For instance, the Crees in Canada "believe that self-determination is compatible with the territorial integrity of the state they live in. Self-determination need not be absolute; it need not imply formal statehood, flags, seats in the United Nations."[5] The Crees want to stop hydroelectric development that would surround their land and turn it into a prison of sorts; the Canadian constitution, a contemporary rendering of rights, honors the territorial, civil, and cultural rights of indigenous groups, so that the Cree have rights of equality in the Canadian state. The Cree will have standing in the law to stop the development that would destroy the quality of their lives and the integrity of their place in Canadian society.

The Crees are increasingly in charge of their own local government, police, and law: "Already, in many native communities of the north, justice is jointly administered by native elders and magistrates from the south."[6] It is not naive to note that within countries there need to be ways in which enemies can make peace, which means to find ways of association that are syncretic. Governance and self-determination do not require a state, a nineteenth-century invention like nationalism itself; but if you have one, I need two.

The state is curiously abstract unless it is in one's face. The state begins with the police; the more stuff that intervenes between a citizen and the police, the freer that citizen is. Much state apparatus exists either to bring the police closer or to create obstacles that keep them farther away. The state includes bureaucrats, civil servants, judges, prosecutors, bankers, a military, and the big guy, a president or prime minister or monarch or dictator. Police enforce laws; without police there is no state. The state is owed taxes, loyalty, and compliance. The state is too complicated for an individual to understand; and both taxes and law are complex diversions that make the state look smart and the individual feel stupid. The state is supposed to have some regard for its citizens and it is supposed to act for their welfare as well as in behalf of their values. The state makes and enforces rules; and in particular it regulates and mandates the rules of nature, which may be hallucinatory, crazed, or sociopathic: for instance, the differences between men and women; or the differences between so-called Aryans and Jews; or the differences between white and black; or the differences between heterosexual and homosexual; or the differences, under Stalin, between workers and *kulaks* (so-called rich peasants, whom he tried to kill off). The state is built to put everything, everyone, in their natural place; nature is part of the authority that grounds state power so that hierarchies, polarities, and discriminations that the state sanctions will appear natural. The assumptions about the nature of the world—people, society, money, property, rights—inhere in how the state does business.

The state's premises are taken for granted by the state's citizens, which contributes to both stability and stasis. Those who argue with the state's construction of reality—who should do what, when, to whom—are dissidents. The punishment for being a dissident can range from the horror, the absolute horror, of not being invited to A-list parties (U.S.); to the gulag, the penal colony, prison, exile, torture, and death. Punishment confirms the rightness of the state's premises.

At the heart of the democratic state is the citizen, the person, the sentient human being; the U.S. and French revolutions (1776 and 1789) and the Enlightenment philosophy that originated in France especially gave rights to individuals that states were supposed to support and that states were forbidden to abrogate. The citizen, in the U.S. promised freedom and in France promised equality, had a new and novel dignity, a sovereignty that guaranteed self-rule and repudiated class-based submission or subordination. There was a sovereign state, and in it lived citizens with their own sovereignty. Women were not included in this civic largess; and in the U.S. slaves also were not included. But the notion that the ruling entity—kings with respect to America and France—had a natural right to domination was now supplanted by a new idea of the state and thus a new idea of nature itself: citizens had rights.

The states themselves did not have natural boundaries. There was nothing self-evident about a state's including these people but excluding those people, or including this land but excluding that land. The state may have incorporated a natural social order of roles and hierarchies, but the state itself had accidental or contested boundaries in nature, in geography, on the earth. Little wars and big wars changed boundaries and so did imperial powers. The borders of nation-states were not the work of either God or Charles Darwin.

The State of Israel goes the Enlightenment one better: it makes a distinction between citizenship and nationality. Put simply, "Israel is not the state of its citizens, but the state of the Jewish nation."[7] In other words, Israel is the state that represents the Jews that live inside its borders and Jews all over the world. This is the State's purpose, its burden, its responsibility. "There is no Israeli nation apart from the Jewish people," said the Israeli Supreme Court, "and the Jewish people consists not only of the people residing in Israel but also the Jews in the Diaspora . . ."[8] One might say that this redistributes not wealth or power but sovereignty, the kind of sovereignty a citizen has. It takes from the Arab who lived in Palestine and gives to the Jew who lives in New Jersey. Israeli soldiers are taught that "[a]

strong State of Israel means a state possessed of military, diplomatic, social, and economic strength, and moral character which can respond
properly to every threat from outside and provide assistance to every persecuted Jew wherever he [*sic*] is."⁹ This is a staggering commitment, with
roots in the Holocaust when the world did nothing to stop the genocide
of the Jews. Is it grandiose, deluded; do the Israelis think they are
Napoleon?

In May 1991, the Israeli Defense Forces "in an operation spectacular
even by their standards airlifted almost 15,000 endangered Ethiopian
Jews to Israel"¹⁰; where else would they have gone? who else would have
rescued them, "people suffering from intestinal parasites, infants and aged
people without means of support, a population that had not been introduced to cutlery and indoor plumbing, much less computer technology."¹¹ Not suffering fools gladly, Ruth R. Wisse goes on to draw what
should be, but is not, the obvious conclusion: "If the nations of the world
were capable of recognizing political truths, they might have seen that for
the first time in history African blacks were being brought westward for
purposes other than slavery."¹² Wisse calls this Israeli sense of responsibility "familial."¹³ Every Jew, however situated, thinks: someday I will need
them. No matter that once in Israel the Ethiopians became the lowest of
the low.

Yet the sense of responsibility cuts another way, too. Those Jews who
are part of the nation but not citizens of Israel, those Jews represented by
Israel as part of its mission, its purpose, have an obligation back: not to
accept the corruption of the Jewish state. "What happened," asks Moshe
Leshem in *Israel Alone: How the Jewish State Lost Its Way and How It Can
Find It Again*, "to the Zionist dream of creating not simply a Jewish state
but a model nation imbued with a new form of ethical nationalism . . .?"¹⁴
What is "ethical nationalism"? It must mean that I care for Israel and Israel cares for me; but then, is not my foot, too, on the neck of the Palestinian? Doesn't "ethical nationalism" suggest a pride that is the opposite of
nationalist or imperial pride, at the least a commitment to do no harm?

Amos Oz claims that "the dreamers were right in asserting from the
start that statehood is a vehicle, not a goal in itself"¹⁵—an astonishing
misstatement of the politics of Ben-Gurion and the other founders, for
whom Jewish statehood was everything, an absolute end; they wanted a
Jewish state without hesitation or ambivalence; they were ruthless enough
to allow no other value to divert them; they believed in the necessity and
even the inevitability of a Jewish state long before the Holocaust, for the

most part before the First World War. Despite the nearly universal contemporary conviction that the Holocaust established or led to the establishment of the Jewish state ("the Nazis gave the Jews Israel, you should be glad"), Ben-Gurion and his cohort arguably would have achieved the State without the Holocaust; they were too formidable to fail. What would a state be a vehicle to? Freedom, perhaps, or equality, or the early North American "Don't Tread on Me." But the claims of the Jewish state were broader: don't tread on me; or her; or them; they don't live here but they are part of the nation, so don't tread on them.

This could have been an ethical nationalism, a step toward a global family, an obligation of honor to a global community; a first step to making the unit of the state archaic, a nonimperial state with a particular human rights agenda, a state with metaphysical borders rather than military borders, a state beyond the constraints of geography: Israel, the safe harbor for the family. But Jews also wanted "normalization; the creation of conditions in which the Jews could live as a nation, like the others."[16] This goes to the heart of the problem: for the others, the state is the nation; the citizens of the state are the nation; the nation is not extraterritorial. Israel is not a so-called normal state, which is simply a fact, an obvious consequence of how the state defined itself: its citizens are not coterminous with the state, nor is the nation a synonym for the citizenry. What is the state? What are its premises? Which roles and polarities does it reify and endorse?

The first fact about the State of Israel is not that it exists as a result of conquest. As Wisse says: "Every country, emphatically including every one of the many Arab countries, can be said to exist at the expense of another. Arabs, having conquered more civilizations than any other people in history, are in the weakest position of all to deny the rights of conquest to a single, tiny Jewish state."[17] With respect to the Arab states, their borders for the most part were determined by the British and French; states do not exist in nature; states do have a view of what is natural: in Israel Jews are natural, Arabs are not; militarism is natural, pacifism is not; male dominance (Jewish) over women (Jewish) is natural, equality is not; class divisions among Jews by color or origin are natural, equality is not; exploited Arab labor is natural, equality is not.

This was a state preceded by the establishment of collective communities: kibbutzim, in which work was supposed to be shared and have a predetermined dignity; and the lesser known *moshavim,* collective communities for work that were inhabited by poorer, darker Sephardic immigrants, sometimes called Oriental Jews, who were not ideologically driven: "The left-wing kibbutzim didn't want any blacks. They were elitists and not eager to take any of us in. Those leftists liked to talk of a new society, but reality was something else."[18] The State developed a military from disparate militias, some underground and criminal, some terrorist. Ben-Gurion demanded a unified army—a demand that included the use of force against recalcitrant guerrillas—because he knew, as Neal Ascherson writes in *Black Sea,* that "[f]orce, race and maleness are seldom the values of a stable and traditional society, but rather of bandits."[19] Ben-Gurion wanted Jewish sovereignty in a Jewish state; and he knew that states have armies, not gangs.

The military ethic might have reigned in Israel even without Arab hostility and aggression, since part of Israel's purpose was to erase from memory the weak Jew, the unarmed Jew, the nonviolent Jew, the gassed and ash Jew—the Jew called by the Israelis themselves *sabon* (soap). (Adolf Eichmann's trial in Israel in the early 1960s seems to have changed the Israeli relationship to both Diaspora Jews and the Holocaust; rather than dissociate themselves from, they began to connect to.) But Arab warfare became what defined the social environment and gave a special standing and importance to Israeli defense: army, air force, navy, and intelligence. Survival, not psychological comfort, depended on a military that was not only strong but also brilliant; what the Israelis lacked in numbers they made up in daring strategy and fearless execution. The condition of permanent hostile threat and military aggression had its own impact: "It is the nature of war to diminish every value except war itself and the values war requires: patriotism, discipline, obedience, endurance. . . . Even the idea of civilization itself will shrink, from a community of culture embracing the world, to that part of culture that is on *our* side."[20] The Israeli Defense Forces, as the military was called, were armies of citizens whose military skills were going to have to last for a lifetime; a citizen-army either changes the army or it changes the citizen. In the case of Israel, the citizens, at first male and female, then male soldiers with females segregated into menial desk or service jobs, became warriors: crack shooters, SWAT teams, parachute units, pilots, infantry; and the military itself became the touchstone and the prerequisite for any ordinary life: "The army is the foundation for adulthood in Israel. Army service has a direct effect on future employment and career prospects. Many jobs and sometimes housing are available only to army veterans, as are many state benefits....In practice beneficiaries include children of Jewish Israelis who have not served in the forces."[21]

Military service, including military intelligence, was the hallmark of virtually every Israeli politician and leader once the state formally existed in 1948. Arabs, not accepting partition, attacked the new state, which won the war. But when the dust settled and the borders were determined in armistice agreements in 1949, there were 160,000 Arabs inside the borders of Israel; they were approximately 17 percent of the population. Of course, the Israeli military was not open to them; thus they were deprived of rights and benefits. From 1948 to 1966, Arabs inside Israel were under military rule "that forbade them to leave their areas of residence without special passes and placed other restrictions on their personal liberties. Large tracts of land were expropriated from them, by means of legislation and administrative fiat, and Jews settled them."[22] Legislation was passed in 1950, the Absentee Property Law, that allowed the Israeli state to confiscate any abandoned property, in particular property that Arabs had fled during the 1948 war: "This land was reallocated for Jewish use. The total quantity of 'absentee' property amounted to some 300 abandoned or semi-abandoned villages with over 16 million dunums of land. State seizures included virtually all the property of the *waaf*, the Islamic institution of religious endowments, the principal property owner in Palestine."[23] People often try to return to their homes after a war; the Israeli state kept the Arabs out; and the Arabs inside the borders of the state in 1949 were eventually given citizenship, though they are not part of the nation. This was a hostile, subordinate, second-class citizenship fraught with insult. Inside the Israeli parliament, it was the Communist Party (which included Jews and Arabs) that "made a decisive contribution to this posture of enabling the Arabs of Israel to take part in the [s]tate's democratic processes and wage a determined struggle for equality."[24]

The militarism of Israeli Jews and the civil subordination of Arabs inside Israel made Israel a sometimes mean place and compromised the democratic ambition of the state. It took something from the Jews—call it conscience or empathy. There was an Arab village called Kfar Kassem, under military law as were all Arab sites within the state. The military authority had made the curfew earlier than usual, but Arab workers returning to their village did not know that. The Israeli soldiers identified the Arabs as residents of Kfar Kassem and then lined them up and shot them, in keeping with this order: "Cut them down." As villagers arrived,

they too were shot and killed. Nearly fifty people were executed, including ten women and seven children. Those who survived had been
wounded but played dead. When the killings became public knowledge,
an Israeli newspaper asked: "How can it be, then, that normal people, our
own boys, would commit a criminal act of this sort?" The paper concluded: "[N]ot enough has been done to inoculate this nation against the
dulling of the moral sense, against the tendency to ignore the holiness of
human life when speaking of an enemy or a potential enemy."[25] The
country was still sensitive enough to recognize the atrocity and not defend
it; but Israeli soldiers had just followed orders. They had not stepped over
a line so much as lost the line altogether; force, racism, and maleness are
the values of bandits.

And when the State of Israel conquered and then occupied the West
Bank and Gaza (1967), the die was cast: "ethical nationalism" could not
have truck with unenlightened imperialism; nor could it withstand being
a military oppressor. The citizen-army, mostly boys, barely men, had to
become cold, heartless, an enemy to civilians. With the intifada (1987), in
which younger boys threw stones at the soldiers, there were reprisals, punishments, rubber bullets; the soldiers had to learn to hate. There were no
innocents in the occupying army, though there were conscientious objectors who would not accept being part of the military occupation. They
said no; the Israeli state sent them to jail; the state, not the nation, sent
them to jail.

In the occupied territories, Palestinian women also fought the Israeli
soldiers, an experience that mirrored the militancy of Algerian women in
the war against the French. In that prior war, "Muslim women also carried weaponry under their clothing and sacrificed their freedom and lives
for the cause. After independence was won, however, the men made sure
they went back into the home . . . even to the extent of being forced to
wear the veil once more."[26] Palestinian women do not intend to be pushed
back: "One thinks of ETA women and their determination to destroy the
machismo that is so deeply ingrained in their men. The IRA women, too,
have realized that the struggle for women's rights has to go hand in hand
with their fight to evict the British presence from Ireland."[27] This political
insight is missing: the liberation-state, like any state, wants to recognize
and institutionalize what it deems natural hierarchies, in the case of Palestine perhaps Arab supremacy and male supremacy. Only a state made up
of women, a state women make and own, a state that is women (rather
than women being an influential constituency or tokens), a state that is a

synonym for *woman,* will see the male-female hierarchy differently: imposing either equality or female supremacy. Short of the state's being female, it can rescue Jews or Palestinians or New Yorkers; it can grant citizenship to women and children only; it can make any rapist, pimp, or batterer pay with his life; but the male-dominant hierarchy will push women down. That is why, in the end, every single successful liberation movement has betrayed women: women either are the state or women are resubordinated. If the state were female, who and how many would it need to kill? And who and how many would it need to save?

The Nazi state spread like a virus; force was used in every conquered state but Austria, which welcomed the Nazis and immediately and spontaneously assaulted and humiliated Jews. But in Eastern Europe—Latvia, Lithuania, Poland—Jew-hating and the right to hurt Jews was the carrot while Nazi violence was the stick. Wherever German pride marched, it was license for Jew-haters in the conquered countries to kill, rape, batter, and pillage Jews; so that the Nazi state spread and spread, creating instrument after instrument for the carrying out of mass murder, starvation, deportation, and, eventually, genocide. The Nazi state was wherever its soldiers, police, SS, shooters and looters were; and the Nazi state traveled on the backs of the indigenous Jew-hating in conquered countries and territories. The Nazi state was not a centralized, totalitarian entity in Berlin that fused terror and control so that German citizens cowered and complied. The Nazi state went wherever there were Jew-haters who would carry out its anti-Semitic policy of destroying Jews. Denmark, under Nazi occupation but actively saving Jews, was not part of the Nazi state. The particular responsibility of the Nazi state was to determine who would die, how, when, where: and then to murder. That state was physically present in the ghettos and in the killing fields, in mass shootings and in mass deportations, in Dachau, Ravensbrück, and later in Auschwitz and Bergen-Belsen. The Nazi state refused abstraction; yet its animating dynamic was huge, ambitious, and demonic: the destruction of all Jews.

It is important to understand that hostage Jews also became part of the Nazi state when they acted in the capacity of police in Nazi-created ghettos. The efficacy of the Jewish police for the Nazis was, in part, that "the Jews would certainly have run away from the Germans, but, when they saw a Jewish policeman, it didn't occur to them that he would lead them to their death."[28] The project of destroying Jews would perhaps have been a little slower, a little harder, without the cooperation of Nazi-appointed Jewish police.

In the Warsaw ghetto resistance, which was phenomenally complex, including as it did education, housing, food, as well as sabotage and assassination of Nazis, Jews who were making money out of the occupation were targeted by the resisters, though not killed. But, said one of the few survivors, the late Yitzhak Zuckerman, code-named Antek, it was wrong not to target the Jewish police: ". . . the Jewish police were armed with rubber truncheons and knives. That is, they didn't have guns. All we had to do was kill them. If a few of them had been killed, others would have been afraid to join the police. They should have been hanged on lamp poles at night; but we didn't." Zuckerman concludes that "it would have been enough to execute a few of them, really execute and scare them. This way, we would have forced the Germans to come into the ghetto and do the job with their own hands."[29] Of course the Nazis would have; Zuckerman knew that. (See Yitzhak Zuckerman, aka Antek, *A Surplus of Memory: Chronicle of the Warsaw Ghetto Uprising.*)

The fact that the Nazi state was more contagion than governance, more plague than policy, led novelist Günter Grass to argue against the reuniting of what, after Hitler's war, had become East Germany and West Germany: "A unified German state existed, in varying sizes, for no more than seventy-five years: as the German Reich under Prussian rule; as the Weimar Republic, precarious from the outset; and finally, until its unconditional surrender, as the Greater German Reich. . . . This state laid the foundation for Auschwitz. It formed the power base for the latent anti-Semitism that existed in other places as well." His conclusion was that Auschwitz, "that place of terror, that permanent wound," makes a unified Germany "impossible. And if such a state is nevertheless insisted upon, it will be doomed to failure."[30] Now, of course, the two Germanies are united. Ernst von Weizsäcker, father of the first president of a reunited Germany, Richard von Weizsäcker, wrote in 1933: "It is extremely difficult for foreigners to understand anti-Jewish acts because they themselves do not get swamped by Jews."[31] That is not a problem his son, an officer in the Wehrmacht and part of his father's defense team at Nuremberg, has had to face.

Camus's *The Plague* is the parable of antifascism, a warning that fascism kills and then it hides. The Nazi regime is gone and yet there are outbreaks of fascism here and there, genocidal fascism in Rwanda or the former Yugoslavia; or the more pervasive and systematic sexual fascism against women: for example, the trafficking in women and the use of women in pornography; mass rape, serial rape, and marital rape.

"Without a country," said Italian nationalist Guiseppe Mazzini, "you have no name, no vote, no right, no baptism of brotherhood between the peoples. You are humanity's bastards, soldiers without a flag. Israelites among the nations, you will win neither trust nor protection: none will be your sureties."[32] When the state and nation are one entity, what are the citizens? In the eighteenth century, France was a nation "bound by the ideals of the rights of man and of the French Revolution; to be a Frenchman meant to make a choice, and in fact foreigners would proclaim themselves Frenchmen because they shared the revolutionary ideal."[33] It was the Enlightenment drive toward brotherhood and equality, with its emphasis on the freedom of the individual, that created the modern idea of citizenship. In the later romantic era, citizens were created by birth, not choice or allegiance to ideals. What signified was "the notion of the ineffable national soul that supposedly determines a given man's belonging to a nation. . . . One was a member of a given nation by virtue of being born on a given soil, from parents of the same language as their ancestors, also because one shared the destiny of a tribe, or a race, or, as some would say, of a common historical fate."[34] Romanticism, says Czeslaw Milosz in *Beginning With My Streets*, "was nothing else than nationalism."[35] Love of the land, love of one's own people, the desolation of exile, parsing or celebrating or bemoaning the soul of one's nation, the particularism of an ethnic identity: these are the elements of a great romance; and romance means infatuation, obsession; nationhood becomes the romance of a people with itself.

In the Middle East, most nations are creations of the British or French. "There is no Arab nation, as such," writes William Pfaff in *The Wrath of Nations: Civilization and the Furies of Nationalism*. "The historical experience and reference of the region is not to nation but to religion, commune, empire, caliphate. The states which exist there today do so because it is now considered appropriate that people live in nation-states, not in multi confessional and multinational empires."[36] The collapse of the Ottoman Empire and the success of British imperialism allowed for a European drawing of borders. As Peter Theroux says, "Many Arab coun-

tries seemed to define themselves by the lone political dogma of their opposition to Israel."[37] On the other hand, Egypt has had the same borders
for 7,000 years; there is an Egyptian culture that is both traditional and
modern, an intellectual and artistic life, and some degree of personal freedom; all this is now being threatened by Muslim fundamentalists. The
Egyptian writer Naguib Mahfouz, himself physically attacked by fundamentalists, stabbed, captures the citizenry by parable: "Only the gangsters
lived in comfort and luxury; above them was their boss and above everyone was the overseer; the people were crushed beneath all of them. If any
unfortunate man was unable to pay his protection money, revenge was ex-
acted against the whole neighborhood, and if he complained to the boss,
he was beaten and turned over to the local gangster to be beaten again.
. . . The poets of the coffeehouses in every corner of our alley tell only of
heroic eras, avoiding public mention of anything that would embarrass
the powerful. . . . We look toward a future that will come we know not
when, and point toward the mansion and say, 'There is our venerable father,' and we point out our gangsters and say, 'These are our men; and
God is master of all.' "[38] There is a fatalism in all Mahfouz's fiction (translated into English); a perception of the corruption of the nation-state and
what that corruption means to the lowly; and that fatalism suggests an
Arabism that is in itself corrupt.

After the Gulf War, the poet Abu Deeb wrote: "We cannot but be with
the nation. . . . The nation may be a gargantuan tyrant. . . . The nation
may be a policeman whose dogs chase us everywhere inside its walls. The
nation may be the cave of our disillusionment, or the slaughterhouse of
our sweet dreams, or the grave of our freedom and honor. . . . And the nation may be a thousand worse and even more terrible things. Still, we cannot but be with the nation."[39] The romance is to say "the nation"; "the
state" is more prosaic but truer. The state, then, "may be a policeman
whose dogs chase us everywhere inside its walls." To say one loves or is
loyal to a nation is to claim a human kinship, a loyalty to all the others
like oneself or close to oneself; to be loyal to a state without conditions, or
to love a state that hurts its citizens, is either fascism or ordinary despair,
lethargy in the place of conscience. The state has responsibilities, obligations, and in Deeb's prose a view of the nature of human beings that
makes them subservient to the state, low, expendable, pitiful, creatures to
torment. In the state of Deeb's prose, citizenship is pain; or maybe the
state is a boy and the citizen is a girl. The boy is a nasty piece of work; the
girl, in love, in passion, in fear, is submissive without recourse. But this is

metaphor. In the lives of real women,* the state has a dual personality:
"Traditionally the state ignores women, except in times of crisis, when it
fiercely attacks them. Muslim women do not have a government that protects them. This is the basis of their tragedy during this very slow transi-
tion from the despotic medieval state to the modern state. For them, the
modern state has still not yet been born."[40]

So women—even though forced—try to prove their loyalty through
self-abnegation, covered, often enclosed; in segregation there is a community of women, a family of women; and it is the state that imprisons half
of the population; each male autocrat is part of the state; and the gangs
that attack and harass women on the street are the state's voluntary and
eager enforcers, self-righteous and swollen with male pride; and women
not only have no state to protect them—they have no nation; the nation
is built on their backs but excludes them from civic life: they are not part
of the nation of boys, except as property. The love and loyalty of kinship
expressed in the love of the nation leaves them out. They are—how did
Mazzini put it?—"humanity's bastards . . . Israelites among the nations,
you will win neither trust nor protection: none will be your sureties."

Does the state think? What does the state think? Who does the state protect? Who does the state cannibalize? Is nationalism a romantic diversion
from facing the way the state works, moves, defines, draws lines, pushes
some up and some down and some away? Can one love the nation but abhor the state? Is nationalism a passion, an emotion, an indelible chauvinism that provides cover for the state: keeps the state from being naked,
seen as it is? "In the name of freedom, justice, and independence," says
Paul Breines in *Tough Jews*, "nationalism has invariably bred conformity,
an ideology of toughness, paranoia in the face of difference, and violence." He is talking about "the nationalism of the so-called great powers,
but also that of the smaller, victimized peoples such as Jews or Palestinians
. . ."[41]

It is injustice that creates the demand for a state to ennoble the nation:
there is the innocent, naive, historically worthless belief that one's own
will not hate, exploit, injure or insult kin, social kin, ethnic kin, those

---

*For the record: there is a Palestinian-drafted secular law that would keep women from falling
under the power of the religious authorities.

who share a history, hardships, experiences; or is it simply that the humiliation is less—to be hurt by a victor, an outsider, is more shameful? Are we a nation because we are all the same, or more the same than different; or are we a nation because we have an idea of citizenship: rights and responsibilities? Wole Soyinka, writing about Nigeria, insists that "we must also not neglect to decide the precise nature of the *problématic:* That is, are we trying to keep Nigeria a nation? Or are we trying to make it one? The difference is crucial. It outlines the magnitude of the task and qualifies the methodology to be adopted. It returns us again and again to our commencing question: When *is* a nation?"[42] The borders of the African nation-states were drawn by the imperialist powers as they abdicated or were forced to abdicate. "In the politics of this continent," says Soyinka, "I have no patience with any national strategy which in any way, overt or covert, solidifies the meaningless colonial boundaries which have created and are still creating such intense havoc . . ."[43]

In South Africa, the Afrikaners, "the white tribe of Africa, arrogant, xenophobic, and 'full of blood,' as the Zulus say of tyrants,"[44] found authority for the apartheid state in the Old Testament—"a whip for the horse, a bridle for the ass, and a rod for the fool's back."[45] In a war with Britain at the end of the nineteenth century, "Afrikaners proved so determined that the British invented concentration camps* in order to subdue them: they herded women and children into such unsanitary prison camps that some twenty-six thousand died. The experience completed Afrikaners' pride in being white Africans, a tough people who embraced the dark continent, who resisted colonial European intervention to the last."[46] Earlier the Afrikaners had refused European cultural influence; when "rumors of the Enlightenment penetrated their wilderness, the Afrikaners considered them, consulted their Bibles and preachers, and reached a consensus . . . They called themselves Doppers because they were deliberately and consciously extinguishing the light of the Enlightenment, so that they could do what they had to do in darkness."[47] Totalitarian states, especially those based on race-hate, fear the light of day: scrutiny of the state will lead to police who torture, judges who acquiesce in the abrogation of human rights, political leaders who create a national

---

*Another origin of the concentration camp is given by Guillero Cabrera in *Mea Culpa,* translated by Kenneth Hall and the author (New York: Farrar Straus Giroux, 1994, p. 270): ". . . [W]ho invented the concentration camps? . . . It was Valeriano Weyler, Governor-General for Spain of the Always Faithful Island of Cuba—in 1896 to be exact. . . . Later the English would perfect this Devil's invention during the war against the Boers in South Africa."

fiction—a nationalism—in which the security of the state depends on se-cret trials, secret verdicts, false accusations that lead to dark, dirty, blood-on-the-floor prisons. Does the state torture? As Kate Millett writes in *The Politics of Cruelty: An Essay on the Literature of Political Imprisonment,* "Torture is the ultimate act of state power. In arrogating to itself the ca-pacity to torture its citizens, the state has assumed absolute power over them. If, in addition to its other powers over the person—arrest, con-finement, trial process, judgment, and sentence—it adds torture as well, it annihilates. Because torture cannot be withstood. It was for this rea-son, perhaps above all others, that the reforming spirit of the Enlighten-ment and the movement for the rights of man outlawed torture categorically."[48]

In 1997 Amnesty International published two reports in July and Au-gust on Israel: *Israel/Lebanon: Unlawful Killings During Operation "Grapes of Wrath"* and *"Under Constant Medical Supervision": Torture, Ill-treatment and the Health Professions in Israel and the Occupied Territories,* the latter of which expressed "concern about the role of medical professionals in inter-rogation centres where detainees suffer torture."[49] The Enlightenment freed European Jews from legal discrimination and made Jews citizens; and the Enlightenment outlawed torture. Is there a Dopper population ensconced in the Israeli state—does it set human rights policy; or is the defense of torture located in the immediate present, impervious to social history—they're only Arabs? And doctors, using doctors—to determine how much torture a prisoner can stand, to stop it and start it: was that not the modus operandi in Argentina during the reign of the military-terror-ist state? There is no reason to bring up Auschwitz; Argentina will do nicely.

For women, the family is the equivalent of the state; all power and au-thority traditionally reside in the head of the family, male; and religion, law, culture, art, and money delineate and reinforce his sovereignty over women and children. In the family, the woman looks for love and mean-ing; in the family she has work, necessary though unpaid; she raises chil-dren who may or may not acknowledge her; in the family it is her special duty to socialize the girls, her own daughters, to accept subordination, humiliation, and often physical pain (from Chinese foot binding to fe-male genital mutilation to wife-beating and marital rape). She fights—either politically or individually—for dignity as she imagines it; respect as she understands it; love as she hopes for it. But even when she achieves a measure of dignity or respect or love, the ground is not solid under her feet. "One of the worst aspects of oppression is that it never ends when the oppressor begins to repent," says Shelby Steele in *The Content of Our Character.* "There is a legacy of doubt in the oppressed that follows long after the cleanest repentance by the oppressor, just as the guilt trails the oppressor and makes his redemption incomplete."[50] The female fear of men has roots in men's physical contempt for women, expressed in kidnapping, killing, forced marriage, rape, prostitution, genital mutilation, battery, and imposed separation or segregation. The male fear of women may come from the birth trauma, fear of castration, infantile dependence, or the tooth fairy; but it is a fear that is old and big. Or maybe men know that they deserve retaliatory violence from women and keep expecting it. If so, they have been expecting it for a long time.

As Knox says about the men of ancient Greece: ". . . in their myths women appear repeatedly either as the willing sacrificial victim at the altar or as the killer, the murderer of the male."[51] He names Medea, Procne, Clytemnestra, Deianira, Stheneboea, and in a draft by Euripides, Phaedra. He notices that "[t]he myths even provided dangerous women in large groups, like the amazons who fought against men on the battlefield, the fifty daughters of Danaus, forty-nine of whom slaughtered their husbands on their wedding night, or the women of the island of Lemnos who went to the extreme limit of defiance of the male hierarchy by murdering their husbands and marrying their slaves."[52] There is always the hope that these myths had some basis in reality somewhere, a factual rather than teleological reality, which may be the case. As Neal Ascherson writes in *Black Sea:* "Among the nomads of the Pontic Steppe, women were at times powerful: not in the condescending male sense of silky persuasiveness in beds or over cradles, but directly. They ruled; they rode with armies into battle; they died of arrow-wounds or spear-stabs; they were buried in female robes and jewellery with their lances, quiver and sword ready to hand. In their grave, a dead youth sometimes lies across their feet. A man sacrificed at the funeral of a woman?"[53]

Inside the family, direct power is experienced only over children; and in many cultures, male children when they are teenagers have more authority and standing than their mothers. Even the 360 goddesses that Arabs worshiped before Muhammad brought monotheism as Allah's prophet—goddesses not unlike Kali in India, goddesses who "wallowed in the bloodbaths of the sacrifices they demanded"[54]—never represented direct female power on earth; thus the many claims based on liturgy that Islam raised the status of women in a material way from what it had been in "the pre-Islamic disorder."[55]

Patterson credits the invention of personal freedom—its value, its importance—to women, because, he says, "[w]omen . . . came to the value of personal freedom out of an inevitable empathy with the slave condition. . . . By empathizing[,] . . . women became more conscious of freedom by the ever-present experience of powerlessness, natal alienation, and dishonor."[56] Of course, women who were slaves did not need empathy but rather courage to think about freedom, to value it, to want it. There were women slaves, usually as a result of conquest, and all the women were enslaved, enclosed, disenfranchised, powerless except perhaps with respect to this tiny hierarchy in the domicile: enslaved woman over woman slave. Women's political tragedy may have started there—an inability or a refusal to bridge the gap between wife and slave (often concubine), or even inside the female area of the home to play at or materially create equality. John Berger describes the Greek landscape now, a landscape that suggests what may have been an old question: "Then suddenly as the light goes and I look over the cemetery towards the sea, I ask myself: What can flesh mean here? *Sarka* in Greek. . . . Flesh here is the only soft thing, the only substance that can suggest a caress; everything else visible is sharp or mineral, shattered or gnarled. . . . Consequently the body is aware of a cruelty even before it is aware of pleasure, for its own existence is cruel. . . . There's nobody here who isn't an expert in longing, in the long drawn-out desire for a life a fraction less cruel."[57] This, too, is why women—in this landscape 2,000 years ago—developed an idea of personal freedom; in a harsh place, humans need freedom; with it comes the chance for survival on one's own and the possibilities of solitude, creativity, physical strength, and a desire for physical love that is the opposite of captivity.

The family has been the site of captivity for women. In the family, the law has required a woman's submission in intercourse and childbearing. In the family, she can be legally punished for disobedience or noncompliance; her action is restricted; force is sanctioned as is unwanted pregnancy and civil insignificance if not erasure. The family is at the same time the site of male absence: there is a grander life outside, in bars, coffeehouses, brothels, pool halls, bowling alleys, casinos, athletic competitions, even paid labor. In the family the woman learns loneliness: where is he and why? Women are not myths of good or evil; nor goddesses wallowing in blood or symbols of fertility; nor are women so lethal, so dangerous, that they need to be locked up or locked in, pushed down or pushed out.

Women in families have real lives that are distorted by men's hallucinatory, cowardly projections and the appropriation of public space by men: a woman walks down a street anywhere in the world at her own peril, although she is more likely to be injured (hit, beaten, set on fire, raped, tortured, killed) in her own home, inside the family: when he is not absent, a woman can learn the deepest loneliness.

Women are raised to be incomplete however accomplished; the need for completion is the need for a man. Women are raised to be physically dependent on men, no matter how weak the man or how strong the woman; thus, a woman needs a man. Women's worth and status are determined by men; a woman needs to have a man in order to count. Single women, widowed women, divorced women, lone women, lesbian women, are derided and marginalized; old women are mostly poor, across lines of class and country. Without a man it is virtually impossible for a woman to stand inside the privileged circle of women with men. Without a man, a woman has less money. Men validate that women are women, give the gold star. Nature does not make a woman into a woman—male perception and a colonized body do. It is in the family that a girl gets taught her place and the strategies of manipulation and manners that will give her a chance of getting a good-enough man; it is in the family that a woman has to teach her sons their superiority to her; it is in the family that the woman must be a wife—she is expected to follow the man, sacrifice for him, and take comfort from assault, which continues to be misconstrued as love, desire, intensity of passion, animalistic vitality, vibrant macho sexuality. It is hard for a woman to have a self-defined, self-motivated sense of honor if she must get a man first; it is hard to make art or music or write books; it is hard to love or climb a mountain or take a stand; it is hard to have a sense of dignity or self-respect or even to have a self at all. So when one hears from politicians that the family is the building block of society or that the family must be intact and headed by a male for the nation to survive, understand that the family has in it a woman; and that it is the family that makes a woman act against her own self-interest, talent, ambition, calling, capacities, potential, and also in opposition to her own civil and political equality. As Simone de Beauvoir saw, women are made, not born.

Often, to keep the family together, the woman will accept repeated beatings and rapes, emotional battering and verbal degradation; she will be debased and ashamed but she will stick it out, or when she runs he will kill her. Ask the politicians who exude delight when they advocate for the so-called traditional family how many women are beaten and children raped when there is no man in the family. Zero is such a perfect and encouraging number; but who, among politicians in male-supremacist cultures, can count that high?

In the traditional Jewish family, in which religion was central, the wife often conducted business for profit as well as doing all the domestic work while the husband and male children studied. The center of the Jewish world was study: Torah, Talmud, Mishna, and on the farthest edge, Kabbalah, the mysticism of Judaism. This world of study, of learning, was a male world. Indeed, girls were not supposed to be taught how to read the holy books, a banishment from the center of the Jewish world to its margins. Virility in the world of the Jews was scholarly, learned, quick-thinking, and fluent in the opinions of the great rabbis. Assimilated Jewish families were more likely to take on the social roles of the dominant culture: men earned money; women cooked and cleaned and took care of the children, except in rich families, in which women were to some degree decorative. Rich assimilated Jews, often with strong ties to the Jewish community, for example the Warburgs, could be appropriated to fill out the stereotype of the powerful Jew, especially banker; the religious Jews, often living in essentially closed communities, were stereotyped as wimps, cowards, not so much effeminate males as feminine and therefore alien creatures. The point of the Jewish family in traditional religious terms was to support the learning and praying of the men; the power was with the male, because the Jewish purpose was study, prayer, and fulfilling the religious law, of which 613 applied to men and 2 to women. It assumed, say some authorities, that the rabbis expected the women to be busy with the children and cooking and housekeeping and thus not have time for 613 laws; but in the Jewish community power was where the religious law was—with the man. In the synagogue, women were segregated in the back, usually on a balcony with a closed curtain—to hide the women in order to protect the men from arousal. Physical fighting, guzzling alcohol, and farming were not part of the male role in the traditional religious family; nor were they a part of Jewish culture in urban, largely assimilated families. The Nazis wiped out a whole way of life when they exterminated virtually all the Jews of Eastern Europe: the traditional, religious Jews. They killed the people; they killed the practice. The fundamentalist Jews of Israel and Crown Heights are a later and different social phenomenon.

After the Holocaust, the Jewish family took on a new meaning; each Jew was part of it; so many families had been destroyed that family itself became a metaphor, barely harnessed to a literal reality. "The family is Jewish history writ small," writes Appelfeld. "Within it there were the surviving believers, those who still believed out of habit, those who were alienated without realizing it, and those who were consciously alienated. Every phenomenon that had taken place during the past hundred years was represented within the family: there were anarchists, communists, Zionists, and Bundists. And the more extended the family, the deeper were rifts within it."[58] After the Holocaust, Jewish law on the Jewish family was lost history, a people's past that was no prologue to any known future. The history had some undisputed elements to it, for instance, "matrilineal descent is what determines the Jewish kinship group";[59] this actually reinforced the sexual double standard—"Because men in ancient Israel produced children by relations with Gentile slaves and concubines, the only way in which the purity of Jewish blood could be scrutinized was by the rabbinical ruling that Jewish descent had to go through the legitimate Jewish wife."[60] Blood: Jewish blood. This is hardly different from the *limpieza de sangre* of the Inquisition, and matrilineal descent was hardly an honor: adultery by the Jewish wife was treason; it compromised the blood line.

The double sexual standard was protected by the Jewish reading of the adultery laws, which had "different implications for men and women: [f]or the man, only intercourse with someone else's wife was adultery; for the wife, intercourse with anyone but her husband was adultery."[61] By the Middle Ages, Jewish law had been interpreted to "specify that a man may engage in sexual relations in any way he pleases with his wife, but he should not force her against her will."[62] Jewish men, of course, like other men, seduced and abandoned; but because only the male could grant a divorce, sometimes a man would marry and "extort large sums of money from the bride's family before giving a writ of divorce"[63]—this was especially true of men who traveled looking for mates, a kind of bogus marriage scam.

According to David Biale in *Eros and the Jews: From Biblical Israel to Contemporary America,* "Sexuality was a central issue in [ancient] Israel's self-conception, with adultery and fidelity the dominant metaphors both for Israel's relationship to God and for national identity. The prophet Ezekiel combines the two explicitly in his accusation that Israel is whoring with her neighbors, the 'well-endowed Egyptians' (16:26); Israel's depravity, he explains, derives from her origins: 'You are daughters of a Hittite mother and an Amorite father' (16:45). Sexual anxiety," concludes Biale, "is thus at the very heart of the struggle with this ambiguous identity."[64] Biale pinpoints the predominant expression of that anxiety as an aversion to semen: "Know from whence you come—from a smelly drop"[65] (semen); or, according to another story, the snake is the first to have had sex with Eve and it ejaculates "filth."[66] Women's bodies still bear the brunt of sexual anxiety or ambiguous identity: "Although a woman is a vessel filled with excrement and her mouth is filled with blood, everyone runs after her."[67]

In this same history, a fetus does not have a right to life until the actual moment of birth, and "[o]nly at the moment of birth does the mother's health cease to take precedence over that of the fetus."[68] Jewish law, however, "does not allow abortion for feminist reasons, nor does it believe that a woman has the right to control her own body in that sense. . . . Neither men nor women are thought to fully own their own bodies, and their behavior toward their own bodies is governed by Jewish law."[69] There is, in fact, much restriction on male sexual behavior in Jewish law; but because a man can commit adultery in the legal sense only if his adulterous partner is married (he is destroying another man's property), Orthodox Jews, post-Holocaust and in Israel, are major users of prostitutes. The sexual restrictions on a man have to do with when he can come into carnal contact with his own wife. He is not forbidden to use unmarried women or prostituted women. In Eastern Europe religious communities before the Holocaust, he would not have; he would have been disgraced in his community. Isaac Bashevis Singer wrote frequently in protest of the sexual restraint required of men in these East European communities. In Israel there is no such restraint.

The Nazis not only destroyed all the Jewish families they touched; they created a new definition of the Jewish family, in particular for the SS. As Thomas Keneally evokes in the fictionalized *Schindler's List:* "SS training documents, written to combat these futile casualties [SS officers who committed suicide], pointed out the simplemindedness of believing that because the Jew bore no visible weapons he was bereft of social, economic, or political arms. He was, in fact, armed to the teeth. Steel yourself, said the documents, for the Jewish child is a cultural time bomb, the Jewish woman a biology of treasons, the Jewish male a more incontrovertible enemy than any Russian could hope to be."[70] Jews, in other words, were biological weapons. The warning is not to perceive the man, the woman, and the child as a human family, unarmed, civilian; but to believe that SS men's survival was at stake in the face of this Jewish biological poison. The SS had to strike first or "a biology of treasons" would engulf and destroy them.

And so the SS did attack the Jewish families, tore them apart with death and disease, transport and starvation, gas and cremation. But the SS did not have an easy time of it in that families stayed faithful to each other; this kept them in the German-gerrymandered ghettos. "Even young people," writes Nora Levin in *The Holocaust: The Destruction of European Jewry 1933–1945*, "who had the best chance to survive, refused to leave their parents or their fellow Jews in the ghetto. . . . The more robust ones could not or would not desert the ghetto. The dilemma, whether to escape or share the fate of the ghetto, was debated passionately in all of the ghettos where resistance was organized, and, in almost every case, the decision ultimately was to remain with the ghetto—to try to organize the ghetto for resistance in the final struggle, but to remain in the ghetto. This was the decision of the young fighters in Warsaw, Bialystok, Lodz, Krakow, Bendin and Vilna."[71] And the family changed: mass arrests of the men as well as group murders stranded traditional patriarchal figures in a nightmare world, where they had no means of keeping the family safe or even alive from day to day. The women and children were stretched thin: how to keep the father from desperate, empty depression; how to get food and shelter; how to get false papers; how to keep warm and dressed and clean. Children were heroes, "indispensable to smuggling food . . ."[72] And later, two years, three years, four years, Jewish parents and children from all over Europe were being transported to the East for slaughter: for instance, in 1942, "[o]n July 31 and August 3, 5, and 7, more than 4,000 parents and their older children were marched through Pithiviers and Beaune-la-Ronde [France], in full view of local residents, and loaded onto four trains for Auschwitz. From the first train, all 1,183 people—693 men, 359 women, and 131 adolescents—were admitted to the camp. Sixteen were alive at the end of the war. Passengers on the other three convoys experienced selections for mass murder; about 2,000, including at least 500 adolescents, were promptly gassed. The others— about 1,150—were admitted to the camp. Nineteen of them are known to have survived."[73] The children who grew up during the Holocaust "knew man as a beast of prey, not metaphorically, but as a physical reality with his full stature and clothing, his way of standing and sitting, his way of caressing his own child and of beating a Jewish child."[74]

After the Holocaust, it was all mimicry: the Jewish family had died, been slaughtered, sadistically pulled apart and broken, smashed to pieces, murdered and burnt. Its bones were broken and its collective heart buried in an unmarked grave somewhere in Russia or Poland, probably Poland. Its bones were broken, the pain being past sadness or anger or grief; and that is a legacy: each living Jew has got broken bones from the family; and can't be healed.

The newspaper headline read: THE SON OF CAPTAIN DREYFUS STRONGLY CONDEMNS NAZI PERSECUTION. Having seen his father destroyed by the anti-Semitic carnage of the French, Pierre Dreyfus reacted to the *Kristallnacht* pogrom in November 1938: "All decent people should have their nights haunted, as mine are haunted, by the abominations . . . inflicted by a government of assassins and sadists."[75] (See Michael Burns, *Dreyfus: A Family Affair, From the French Revolution to the Holocaust*.) As usual, all decent people were busy elsewhere; but Pierre Dreyfus had seen cultured anti-Semitic gangs who wrote and published operate like sharks, the smell of Jewish blood rousing them to feed. This, too, was part of being in a Jewish family: childhoods disfigured by anti-Semitism along with sharp eyes for the sadism of Jew-hating, especially public sadism, the sadism of the neighborhood, the sadism of civilized attackers and vandals; and a sense of outrage that presupposes the decency of others, even though one has witnessed malice and indifference. A sense of outrage, of course, is innocence: always.

By 1938 Jews and the Jewish family had been under attack, severely wounded, intimidated, as had individual Jews, for instance, Jews who married non-Jews. In October of 1935 Julius Streicher's vicious rag *Der Stürmer* was publishing names, addresses, professions, and birth dates of those who had intermarried, even suggesting "that local party cadres in charge of housing should look into the situation of these 'race defilers.'"[76] Jewish women married to blessed and beautiful German men were most vulnerable, called "Jew whores" by the Nazis and attacked or assaulted with impunity. Jews inside Germany tried to get out, to find safe haven in other countries in Europe or in Palestine or in the United States. "Who was left behind?" asks William D. Rubinstein in *The Myth of Rescue: Why the Democracies Could Not Have Saved More Jews From the Nazis.* And he answers: "Disproportionately, they were the elderly and women, although just before the war working-age women emigrated in large numbers as domestic servants."[77] The elderly tried to get their adult children to leave; women tried to get men to leave. One can see clearly the internalized hierarchy, whose life was worth more. Still, what prevailed was the attachment within families; children wanting to be with their parents; parents wanting to be with their parents. Children begged the Gestapo to let them be with their mothers. Said one such survivor, "We still believed that nothing could happen to us as long as we weren't torn apart."[78] In Vienna where Sigmund Freud's office had been ransacked by storm troopers and his daughter, Anna, arrested once and released, with another arrest forthcoming, Anna asked Freud, "'Wouldn't it be better if we all killed ourselves?' . . . [to which] her father answered . . . 'Why? Because they would like us to?'"[79] Freud died in London of cancer of the jaw a year later. His four sisters were killed by the Nazis.

In the ghettos women, like men, were required to do heavy labor; and pregnancies and births were forbidden by the Germans. Many hid their fathers, brothers, or husbands, especially if the men were religious and according to orthodox practice wore beards and sidelocks. Then there was the monstrous horror, described by Anne Michaels in her novel, *Fugitive Pieces:* "I think of the Lodz ghetto, where infants were thrown by soldiers from hospital windows to soldiers below who 'caught' them on their bayonets. When the sport became too messy, the soldiers complained loudly, shouting about the blood running down their long sleeves, staining their uniforms . . . A mother felt the weight of her child in her arms, even as she saw her daughter's body on the sidewalk."[80] In the camps, women invent a new dictionary: "Vitamin J, of news about the war, is the Jewish vitamin. 'Angel-makers' are abortionists. The 'market' is the animated bazaar where the trick is 'to get rid of a piece of merchandise that nobody needs, at a price (usually bread) that you think is scandalous. The latrine in Auschwitz is the 'club,' international but not cosmopolitan."[81] And women make something resembling a family, except that what they make is a sisterhood in the camp, to watch out for someone else, to flex practical and moral muscles: "'Camp sisters' accepted responsibility for each other's survival, including sharing food, risking punishments, and encouraging each other in the face of hopelessness."[82] In Auschwitz women used domestic experience to maintain the will to live; as Ruth Elias writes in *Triumph of Hope: From Theresienstadt and Auschwitz to Israel:* "We talked about food constantly. Every day after work we ate the meager supper that had been provided, devouring our entire daily bread ration. Then a few young women would get together up on the third tier and start 'cooking'—that is, we talked about all the various foods and dishes we had known back home. These conversations were like self-inflicted torment, but they gave us a feeling of having eaten our fill. We cooked in our imaginations for hours at a time, even though most of us were too young to have had much experience with actual cooking. This cooking also affirmed the ties to our families and strengthened our will to survive . . ."[83] And after the war, in Holland, for instance, Jewish agencies were faced with a new problem: the numbers of Jewish children who had been sexually abused in hiding, "sexually abused by their protectors."[84] Was this sexual abuse familial or was it the most egregious stranger-rape?

After the war, some Nazis of high rank were imprisoned. The arrogance of high-ranking Nazis was truly astonishing, none more so than that of the commandant of Auschwitz, Rudolph Höss, who wrote a memoir before the Poles hanged him. In it he expresses a lot of self-pity, sentimentalizing the great burdens on him in his important but thankless job; in particular, he felt such empathy for the prisoners that, in retrospect, he realized that he should have told Himmler that he, Höss, was too sensitive to do this job. His sensitivity is most apparent when he speaks as a sociologist of sorts. On the Jewish family he had this to say: "As I have said repeatedly, the Jews have a very strong sense of family. They cling to each other like leeches, but from what I observed, they lack a feeling of solidarity. In their situation you would assume that they would protect each other. But no, it was just the opposite."[85] Höss was known to have (in the parlance of the time) "had an affair with" a Jewish inmate, then killed her when he was done with her. Questioned by his captors about his sexual relationship with his own wife, he revealed, "Well, it was normal, but after she found out what I was doing, we rarely had the desire for intercourse. Things looked normal outwardly, I guess—there was an estrangement."[86] Who was she? Who was Mrs. Commandant Höss? Is it even possible that she had a conscience? If she had not been brought up to need a man, any man, might she have done something active, oppositional, subversive rather than passive, absent, indifferent? Is the wife of a perpetrator a moral nullity, or should she be accountable—for her loyalty to him, for what she knew and what she saw? Can a good woman be married to a genuinely bad man and not rebel, revolt? Or does the place of the wife in the family require an absence of integrity, ethics, fairness, and human dignity? Are wives—by virtue of their function in the family—enablers for killers, rapists, torturers? Is that the meaning of being a wife? If he is good, a wife enables him to become better; if he is bad she enables him to become worse? Or is it simply that this Nazi wife and hosts of lesser German and Austrian Nazi wives were up against a rival they could not surpass: "Once you have seen mountains of naked corpses, women among them, the charms of your housewife back home offer no more than a paltry temptation."[87]

The Arab practice of the family keeps women from being seen by both covering and segregating the female body. Honor (*sharaf*) governs the place of the female; she must be chaste, a virgin, until married; a woman whose hymen is broken from rape will find herself disgraced; thus, there is the underground in which surgeons will restore the hymens of raped women. Uniquely, in Arab societies the brother is the presumed enforcer. If a sister is promiscuous or not chaste, the family honor is compromised and it is the brother's responsibility to kill her. The mad genius of this is that in a male-supremacist society the only possible experience of equality for a female might be with her brother—his role as potential executioner would make him an unreliable ally in her quest for freedom or education or love. One Palestinian writer narrates the story of his own sister's honor killing: forced by the oldest brother to drink poison in the family home. (See Fawaz Turki, *Exile's Return: The Making of a Palestinian-American.*) Another Arab writer describes an honor killing in the Gaza Strip: ". . . a man who had just discovered his Islamic roots locked up his four sisters, whom he was convinced were whores. He then set the room on fire while he sat outside reading passages from the Qur'an to himself."[88] In Amman, Jordan, police arrest young women who are with men not related to them. The woman is tested to see if the hymen is intact; if not the police notify both families who then try to force a marriage: "Should the man refuse… both are charged. The sentences are light, and within two months the man is released. But the women are compelled to stay on . . . [b]ecause they needed protection from their own families. The Jordanian police [are] unwilling to take responsibility for a girl being shot or stabbed to death on the prison steps on the day of her release (an actual incident)."[89]

In *Sexuality and War: Literary Masks of the Middle East,* Evelyne Accad describes interviews with Arab maids at a hotel in Algeria—"Most of them lived in polygamous relationships and had to wear the veil . . . Most of them expressed revolt . . ."; and women in the United Arab Emirates— "They too expressed to me revolt against their condition—having to produce a child every year with the threat of repudiation or of their husbands taking a younger wife if they did not, and wearing the *burga* (a stiff, mask-type face cover that leaves purplish-blue marks when one sweats)"; and women in the Sudan—"[t]hey expressed unhappiness with the practice of infibulation, their suffering from it, their desire to change customs that mutilate them."[90] Accad asks herself a fundamental question of feminism: "I wondered, as I listened and talked with women, why there was so much pain in remembering past events in their lives connected with sexuality, yet so much resistance and denial around a political analysis of sexuality?"[91]

This question takes on a great sadness because each group of women wanted change for their daughters; and yet nationalism or Arab chauvinism continues to trump gender equality, in the recognizable and common pattern of first things first; first we rescue the nation, and then, sisters, we promise, we will rescue you. Gloria Emerson in *Gaza: A Year in the Intifada—A Personal Account From an Occupied Land* describes the loss of male pride: "That year, as in the year before, the husband or father could not provide protection to his own parents, wife or children. In the eyes of Muslim men, their own immense value diminished when they were beaten in front of women or children or could not protect or rescue members of the family from attack. The man knocked to the floor and kicked was no longer the strong commanding head of the family. The arrested man, being prodded and tied up, was no longer the father who can keep harm away. It ate into some men deeply and they did not know how to relieve their own shame."[92]

In Lebanon in 1975, according to Yolla Polity Charara, "the party and ideological loyalties made women loath to complain about their fate to other unknown women . . . The militants among them, when conscious of the discrimination women faced, when they were not themselves token women in the party, preferred to wash their dirty laundry within the family; they refused to question publicly the men of their party . . ."[93] Even the Gulf War, fought with Arab allies, presented a terrible problem of conscience to Arab feminists, indeed especially to Arab feminists. As Fatima Mernissi asks in *Islam and Democracy: Fear of the Modern World:* "How can an Arab woman . . . insist on raising with her own group her problem, which is the *hijab?* How can she demand the negotiation of new boundaries for the sexes if her group feels naked and vulnerable in a world where bombs in a fury of passion can single out Baghdad?"[94] To the colonized woman, boundaries are always the issue and one seeks reforms that move but do not destroy gendered boundaries.

In every male-supremacist country, the woman's status is always overshadowed by the demands of ethnic loyalty, as if, for instance, the humiliation of Palestinian men being beaten by Israeli soldiers is a real devastation but wife-beating is not. Even in countries with sadistic totalitarian rule, a nationalist enemy is always the real enemy. Police-state rule of one's own kind is favored over even benign foreign occupation and is often experienced as less destructive, less demeaning, even less cruel.

In Gaza and the West Bank, Israel was able to use the Arab honor code to force confessions from women under arrest, to taunt male resisters, to threaten both male and female activists. In addition, the demolition of houses (or the sealing off of rooms), a practice that originated with the British when they controlled Palestine, is used to punish the Palestinian family: "When Israel took over the territories after the war Dayan soon employed demolition in the face of P.L.O. guerrilla terror warfare. Through 1977, 1,224 homes had been destroyed under this policy."[95] Under U.N. pressure Israel allowed the United Nations Relief and Works Agency (U.N.R.W.A.) to improve education in the occupied territories (no colleges or universities existed when Jordan and Egypt had control of the same territories); the colleges and universities became hotbeds of radical activism for Palestinians, so Israel closed these institutions, sometimes for up to a year. In Gaza and the West Bank "both mortality rates and malnutrition tended to be higher among girls than boys, a fact which could not conceivably be ascribed to the occupation but reflected traditional attitudes that damaged the health of the community."[96] All of this is an old story, but this old story has two new elements: Palestinian and Israeli women have found ways to work together to help women and children; and the occupying soldiers, the controlling soldiers, the armed and trained soldiers are Jews. This primacy of the Jewish military stays true even under the apparent rulership of the Palestinian Authority.

There are other questions about the family. How do the great haters become effective mass or genocidal killers? Some consider the tremendous brutality in their childhoods, especially beatings at the hand of their fathers, to have a momentous role in forming cruelty. Stalin's anti-Semitism may have been a legacy of child-abuse—"perhaps from his drunken, brutal father, who liked to put his wine-drenched fingers into his infant son's mouth; perhaps from his mother, who consecrated her son to the Orthodox Christian church and who believed implicitly in the legend that the perfidious Jews had murdered the 'Messiah.'"[97] One of Stalin's childhood friends characterized the beatings Stalin endured from his father as "undeserved, frightful beatings."[98] Stalin later "brutalized and lashed"[99] his own children. Hitler's stepfather also beat him; he was born out of wedlock and he lived with the still up-and-kicking rumor that his real grandfather was a Jew.

The grown children of Nazi leaders ask questions and, with some exceptions, feel either guilt or some kind of responsibility for what their fathers did. "How could he be so cultured and good to me," asked one son of Hans Frank, who was master of German-occupied Poland, "and then say things so stupid and hateful."[100] Another son recalled that when he was in school a classmate drew a picture of a Jew being turned into soap, which the teacher complimented and showed to the whole class: "Already rebuffed by his father when he tried to ask about the shooting of Poles, Norman did not mention the drawing to his father. 'But I felt then that something terrible was happening,' he recalls."[101] A third son says, "I would like to go to Israel, but how can I go? I am ashamed to meet these people."[102] Norman Frank refuses to have children because, he says, "after what my father did, I don't think the Frank name should go on."[103]

Fascism creates its own legacy. For instance, Alain Robbe-Grillet and Michel Foucault—each having had remarkable influence in western art and thought—share a set of compulsions rooted, at least in part, in the Nazi occupation of France, and in this they are more the norm than deviant. Robbe-Grillet's parents were "virulent anti-Semites" and had "avidly collaborated with the Nazis after 1940."[104] Foucault and Robbe-Grillet were "haunted . . . by a dream of apocalypse. From the early 1940s on, [Robbe-Grillet] was obsessed by the fantasy of being 'sucked reluctantly into the heart of an unknown, unstable, irrational liquid universe ready to engulf me, its ineffable face at once the face of death and desire.'"[105] For Foucault, sex became the annihilation of the self through pain; for Robbe-Grillett a sexual voyeurism that increasingly involves film of women murdered, cut, mutilated—art, of course.

There is also an emergent profile of families that hid Jews during the

Nazi terror: in general, parents discussed rules and used inductive reasoning "instead of harsh punishment";[106] "[m]ost Holocaust rescuers came from loving families that instilled in them a sense of self-worth and love";[107] or there was "a nurturing, loving home [or] an altruistic parent or beloved caretaker . . . [or] a tolerance for people who were different [or] a childhood illness or personal loss that tested their resilience and exposed them to special care [or] an upbringing that emphasized independence, discipline with explanations (rather than physical punishment or withdrawal of love), and caring."[108] These were the families who, in the main, rescued Jews. Yet rescuers have been sentimentalized. What accounts for the rescuers who sexually abused children?

5

MASCULINITY/FEMININITY

The Nazis called National Socialism "a male event."[1] Brutality was a synonym for strength, order for society; respect for human life was a weakness, feeble and fatal. For the most part hard-core Nazis were "recalcitrant and demobilized soldiers who could not reconcile their inherited militarism with the democratic beliefs of the Weimar Republic."[2] Democracy was feminine, subject to the will of citizens who were perceived as a mass, a crowd, infiltrated by communists and poisoned by Jews; democracy had sickness running through it. To Hitler the masses were "feminine"—in the words of Walter Laqueur describing Hitler's and Goebbels' view, "slow and lazy; their memories were weak; and they reacted only to the thousandfold repetition of the simplest ideas. . . . [I]n their activities and thought [they] were motivated by emotion rather than reason."[3] Hitler shrewdly bypassed intellectuals; he wanted a dumb mob, which he got. The men in the mob felt more male, more German while their leader was, in his mind, treating them like a girl. They were stupid, simple, seduced; and the morning after, they were deployed. Every *Sieg Heil* announced a romance—with Hitler cast as Rhett. Surely the Germans went mad, but there was an anatomy (not a biology) to their madness. This was a homoerotic frenzy in which Hitler was the maximum male; he knew it and his girlfriend soldiers knew it too. The literal homosexuality of Ernst Röhm and his SA (a paramilitary Nazi police force) became intolerable in what it revealed about the cult of masculinity Nazi-style: iconic, baroque, debauched, anal but messy with promiscuity, partaking in sadism and pedophilia, it subverted the identity of the maximum male, challenged the loyalty of his girls to him, and implied an absence of literal potency. Hitler had Röhm and his cohort killed, an assertive declaration of his own male preeminence. In fact, Hitler was seen by many both inside and outside Germany as a pure, spartan, modest man of iron and steel. In England, profascist novelist Wyndham Lewis spoke for many aristocrats in admiring "the Führer's rigorous, clean-living masculinity,"[4] while opposing and stigmatizing the "'softness' and 'flabbiness' of the female flux."[5] England's elites in art, society, and government flirted with Hitler, a crush rivaled only by those who swooned for Mussolini. It was a vicarious experience of manhood uncompromised by British manners.

In the German paradigm, manhood was peasant, not aristo: land, soil, ethnic Germans on German soil, the soil itself as German as the Germans. This was the Fatherland, not girlie Mother Russia (the bolshevik menace). It was the peasant who worked the soil, who had dirty German soil on dirty German hands; it was the peasant who did the real work of producing food and it was the peasant who was unequivocally German, not Jewish. For the Nazis, "peasants represented everything that was healthy in German tradition; they were the life source of the nation; and their strength was essential to the racial hygiene of the Nordic race."[6] This may be why, in Poland, the educated were targeted and annihilated. Polish peasants, Hitler believed, could work as slave labor for the Germans; but teachers and clergy, for instance, had to be destroyed—as if education too was in the blood, passed on by biological inheritance.

Clearly German peasants were higher on the food chain than either Polish peasants or educated Poles. But the food chain itself has to be understood as devolution from male to female, each ratchet down closer to the feminized, the feminine. In cultural terms, hatred of Jews and women had been synthesized, the result of a mix of Nietzsche, Weininger, and Strindberg. Both women and Jews were defined as parasites who live off the vitality of the so-called Aryan male. This was a new kind of misogyny in that it imparted to women the stereotypical evil, cunning, and power of the Jew while at the same time insisting on the parasitism of both groups. This synthesis of Jew-hate and woman-hate made both the woman and the Jew more repugnant—and made the burden of a feminized male more unbearable. The scapegoating of the Jewish body, the feminized body, and the woman's body became a necessity for men in constant fear of descending—or being shoved—into the anti-Aryan abyss of the Jew, abhorrent and despised.

In Nazi Germany masculinity was a matter of life and death; the masculine standard was murderous, coldblooded, heartless. Imagine the relief in using a Jew's body as a line of demarcation—step on the Jew, crush him underfoot, be without remorse—and the women and children: crush them or become like them. Could boys have stood against Himmler and Heydrich when imitating them was so much easier—a uniform and the hardened penile arm? The promise of militarism is that masculinity will be affirmed. The promise of Nazi militarism was that the murderer would live in honor and glory, rewarded: Hitler's progeny would triumph over the weak, the conquered, the parasitic, the vicious—murder would make them men. The men who embraced Hitler embraced murder, even under the guise of conventional warfare: not just the SS or the Wehrmacht but the grunts too—they were all Hitler's sons.

The dynamic Hitler exploited was written about in the Hebrew Bible: Abraham obeyed an omnipotent father and prepared to sacrifice his own son Isaac; just in time God provided a scapegoat for Isaac, a lamb to take his place. This is often understood as a parable of human progress: moving from human to animal sacrifice. But, in fact, this is a story of male fear of the more powerful male: Abraham fears the male God; Isaac, the son, has to fear both of them. In *The Untouchable Key*, Alice Miller describes the cost of this patriarchal dynamic to the sons: "How can a person lying on a sacrificial altar with hands bound, about to be slaughtered, ask questions when his father's hand keeps him from seeing or speaking and hinders his breathing? . . . He has been dehumanized by being made a sacrifice; he no longer has a right to ask questions and will scarcely even be able to articulate them to himself, for there is no room in him for anything besides fear."[7] For German men, the lamb was a Jew. For Hitler's gang, the lamb was a Jew.

Another way to put it is that Hitler harnessed the masculinity, the virility of men, organized it, trained it to kill. He organized the violence of men, especially young men, who then became canon fodder; he harnessed the sadism of men, middle-aged, fully adult men, who then murdered both systematically and on whim. He used male violence in a game called More-Male-Than-Thou: the "Thou" was a Jew. He provoked, antagonized, and terrified men, younger and older, to create in them an anxiety that only killing could cure and only hate could pacify. He used that anxiety to make men killers with the opposite of a conscience, in effect an anticonscience in which softness or kindness or any regard for human life was a moral flaw, a corruption of the German spirit. Hitler fought a racist war dressed up as nationalism and designed to make the male organ swell; its point was to destroy civilization as embodied in the Jew, to savage the ethical codes of armies and citizens, to wreck the decency of ordinary human beings. Hitler parlayed men's fear of other men into an aggression that degraded and destroyed most of Europe, including, of course, Germany itself. Hitler abandoned Germany before he died; he wanted Germans to suffer because they had not been strong enough, brutal enough to win the war: he died with resentment and bitterness in his heart (so to speak) and with a contempt for the German people that both betrayed and denied their loyalty to him. Where was the *Volk* now that he needed them? He was a sociopathic killer with a social policy of mass murder and genocide. The German people, male and female (although all female in relation to him), adored him. The only sheep led to the slaughter in World War II were the Germans.

In the devastating nationalist—or ethnocentric—wars that dot the planet now, hypermasculinity is more democratized than it was under Nazi rule. In *Blood and Belonging: Journey Into the New Nationalism,* Michael Ignatieff says, "As everyone can see on his [*sic*] television screen, most nationalist violence is perpetrated by a small minority of males between the ages of eighteen and twenty-five. Some are psychopaths but most are perfectly sane."[8] These are, he says, "young males, intoxicated by the power of the guns on their hips"; he had not, he says, "understood how deeply pleasurable it is to have the power of life and death in your hands."[9] He suggests that "liberals have not understood the force of male resentment" at peace: "[l]iberals have not reckoned with the male loathing of peace and domesticity or with the anger of young males at the modern state's confiscation of their weapons."[10] He sees the state as "the order of the father," and "nationalism is the rebellion of the sons."[11] The savageness of these wars, "the staggering gratuitousness and bestiality," suggest to him "that nationalism exists to warrant and legitimize the son's vengeance against the father."[12] The state has taken the power of the gun from the male; nationalism gives it back. Ignatieff is positing a biological male violence that is angry at both order and civilization; and the great achievement of peace in Europe (now threatened by Balkan atrocities) is one source of this violent discontent.

In *The Warrior's Honor: Ethnic War and the Modern Conscience,* Ignatieff advocates disarmament of these same violent, resentful young men— "Militias must be disarmed; weapons must be confiscated"; "these societies need states, with professional armies under the command of trained leaders."[13] Either the cycles of male violence are definable (and predictable) or in metaphysical terms this is the chicken-and-egg question: are these young men violent and in love with killing because there is a state, or do they need a state to pacify them, at which point another co-hort of young men can start shooting their neighbors (can and will)? Is hypermasculinity a young man's game; or is it masculinity itself that both causes and motivates violence? Is the pleasure in killing a male pleasure? In the United States are ten- and eleven-year-old boys discovering this male pleasure—are they just precocious (and armed)? How much of the pleasure is in the power per se, especially in humiliating a designated en-emy, creating terror, lording it over the less powerful? Is power the fore-play and killing the act?

The rape and murder of women and children have also been part of the fun; might it be that epidemic rape, saturation rape is needed as much or more than the gun to make the violent boys feel genuinely unpacified, genuinely undomesticated, full-body violence in conjunction with gang violence being the most eloquent expression of masculinity? "The pre-ferred victims of today's civil wars," writes Hans Magnus Enzenberger in *Civil Wars: From L.A. to Bosnia,* "are women and children . . . [I]t seems that everywhere the aim is to dispose of the defenseless."[14] Enzenberger blames the violence on the breakdown of patriarchy: "The young protag-onists are almost exclusively young men. Their behavior demonstrates the extent to which the patriarchal system has eroded."[15] He regards patri-archy as a system in which the energy or violence ("testosterone-fueled en-ergies"[16]) was socialized by a code in which men tested their strength against the strongest, not the weakest; this was a masculinity that had as an intrinsic part of it a code of honor. Instead, "[a] new manliness has come to the fore. It may seem to glory in cowardice; but that would be an exaggeration, for it is unable to distinguish between bravery and cow-ardice."[17] Walter Laqueur in his study of fascism finds the same dynamic in the radical fundamentalism sweeping the Middle East: "Like fascism, radical fundamentalism is a movement of young males, in the Middle East as much as in Sri Lanka and elsewhere."[18]

Is the problem violent men, or is the problem masculinity outside bi-ology (whatever the biology might be)? For women, the question is ur-gent: with patriarchy intact women are raped and murdered; with patriarchy "eroded" women are raped and murdered. Why do young men have a crazed fear of being feminized—pacified and domestic? Could the reason be that women are raped and murdered? For men, doing the rape and murder puts them on top: the weak are under them, literally and fig-uratively. "They belonged," writes Hanan Al-Shaykh in *The Story of Zahra,* "to a world that was not my world, not a world for those who dared not lift a gun. Always, to my great surprise, they would be laughing like young men in a dormitory. I could never understand their logic. It was a logic that confused war with life."[19] Will violent young men always confuse war with life, or is it masculinity, the need for it, that is the root cause of the violence? Make no mistake; these are not rhetorical questions—they need to be answered.

After Masada, when Jewish resisters to Roman rule killed every last Jew including themselves so as not to be made slaves, Jewish history has been perceived as a history of weak and impotent men, scholarly, passive. Jewish history is also the story of Jews being everywhere, belonging nowhere, locked in ghettos, expelled from countries, killed in pogroms, dying in or surviving legal and violent persecution. The martial Jew in the Hebrew Bible disappears from sight altogether, as if Jewish men were pacifistic by nature, a kind of biological mutation among men, gentle, nonviolent, all these descriptions being pejorative: sissies, wimps, incapable of fighting; cowards, almost clowns.

The overwhelming Jewish self-conception was the same. It was in part this antimanliness on the part of Jewish men that kept Jews separate and disparaged. Even in considering civil emancipation, opponents argued "that Jews could not become true citizens because they were worthless as soldiers due to their physical stature."[20] And yet, the history of Jews in their countries of residence was one of military participation and distinction: in Germany, Jews were given civil equality in 1871—"Jews were only 1 per cent of the population, but grossly over represented among the upper classes. They repaid the German fatherland with fervent patriotism, and 12,000 died in World War I"[21]; in Russian-occupied Poland, "[t]he Jews participated in two armed uprisings against the Tsars in 1830–31 and 1863–64"[22]; in France, "[t]en thousand foreign Jews are believed to have enlisted from a total immigrant Jewish population in France in 1914 of perhaps 40,000. Some 46,000 native and foreign Jews were mobilized and 6,500 were killed, from a population in 1914 of about 120,000"[23]; and in France by May 1940—"[o]f about 100,000 foreigners who had volunteered or been drafted into the French army . . . about 30,000, or 30 percent—a number enormously in excess of their proportion of the immigrant population—were non-French Jews"[24]; throughout Europe in World War II—"[i]n many countries—France, the Soviet Union, Holland, Belgium, Greece—a million or more Jews fought in the nation's army or resistance forces . . ."[25]; and in the Soviet Union, "Jews in fact earned the most disproportionate number of military awards of any Soviet nationality during the war, distinguishing themselves in every branch of the Soviet military."[26]

John Weiss notes that in World War I, German-Jewish officers "were often amazed when their orders were obeyed."[27] It is an odd fact that Jews could be fighting and dying virtually invisible to the societies in which they lived. They were invisible, too, to Jews who adopted Zionism as a fix for manhood denied in these same societies—we are strong, not weak: "The decades around 1900 in Europe constituted a turning point . . . Zionism amounts to *the* historic break with the culture of Jewish meekness and gentleness and the beginnings of a tough Jewish counterculture."[28] While many Zionists wanted to turn Jews into peasant-farmers, the father of military Zionism, Zeev Jabotinsky, wanted to turn Jews into soldiers: "Because the Yid is ugly, sickly, and lacks decorum, we shall endow the ideal image of the Hebrew with masculine beauty. The Yid is trodden upon and easily frightened and, therefore, the Hebrew ought to be proud and independent. The Yid is despised by all and, therefore, the Hebrew ought to charm all. The Yid has accepted submission and, therefore, the Hebrew ought to learn to command. The Yid wants to conceal his identity from strangers and, therefore, the Hebrew should look the world in the eye and declare: 'I am a Hebrew.'"[29] This is an extraordinary expression of Jewish self-hate.

Hatred of the "Yids" is not mitigated by any knowledge or recognition of Jewish participation in wars and uprisings in the record of the time. Anti-Semites were successful in destroying the self-worth of Jews by creating a portrait of effeminate males; but without the misogyny that made the feminization of any male stigmatizing, anti-Semites could not have elicited shame in the Jewish male: the shame of preferring peace to war; the shame of appearing gentle, not brutal; the shame of reading, writing, thinking as male vocation. And in the most desperate days of Hitler's rule, a few good men and women discovered for themselves—since it had not been handed down to them—the beauty and power of a gun. Amid the Jewish partisans who fought the Nazi slaughter of Jews from forests, "a man could change his situation by acquiring a gun . . . No such opportunities were available to women, who were discouraged from carrying arms. . . . In the very rare instances when a woman with a weapon reached [the partisans,] it would be confiscated. Guns belonged to men, not to women—this was the law of the forest."[30] This particular partisan group was founded by the Bielski brothers, who had, in fact, been Jewish peasants. They had the skills and strengths of peasants, not scholars; this when joined to their Jewish identity produced a physical resistance. The Bielski brothers and their families were at the top of the guerrilla hierarchy; "next in importance were young men with guns."[31] (See Nechama Tec, *Defiance: The Bielski Partisans.*)

In the Warsaw ghetto, both men and women organized the resistance; the role of the women was anything but subordinate. These resisters "all dreamed of having weapons to be able to shoot our oppressors if we were caught and not to be taken alive. We had light weapons, grenades, and revolvers, our major weapons, which we had also used in the Uprising. Everyone had somehow managed to take his [or her] pistol out with him [or her] through the sewers."[32] The longing for a gun was a dream shared, surprisingly perhaps, by Sigmund Freud who "identified with the life of the soldier. Particularly attached to Hannibal, the great Carthaginian general, Freud precisely plotted out Hannibal's battles and remarked that had he himself not been Jewish (and therefore prohibited from military leadership), he would have pursued the career of a military officer."[33]

The Jewish male, emasculated by anti-Semitism, shamed by the stigma of the feminine, was overrun and overpowered by the carefully cultivated brutality of the Nazis; but, for those who did resist, as Eva Hoffman says in *Shtetl: The Life and Death of a Small Town and the World of Polish Jews,* "It is a consistent element of all the testimonies by and about the Jewish fighters that, despite the devastating personal losses they sustained, their morale improved as soon as they got weapons and learned to use them. The arms, of course, literally made it possible for them to defend themselves, but the weapons also lessened their sense of humiliation and helplessness, of being turned into pure victims."[34]

In the Warsaw ghetto itself, says Nora Levin, "the fighters and the Ghetto as a whole had crossed over a big psychological block: a Jewish fighting arm was now permitted to place Jewish lives in the balance, to go to war knowing that it had the full support of the Ghetto." This was important, says Levin, because it restored "[t]he uses of sovereignty to which Jews had been unaccustomed for two millennia . . ."[35] It cannot be surprising that sovereignty attaches to the use of force; nor that organized violence as a form of self-defense provides self-respect. For Jews after World War II, guns mattered: U.S. Jews bought and sent guns into Palestine, then Israel; and in every still existing Jewish community pacifism was dead, killed by the Nazis along with the six million. There would be no more feminized, gentle Jewish male, no more "Yid."

Even Jewish-American gangsters got into the pro-Zionist spirit and provided some material help to Israel; the relationship started in 1946: "Reuven Dafni, an envoy of the Palestinian Jewish underground, had a meeting with Bugsy Siegel in a Los Angeles restaurant as early as 1946. 'Do you really want to tell me that the Jews in Palestine have taken arms, shoot, fight?' asked the gangster with some surprise. 'Yes,' answered the Israeli envoy. Bugsy looked him straight in the eyes. 'When you say "fight," you mean "kill"?' Again, Dafni answered in the affirmative. 'Then I'm your man,' responded Bugsy."[36]

Like it or not, Israelis became martial Jews, proud Hebrews: the army not only of Israel but of the Jewish nation. And once Israel occupied the West Bank and Gaza, the shoe, so to speak, was finally on the other foot: "Without a physical environment of their own in which to chart their progress as a people, the Palestinian refugees instead take pride in their ability to suffer."[37] The irony is overwhelming. First there were stones thrown by young men: "The adrenaline-filled battles of the intifada release pent-up frustration, rage, and testosterone of the *shabbab* (young men) . . ."[38] Now Arafat has a Palestinian police force in place, with guns. What will the *shabbab*—with their analogues in Bosnia and Zaire—do? What will the violent young men do?

Of course, once Jewish men became physical, no longer gentle or weak, they had to own Jewish women in a new roughhouse sort of way: in Israel Jewish women have no civil equality with Israeli men, who are the fighters, the army, the men. Under religious law, equality is proscribed. In Israel, women live under the ancient laws of their religion: Jewish, Druze, Muslim, or Christian. The religious courts have jurisdiction over the so-called private sphere, the sphere in which women, driven from history, live. The religious courts have authority over child custody, reproduction, marriage, and citizenship per se. In those courts a woman cannot be a witness; if she is granted a divorce, entirely at the pleasure of her husband, she must back out of the courtroom bowing (to him, no less). Women whose husbands deny them divorce are called *agunot,* chained; they include battered women, betrayed women, raped-in-marriage women, and they are in internal exile in the Promised Land with no rights, usually also no shelter and no money. In 1988 there were an estimated ten-thousand *agunot.*

The military is the backbone of the nation. The Israeli military in its early days had women combatants; but as Israeli masculinity grew in size and ambition, the women were driven out, recolonialized as the "weak Jews" the men no longer were. As Simona Sharoni describes in *Gender and the Israeli-Palestinian Conflict: The Politics of Women's Resistance:* "Women serving in the Israeli military belong to the Women's Corps, which is known in Hebrew as *chail nashim* but usually referred to in its abbreviated version, *chen,* which translates literally as charm and grace. . . . In fact, during their basic military training, women are coached to emphasize their femininity and neat appearance; they even receive cosmetic guidance as part of their official basic training. . . . Women in the military are expected to raise the morale of male soldiers and make the army a home away from home."[39] This required military service makes second-class status an order: commanded to be feminine, the women (like the women in the forests with the partisans) are kept from bonding with the gun, from owning violence, even disciplined violence. The presumption is made that this class of "weak Jews" is better off weak, vulnerable to attack, not entitled to self-defense: the State and its interests are defended by men with guns, which finally does away with the emasculating stereotypes of anti-Semitism. Sharoni says that "[t]his gendered division of labor and power was institutionalized in February 1981, when the Israeli military attorney general ruled that coffee making and floor washing are within the legitimate duties of military secretaries, the majority of whom happen to be women."[40] This purposeful dispossession of women from equality, self-sovereignty, and independence, this official trivialization, socializes women to accept inequality. As Yaron Ezrahi says in *Rubber Bullets: Power and Conscience in Modern Israel,* "Considering the central role of the Israeli army in shaping social values and in defining cultural patterns, designating women soldiers to serve in secretarial jobs or as telephone operators, nurses, and parachute folders has defined them as a supporting cast even beyond the army context. . . . In the army, to be a male qualifies one to expect obedience from a woman."[41]

The language itself provides a pornographic underbelly for Israeli statehood and nationalism: "The Hebrew word *kibush,* which is the most commonly used term for the Israeli occupation of the West Bank and Gaza Strip, is also used to describe conquest either of a military target or of a woman's heart. This conflation of women and military targets is not merely linguistic . . . During military training exercises, for example, strategic targets are often named after significant women in the soldiers' lives. This common practice implies that women, like military targets, must be protected so that they will not be conquered or controlled by the enemy."[42] Significantly, it also means that women must be conquered and controlled by the Israeli male. There is the racist evocation of conquered Arabs, which, when in the sphere of sexuality, raises the temperature of the conflict; and there is the misogyny of turning women into objects, targeting women for violence. This means that Israeli soldiers colonize two groups: "weak Jews," in this case Jewish women, and the indigenous Arab population. This is a staggering, if unoriginal, assertion of masculinity. As Ian Buruma writes (paraphrasing an Israeli living in Bonn, Germany): "Before the war, Michael said, Jews were seen as gentle, bookish pacifists. The Germans, on the other hand, had Prussian discipline. They were 'hard as Krupp steel' . . . But now Israelis had become the disciplined, hardworking warriors. Many older Germans admired them for this, as much as they despised the Arabs for being lazy and dirty. Now it was the Germans who had become pacifists. 'We Israelis laugh at German soldiers now,' said Michael."[43]

The masculinity of Israeli soldiers frankly goes off the charts: normalizing Jewishness has meant normalizing violence—ordered and disciplined violence, which distinguishes young Israeli soldiers from the *shabbab* or the other violent young men in contemporary nationalist wars. Israeli virility has changed the meaning of being a Jew so profoundly that the enemies of Israel do it honor. "Every sect and nationality in the Arab world," says Peter Theroux in *Sandstorms: Days and Nights in Arabia,* "was known as 'the Jews of the Arab world.' It was a boast. In Saudi Arabia's agricultural province, Gassim, a wealthy farmer proudly told me that his tribe were 'the Jews of the Arab world.' I heard it from Druze, Palestinians, Copts, even from an ethnic Persian in Iraq; from everyone, naturally, except Arab Jews. It implied wily, moneyed machismo and had no overtones of religion, suffering, or dispersal."[44] This might be called Jew-envy—evidence that the revolution happened: Israeli men are admired for being hard, cold, cruel; the stigmatized smartness of the Jewish scholar has been transformed into strategic skill and an unnerving capacity to use force, including torture and assassination, against a perceived enemy.

Arab recognition of Israeli virility, or, if you will, military superiority, has caused an Arab crisis: there may be many Arab states but none of them nor all of them have been able to defeat the Israeli military. This is King David's army. The Israelis have won war after war; and the warrior ethic informs all the values of the state if not the Jewish nation. Terrorism, especially suicide missions, is the war of the weak Arab, the stateless Arab, the emasculated Arab: the Arab male now feminized by the Israeli soldier; especially the Palestinian male, who has been defeated utterly. Terrorism makes a powerful society afraid: witness terrorism in the United States. "Terrorism," says William V. O'Brien in *Law and Morality in Israel's War With the PLO,* "may have an enormous psychological impact on a target society, forcing it to exist in a perpetual state of emergency. This is its genius as a means of coercion."[45] Terrorism against a powerful, militarist opponent can turn that opponent into a girl; in fact it is not unlike rape used to conquer and destroy women: it is sudden force, incomprehensible violence, intense hate; it proves masculinity by creating fear, chaos, and pain. Terrorism takes over the minds of those who use it just as militarism does; the strategy itself creates a moral universe of catastrophe, emergency, and despair. The violent young men kill enemies—the nationalist enemy and also the female enemy among themselves—women of their own group become targets for extreme aggression, control, and domination. The nationalist enemy will try to find collaborators in the feminized population and the violent young men will kill their own: "In their latest genesis as masked and hatchet-wielding ninjas, the *shabbab* are Palestine's nocturnal enforcers of law and order, the self-appointed judges, juries, and executioners . . . Now, more Palestinians are being executed by other Palestinians than are being killed by the Israeli army."[46]

In particular, a growing number of women are "being targeted as spies by the fundamentalist *shabbab* . . . The phenomenon is linked to the rise of militant Islam"[47]—which is linked to the feeling of impotence. Endangered masculinity requires a deeper, stricter colonization of one's own women; and it is not only Palestinians who are motivated by a driving need not to be seen as weak or feminine up against the Israelis. "The problem for the Muslim states," says Fatima Mernissi in *The Veil and the Male Elite: A Feminist Interpretation of Women's Rights in Islam,* "after their quasi-disappearance during the colonial period, was that they found themselves almost feminized—veiled, obliterated, nonexistent."[48] The power of the stigma of feminization seems indelible: it touches and corrodes states as well as groups of men; its reach can countenance any crime; at the same time scapegoating women per se provides relief from the anxiety created by perceived weakness and it is easy to do: "The *hijab* is manna from heaven for politicians facing crises. It is not just a scrap of cloth; it is a division of labor."[49]

In societies that cannot tolerate any deviation from hypermasculinity, the drive to push women down is obsessive: this the Israelis and their Arab neighbors have in common; but Palestinian men are seen as a group purposefully humiliated by Israeli soldiers, "continuously pushed around, humiliated, treated very badly by the security forces"[50]; "[m]uch of this belittling has taken place in front of their children and their womenfolk"[51]; "[f]or Arab men, that is the same as losing their masculinity . . ."[52]

Palestinian men also do menial labor throughout Israel, including women's work such as cleaning hotel rooms. QED: the rise of Hamas and a mean fundamentalism that wants Palestinian women—the best educated among the Arabs—lower than the demeaned men. Some Palestinian men "who grew up as the children of refugees" claim a sensual and even sexual relationship with the land—"Shehadeh walks on the soil of the little hills near Ramallah, unconsciously enjoys the touch of the hard earth under the soles of his feet, smells the thyme, looks for a long time at the olive trees. Desire for the earth which the Jews threaten to take over arouses such physical jealousy within him that he calls himself the country's pornographer."[53] This sentimentality is a sophisticated form of sexualized self-pity gendered male, a sentimentality shared by men who have been defeated; it is a phony narrative of dominance. An East German neo-Nazi explains: "You always thought about it from the perspective of an embattled German man. There was a world conspiracy against the Nazi Party, which made us the most persecuted group in history—'today's Jews,' as some neo-Nazis ironically put it. . . . We were the most persecuted minority in Europe, so there was hardly a moment to stop to think objectively, when every minute had to be spent in a defensive struggle against our enemies."[54]

The emotional landscape of the defeated male is one of rage, stupidity, and delusion. The Zionists who built the Israeli state never allowed themselves either self-pity or sentimentality; nor do Israelis now. That is why they won; and win. Clarity and discipline are great strengths; once lost or compromised, the effect will be defeat or an increasingly grotesque use of force to patch over failures in objectivity: not seeing the world, including the men and women on the ground, except through a distorting lens.

Any warrior has to be unsentimental. The situation of the Israelis raises, in part, this question: is masculinity master over human intelligence, never satisfied, always arrogant, a kind of delusion that grows with power until the too-strong are as dumb as the too-weak?

Inside the male soul there are hallucinations about one's self that beggar description: the jackal is tender, sensitive, wise; the vulture is tender-hearted. Consider the self-view of Höss, the commandant of Auschwitz, as an example of a defeated male's sense of self but also the conqueror's sense of the very same: "Even though I became accustomed to all of the occurrences of the concentration camp, I never became insensitive to human suffering. I always saw it and felt it. But I always had to walk away from it because I was not allowed to be soft. I wanted to have the reputation of being hard. I did not want to be thought of as a weak person."[55] Poor baby. In fact, Höss was just one of the boys: deluded, dangerous, and self-justifying.

There is a commonplace analogy, pre-Israel, between Jews and women. This analogy is based on the perceived nature not of Jews but of women as such; H. L. Mencken's biographer paraphrases him, but this formulation of the analogy is widespread in pre-Israel literature, psychology, and philosophy: "Jews, like women, are cunning in the attempt to make weakness overcome strength. Their moral code was framed to protect the weak, condemning, for instance, 'the quite natural act of destroying one's enemies.'"[56] The nature of women is taken to be predetermined, immutable, a fixed fact of life taken for granted, and therefore a touchstone that could always be invoked. As Jung said in 1934: "Freud and Adler have beheld very clearly the shadow that accompanies us all. The Jews have this in common with women; being physically weaker, they have to aim at the chinks in the armour of their adversary . . ."[57] Contempt for Jews is warranted because contempt for women is normative; both Jews and women have been locked in at night, Jews in ghettos, women in houses. Because, like women, Jews have not fought back, the men are taken to be biologically deviant in having none of the violent pride that distinguishes men from women. There was no literature pre-Israel that said, "Jewish men are peaceful, not violent; how can we be like them? If Jewish men are not inherently violent, maybe male violence is not a biological inevitability." But because the stigma of being a woman is deadly as well as dangerous, the Jewish male had to die or evolve in the opposite direction: move toward public violence, move away from women. Hitler made the necessity convulsive and universally accepted, but these simultaneous movements—toward violence, away from women—began nearly half a century before in Russia and Eastern Europe, especially Poland.

Coincidentally, the feminism of the nineteenth and early twentieth centuries was careful not to bring into question biological imperatives in order to concentrate more directly on attaining specific rights for women, including suffrage and the right of married women to own property. Because Jewish men were enfranchised during the Enlightenment, their civil situation should have pushed them across the boundary line between male and female into male. But civil recognition did not reify the maleness of Jewish men; in fact, their refusal to assimilate when given the opportunity reified their deviance. The Jewish problem and the Woman Question became twinned in the European consciousness and made the association political as well as psychological and perceptual.

Virginia Woolf, part of the feminist ferment, still lingered on the oddness of Jews in her 1918 diary: "There is something condensed in all Jews . . . as about some women, . . . unnatural repressions have forced unnatural assertions."[58] She seemed to mean that male Jews, like some women, were pushy and vulgar, lashing out with socially aggressive behavior in society; her context was the British upper-middle class. She is pointing to the self-consciousness of the outsider and she had a keen eye for the deformations caused by the absence of freedom and socially reified worth. She anticipates the eroticization of that entirely outré combination: the Jewish woman.

In *Memoirs of an Anti-Semite: A Novel in Five Stories*, Gregor von Rezzori describes that creature: "I would have been lying if I had not admitted that the aura of her lowly origins was what made my love for the Black Widow as rotten as if it were crawling with maggots . . . It was not just the way she spoke—she could not, of course, deny that she was Jewish. Her race was written in her features."[59] The black widow characterization—deadly, abnormally powerful, avaricious—applies to money as well as sex. As José Donoso writes in his novel *The Garden Next Door:* " . . . I started to explain that despite its reputation, Chiriboga's work is lifeless; that it's really an invention of that financial wizard Núria Monclús; that its quality is weighed down by its shortcomings; that it was invented by Núria to fill her already well-lined coffers; that she's a money-hungry, avaricious Catalan, a Jewish shark, a Fagin in skirts, and Latin American novelists are used by her the way Fagin used his little boys."[60] Fagin is more cruel than Shylock, more exploitative, more criminal, more heartless, without love or redemption. (Shylock loves his daughter.) This is the Jew in skirts, an anatomically correct woman as opposed to a feminized male; and she strikes double terror because she is imprisoned by a double contempt.

Unlike the male Jew, the Jewish woman cannot assimilate: because there is no sphere—public or private—in which she is free; she stays woman, caged by male perception and by male violence.

Male perception has a materiality to it: operating as if it were a metaphysical law that sets boundaries for women; and male violence is both public and private and even existed in the domiciles of the so-called weak Jews. Those homes were patriarchal homes in every sense of the word: the father was the master, and while the scholar might have been weak to outsiders, inside Jewish life the scholar was the center of the universe. In other words, he had dominion over his wife and children and nothing about the valuation of him as weak by non-Jews compromised his place. Because the violence of the male Jew pre-Israel was private, not public, it did not exist; it could not be seen or documented, since women were neither socially articulate nor inside history. Any violence inside the home—among Jews as among others—could be denied and sheltered behind a wall of privacy and male legitimacy.

It is hard to find women's voices in the long history of Jewish dialogue and discourse. Judaism may have been sex friendly if one followed the rules, but women did not get to argue with God about any aspect or dimension of their lives. "With very few exceptions," says David Biale in *Eros and the Jews: From Biblical Israel to Contemporary America,* "what we know of women's sexuality was filtered through male eyes; even the *tekhines,* women's prayers written in Yiddish, were often composed by men, sometimes masquerading as women."[61] The fact is that the pre-Israel Jewish man constructed the category *woman* as did non-Jewish males. In writing about Franz Kafka, the secular prototype of the weak Jew, biographer Frederick Karl says of Kafka's tortured relationships with women: "The role he chooses for her is one in which she must act out his own debased view of what a woman is. She, accordingly, loses whatever identity she may have in that particular relationship, and takes on role-playing that justifies the man's debased view of women as destructive, abusive, cruel, traitorous creatures."[62]

Women get blamed a lot for not protecting men from their cruel fathers (Kafka's situation); the blame is both in the form of cultural libels and physical punishment, especially degrading sexual use. Consistently, under the so-called passivity of women there is hidden a monster. She manifests as succubus or dominatrix or avenger (that being the stereotype of the feminist). It is surely a circle in hell for women: never perceived as human, a bit of this and a bit of that; instead always the ingenue under which is the bitch who deserves (and wants) the pain she gets. It is precisely this dimension under the passivity that justifies male cruelty toward women. The wheel can turn in any direction; for instance, "In Claude Morgan's early postwar novel *La Marque de l'homme,* the would-be collaborator (female) is tempted to yield to the charms of (German) seduction, illustrating a view of collaboration as an activity essentially restricted to and indulged in by women influenced by the strong masculine appeal of the dominant occupier. This association of collaboration with the female gender was a widespread myth of these years."[63] In collaborating, she becomes venal, the active agent of betrayal, the active agent of Nazism, the active destroyer of good men hurt by bad men with whom she colludes; her sexual appetite victimizes honorable men. The wheel also turned in the other direction, to the same effect for women, in Germany. According to Richard J. Evans in *Tales From the German Underworld: Crime and Punishment in the Nineteenth Century:* "In the early 1900s . . . the pornography of violence was overwhelmingly a pornography of women inflicting violence on men. The figure of the powerful, seductive and destructive woman, central to Sacher-Masoch's work, featured . . . in other novels of the time, such as Heinrich Mann's *Dr. Unrat* . . . These fantasies of violence were an aspect of the fascination of the new modernist art . . . with the marginal and the forbidden. They also represented . . . a masculine reaction to the emergence of a powerful, prominent, active and radical Feminist movement in the public sphere of Wilhelmine Germany in the middle of the 1890s onwards."[64] This abreaction to feminism, which will be familiar to contemporary feminists, actually reversed itself in reaction to "[d]efeat in the First World War and the collapse of the Wilhelmine empire"—then men preferred "the exercise of violent and sadistic impulses against women carried out in the name of an injured masculinity."[65] The violence was, in Evans's words, "real or imagined."[66] His concern here, happily, is male reality and male imagination; he is not suggesting that women imagined the violence.

In male culture, the nature of women is simply a movable feast from whip wielder to abject victim: but both justify eventual male violence. The choice for women seems to be punishment at the hands of "injured masculinity" or projections of sadism from a dominant masculinity; or is it that the injured men project the sadism onto women, for example Kafka, and the dominant men beat the shit out of women? Whichever. It is called "whatever works for him"; and most women at some point have "been there, done that," though many do not survive his pleasure. The question is how to get off this wheel constructed for the comfort and solace of men altogether; and then, the wheel itself badly needs burning. Women on the Indian subcontinent, who face being burned to death by husbands who find their dowries insufficient and being burned to death when widowed, should have the honor of the first arson.

One difference between women (including Jewish women) and male Jews was that women were forbidden study, scholarship, formal education. "In general," writes Gerda Lerner in *The Creation of Feminist Consciousness From the Middle Ages to Eighteen-seventy,* "education becomes institution- alized when elites—military, religious, political—need to assure their po- sition in power by means of training a group to serve and perpetuate their interests. Whenever that has happened, historically, women were discrim- inated against and excluded from the very inception of each system. The earliest example is the exclusion of women from training in the newly dis- covered skills of writing and reading in Sumer and Babylon of the 2nd millennium B.C. . . ."[67] There were exceptions, for instance, the surprising example of Sparta, the militarist utopia in ancient Greece; but even "[ed- ucated] girls were disadvantaged in every known society of the Western world in regard to the length of their training, the content they were taught and the skills of their teachers."[68] This was certainly also true of Asian, African, and Arab societies. So: there was nothing feminine about reading and writing; and there is no reason other than the role of violence in masculinity for stigmatizing Jewish men as if female. Reading and writ- ing were as distinctively male as plundering and killing. The exclusion of women from education was part of a strategy of erasure and captivity: sep- arate, segregated bodily or by social role, publicly invisible, women could not cross the boundary from the feminine sphere into power, especially civic power, the power of a distinct and sovereign citizen.

Ignorance and femininity are affirmed as virtual synonyms through an iconography of stereotype and disparagement: from the exposed and of- ten prefabricated dumb blonde of U.S. celebration to the Arab woman hidden in *hijab.* Fatima Mernissi in *Islam and Democracy: Fear of the Modern World* boldly describes the association of ignorance and feminin- ity in the Arab world: "Our pre-Islamic past is called the *jahiliyya,* 'the time of ignorance,' and as a result is subjected to the *hijab* that also veils the feminine. But who knows better than the Arabs the haunting power of that which is veiled, of that which the *hijab* hides?"[69]

However configured, women are separated because of their bodies, which are posited as an absolute other. As the rabbis of old said, "Anyone who looks at the little finger of a woman is as if he looked at [her genitals] . . . the handbreadth of a woman is [like] her genitals, and even that of his wife."[70] Hiding women through distortion and separation creates a fear that cruelty suppresses; and the French Revolution and the Enlightenment did nothing to ameliorate "the pervasive fear of women as a threat to the body politic" such that "even nonfeminist historians [now] recognize the overlap between Marie-Antoinette's official condemnation to death and the condemnation of her behavior as a reputedly bad woman, wife, and mother."[71] In the women's diaries of the era, as analyzed by Marilyn Yalom in *Blood Sisters: The French Revolution in Women's Memory,* "[A]ll, including Mme Roland, saw themselves as victims, and all, regardless of class, leave records of the connection between victimization and gender. . . . They describe their resistance to . . . jailers offering freedom for sexual favors. They remember the threats of brutal soldiers and the intervention of unexpected saviors as they and their children fled for their lives."[72] The diaries were acts of self-consciousness but this was muted speech, entirely private, engulfed in the isolation from public discourse. Each woman spoke to herself about events of daily life that were common among them as well as about war and persecution. Those who were brave have no public fame, nor is the rescue of children considered (especially by women themselves) a public act.

Some say, as does Tzvetan Todorov in *Facing Extremes: Moral Life in the Concentration Camps,* that "[h]eroic virtues tend to be the province of men, while ordinary virtues are equally if not more characteristic of women (but it is true that the physical abilities required are different)."[73] What exactly are "heroic virtues"? In *Conscience and Courage: Rescuers of Jews During the Holocaust,* Eva Fogelman notes: "Running through all these various inquiries was the assumption, sometimes implicit, sometimes overt, that in dangerous situations men would be more likely to help. I too assumed that women would undertake less physically taxing or hazardous tasks and leave the heroics to men. Time and again I was proven wrong. Women told of how they acted as decoys, couriers, double agents, and border runners."[74] In locked ghettos, while undertaking the support and care of children and men, women committed concrete acts of rebellion and resistance; and also in the camps. These were not acts in public for fame; nor have many historians been willing to recognize women as resisters or rescuers. Instead male writers on the subject do much as Todorov did: men acted on the stage of history on a heroic scale; women did ordinary acts. This is the clear bipolarity of male and female. But what is ordinary, for instance, about saving children? As Debórah Dwork notes: "It is interesting to observe that while much is known about the armed resistance, the history of groups that helped children has not been part of the recognized, legitimate public past. Many of these resisters were women; after the war they disappeared from public life. They did not seek publicity and they had left few records of their activities."[75]

And how does one signify and inscribe the bravery of women in the camps: who could bear what was done to them before murder? how is it possible that the survivors could become teachers, raise children, give birth to more children, make new families in new countries? "A long corridor with pegs on the walls," writes Czech resister Vera Laska about Auschwitz. "SS men with dogs straining their leashes and bearing their teeth. Strip down to the skin. Zebras shave off all hair, top, bottom and middle, whispering . . . SS men looking on with blasé expressions or shaking with laughter, the newer ones glaring at naked females as if judging a contest of ugliness. Each of their degrading glances is an obscenity. A menstruating woman is kicked for messing up the floor. . . . Showers, dozens of showers in one huge room, real water coming from the ceiling. One second it is hot, scorching, then cold, freezing, then it stops. Cursing it, I do not realize that at the same time in another shower room gas is pouring from those shower heads in the ceiling, exterminating those who went [to the] left."[76] Against this background of ordinary life in Auschwitz, to dare to accept being alive was heroic. And the atrocities were part of ordinary life, too: "One doctor," recalls Laska, "bet that he could perform ten hysterectomies in one afternoon and won; the women who were his guinea pigs lost."[77]

Israel insults these women by turning Israeli women into "weak Jews." In the military where the citizen-soldier is trained, each parachute folded, each menial act, is a repudiation of the courage of Jewish women in Auschwitz and disparages the women resisters of Europe, including those who saved children. Every aspect of second-class status for women in Israel degrades and demeans the women who were murdered in the Holocaust and the women who survived it. Every target named for a wife or sweetheart reenacts the murder of a Jewish woman. How can this dishonor be borne?

6

THE CHOSEN/THE EVIL

According to the Hebrew Bible (and its Christian analogue, the Old Testament) Jews are God's chosen people. It is not easy to see the benefits, if any, of this divine chosenness, since the history of the Jews is one of persecution and oppression, more Job than Joshua. An Israeli journalist, unhappy over Israeli remorse for the massacre of Arabs at Kfar Kassem, "computed that, over the previous 2,000 years—some 730,000 days or 17 million hours—at least one Jew had been killed every hour."[1] In the often-joined race for having suffered most, Jews are always the group to beat. To Jews, used to collective mourning, Jesus is just another murdered Jew (which is why the resurrection, not the crucifixion, is distinctively Christian). Jesus' suffering on the cross is familiar, part of a Jewish destiny burdened by chosenness. Christian antagonism to Jews, accused of deicide, rarely considered the Jewishness of Christ nor how, from a Jewish perspective, his murder was—to understate—one of many. The poet Paul Celan, Holocaust survivor, then suicide, articulates this perspective in an ageless way: "We are near, Lord,/near and at hand./Handled already, Lord,/clawed and clawing as though/the body of each of us were/your body, Lord."[2]

This relationship to God, embodied so brilliantly in the Jesus story, is terrifying in its intimacy and perhaps arrogant in its reach; but in biblical terms the Jewish God is the agent of Jewish suffering, the relationship itself being a spiritual paradigm for sadomasochism with the suffering as an empirical synonym for chosenness. God's desire, as it were, works itself out in the tormenting of his beloved: the Jews. As the stories of both Job and Jesus show, this torment did not begin, and arguably will not end, with the Holocaust. But the Holocaust—incomprehensible in both scope and detail—obliterates from recall, if not from memory, earlier mass persecution of the Jews and also mass murder and genocide suffered by other groups.

For the Jews, the Nazis were foreshadowed by the Chmeilnitzki massacres in 1648–1649, which were led by a Ukrainian Cossack whose name attaches to the dreadful events. As Joseph Telushkin puts it, "Although few people today know about it, there was a Nazilike war against the Jews three centuries before the Holocaust. . . . It is estimated that [Chmeilnitzki's] Cossack troops murdered well over 100,000 Jews at a time when world Jewry probably numbered no more than a million and a half."[3] As the Polish nationalist Wladyslaw T. Bartoszewski describes: "Between the 16th and 18th centuries, the Jews entered into what may be described as a marriage of convenience with the nobility. . . . Poland was described as 'heaven for the Jews, paradise for the nobles, hell for the serfs.'" Because of the perceived alliance between Jews and the nobility, "[t]he Jewish community suffered greatly . . . [A]bout twenty per cent of them were killed."[4] After the First World War, in the Ukraine "more than 100,000 Jews were murdered . . ."[5] Perceived as communists three hundred years after the Chmeilnitzki massacres, the Jews were again slaughtered. The Germans did the shooting, but Jews were barely acknowledged or helped by Polish partisans, only to be subjected to pogroms by Poles after Hitler's war. If soil remembers, it remembers the blood of Jews; as Christopher R. Browning describes in *Ordinary Men: Reserve Police Battalion 101 and the Final Solution in Poland:* "By mid-November 1942, following the massacres at Józefów, Łomazy, Serokomla, Konskwola, and elsewhere, and the liquidation of ghettos in Międzyrzec, Łuków, Parczew, Radzyń, and Kock, the men of Reserve Police Battalion 101 had participated in the outright execution of at least 6,500 Polish Jews and the deportation of at least 42,000 more to the gas chambers of Treblinka. . . . Once the towns and ghettos of the northern Lublin district had been cleared of Jews, Reserve Police Battalion 101 was assigned to track down and systematically eliminate all those who had escaped . . . and were now in hiding."[6] It is a fact that not even the common Nazi enemy led the Christian Poles to an alliance with the Jews of Poland, who were seen as a separate entity, a nation of sorts, foreign to the Poles. This division remains alive, even if few Jews do—the Nazis mass-murdered Poles and Jews, two distinct peoples by Christian conviction even if the Jews thought they were Polish.

This continuing bifurcation makes Diaspora Jews heartsick as they try to find the lost culture of their exterminated families; much as Germany's earlier rejection of the Jews devastated the Jewish love of German culture. These matters of heartbreak, while hardly matching murder in importance, still signify as betrayal, a treason to the dignity of Jews.

In the Balkans, too, a shared fate did not unite the persecuted. As Ignatieff describes: "Between 1941 and 1945, trains drew up at the railhead ramp on the other side of a vast, low, marshy field that slopes down to the Sava River. Jews and Serbs, Gypsies and Croatian Communists were herded out of the sealed wagons and pushed down the ramp to the rows of barracks behind the barbed wire. They were put to work in the brick factory, and when they were used up they were burned in the brick ovens or shot in the back of the head and then dumped in the Sava River. No one knows exactly how many people died . . ."[7] Serbs and Croatians still argue about the numbers, but neither Jews nor Gypsies participate in this dialogue now articulated by gunfire because they are gone. Extermination is different from even mass death; it is erasure, disappearance, permanent silence, impenetrable silence. Neither the beginning nor the end can be found. And still, somewhere else, in another time, another place, the chosen people live on side-by-side with the void, the unknowable absence. Perhaps only a writer of fiction could enumerate the consequences, dissect the aftermath; as Andrzej Szczypiorski writes in *The Beautiful Mrs. Seidenman:* "At any rate, the world later started in on others and left the Jews in peace, as if their quota of suffering had become exhausted by then and the quota of suffering of others had not. It even turned out that this strange bond that linked Jews with Germans, hence Heine with Goethe, Mendelssohn with Schubert, Marx with Bismarck, Einstein with Heisenberg, was not the only one of its kind or unsurpassed in its ambiguous madness. For behold, in Vietnam people were falling like flies from gas that exceeded Zyklon B in excellence, in Indonesia the rivers quite literally ran red with human blood, in Biafra people were shriveling from hunger . . . and in Cambodia pyramids were being constructed from human skulls whose numbers exceeded those in the crematoria and gas chambers."[8] Has God abandoned the Jews; is he trying out new partners; is he dancing as fast as he can? Why don't people hide from this crazed lover, this brutal father? Does human life matter to its creator? Or are human beings ants, all of us, with our illusions of identity and importance, our hallucinations of meaning; does he step on us not even knowing we are underfoot? Is he present or absent—was he present at Auschwitz? And why is he worshiped? And how is his existence consoling? Is it even possible that Jews have fulfilled "their quota of suffering"—is it possible to hope that he will be promiscuous enough to keep choosing others: that Cambodia or Biafra were not just infatuations of the moment? How does one ask God to choose someone else?

Shimon Peres writes that "[b]eing Jewish means belonging to a people that is both a chosen and a universal people."[9] Peres may be talking out of both sides of his mouth; but there is a truth hiding in his double talk; which is that the Holocaust is both unique and universal—indelible, indescribable, incomprehensible, and still a plain old genocide, not the first and not the last, the word *genocide* itself being newer than the reality, coined in closing arguments at the Nuremberg trials by Charles Dubost, representing the French as prosecutor—a word created in retrospect, a word not so much definitive as contemplative: what is the murder of a people? what are the constituent parts of this kind of murder? Could it be that Jews are chosen and others just die? In terms of both genocide and persecution, there have been a lot of others; is there a god worth having who is not a rescuer as well as a redeemer? Did the Christians conjure the divinity of Christ and the Muslims submit to Allah in order to have a god who loved them whatever the cost? Is the hatred of Jews a purposeful repudiation of the wrathful God who chose the Jews, and do Jews die in his place: scapegoated, substituting for the Hebrew God himself?

So many have suffered without the consolation of special biblical status. Slavery, known in many societies, is described by Orlando Patterson as "the permanent, violent, and personal domination of natally alienated and generally dishonored persons. . . . [T]he slave is always an excommunicated person."[10] Simply the transport of Africans for use as slaves is estimated to have cost millions of lives. And still, as David E. Stannard writes in *American Holocaust: Columbus and the Conquest of the New World,* "[t]he destruction of the Indians of the Americas was, far and away, the most massive act of genocide in the history of the world."[11]

This genocide, as J.M.G. Le Clézio says in *The Mexican Dream Or, The Interrupted Thought of Amerindian Civilizations,* "engulfed the Indian world from 1492 to 1550, and reduced it to a void. . . . To carry out such destruction it took the power of all of Europe . . . The Conquest was not just a handful of men taking over . . . seizing the lands, the food reserves, the roads, the political organizations, the work force of the men and the genetic reserve of the women. It was the implementation of a project, conceived at the very beginning of the Renaissance, which aimed to dominate the entire world."[12]

The genocide of indigenous populations continues in both South and Central America: for instance, "[a]s recently as 1986, the Commission on Human Rights of the Organization of American States observed that 40,000 people had simply 'disappeared' in Guatemala during the preceding fifteen years. Another 100,000 had been openly murdered."[13] Imperial domination and exploitation are one source of murder; and intraethnic violence another, as, for instance, inside the Indian populations the Spanish conquered. Richard Lee Marks in *Cortés: The Great Adventurer and the Fate of Aztec Mexico* claims, perhaps rightly (certainly about the Aztecs), that "tribe to tribe, the Indians were infinitely cruel to one another in ways that had no counterpart in anything the Spaniards had done or ever did. For example, the tribute [paid to Aztecs] . . . included as part payment young males and females for sacrifice. The Aztecs never sacrificed their own . . . and, because the Aztec need for sacrificial victims was so enormous, the Aztecs had to amplify the collected tribute with captives . . . and wars of exploration and conquest."[14] Aztec human sacrifice might be matched by, for instance, the Soviet famine under Stalin in which "millions starved to death," and "it was simply denied that any famine existed."[15] World history suggests that mass murder and intentional death are the rule, not the exception.

In contemporary terms, the most important modern genocide may be the Turkish massacre of the Armenians begun in the late nineteenth century with pogroms and executed by state terror from 1914 to 1917. First, Hitler took this genocide as encouragement; no one remembered it, he said. But second, it was in direct response to the 1914–1917 genocide that the concept of crimes against humanity began to be articulated in the international sphere. As Christopher Simpson says in *The Splendid Blond Beast: Money, Law, and Genocide in the Twentieth Century*, "[t]he new definition included domestic campaigns to exterminate a particular ethnic or religious group as well as institutionalized slavery, even though neither of these was considered a war crime under the Hague or Geneva covenant"; the definition also included "atrocities committed by a government against its own people."[16] The pogroms at the end of the nineteenth century took the lives of "tens of thousands [of] Armenians";[17] in 1914 Armenian men were used for forced labor, "worked . . . to death building a trans-Turkish railway for German business interests," after which any survivors were killed; in 1915 the Turkish government "secretly ordered mass executions of Armenian intellectuals and political leaders . . . The state also uprooted Armenian women and children from their homes and drove them into vast resettlement camps that were barren of supplies or shelter"; the populations in these camps were eventually pushed into the desert where "[h]undreds of thousands of Armenians died from shootings, starvation, exposure, and disease."[18] The ruling Turkish political party "expected to strike quickly, to keep the deportations and massacres secret, and to exterminate the Armenians *as a race* before the outside world learned of the atrocities."[19] [Italics mine.] Each detail of this genocide was noticed by Hitler as was the failure of European states to stop the killing; and virtually every element of genocide except for mass death by gas was rehearsed by the Turks to the later benefit of the Nazis.

In an earlier incarnation, when the Turks were the head and body of the Ottoman Empire, persecution of Christians included saturation rape; as Andrew Wheatcroft describes in *The Ottomans,* "Byzantine eyewitnesses told how young girls and boys were raped on altar tables . . ."[20] The rape was so vicious and extensive that "[m]any felt that the worst violation was not the killing, which was an outpouring of blood-lust quickly assuaged, but the ravishment of defenceless women and children, and the pillage of homes and churches. All the eyewitnesses talked of women 'dragged by force from their chambers' . . ."[21]

Are there national characters, traits inscribed on persons by nationality: for instance, are the Turks and the Germans natural predators? Or is domination the enticement to cruelty; and is power once achieved the crucible of sadism? Who chose the Armenians to be Hitler's rough draft; and was God present or absent; and where is he when children are being raped?

In the Hebrew Bible God is deeply involved in the fate of the Jews. He watches, he waits, he has conversations. In the beginning he sometimes appears to be elsewhere (for instance, when Eve eats the apple). He is unequivocally a god of retribution. He punishes disobedience, whether by turning Lot's wife into a pillar of salt or sending a flood. There is no biblical narrative in Jewish tradition in which God does good and the devil does bad. The emasculation of the Hebrew God—by limiting him to being responsible for all that is good—is no doubt a Christian improvement, a reconstruction of his character. As God is limited to good, Satan's domain expands. But Jews had to obey and worship a God who could be cruel—and not only to Jews: God strategizes military tactics when Israel makes war. The involvement of God with the collective fate of the Jewish people as opposed to the fate of individuals creates in Jewish consciousness a cause-and-effect relationship: God causes events, including bad events. As Elie Wiesel writes in the novel *A Beggar in Jerusalem:* "I question my Master: 'I can conceive of God's wanting to punish us for reasons that are His and not necessarily ours; but why do entire nations, so many nations, aspire to become His whip, His sword?' And my Master, his body emaciated by fasting, answers . . . 'The Jews are God's memory and the heart of mankind. We do not always know this, but the others do, and that is why they treat us with suspicion and cruelty.' "[22] It is God, not the devil, who is implicated in the Holocaust; because he determines the fate of the Jews. This is the ultimate meaning of chosenness and the core of Jewish sensibility.

The covenant between God and the Jews is signified on the flesh of Jewish men in circumcision—there is no human or animal sacrifice to commemorate the covenant, only the giving up of the male's foreskin. Because this covenant marks the Jewish male, many Holocaust survivors tell the same story: "For some time now I had known that whatever happened, I must never let anyone remove my pants or watch me while I was peeing."[23] The exposed penis reifies the vulnerability of the Jewish male; the exposed penis itself—exposed by circumcision—is vulnerable, and in its sanctification noncircumcised males are threatened: who are these men who have cut penises? what are they? The cutting is taken to be a partial castration, to mean less male, or to mean female in relation to the Jewish God. The circumcised penis amounts to the creation of a new genital, antinatural, antipagan, eventually anti-Christian. The circumcised penis denotes both chosenness and submission: the chosenness antagonizes; the submission feminizes.

In the West now, male circumcision is widely normalized as a so-called hygienic practice; but in the ancient world and until the modern era it must have seemed monstrous, a sinister form of penile mutilation that created overwhelming fear and anxiety in other men. There is no doubt that Jewish separateness—in circumcision, in diet, in devotion to one god, in following a divinely given legal code—was a source of resentment and hostility toward Jews. The blood-libel itself, which precedes Christianity, derives from a nightmare perception of the bleeding penis, the menstruating male.

Cut genitalia aside, the Jews were, as Lucy S. Dawidowicz says in *The Holocaust and the Historians,* "[t]he quintessential people of history"; the Jews "originated the idea of the God of history and they produced a written record of the past at least four centuries before Herodotus, whom the Western Christian world called 'the father of history' "; the Hebrew Bible "resounds with the word *z'chor,* elaborating the concept of memory and remembrance, the stuff out of which history is constituted."[24] In *The Sacred Chain: The History of the Jews,* Norman G. Cantor notes that "antimagicality is the distinctive quality of the Hebrew covenant religion as it took its definitive form toward the beginning of the Common Era."[25] This "antimagicality" is rooted in the demands of historicity and law, or time and duty; the Judaism of the Hebrew Bible is unsentimental in what is required from Jews, and faith cannot substitute for practice, the demands of the daily life. In addition, the Jewish God cannot be visually represented or imagined; his name must be neither spoken nor written. Distinct, on "a radical course different from religion of all other Mediterranean communities,"[26] memory and word oriented, the doctrine of chosenness fit like a glove; and when attacked in pogroms or by virulent anti-Semites in Hellenic and Roman times, when Jews started dying for being Jews, chosenness became the refuge for the question *why;* and, as Wistrich says, there was a "self-conscious pride in their special vocation as a people covenanted by God."[27]

Peter Gay in *The Cultivation of Hatred* sees chosenness as the garden-variety creation of an other: "Nothing seems more natural than the ease with which humans claim superiority over a collective Other. It is an immensely serviceable alibi for aggression . . . The Hebrews of the Old Testament times believed that Abraham's covenant with the Lord set them apart from lesser mortals. The Egyptians of the Old Kingdom took their fertile land as proof that the creator-god Re had singled them out in preference to the miserable Asians. The Greeks thought themselves better than the barbarians. . . . The animus was always the same: . . . the more one loved one's own, the more one was entitled to hate the Other."[28] But chosenness encompassed suffering and punishment: not the self-regard of civilization's various victors. It was "difference" in a multicultural world when "difference" wasn't cool. In maintaining this difference, Jews became enduring targets. Only after the Holocaust, for instance, did Christians of virtually every stripe, including Catholics, grant that the chosen people were not going to change, to convert and eradicate themselves, thereby voluntarily ending "the Jewish problem" (as if the Inquisition had not proved the futility of any such strategy). But finally, post-Holocaust, there was a begrudging respect: if these mad people were still Jews after the Nazi slaughter, evangelism would hardly make them sane. And well, okay, the Jews did not kill Christ—we got that wrong, sorry. In fact, there was some real introspection about the role of Christian anti-Semitism in informing and legitimizing Nazi anti-Semitism; there were real investigations into papal collusion with the Nazis in targeting Jews; and biographical narratives of Luther and Calvin were amended to take anti-Semitism into account. Among evangelical Christians in particular there was an acknowledgment of Jewish chosenness as the will of the creator; and a new regard for Jews as the people from whom Jesus came.

Late twentieth-century Christology took the position of Philo (c. 39–40 C.E.), who "wrote a series of tracts attacking Flaccus, a Roman governor of Egypt, and even Caligula himself for their persecution of the Jews. He argued that rulers prospered only so long as they protected the Chosen People."[29] Christians, it is now argued, need the Jews, especially the Jews in the Israeli state: the new existence of Israel is a step in bringing the Messiah back to earth; the urge to convert through violence or insult or contempt seems to have surrendered to a kind of apocalyptic pragmatism—without the Jews gathered together again in their homeland, the end of days will not come. For that reason, evangelicals support the Israeli state with money and spiritual fervor. Before, Jews could not get into heaven; now, without Jews, heaven cannot (or will not) relocate to earth.

Chosenness remains a key tenet of orthodox Judaism, but it is more problematic for less literally observant Jews and it is a minefield for secular Jews, especially those who pursue social justice. In *Jews: The Essence and Character of a People,* Arthur Hertzberg and Aron Hirt-Manheimer say: "The chosenness of the Jews is a mystery. Only God knows the purpose of setting apart an obscure tribe to suffer and to achieve more than could be expected from so small a band on so stormy a journey."[30] Humans cannot know the will of God; as Wiesel also affirms, it is a mystery. But Hertzberg and Hirt-Manheimer go on to make secular claims for chosenness: "Chosenness is the ever-present, and inescapable, discomfort caused by conscience";[31] "It does not really matter who chose the Jews. What does matter is that they have this angel or demon, conscience or neurosis, always riding on their back";[32] "We Jews know why we suffer. Society resents anyone who challenges its fundamental beliefs, behavior, and prejudices. The ruling class does not like to be told that morality overrules power. . . . The Jew, therefore, must stand up for a society that is bound by human morality and speak truth to power."[33] It is common, at least among Jews, to assert that there is a distinctly Jewish social conscience; it is also common among anti-Semites to point out the consistently high proportions of Jews in left or liberal social movements; these are two different values put on the same fact, which is that Jews were and are prominent in movements for social change that range from socialism to Marxism to civil rights agitation to feminism. By both Jews and those who hate them, there is an assertion of Jewishness separate from religion that manifests in political behavior motivated by a construct called conscience. This conscience is not developed through religious discipline or study; it is free-standing—anti-Semites would say in intrinsic combination with race, and Jews would say what? I am, therefore it is? As George Steiner says, "Earlier today I heard . . . the moving, poignant remark that oppression is not in the tradition of Judaism, and I wondered whether once again I was witnessing that very frequent privilege of the Old Testament, which is not to be read anymore. The Book of Joshua is one of the cruelest books ever written; it is a book of savagery and triumphalism which puts beyond doubt who are to be the hewers of wood and the drawers of water."[34] It is partly the conviction among Jews that Jews are a people with a conscience—having been powerless, having suffered—that has given the Israelis carte blanche: Jews are not, cannot be cruel or brutal. As an immigrant to the United States from Czarist Russia said in 1962 or 1963, "Jewish police. You can't imagine. Just think. Jewish police."[35] He did not know about the Jewish police under the Nazis; he knew the Russian Czar's police. The Jewish police in Israel, he thought, would be good, honorable, even gentle; there would not be bullies and curs, no mangy dogs among them; and no torture, never torture: how could a Jew torture?

The logic of chosenness is a moral logic: suffering creates an abhorrence of suffering, and God picked the Jews to carry this burden. Gerald Early notes the same moral logic in Afrocentrism: ". . . those black students confronted me with the conundrum of blackness as theodicy: that is, in their Afrocentrism . . . those black students wanted to know why God would give to them, to us, such a history of suffering and degradation, such a burden of warped consciousness, if blackness did not mean something, nay, everything in the beginning and the end."[36] How does a people bear undeserved suffering; how do individuals find meaning for themselves as part of a people denied dignity? Chosenness is the Jewish strategy, religious and secular. The secular lexicon is expressed by historian Simon Dubnov at the end of the nineteenth century: "I myself have lost faith in personal immortality, yet history teaches me that there is collective immortality and that the Jewish people can be considered as relatively eternal, for its history coincides with the full span of world history. The study of the Jewish people's past, then, also encompasses me in something eternal. This historicism admitted me into the national collective . . . National sorrow became dearer to me than the sorrow of the world."[37]

Even under the Nazis there were heartfelt assertions of chosenness. In *Surviving the Holocaust: The Kovno Ghetto Diary*, Avraham Tory wrote on July 30, 1942: "The Jewish genius, and the talent displayed by the Jewish people for adapting themselves to any conditions, have been given an expression in the form of cultivation of vegetable plots and fields in the Ghetto."[38] "Jewish genius" along with "Jewish conscience" are euphemisms for chosenness—and it must have been very hard to grow vegetables by 1942 in the Kovno ghetto: genius may be the word for it.

In the camps, where life was inside out and upside down, chosenness came to have a new meaning. As Wolfgang Sofsky writes in *The Order of Terror: The Concentration Camp:* " . . . prestige was not a function of education and profession, but of possession, power, and violence, the elementary criteria of survival. The first sign of the Prominents was brute violence. It documented the prerogative they enjoyed to beat, torment, and kill. . . . [T]he violence of [this] aristocracy had a clear social meaning. It demonstrated the priority of the Prominents over the superfluous. . . . To kill is to feel that you still exist, while your fellow does not. The killer experiences an exceptional strength: the power of being someone chosen."[39] Even the Jewish kapos beat and killed Jews; and the concentration camp inversion of chosenness was a sadistic mockery of God's covenant with the Jews; the violence also made a mockery of Judaism as the inmates knew it—nonviolent, moral, law- and word-centered, God-centered. But Nazi genius, an oxymoron, was the first inversion: the idea and practice of humans as superfluous; and it was Nazi skill that organized the murder and disposal of those superfluous humans.

The Nazis went far beyond hate in making Jews superfluous—as Pierre Vidal-Naquet says in *Assassins of Memory: Essays on the Denial of the Holocaust:* "What the Nazis wanted (and this is perfectly expressed by the ideology of the SS) was to replace the Jews in their mythological role as the chosen people, which had been a subject of fascination for nations on the rise ever since the time of the Enlightenment. In that sense, Nazism may be said to be a *perversa imitatio,* a perverse imitation of the *image* of the Jewish people. It was a matter of breaking with Abraham, and consequently also with Jesus, and searching for a new lineage among the Aryans."[40] Indeed, George Steiner has gone so far as to suggest, in his novel *The Portage to San Cristobal of A.H.,* that Hitler took the concept of the master race from chosenness: "It was Adolf Hitler," says his narrator, A.H., "who dreamed up the master race. Who conceived of enslaving inferior peoples. Lies. Lies. . . . It was in the doss house . . . that I first understood your secret power. The secret power of your teaching. Of *yours.* A chosen people. Chosen by God for His own. The only race on earth chosen, exalted, made singular among mankind."[41] It was Steiner, Jewish-born, who attacked the poet Sylvia Plath for her poem "Daddy," in which she conflates a father's power with Nazi power: bad, said Steiner, wrong, said Steiner, cheapens the Holocaust, said Steiner. Yet he defends his fictional exercise in moral equivalency to Ron Rosenbaum in *Explaining Hitler: The Search for the Origins of His Evil:* "The thousand-year reich, the nonmixing of races, it's all, if you want, a hideous travesty of the Judaic. But a travesty can only exist because of that which it imitates."[42]

This is the haute-intellectual version of blame-the-victim. Could there be an insult that is more morally and intellectually lazy?—perhaps this one, said to an Israeli journalist by Bruno Kreisky, a Jewish-born socialist who became Austrian chancellor in 1970: "If the Jews are a people, then they are a lousy people."[43] The Jewish-born socialist had three former Nazis in his cabinet and had used anti-Semitic messages in his campaign. In behalf of Steiner and Kreisky one must say: it is hard to be born Jew. Of course, it was harder in Europe from 1933 to 1945.

Envy and insult seem to be two sides of the same coin; and the metaphoric labeling of various groups as "the Jews of . . ." is commonplace and expresses either insult or envy.

For instance: in the words of John Steinbeck in a 1930 letter: "We went to a party at John Calvin's in Carmel last week. These writers of juveniles are the Jews of literature. They seem to wring out the English language, to squeeze pennies out of it. They don't even pretend that there is any dignity in craftsmanship. A conversation with them sounds like an afternoon spent with a pawnbroker";[44] or:

"Most American reviewers were won over by Melville's paean to Americans as 'the peculiarly chosen people—the Israel of our time; [who] bear the ark of the liberties of the world'";[45] or:

"We heard quite accidentally that Herman had gone to sea: the Melville family resemble the Jews in one particular, they are to be found in every part of the world";[46] or:

"When the king of Siam, Rama VI, first labeled [the Chinese] 'the Jews of the East' in 1914, it was not meant as a testament to their intelligence or industry but to point out their less positive, allegedly 'Jewish' characteristics such as overcompetitiveness, greed, and double-dealing";[47] or:

"The Chinese have been called 'the Jews of Southeast Asia' and the Lebanese 'the Jews of West Africa' ";[48] or:

"The overseas Chinese have often been called 'the Jews of Asia,' but perhaps the Jews might be called the Chinese of the West";[49] or:

"[Camus] would say about Frenchmen from Algeria: 'We are the Jews of France,' and he may have been only half-joking. He meant to say that Algeria's *pieds noirs* were victims of discrimination in Paris";[50] or:

"The major independent contribution of Protestantism to the development of English nationalism . . . had to do with the fact that it was a religion of the Book. The centrality of the Old Testament was of crucial significance, since it is there that one found the example of a chosen, godly people, a people which was an elite and a light to the world because every one of its members was a party to the covenant with God. This message was not lost on England, and . . . brought Englishmen to assert themselves to be the second Israel";[51] or:

". . . Gladstone, in the intervals of serving as president of the Board of Trade, colonial secretary, chancellor of the exchequer, and four terms as prime minister, found time to write a series of books, . . . in which he tried to prove that the Greeks, like the Jews, were a chosen people, entrusted by God with 'no small share of those treasures of which the Semitic family of Abraham were to be the appointed guardians, on behalf of mankind, until the fullness of time should come' ";[52] or:

"To say that by the 1780s the nobility had become 'a marginal minority in the French society, under sentence,' and that 'in 1789 nobles were the kingdom's Jews,' as does Guy Chaussinand-Nogaret, is to go too far";[53] or:

"In the Book of Mormon it is revealed that the American Indians are descended from ancient Jews";[54] or:

"Some of the common Spanish soldiers . . . advanced the suggestion that the Indians might be Jews";[55] or:

"The Jews, whatever be said of them, have a country—the London Stock Exchange; they operate everywhere, but they are rooted in the country of gold";[56] or:

"For, ironically, Poland's identity as a nation perpetually under siege may actually compete with the Jews' traditional sense of themselves as the primary victims of history. As self-perceived 'Christ among the nations,' Poland has exalted its martyrdom to an extent that rivals the place of catastrophe in Jewish memory";[57] or:

"One might go so far as to believe that the rioting French students, who in May 1968, when we were writing these lines, demonstrated with cries of 'we are all German Jews,' were likewise attempting[,] though without realizing it, to dispose of that taboo";[58] or:

"And, of course, American Jews, from whom Miami Cubans had derived so many of their behavioral and political styles, remained obsessed not only with their own dramas of difference and assimilation but with another country, Israel, about which they harbored feelings only slightly less intense than those of *el exhilio* for Cuba. If this kind of self-absorption was all right for the Jews of Miami Beach, more than one exile had been heard to ask plaintively, then why not for the Cubans of Kendall and Calle Ocho?";[59] or:

"Like Israelis, they have fought enemies internal as well as external. Like Israelis, white South Africans have learned from national service the cost of their citizenship, the cost of being a small embattled people surrounded and outnumbered by a hostile race";[60] or:

"They say they are the Arab diaspora, longing for their own homeland. The PLO writes a 'covenant,' a sacred document like the one in the Torah, that promises the land of Israel to them, the Arabs. They launch a ship called the *Exodus* to draw attention to [the] Arab plight. They claim to be suffering a Holocaust at the hands of the Jews. They initiate a United Palestinian Appeal, with the map of Israel as its logo. A spokeswoman of the Palestinian Arabs, widely perceived as a new model of moderation, holds up the picture of a dead Arab girl as the Palestinian 'Anne Frank' ";[61] or:

" 'I am a good Moslem,' [Arafat] likes to say, 'and a good Jew.' Islam incorporates three religions, he explains. 'For your information, to be a good Moslem, you have to be a good Christian and a good Jew.' Leaning back in his swivel chair, he says to his Jewish listeners, 'Judaism is part of my religion.' The references he often makes, to his cousins the Jews, to the Diaspora, to the biblical chapter of Exodus, to the right of return, and to David and Goliath are meant to prey on a sense of moral guilt over the displaced Palestinians";[62] or:

" 'What we need is something like the United Jewish Appeal for Palestinians,' explains Paul Ajlouny, the New York–based publisher of the Jerusalem Palestinian newspaper *El Fajr.* 'Be together like the Jews. That should be our goal' ";[63] or:

"*Roe* v. *Wade* has been the Wandering Jew of constitutional law";[64] or:

"The meeting was called by Pete Peters, a leader of the Christian Identity movement, a sect with its origins in nineteenth-century Britain which holds that Anglo-Americans, not Jews, are the true descendants of the Israelites of the Old Testament";[65] or:

"A complex and bizarre theology also helps Patriots explain their beliefs and justify their tactics. Many subscribe to the Identity religion, which holds that white people are God's chosen";[66] or:

Edward Said—uniquely, it appears—acknowledging yet refusing the characterization of Palestinians as "the Jews of the Arab world": "I suppose there is a sense in which . . . we are 'the Jews of the Arab world.' But I think our experience is really quite different and beyond such attempts to draw parallels. Perhaps its dimension is more modest. In any case the idea that there is a kind of redemptive homeland doesn't answer to my view of things."[67] Before the formation of the Palestinian Authority Said wanted a secular and democratic Palestinian state; he eschewed the sentimentality of the metaphor of the Jew. Even less sentimental now, he wants both peoples to live together in one secular and democratic state.

This I'm-the-Jew sentimentality is a formidable roadblock for Jews, still not normalized despite Israel, still envied and condemned. A wry Israeli girl deflates the mystification—"In the Diaspora the Jews are always the smart ones, but here in their own country one sees very little of their vaunted intelligence."[68] Still, chosen is as chosen does: "Over a period of seventy-five years, Jews have won 16 percent of all Nobel Prizes awarded in the entire world . . . though they are much less than 1 percent of the world's population . . . There are fewer Jews in the world than there are Kazakha or Sri Lankans."[69] This success is overwhelmingly the success of so-called weak Jews, not the martial heroes of Israel; yet this kind of success did not stop the killing of Jews, nor can one hold up a book to block a bullet. Is it romantic to love the creators over the warriors? Each time one wants the Israelis to put down the guns, one must confront the honest and terrifying words of W. H. Auden: "Political and social history would be no different if Dante, Michelangelo, Byron had never lived. Nothing I wrote against Hitler prevented one Jew from being killed."[70]

Still, why do so many want to be "the Jew," "Israel," "the second Israel," when both the Jew and Israel are so despised? Do they want to be chosen? What would they gain? Could they bear surviving their dead? Would they embrace suffering? Would they stockpile guns or Nobel Prizes? And why don't women have either?

"I think I may well be a Jew," says Sylvia Plath in "Daddy." "I may be a bit of a Jew."[71] The analogy between Jews and women came into vogue right after the war, in particular because Simone de Beauvoir used it in *The Second Sex,* published in 1949: this is the classic first text of modern feminism in the West. Subsequently poets like Plath and Muriel Rukeyser made naked, emotional, and imaginative analogies in their art in which the Nazi horror also articulates what is brutal and foul in the lives of women. This analogizing was not literalist nor was it driven by intellect. Plath claims for women what she never ascribed to Jews: "Every woman adores a Fascist,/The boot in the face, the brute/Brute heart of a brute like you."[72] The analogizing was intuitive and instinctive; it was pulled from hidden experience of intimate male violence; indeed, the revelations about the fate of Jews in the concentration camps touched a deep and possibly irrational nerve; the photographs, the few texts exploded in the female consciousness without any intellectual argument.

In *No Man's Land: The Place of the Woman Writer in the Twentieth Century,* Sandra M. Gilbert and Susan Gubar see the origins of the analogy this way: "Because so many literary women viewed fascist ideology as a form of masculinism, because they suffered militarism as an assault, because they were imbued with the guilt of victimization, and because they saw themselves caught in a threatening assimilation process, not a few of them identified the vulnerability of women with the extermination of the Jews." Gilbert and Gubar say that "even as they examined the metaphorical relationship between womanhood and Jewishness, they confronted the immorality of the analogy."[73] But was the analogy immoral or was it, from the poet's point of view, virtually involuntary (even as the art of the poem was intentional)? Was the shock of recognition so raw and so visceral as to make its expression necessary and inevitable? Did Nazi brutality so resemble male brutality, did Nazi sadism so resemble male sadism, that the identification of one with the other simply was the emotional truth? How did the starved bodies—starved to the skeletal frame, starved past gender—look to women who had the experience of male brutality on and in a shrunken body? How did the bones jagged through the stretched skin look to women who felt that their bodies might break under the weight of someone cruel? Was the physical fragility familiar, or when they looked at the cadavers were they looking in some kind of fun-house mirror but a mirror nonetheless? Did they see punishment because they knew punishment through and against the body? Did the exposed atrocities provide an illumination of similarity, except that for these women it was

private, isolated, each woman alone? Was the sense of shame when looking at the photographs a familiar sense of shame: had she too been tortured? Did the Jews force self-consciousness; was there a recognition of
humiliation, violence, despair? Plath killed herself: gas, an oven; but alone
and in private. Was it the worthlessness that was the same; or the impotence; or being judged by an enemy?

When women are chosen, it is one by one, individual; the man doing
the choosing begins to shape her life through his desire; just to say "I love
you" is to mark her as his; and the taking of her body makes her his. Yet
running under the etiquette of his choice and his desire is a stream of unspoken knowledge about the nature of women as such: whorish, carnal,
provocative, wants it, says no but means yes, likes aggression, wants to
submit but pretends otherwise, forced she finally gets what she wants,
huge sexual appetite but pretends otherwise, likes pain but pretends otherwise, likes being hit but pretends otherwise: she's bad because her sexuality is bad; she's dirty because her genitals are dirty and she bleeds; she's
evil because her vagina eats up the penis, temporarily castrates, in her the
penis becomes part of her, part of her filth; she's diseased, she spreads disease; she smells, her genitals, her sex; she deserves rape; she's a whore anyway; slicing her open, penis or knife, might be fun; there's always more
where she came from. All this slander has history and culture behind it;
she incarnates evil; Lilith, in myth Adam's first wife who wanted to be
equal, kills babies; the witches in the Middle Ages and Renaissance stole
men's penises and visited men in their dreams to steal their semen and
their virility; maybe it is simple—"The monotheistic order required that
the feminine should be barred from the sphere of power, which coincided
with the sacred";[74] but women are perceived as carnal and punished for it
as evil; submissive women are dangerous and so are the bitches; Eve was
inferior and did evil and brought punishment down from God, exile from
the Garden, and she was cursed with painful childbirth and eternal obedience to the male; women are traps; women are sewers; it is better to marry
than to burn; women are deep ditches; women are wanton, lethal; Circe,
Delilah, Medusa, Medea; Judith, Artemis, Aphrodite; women are venge-
ful, venal, mean, bitter, angry, shrewlike; virago, witch, and evil step-
mother.

The myth of feminine evil continues to haunt women's ordinary lives;
it is a collective stigma applied in real life one-at-a-time: in the beating or
in the rape or in the court where the woman comes for restitution; in the
United States in 1998 the American President used what is known as a

"sluts and nuts" defense, which is to say, his minions attacked the reputations of women who made sex-related charges against him by spreading rumors and using intimidation to libel them as promiscuous or unstable or stalkers; name any man as a perpetrator, charge him with any form of sexual exploitation or predation, and one will be confronted with the myth of feminine evil: women lie; she's a spurned lover or an erotomaniac or she consented no matter what was done to her. Book after book by putative feminists tries to prove that women are violent, too, as if that were the competition women had to win: no more sugar and spice and everything nice; equality may be found in the capacity to do violence if not in the doing itself. Women appear to experience social coercion into so-called good behavior and want to break those bonds by so-called bad, or brazenly sexual, behavior; but this is not an either/or system. Instead, it scans like this: a bunch of girls are thrown away through pornography and prostitution and in sweatshops and a bunch of girls are raised to be wives and mothers; the wives-and-mothers group can be beaten or raped, but they are rarely prostituted—if or when they show up in a court of law because they were aggressed against, they will find that they are on trial, because the law, culture, men, and other women will view them as hostiles: liars, provocateurs, underneath wanting whatever was done to them; they won't know why this is happening; each one will know she has been wronged but each one will probably not be able to make the case for herself; each one will feel helpless and endangered, threatened and humiliated, and wonder why those who judge her ignore her individuality, her real life, her interior sense of self and dignity; each one will be tainted, exposed in a false scenario of what passes for her sexuality, pornographized, because both Lilith and Eve were guilty—one of wanting equality, the other knowledge; the collective definition of women trumps any individuality a woman might assert, especially against a male exploiter or predator. Jews know that the collective definition however expressed will affect their lives; women insist on an individuality that has no credibility in the face of the rapist, the batterer, the pimp, nor in the media and the courts.

Meanwhile the bunch of girls sent into whorehouses and tape loops will grow up: some will die; some will become adult, of legal age, and suddenly they will have made a choice to do what they have had done to them since they were six or seven or ten, and that perceived choice will reify the conviction that adult women choose pornography, choose prostitution, and some will die, and some will die, and some will die, and then later some will die; the girls in the sweatshops will become adults who do piecework of every kind, and some will die, and some will be prostituted, and some will be married and beaten or raped, and then some of them will die, they will be exposed to environmental hazards of every sort and some will get cancer and some will get asthma and some tuberculosis, and some will die. The prostituted girls and the sweatshop girls will stay poor for however long they live, and they will die younger than women not in poverty. And each girl and each woman will expect some kind of justice somewhere down the line and each girl and each woman will not get it. That's in Pakistan or the United States, for Arab or Jew, educated or not, literate or not, first world, second world, or third.

Women's lives are destroyed by the collective definition circumscribing individual will and meaning; and the collective definition of women is not the famous virgin-or-whore polarity, which has served as a fine diversion, but the whore premise: all women are by nature evil, licentious, dirty, underneath, where the sex is. So each woman says "not me" until it is her turn and other women point and say "it's her, not me." As for genuinely violent or sadistic women: the Nazis may have gotten the ratio just right—there were "6,800 SS men and 200 women who served in the camp [Auschwitz]."[75] The ratio is thirty-four to one.

The distressing impact of prejudice concerning the nature of women distorts and corrupts legal systems, sanctions rape and prostitution, legitimizes battery, encourages incestuous rape, and of course is the foundation of both the pornography industry and the global trafficking in girls and women. There is also the dignity question: do women need dignity? There is the justice question: do women need justice? There is the individuality question: are women discrete human beings or honestly and factually defined by the collective definition and the common practices it supports? Are women complex and unique persons; or do women need men to make them whole? How can women be perceived as whole when the real fascination is for body parts? The good are sometimes acknowledged: in the ingenues of fairy tales, the saints of Catholicism, Maryology itself, stories of martyrdom; but there are neither spontaneous nor reliable perceptions of women as flawed but significant, brave but reckless, driven and therefore insensitive or ruthless. As for concretely bad women, there are the witches of both fairy tale and the Inquisition but the badness of both are fictive. The evil of misogynist prejudice is preferred over a genuine reckoning.

Is every rape victim really a slutty liar; or might one take notice of Hermine Braunsteiner Ryan, an "extradited New York housewife known in camp [Majdanek] as the 'Mare' for trampling women to death under her steel-studded boots"[76] and who was found guilty of complicity in killing by gas more than 1,000 prisoners? Is every battered woman asking for it; or might one consider Hildegard Lachert, known as Bloody Brigitte, who "got twelve years for 'conspiracy to commit murder,' although witnesses testified that she drowned inmates in the latrine, beat others to death with a steel-tipped whip and sicked a vicious dog on a pregnant woman"[77]? Are women who make accusations of sexual harassment "erotomaniacs"; or might one pay attention to Ilse Koch, "who placed orders for lamp shades, book-covers and other 'ornamental' objects to be prepared from the skins of concentration camp inmates"[78]? Are prostituted women on street corners and in pornography carnal and evil enough to deserve the punishment they get; or might one think of retaliation against Irma Grese, the so-called Blond Angel of Hell, hell being Auschwitz and Bergen-Belsen: she whipped women to death and "cut women's breasts open with her whip; when the infected breasts had to be operated on—with no anesthetic available—Grese looked on transfixed, with flushed cheeks and salivating mouth, and swaying from side to side in a revealing rhythmical motion in a sexual paroxysm"[79]—she was hanged in 1945. Of what use is the myth of women's evil up against the reality of it? Is it really bad when a woman wears a too-short skirt; or is this really bad—described by a survivor: "A nearly naked body is lying in front of the barracks. A woman SS is riding a bicycle over it. The body is moving. At one point the bloody head rises, but the young guard standing to the side pushes it back down with his boot so that his lively friend can continue her game. When she passes in front of us I stare at her closely; she's very young, her cheeks are aflame, she's giggling hysterically"[80]? Both cannot be really bad. Even Commandant Höss could not quite reconcile himself to the women guards: "I have a great respect for women in general. In Auschwitz, however, I learned that I had to reserve my general opinion, so that I had to look very closely at a woman before I could consider her with the greatest respect. The above applies to the majority of the female guard personnel. However, there were good, dependable, and very decent women among them, even if they were just a few."[81] Did he "look very closely at a woman"? Certainly, there was at least one Jewish woman whom he used sexually, then killed; did he look very closely at her?

It is hard to characterize Jewish women who collaborated; but some did. In *Stella* Peter Wyden describes a woman he knew who was a *Greifer*, a Jew who hunted other Jews for the Gestapo; she operated as part of the Gestapo's Jewish Scouting Service (*Jüdischer Fahndungsdienst*)—a Jew herself, she was, in the parlance of the ghetto, a "Jew catcher"; but, as Wyden says, "Prey like Stella, survivors of torture, were only physically restored to life."[82] In the often quoted words of Jean Améry, a survivor of Auschwitz who committed suicide in 1978: "Anyone who has been tortured remains tortured. Anyone who has suffered torture never again will be able to be at ease with the world, the abomination of the annihilation is never extinguished. Faith in humanity, already cracked by the first slap in the face, then demolished by torture, is never acquired again."[83] In Zuckerman's account of the Warsaw ghetto, another kind of collaboration is described: ". . . we learned of the existence and activity of the Committee to Aid Jews operated by women from Kraków who worked for the Gestapo. The Germans poured lots of money into this committee . . . The women expanded the circle of those receiving support and turned the names over to the Germans."[84] Given how many Jews were in hiding and how hard the Germans were looking for every single Jew up to and including the last living Jew, these women may have been instrumental in untold deaths. Were they evil, or did they do evil under staggering duress?

Being and doing: the myth of feminine evil is a pervasive belief about being; doing evil is at least marginally different from being evil. Colluding is sometimes different from doing. What is the moral vocabulary for women even if, under the Nazis, it would have had to be discarded? Is there a conception of honor or heroism: is there a standard to meet? Still, the women in the Warsaw ghetto underground had honor and were heroes.

The cruelty of women guards was not an aberration of the Nazi system per se. In *Shoot the Women First,* Eileen MacDonald finds custodial and police violence by women against women in different, more contemporary settings. A woman active in Italy's Red Brigade says, "The female prison warders had no difficulty using violence. In fact, the violence shown to us by the women guards was much worse than that of the male warders . . . The women used violence neutrally, as a type of control, and the amount they used, just doing a normal job, showed what truly violent people they were. . . . [I]t was difficult to accept women behaving in such a way toward women."[85] For women in the Basque separatist movement, says MacDonald, "[t]he maddest and most barbaric of all were the women. Women police officers often took part in the torture of ETA women. All three women remembered that there had been a woman present, hurling obscenities at her broken body; the woman was an 'added psychological torture.' "[86] These were, of course, all political prisoners, which would have affected the ways in which they were treated by guards and police (who, generally speaking, do not mind criminals but hate politicals). Still, the pattern is familiar: women hurt women; women can be brutal, violent, and cruel. Are women equal yet; or does the thirty-four–to–one ratio have to change? Someone should say.

The fact is that discourse about the nature of women rarely refers to history, to real actions in real time. Instead, both fantasy and intellection are built on the first premise of male supremacy: whores cannot be raped and raped women are whores. This contemptuous rule is applied to all women and can be applied to any woman. Only racist superiority of one woman to another mitigates or modifies the blame: all the aspersions will be doubled and trebled when applied to a racially stigmatized woman; and only racist superiority gets the racially stigmatized male blamed for rape in place of the raped woman. Racial superiority whether white or Aryan provides a comfort zone for the superior women—and when they say "he did it" they are likely to be believed. They will still be victimized by intimate male violence—battery or marital rape; but they will have a stake in scapegoating stigmatized males—and they will have a stake in being utterly separate from racially despised women.

Pro-Nazi women lived in a cocoon of sorts: their value as biological conduits for the reproduction of pure Aryan males was high; Himmler provided political and economic support for unmarried Aryan women who produced more little Aryans. Albert Speer wanted German women to work: "In vain did the arms minister point to the examples of Britain, the Soviet Union and the United States . . . Hitler, Goring, Bormann, the generals and many others objected to the conscription of female labour . . . [T]hey believed in the 'three Ks'—*Kinder, Küche, Kirche* (kids, kitchen, [church])—as a woman's proper concerns . . ."[87] Pro-Nazi women accepted "conventional stereotypes about women's special nature" but with this difference: "Women in other political movements took their concerns into the male-dominated political sphere. But Nazi women, like members of nonpartisan Catholic and Protestant organizations, worked outside the political framework altogether. Rather than competing in the men's world, they expanded their own sphere beyond men's direct intervention, relying on men for protection against external enemies."[88] This separatism allowed them to flourish; as long as they stayed inside the sphere of home and family they were strangely insulated from the Nazi Party itself, this because

"Nazi men . . . cared so little about the women in their ranks."[89] This means that they cared little about actual women; they cared deeply about the mythology they created around the pure Aryan woman: Jewish men were rapists who would pollute the blood; Jewish women were whores who could tempt Aryan men into carnality and depravity. The racial scapegoats provided Nazi women with the means to articulate their own loyalty, womanly goodness, and gender-specific drive for racial purity. The only mass demonstration by Germans in behalf of Jews was, according to Goldhagen, "when German women massed in Berlin and demonstrated for three days for the release of their recently incarcerated Jewish husbands"; the result was that "[t]he six thousand Jewish men were freed."[90] There was no retaliation against the women.

Between 1933 and 1938 there was active agitation by German Communist resistance groups against Nazi anti-Semitism. German communists were among the first political prisoners in Dachau and Ravensbrück. Later, the only real and principled demonstration against the Nazis and in behalf of the Jews was organized by a group called the White Rose, which was led by a brother and sister, Hans Scholl and Sophie Scholl, both of whom were beheaded by the Nazis in 1943. Sophie composed her own epitaph when she said: "So many people have already died for this regime that it's time someone died against it."[91]

When they were on the rise politically the Nazis wanted to destroy the German feminist movement, which was the biggest and most important probably in the world at that time. Feminists, socialists, and Jews were all tarred with the same brush: liberals, communists, traitors, polluters of the traditional values of the *Volk;* pro-Nazi women helped erase any sign of the ambitions of feminists by their rush to domesticity and reproduction; pro-Nazi women raced to undo feminist rebellion and to reinforce an earlier status quo; and, as Claudia Koonz says in *Mothers in the Fatherland: Women, the Family and Nazi Politics,* "Far from being helpless or even innocent, women made possible a murderous state in the name of concerns they defined as motherly."[92]

What the pro-Nazi women got from the regime was an independent venue as it were: the home as a separate sphere run by women. By racially scapegoating Jews, these women enabled themselves to look innocent in Nazi eyes: the dominant perception. All the filth was with the Jews; all criminality and depravity were with the Jews; the whole world of rape and prostitution was encompassed by Jewish rapists and Jewish prostitutes. In fact, the pro-Nazi women extricated themselves from the female curse: by accepting segregation based on polar sex-roles, by accepting second-class status as if it were a distinction of pride, they purged themselves of sexual blame; they became good because Jews were bad. The racist escape clause from the burden of being female works better than any other means of escape: blame them, not me.

7

HATE LITERATURE/
PORNOGRAPHY

Humans know, express, feel, learn, wonder, understand, imagine, through language; we use it and when degraded it uses us; as Julio Cortázar said, "Under authoritarian regimes language is the first system that suffers, that gets degraded."[1] In *A Lexicon of Terror: Argentina and the Legacies of Torture*, Marguerite Feitlowitz adds: "I have come to believe that . . . language may be the last system to recover."[2] Humans are the animals of meaning and meaning requires a rigorous but nuanced linguistic palate; language is the fragile but brilliant bridge between reality and human subjectivity; language is not endlessly elastic—if it were it could not carry meaning; language is not indestructible—if it were it could not become a totalitarian tool because bad use would destroy it, wrong meaning would make it break. Like the law, which begins in words, language can be a sword or a shield—it can wound, cut, kill or it can save; but language, like law, can also console, provide dignity in an inner-soliliquy, convey experience outside the bounds of propriety or acknowledged commonplaces; even in silence, language can run through one like a river and language can remove one from one's time and place and circumstance in showing a bigger and different world. U.S. slave owners knew that there was a relationship between language and freedom when they outlawed teaching slaves to read or write. Frederick Douglass's master, Hugh Auld, enumerated the ways in which a slave would be ruined by reading and writing: ". . . he should know nothing but the will of his master and learn to obey it"; "[l]earning would spoil the best nigger in the world"; "if you teach that nigger . . . how to read the bible, there will be no keeping him"; "it would forever unfit him for the duties of a slave"; "learning would do him no good, but probably a great deal of harm—making him disconsolate and unhappy"; "[i]f you learn him how to read, he'll want to know how to write; and, this accomplished, he'll be running away with himself."[3] Auld saw language as an unmitigated, uncompromised good: it was a civilizing influence that was incompatible with servitude. One might say with wonderment that he lived in a more innocent time, participated in a more innocent tyranny than any modern one—because the sacking and pillaging of language, its degradation, is the heritage left by the Nazis and the Communists to so-called free societies in the industrialized West; language has, in fact, never recovered.

Thus in 1949 Heidegger could compare "'the manufacturing of corpses in gas chambers and extermination camps' to mass-production of agricultural goods."[4] In 1945 Heidegger chose to eulogize the Nazis by affirming "the inner truth and greatness of this movement (namely, the encounter between global technology and modern man)."[5] Well, hell. Heidegger's intellectual children—the deconstructionists and postmodernists, especially in France, the home of Holocaust denial—continued the project of turning degraded language in the post-Nazi world into a movement of jargon and abstraction. At least some of Heidegger's kiddies turned on him by deploring his sentimentality: "Nazism is a humanism."[6] This was a criticism.

Paul de Man, comfortably ensconced at Yale University in the United States after the defeat of the Nazis, denied having collaborated, from which sprung a denial that language had any knowable meaning. In 1941 his collaborationist prose in *Le Soir* was smarmy but clear: ". . . it is enough to have discovered several Jewish writers under Latinized pseudonyms for all contemporary production to be considered polluted and harmful. . . . [Yet] it would be an unflattering estimation of Western writers to reduce them to being mere imitators of a Jewish culture that is foreign to them."[7] After the war, de Man became harder to understand.

In fact, a genius for linguistic and intellectual obfuscation descended on Europe after Hitler's defeat: there were so many crimes to hide, so many intellectuals who did the heavy lifting for the Nazis by using words, that to muddle meaning was aggressive self-defense. It allowed intellectuals new identities, new passports as it were; and, most delightfully, new games to play: words were a terrain for hide-and-seek, or a map for the new monopoly, or dice for those who craved risk. In Germany in the 1980s historians were having a self-referential dispute known as *Historikerstreit* (the historians' conflict), the object being an evaluation of the uniqueness of the Holocaust, thus inevitably also an exciting inquiry into their own ranking in the serial-, mass-, and genocidal-killer sweepstakes.

In this case, words were used to focus German consciousness away from the Nazis to a realm, any realm, outside the moral squalor and disgrace of Nazism. Was Stalin worse? They seemed to hope so. Pol Pot must have cheered them immensely.

Over time, Heidegger's membership in the Nazi Party and sincere loyalty as well as de Man's committed collaboration had become undeniable facts; but facts were déclassé, valued only by those simple-minded proles who thought that some things were true and some were not. Deconstructionists and postmodernists were academic royalty; and the emperor's swastika did not embarrass them at all. They had learned the mesmerizing tactic of nothing meaning nothing, everything meaning nothing, nothing being both itself and its opposite as well as the absolute unknowable; they read books written by no one nowhere and, more miraculously, wrote such books themselves. How these nonauthors handled their noncorporeality was kept a trade secret. Some questions did emerge: what was or was not female; what was or was not male; what male and female each were or were not, especially considering that the female was an absence. More analytically, there was a concern that any assertion of sexual ethics, even under the rubric of human rights, amounted to the forbidden expressing itself through the tabooed, which reified repression. "Is the rectum a grave?" by academic Leo Bersani became possibly the world's most obscure and admired intellectual artifact in that it was completely uncompromised by meaning; and nonelite readers and writers, trapped in a false existence (not a false consciousness, Hegel having been taken out by Heidegger), longed for a literate Rabelaisean fart, which would, indeed, signify.

Heidegger and de Man—and through them fascism—have left a legacy. It is hard to use language to convey meaning; it is laughable to try to use language to search for truth; the truth itself is laughable, a partly visible stage on which clowns slip on banana peels. Language has ceased to be human, or part of the human endeavor toward self-determination and dignity; and in 1998, the President of the United States, a lawyer from Arkansas, argued before a grand jury (investigating him for alleged criminal corruption) the meaning of the word *is*. His point was that saying he was not having sex with a given woman (with whom he had been having oral sex, she servicing him) was not a lie (even under oath) because he was not having sex with her right then, at that moment when he or his lawyer used the word *is*. Using language to say nothing is, of course, an exhausting enterprise, and even the virile if adolescent young president looked tired. He also maintained that when this young woman had fellated him (in the past), she was having sex and he was not: thus, he was not lying when he said he did not have sex with her. Jacques Derrida, meet William Jefferson Clinton.

In the United States, language exists in a vacuum as if it were isolated from any community of values or action. A recent thirty-year reinterpretation of the First Amendment to the U.S. Constitution, which protects speech, assembly, and religion from government sanction, fetishizes all expressive language: words become sacred totems, untouchable, an archeology of immutable runes. Pulled away from its context, surgically excised by literalist courts of law, language is the dead corpse at the party—murdered, but by whom and so what? Separated from any perception of its efficacy, language is lifted out of the common life: all speech is purposefully and systematically made immune to meaningful challenge because consequences have become irrelevant. The reigning dogma is that consequences are irrelevant: and so human life is entirely subservient to an abstract, absolutist principle of recent and cynical vintage (the protection of the pornography industry) that guts language by misdefining its very nature; language cannot be severed from acts or motives or slow, lingering, repetitive incitements whether lyrical, innocent, shocking, vulgar, invasive, or malign. Language cannot be frozen, unrefracted, misshapen by legal design and still have value. Language lives in a world in which things happen: sometimes things happen because of language.

It is not hard to see how words determine human destiny: "The Auschwitz syndrome: the enemy must be wiped off the face of the earth," writes George Konrád. "And the enemy is anyone who has been declared an enemy. At age eleven I was an enemy. . . . I had to be removed, much as one removes a piece of garbage."[8] In *Fugitive Pieces* Anne Michaels notices the convergence of language and a human life: "The relation between a man's behaviour and his words is usually that of gristle and fat on the bone of meaning. But, in your case, there seemed to be no gap between the poems and the man . . . [w]ho knew that even one letter—like the 'J' stamped on a passport—could have the power of life or death."[9] How could it be otherwise; and isn't U.S. imperviousness to the consequences of words and letters of the alphabet evidence of complacency, stasis, ignorance, indifference, corruption: the happy stupidity of the well-sheltered and well-fed?

Raul Hilberg, a great historian of the Holocaust, remembers a moment of defining consciousness: "I had just begun to understand what a document really is. Here I could see that it is first of all an artifact, immediately recognizable as a relic. It is the original paper that once upon a time was handled by a bureaucrat and signed or initialed by him. More than that, the words on that paper constituted an *action:* the performance of a function. If the paper was an order, it signified the *entire* action of its originator."[10]

Less introspective, more common, is the obvious recognition of the role of words in riots and sustained racist agitation: after the publication of Émile Zola's *J'Accuse* in defense of Dreyfus on January 13, 1898, "thousands of young people marched through the streets of scores of French cities, calling for the death of Jews, smashing Jewish storefronts, and attempting to break into homes and synagogues"; in letters sent with money contributions to the widow of Major Hubert-Joseph Henry, a suicide as a result of being imprisoned for forging the documents that convicted Dreyfus, the violence continued: "'Death to the Jews' was a restrained expression when compared to pathological calls for roasting, hanging, gassing, vivisection, and massacre, accompanied by references to Jews as kikes, pimps, lice, plagues, cancers, and filthy beings."[11] In long-term conflicts—for instance, the Dreyfus case—words can be nails in any number of coffins.

The line between the violence of words and the violence of crowds is sometimes real; but more often such a line is a product of jurisprudential artifice and fictive sociology. Indeed, it is hard to imagine violent acts surrounded by silence: riots without words; mobs without slogans; threats so quiet they remain unheard; mute masses of vandals. The actions happen but there is no sound.

In Argentina under military rule the language was simply tranquilized, flattened out, a strategy that helped cliché emerge as political principle: "We were defrauded by democracy, which was not what we had expected"; "Recurrent themes in 1978 and 1979 include 'benefits of limits' and 'authority is not dictatorship,' as they apply not only in politics, but also in childrearing and education."[12] Timmerman explained that there was no state censorship during the tyranny. Instead, writers disappeared. He called it "biological censorship."[13]

A contemporary Iraqi dissident says that "[i]n Iraq, words can kill"; a woman taped her husband cursing Saddam in order to get him [the husband] executed; "She inherited his property and lives today in my own neighborhood . . . That is the power of words."[14] This is a venal use of language; but it helps to destroy the fiction that words have no consequences. Collaborating, ratting someone out, entrapment, and blackmail all involve a potentially lethal use of words.

The greatest affront to language is to devalue it entirely—its meaning, its power—as First Amendment absolutism does in the U.S. This degradation of language is now a new phenomenon in Russia; as Andrei Sinyavsky, a Soviet dissident writer, recently explained: "A devaluation of words has taken place, which for an intellectual is more frightening than the devaluation of the ruble. . . . The Russian government, which in the past had had such a serious and painfully sensitive attitude to words that it imprisoned people for them, suddenly realized it was possible simply to spit on everything written in newspapers, magazines, and books."[15] Returning to the U.S. from the former Soviet Union some three decades ago, writer Grace Paley talked about how deeply important, even cherished, writers were in that totalitarian state. "Whatever we write here, it doesn't matter," she said, "but everything that they write matters."[16] Indeed, civil repression heightens the value of expression. Imprisonment or its possibility make writers and writing intensely serious and committed. In the U.S. writers are, at best, entertainers working in a medium—words—that may be a dinosaur in an image-saturated popular culture. But there is a more troubling issue. In the U.S. *Ulysses* is protected and, under the same law with the same logic, so are men pushing money into the vaginas of women dancers. In this descent into legal madness, the court considers itself to be protecting the speech rights of women. Both the pornographers and the U.S. Supreme Court believe in the civic importance of what the pornographers so gracefully call "talking pussy."

There are words that stigmatize and there are words that kill. In ancient Greece, barbarians were "those whose speech sounded like 'bar bar' to Greek ears."[17] The charge of being a barbarian saddles one with inferiority, a perception of stupidity, and the hatred of a xenophobic society. Foreigners are often perceived as barbarians: in Chinese, "*low faan,* an object of fear, distrust, indifference," this being an abbreviation of "*guey low faan,* or 'barbarian.'"[18] With the European invasion of the Americas, tribes were renamed according to the understanding of the white male adventurers: "Typically, Europeans did not ask a tribe for its name, but asked a nearby tribe . . . Relations between adjacent tribes were frequently hostile, and it followed that so were the names given in answer to the question. The word Mohawk means 'man-eater.' . . . The word Iroquois is not found in the Iroquoian languages, but belongs to the other major Eastern language group, the Algonquin, and is a pejorative meaning 'rattlesnake people.'"[19] This pretty much meant that whites were always unknowingly insulting the Indian tribes they addressed by name.

Insulting words for Jews were forged by Jew-haters. Surrounded by anti-Semites, Czar Nicholas "habitually used the coarse and insulting Russian term *zhydi* (kikes) rather than the more polite *yevrei* (Hebrews)."[20] In the 1880s and 1890s in France the rhetoric of choice included "Jewish question," "Jewish problem," and "[m]eteques, a pejorative word for foreigners in general and Jews in particular . . ."[21] In addition, "*Juif*, like 'Polak,' often signified the unassimilated immigrant, while *israélite*, increasingly, though never neatly, stood for French Jews with a religious, rather than a cultural, interest in Judaism."[22] In Bordeaux Jews were promised emancipation "if they freed themselves from the 'dark phantoms of the Talmudists,' and if they abandoned their 'judesco-hebraico-rabbinical jargon . . . '"[23] Many years later the writer Colette, who also was a stage performer, said about a colleague: "She must be a sordid Jew who doesn't wash."[24] Rilke, in rejecting a young poet whom he thought had genius, explained: "The Jew, the Jew-boy, to say it straight, would not have made a difference to me, but his decidedly Jewish attitude toward his work must have made itself felt."[25]

Benjamin Disraeli, baptized when he was twelve, was pursued by the language of Jew-hate throughout his political career (he became Prime Minister of England). "A Jew is bad [enough]," wrote Carlyle at the beginning of Disraeli's career, "but what is a sham-Jew, a Quack-Jew? And how can a real Jew . . . try to be a Senator, or even a citizen, of any country except his own wretched Palestine?"[26] Disraeli's eventual close relationship with Queen Victoria was a cause for alarm: "Matters seem very critical—a woman on the throne, and a Jew adventurer who found out the secret of getting around her."[27] His lifelong political opponent, Gladstone, said Disraeli had "Jew feelings"; by others he was called "loathsome Jew," "Eastern Jew," "under all his trappings, the absurd Jew-boy" (Lytton Strachey), "the tawdry old Jew" (Henry James).[28] Vita Sackville-West, reading Virginia Woolf's diary, noted Woolf's distaste for "the Jew side of Leonard."[29] D. H. Lawrence's poetry abandoned him when he turned to the subject of Jews: "I hear Huebsch is a Jew. Are you a Jew also? The best of the Jews is, that they *know* truth from untruth. The worst of them is, that they are rather slave-like, and that almost inevitably, in action, they betray the truth they know. . . . [T]hey cringe their buttocks to the fetish of Mammon, peeping over their shoulders to see if the truth is watching them."[30] The Jew kept obsessing Lawrence: "Nobody has any money any more except the profiteers, chiefly Jews"; "his Jewship"; "Are you a Jew?"; "If Seltzer deals decently with me . . . then I don't mind if he is a Jew and a little nobody, I will stick to him. I don't really like Jews."[31] Similarly, the Irish were condescended to, called "Paddy," and considered "'babies' who could never govern themselves."[32] It took Disraeli to articulate the condition of the Irish to the English: "I want to see a public man come forward and say what the Irish question is. One says it is a physical question, another a spiritual. Now it is the absence of the aristocracy. Now it is the absence of railways. It is the Pope one day and potatoes the next. A dense population inhabit an island where there is an established church which is not their church, and a territorial aristocracy, the richest of whom live in a distant capital. Thus they have a starving population, an alien church, and in addition the weakest executive in the world. Well, what then would gentlemen say if they were reading of a country in that position? They would say at once, 'The remedy is a revolution.' . . . The connection with England became the cause of the present state of Ireland. If the connection with England prevented a revolution and a revolution was the only remedy, England logically is in the odious position of being the cause of all the misery of Ireland. What then is the duty of an English minister? To effect by his policy all those changes which a revolution would effect by force."[33] And it was left to George Eliot—writing to Harriet Beecher Stowe—to take on the verbal anti-Semitism of the English: "Can anything be more disgusting than to hear people called 'educated' making small jokes about eating ham, and showing themselves empty of any real knowledge as to the relation of their own social religious life to the history of the people they think themselves witty in insulting? They hardly know that Christ was a Jew. And I find men educated at Rugby supposing that Christ spoke Greek. To my feeling, . . . this inability to find interest in any form of life that is not clad in the coat-tails and flounces as our own lies very close to the worst kind of irreligion. The best that can be said of it is, that it is a sign of the intellectual narrowness—in plain English, the stupidity, which is still the average mark of our culture."[34] Intellectual clarity and empathy sometimes find each other.

There was no intellect or clarity or empathy in the Nazi lexicon. The name of Julius Streicher's *Der Stürmer* has variously been translated as "slang for 'lady-killers'"[35] and "The Assailant."[36] According to Goldhagen, "[t]he Germans' use of the term 'Jew-hunt' was not casual. It expressed the killers' conception of the nature of their activity and the attendant emotion . . . [T]he word '*Jagd*' has a positive *Gefülswert,* a positive emotive valence. Hunting is a pleasurable pursuit . . . and its reward is a record of animals slain—in the case of the men of this police battalion and other German 'Jew-hunters,' a record of Jews ferreted out and killed."[37] Isaiah Berlin identified one word that stigmatized and killed: "The Nazis were led to believe by those who preached to them by word of mouth or printed words that there existed people, correctly described as sub-human, *Untermenschen,* and that these persons were poisonous creatures . . . [I]f you believe it, because someone has told you so, and you trust this persuader, then you arrive at a state of mind where, in a sense quite rationally, you believe it necessary to exterminate Jews . . ."[38]

Among Jews, inside the world of Jews, there were words of contempt inseparable from death and ruin: for the partisans, "the bulk . . ., the unarmed, were placed into a less valued category disdainfully called 'malbush.' 'Malbush' is a Hebrew term for clothes. No one seems to know how the term acquired its negative meaning."[39] In Israel German immigrants were called *yekkes,* a term of contempt also with no known origin; and *sabon,* soap. Inside Israel "[e]thnic tension led to the coining of such expressions as *Ashken-Nazis.*"[40] Protesting Israeli military actions in Lebanon, one Israeli writer coined the term *Judeo-Nazis.* Novelist Amos Oz responded, rightly: "That is a demagogic and corrupt comparison."[41] The uniquely troubled self-consciousness of the Israelis—a combination of rage, shame, and self-blame—made bitter hyperbole easy.

In *The Seventh Million: The Israelis and the Holocaust,* Tom Segev analyzes this same phenomenon: ". . . the political extremism that gave birth to Kahanism on the one hand, and to the refusal to perform military service on the other, made Israelis of the 1980s more prone to compare themselves with the Nazis. That shift was a result of, among other things, the extensive rhetorical use to which Begin had put the Holocaust."[42]

Nightmares and hate were created and reified through words. There was no sacred, separate place where words could be both hidden and worshipped in and of themselves; words were not pristine artifacts; words had human behavior all over them. It was an Israeli Holocaust survivor who, during the Gulf War, captured the rapier dynamic of words intended to cause pain: "Here is my problem: As I dwell on the fate of my family during those darkest of days in Europe, Baghdad Radio is boasting that Iraqi Scud missiles have turned Tel-Aviv into a 'crematorium.' That was their exact word, aired today, January 19, 1991. They could have phrased it differently . . . devastation, misery, defeat, desert, wasteland, destruction, ruin, fall, havoc, or even fire from hell. But the word they chose, taken from the unholy vocabulary that dominated my childhood, was targeted to hit the most vulnerable part of their victims' souls, with a precision exceeding by far that of the missiles themselves."[43] If one wants a word to draw blood, one simply has to point it in the right direction at a vulnerable target without sentimentality or remorse.

U.S. poet Ezra Pound, propagandizing for the fascists in Italy during World War II, called Jews *yitts;* President Roosevelt was *Jewsfeldt* and *Stinkie Roosenstein.* Writing about the anti-Semitism of his own father and his father's peers, William H. Gass distinguished the different kinds of socially legitimate Jew-hate: "There was the anti-Semitism of the snob, who viewed Jews with the faint distaste reserved for every *nouveau riche* and social climber; there was the economic anti-Semite, who associated the Jews with money-lenders and shylocks . . . from simple shopkeepers to munitions czars; there was the religious Jew-hater, who still thought of them as Christ-killers; there was the political Jew-baiter, who felt they infiltrated the system secretly, seized control of it, and, in effect, went about poisoning wells; and there was the racial purist, the blood-taint anti-Semite . . ."[44] All these persons used language; language was implicated in all their ideas, convictions, and views; through words they learned and they taught; they used language to create the social reproduction of their prejudices and behaviors of exclusion and contempt.

The PLO leadership is characterized by fundamentalist critics to the right as "[p]ork eaters and wine drinkers," and treated with contempt because "a woman's voice is indecent."[45] The Provos in Northern Ireland "had a response to any peace without justice: the organized harassment of many of the women. A large group of Provo supporters, mainly young men, shouted and cursed. There were tussles, screams, howls: 'Whores! Traitors! Brits Out! Provos Rule!' "[46]

One of the deepest strains of language and contempt and obliteration comes from the vocabulary of the Enlightenment itself: "Light over dark. Enlightened over savage. We over they. Think of all the light-type words with favorable connotations—'enlightened,' 'brilliant,' 'insightful.' . . . *they* are benighted, ignorant, superstitious, mired in darkness."[47] Light over dark is one of the major metaphors in discourse of all kinds.

Instead of recognizing the power of language, which is complex and difficult to untangle or understand, the notion that words have consequences is ridiculed; any attempt to try to understand the linguistic dimensions of hate is treated as if the effort itself were a form of fascism. But words live and have their most profound meanings in ordinary conversations, trivial conflicts. Klaus, a son of Nazi leader Karl Saur, had an argument with his mother, described by his younger brother: "It was between Klaus and my mother. They had seen a discussion on television about the war and a Jewish person had been interviewed. My mother had said a typical German expression, 'That is one that should have gone to the gas chambers.' And my brother was furious and told her it was stupid to say such things. And she was really shocked that he was so angry. 'It's just an expression, it doesn't mean anything,' she told him. 'You know I don't mean any harm by it.' But Klaus was very firm with her. 'Those stupid sentences are what eventually led to the types of things that happened in the war,' he told her."[48] One might wish that Klaus had been less enigmatic in verbally confronting what had happened in the war; but he was right that "those stupid sentences" bear the burden of genocide.

There are bad words. Words become bad precisely because or when they cannot be separated from the shedding of human blood. The delusion of separation is, of course, consoling.

Hate propaganda has themes; for instance, "Apion's portrait of the Jew as a carrier of disease was often repeated in the Middle Ages by Christians, who accused the Jews of poisoning wells and spreading the Black Death. It was repeated by Hitler and Goebbels, who portrayed Jews as bacillus; it was repeated by Stalin, who believed Jewish doctors were plotting to poison him; and it is repeated today by Black Muslims, who charge that Jews are infecting them with the HIV virus."[49] These themes travel through the long tunnel of history riding on the backs of words; there is a toxic vocabulary characterized by longevity and repetition; it plays on fear by creating horror. In *The Origins of the Inquisition in Fifteenth Century Spain*, B. Netanyahu describes "the anti-Marrano works produced by Spain's racists in the 15th century" as a subset of "writings called by the Germans 'atrocity propaganda'—that is, agitation that ascribes to an opponent such loathsome improprieties and such deeds of horror that the general public is moved to view him as both despicable and frightful."[50] The Spanish propaganda, like the Nazis', calls Jews "false, hypocritical, deceitful, treacherous, cowardly, shameless, pompous, boastful, arrogant and, above all, wicked, cruel, and merciless. [So, too,] they are defined as tyrants, oppressors, idol-worshipers, sodomites, false prophets, thieves, robbers, murderers and, needless to say, heretics and Judaizers. . . . The Marranos are evil incarnate."[51]

Entertainment and art make the charges seem more true, more real; think of Marlowe's Barabas, an early evil Jew of literature: "They say we are a scattered nation—/I cannot tell—but we have scrambled up/More wealth by far than any Christian."[52] Two centuries later, John Maynard Keynes could see the Jews as the people of capital: "Perhaps it is not an accident that the race which did most to bring the promise of immortality into the heart and essence of our religions has also done most for the principle of compound interest and particularly loves this most purposive of human institutions"; the Jews, said Keynes, had "sublimated immortality into compound interest."[53] This conception moved through history from Marlowe to Keynes. Isn't Marlowe a poet to be feared? If not, why not?

Shakespeare's Shylock in *The Merchant of Venice* communicates not so much ideas about Jews but a figure of heroic, essentialist, Jewish evil; the power of the play has never lessened. "It must also be borne in mind," writes John Gross in *Shylock: A Legend and Its Legacy,* "that most people first get to hear of Shylock at an early age, when the seeds of prejudice are most readily sown"; citing a 1950s study, Gross notes the finding that "children colloquially refer to a Jew as a Yid, Shylock or Hooknose"; in a study conducted during World War II, "*The Merchant of Venice* was regularly cited by respondents who were asked to name the influences that had done most to shape their attitudes to Jews when they were young."[54] There really is not a way around the fact that the Nazis loved *The Merchant of Venice:* In Germany in 1933, "there were no less than twenty separate productions; between 1934 and 1939 there were another thirty."[55] Surely one must contemplate the possibility that the influence of art is enhanced by its greatness for better or worse; and that so-called censorship is a lazy diversion for those who support it and for those who oppose it. To argue about whether or not *The Merchant of Venice* should be performed is to short-circuit any understanding of what happens when it is performed.

Shylock wants his pound of flesh, this hearkening back to the blood libel. In 1255, following on accusations of a ritual murder of a boy by Jews, eighteen Jews were killed: ". . . the folklore which sprang up around it included the belief that the boy had been lured to his death [by] a 'Jew's daughter.'"[56] Folklore is often the deepest expression of fear, beliefs, hatreds. Synthesizing sex and murder ups the ante: the Jew's daughter eroticizes the blood libel. In creating Jessica, Shylock's daughter, Shakespeare takes a step away from the dizzying carnality of murder. The step, however, was not big enough to make the play either useless or repugnant to the Nazis. The beauty, the power, the complexity, of *The Merchant of Venice* requires one to ask the question: for how many Jewish corpses of Nazi origin is Shakespeare responsible? one? ten? fifty? And which does one value more: the play or the human lives? It is vile to refuse to confront this great and troubling dilemma, this terrible sadness, the offspring of art and history.

In the English tradition, Shylock is followed by Fagin, Svengali, and Count Dracula: "Svengali and Count Dracula—both looming mesmerists and demon lovers—join Mr. Hyde, Iago, Claggart, and Professor Moriarity as enduring evil icons. . . . Svengali is described as an 'Oriental Israelite Hebrew Jew.' Dracula has a 'hook' and 'beaky' nose. By featuring a sinister foreign seducer, [the] authors reveal a prevalent xenophobia over the influx of Eastern European Jews . . . but only *Dracula* elevates the desire—and fear—of the pristine middle-class to be violated by a dark outsider."[57] Finally one understands why Dracula drinks blood and why a cross deters him: he incarnates the sexual demonism of the Jew. All of these popular villains of heroic size, corrupted by evil appetites, corrupters of innocent women (and in Fagin's case, boys) communicate the logic of anti-Semitism but hide that logic in romantic hyperbole and the zest of good storytelling. Svengali, Dracula, and Fagin are carriers of the disease: Jewish evil. Once again, words push prejudice forward in time; words evoke evil and the need for punishment; words carry repugnance: and suddenly Fagin is on the stage in London's West End or on New York's Broadway singing.

Who teaches language? Who is its guardian? Which ideas reach the schools and is Timmerman's "biological censorship" not at all unique to the recent Argentinean terror? In German and Prussian schools, such a censorship was imposed long before Hitler—without force, using no guns, burning and gassing no one. As John Weiss says in *Ideology of Death: Why the Holocaust Happened in Germany,* "Although millions of Germans supported liberalism and socialism, their ideas were not to be found in the schools. Jewish teachers might have contradicted stereotypes, but of some eight thousand teaching appointments from 1875 to 1895, about forty went to Jews. Prussia never had more than twelve Jewish secondary school teachers."[58] In the universities, the landscape was equally barren: "The universities made every effort to avoid hiring or promoting

Jews, though it meant ignoring the brilliant achievements of many. In 1900 about 2 percent of German academics were of Jewish origin, but in lower ranks and with dim prospects."[59]

Jewish absence in schools was matched by anti-Semitism in popular newspapers; for instance, from a Munich paper of 1919: "Dreadful times in which Christian-hating, circumcised Asiatics everywhere are raising their bloodstained hands to strangle us in droves! The butcheries of Christians by the Jew Issachar Zederblum, alias Lenin, would have made even a Genghis Khan blush. In Hungary his pupil Cohn, alias Bela Kun, marched through the unhappy land with a band of Jewish terrorists schooled in murder and robbery, to set up, among brutal gallows, a mobile machine gallows and execute middle-class citizens and peasants on it. A splendidly equipped army served him, in his stolen royal train, to rape and defile honorable Christian virgins by the dozen. His lieutenant Samuely has had sixty priests cruelly butchered in a single underground room. Their bellies are ripped open, their corpses mutilated after they have been plundered to their blood-drenched skin. In the case of eight murdered priests it has been established that they were first crucified on the doors of their own churches!"[60] This was a mainstream expression of popular German culture too easily characterized as the culture of Goethe and Beethoven. It was, it had been, it continued to be, the culture of venal Jew-hate; and the first cultural product of Germany was not art but anti-Semitism. In the well-fertilized field of German culture, Goethe's influence was down on any honest list. If the Holocaust could happen—if it were possible—how could it not have happened in Germany?

By 1919 Adolf Hitler "began to proselytize among angry veterans in Munich beer halls. At Berlin University, Eric Warburg heard Albert Einstein deliver lectures on relativity amid repeated heckling from anti-Semitic students."[61] Leaflets were distributed at the stock exchange blaming Max Warburg for the Versailles Treaty, called the "Warburg Jewish Peace."[62]

The slaughter of World War I—the waves and waves of young men cut down, each side's experience of the awfulness of such loss—left Europe sick and weary; the Treaty of Versailles provided cause for the Germans, the original aggressors and the losers of that war, to wallow in self-pity, to romanticize themselves as abject victims, and to maintain an inner sense of hostility and rage toward the victors, in particular England and France. In *The Sense of Sight*, John Berger identifies 1914 as a turning point in consciousness: there was a "new kind of suffering . . . an inverted suffering. Men fought within themselves about the meaning of events, identity, hope. . . . The life they experienced became a chaos within them. They became lost within themselves."[63] Berger notes that this "new and terrible form of suffering . . . coincided with the widespread, deliberate use of false ideological propaganda as a weapon. Such propaganda . . . transforms [people] into puppets—whilst most of the strain . . . remains politically harmless as inevitably *incoherent* frustration. The only purpose of such propaganda is to make people deny and then abandon the selves which otherwise their own experience would create."[64] This gets to the heart of modern scapegoating, because the abandonment of a self created by experience requires the creation of a self composed of bits and shards of other people, other identities, a collection of fantasies culled from garbage prejudice. In Germany the national self had been gutted; given that Jews were linked in the German mind "with prostitution and all forms of sexual depravity" and were charged "with defiling unsuspecting German virgins," a scapegoat was not hard to find: "Ritual murder accusations, the age-old antisemitic canard, and trials continued to haunt the Jewish community; in Germany and the Austrian Empire, twelve such trials took place between 1867 and 1914."[65] The cultural ground saturated with hate, "[e]ven liberal newspapers took to printing all manner of rumors and accusations against Jews, including ritual murder charges, as if they had been proven facts."[66]

While any number of ghouls might have become Goebbels or Himmler, Ribbentrop or Goering, only Hitler could have become Hitler; and the questions persist—why? how? Yes, he was savagely beaten as a child; he was illegitimate; his biological grandfather may have been a Jew; his formative years were filled with brutality and deprivation; he was a loner, isolated, fitting in nowhere; he lived in a society in which anti-Semitism was the first principle of nationalism and of ethnic pride; in his Vienna years "[a]lmost every gentile in the Austrian capital was an anti-Semite."[67] They spoke; they used words; they communicated; they inculcated; they indoctrinated; they intimidated. Words were not innocent; language was not neutral. In this rich diet of anti-Semitism what did Hitler consume?

First, he was a citizen of Berger's 1914: nothing inside; the skin and bones of degraded others as the building block of the self; a mind looped with anti-Semitic, sexually morbid scenarios. (See Adolf Hitler, *Mein Kampf.*) Second, in Vienna "[o]rganized groups worked tirelessly to spread hate against Jews and young Hitler became an avid reader of the trash literature which filled the newsstands."[68] He was known to have read the magazine *Ostara,* "a concoction of the occult and erotic, its editorial policy 'the practical application of anthropological research for the purpose of . . . preserving the European master race from destruction . . . ' "[69] *Ostara* "abounded in lurid illustrations of Aryan women succumbing to the sexual power and allure of these hairy, apelike creatures [Jews]."[70] In his youth, "Hitler's fundamental anti-Semitic attitudes undoubtedly came to him through his old schoolmaster."[71] He was known to have read an anti-Semitic satirical magazine, *Der Scherer,* and also the locally published (in Linz) *Illustrierte Tiroler Monatsschrift für Politik und der Laune in Kunst (Illustrated Tyrolean Monthly for Politics and Entertainment in Art and Life):* "It had a good deal to say about the decline of morals and the evils of alcoholism, but it specialized in attacks on the Jews, the 'papists,' the suffragettes and members of Parliament."[72] Long before Hitler read it (its first issue was in May 1899), "it carried a picture of a swastika . . ."[73] In the great tradition of garbage in/garbage out, he himself wrote *Mein Kampf,* which was published in two volumes. In celebrating the publication of the second volume in 1924, Hitler likened himself to Christ: "Christ was the greatest early fighter in the battle against the world enemy, the Jews. . . . The work that Christ started but could not finish, I— Adolf Hitler—will conclude."[74] (Christ's lineage was not Jewish as Hitler reckoned these things; because of immaculate conception, he had only "two Jewish grandparents."[75])

From a neophyte who swamped his consciousness with anti-Semitic, often pornographic images, slogans, and words, he became a master propagandist. Distinguishing as he did between emotional anti-Semitism, which produced riots, and rational anti-Semitism, "which would result in a series of legal measures aimed at the eventual elimination of the Jews,"[76] Hitler discarded all sentimentality to pursue his political objectives. Asked if it was necessary to eliminate the Jews, Hitler said, "We should have then to invent him. It is essential to have a tangible enemy, not merely an abstract one."[77] His anti-Semitism as a political leader was cold, purposeful, immovable. His own political rhetoric used the metaphor of disease to justify eliminating the Jew, except that for Hitler it was no metaphor: "The discovery of the Jewish virus is one of the greatest revolutions the world has seen. The struggle in which we are now engaged is similar to the one waged by Pasteur and Koch in the last century. How many diseases must owe their origins to the Jewish virus? Only when we have eliminated the Jews will we regain our health."[78]

He understood propaganda from the inside out—it must be popular and accessible, easily understood by the masses, "adjusted to the most limited intelligence among those it is addressed to."[79] Even though policy was built on scientific or rational or logical anti-Semitism, propaganda must reach the emotions of a crowd; it must present "love or hate, right or wrong, truth or lie, never half this way and half that way."[80]

Many noted that "[a]t the beginning of his political career Hitler had a beautiful voice, which fascinated admiring women. But electronic amplification was unavailable till the end of the twenties, and he progressively made himself hoarse by shouting."[81] He would begin his speeches "in a low, slow tenor voice, and after about fifteen minutes, something occurs that can be described only by the ancient primitive metaphor—the spirit enters into him."[82] One writer "compared his oratory to rape and murder. Using repetition and insistent rhythms, he would pummel the audience's emotions, pushing it relentlessly toward a climax that has often been called orgasmic."[83] Without words, in particular Hitler's words, not one Jew would have been gassed.

In fact, the younger Hitler was trained for propaganda and speaking. According to Captain Karl Mayr, Hitler the soldier "was like a stray dog looking for a master."[84] After doing guard duty at a prisoner-of-war camp, he was assigned to the propaganda department and in 1919 took a political training course. According to some of his peers, Hitler was a socialist, on the side of the Bavarian Reds. When the socialist Hans Eisner was killed, Hitler "marched in the funeral procession following the coffin. (Later these facts were suppressed, and it was not until 1995 that German television audiences saw a sequence of film showing him in the procession.)"[85] Mayr then commanded an intelligence unit designed to "counteract the influence of Marxist ideas on soldiers returning to civilian life."[86] Having taken Hitler's measure, Mayr assigned Hitler to inform on his comrades; and then "Mayr selected him for an anti-Communist political education, together with a training in agitation and public speaking."[87] Needless to say, "[a]s a trainee speaker, Hitler made rapid progress."[88] This makes clear that Hitler did not simply emerge out of thin air, an excrescence of evil. He had military training and he emerged from the army an educated speaker, a propagandist, and a strategic thinker.

In 1920 the Nazi party had its first official house organ: a rag called the *Volkischer Beobachter.* It had been the *Munchener Beobachter,* a product of the Jew-hating Thule Society; as the official Nazi newspaper "it played a major role in manufacturing and propagating the Hitler myth."[89] In 1924 Hitler collaborated with the newspaper's editor to write *Bolshevism*

From Moses to Lenin: "It was one of the main premisses of their anti-Semitism that Communism was part of the Jewish conspiracy to take control of the world."[90] The accusations that Jews were Bolsheviks and also capitalist bankers running the world defied the law of physics: both could be in the same place at the same time. In fact, it was Hitler who had been both faux-communist and proto-fascist; and also a parasite who produced nothing except, eventually, mountains of corpses. And, transparently, it was Hitler who wanted to take control of the world.

The Nazi party and then the Nazi regime never overlooked or neglected the importance of propaganda, even when fighting a war on two fronts and annihilating millions. Joseph Goebbels, who eventually headed a ministry for propaganda, had his own newspaper, *Der Angriff* (*The Attack*): ". . . it was ruthless and relentless against its main target, the Jews. As the symbol of the Jews' evil machinations and misuse of power, Goebbels chose Dr. Bernhard Weiss, vice president of the Berlin police, whom [Goebbels] dubbed 'Isidor.' "[91] Goebbels published the articles and cartoons in a book, *Das Buch Isidor* (*The Isidor Book*) in 1928. The deputy police chief sued for libel; and the liberal courts found for Goebbels on the logic that there was nothing wrong with calling someone a Jew. Julius Streicher produced *Der Stürmer,* usually described as pornographic. *Der Stürmer* pretended to be a journal that documented Jewish sexual depravity: the whorishness of the women; the rapist nature of the men; both played off against innocent young blonde girls. The effectiveness of *Der Stürmer* as hate literature came precisely from its sexualization of contempt, the attribution of sexual filth to Jews, the dehumanization of the alleged rapers and sluts. Jewish carnality was used to evoke aggression in the reader or consumer: hostile sexual excitement. There are those who argue, as does Gitta Sereny in her biographical investigation of Albert Speer, that "[i]t was not in *Der Angriff* or Julius Streicher's disgusting anti-Semitic tabloid *Der Stürmer* that the ground was prepared, but in small, slanted items in the quality dailies; long, learned articles in specialist papers; fictionalized stories in popular magazines; and finally—Goebbels's principal weapons—radio and films."[92] It makes sense to say that it was both, or all. And with the Nazi regime, words proliferated, words that were actions: "The quantity and intensity of verbal violence, which included the widespread posting of signs (which Germans and Jews saw daily) that forbade Jews' physical and social existence among Germans . . . should be seen as an assault in its own right, having been intended to produce profound damage—emotional, psychological, and social . . . The wounds that people suffer by having to listen publicly (particularly in front of their children) to such vituperation and by not being able to respond—can be as bad as the humiliation of a public beating."[93] Many who experienced both the physical and verbal violence prayed for respite from the latter; as Dawid Rubinowicz, twelve years old, wrote in his diary: "In the third picture a Jew is shown stamping dough with his feet and worms are crawling over him and the dough. The heading of this notice reads: 'The Jew is a Cheat. Your only Enemy.' And the inscription ran as follows: 'Dear Reader, before your very eyes, Are Jews deceiving you with lies. If you buy your milk from them, beware, Dirty water they've poured in there. Into the mincer dead rats they throw, Then as mincemeat it's put on show. Worms infest their home-made bread, Because the dough with feet they tread.' When the Village constable had put it up, some people came along, and their laughter gave me a headache from the shame that the Jews suffer nowadays. God give that this shame may soon cease."[94] Words—signs, warnings, threats, hate-based laws, insults—were all part of the terror; as Laqueur says, "The terror of fascism differs from that of other dictatorships not just because it applied terror on such a massive scale, but because it combined the use of terror with widespread, all-pervasive propaganda."[95] The terror of the Nazis and the Italian fascists was "always in combination with political propaganda."[96]

It was proven over and over again by the Nazis that words were necessary in order to create terror, to coerce compliance, and even to enable killers to continue committing crimes: the German police surrounding the Warsaw ghetto were "openly encouraged" to shoot Jews; "[t]he company recreation room was decorated with racist slogans, and a Star of David hung above the bar. A mark was made on the bar door for each Jew shot, and 'victory celebrations' were reportedly held on days when high scores were recorded."[97] Call it atmosphere or milieu or fraternity—use any euphemism: but the signs and slogans were incitement, a continuing agitation to normalize killing, an encouragement to kill more tomorrow and the day after. An order (words) was not enough; the social environment, including artifacts and words, had to cosset the shooters in contextual support, which made them heroes or good soldiers or good Germans or just one of the (Aryan) boys.

The Nazis understood saturation propaganda: every element of reality would reinforce Jew-hating; the deviant (in sociological terms) would then stand out in bold relief; hating Jews would be, in effect, the spiritual high-water mark of the society toward which people would strive; every vulgar expression of that hate in words or acts would be sanctified, part of a national project of self-improvement, self-cleansing.

The Russian Czar's secret police took another tack: the creation of one piece of poison so toxic yet so compelling that it would slander the Jews century after century. They created *The Protocols of the Meetings of the Learned Elders of Zion,* the secret plan of a cabal of Jews to control the world: "We shall create an intensified centralization of government in order to grip in our hands all the forces of the community. We shall regulate mechanically all the actions of political life of our subjects by new laws. These laws will withdraw one by one all the indulgences and liberties which have been permitted by *goyim* [non-Jews], and our kingdom will be distinguished by a despotism of such magnificent proportions as to be at any moment and in every place in a position to wipe out any *goyim* who oppose us by deed or word."[98] The so-called protocols outline plans for the economic, legal, and social domination by Jews of non-Jews, derisively called "goyim." The protocols outline an internationalist plot to destroy all the values of Christian civilization. The evil of the Jews is not a magical evil; it is instead a marshaling of will to domination that has behind it a strategy of pollution and deceit. This plan for dominance is by a group at once too smart to be human and too vile to tolerate. "Do not suppose for a moment," say these fictive Jews, "that these statements are empty words: think carefully of the successes we arranged for Darwinism, Marxism, Nietzsche-ism. To us Jews, at any rate, it should be plain to see what a disintegrating importance these directives have had upon the minds of the *goyim.*"[99]

These Jews not only want and have all the money; they are also the source of democratic ideas of liberty and equality, disseminated to cause chaos: "Far back in ancient times we were the first to cry among the masses of the people the words 'Liberty, Equality, Fraternity,' words many times repeated since those days by stupid poll-parrots who from all sides around . . . carried away the well-being of the world, true freedom of the individual, formerly so well-guarded against the pressure of the mob. The would-be wise men of the *goyim,* the intellectuals, could not make anything out of the uttered words in their abstractness; did not note the contradiction of their meaning and inter-relation: did not see that in nature there is no equality, cannot be freedom; that nature herself has established inequality of minds, of characters and capacities, just as immutably as she has established subordination to her laws: never stopped to think that the mob is a blind thing, that upstarts elected from among it to bear rule are, in regard to the political, the same blind men as the mob itself . . ."[100] The Czar must be credited with having politically sophisticated police; it is hard to think of Brooklyn cops being so politically literate.

Hannah Arendt makes the point that "one should remember that the first anti-Semitic parties on the continent in the 1880s had already (in contrast to the practice of all other rightist parties) combined on an international scale. In other words, modern anti-Semitism was never a mere matter of extreme nationalism: from the very beginning it functioned as an International."[101] *The Protocols of the Meetings of the Learned Elders of Zion* was translated, distributed, and read internationally as well, "whether there were many Jews there, or few Jews, or none at all. Thus, to cite a little noted example, Franco had his *Protocols* translated during the Spanish Civil War, even though Spain for lack of Jews could claim no Jewish problem."[102]

Many have noted the remarkable resemblance of the strategies and goals put forth in *The Protocols* to the strategies and goals of fascism itself—a point that Arendt says was first made by Alexander Stein in the 1930s. *The Protocols* as a guidebook for creating Fascism Now! may be what accounts for its staggering international success: "not primarily Jew-hatred, but rather, boundless admiration for the cunning of an allegedly Jewish technique of global world organization . . .; and . . . that the international global conspiracy which [*The Protocols*] describe has an ethnic and racist foundation, enabling a people without a state or a territory to rule the whole world by means of a secret society."[103] The Czar, needless to say, had a stake in smearing socialists and communists as Jews and vice versa; the whole point of the police conspiracy that resulted in *The Protocols* was to create a common scapegoat enemy that would unite Russians behind the legitimacy of the royal family. When the Czar was deposed, it was taken as a truism (one neatly reinforced by *The Protocols*) that the Bolsheviks were Jews: "Inflamed by a flood of pamphlets highlighting the Russian Jews among the Bolshevik leadership, the public did not know that only some 7 percent were of Jewish origin, though Jews composed some 12 percent of the populations from which Bolshevik leaders were drawn. . . . In 1920 the highest proportion of minority peoples in the Bolshevik leadership were in fact Russians of German origin . . ."[104]

Many believe that paranoia is a dynamic of anti-Semitism; according to Louis Rapoport in *Stalin's War Against the Jews,* anti-Semitic paranoia was "epitomized by *The Protocols* forged by the Czarist secret police and by the Doctors' Plot as fabricated, staged, and directed by Joseph

Stalin."[105] Arrested, exiled, and killed by the Czarist police, Soviet Jews then faced the anti-Semitism of the left, no less murderous. Still, throughout Eastern Europe Jews were perceived as socialists, communists, and Bolsheviks, no matter how few were in the leadership; in Germany Jews were perceived as the bankers of capital and also socialists, communists, and Bolsheviks. After the end of the Soviet occupation of Poland, elections were a novelty but some of the propaganda was not: "A small conservative Catholic party with the backing of Polish Primate Jozef Cardinal Glemp produced a poster that showed a happy worker tossing out a barrel-load of people bearing the sinister rapacious faces that have become the standard anti-Semitic stereotypes for Jews. The caption said, 'Enough of socialism, comrades.'"[106]

The Protocols themselves had been based on "an anti-Bonapartist tract of the 1860s,"[107] and "[s]ignificant parts of the document . . . are virtual word-for-word copies of an obscure French satire, John Robinson's best-selling *Proofs of a Conspiracy,* which popularized the role of Freemasons in causing the French Revolution."[108] Because French Jesuits exposed *The Protocols* as a forgery when it was published in 1920 in France, "*The Protocols* never had a following in France similar to that received in Germany and Great Britain"[109]—and in the United States, where "[o]n May 22, 1920, an article entitled 'The International Jew: The World's Problem' reproduced the essence of *[The] Protocols* and dominated page one of Henry Ford's newspaper, *The Dearborn Independent.*"[110] Radio preacher Charles Coughlin, partially funded by the Nazis, blamed the 1929 stock market crash on the Jews and "linked the event to the ideas of 'Karl Marx, a Hebrew.'"[111]

But the power and reach of *The Protocols* survive Ford, Coughlin, Hitler, and the Bolsheviks; now the material appears throughout the Arab world, hand in hand with *Mein Kampf* and Holocaust-denial literature. According to Wistrich, anti-Semitic propaganda had "begun to penetrate the Arab world in the 1920s and 1930s, especially as a result of Nazi propaganda and influence. After 1948 they were deliberately utilised by Arab governments and by all those many forces in the Arab world interested in mobilising the semi-literate masses against a common enemy, the Jewish state."[112] According to Riva Yadlin, an expert on Jew-hate in contemporary Egypt and cited by Wistrich: "Egyptian writing of the 1980s is permeated with the evil spirit of antisemitism. . . . Israel, in political cartoons, is depicted by hooked-nosed and hunchbacked figures with wispy beards and skull caps or black hats, reminiscent of *Der Stürmer* caricatures."[113] In 1989, the Egyptian weekly *October* said, "It has now become clear that perhaps Hitler did have justification for gassing the Jews. Because if the Jews were allowed freedom of action they would have eaten others."[114] Jews are accused of flooding Egypt with drugs. In 1989 at a conference on drugs in Jordan, one speaker "quoted *The Protocols* as advising Jews to distribute drugs in order to blind other people."[115]

Even in what appear to be intellectually substantive pieces of work, "[t]he Arabist Norman Stillman has pointed to the ubiquity of the blood libel even in seemingly scholarly tomes by Muslim writers like Ali Abd al-Wāhid Wāfi, Muhammad Sabrī, Hasan Zāzā, Mustafā al-Sa'danī and the prominent Egyptian writer, A'isha 'Abd al-Rahmān (pen-name Bint al-Shāti')—a literature that, *inter alia,* treats the draining of children's blood at Passover as a recognized Jewish ritual."[116] Additionally, Arab propaganda "attacked the Jews in democratic countries with charges of corrupt association . . . The more unpopular the Arabs were able to make Israel, the more Jews outside Israel tried to win back their own popularity by proving their innocence."[117]

Laqueur in his study of fascism shows "the political aspects of Islamic radicalism and the features it shares with fascism. These features include Islamic radicalism's anti-Western, anti-Enlightenment character; its renunciation of the values of a liberal society and of human rights; . . . its widespread use of propaganda and terror . . ."[118] The reasonable fear is that the Arab world is on its way to saturation propaganda so that contempt for Jews is the norm and any humanizing characterization is deviant. If there is not a German gene that causes anti-Semitism, there is unlikely to be an Arab one. In the absence of genetic inevitability, words matter, speech matters, expression matters; and none are distinct from acts. A former neo-Nazi, originally an East Berliner, describes these expressive activities: "painting a swastika, . . . desecrating Jewish cemeteries and throwing darts at Jewish faces and pissing on Jewish stars."[119] Indeed, these are all political expressions—eloquent expressions—of a familiar point of view. In *The Irish Troubles: A Generation of Violence 1967–1992,* J. Bowyer Bell describes the organization of a so-called Third Force by Protestant Ian Paisley: "five hundred marching men." Because of British laws against violence and sedition, "the Third Force was limited to rhetoric, a rhetoric the responsible feared as much as the marching men."[120] The responsible were right to fear rhetoric as much as they feared marching men: words make killing easier, legitimate, or inevitable. Words can kill; and one cannot find killing without finding the words that accompany it.

In the United States, the right-wing militia movement, or the Free Militias as they call themselves, are in alliance with homegrown Nazis and a resurgent Ku Klux Klan. As Elisabeth Young-Bruehl says in *The Anatomy of Prejudices,* "The basic Klan message remains white supremacy, but there is much talk about the ZOG [Zionist Occupational Government] that controls the African Americans and all other 'mud people' (non-whites). And, in keeping with a general movement on the American right, current Klan propaganda contains extensive antifeminism and homophobia. The slogan that feminism is a 'Jew-dyke conspiracy against the White Race' catches the syncretistic flavor of the current movement, packaging, as it does, so many prejudices in one phrase."[121] No mainstream politician has suffered quite as much from the influence of the right-wing haters as has Jack Kemp, as described by David Frum in *Dead Right:* "A right-wing Republican who hated communism and despised arms control, but who also cared about black America; a nostalgic for the gold standard who also believed in unionism, immigration, and the defense of Israel—Kemp was an unpredictable man who delighted in stringing together unlikely modifiers . . ."[122] While Kemp might not have minded being referred to as a "bleeding heart conservative" or a "classical liberal of the twenty-first century," he may well recoil from the conservatives in his own party who refer to him as "Yitzhak Kemp."[123] In U.S. conservative ideology, it remains a truism that immigrants, unions, antidiscrimination initiatives, and defense of Israel continue the contagion of so-called Jewish ideas. Of course, the right is not without its sectarian critics. Tom Metzger of the White Aryan Resistance (WAR) has contempt for the more polished and literate conservatives: "Right-wingism is one of the most dangerous weapons used against our race, since their spokesmen give us lip service and now and then they use a racial code word. They are all liars and hypocrites deserving a Pol Pot solution."[124] Metzger considers the Jews a diversion: "Don't worry about the Jews, they would voluntarily leave the country in no time. They can take all their Juaised [*sic*] Aryans with them too."[125] Metzger is fighting a losing battle, however: not against blacks but against the current underbelly of conservatism, the haters of Jews, the famous international Jewish conspiracy, and Israel, a demon incarnation of Jewish deceit and treachery—with guns.

In material sold in antiabortion, antitax, proto-Republican venues, Cincinnatus, author of *War! War! War!,* gives a history lesson: "The fact that it was Jewish help that brought the United States into the War on the side of the Allies has rankled ever since in German—especially Nazi—minds and has contributed in no small measure to the prominence which anti-Semitism occupies in the Nazi program."[126] Imagine: Nazi minds "rankled." Also present in the same legitimate venues is *The Turner Diaries* by the pseudonymous Andrew Macdonald (neo-Nazi William Pierce). This was the book that appears to have led U.S. soldier Timothy McVeigh to blow up a Federal building in Oklahoma City on April 19, 1995 (the day before Hitler's birthday); 168 people were killed. *The Turner Diaries* is a book advocating not only right-wing revolution but also strategies, tactics, and armed scenarios. It appeals especially to young men who are idealistic and trained military personnel; their idealism is white-only, Christian-only, and fashioned as part of a cult that continues to develop hallowing the Second Amendment to the U.S. Constitution: which calls for armed state militias. This movement is a precise analogue on the right to First Amendment fetishism on the left. The left claims words; the right claims guns; the founders claimed both. *The Turner Diaries* is written as political science fiction: "There was a time when we were better—and we are fighting to insure that there will be such a time again—but for now we are merely a herd, being manipulated through our basest instincts by a pack of clever aliens. . . . We will suffer grievously for having allowed ourselves to fall under the Jewish spell."[127] The white men want to win a war against the aliens. The back cover of *The Turner Diaries* gives the gist of the story: "The hated Equality Police begin hunting [white men] down, but the patriots fight back with a campaign of sabotage and assassination. An all-out race war occurs as the struggle escalates."[128] And escalate it does: from the early days when "the Cohen Act had outlawed all private ownership of firearms in the United States"[129] to the apocalyptic end: "Within 24 hours after we hit Tel Aviv and a half-a-dozen other Israeli targets last month, hundreds of Arabs were swarming across the borders of occupied Palestine . . . Within a week the throat of the last Jewish survivor in the last *kibbutz* and in the last, smoking ruin in Tel Aviv had been cut."[130] So, too, in Moscow, Leningrad, London, Paris, Brussels, Rotterdam, Bucharest, Buenos Aires, Johannesburg, and Sydney. One theme of *The Turner Diaries* is a familiar part of mainstream discourse: "None of the politicians are willing to face the real issues . . . one of which is the disastrous effect Washington's Israel-dominated foreign policy during the last two decades has had on America's supply of foreign oil."[131] Most Republicans, for now, do not go where *The Turner Diaries* leads: ". . . why didn't we rise up three years ago, when they started taking our guns away? Why didn't we rise up in righteous fury and drag these arrogant aliens into the streets and cut their throats then? Why didn't we roast them over bonfires at every street-corner in America? Why didn't we make a final end to this obnoxious and eternally pushy clan, this pestilence from the sewers of the East, instead of meekly allowing ourselves to be disarmed?"[132]

After the Federal disaster in Waco, Texas, where Federal authorities, going after an arsenal of weapons, were perceived to be responsible for the incineration of dozens of men, women, and children, Timothy McVeigh decided not to be meek. Indeed, in *The Turner Diaries,* as with McVeigh, political introspection leads slowly but surely to armed insurrection against the U.S. government, called *the System,* which is a tool of the Israelis: "From our contacts inside one of the Federal police agencies we learned that our people are being killed by two groups: a special Israeli assassination squad and an assortment of Mafia 'hit men' under contract to the government of Israel."[133] Israelis work in Washington, D.C., as "torture specialists."[134] This seems to be a race-based claim that Israelis are especially sadistic and ruthless.

The patriots are referred to as *the Organization;* and they are never happier than when Israelis die: "As we were driving home this evening, we heard the news on the radio which capped a perfect day: the Organization hit the Israeli embassy in Washington . . . For months an Israeli murder squad, working out of their embassy, has been picking off our people . . . We struck with heavy mortars while the Israelis were throwing a cocktail party for their obedient servants in the U.S. Senate. A number of Israeli officials had flown in for the occasion, and there must have been more than 300 people in the embassy when our 4.2-inch mortars began raining TNT and phosphorous onto their heads through the roof."[135]

The crossover from Jews to blacks is easy enough: "These swarthy, kinky-haired little Jewboys . . . had the mob screaming with real blood lust for any 'White racist' who might be unfortunate enough to fall into their hands."[136] The so-called Human Relations Councils are staffed by African Americans under Jewish domination, but the Organization sows the seeds of conflict: "The 'Toms' will eventually get their more militant and resentful brethren back into line, but meanwhile Izzy and Sambo are really at one another's throats, tooth and nail, and it is a joy to behold."[137] Blacks are characterized as angry brutes, stupid, and, by nature, rapist. Early on, blacks from the equality offices of the government "have been hauling some White women into their 'field headquarters' for 'questioning.' There they are stripped, gang-raped, and beaten—all in the name of the law!"[138] That would be equality law.

As the Organization becomes more successful as an underground creating chaos, the portrayal of blacks becomes more frenzied: "We also found gruesome evidence of one way in which the Blacks have solved their food shortage: cannibalism. They began by setting up barricades . . . unfortunate Whites are dragged from their cars, taken into a nearby Black restaurant, butchered, cooked, and eaten."[139] The vile imagery conjures up primitive headhunters and Idi Amin: in a black-controlled building, the patriots find "a human slaughterhouse . . . There were washtubs full of stinking entrails, and others filled with severed heads. Four tiny, human haunches dangled overhead from wires. . . . I saw the most terrible thing I have ever seen. It was the butchered and partially dismembered body of a teenage girl. Her blue eyes stared emptily at the ceiling, and her long, golden hair was matted with the blood which had rushed from the gaping wound in her throat."[140] This is the old U.S. racist hallucination, this time revivified by graphic, violent detail.

As Young-Bruehl would have predicted, feminists do not do too well in *The Turner Diaries,* which contributes to the toxic representation of the women's movement, especially by conservatives. The earliest underground patriot group in which the diarist participated had one woman member: "She complained that she had not yet been given a chance to participate . . . She had no intention, she said, of being nothing but a cook and housekeeper for the rest of us. We were all under a bit of tension following the big bombing, and Katherine came across a bit shrill—almost like a women's libber."[141] The editor of the *Diaries,* presumably Andrew Macdonald, inserts a note to the reader: "'Women's lib' was a form of mass psychosis which broke out during the last three decades of the Old Era. Women affected by it denied their femininity and insisted they were 'people,' not 'women.' This aberration was promoted and encouraged by the System as a means of dividing our race against itself."[142] Poor Katherine; just like her peers in the Weather Underground or Baader-Meinhof: she wants to blow up buildings but has to keep the secret lair clean.

The Turner Diaries introduces the perfidy of women slowly, so that the reader will understand the revolutionary necessity of killing white women: "In thinking over Saturday's events, what surprises me is that I feel no remorse or regret for killing those two White whores. Six months ago I couldn't imagine myself calmly butchering a teen-aged White girl . . . But I have become much more realistic . . . I understand that the two girls were with the Blacks only because they had been infected with the disease of liberalism . . ."[143] White girls slaughtered by black men are used to incite fury at the blacks; white patriot murder of white girls is just another heroic necessity: the culprit is the contagion of liberalism. The white girl in white-supremacist literature or propaganda is raped and killed, then raped and killed again: the incitement of violence against black men requires the pornographic dissection, the ravaged violation, of white women. Justice, one discovers from *The Turner Diaries,* is when white men kill corrupted white women.

The Turner Diaries is a book with a future; it is the closest analogue in toxic hate to *The Protocols of the Meetings of the Learned Elders of Zion* that is currently in circulation. It offers white men a model of military purity and spartan self-sacrifice, especially in the form of a shootout, that classic U.S. form of armed combat. It presents an argument against the U.S. government that has some constitutional validity; it exploits common U.S. beliefs in conspiracies, especially conspiracies designed by the U.S. and Israeli governments; blacks, Jews, Israelis, and feminists are the villains, consonant with the argument concurrently being made in a higher, more literate spate of books denouncing equality strategies by blacks and women in particular; it sexualizes the hate it expresses, which gives that hate a more intense emotional valence. It calls on patriots to act against the government much as McVeigh did and to respond to capture in the same way: he had nothing to explain; he refused to enter into a conversation about what he had done and why; he did not need or want psychological succor or public understanding; he was a soldier, trained by the U.S. Army and then pointed by *The Turner Diaries* at a Federal building filled with so-called mud people, Jews, white women, who were collaborators with or agents of a contemptible Federal government. He was prepared to kill in order to act against what he considered an invasive, contaminated, contagious, outlaw Federal government and he did; he was prepared to die and he will—a martyr like the fictional Earl Turner of *The Turner Diaries.* There is no special tragedy in executing a mass murderer who has committed treason; but if the innocents matter, unhappy questions must be asked. How many more will die because of the influence of *The Turner Diaries?* The old libertarian canard is that no girl was ever ruined by a book; but in fact boys have been—they learn whom and how to kill.

The Nazis really liked taking photographs. They loved documenting how they hurt those they were about to kill: for instance, early on, imperfect or disabled or mentally impaired Germans whom they were about to euthanize. Photographs collected at the U.S. Holocaust Memorial Museum in Washington, D.C., display thin, white, fragile children, half-undressed, bodies languid from slow destruction: a perfect pornography of pain. The Nazis filmed their medical experiments on humans: surgeries, castrations, induced infections and diseases, wounding and maiming, eventual evisceration and decapitation. Like lonelier serial killers, they wanted trophies, memories, proof, and the pleasure of owning the victim, flattened and caged in the photograph, kept the same forever, while the flesh-and-blood original was rotting in a mass grave or was ash rising out of a chimney. The photographs are variously war mementos, personal diaries, and a private pornography of sadistic conquest. The use of the camera was an oppressor's privilege: photographs taken (and hidden) by the victims do exist but are rare and few. They are qualitatively different from the photographs by the tormentors. A viewer is compelled to search faces, infer individuality, see whole persons however degraded by circumstance. The photographs by the victims show suffering, confusion, and endurance, not violence. (See, for instance, *The Auschwitz Album,* with photographs found by Auschwitz survivor Lili Meier.) In the hands of the innocent, the camera was not a weapon of sadism or dehumanization.

The murderers certainly got private pleasure from the photographs they took of their work; but there was also another dimension—public entertainment, killing and the cameras united together: "The most horrible photographs, and some of the most horrible narratives . . . record [that] . . . the first massacres, especially those in the Baltic states, were carried out in public. In Kaunas, Lithuania, where Einsatzkommando 3 operated, the Jews were clubbed to death with crowbars, before cheering crowds, mothers holding up their children to see the fun, and German soldiers clustered round like spectators at a football match. At the end, while the streets ran with blood, the chief murderer stood on the pile of corpses as a triumphant hero and played the Lithuanian national anthem on an accordion."[144] Published first in Germany in a book called, with mordant wit, *"The Good Old Days": The Holocaust as Seen by Its Perpetrators and Bystanders,* these photographs might as well be documenting a state fair: "The public mass executions were in many ways a festival. In Kovno (Lithuania) locals—among them mothers with their children—applauded as each Jew was beaten to death in front of them. Cheers and laughter rang out. German soldiers stood by and took photographs. The military authorities were aware of this but did not intervene. German soldiers were sometimes prepared to travel long distances in order to obtain the best places at the bloody 'shooting festivals.' "[145] The editors and compilers of *"The Good Old Days"* call this phenomenon "execution tourism";[146] indeed, some couples spent their honeymoons at these convivial celebrations and, like all honeymooners, took photographs. *"The Good Old Days"* serves the purpose of documenting "how mass murder was carried out in full public view over a long period of time."[147]

The photographs themselves require explanation: they are a wretched pornography of brute bloodbaths, enjoyed by crowds who cheered on the killers and immortalized them in the amateur photography of soldiers and tourists as well as locals who were themselves under Nazi occupation. One can barely stand to look at them.

According to Goldhagen, similar photography in Poland proves the pride Germans took in killing Jews: ". . . Police Battalion 101 took [photographs] memorializing their time in Poland, of which only some unknown percentage has come to light"; he sees the willingness "to make an extensive photographic record of their deeds, including their killing operations," as evidence that they were unaware of their criminality; he describes the Germans in the photographs as having "cheerful and proud demeanors . . . entirely comfortable with their environment, their vocation, and with the images that are being preserved . . ."[148]

In addition, the Germans used the camera to make filmic propaganda starring real Jews as well as German actors "made up like Jews."[149] Ringelbaum, the contemporaneous historian of the Warsaw ghetto, described a German movie being shot in that ghetto on May 19, 1942: "This film seems to be designed to represent all the bad features of the Jews as 'subhumans.' . . . After photographing scenes of misery in the streets, begging, etc., special scenes are set up in which German actors, made up like Jews, play their parts. Moreover, Jewish people, seized at random in the streets, are forced to participate. Thus, when a picture of a ritual bathing-establishment, the so-called *mikva,* was to be taken, fifty people were seized in Gesia Street and transported to a *real mikva* . . . There all these people were ordered to undress completely and they were driven, both men and women, into a pool, so that pictures might be taken."[150] The *mikva* was a bath in running water for the purpose of a ritual cleansing: men and women separate, of course, with the schedule determined by religious obligation. But both the pornographic degradation and sacrilege were not enough: "A few days later the same film team arrive in the so-called 'refugee' centers, which accommodate Jews driven out from the towns in which the ghettos had been liquidated. There unimaginably pornographic pictures were taken. Old bearded Jews were ordered at pistol point to commit lascivious acts with children, with young girls, etc. On Sunday, the 17th of this month [May], the movie people filmed the ceremony of circumcision of a Jewish infant."[151] This use of Jews was then reported as a social policy victory of National Socialism; as Levin describes, "While the large trucks with motion-picture equipment were grinding cameras to film the Ghetto, an enthusiastic article appeared in the official German *Warschauer Zeitung* describing how 100,000 Jews in Warsaw who had been social parasites were 'now productively working for the Germans.' This appeared one month before the deportations to Treblinka."[152]

But no newspaper, even with pornographic drawings, cartoons, and illustrations, as in *Der Stürmer,* could take the place of the camera in the killing project. Even Himmler took the trouble to collect and publish a book of photographs: "Himmler took considerable pride in the book, entitled *The Subhuman (Der Untermensch),* filled with pictures of threatening, un-European visages supposedly of the enemies to the east."[153] Hitler liked Himmler's book.

The Nazis also photographed and filmed the torture and eventual murder of the German officers who tried to depose Hitler and failed. This group of soldiers is often designated "the German resistance," a hyperbole of astonishing magnitude. They were anti-Semites, German supremacists, and loyal patriots who considered that Hitler himself—with his erratic decisions and appalling two-front war—should be replaced by a military government, which is to say, them. Setting off a bomb at the Wolf's Lair, Hitler's bunker hideaway, failed to kill Hitler; and the conspirators were soon found out and brought to Nazi justice, which consisted of slow, vile, filmed torture to death: "Hitler's revenge was bestial. Nearly 200 men, including officers, members of the Kreisau Circle and other prominent dissidents, were subjected to Gestapo torture in many cases by strangulation or hanging from meathooks by piano wire in front of a movie camera."[154] Goebbels's idea was to take the movie footage and make a propaganda film, which he did. It was shown once in Berlin. Full-dress Nazis were nauseated and made physically ill. It was fine to photograph Jews being clubbed to death in public; but watching adult, Aryan, military men die was another thing altogether, which suggests that torture as entertainment requires dehumanization of an enemy and that enemy's stigmatized powerlessness. Torture adult male soldiers of rank and other adult male soldiers will throw up. There but for the grace of Hitler go I. Enjoyment in the debased photographic object requires that the viewer never identify with the victim so that, whatever his future, the viewer knows that he will never be that abject and soiled.

Albert Speer, the only Nazi leader to feign repentance after the Holocaust, was, at least, no Goebbels: "For Speer the single most devastating incident was to see photographs lying on Hitler's desk . . . of men, dressed in striped convict suits, unrecognizable in their death agony, hanging from meat hooks. One of these, an SS officer told him, inviting him to a showing that night of a film of the hangings, was Field Marshall von Witzleben. Speer declined the invitation. 'The very thought made me sick,' he wrote in Spandau prison. 'Many SS leaders attended but no army officers.' "[155] Maybe Speer was, as one biographer hazarded, "the good Nazi";[156] or he saw himself in the photographs on Hitler's desk. The camera, like the gun, could shoot in any direction, be aimed at anyone, but not with the same predictable effect. There is a dispute by writers on the subject about wire: was it piano or chicken wire? There is no dispute about the meat hooks, the prisoners "squirming and wiggling in agony until they died."[157] There is also no dispute that this long, awful dying was filmed.

Of course, the Nazis also made more conventional propaganda films, the most famous being, perhaps, *The Eternal Jew*. This is a film of unmitigated anti-Semitic propaganda that has spliced into it part of a Fritz Lang movie about a real-life serial killer of the Weimar era: "The Nazi film . . . contains a film clip of Peter Lorre enacting the panicked response of the murderer Franz Beckert to his capture. This cinematic moment, transplanted to a document of virulent anti-Semitic propaganda, is intended to assert the identity of the foreign-born Jewish actor with his role: the Jew who *plays* at being a criminal also *is* the criminal. . . . Franz Beckert and the actor-criminal-alien-Jew Peter Lorre are cast as pathogens—as sources of fatal contamination that must be eliminated before infecting the general population."[158] East Germany's neo-Nazis also appreciated the movie: "And that's why we watched *The Eternal Jew* . . . It showed all the Nazi stereotypes of the Jews: they were rats, parasites, they knew how to get money. . . . The idea was not to buy from the Eternal Jew the idea of his truth, the idea of his importance as a human being. The Eternal Jew was a piece in our board game who needed to learn not to take so seriously what we'd done to him."[159] *The Eternal Jew* has since changed technologies; it is buttressed and reinforced by anti-Semitic computer games widely distributed in Germany and Austria. The idea is for the player to win: in a concentration-camplike setting to kill Jews.

The old Nazis were truly incorrigible: about cameras as well as about Jews. At the Nuremberg Trials, the prosecutors showed a documentary film called *The Nazi Plan:* ". . . it was a compilation of 'films made by the Nazis themselves' which had been given continuity by their assemblage chronologically . . . The reaction of [the accused Nazis] surprised many of us. Far from viewing the film as another nail in their coffins, they enjoyed it hugely. . . . 'Goering was visibly delighted to see himself once more "in the good old times," Ribbentrop spoke of the gripping force of Hitler's personality, another defendant declared himself happy that the Tribunal would see him at least once in full uniform, and with the dignity of his office.'"[160] That night back in jail, Goering was "cocky and gloating over his own past accomplishments"; Hess was "predicting that Germany would rise again"; and Ribbentrop was "half moved to tears."[161] Gas, cameras, and sentimentality: the old Nazis loved their trophies; in the carnage they saw images of themselves that were heroic; they experienced self-love; the subhuman garbage made them, by contrast, human giants, admirable and omnipotent. Since so much of the footage showed skeletal, debased human bodies, the Nazi films need to be understood as a sexually aggressive and depraved pornography of power.

Is the question what constitutes pornography, or what makes a pornographer? The invention and then advancing technology of the camera made it possible to distribute documentary replications of debased, dirtied, dehumanized, and violated human beings; the circle of accessibility got bigger and more democratic as the technology itself got cheaper and more democratic. But pornographic artifacts—from drawings and writings to film and Internet exploitation—are no more distinct from the ongoing reality of life than are words per se. Prostitutes were required by pimps and johns to act out pornographic scenarios in brothels and fraternal clubhouses, in carriages and cars, on street corners and under bridges. In homes wives and slaves were sexually used without consent, forcibly raped, beaten, or tortured: children were raped. Inside the violence there was a coherence of hate and annihilation articulated by and as pornography; pornography was the inner logic of any sexualized dominance and the reigning iconography of dehumanization. Pornography was acted out on prostituted women and on married women by men who wanted sexualized dominance or had an inner map that required dehumanization of others as a predicate for pleasure. Needless to say, Hitler was such a man. He was known to collect "editions of a semi-pornographic nature . . . discretely shrouded in Edgar Wallace thrillers. Three of these well-thumbed volumes consisted of the curious studies of Edward Fuchs—the *History of Erotic Art* and an *Illustrated History of Morals.*"[162]

Hitler also liked watching women boxers: "This seemed to appeal to him, so in we went and watched several matches . . . with the women in abbreviated trunks and vests, mincing around and landing the occasional tap. It was all pure circus, but Hitler was riveted."[163] He had a perceptible sexual interest in teenage girls; he met the young Eva Braun through a pornographer he knew—the pornographer was upset with Hitler's obvious sexual interest in his own even younger niece so he foisted Eva Braun, his shop assistant, on Hitler: ". . . much of his business had been in pornographic postcards and photographs of nude dancers. His models had been girls who worked in second-rate bars—including Braun, who had become both his assistant and his mistress. He had happily handed Eva over to the Führer."[164] A secret OSS report had concluded "that Hitler practiced an outre sexual perversion so repellent it drove women to suicide."[165] The probability that Hitler's sexual practice was coprophilia, or defecating on a sexual partner, is given weight by a staggering statistical aberration: ". . . of the seven women who, we can be reasonably sure, had intimate relations with Hitler, six committed suicide or seriously attempted to do so."[166] The facts are remarkable. The love of Hitler's life was his teenage niece Geli Raubal. Her death appeared to be a suicide though murder by Hitler cannot be ruled out: she was killed with Hitler's gun. They lived together in his apartment; he was obsessed with her—maybe he was a little bit controlling, as we say?; she was trapped in what might have at first looked like a gilded cage. If Geli was not a suicide, hers would be the first life Hitler took: she would be his first murder victim. This is possible because it is common for men to practice violence on women they know; this violence foreshadows more public destructions. But suicide is also plausible because Geli was unable to escape her uncle's love for her and sexual use of her. Then there were the others: "Mimi Reiter tried to hang herself in 1928; . . . Eva Braun attempted suicide in 1932 and again in 1935; Frau Inge Ley was a successful suicide, as were Renate Mueller and Suzi Liptauer."[167] The seventh is believed to be Leni Riefenstahl; camera in hand, she had the sensibility of a perpetrator, not a suicide.

It is also documented that Hitler's henchman, the exceedingly cruel Reinhard Heydrich, engineered two episodes of sexual blackmail to serve Hitler's political purposes: "First, pornographic photographs of General Blomberg's new young wife illustrating her recent past in the sexual demi-monde were dredged up and presented to Blomberg, then the highest ranking officer in the Reich. He resigned rather than face scandal. And then a homosexual prostitute known as 'Bavarian Joe' materialized to make secret accusations to army authorities that he had observed General Fritsch, the second highest officer in the army, paying for the services of boy prostitutes in Berlin dives. Although this accusation (unlike the photographs of General Blomberg's wife) seemed to have been fabricated from whole cloth, General Fritsch . . . promptly resigned as well."[168] This enabled Hitler to make the army his own. There would be no principled high-authority dissent from the war plans of the Führer.

For the Nazis pornography was a verb. They were always doing it no matter what they were doing. Concentration camp prisoners were the pornographized population, sometimes occasioning awe; as Höss, who was at Sachsenhausen (not yet a commandant), relates: "The minute he arrived he attracted my attention . . . The way his eyes roamed everywhere, the way he jumped at the slightest noise, and his feminine, dancer-like movements made me suspect he was a true homosexual. He started to cry when the Kommandant barked at him in a very harsh tone . . . He didn't want to shower because he said he was afraid to undress. We discovered rather quickly why, when he undressed. His entire body, from his neck to his wrists and ankles was tattooed with pornographic pictures. These tattoos depicted every kind of social perversion . . . even, curiously, normal sexual intercourse with women. He became sexually aroused, especially when someone touched him, as when his sexual tattoos were being photographed by the police."[169] In Buchenwald Commandant Koch and his wife, Ilse, had a policy on tattoos: "Koch had ordered all tattooed prisoners to report to the dispensary. Those with the most interesting and artistic tattoos were put to death by lethal injection. . . . Ilse Koch . . . liked to have the tattooed flesh tanned and fashioned into household objects like lampshades."[170] This was a pornographic aesthetic shared by husband and wife, interior design in which every object was felicitously tactile; at Nuremberg, photographs of "[t]he exposed, pale, leathery objects with the designs of ships and hearts still visible"[171] were evidence. The photographs, however, could not possibly expose or express the pornography of the objects themselves; only the processing of the skin on the one hand and the touching of the artifact from it on the other could; and how many have done that? In the absence of experience, one is forced to think about the wretchedness of this assault on the body, this appropriation of tattooed skin, this expressive cannibalism. Those less resourceful, like Höss at Auschwitz, "would watch the beatings and hangings as if he were watching a movie, but with no reaction showing on his face."[172] This was the Nazi reality: Höss could watch pornographic loops in real time because he never ran out of the raw material: the Jews to beat and hang. The Nazis kept the masses of inmates nearly naked or naked: "Before being killed, they are stripped naked. Human beings tend not to congregate naked, they do not move about from place to place naked; to deprive them of their clothing is to make them like animals. Guards have testified that it became impossible for them to identify their victims once those people became a mass of nude bodies: clothes are a mark of humanity."[173]

The pornographizing of the inmates deprived them of dignity: "*Dignity:* this, then, . . . simply means the capacity of the individual to remain a subject with a will; that fact, by itself, is enough to ensure membership in the human race."[174] Taking dignity away, robbing someone of it, making the body an object for use by a hater, sexualizing that use through any number of strategies including nudity or fetishism: these are the common elements of pornography. As Elfriede Jelinek says in her novel *Wonderful Wonderful Times:* "His one-time enemies got away through the chimneys and crematoria of Auschwitz and Treblinka or littered Slavic earth. Nowadays Rainer's father crosses the petty frontiers of today's Germany anew whenever he takes his artistic photographs. Only a philistine recognises those frontiers in his private life. In photography, the bounds are fixed by clothing."[175] When a model asks for a break, "Herr Witkowski says he'll break something of hers in a minute, and throws something hard that hits her shoulder and makes her start. She'll have a bruise there. Ready yet, you whore? . . . Now get your legs apart!"[176] The pornographer is the user, the abuser, the perpetrator in his role as commandant or artist. He uses human bodies with contempt.

In Israel there is a genre of pornography defined by the theme of the Holocaust: women's bodies in pieces run down by trains or skeletal standing by open ovens.* In Israel there are no "weak (male) Jews," Jews who

---

*I have written in detail about Holocaust pornography in "Israel: Whose Country Is It Anyway?" in *Life and Death: Unapologetic Writings on the Continuing War Against Women,* The Free Press, New York, 1997.

repudiate the perpetrator, Jews who refuse to accept a pornography of using the skin of Jewish women, attacking the dignity of the bodies of Jewish women; instead there is an acceptance of the sexual hostility of the one who dominates through the subordinating of women and Arabs. The Israeli pornography that invokes the themes and scenarios of the Holocaust is a death threat: the camera works for the oppressor and against the innocents.

Many Israelis recognize the Zionism of Meir Kahane as "racist and pornographic."[177] Kahane and his gang raised the specter of Arabs expressing their hatred of Jews "by raping women and children; a series of murders and rapes that enraged the country at that time—some of them perpetrated by terrorists, some by common criminals, and some of which remain unsolved—fed his propaganda machine."[178] Israelis have also used pornography as a weapon against the Palestinian population: "The *shabbab* . . . say that one of the most effective methods used by Israel's security police to coerce devout Palestinian youths into collaboration with them is to arrest them and then produce doctored pornographic photos of their mothers, sisters, or wives. 'It is terrible . . . These photos show the bodies of naked women, doing all kinds of bad things, with the faces of *their* women attached. . . . The Israelis tell them they will make the photos public if they don't cooperate with them.' "[179] A consequence of this use of pornography as a weapon of humiliation and disgrace is to push Palestinians further to the right: "The Israelis would not have *any* photos of these Palestinian women if they were kept at home, as Muslim women should be. . . . [W]omen are perceived by fundamentalists to be the cause of men's weaknesses and ultimately, their downfall."[180] This puts Palestinian men in the position of having two mortal enemies: Israelis and Palestinian women.

Other women in left nationalist or quasi-nationalist fights have been subjected to the misogyny of their own side: Andreas Baader, famous as a pornographer, called all women "cunts"[181] and "[f]ar from being a leader, Ulrike [Meinhof] was the whipping boy."[182] So in later movements women created and put into practice their own agenda: in Italy, "[s]ome feminists formed vigilante squads, attacking doctors who spoke out against abortions, cinemas showing sex films, and shops that displayed live models of women in their windows";[183] for the Basque separatists, "[i]ndustries perceived as threatening the environment are attacked, cinemas showing sex films are bombed, and drug dealers are kneecapped or killed."[184] Women in revolutionary movements have to resist the misogyny of the dominant group of men and the intrafamilial hatred and dominance of their own men.

There is a pornography of women in the Arab world as well as sexualized propaganda against Jews; but in the U.S., where the publication and use of pornography is considered a freedom, defenders of pornography use rhetorical intimidation based on wrong facts to suggest that in countries where women's status is low, for instance, in Saudi Arabia, there is no pornography. But there is, in Saudi Arabia, too. First, there is the living pornography, the women in captivity. Second, there is the imported prostitute pornography—prostitutes flown in, used, and flown out. Third, there are the pornographic artifacts; as the unnamed Saudi princess writes, ". . . I had located Ali's [her brother's] collection of *Playboy* and other similar magazines . . . I had discovered a new collection of photo slides. Curious, I had taken them to my bedroom; perplexed, I viewed them on the slide projector. Naked men and women were doing all kinds of strange things; one group of pictures even showed animals with women. Ali had obviously lent them to other boys on occasion, for he had clearly printed his name on every forbidden article."[185] The apparent absence of pornography is a highly charged and dangerous presence; in reality, it trains men to hate women and contributes to the conviction that women need prisonlike separation from men: from men like them. Sometimes the men will claim that they themselves need the protection of female segregation because women are sexual provocateurs.

For women turned into pornography, especially through rape or other sexual torture, the consequences if they survive are an internalized shame immune to rescue; as a distressed survivor from Argentine torture said, "[her] voice . . . subsumed by that of a man: Gruffly and in a low, growling register, she berated herself in the filthy language they had used when they searched her vagina for contraband."[186] The woman becomes pornography to herself: the worst alienation.

John Berger says about nakedness: "Nudity with its thrill for puritans and its superficial promise for hedonists is still far too exterior . . . It is necessary to go further into the interior of the being until, ideally, we touch not the body but the experience of the body."[187] This expresses an ethic that repudiates the pornographic and explains it at the same time.

8

RELIGION / MATERNITY

The difficulties (to understate) of being either a Jew or a woman are arguably more than made up for by the value of religion and of maternity per se: each a special and unequivocal gift of substance and spirituality. Jews have God; women have children. A gift need not be accepted; a capacity need not be used. God and children go to the heart of humanity's deepest, most discomfiting mystery: origins—who are we and how did we get here? It is never enough to know what mommy and daddy did in the dark: individual existence does not mean enough to put questions of origin to rest. One wants to know about the beginnings of the group or tribe or people. One wants to know about the beginnings of existence itself, the story of which will begin to enunciate a narrative of meaning, of inclusion and exclusion, of reality and romance, of true and false. Stories of origin are mythologies of lineage and prehistory that define the heroic: only heroes make something out of nothing, transform existence by existing, compromise the void irredeemably, annihilate the vacuum. Where do I come from? is the question one is socialized to try to answer. Where do we come from? is the first question articulated by birth itself, by the fact of becoming. Armenians, for instance, "trace their lineage to a common mythological ancestor, Haig, and later to a series of kingdoms that were among the first to espouse Christianity";[1] experiencing a vision of Christ is part of the Armenian myth or history or origin. In *Tribes: How Race, Religion, and Identity Determine Success in the New Global Economy,* Joel Kotkin notes how stories of group origins provide a basis for social and economic cohesion: "For Indians [on the subcontinent], their origination myths derive from the ancient stories of the Vedas, 'the first Bible of the Hindus'; the legends associated with the rise of the first 'Yellow Emperor' serve as the mythological basis for the unique sense of venerable and noble beginnings of the Chinese; the Japanese concept of the 'divine' origin of their land and the Yamato race underlies a particularly well developed sense of their tribal uniqueness."[2] Myths of origin do not have to be sui generis: "In the case of the British, much of the mythology of unique-ness—including the myth of King Arthur and the Holy Grail—draws on themes derived from the Jewish Holy Land."[3]

In Africa, Islam became a force in 639, "when Arab armies invaded Egypt and defeated the Byzantine garrison."[4] It would have been known as *din Allah*, "the religion of God."[5] According to Roland Oliver in *The African Experience: Major Themes in African History from Earliest Times to the Present*, the *din Allah* existed "at least a century before the develop-ment of a literary tradition in Arabic, and nearly two centuries before the earliest written codifications of the Shari·a, the law of Islam, and the Ko-ran, the book of God . . . The *din Allah*, then, was purely an oral tradi-tion, not yet defined and guarded by any class of learned specialists . . ."[6] In fact, in Africa early on, oral Islam was experienced as a "military disci-pline imparted by commanders to their Arab soldiers, the *muhajirun*, and to the local levies, the *mawali*, recruited among the conquered peoples."[7] For Muhammad himself, divine revelation was oral, not written. There are two nationalist points to be made: one, the oral revelations were in Arabic; second, these revelations were to supersede the texts and practices of both Jews and Christians. Dostoevsky was interpreting narrowly by omitting conquest when he said, "The object of every national move-ment, in every people, and at every period of its existence, is only the seeking for its god who must be its own god, and the faith in him as the only true one."[8]

In what became the holy book of written Islam, the Koran, there are "114 suras of varying length, from a few lines to several pages. According to Aman Ibn Kathir, there are 6,000 verses in the Koran, 77,439 words, and not less than 321,180 letters."[9] If there were no other virtue to it, re-ligion does begin to demand literacy: laws must be read and interpreted; stories must be communicated with accuracy; prohibitions must be un-derstood and accepted collectively; "people who will never meet in the flesh [must] absorb the same fundamental ideas by using as nearly as pos-sible the same words"; "[t]ranslation from one language to another need not be an impediment, provided that it is the translation of written texts"; "[l]iteracy may be confined to a small minority of those who participate," although that small minority will become a ruling elite; "[t]he written word exercises its control not only through space but through time";

"[i]nspiration and genius can speak to future generations . . ."[10] Written language creates cohesion by generating a common set of experiences: those who do this and do not do that are related through the imperatives of religious literacy. Written language also creates boundaries: there are those who honor the words and those who do not; one community lives a common vocabulary, another does not. Inside written language, conflicts and differences are made indelible; once consciousness includes writing, arguments continue over centuries; someone in conflict with his or her indigenous community will write down how and why, possibly generating a new community, a new tradition, out of the old one. Exile as stigmatized punishment becomes an opportunity for a new literature: the outsider, the newly excluded, the dissident has writing with which to fight banishment or imposed isolation: these are the real facts, he or she will say, a new articulation of events, a new history; this is the true story.

The earliest Greek historians were exiles, "men with the leisure to write and the detachment . . . to explain; many of their successors also lived outside their home cities."[11] For Jews, exile became the common condition; as Robin Lane Fox says in *The Unauthorized Version: Truth and Fiction in the Bible,* "the Exile occurred as a shared catastrophe . . . It left some [Jews] asking why, and what, if anything, was next. Others wished to maintain tradition, to keep alive the past and its practices, to idealize them, even, in order to bridge this great interruption in their lives."[12] It was the high literacy of the Hebrew religion that allowed for the replication and idealization of religious practice; and it was the pain of exile that led to new writing: ". . . the Jews' songs and writings of this period are the great literary achievements of the mid to late sixth century BC, an age which was one of relative mediocrity among the world's writers elsewhere."[13] Exile introduced the lyricism of dispossession into religious writing: who were we and where are we now and why? Why are we here, not there? Are we hated, inferior, subjugated, degraded; are we cowards; were we abandoned by God; why did we lose?

The individual dilemma of rootlessness or homelessness in itself had no importance. The questions were collective, communal. Why did they push us out? What are we going to do about it? Self-consciousness derives to a remarkable degree from group consciousness. The urgent epistemological themes of the tribe are experienced inside the tribe, by virtue of being part of the tribe. Along with a common origin, the group begins to experience a common pain: the suffering of separation from who and what they were; the humiliation of being less.

Religious inferiority can be imposed from outside the group through conquest or colonialization or a hierarchical imperialism; or the group itself can designate inferiors inside it—usually women and slaves or foreigners. The second-class citizenship of women within religious communities is expressed concretely through separation and segregation, male priests and grand dragons, sacrifice of the person herself, ritually hallowed. The practice of *sati* is one example. Arguably rooted in ancient Vedic texts, *sati* was outlawed by the British during their rule over the Indian subcontinent; but the practice continues, its point being "to turn what is in fact murder, into a mystical act."[14] The bride, often a child, makes an apparent choice to be burned alive in the fire that is cremating her dead husband; *sati* is justified now precisely as an issue of choice, female self-determination, and yet eyewitnesses repeatedly testify that the child/wife is pushed into the fire or that her egress is blocked. As a *sati,* she will be memorialized as a saint, an iconic martyr; should she "choose" to live—or evade the male relatives and often armed soldiers who box her in—she will be considered inauspicious: basically responsible for the death of her husband and unfit to have any contact with her own children. She will be treated as if she is dead: dead without honor.

The inferiority of Irish Catholics has been a theme of British repression in Northern Ireland: "First the British, not simply the Ulster Protestants, assumed that the Irish—this usually meant all Irish in London and Catholics in Belfast—were innately inferior by culture if not by birth. In 1971 a majority study on race and intelligence by a British psychologist claimed that the Irish were an inherently and intellectually inferior racial group."[15] (See Richard J. Hernnstein and Charles Murray, *The Bell Curve: Intelligence and Class Structure in American Life;* they made similar claims but about Americans of African descent.) The most important point—for both Irish Catholics and African Americans—may be the one made by Bell in *The Irish Troubles: A Generation of Violence 1967–1992:* ". . . many, perhaps most, Catholics in Northern Ireland accepted that they *were inferior.* Whether this was by birth or not scarcely mattered; they had less education, less capital, poorer prospects, worse leaders, and none of the signs of success. They were inferior and felt so . . ."[16]

The stigma of religious inferiority moves the burden of hate from men to God, thus ensuring that the inferiority is both eternal and omnipresent: inescapable because one carries it inside one. Religious inferiority, however it saturates the host society, has a long half-life. Add race into the mix—either by beleaguered metaphor or because racial difference is a fact or as an emphasis on how primal the inferiority itself is and one creates the perfect political diversion: often the conflict between religious groups is about land—call the land holy or profane. The issues can have to do with sovereignty or natural resources or just plain greed, an acquisitiveness encouraged by the exercise of power over a group defined as religiously or racially inferior. For instance, Native Americans in the United States want "their land and their religion; the two converged . . . in a world view that understood the natural environment not as an object of manipulation but as an extension of the tribe."[17] (See Vine Deloria, Jr., *God Is Red*.) This holistic convergence notwithstanding there is nearly everywhere a long history of wars of conquest, for land, motivated by religious zealotry, which amounted to an assertion of religious superiority: being nearer my God to Thee.

In opposition to this commonplace congruence of land and religion, Jews in modern times (from the Enlightenment to the Holocaust) were reluctant to attach religion to land—let alone to claim superiority: difference, yes; superiority, no. Exile itself became the Jewish landscape; and the geography of exile kept changing according to the limits of non-Jewish tolerance. Jews became known for "their passivity and spirituality which, over the course of generations, had stamped itself on the Jewish people until it had become second nature."[18] An acquired trait was turned into a biological fact: believed by non-Jews and Jews alike. The rabbinic philosopher of the German Enlightenment, Moses Mendelssohn, rejected tentative Zionist ideas (in which religion and land were associated with each other) by saying: "The greatest obstacle in the way of this proposal is the character of my people. It is not ready to attempt anything so great. The pressure under which we have lived for centuries has removed all vigor from our spirit . . . [T]he natural impulse for freedom has ceased its activity within us. It has been changed into a monkish piety, manifested in prayer and suffering, not in activity."[19]

In this view, which was nearly universal for centuries, Jews, like women, take the beatings, rape, plunder, murders, and are ennobled by them. Survival will be luck or God's will but not a consequence of strategy, martial or not. Each violation will be another opportunity to thank God for making us better than *them*. To fight back would mean changing sides in the moral sweepstakes: we'd cross over to the victor side, a corruption for the poor, the downtrodden, the oppressed; to fight like them would mean being like them, moral monsters. Jews, like women, were passive, pure, and frequently martyred: world-class champions at suffering.

Nor could Jews or women get entangled with making new versions of God's earth: imitating him in paintings, sculptures, drawings, a visual, human re-creation of existence. Jews had God; women had children. In the second of the Ten Commandments, God ordered the Jews: "Thou shall not make unto thee any graven image, any likeness of anything that is in heaven above, or that is in the earth beneath, or that is in the water beneath the earth."[20] Politically, this means that painting is theft. The second commandment is a militant copyright law: it's Mine, not yours, I don't want to see your pathetic imitations. In *Amusing Ourselves to Death: Public Discourse in the Age of Show Business,* Neil Postman wonders "why the God of these people would have included instructions on how they were to symbolize, or not symbolize, their experience. It is a strange injunction to include as part of an ethical system *unless its author assumed a connection between forms of human communication and the quality of a culture.*"[21] In fact, the Hebrew God did assume just that: that existence was diminished by the pictorial but made richer with words; the first debased because it required objectification; the latter enhanced because it required subjectivity. As Postman says, "The God of the Jews was to exist in the Word and through the Word, an unprecedented conception requiring the highest order of abstract thinking."[22]

God left the water lilies to Monet but wanted from the Jews (male persuasion) reading, writing, thinking, arguing in words about laws, ideas, and meaning; God wanted storytelling, contemplation, introspection, learning, engagement—an active and thinking morality with a dialectic inside the (rather wide) boundaries of moral law: no graffiti allowed. But this abstract thinking, this reading and writing, had its own requirements: humans who were at least nearly whole, perhaps wounded but not egregiously degraded and shamed: "Within days of their liberation, former concentration camp inmates at Dachau, Buchenwald, and Bergen-Belsen had fashioned makeshift memorial towers from bric-à-brac of their dismantled prisons."[23] Who were these new Jews, ready to use fascist artifacts as the fundamental materials of celebratory art; were they unmindful of the God who had been so very unmindful of them; since the waste, the garbage of Dachau and Buchenwald and Bergen-Belsen included them, do they have to redefine their origins; were they children not of God but of Hitler's death camps? And if they could break the second commandment using Nazi detritus, could they also kill? Did the Jews from the ashes have a new nature, one born as much in Auschwitz as in Palestine?

Meir Kahane, the fascist Jew from Brooklyn who began a racist, anti-Arab political party in Israel, argued against the old pacifist Jew: "Once upon a time, the Jew was not a member of the [Anti-Defamation League]—neither in form nor in spirit. It was not in the role of Mahatma Gandhi that the Jews fought at Masada; the men of Bar-Kockba and Judah Macabee never went to a Quaker meeting. The Jews of old—when Jews were knowledgeable about their religion, when they turned the page of the Jewish Bible instead of turning the Christian cheek—understood the concept of the Book and the Sword. It was only in the horror of the ghetto with its fears, neuroses, and insecurities that the Jew began to react in fright rather than with self-respect."[24]

Kahane's words might be thought of as a musical score accompanying his actions: "Passing provocatively through the Arab section of the Old City, Kahane's excited followers smashed through the market, overturning vegetable stalls, hitting bystanders, punching the air with clenched fists, and telling frightened residents that the end of their stay in the Holy Land was near, a kind of street brutality that has often been repeated since then . . . But instead of being shocked by the violence—until then seen only in old newsreels of pre-1945 central Europe or in modern scenes from Teheran—some Israelis liked what they saw. In fact, support for Kahane increased substantially."[25]

Is this fascism? Find the congruence between Kahane's words and acts; see the violence in words and in acts of brutality; search for a threat—is it encapsulated, words and acts, in hate? There is no antifascism gene that the Jews have but the Germans do not. But a people can refuse to be held hostage by hate: for instance, the Israeli Knesset (parliament) created a hate law that made Kahane's party illegal because of the pro-genocidal race-hate it promulgated. Still, says Moshe Leshem in *Israel Alone: How the Jewish State Lost Its Way and How It Can Find It Again,* "[t]hese days in Israel true Jewish nationalism is held to be inseparable from Orthodox Judaism. Any other form of nationalism is necessarily suspect as being tainted by alien sources."[26] Kahane's hatred of Arabs, expressed in pro-genocidal policy demands, legitimized the orthodox nationalism now passing for authentic love of God and country: and whose religion becomes inferior? Inside Judaism, liberals are suspect; rocks are thrown at

Jewish women in Jerusalem whose arms are insufficiently covered according to the shadow government of orthodox rabbis; Jewish women cannot testify in religious courts (which adjudicate so-called private issues having to do with marriage, reproductive rights, and divorce); and Islam, the religion of a despised people, becomes stigmatized—the inferior religion of an inferior people. (Partly in response to the increasing political power of zealot Jews—and not for the sake of women—Israel's Supreme Court has recently released decisions "clearing the way for seminary students to be drafted, and challenging Orthodox control of marriage, burial, Sabbath travel and other personal-status issues."[27])

Everyone, of course, prefers to be brutalized by their own home-grown fascists. As the problem is currently defined in the Middle East, foreign fascists for the sake of God and country (different God, wrong country), injure and kill those not-their-own, an insufferable offense. Even modest self-determination requires that Palestinians be killed by Palestinians and Israelis by Israelis. Each side can hate as it sees fit but the guns, bombs, and demolitions should be targeted against one's own. Each group can think the other religiously inferior; but peace requires that when weapons go boom in the night, each side has shot itself in the foot. One need not take away the gun to have it pointed in a different direction; and each side, thankfully, has women waiting for the other shoe to drop: so the violence can continue unabated and the international community can have the pleasure of having made a peace as good as any other peace.

Though feminists have worked very hard on principles of international law, including the Convention Eliminating Discrimination Against Women, Convention on the Rights of Children, International Convention on Civil and Political Rights, Universal Declaration of Human Rights, International Declaration on Trafficking, and the Beijing document from the 1995 UN Fourth World Conference on Women, the United Nations, NATO, the IMF, and Amnesty International in fact never interfere with the beating, raping, torturing, murdering, of one's own women, especially if they are family: there will be no bad consequences and no bad publicity. It is true that the Taliban in Afghanistan have gone a little too far—what with letting women starve to death rather than work or be seen outside of the hut—but no international or western or United Nations or NATO soldiers are marching in to save them: are they? Peace is easy: just let your own women be your Palestinians and Israelis as you see fit—that's what they're for. It works. The beauty of it is that it works.

Language is hard; and the Tower of Babel made it harder. Translation is a beast. As Karen Armstrong points out in *A History of God: The 4,000-Year Quest of Judaism, Christianity, and Islam:* ". . . the masculine tenor of God-talk is particularly problematic in English. In Hebrew, Arabic, and French, however, grammatical gender gives theological discourse a sort of sexual counterpoint and dialectic, which provides a balance that is often lacking in English."[28] Just as verb tenses shape cognition, gendered language changes the experience of gender. How does one compensate for a dimension of meaning left out of one's own language? There is the humility of recognizing that one's language includes an absence; but there is no way to replicate the formal meaning of the missing element or to discern how that formal meaning narrows imagination, especially one's sense of possibility. God literally becomes bigger, more inclusive, less literal. *Elohim,* the Hebrew word for the God whose name may never be said, "is composed of a feminine noun and a masculine plural ending."[29] Armstrong gives an example for the Arabic: ". . . *al-Lab* (the supreme name for God) is grammatically masculine, but the word for the divine and inscrutable essence of God—*al-Dhat*—is feminine."[30] Realistically speaking, no actual woman has ever been helped one iota because her language was gendered; but that is because his fist in her face is its own language, the triumphalist expression of gender. Nuance never trumps brutality.

The name *Israel* appears in Genesis (32:28) when God says to Jacob, "Your name shall no more be called Jacob, but Israel for you have striven with God and with men, and have prevailed."[31] My angel attacked you when you were sleeping and you put up a hell of a fight; you cheated your brother out of his birthright; you worked seven years to get Leah, whom you did not want; and another seven years to get Rachel, whom you did want. You're a spunky, contentious sort of guy so I name you "Israel," which Leshem translates as "one who has striven and wrestled with God."[32] Leshem quotes "the sages" who "saw an additional meaning in the divine change of name. The root of the name 'Ya'acov' [Jacob] is related to the word for 'crooked,' while 'yisrael' is related to 'straight.'"[33] Israel the country might have done better to call itself "Ya'acov." Crooked or straight, Jacob always won.

In secular cultures, Christians and Jews speak about the Old Testament as if it were the same book Jews use, the Hebrew Bible. Jack Miles in *God: A Biography* explains the differences with rare clarity. First, "[t]he Hebrew

Bible and the Old Testament are not quite two different works but, to speak more precisely, two very different editions of the same collection."[34] Second, the editions are arranged differently: "The distinctive broad movement of the Hebrew Bible from action to speech to silence is not matched in the Old Testament, whose movement is from action to silence to speech. . . . The Old Testament shifts the great prophetic collections—Isaiah, Jeremiah, Ezekiel, and the twelve minor prophets—from the middle to the end, leaving in the middle . . . the books of silence, including Job, Lamentations, Ecclesiastes, and Esther."[35] Miles bases his biography of God on the Hebrew Bible, "or, to use the standard Hebrew word for the collection, on the Tanakh. The word *Tanakh* is a postbiblical acronym derived from the Hebrew equivalents of the letters *t*, *n*, and *k* . . . standing respectively for the Hebrew words *torah*, 'teaching'; *nebi'em*, 'prophets'; and *ketubim*, 'writings.'"[36] It makes both formal and substantive sense that the Hebrew Bible moves toward silence as God moves further and further away from the Jewish people; and as Christians, through Jesus, establish their own singular relationship with He-Who-had-been-the-Jewish-God, they rearrange the holy book so that it moves from silence to speech. *Old Testament* is now common parlance for both the Christian and Hebrew editions of this book. Many Jews are offended by the common usage but most are desensitized to it.

There are other problems of language: "For example," says Liah Greenfeld in *Nationalism: Five Roads to Modernity*, "there are no exact equivalents of the word 'nation' (especially in its modern sense) in either biblical Hebrew or Greek. Yet all the English bibles use the word. . . . The King James Bible uses 'nation' as the translation of the Hebrew *uma, goi, leom*, and *am*, which in most cases are translated as *populous* in the Latin version . . . In one case (Isaiah 37:18) the English Bible translates as 'nation' the Hebrew *aretz*, which means 'land' or 'country,' and which is correctly rendered *terra* in the Vulgate."[37]

This may all seem inconsequential, but since many thousands have died and probably will die for nations or land or the Old Testament or the Hebrew Bible or the *al-Lab* and the *al-Dhat*, it might be honorable (if not useful) to tell each boy and each girl what the words at the heart of the conflict mean. Then there could be questions and discussions, which leaves plenty of time for killing. For instance, in *The Creators: A History of Heroes of the Imagination* Daniel J. Boorstin describes the origin of the word *synagogue:* "'Synagogue' for the Jews' ancient gathering place, a place of worship and study, came from the Greek word 'to bring together' (*synagein*)."[38] Boorstin's statement is simple, clear, correct, respectful, and true. Yet the word has another meaning for Leon Wieseltier: ". . . the term 'synagogue' became a linguistic and iconographic abbreviation for the degradation of the Jews. In my own mind, I have never been able to divest the term of the connotations that were conferred upon it by the centuries-long conflict between *ecclesia* and *synagoga,* in which the latter was represented, with varying degrees of crudity and refinement, as an old and defeated woman, mocked, trampled, blinded by a snake, run through by a sword, ridden by the devil, her staff broken, her law turned upside down. I prefer to call the house of worship a shul."[39] The demeaning iconography is deeply misogynist: it is the turning of a sacred place where men meet into a broken old woman that insults and debases; if only the synagogues had been filled with such women, mocked, trampled, blinded by a snake, run through by a sword; but the synagogue never was a safe house for dispossessed women, for used and broken old women, each of whom, no doubt, had been ridden by the devil. When does the religious man, the Jewish man, the man saying *kaddish* for his deceased father, the man of wit and scholarship, stand up for the debased old woman; how honored and holy and sacred the synagogue would be had she been its authentic symbol.

The God of the Jews cannot be understood, approached, or loved. He is wrath and terror; he is not a god of kindness and love (a good enough reason for cherishing his kinder, gentler offspring). Every Jew experiences the Jewish god, not the Christian one; he rips right through the heart. Is it the sacrifice of Isaac—an indelible nightmare for the Jewish child—or the flood or Joseph being sold by his brothers or Joshua being ordered by God to exterminate the enemy or Solomon wanting to cut the baby in half or the Red Sea parting but then drowning the Egyptian soldiers or Lot's wife being turned into a pillar of salt or God's inexplicable hostility to Cain, who then murders Abel, or God's curse on Eve or Jonah inside a whale or Job, punished for his righteousness? In *A Feast in the Garden,* Holocaust survivor and novelist George Konrád says, "The fierce spirit of the Jews has separated God from the world. They have understood that the more inhuman the Lord, the more divine he is."[40] Jews brought up on the Hebrew Bible do have a fierce spirit, but it is a defensive spirit, designed to survive a ruthless divinity. In the Temple animals were eviscerated for worship, to appease the Hebrew God, all of this described in the Hebrew Bible. According to Donald Harman Akenson in *Surpassing Wonder: The Invention of the Bible and the Talmuds,* "these descriptions were immensely comforting to those who remembered them, put them in a coherent order, repeated them, and eventually wrote them down . . . The act of remembering . . . guaranteed that the Temple continued to exist . . ."[41] Judaism is a religion of law, not faith. Each day from morning to nightfall, each human activity is delineated: do this in this way, do not do that. Judaism is a way of life in which awe of God is expressed through behavior. Authoritative law, called *halakhah,* "governs not only the complex ritual requirements of religious practice—when and how to pray, what blessings to make over myriad daily activities—but all social existence as well: diet, sexuality, business ethics, social life, entertainment, artistic expression, clothing, personal appearance, and so on."[42]

Men are expected to fulfill 613 laws; women 2. The deep metaphysical premise behind this series of rules is that by conformity to the demands of Jewish law one will lead a sanctified life, a holy life: a life that is good in the eyes of God. In the United States, "only Orthodox Judaism has retained its belief that Judaism is synonymous with the *halakhah,* a divinely given and inspired way of life."[43] In effect, *halakhah* is the law of rabbis who undertake to comprehend God's ways. This rabbinic Judaism "had its origins in Greco-Roman Palestine in the first three or four centuries of the Common Era and it both participated in and resisted the wider culture of Hellenism."[44] In other words, contemporaneous culture (Greek, Roman) would challenge Jewish practice or conviction based on the Hebrew Bible; rabbinic sages would try to discern God's meaning in a cultural context that was not Jewish; a dialectic would be implicitly established between the wider intellectual and cultural world and the world of Jewish study. Thus, rabbinic law kept Jewish law a living entity, on the cutting edge of moral and ethical questions. Rabbinic Judaism was rooted in Talmud, not Torah. Torah is God's law; Talmud is human commentary, exegesis, interpretation, intellection, arguments, and dialogues about God's words and God's meanings. This legacy of complex and scholarly speech, not the rote practice of ritual, has kept Judaism vital: intellectually and creatively alive. As Beit-Hallahmi says, "What we have known as Jewish culture, or Jewish genius, over the past 1,500 years, can be directly attributed to the Talmud . . . [The legalism of the Talmud] led to the unique Jewish emphasis not only on literacy, but also on learning, since studying the law was not just a religious duty, but the most important one. Synagogues in Eastern Europe were known as houses of learn-ing; prayer and study were always related."[45]

The development of Judaism toward learning, study, and prayer was not inevitable or even likely. As Robert L. Wilken makes clear in *The Land Called Holy: Palestine in Christian History and Thought:* "The Bible does not disguise the embarrassing historical fact that the land of Israel once belonged to other peoples and had to be taken by conquest. Even later writings within the Bible make no effort to conceal the earlier history of the land: 'It was [the Lord] who smote many nations . . . and all the kingdoms of Canaan, and gave *their* land as a heritage, a heritage to his people Israel' (Ps135:12)."[46] God promises the Jews a gift "but paradoxi-cally God's largess could be acquired only through military conquest,"[47] which there is plenty of as Hittites, Canaanites, Amorites, Perizites, and Jebusites are displaced. The clearest, saddest, most unrepentant and un-troubled statement on this divinely inspired military carnage and dispos-session is in Joshua 24:13: "I gave you a land on which you had not labored, and cities which you had not built, and you dwell therein; you eat the fruit of vineyards and olive yards which you did not plant."[48] Fox enumerates a series of conquests from Numbers and the Book of Joshua: "The text describes a series of memorable conquests: Heshbon, city of Si-hon king of the Amorites, was taken and occupied by the Israelites (Num-bers 21:25); Dibon is implied to have suffered a similar fate (Numbers 21:30 and 32:3); Joshua made the walls of Jericho tumble (Joshua 6:20), whereupon the Israelites slaughtered every man, woman and child except the household of Rahab, a friendly harlot . . ."[49] This is a myth of origins designed to produce storm troopers. According to Kotkin in his book on global tribes, Nietzsche (who despised the Nazis but was enchanted by or infatuated with Wagner) saw the Old Testament as "more than a religious text; it was a national epic."[50] Nietzsche also "saw the Jews' adherence to their biblical legacy not as religious piety but as a demonstration of 'the toughest life-will that has ever existed in any people on earth.' "[51] Even with the Hebrew Bible's being the most read book, the most studied book, the most respected book, the most recited and learned-by-heart book, the martial legacy died and what superseded it was an introspective learning: the subjectivity that God defined as intellectual vitality reading God's law: for which these descendents of killers were themselves killed. It seems that it was the exile that transformed Jews from martial heroes into lovers of learning: the exile broke the hearts of the warriors and made lit-eracy and literature sacrosanct; and it was literacy itself that made the Jews gentle, with a gentler view of God: "In the words of Maimon the Dayan (father of Maimonides), 'While the stream destroys walls and sweeps away stones, the pliant object remains standing. Thus is the Exile . . . The Holy One, blessed be He, saves the pliant nation.'"[52] It was not that the Jews over centuries became lazy or weak or cowardly; but a new ethic did develop: that the pliant object remains standing; or that the way to victory is "not by force but by strength of spirit."[53] This was almost Buddhism in Jewish hands: "The guiding principle is that the evil of the world should not be fought; that the struggle between good and evil will be decided elsewhere, by Divine Providence. In accordance with this view, the true weapons of resistance are conscience, prayer, religious meditation, and devotion—not military arms."[54]

One might say now that Judaism is a stream that runs in two directions: toward the martial Judaism of the Hebrew Bible, reflected not only in the defense forces and intelligence operations of the Israelis but also in the rabid Arab-hate of Israel's orthodox Jews, who want Israel's land mass enlarged and have planned or participated in vigilante violence; and what is wrongly considered a secular, atheistic Judaism more rooted in the Enlightenment than in Torah, Talmud, or Midrash. Eliot Abrams in *Faith or Fear: How Jews Can Survive in a Christian America* maintains that "the very individualism of the Enlightenment philosophers subverted the spirit of Jewish peoplehood. The free individual choice of which those thinkers wrote, and which was sanctified in the U.S. Constitution, was absolutely contrary to the Jewish idea of covenant and commandment."[55] And yet it was the great Hillel "who responded to the scoffing request of a heathen to teach him the whole Torah while the heathen was standing on one foot: 'What is hateful to you, do not do to your neighbor: that is the whole Torah; the rest is commentary.'"[56]

There is an ethical tradition rooted in Jewish law that bypasses *halakhah* and the 613 rules for men. Konrád paraphrases Hillel after the Holocaust: "I must make good decisions. With a bad decision I can destroy myself. I do not need a mediator to speak to God. A crowded subway car, too, can be a temple. I am trying not to do unto others what I don't want done to me. That is the essence of the Torah; the rest is commentary."[57] This ethical Judaism is old, traditional, and has many sources in the literature of Judaism. Vidal-Naquet quotes one such story "from a *midrash* (or ancient rabbinic commentary) of Leviticus 27:5. . . . 'God is always on the side of the persecuted. One can find a case where a just man persecutes a just man, and God is on the side of the persecuted; when an evil man persecutes a just man, God is on the side of the persecuted; when an evil man persecutes an evil man, God is on the side of the persecuted; and even when a just man persecutes an evil man, God is on the side of the persecuted.'"[58] Ethical or social-justice Judaism is not some vaguely New Age lapse into the ether; Judaism does have or require or include a social conscience that is as Jewish as the slaughter of a lamb or not eating shrimp.

According to Armstrong's reading, "Amos was the first of the prophets to emphasize the importance of social justice and compassion."[59] In a 1989 survey by the *Los Angeles Times,* "half the Jews polled locally cited 'a commitment to social equality' as the chief characteristic of their Jewish identity as against only 17 percent who chose religious observance and about the same number who cited support for Israel."[60] This is not a repudiation of Judaism but a recognition of Judaism's greatest gift: subjectivity through language that allows for rigorous social engagement and mandates a search for justice. In *Saving Remnants: Feeling Jewish in America,* Bershtel and Graubard define Judaism's most important ethical imperative, *tikkun olam,* as "the repairing of human society and the world."[61] It is a bad habit to refuse to acknowledge the roots of Jewish social activism in Judaism itself. Judaism's textual sources are rich in ideas of fairness. It is particularly the ethical subjectivity of Judaism, the fairness demanded of the person who is and who will remain the subject—who will never be exploited or demeaned as if an object—that makes Judaism anathema to such a wide range of haters.

But sometimes ethics and religion collide: "At this moment," write Hertzberg and Hirt-Manheimer in the late 1990s, "the great issue for Jews who want to live within the tradition is equality and dignity for women. This can be achieved only if every aspect of Jewish law and practice that demeans women is nullified."[62] Once one excises each and every law and practice that keeps women second-class, what is left? One might have to lose the religious community in order to create the ethical community, the fair community. Jewish women, say Hertzberg and Hirt-Manheimer, "have been at the forefront of this struggle for the past three decades . . ."; therefore "[t]his effort will succeed."[63] But in these last three decades, which women used the word *nullified?* Has any woman articulated what is transparently true: that equality and dignity for women can be achieved only *if every aspect of Jewish law and practice that demeans women is nullified?* "For over a thousand years," says Gerda Lerner in *The Creation of Feminist Consciousness,* "women reinterpreted the biblical texts in a massive feminist critique, yet their marginalization . . . prevented this critique from ever engaging the minds of the men who had appointed themselves as the definers of divine truth and revelation."[64] In the United States, there is Elizabeth Cady Stanton's *The Woman's Bible,* a stunning nineteenth-century repudiation of androcentric biblical texts; and more recently there is the critic Harold Bloom, who did insist that the most important parts of the Hebrew Bible, the so-called "J" source, were written by a woman. (See Harold Bloom and David Rosenberg, *The Book of J.*) One can see her, a desert-woman Jane Austen, writing both alone and in secret between chores and hard labor, leaving behind for us in writing the ultimate feminist exposé: how the men of her tribe, sociopaths who listened to divine voices, conquered and killed.

An old song of the Polish resistance says that "when a German puts his foot down, the soil bleeds a hundred years."[65] But women know blood not associated with violence. It is normal to bleed every month and to push out blood and placenta in childbirth. Men fear blood the way that Central and Eastern Europe feared the Germans; women fear pain, not blood. Women are closer to the animals sacrificed in the Temple of old than are men; women wash their hands in blood, feel its textures (which change), know the range of colors in what men call red; it is confusing to bleed and still live, to bleed and be strong, not weak; men have a terror of women's blood even though each and every one of them slept in it; for most the blood was the ocean that carried them to the shore, a drier place; even with cesarian section, the baby's skin is his mother's blood. The courage of pregnancy and childbearing is trivialized: second-class citizens have second-class courage. There is not a man alive who could stand it. Women's blood is the blood of life, not death; the pain is hers, not inflicted on someone else. Men can climb a million mountains and still that physical act does not begin to approach the will to live expressed doubly in childbirth: two living humans sharing the same blood—hers; and each gasps and cries and then sleeps. This is the deeper mystery of origin: she is blood inside and out, the baby is swathed in blood, shielded and fed through blood, carried by blood out of the uterus, through the vagina: each boy owes his mother the blood he used. Being of women born is an obsessive problem for men who consider women inferior, stinky, moldy, dirty, polluted: and then there is the scary part of the blood, its viscosity, and the fact that God has cursed this very blood: punished Eve for eating the apple of the Tree of Knowledge by saying (in that special way) that women would conceive under the dominance of men and always with pain. It is a kind of pain that men do not experience and do not imagine. Pure men, warrior men, proud men, owe life itself to the blood stigmatized and denounced by an omniscient father. In the great religions of monotheism—Judaism, Christianity, and Islam—the child needs to be taken from the woman, washed clean, reborn as a figure of a divine, authoritarian father. In Christianity there is the water of baptism: the water washes away original sin (being born in Eve's line; being of woman born). Even in Jewish tradition, after circumcision "[i]mmersion is [a] rebirth into being Jewish. It's like coming out of the womb"[66]—doing it right this time: no female blood; no female is a card-carrying member of the covenant with god. And in Islam, "*Al-ba'th,* resurrection after death, gives the Muslim immortality. It accomplishes two miracles with one stroke: It ties the life of the individual to the trajectory of the stars, and it effaces the uterus. A man born of the uterus of a woman is inevitably mortal."[67] In other words, in all three monotheistic religions, the blood of the mother must be superseded. In Christianity and Judaism the infant needs to be washed clean of his origin so that the mother's blood no longer contaminates him and so that his masculinity is uncompromised: if female blood gets near him he is too near to be accepted as a man. In Islam as his mother's child he is mortal (read: powerless like her); as Allah's child he has immortality.

It is easy enough to transform the religious insult to women into a political one: on Stalin's fiftieth birthday, he thanked "the great Party of the working class which bore me and reared me in its own image and likeness."[68] As Edvard Radsinsky writes in *Stalin:* "The use of biblical language—'in its own image and likeness'—was deliberate. So was the statement that he was born not of woman, but of the Party."[69]

In the Western Sahara, guerrilla fighters declare themselves citizens but women and children are dependents; fighters cannot tolerate an equality with the bloody, animal-like creatures who gave birth to them: "'We could obviously have built houses for the people if we had wanted,' says Alie Beiba. 'But this isn't our home; our home is in the Western Sahara, and so we have stayed in tents to emphasize the temporary nature of our exile. And finally, from the very beginning it was laid down that only women, children, and old people were refugees. The man isn't a refugee. He is a Saharawi soldier, fighting inside liberated territory.'"[70] To be a shedder of blood, an agent of slaughter (which is synonymous with citizenship), gets rid of the blood taint—the more blood of enemies that he sheds, the more different he is from her: his gun means death, the good blood, the clean blood; her blood means life—this is the abhorrent blood, the repugnant blood.

In *The Double Flame: Love and Eroticism* Octavio Paz exonerated Judaism from religion's vast negativity toward sexuality: "Contempt for the body . . . does not appear in Judaism, which always exalted the generative power: *increase and multiply* is the first Biblical commandment."[71] This is the exact moment when the schism between women and men on sexuality becomes apparent: God cursed Eve into painful and male-dominated childbirth and sex. Exalting male potency may be a dazzling token of good will to the men but in fact *increase and multiply* requires self-abnegation and pain for the woman. She bleeds, and then she bleeds some more. The more of herself that she gives, the more the child must be washed clean, sanctified. Scrub him, rub him, make her stand for every dirty woman, make him hate her for polluting him and at the same time, in reacting against that pollution, make him want to shed blood, renounce the blood of life (her blood) and embrace the blood of death (his). "Sons are the provision of the Lord; the fruit of the womb, His reward, Like arrows in the hand of a warrior are sons born to a man in his youth. Happy is the man who fills his quiver with them; they shall not be put to shame when they contend with the enemy at the gate"(Psalms 127:3–7).[72] In "Requiem," Anna Akhmatova writes of the arrest of her son: "They took you away at daybreak. Half waking, as though at a wake, I followed. In the dark chamber children were crying, In the image-case, candlelight guttered. At your lips, the chill of an ikon, A deathly sweat at your brow. I shall go creep to our wailing wall, Crawl to the Kremlin towers."[73] For seventeen months Akhmatova stood in lines of women at the prison trying to deliver food or cigarettes or notes to their kin; also trying to find out if they were still alive. "One day," writes Akhmatova, "somebody 'identified' me. Beside me, in the queue, there was a woman with blue lips. She had, of course, never heard of me; but she suddenly came out of that trance so common to us all and whispered in my ear (everybody spoke in whispers there): 'Can you describe this?' And I said: 'Yes, I can.' And then something like the shadow of a smile crossed what had once been her face."[74] Maternity, like poetry, is a place for heroes: others need not apply. Even with all one's blood gone—used, squandered, spent lavishly or stupidly or with dreams of love—one continues to be faithful to the child of one's blood: this is not the collective blood-and-soil of men; this is the blood of one person, a single person, largely unregarded, her own real bloodletting ignored in the male rhetoric of blood as war: she gives life. The giving of life may not make her virtuous but it does make her significant. The significance, like the blood, is hers: hers alone; from her individual will and act and courage: if maternity requires less, it is coerced. She is, however fragile or brutish, the homeland for everyone to whom she gives birth; yet where is the nationalism? where is the national pride? This is an authentic origin without myth; it is an origin of fact. Sometimes disgraced by pregnancy, sometimes needing to abort, sometimes taking all the risks so that the child will survive, an individual woman becomes a new continent with new life there, life Darwin never saw. It is all right for the woman just finished with childbirth to feel enfeebled or wounded or weak with fatigue; but still she is treated like a canine bitch: lick your pups clean and do not make a mess on the rug. All celebrations honor the boy newly born, superior to the person who gave him life, who birthed him, in rights, in opportunities, in recognition, and in value. When a girl is born, one hears the whispers: next time. In Auschwitz Ruth Elias asked a universal but unspoken question: "How, in my loneliness, could I give birth to a child?"[75]

This great gift to women—this significance—comes from between spread legs; with the lascivious participation of thighs, pubic area, labial lips, clitoris, vagina, and uterus: all these very dirty places according to the lexicon of men who exploit women. These words are dirty because they correspond to real places on the bodies of women who have been captives for the most part; words do not free captives, because captivity and not freedom has been inscribed on the body. Women were the first slaves and every contact with a woman had its meaning in money: brides needed to be rich; concubines needed to consort with rich men and pluck at their wealth; slaves themselves were a kind of capital, whose worth included their sexual worth to the owner. Marriage contracts embedded in statutory law and interpreted as part of the common law became just another regulation of a different order of slave: her body was his and her children had better be his. But even in slavery, women came up with relationships unimagined by men in power; as Patterson says, "One of the earliest manumission contracts on record . . . comes from the first dynasty of Babylon, and concerns a slave who used the traditional legal method of entering into a daughtership with her owner, agreeing to support her for the rest of her life. When the owner died, the slave became free."[76] This woman-to-woman arrangement suggests trust and friendship. As Bernard Williams points out in *Shame and Necessity*, "In their own persons slaves had no legal rights, and in particular none in the area of marriage or family law."[77] This is the same conception of marriage and family law that governed so-called free women: the wives and daughters not allowed out of the residence, which could be sumptuous, making the captivity not one whit less noxious. These were the laws that outlasted slavery itself—repeated and repeated again as ownership of women as such. Force was legally enshrined as a right of a husband; it was the legal responsibility of the wife to comply with the carnal desires of the husband. That force—intimacy backed up by state power—is still legally in place in most parts of the world and was only eliminated from New York State's laws by judicial fiat (rather than legislative activism) some twenty years ago. In the Arab world, the substance of the law was the same; only the details were different. As Nawal El Saadawi writes in *God Dies by the Nile:* "The wife of Sheikh Hamzawi, as he had explained to her father, was not like the wives of other men. Her husband was responsible for upholding the teachings of Allah, and keeping the morals and piety of the village intact. The wife of a man like that was not supposed to be seen by just anyone. Her body had to be concealed even from her closest relatives, except for her face and the palms of her hands. She was expected to live in his house surrounded by all due care and respect, never to be seen elsewhere except twice in her life. The first time when she moved from her father's to her husband's house. And the second when she left her husband's house for the grave allotted to her in the burial grounds."[78] Herodotus also wanted women to be seen only twice: the same two times. What happens between the legs of a woman obsesses men: and so the woman is imprisoned, segregated, denied freedom—denied the most basic elements of liberty; there is no sanctification of her that celebrates the great power of her body in originating life. She is not the husband or child or sacrificed lamb; she is wanted as a means to an end—ejaculation that promises the eventual birth of a boy.

Ailbhe Smyth, in "Seeing Red: Men's Violence Against Women in Ireland," notes the role of the state in using violence to control women: "The State tolerates a certain level of violence by *limiting* the number of women it is prepared to support."[79]

In India, as Sakuntala Narasimhan shows in *Sati: Widow Burning in India,* to be born female means living near her own potential murderer her whole life: "Smothered or poisoned at birth, given away in marriage at a tender age, bargained over like some commodity by dowry hungry in-laws, secluded in the name of chastity and religion, and finally burned for the exaltation of the family's honour, or shunned as inauspicious widows, oppression took different forms at different stages of a woman's life, from birth to death, in a chain of attitudes linked by contempt for the fe-male."[80] The Dowry Prohibition Act was passed in 1961: this made it "il-legal to demand gifts in cash and kind from parents of a girl in consideration of marriage. Twenty-nine years later, the custom still per-sists . . ."[81] Young women, sometimes married girls, continue to be burned alive in "kitchen accidents."[82] India and China are particularly important because in both countries—free-market India and state-controlled China—female fetuses are aborted or, if born, killed. India shows the su-perficiality of so-called choice as a political strategy or as a right; China shows the extraordinary damage created by the state when it imposes abortion on women. In India, two woman-hating practices are defined as choice for women: abortion of female fetuses and sati. Because of the low value of the female, in India she is likely to be aborted or killed or sold—trafficking in Indian women now emerges as a new fact on the ground; in China aborted, killed, or sold.

A recent United Nations report says that "violence against women is the world's most pervasive form of human rights abuse."[83] In the United States, the Justice Department says that "one out of 12 women will be stalked at some point in her lifetime."[84] The American Medical Associa-tion concludes that "[s]exual assault and family violence are devastating the United States' physical and emotional well-being"; in 1995 the AMA reported that "[m]ore than 700,000 women in the United States are sex-ually assaulted each year, or one every 45 seconds."[85] A study by the Alan Guttmacher Institute, in a report researchers said was the most compre-hensive extant, finds that "[a]t least half of the babies born to teen-age girls are fathered by adults"; this "implies that a startling number of teen-age girls are having sex with men who are breaking state laws on statutory rape."[86]

What the statistics in the United States suggest is that teen-age girls have to carry the burden of incest or other sexual abuse, statutory rape, and unwanted pregnancy. A recent report in *The Washington Post* con-cludes that "[n]early a quarter of teenage girls who have had sex indicate their first experience was 'voluntary but not wanted.'"[87] There are many ways to interpret this staggering piece of news. Kristin A. Moore, a coauthor of the study, argues that "[i]n the whole discussion about teen sex, there is always the pressure to make it either-or . . . For some kids, there are issues of predatory men. For some, sex is voluntary. And for some kids, it's very much in between. . . . It's a continuum."[88] Any such reading essentially regards female desire as passive and female compliance as normative. The real question is: how many of this population of teen-age girls wanted to have sex? Is it really so much to ask that researchers surgically investigate the sexual double standard and seek not to replicate it in the questions they ask and the conclusions they offer? What is striking in new statistics from the Justice Department is that rape victims are younger and younger: "Convicted rape and sexual assault offenders serving time in State prisons report that two-thirds of their victims were under the age of 18, and 58% of those—or nearly 4 in 10 imprisoned violent sex offenders—said their victims were aged 12 or younger. In 90% of the rapes of children less than 12 years old, the child knew the offender, according to police-recorded incident data. Among victims 18 to 29 years old, two-thirds had a prior relationship with the rapist."[89] It is likely, of course, that rapists of children are arrested more and imprisoned more than other rapists; and that earlier profiles of rape showing that women in every age category are targets are right.

In Ireland, data have been gathered that show the increasing gravity of the sexual assault: the increasing sadism of the assault: for example, "A woman's back was broken and she is now confined for life to a wheelchair"; "Limerick woman, kicked in the face, thought 4 men, raping her, would have killed her had the Gardia [police] not arrived"; "A teenage rapist said only after being beaten in prison did he realise rape was wrong"; "Blackrock woman raped and beaten for 6½ hours"; "Waterford woman, 22, unconscious for 'some weeks' after rape, still too ill to be interviewed by Gardai."[90] Irish reports on sexual assault are not shy about reporting "on pornography as an assault causative."[91]

In her book about why she did not have children, poet Molly Peacock recalls an interchange with her younger (but adult) hippie sister: Says the sister about their mother—"That *cunt*, she could have sent me the money. Hey, Molly, I need a few bucks now. You got any money? This is a really nice apartment"; and Molly thinks—"She called Polly a *cunt*. Had I ever heard the word I'd only read in D. H. Lawrence spoken out loud? Oh, yes, I heard it in my father's voice. Ted calling Polly cunt. You cunt. Bitch.

It was Ted speaking through Gail's lips, like a mass of something, bruise-colored, growing. . . . He was coming out of her mouth like pus."[92] Words are different for women: inside them we hear our legs being spread open, then bile shot through. Says Peter Theroux in *Sandstorms: Days and Nights in Arabia:* "The Palestinian and Lebanese dialects had a staggering fund of obscene expressions, almost all explicitly sexual, though the word for fuck was rarely used, only the body parts—"My prick-in-you!' 'Damned-sister's-cunt!' "[93] Says novelist Simon Louvish, an Israeli: "Four were killed in a village near Bethlehem, where Border Police had opened fire indiscriminately and had to be held back by regular army units. As the army medics tended to the Arab wounded, the Border Policemen shouted insults at them, culminating in their worst epithet: 'leftists!' The police units, apparently, had been entering the village daily, calling out through their loudspeakers: 'Bring out your wives so we can fuck 'em.' The villagers finally responded to this provocation with predictable results. My country, my people."[94] What is between our legs, that small piece of darkness, the thighs making shadows that keep the cut hidden, is implicated in political abuse or marital terrorism: "The scenario deserves elaborating. The most beautiful, desirable woman of her time, focus of tens of millions of erotic fantasies, is cast as guardian angel of the most destructive weapon in history. She sits astride a gigantic penile missile that will produce the most powerful male orgasm ever—the atomic explosion. The rape of an entire city is between her legs."[95] The author, Edwin Mullins, is referring to a photograph of Rita Hayworth—a pinup on the bomb used on Hiroshima in 1945. The appropriation of every cell from thigh to labia and inside is an imperialism of hate. As Michael Lind writes in *Up from Conservatism: Why the Right Is Wrong for America,* "The major form of terrorism in the United States since the 1970s, it should not be forgotten, has been the right-wing terrorism perpetrated by the violent wing of the anti-abortion movement."[96] This right-wing terrorism has used assassination and bombs: there is a hit list on the Internet of pro-choice advocates—mostly doctors who perform abortions—a line is drawn through their name when the person is murdered.

Gender neutrality is one lesson the antiabortion terrorists have learned, as did Timothy McVeigh in Oklahoma City. As *The Turner Diaries* say: "It is a terrible thing to kill women of our own race, but we are engaged in a war in which all the old rules have been scrapped. We are in a war to the death with the Jew, who now feels himself so close to his final victory that he can safely drop his mask and treat his enemies as the 'cattle' his religion tells him they are. . . . [I]f they adopt the Jew's attitude toward *our* women and children, then they cannot expect their own families to be safe."[97] Questions of birth and life transform like quicksilver into loss and revenge: "If you ask me what I want to receive from the German people," says one survivor, "I would say, a mother for a mother, a father for a father, a child for a child. My soul would be at rest if I knew that there would be six million German dead to match the six million Jews."[98] It is the woman who creates the vulnerability for both love and hate: she makes the family literally as if she had knitted it from bone and blood in her own skin.

In Iraq, the goal of using rape to punish a whole family had to do with asserting an unbreakable political control: "'To break someone's eye,' is an old Bedouin expression, which was turned into state policy in Iraq through the employment of [rapists] . . . The newly appointed governor, along with his wife and children, would be invited for a welcoming feast in the house of a local notable. On the way back, the party would be ambushed by a group of armed masked men. The governor would be forced to watch his wife being gang-raped, after which the men would whip off their masks, show the governor their faces, and disappear into the night, killing no one. . . . By the late 1970s, the most famous 'aristocratic' Baghdadi families were having their eyes 'broken' by the new upstart Ba'thi rulers . . . Young women from such families were kidnapped off the streets on their way to and from some of the most famous clubs of Baghdad. They would disappear for a few weeks, and then reappear."[99] It is fair to say that rape everywhere is pissing on the woman's maternity: her capacity to have children and to love them. What is generative—her ability to be the origin of a human life, now closer to God than to man—is physically injured—attacked and punished for the crimes of existing and being able to bring forth existence. In *Lustmord: Sexual Murder in Weimar Germany,* Maria Tatar notices "[t]hat the targets of assault for sexual murderers since Jack the Ripper [presumed by many to be a surgeon] have been not only the genitals of the female body, but the interior reproductive organs as well. [This] reveals the degree to which the murderers are driven by something more than the perversion of sexual desire."[100]

One might think that such sadistic attack, so contemptuous and so angry, presumes a connection between reproduction and power, or reproduction and an authentic moral superiority. This is not an ideological assertion. The poet Joseph Brodsky in conversations with Solomon Volkov claimed "that women are more sensitive to ethical transgressions, to psychological and intellectual morality. And universal amorality is precisely what the twentieth century has offered us in abundance."[101] Todorov considers the difference between heroic and ordinary virtues; women, he believes, manifest the ordinary virtues: "Caring, or concern, is the second ordinary virtue: acts of ordinary virtue are undertaken not in behalf of humanity or for a nation but always for the sake of an individual human being."[102] In ghettos, in concentration camps, in Argentinean jails, women found ways of sharing and caring for each other: not all women; but more women than men.

Author Leon Uris, whose book *Exodus* presented a popular romance of escape from the Nazis and the founding of Israel by Jews, remembered why he wrote the book: "It has been the fulfilling experience of my life as a writer. I was just plain pissed off about the Holocaust, and I wanted to hurl that in the face of the Christian world. And when I went to Israel, I saw I had a lightning story in my hands. So I wanted to use it to light a fire under the Jews, to tell them we were better than the other Jewish writers would have you believe with all their self-pitying writing that made 'Jewish mother' a dirty name."[103] Roth, Bellow, Mailer, Ginsberg: they all had a malign paradigm for that Jewish mother: a hatred for her ability to bring life into the world; a self-hatred that they themselves were bound by *her* legacy to the Jewish people. She had "ordinary virtues," which were despised by her literary sons who were good with dead words from which nothing would ever be born. Their contempt for women brought the sons worldly honor; but spiritually they had only a corrupted sense of self-importance. Honor requires knowing whose blood built your bones. One owes her honor: how much blood did she spill, just for the sake of you? With respect to Jewish American male writers, she shed too much.

According to *The World's Women 1995: Trends and Statistics,* published by the United Nations, the low sex ratios of female to male "might be explained by female infanticides, underreporting of female births and increased availability of technologies that facilitate sex-selected abortion."[104] The UN confirms that "[g]ender-based violence against women crosses all cultural, religious and regional boundaries and is a major problem in every country in which it has been studied"; and that "[t]he most pervasive form of gender-based violence against women is reported abuse by a husband or an intimate partner. National studies in 10 countries estimate that between 17 and 38 per cent of women have been physically assaulted by an intimate partner. More limited studies in Africa, Latin America and Asia report even higher rates of physical abuse among the population studied—up to 60 per cent or more of women"; "[s]exual assault is also common, but only a small fraction of rapes are reported to the police . . . In the United States more than 100,000 attempted and completed rapes of women and girls were reported to the police in 1990. But a national survey found the rate was more than six times greater, even when considering only adult women and completed rapes."[105]

The United Nations also found that "[m]ost sexual crimes are committed by individuals known to the victims. Criminal justice statistics and data from rape crisis centres from six countries (Chile, Malaysia, Mexico, Panama, Peru and the United States) have been used to estimate that in more than 60 per cent of all sexual [abuse] cases the victim knows the perpetrator"; moreover, "[i]n national sample surveys in Barbados, Canada, the Netherlands, New Zealand, Norway and the United States, 27 to 34 per cent of women interviewed reported sexual abuse during childhood or adolescence. Lower rates of abuse were reported in Great Britain (12 per cent) and Germany (17 per cent)"; and "[i]n a study of 450 school girls aged 13 to 14 in Kingston, Jamaica, 13 per cent had experienced attempted rape, half before age 12 . . . In India, close to 26 per cent of 133 postgraduate, middle- and upper-class students reported having been sexually abused by age 12. From 40 to 60 per cent of known sexual assaults have been found to be committed against girls 15 and younger, regardless of region or culture."[106] It is in this context of rape and assault that maternity exists, girl child and mother separated rather than brought together by the terrorism of rape and assault at the hands of an intimate or acquaintance. One solution is to lock the women up, a strategy tried unsuccessfully in Arab, Persian, and Byzantine societies: unsuccessful because rape and assault are acts of hostility and ownership committed mostly by intimates—behind the walls where the women are kept. The opposite strategy has not been tried on any scale other than the random and the accidental: locking up men. This is the way women live: "How well, indeed, do I remember the day on which the order was issued for everyone in the Ghetto to bring their dogs and cats to the synagogue on Veliuonos Street. Animals not brought were hunted down in the streets and then taken to the synagogue, where all the assembled animals were then shot. It was a cruel and sadistic spectacle: wounded dogs and cats running about in the synagogue, wailing and shrieking."[107] Unbearable: and the mothers, daughters, and sisters of men live like that: hunted down, confined, then there are random shots; assembled, shot; captured, random fire; touched everywhere by men's blood, the blood of death.

Each man is half woman: the X chromosome. Is that luck, common ground, a universal link from which one can articulate biological sameness as well as anatomical difference? How far need one go to obliterate any sameness with women? How much does blood function as a discourse of difference rather than as a fact of sameness: one bleeds, one dies—except for XX—she can bleed for days each and every month and she does not die. How deep is the envy of the female procreative capacity, the truly awesome splendor of being the origin of a human life? Proving manhood, one might say, is a sickness; and the Nazis were the sickest motherfuckers ever to stomp on this planet: "when a German puts his foot down, the soil bleeds for a hundred years." The Nazis did not just attack Poland or the Soviet Union or France or sovereign countries with populations of so-called ethnic Germans: they attacked procreation. They used death—pioneered a technology of death—to defeat both life and the living. They set out to sterilize and castrate, odd preoccupations for a regime committed to murder by starvation, shooting, gassing. Before the Second World War, Germany killed "close to 400,000 people, most of whom were judged feebleminded, schizophrenic, epileptic, or alcoholic. The sterilizations themselves required the services of physicians in gynecology . . . After the consummation of the program . . . there was some hope that Slavic populations in German-occupied Europe could be brought to extinction by mass sterilizations. To this end, thousands of Jewish women and men in Auschwitz were sterilized in medical experiments designed to find an efficient method of performing the procedure quickly and without the knowledge of the victims."[108] This was Nazi science; so "the extensive sterilization and castration experiments conducted at Auschwitz by doctors Carl Clauberg and Horst Schumann received official encouragement as direct expression of racial theory and politics."[109] When Clauberg came to Auschwitz in 1943, "more than two hundred women were installed in Block 10 and placed at his disposal. Clauberg injected various chemicals into their Fallopian tubes. His formulas were kept secret, but the main ingredient was apparently a formalin solution. This stopped the women's menstruation. Clauberg pronounced his system a great success. He boasted to Himmler that his method would enable one skilled physician with ten assistants to sterilize several hundred women a day."[110]

The use of women as guinea pigs expanded to include four hundred women: "They were of many different nationalities, but the Greek girls were extremely young, between sixteen and nineteen years of age. They were divided up among the doctors. There were Dr. Wirths' 'specimens'; Clauberg's women who had a caustic fluid injected into their uteruses; Dr. Weber's sputum and blood guinea pigs and the Greek girls who belonged to Dr. Schumann. The latter all had deep x-ray radiation burns on their bodies, since their ovaries had been irradiated and their skin was covered with suppurating blisters and ulcers."[111] One promising experiment was initiated by an SS official, Viktor Brack, who "was urging Himmler to have all able-bodied Jews sterilized by x rays. Brack's theory was that the unwitting victims should be made to line up at a counter: 'There,' he wrote, 'they would be asked questions or handed a form to fill in, keeping them at the counter for two or three minutes. The clerk behind the counter would . . . start an x-ray apparatus with two tubes to irradiate the persons at the counter . . . ' "[112]

In the same spirit, Dr. Horst Schumann "exposed a batch of several hundred Dutch and Greek Jews to fifteen minutes of radiation of the genital area at a rate of thirty prisoners a day. Many victims suffered severe burns. After three months, Dr. Schumann removed parts of the women's sexual organs to be sent to Berlin for analysis. The men were castrated. Records of these experiments were partially destroyed, but one surviving report from one day in the surgical ward, December 16, 1943, records ninety castrations."[113] Block 10, where the female guinea pigs were held, "resounded with the constant screams of these women. Many had one or both ovaries removed; these organs were shipped to Berlin for further research. The women's blood was frequently taken, including that of Jewish women. Other experiments consisted of the castration of males and the artificial insemination of females. The main purpose of this research was to find the fastest ways of limiting and eventually exterminating 'inferior races,' and to raise the birth rates of the 'pure' Nordic race."[114] A Jewish doctor in captivity was forced to participate in "the surgical removal of the cervix from a considerable number of women who were part of the 'research project' conducted by Eduard Wirths on precancerous growths . . ."[115]

In Ravensbrück, a women's camp, women "unworthy of reproduction" were sterilized and/or vivisected; as one survivor characterized the vivisections—"and the vivisection of those most pitiful of all pitiful victims, the human guinea pigs nicknamed the 'rabbits.' "[116] At Ravensbrück, inmates were "inflicted with gangrene wounds"; Polish women, "laughingly called 'rabid girls,' were given bone grafts."[117] Gypsies were used in other experiments: "[A]t Sachsenhausen they were used to determine whether seawater was drinkable, were pumped full of poison bullets, and were injected with contagious jaundice."[118]

There was no better or worse, no more suffering or less suffering: but was there any logic in this sadistic Nazi foreplay? The Jews were, in fact, attacked in such a way as to stop, injure, and insult reproduction. Like Jack the Ripper, the Nazis wanted to get further into a woman's body than sex could provide: the Nazis wanted to destroy her internally, plunder her body for reproductive material. Certainly, the Nazis wanted the destruction of the Jewish male: castration, later death. But they pillaged the bodies of Jewish and other women: vivisection, removing ovaries, cutting away cervixes. In addition, every procedure was done in such a way as to enhance pain: "Dering removed ovaries and testicles of about two hundred Jewish inmates after these organs had been subjected to radiation, to make them available for pathological examination to determine whether the radiation had been effective. He administered spinal anesthesia in a crude and painful manner (rather than following the usual procedure of first anesthetizing the track of the main injection) often while patients were forcibly restrained. Operations were done without sterile procedures for hands and instruments, were performed extremely rapidly, and were followed by hasty and rough suturing."[119]

Most pregnant women or women accompanying small or young children were immediately killed. The children hugged the legs of their mothers; the mothers tried to hold them tight: wherever they were going, they were going together. But life is hard to defeat: "During roll call a child began to cry. My blood froze. A Kapo ran into the block and in one of the cages he found a small child lying in a basket, crying bitterly. . . . Somehow [the mother] had obtained sleeping pills . . . and had given one to the child. All through the selection, therefore, the infant had been fast asleep. . . . But the effect of the sleeping pill wore off, and that's how the bestial Kapos discovered the body. . . . Shortly thereafter they came for her and the baby. They took them back to the family camp, where they were put to death in the gas chamber."[120]

Each story is different, and unbearable: "Frames of the laterna magica of my mind: a pregnant girl pulled out at [the selection]; we never see her again. Pregnancy . . . is verboten. A woman ran to the electric fence and is hanging there by her fingers cramped by death. The SS in the guard tower does not even bother to shoot."[121] While still in the ghettos, "there are hardly any contraceptives available anymore, and they are very expensive.

But then, having children is probably contagious, the result of the endless propaganda for large families. After all, there's nothing more beautiful than a healthy, laughing baby. All the Aryan women have some . . . In this hopelessness, the Jewish women, who no longer have anything else, at least want to have a child . . . so that their life has some meaning."[122] While still in the ghettos, some Nazis used their position and power to extort money, some to extort sex: "One bureaucrat, eyeing a Jewish woman who had come to his office several times for emigration visas for her husband and family, told her, 'We know each other very well by now, don't we. I can see, you are wearing a different blouse today. You really look very attractive in it. . . . [S]he told her daughter: 'It is written all over his face . . . how appetizing she [looks]. How good she will taste.' Another woman is still thankful today that her mother saved their lives by having sex with a bureaucrat who then provided their exit papers."[123] Women suffered for and with their children: this is not to say that fathers and brothers did not care; but that there is meaning to the fact that the fetus lives inside the mother—not a metaphorical meaning but a literal one.

In Theresienstadt, for instance, which the Nazis tried to pass off to the world as an ideal resort for rich and cultured Jews, "[b]y Nazi decree there was no choice for a pregnant woman . . . but to abort. The daily bulletin of 21 August 1943 carried a formal notice instructing doctors to abort all pregnant women, otherwise both parents would be held accountable if a pregnancy were not reported. Adler gives a figure of 350 as the number of abortions but claims that there may have been as many as 230 births."[124] Survival was the anomaly; death was the norm. But even survival was contaminated by the Nazi project: "The fact that I had the toughness to live, to function, to keep my health and my sanity, after and despite the loss of my family, meant that—as illogical as it may seem—I carried, and still carry, the weight of a solitary crime: having lived. Absurd, you say; but it has never been erased from my conscience, and never pardoned by it."[125] It will never be pardoned, at least by her, because her family died and because children died. If a woman, the children need not be your own to be yours: women are a group with a relationship to children not their own; women are the protectors of children, much as God is the father of the Jews—in other words, were women as irrational as the Jewish God, children would be victims of a distinctly female sadism. But women in general suffer for hurt children: a suffering with no magical efficacy to wipe clean all hurt, all pain. Every woman fighting for herself is fighting for the girl she was and the girls who recognize her as their origin, biological or not. And when the children starve and die, the women feel shame.

What happened to the children? "Out of two hundred of my school-mates," writes George Konrád, "only seven of us survived. One hundred and ninety-three were gassed by the Germans and their vassals of this region. My schoolmates were rounded up, put into the ghetto, and then packed into deportation trains by the Hungarian police. At the border of the Hungarian Kingdom and the German Empire they were turned over, in exchange for properly filled-out receipts, to the Waffen SS."[126]

The children had to keep the ghetto from starvation: "Children had an advantage on dangerous errands because they could run and hide more easily than adults, and often they became providers for the entire family. Many were forced to work all day at very young ages in the ghetto, while others sold small items in the streets—radishes, cigarettes, candy—to provide a bit of food for their relatives. They knew no other life and were unaware that they had had no childhood."[127]

Says one child of those days: "I can still picture some of our neighbours and townspeople—whole families—and not even *one person* survived."[128] Says another child from then in a contemporaneous diary: "I think of nothing: not what I am losing, not what I have just lost, not what is in store for me. I do not see the streets before me, the people passing by. I only feel that I am terribly weary, I feel that an insult, a hurt is burning inside me."[129] Heroism was upside down, inside out: "Jurek killed his sister, at her own request. They wanted to send her to the front, to a brothel for the soldiers. "[130] Everything was upside down, inside out: it is good to be appreciated, but to be appreciated by Dr. Josef Mengele, the Angel of Death, meant undergoing forced slow and painful steps toward death. Mengele never missed a selection, because there he got to pick his experimental material: women and children. He was interested in twins, a consequence of which was that "[i]n addition to keeping their clothes and hair, some of the twins, especially the boys, recall receiving somewhat better rations than the other prisoners."[131] Hedvah and Leah Stern understood that "Mengele was trying to change the color of our eyes. One day, we were given eye-drops. Afterwards, we could not see for several days. We thought the Nazis had made us blind. We were very frightened of the experiments. They took a lot of blood from us. We fainted several times, and the SS guards were very amused. We were not very developed. The Nazis made us remove our clothes, and then took photographs of us. The SS guard would point to us and laugh. We stood naked in front of these young Nazi thugs, shaking from cold and fear, and they laughed."[132]

Mengele's cruelty toward children does not have a name. Neither sadist nor pedophile communicates his breathtaking cruelty: "One day, my twin brother, Tibi, was taken away for some special experiments. Dr. Mengele had always been more interested in Tibi. I am not sure why—perhaps because he was the older twin. Mengele made several operations on Tibi. One surgery on his spine left my brother paralyzed. He could not walk anymore. Then they took out his sexual organs. After the fourth operation, I did not see Tibi anymore."[133] What does one call this savage war against the bodies of children?

As Debórah Dwork says in *Children with a Star: Jewish Youth in Nazi Europe,* "Perhaps it is well to remember that a mere 11 percent of European Jewish children alive in 1939 survived the war; one-and-a-half million were killed."[134] Still, it is best to remember the children in the picture Abraham Lewin paints in *A Cup of Tears: A Diary of the Warsaw Ghetto:* "Once again we can observe scores of Jewish children from the age of ten to 12 or 13 stealing over to the Aryan side to buy a few potatoes there. These they hide in their little coats, with hems swollen so that the children look like balloons. Whole hosts of them can be seen climbing over the walls, crawling through the gaps or so-called 'targets' and passing through the official entrances where gendarmes and Polish police stand guard. There are some Germans who show a little mercy . . . There are also vicious guards who hit the children with murderous blows, take away their potatoes, and often even use their weapons."[135] Dwork points out that "the majority of the resistance workers who undertook to save and sustain life were women, and the people for whom they cared were children—Jewish children. In other words, the disparity between this and other resistance work is the difference between the nursery and the battlefield."[136] How long before women are honored for their values of caring and consoling? How long before we put public life in the hands of those who make life? Writing about a school for troubled and troublesome teenagers, novelist Peter Høeg describes the experience of the lost child: ". . . once someone has stood under the cold shower just so that you can stay under the warm one, then you can never really be totally alone again."[137] That is the maternal responsibility of the woman, whether or not she is a mother: stand under the cold shower so that a kid can have a warm one. Showers without gas, of course.

9

ZIONISM/WOMEN'S LIBERATION

One must approach both Zionism and women's liberation from the context of urgency—what the militants felt and why—and also with rigorous common sense. The common sense will be dismissed as if it were frenzy but only because it is the common sense of the unincluded defined as lesser. As Isaiah Berlin said: "You must have a view of what justice is, what freedom is, what social bonds are; you have to distinguish types of liberty, authority, obligation and the like. Political theories often differ in the way they answer a central question—'Why should anyone obey anyone?'—not why do they obey, but why should they; and how far."[1] To treat these issues and questions as already resolved is to abandon them at best in the eighteenth century, a lovely place but far away and too long ago. Fundamentally different was the place of women, the presence or absence of speech from women, Jews, people of color: in the United States, slavery, a chattel status based on race. The eighteenth century answers are the handiwork of white men; more important, so are the questions. One is entangled in a social system that has deep roots, hidden premises, framed inevitably by those who had status, power, and wealth.

Obedience of women or, for instance, African slaves was essential to the well-ordered world, a civilized world of the owners and the owned. Even the emancipation of Jews in Europe from the official margins of the ghetto—ciphers in shadows made more monstrous by being nearer—reified hate and created the silencing imperatives of assimilation. Women, Jews, and blacks in the cage of imperial power were either entirely foreign or had to try to fit in. Women were an absolute other; to fit in was to accept one's station and role among Jews or blacks or the imperial white. Not having asked or answered political, civil, or economic questions—being exiled and prohibited from articulation and power—outsiders were

disabled in the exercise of self-sovereignty; obedience modified by incapacity was the rule of law for the disenfranchised. Obedience was expected; more sadly, obedience was the norm. The whole edifice of
citizenship and rights in Europe and in North America was built on top
of a murderous silence; in the Americas, the genocide of the indigenous
population was the foundation at the bottom, concrete and with an awful
stench, millions of dead bodies rotting. Throughout Europe and Asia
Jews never were white; even during and after the Enlightenment, emancipated Jews were dark, foreign, contaminating, still hated even by the
philosophes themselves: Voltaire was a world-class anti-Semite.

In that world of hierarchy and hate, as now, the victim of the hate was
to blame: "If lynching was not taboo as a topic, the victim was usually
portrayed in the mainstream press as someone owing the lynch mob an
apology for its sadism. How often had Booker Washington not regretted
the harm done by lynching to the morals of the perpetrators?"[2] This
theme was elaborated on by James Baldwin in the 1960s and 1970s—
with substance, grace, and merit. (See James Baldwin, *The Price of the
Ticket.*) Indeed, if there is any moral logic in the universe, lynching, raping, plundering, or simply hating must degrade, stupefy, dehumanize; has
anyone stopped because it hurts him to do it? Strangely, the Nazis made a
similar argument: that the gas chambers were a necessity because shooting
Jews into open mass graves early morning to night demoralized and disturbed the shooters. There is a missing synapse, of course: Nazi, lyncher,
hater, or rapist could just stop—so perhaps one might generalize that the
perpetrator gets more out of doing the violence than he would out of not
doing it—whatever distortions of his heart and mind, whatever distress, it
is easier to do it than not to. Why?

And there is more bad news: as Sebastian Mallaby writes in *After
Apartheid: The Future of South Africa,* "Independence movements all over
the world have united different factions in the struggles against whites.
Their leaders believed that division had been conquered; but on the day
of independence, they were nearly always proved wrong. In the Indian
subcontinent the campaign against the British gave way to a new fight between Hindus and Muslims. In the southern Caribbean the passing of
white dominance opened a new conflict between blacks and Indians. In
Zimbabwe the Shona and Ndebele people united briefly against white
Rhodesia in the Patriotic Front; after independence the Shona-Ndebele
bloodbath cost over one thousand lives."[3] In part, the question is one of
moral authority and political accountability: who or what embodies or

represents for people their honest sense of who they are, including who they were and who they want to be. "Almost everywhere in Africa," says Mallaby, "the chiefs retain the loyalty of their people despite the efforts of modern rulers to promote the authority of the state."[4]

This question of civil sovereignty is not a simple one: the Palestinians want their state and many, if not most, Africans want their tribe; Jews wanted a nation and a state and a land and the inalienable rights associated with sovereignty. One fights for the liberation from one enemy, only to be confronted with other blood-soaked disputes and the flowering of hates that have been quiescent. Sometimes this is because fighting an oppressor—fighting for liberation from dominance or brutality or fighting to take back what has been given or stolen away—is different from the governance that must follow the fight.

The fracturing of identity in areas plundered by conquest can push self-consciousness to the brink of self-destruction; as South African writer Breyten Breytenbach writes in *Return to Paradise*: "What right have these 'foreign intruders' [tourists from Europe] to strut so arrogantly, as if this country belonged to them, even if they have been living off the fat of the land for years? But then, since when is this 'my' country? Who am I? and my kind, those who look and speak like me? And the blacks? Of course the country is theirs, that's what the struggle has been all about and am I not black too? Yes, but actually the land belongs only to those who are locked in a battle of life and death. Can there be degrees of nativeness? Black and Boer and brown, OK, Indian? Come now, do I really see them as fully South African? And the Anglo-whites? . . . The other white immigrants then—Greeks, Dutch, Polish, Italian, German, Portuguese? How long before they can qualify as African? And the black immigrants from Mozambique and Botswana and ever further north? Should they have a better claim than the pale Europeans?"[5] This fractured self-consciousness is a broken mirror with shards and slivers spread like sand under the feet of ordinary human beings—to whom the fighter for liberation claims a fidelity that he will almost inevitably betray: because to fight for freedom is not to govern.

Sovereignty poses questions that are both large and delicate and that rarely can be adequately addressed by guns on the hips of swaggering men. There are exceptions: where a revolutionary vision and conflict accompany the building of a new political ethic; for instance, as Rupert Christiansen writes in *Paris Babylon: The Story of the Paris Commune* (quoting Arthur Arnould's 1878 history of the Commune): "[D]uring its short reign, not a man, child or old person was hungry, cold or homeless, even though no government can have been more scrupulous on matters of money, even though it never touched any of Paris's countless riches, belonging to the [Commune's] most implacable enemies. Never was more done with less."[6] Does the fighter fight in order to rule? If so, liberation is likely to be a body-strewn path to dictatorship and ethnic conflagration. Does the fighter fight knowing that governance must be an exercise in fairness, principle, and law or it is nothing? If so, there is a chance.

Zionism, often called the liberation movement of the Jewish people, is Jewish nationalism moving against the oppression of Jews, which has a historical specificity; as Stephen L. Carter writes in *The Culture of Disbelief: How American Law and Politics Trivialize Religious Devotion*: "Every one of the world's great oppressions is unique, which is why each might demand a different solution. . . . So it is quite plausible that the unique circumstance of the oppression of Jews might demand the careful nurturing of a place—an actual physical location."[7] Zionism is, indeed, the fight of the Jews as a people for land that in and of itself has highly charged meaning; but Zionism is not governance, nor could it be. As Israeli pioneer Yigael Yadin said in 1973: "In two thousand years of exile we never had to face the actuality of questions of sovereignty. . . . Only three times in history have Jews had to accommodate themselves to independence: in the time of David, during which a real revolution occurred and ways of life were determined that would last for hundreds of years of monarchical independence; [second] when the Jews returned from Babylon . . . And the third time—when the Maccabees achieved independence—Judaism changed the character of Torah in the greatest revolution that has ever taken place in Jewish history."[8] Yadin was proposing the creation of what he called a "new torah" that would "help us lead our lives."[9] Even with Israel's military ethos, which Yadin had a part in building, he recognized that Zionism was failing as governance; that "[a] democratic-Jewish state can arise only when everyone has the feeling that opportunities are equal for everyone. . . . [W]e have not learned in the twenty-five years of the state to give the weaker and disadvantaged strata of society a feeling of equal worth. This is no less important than matters of national defense. In this area we have failed."[10] However modest the rhetoric, this is a tremendous recognition that in Israel the means have not been adequate to the end, that being—in the lexicon of the founding fathers—a secular Jewish state in which Jews are the majority of citizens and have rights to social and political liberty and equality. Zionists wanted a state that would embrace Jews (though not Judaism), a refuge for Jews, a new sovereignty for Jews, that sovereignty being the essential purpose of the state, its logic, its heart, its moral and ethical center.

There is nothing simple or self-evident about sovereignty, except for the fact that thugs cannot govern with fairness or delicacy; also, governance cannot be compromised by the abuse of state power or corruption for personal benefit. Fundamentally, the state must abhor exploitation and it must, at the same time, advance both liberty and equality through institutions and infrastructure that respect the self-sovereignty of individual citizens. These are simple—but not simple-minded—goals. The inclusion of women in both abstract and pragmatic principles of integrity and rights—originally part of the Zionist project but jettisoned by the Israelis—is required by the moral arithmetic of Jewish history if nothing else: women were tortured, women were murdered, women died too. Women were hunted and killed by Cossacks and by Nazis; and women fought the Zionist battles on the ground that established the state of Israel: after which women's equality was dumped from the vision and as a principle of governance. In other words, pre-Israel Zionists considered Jewish women to be Jews, which meant that Jewish women were entitled to equal participation in creating the Jewish state, the homeland; Israelis, on the other hand, have a distinct hierarchy—the subordination of Jewish women to Israeli men and the racial stigmatization of Palestinian Arabs. The domination of women and the degraded status of Palestinian Arabs give the state a testosterone-driven identity: Israel is strong and dangerous. Without this subversion of the integrity of Jewish women and Palestinian Arabs, Israeli men would run the risk of being perceived as Jewish men, with which comes the stereotype of weakness, passivity, pacifism, and also the reality of having been literally castrated: male currency requires inferiority on the part of women and a racial or ethnic other to have value—otherwise it is counterfeit.

Even without the complicating difficulty of freedom for women, Zionism was filled with contradictions that inevitably would implode: is there such a thing as secular Judaism? is being Jewish a basic entitlement to citizenship at the cost of second-class status for Arabs, including Arab citizens of Israel? what distinguishes a Jewish state from an apartheid state? can the Jewish state sustain itself without the use of torture on a subject population? can a secular Jewish morality—which tends to be left-wing and rights-based—withstand the imperatives of militarism? can separatist orthodox practice coexist not only with Arabs but also with secular

Jews? how can orthodox Jews who do not recognize Israeli sovereignty (and there are many) keep being included in both conservative and labor governments, especially when orthodox conviction mandates women's and Arab's inferiority? how can a Jewish state—that refuge, secular but sanctified in the Jewish imagination—be a fair state?

Moshe Leshem raises related questions: "How to reconcile the evident Israeli distinctiveness with Jewish peoplehood is at the root of the so-called Israeli identity crisis, a problem that escalated after 1967, when Eretz Israel became 'whole' [with the occupation of the West Bank, Gaza, and East Jerusalem]. To be sure, it is a crisis that afflicts mainly intellectuals. The vast majority of the population whose identity cards list their 'nationality' as 'Jewish' have more mundane preoccupations. But though the mere fact of being Israelis provides them with a self-evident Jewish identity, Israelis do have a difficulty with the notion of being Zionists. After all, with the establishment of the state, Zionism had attained its principal political goal . . . In many ways, a Zionist in Israel today is very much like an American abolitionist after the Civil War."[11] Right: and please read about Reconstruction—the abolitionists won the war metaphorically speaking and lost the peace, as a result of which the United States remains mired in social conflict based on race. This is a good example of how a liberation movement can make a mess because of its failure to recognize the new exigencies created precisely by victory.

The near irrelevance of Zionism to governance is savagely mocked by Gore Vidal in Live from Golgatha: "I was a dedicated Zionist, largely because I had been brought up as a Presbyterian in New Jersey and so I felt personally responsible for the Holocaust. Many of us did—and still do—in the Oranges. . . . Well, the more I got about, the more I realized that the world would have been a better place without Christianity, as invented by Saint Paul. I also wanted Israel to be supreme. I joined B'nai Brith, and I started to read The New York Times—between the lines."[12]

The great hatred for Zionism in which political people feel free to indulge suggests that Zionism is frequently experienced as if it were the equivalent of The Protocols of the Meetings of the Learned Elders of Zion in real time, a fictive frenzy of fanatical cunning. Concurrently the North American appreciation of Zionism as the substance of political Judaism is nearly as warped in that Zionism has never meant the absolutist support of an existing state but rather the fight to establish a fair Jewish state. Perhaps "fair state" is an oxymoron. Regardless, the fight for statehood is over. Jews won. Israel exists; and even more shockingly so do Israelis, who cannot be mistaken for European shtetl Jews nor for New York's urban Jewish population. The fact is that even defending an already existing state facing rhetorical extermination and angry neighbors is different from fighting to create a state. All political conflict, issues, and problems are subsumed under the category "Zionism"; while the difficulties of authentic and ethical governance are not being addressed—certainly not by Israel's supporters in North America; nor by intellectuals—U.S., British, Israeli, Arab—who fulminate one way or the other about Zionism but avoid the moral and political questions about good government in the here and now. The fear of losing land—that tiny sliver of land—comes from a legacy of homelessness and dispossession: expulsions from countries; being taxed for practicing Judaism (including in Arab principalities); confinement in ghettos; assaulted by soldiers, mobs, and then the elegantly sadistic doctors and SS elite in concentration camps. There is a collective anxiety about being thrown out, whether into the sea or into gas chambers; that anxiety is necessarily fierce, a near hysteria not unlike the terrible trauma of individuals who have lived without shelter or food and as targets of violence. In fact, take away Israeli weaponry and one has naked Jewish men, vulnerable to castration, assault, rape, and mass murder. Take away that little piece of land and the collective is homeless again: destroyed.

The hypernationalism of right-wing Israelis who want to expand the territory of the state to its original biblical borders is an expression of that same fear: transformed into hatred of Arabs. Arabs are the enemy; fear is not. Call everything Israeli "Zionism" because inevitably everything developed from a time when there was no Jewish state—but Israeli state and social policy has virtually nothing to do with Zionism nor can "Zionism" solve Israel's international or domestic problems. But men with guns do not like to acknowledge fear, in this case a fear of homelessness that would turn Israeli men back into so-called weak Jews: like Cinderella at the ball when the clock strikes midnight. Israeli men would become unarmed, Wandering Jews.

In biblical antiquity Jews "had worked as shepherds, farmers and vintners, but they had become highly urbanized in the modern world, shunted into trading, peddling, or moneylending."[13] Jews had been widely prohibited from owning land; Jews had been robbed repeatedly, not only of shelter but also of skills—how to grow food, how to have a direct relationship with the earth under one's feet—a relationship not mediated by hostile and punishing anti-Semitic governments. The question seemed to be: where can these people with no land be put? In czarist Russia "the Russian Jews hadn't been allowed to buy or manage land beyond their tumbledown shtetls. A czarist plan to resettle them on the land had turned into a wretched hoax, hobbling its recipients with myriad rules."[14] What piece of land can harbor these Jews who read and write, who study, who do not ride on horses to rape and pillage, which makes them different and strange?

Even before World War II, resettling the Jews was in the political air: where could they be put? ". . . Roosevelt suggested opening Ethiopia to Jews. Mussolini countered by suggesting the Soviet Union, Brazil and the United States";[15] "The plan for mass Jewish migration to Africa was the best bet";[16] "A leader of New York's Jewish laity, he dreamed of building a Jewish homeland (which he called, fittingly, Ararat) on Grand Island in the Niagra River";[17] "In a dozen years . . . more than a quarter-million Soviet Jews [were transplanted] to 215 colonies spread over two and a half million acres of land. They rode a thousand American-made tractors and tended twenty thousand cows, twenty-five thousand chickens, and even eighty-five hundred pigs. In time, four hundred vocational schools also sprang up to teach Jews metal, woodworking, printing, and other trades";[18] ". . . Max [Warburg] urged Jews to stay and fight while also making clandestine overtures to have them admitted into Syria, Cyprus, Turkey, Egypt, and Latin America. He helped start the Parana Project, which settled a small number of German Jews as coffee planters in the Brazilian jungle. He explored prospects for Jewish settlers on a coffee farm . . . in Guatemala";[19] "As war neared, FDR and his aides increasingly turned toward a land resettlement solution to the Jewish persecutions in Europe. A number of locations were considered, including Palestine, Madagascar, and even Alaska. An Alaska plan [was] developed by Interior Secretary Harold Ickes . . ."[20] This fever to relocate Jews—of course motivated by apparent German hostility toward Jews—gave the Nazis' ideas of transport some legitimacy: "Nazi propagandists could maintain that the Third Reich was merely carrying out an idea developed by other Europeans."[21] Zionists especially were accused of conspiring with Nazis to bring Jews to Palestine; the bargains—minimal though they were—were both odious and necessary because the Nazis were holding the Jews hostage.

Early on, "Eichmann, in fact, stood ready to expedite the emigration from Austria . . . This relationship was the precedent for Eichmann's unsuccessful attempts toward the end of the war to trade Jewish lives for dollars and vehicles in Eastern Europe."[22] These efforts were not malignant, dishonorable attempts to join the Nazi Party by Zionists who wanted to settle Jews in Palestine; as Jews had collected money to ransom Jews who were slaves, so Jews tried to ransom Jews endangered by Nazi hegemony. As Friedländer writes, "In one instance only were the economic conditions of emigration somewhat facilitated [by Nazis]. . . . The so-called Haavarah (Hebrew: Transfer) Agreement, concluded on August 27, 1933, between the German Ministry of the Economy and Zionist representatives from Germany and Palestine, allowed Jewish emigrants indirect transfer of part of their assets and facilitated exports of goods from Nazi Germany to Palestine. As a result, some one hundred million Reichsmarks were transferred to Palestine, and most of the sixty thousand German Jews who arrived in that country during 1933–39 could thereby ensure a minimal basis for their material existence."[23] Even while Eichmann flirted with Zionists and emigration of Jews was arguably encouraged, Eichmann knew that "[t]he policy of the Reich is . . . to hinder the development of a Jewish state in Palestine."[24] The Nazis "did not want a Jewish state that would always represent a danger, and German policy was to prevent strengthening the Jewish position. Furthermore, [according to Nazi logic] the flooding of Jews to countries all over the world would result in an increase of anti-Semitism, the best propaganda for the Reich's Jewish policy."[25]

What can be deduced in retrospect is supported by then-contemporary evidence: "A number of contemporary sources indicate that there were only two possibilities for German Jews: emigration or death. In this situation, Göring was a moderate, because he was willing to bargain with the Intergovernmental Committee on Refugees over a large-scale emigration, whereas Goebbels, Ribbentrop, Heydrich, and Himmler were not. Well-informed diplomats perceived this alignment among the Nazi leaders."[26] To make Germany Jew-free, a euphemism accepted by the community of nations, Jews were forced to "emigrate": in cattle cars to Poland and Eastern Europe: ". . . to make Germany free of Jews was a goal that did not sound so criminal. There were various ways to rid Germany of its Jews, but the SS had long since possessed a plan to kill as many as possible. Himmler had taken the same approach for Poland: forcing adult male Jews to work under conditions where many would die, ghettoization as preparation for the elimination of as many of the rest as possible."[27] As Browning points out: "In mid-March 1942 some 75 to 80 percent of all victims of the Holocaust were still alive, while 20 to 25 percent had per-

ished. A mere eleven months later, in mid-February 1943, the percentages
were exactly the reverse. At the core of the Holocaust was a short, intense
wave of mass murder. The center of gravity of this mass murder was
Poland, where in March 1942, despite two and a half years of terrible
hardship, deprivation, and persecution, every major Jewish community
was still intact, and where eleven months later only the remnants of Polish
Jewry survived in a few rump ghettos and labor camps."[28] Nazi-occupied
Poland was a graveyard for Jews, first shot, later gassed: "The policemen
in the shooting commandos marched their Jews to the crest of one of the
mounds of waste material in the area of the gravel pits. The victims were
lined up facing a six-foot drop. From a short distance behind, the policemen fired on order into the necks of the Jews. The bodies tumbled over
the edge. Following each round, the next group of Jews was brought to
the same spot and thus had to look down at the growing piles of corpses
of their family and friends before they were shot in turn. Only after a
number of rounds did the shooters change sites."[29]

As a showcase for monitoring done by the Red Cross, the Nazis developed Terezin, which Jews were told was "an alternative to the camps in the
East and so welcomed the chance to live in a wholly Jewish city."[30] Jewish
children attended school; there were concerts and lectures; it was the
Nazis' model community; sometimes Jews were dressed in suits and
dresses and sat at fancy round tables for dinner, resort-style; the Red Cross
did not look any further. In fact, "Terezin was little more than a transit
camp—a way station—on the road to Auschwitz. Thus masked, the Final
Solution was that much easier to accomplish: of the nearly 150,000 men,
women, and children who passed through this 'model ghetto,' only
12,000 survived the war. Some 33,000 people died in Terezin between
1941 and 1945 of disease, starvation, beatings, and shootings. Another
90,000 were eventually murdered in Auschwitz."[31]

Laqueur asks, "What did it mean to grow up in Germany as a young
Jew? I was born in Germany and my ancestors had lived there as far back
as one could trace them. Yet those in authority told me after 1933 that I
did not belong . . . But the adults were saying that it was by no means
clear how long the government would last, and there were proverbs to the
effect that dogs who bark do not bite."[32] But these were rabid dogs and
they did bite. Still, only Nazis could begin to imagine what they, the
Nazis, would do: the perpetrator always understands the crime better—
and sooner—than the victim. One longs for the historian who can tame
history: organize it, see a pattern, show a continuity; one longs for a his-

torical determinism that one can grasp as if it were law. One longs for the peace of retrospection—signs, patterns, order, reasons, cause and effect. For instance, in *A History of Civilizations* Fernand Braudel finds an animating principle: "Every civilization, then, is based on an area with more or less fixed limits. Each has its own geography with its own opportunities and constraints, some virtually permanent and quite different from one civilization to another. The result? A variegated world, whose maps can indicate which areas have houses built of wood, and which of clay, bamboo, paper, bricks or stone; which areas use wool or cotton or silk for textiles; which areas grow various food crops—rice, maize, wheat, etc."[33] This is restful with a measured beauty; and the Jews are nowhere in it nor is the reckless hate that has driven them from one place to another in an effort to escape murder. There is horror in Jewish history; the pages of history books are visibly stained by blood. The persecution has been monstrous. Zionism changed the terms by establishing Jewish sovereignty: a boundary around Jews to safeguard the Jewish body—there would be a cost to the aggressor to cross that boundary; the further the boundary could be from the body, the greater the distance would be between hate and what or whom it could touch. Zionism was a means to an end: "We will be a normal state," said Chaim Nachman Bialik, "when we have the first Hebrew prostitute, the first Hebrew thief and the first Hebrew policeman."[34] By this measure Israeli men set the standard for normal, a state of grace that enhances the virility of Jewish men outside Israel too. As Paul Breines writes in *Tough Jews:* "The Jewish desire to enter the world of bodies is the desire of an excluded, beleaguered minority for what the dominant majority considers normalcy. Zionism has been straightforward in its contention that a Jewish state is the key to normalization of the Jewish situation and that the abnormality of the Jews was a political problem caused by statelessness. And statelessness, according to Zionism, is the cause of meekness, frailty, passivity, humiliation, pogroms, futile appeals to reason and dialogue—in short, Jewish weakness and gentleness."[35]

Was it statelessness or was it cowardice or did shtetl Jews have a better life, qualitatively better, than men in the foreign domain of normalcy? And was it normalcy, then, that required the subordination of women and the stigmatization of Arabs, through which one creates a male hierarchy with Arab male menials on the bottom? The arrangement itself is not Zionism, though some Zionists foresaw conflict between Jews and Arabs in a future Jewish state. And: Zionism advocated for equality of the sexes; a principle cannibalized by the Israeli state when it gave religious courts authority over the private and family lives of women and children. The arrangement—male over female, Jew over Arab—is Israel, nearly an apartheid state, its own women hostages to a machismo designed to make up for centuries of political and social emasculation and especially to make up for the Nazi castration of Jewish men; some literally, all metaphorically. In Auschwitz the castration of Jewish men was real: this is the elephant standing in the middle of the room, the unmentionable, vile crime against Jews, for which Israeli men punish Israeli women, as if Jewish women had not been reproductively mutilated or annihilated. Wife-beating in Israel is ubiquitous, according to grassroots activists, though the current official figure is one-in-seven; how many does it take is the unspoken question raised by statistics on violence against women in every country—there are either too many to be able to do anything about it or too few to warrant action. In Israel wife-beating is aggravated by religious law, which makes the husband the sole dispenser of divorce and turns women who leave husbands without divorce into refugees, *agunot*, chained: not entitled to food or shelter or welfare or any of the prerogatives of citizenship; pushed from intimate violence backward in Jewish history to homelessness but inside the Israeli state. A news report from Jerusalem dated November 25, 1998, notes that "[d]uring the past eight months, 112 women have been killed by their husbands."[36] In both religious and civil courts there is an across-the-board tolerance for male violence against women: "The problem," says Yael Dayan, "isn't beaten women but men who beat and who then benefit from judges' laxness."[37]

A UNICEF report in 1997 said that violence against women "is so deeply embedded in cultures around the world that it is almost invisible."[38] This invisibility attaches to violence against Palestinians, too: "According to a report submitted to the Attorney General in the late 1980s, hundreds of suspected acts of aggression by settlers against Palestinians remained unresolved, including several killings and numerous instances in which Palestinians have been wounded or beaten. Since then, there have been many more."[39] Once a culture gets its masculinity from contempt for women, which is then reified by ethnic hatred, the very identity of the dominant men depends on having an implicit right to hurt, to injure, to assault, to control using physical force. That right is visible even if the harm it allows is not. The cost to subordinates who are by definition lesser—less valuable, less human—either cannot be seen or does not matter. Male domination becomes like gravity: it holds everything and everyone in place but is not visible to the naked eye; it pushes down relentlessly; it is not violence per se but the force of the natural: it need not be understood to be experienced and, in fact, it is impossible not to experience it. If it is invisible and everywhere, how does one notice it, name it, define it, examine it, challenge it, change it? For certain, its name is not "Zionism." For certain, Israel is a nation-state; for certain, no one kicks sand in the faces of Israeli men; for certain, hatred of Arabs is useful in sustaining male rage and a willingness to injure and kill; for certain, militarist heroes do not get bashed by the international community or Amnesty International or human rights groups for beating their wives or for killing them; for certain, Israeli men are normal. Each battered, raped, or prostituted woman is normal too.

The English politician and eventual prime minister Benjamin Disraeli— slandered as he was by anti-Semitic hate literature—may have been the first public Zionist. Disraeli was born into a Jewish family, his father a writer and scholar who had a falling out with the Jewish community and so had his son baptized when he was twelve; a radical who made his way in the Tory party; an anomaly, not unlike Margaret Thatcher, in that the group from which he came was marginal and stigmatized. According to Stanley Weintraub, one of Disraeli's many biographers, "fifty years before the term Zionism first appeared in print"[40] Disraeli wrote in one of his novels, *Tancred or the New Crusade:* "The vineyards of Israel have ceased to exist but the eternal law enjoins the children of Israel still to celebrate the vintage. A race that persists in celebrating their vintage, although they have no fruits to gather, will regain their vineyards."[41] In 1830–1831 he made a tour of the Middle East and, according to Jane Ridley in *Young Disraeli 1804–1846:* "He returned to England and publicly demonstrated the superiority of the Jews, himself included. Stressing his own ancient descent made him feel the equal, if not the superior, of the aristocrats who ruled Victorian Britain."[42] To embody the so-called vulgar Jew, Disraeli dressed in "ornate suits laden with golden chains so as to remind everyone of his noble Oriental—that is, Jewish—descent."[43]

In Disraeli's first novel, *Alroy,* "the Jewish hero leads a rebellion to re-conquer the Holy Land from the Babylonians. Alroy's lust for power leads to the defeat of his army. But he achieves personal redemption by refusing to commit apostasy."[44] Hertzberg and Hirt-Manheimer think that "[t]hrough the character of Alroy, Disraeli casts himself as the leader of

the Jews who would bring his people back, sword in hand, to Palestine";
no doubt, as they say, "[t]here is defiant boldness in Disraeli's publishing
such a novel at a time when he was striving to launch a political career and
win a seat in the British Parliament."[45] He was always bold, facing, as he
did, "anti-Semitic attacks of a more dangerous kind than the pieces of
stinking pork that the mob thrust in his face as he stood on the hustings
at elections."[46] It was Disraeli who, for better or worse, "brought England
into the sphere of Middle East politics by arranging with Baron Lionel de
Rothschild to finance the Suez Canal project."[47] There had been an ongoing battle in Parliament about seating Rothschild, who refused to take the
oath of office on the New Testament; the members would not allow an
oath sworn on the Hebrew Bible. Only Disraeli would have—and did—
make this argument in Parliament for the seating of Rothschild: "I cannot
sit in this House with any misconception of my opinion on this subject.
Whatever may be the consequences on the seat I hold . . . I cannot, for
one, give a vote which is not in deference to what I believe to be the true
principles of religion. Yes, it is as a Christian that I will not take upon me
the awful responsibility of excluding from the legislature those who are
from the religion in the bosom of which my Lord and Saviour was
born."[48] Indeed, he was hated for his cunning; but implicit in that and
many other speeches was the argument he articulated most fully in his
1847 novel, *Tancred or the New Crusade*: "Why do the Saxon and Celtic
societies persecute an Arabian race [the Jews] from whom they have
adopted laws of sublime benevolence, and in the pages of whose literature
they have found perpetual delight, instruction, and consolation? That is a
great question, which in an enlightened age, may be fairly asked."[49] His
attack on English oppression in Ireland was no less daring.

And twenty years before Theodor Herzl "deserted German nationalism for Jewish nationalism"[50] British novelist George Eliot wrote her last
novel, *Daniel Deronda,* published in serialized parts in 1875–1876.
Daniel Deronda told two stories: the first, in intricate detail, the cruelty of
an upper-class husband to his entrapped wife, befriended by the kind and
beautiful Daniel Deronda; the second a saga of a Jewish family torn apart
in the Diaspora, which ends with the emigration of the heroic and now
clearly Jewish Deronda with his love to settle in Palestine: "The most important of the dreams that the plot realizes is Daniel Deronda's desire to
be a Jew. His mother makes it true by telling him her life story: her word
legitimizes his flesh, and significantly qualifies it. . . . [T]he novel asks
whether the 'natural' qualities seemingly lodged in the flesh—the race, the

sex—are not rather formed and informed, created as it were, by desire and dreams and language, the uncontrollable imagination and the conscious will, awkwardly collaborating."[51]

For a British novelist with an Evangelical Christian background to make a sympathetic Jew the heart and soul of her epic story was auda-cious; to romanticize Palestine as the Jewish homeland was visionary. It is likely that Daniel Deronda as a character was based on Emanuel Deutsch, a young man who helped Eliot with research and taught her Hebrew: "Deutsch was an enthusiast for a Jewish homeland; when he visited Pales-tine in 1869 he wrote that all his 'wild yearnings' had been fulfilled. . . . Deutsch and his experience, including his painful decline and death from cancer in 1873, were etched in George Eliot's mind as she wrote about Daniel Deronda and his Jewish mentor Mordecai . . ."[52] In the novel, "[t]he ailing Mordecai, steeped in Old Testament prophecy and Hebrew teaching, seeks a friend to carry out in the East his political dream of founding a Jewish community, separate from non-Jews yet communicat-ing with them, in a Palestinian homeland. It is a remarkable fictional prophecy of the influential work twenty years later of the Zionist Theodor Herzl . . . published in German and English in 1896."[53]

But Daniel Deronda is even more astonishing in its political reach: it links the powerlessness of women (in the marriage story) with the power-lessness of Jews: women in being the property of men; Jews in being dis-placed. Eliot and Disraeli were each displaced persons in their native Britain; each had a deep experience of the distress, danger, and pain of homelessness. Eliot reached the apex of British literature, her genius un-touched by Dickens or the Brontës or Austen. Disraeli, too, reached the top of the British political system: what he called "climbing the greasy pole." Both rejected or sought to undermine Jew-hating stereotypes; both demanded social standing for Jews among the English and a homeland for Jews in Palestine. Both boldly presented Jews as worthy human beings: the homeland in Palestine is not tied to nor contextualized by expul-sion—a desire to get rid of Jews, move them somewhere else, out of sight/out of mind. Eliot took her own situation—a woman living with a man she could not marry, shunned, left alone when her intimate went to dinners she could never join, boycotted by women (except for her one feminist friend)—and she matched her desolation to the homeless, place-less Jew. Disraeli's aggressive tactics and Eliot's vision and daring were characterized by empathy, a sympathy that did not condescend or slander.

But the Zionism of Herzl and those who came after him was deeply informed by the anti-Semite's valuation of the Jew. Herzl was a Viennese journalist who "was out to prove that a Jew could be a perfectly modern gentleman imbued with the highest European values without ceasing to belong to a distinctly separate national collective—the Jewish nation."[54] As a journalist he covered the Dreyfus trial in Paris, where the whirlwind of anti-Semitism had the force of a public lynching; seeing Dreyfus convicted of treason because he was a Jew was the injustice that changed Herzl—he knew that Jews needed rescue. In fact, the ferocity of French anti-Semitism was such that even native-born French Jews embraced it: "The brutal antipathy between French and immigrant Jews was longstanding. As early as 1890, the French Jewish writer and journalist Bernard Lazarre (1865–1903), soon to become a staunch Dreyfusard, referred to East European immigrants as 'these predatory Tatars, coarse and dirty, who come in huge numbers to graze in a country which is not theirs.'"[55] Zola would defend Dreyfus in his famous *J'Accuse* and, under threat of arrest for criminal libel, be forced to flee France for political refuge in England. Herzl concluded that only a separate self-governing territory could safeguard the Jews from the furies of anti-Semitism. "We have honestly endeavored everywhere," he wrote in *The Jewish State,* "to merge ourselves in the social life of surrounding communities and to preserve the faith of our fathers. We are not permitted to do so. In vain are we loyal patriots, our loyalty, our loyalty in some places running to extremes; in vain do we make the same sacrifices of life and property as our fellow-citizens; in vain do we strive to increase the fame of our native land in science and art, or her wealth by trade and commerce. In countries where we have lived for centuries we are still cried down as strangers, and often by those whose ancestors were not yet domiciled in the land where Jews had already had the experience of suffering."[56] Herzl experienced the Dreyfus case as an example of how disenfranchised the Jews were in Europe, and, of course, he was right.

Back in Vienna Herzl started a newspaper that he made clear was a *Judenblatt,* a Jews' paper: "It was a deliberate choice. In German, in Herzl's time at least, to place Jude in front of another noun turned the combined word into a term of contempt and contumely. 'We take this word,' Herzl wrote . . . , 'which is meant as a slur and turn it into an expression of honor.'"[57] Herzl particularly blamed emancipation for the immovability of anti-Semitism: "When civilized nations awoke to the inhumanity of discriminatory legislation and enfranchised us, our enfranchisement came too late. It was no longer possible to remove our disabilities in our old homes. For we had, curiously enough, developed while in the Ghetto into a bourgeois people, and we stepped out of it only to enter into fierce competition with the middle classes."[58] The sociology may be right; the economic analysis may be precisely on point; but Herzl's purpose is to say that Jews had the qualities anti-Semites alleged. He is more ambivalent about assimilation and emancipation than the above passage indicates, because he also holds that "prosperity weakens our Judaism and extinguishes our peculiarities. It is only pressure that forces us back to the parent stem; it is only hatred encompassing us that makes us strangers once more."[59] In other words, he was heartsick that assimilated Jews like Dreyfus in France and himself in Vienna were still hated in the cultures and countries they themselves loved. No one so embodies the sad love affair between Jews and the world as did Herzl, who denounced a Europe "provoked somehow by our prosperity, because it has for many centuries been accustomed to consider us as the most contemptible among the poverty-stricken"; he denounces the world's "ignorance and narrowness of heart."[60]

But Herzl acted and his actions had an astonishing efficacy: the first Zionist congress took place in Basle, Switzerland, on August 29, 1897; there were 197 delegates. Herzl had been trying to get the Sultan of Turkey to give the Jews what the British would later also refuse them: a piece of Palestine; and so the congress first passed a resolution thanking the Sultan of Turkey. "Then Herzl rose and walked over to the pulpit. It was no longer the elegant Dr. Herzl of Vienna, it was no longer the easy-going literary man . . . As one reporter said: 'It was a scion of the house of David,' risen from among the dead, clothed in legend and fantasy and beauty.'"[61] Herzl said: "We are here to lay the foundation stone of the house which is to shelter the Jewish nation."[62] In the end, the congress adopted this resolution: "Zionism seeks to secure for the Jewish people a publicly recognized, legally secured home (or homeland) in Palestine."[63] With seerlike foresight, Herzl wrote in his diary: "If I were to sum up the Basle Congress in a single phrase I would say: In Basle I created the Jewish State. Were I to say this aloud I would be greeted by universal laughter. But perhaps five years hence, certainly fifty years hence, everyone will perceive it."[64] It took fifty-one years.

Herzl saw the state as an abstraction, the territory as a material base; he claimed to have invented the abstraction, "which, as such, is invisible to the great majority."[65]

There were other Zionists who explicated at length the distinctive qualities of the Jews implicit in Herzl's confusion about emancipation and assimilation. Moses Hess, a German Jew and author of *Rome and Jerusalem* (1862), saw his own Judaism fused with Palestine and, in particular, Jerusalem; of the need to return he said, "Without soil a man sinks to the status of a parasite, feeding on others."[66] This was one anti-Semitic characterization that became part of the Zionist iconography of the Jew in exile (the Diaspora Jew, residing outside of Palestine). A little after Hess, Aaron David Gordon, called "the Tolstoy of Palestine,"[67] described Jews as "broken and crushed . . . sick and diseased in body and soul"; "we are a parasitic people. We have no roots in the soil; there is no ground beneath our feet. And we are parasites not only in the economic sense but in spirit, in thought, in poetry, in literature, and in our virtues, our ideals, our higher human aspirations. Every alien movement sweeps us along, every wind in the world carries us. We in ourselves are almost nonexistent, so of course we are nothing in the eyes of other peoples either."[68]

This charge of parasitism required refutation by developing a new kind of Jew: feet planted in the ground; farmer or artisan; in Palestine. Under Hitler the parasite analogy became a literal Nazi fact: the healthy Aryan body had been made sick by the Jewish parasite that uses its host for sustenance but creates nothing itself; "Jews were essentially a foreign people, one who could never be absorbed by the nations they dwelled among."[69] In addition, Jews were feminine: weak, passive, cowardly, non-violent in the face of aggression or imminent harm. To change this, Jews needed guns and a new martial spirit. As Wheatcroft says in *The Controversy of Zion: Jewish Nationalism, the Jewish State, and the Unresolved Jewish Dilemma*, "Zionism wanted to make men of the Jews. Gordon and the Labour Zionists wanted the Jew to become a farmer and an artisan; Jabotinsky and the Revisionists wanted the Jew to become a soldier. Those projects have succeeded almost to a fault—the latter more than the former. The heroism among the descendants of the Maccabees of which Macaulay spoke in 1833 has been seen on a scale he could not have dreamt of."[70]

But what went into the creation of the Zionist's new man? His body had to change: "Elias Auerbach's evocation of sport as the social force to reshape the Jewish body had its origins in the turn-of-the-century call of the physician and Zionist leader Max Nordau for a 'new Muscle Jew.' This view became a commonplace of the early Zionist literature . . . Nordau's cry that we have killed our bodies in the stinking streets of the ghettoes and we must now rebuild them on the playing fields of Berlin and Vienna, is picked up by the mainstream of German-Jewish gymnastics."[71] In Germany and Vienna Jews took up fencing to defy their Prussian brothers for whom fencing was the ultimate male sport and the scars from it, especially visible scars on the face, were a reward, a proof of steely masculinity.

Damning Jews who had fallen under or survived persecution and oppression, "Zionism wanted to hark back to the glories of Jewish kings and the national rebellions against oppression"; this meant wanting "to efface the image of the 'trading Jew' grubbing for profit in undignified, unhealthy Galut [exile] occupations."[72] Zionists were particularly humiliated by the passivity of Jews, passivity being in Zionist usage a synonym for pacifism; in Zionist interpretation, Jews settled for peace at any price. Jews had, under the most vicious circumstances of assault and predation, held fast "to their faith and identity . . .";[73] this kind of courage carried only shame, so much so that Jews themselves berated Jews caught in the Nazi killing-machine: they went like sheep to the slaughter. But, as Leni Yahil writes in *The Holocaust: The Fate of European Jewry, 1932–1945:* "We know of almost no cases of uprisings in concentration camps, although the proportion of non-Jews and the mortality rates were high there. It is interesting to note that of some 5.7 million Soviet POWs, the Nazis liquidated between 65 and 70 percent. Nobody would cast aspersions on the courage of Soviet soldiers who fell into enemy hands; yet we know of no revolts of Soviet POWs, with the exception of isolated escapes. Furthermore, this phenomenon of acquiescence—acceptance of one's fate on the threshold of death—can be found in Soviet detention camps as well."[74] Or consider this description of 7,000 Chinese soldiers in Iris Chang's *The Rape of Nanking: The Forgotten Holocaust of World War II:* "The prisoners were a ragged assortment of men wearing blue cotton military uniforms, blue cotton overcoats, and caps. Some covered their heads with blankets, some carried mat-rush sacks, and some carried futons on their backs. The Japanese lined the prisoners up into four columns, with the white flag at the head. This group of thousands of Chinese soldiers had waited patiently for the Japanese to fetch them and direct them to the next step in the surrender process."[75] Both the Soviets and the Chinese were trained soldiers. As Bronia K., a fighter in the uprising in the Bialystok ghetto, saw the situation: "We were brought up in too humanistic [a] way. We learned how to love, but not how to kill. And now we have to learn how to kill, how to fight. And it was very difficult."[76] Before Hitler Zionists wanted Jews to learn how to fight, how to kill; after Hitler the imperative to fight, to kill, turned Jews into Zionists.

Hannah Senesh went from Hungary to Palestine to help build a Jewish nation. Assigned to agricultural work, she wrote in her diary: "My thoughts are generally motivated by existing conditions and return to 'idealism.' For example, while sorting grapefruit in the storeroom, selecting the beautiful, good ones on top, the comparison ran through my mind that this is the way God arranged our people. He piled the strong at the bottom so they could bear the pressure which represented the weight of a developing country, while the battered remain for the top. And within me a request was born: My Lord, may our people be like wholesome, faultless, stainless fruit so Your hand won't have to search among those which will bear the weight and those which are weak. Or, if possible, let there not be a lower and an upper level, but rather a great, wide shelf upon which everyone is placed side by side."[77] Senesh was among the thirty-two parachutists trained by the British in Palestine and sent to Hungary and the Balkans as saboteurs. Senesh was arrested by the Nazis as an enemy soldier and held in a military prison by the Gestapo, who also arrested her mother, who had not repatriated and was still living in Hungary. Senesh was threatened with the torture of her mother; she herself was tortured over a five-month period and then executed on November 7, 1944. She wrote: "I could have been twenty-three next July;/I gambled on what mattered most,/The dice were cast. I lost."[78] (See Hannah Senesh, *Hannah Senesh: Her Life and Diary*.) Senesh was a Zionist who wanted to build a homeland for the Jews in Palestine; her sense of the value of Jewish life sent her back to Hungary to try to defeat the Nazis. There was no room in the ethic of her Zionism for contempt of Jews like her mother, Catherine, bound by ties of loyalty and familiarity to Europe. Her actions were dictated by love and self-respect, not contempt. But for many Zionists—and the main speakers and notables were men—contempt was an essential dynamic: erase the Jewish past to build a Jewish future with new Jews. Said one survivor of the Holocaust: "For years after the war, the popular line was that we, the survivors, had allowed the Germans to lead us 'like sheep' to the slaughter. When I joined the Israeli Army, for example, I was surrounded by many so-called heroes. They were all tough guys. They constantly boasted about all the Arabs they had killed. And they really looked down on me for having been a camp victim. When I tried to tell them what I had gone through, my army buddies would ask, 'How could you have let the Germans do this to you?' It's taken me years to come up with the answer. When we were liberated from Auschwitz, I remember the Russians captured some five thousand Nazi SS men. I saw these two . . . Jewish inmates, thin as skeletons, who had been left to die—take the guns away from these SS men and start shooting. And you know what? Not a single one of the Nazis even tried to run away. I watched as the Germans sat, awaiting their turn to be killed. There were only these two frail little [skeletons]. Yet the Germans sat there—like sheep. . . . And today, when I am asked that question, I tell people it doesn't matter whether you're Hungarian, Polish, Jewish, or German: If you don't have a gun, you have nothing."[79]

According to Appelfeld, "Only a few of the Holocaust survivors reached Israel. Most of them preferred to be scattered throughout the world, to distant and remote places. The land of Israel was considered, and not incorrectly, to be Judaism, a danger that must be fled."[80] Indeed, the strategy of never being all in one place at one time made a certain rough sense, apparent to many Holocaust survivors but not to other Jews or Israelis until Saddam Hussein aimed his missiles at Tel Aviv during the Gulf War. Yet, the Zionist repudiation of Holocaust survivors, particularly in Palestine and later in Israel itself, remains a shocking fact. One of Senesh's fellow saboteurs who lived tells of going to a club for soldiers in June 1945; according to Tom Segev in *The Seventh Million: The Israelis and the Holocaust*, "Everyone received him warmly . . . But no one was interested in accounts of Jewish suffering. They wanted a different story, about the few who had fought like lions. 'Everywhere I turned,' [the soldier] wrote, 'the question was fired at me: why did the Jews not rebel? Why did they go like lambs to the slaughter? Suddenly I realized that we were ashamed of those who were tortured, shot, burned. There is a kind of general agreement that the Holocaust dead were worthless people. Unconsciously, we have accepted the Nazi view that the Jews were subhuman.'"[81] This repudiation of Holocaust Jews is the great stain on Zionism, its first corruption and dishonor. "This people is ugly, impoverished, morally suspect, and hard to love,"[82] said a woman writer in a meeting Ben-Gurion had with writers. Appelfeld, with great wisdom, understands that "[e]normous catastrophes are often perceived as bitter failures, and they bring into being, consciously or unconsciously, accused and accusers."[83] But there is a callousness here that predates the Holocaust. Ben-Gurion refused his own sister in Russia entry to pre-Holocaust Palestine: "I do not believe she will be able to work or to find work she is fitted for."[84] Somehow he was also able to say: "If I knew that I was able to save all the children in Germany by transporting them to England, but only half of them by transporting them to Palestine, I would choose the second—because we face not only the reckoning of those children, but the historical reckoning of the Jewish people."[85] Was this just rhetoric? No.

Yet it was Ben-Gurion's pragmatic ruthlessness that gave the state its character: tough. Ben-Gurion clashed with the elite Jewish banking families, whose monies to Jewish Palestine had not been negligible, over self-defense groups, military training, and violent underground strikes: these were the early forerunners of what became the Israeli Defense Force. According to Chernow in his biography of the Warburg banking family, "The Zionist movement was, in part, a populist revolt against Jewish banking royalty."[86] Ben-Gurion thought that a Jewish state "would supplant the old elite" and would challenge its "property, status, rights, and influence."[87] As Ehud Sprinzak says in *The Ascendance of Israel's Radical Right*, ". . . Ben-Gurion and his colleagues understood that unrestrained Arab violence was politically useful for the Jews. It alienated the Arabs from the British, damaged their cause internationally, and forced the Mandatory government to use military means against the Arabs."[88] It was Ben-Gurion's strategic use of Arab violence that achieved an armed Jewish force under British rule: "[T]he British granted a semiofficial status to the military wing of the Histadrut [the official labor organization for Jews in Palestine], the Haganah, which was allowed to create a mass defense system that later became the foundation of the Israeli army."[89]

It was Ben-Gurion's economic strategy to include the southern Negev as part of the Israeli state: "that slender triangle of desolate desert mountains jutting southward between Transjordan and Egypt toward the Gulf of Aqaba. Ben-Gurion . . . was intent on gaining full control of this direct passage to the Indian Ocean and the Far East."[90] Ben-Gurion could parse events, tendencies, conflicts, and possibilities for the elements that would support the state; he stood against any plan or act or tendency that supported what he considered a ghetto mentality. He had an immense understanding of reality and a vision, no less than Herzl but never abstract, of winning: creating a new Jew in a new Jewish state. With this came a disdain for European Jews—as expressed by author Yehudit Hendel: "People we saw as inferior who had some kind of flaw, some kind of hunchback, and these were the people who came after the war. I was taught in school that the ugliest, basest thing is not the Exile but the Jew who came from there."[91] So what chance did Arabs have?

Ben-Gurion declared Israel's existence as a state on May 14, 1948, "to be effective at midnight, Israeli time, and eleven minutes later the White

House announced that 'the United States recognizes the provisional government as the de facto authority of the new State of Israel.' On the following day, the Arab states of Lebanon, Syria, Jordan, Egypt and Iraq attacked Israel. Israel had only the most rudimentary army, which evolved from the Haganah, and virtually no air force. . . . Israel sacrificed 6,500 lives—1 percent of its population in 1948."[92] Israel won. With the Jewish state secured, there were still Zionist imperatives, especially a sense of responsibility for Jews everywhere except what had been Nazi Europe. To Diaspora Jews, Israel was the waiting refuge in any time of need; Russian Jews struggled for the right to emigrate; Ethiopian Jews were airlifted to Israel in a secret and magnificent act of rescue; Jews hijacked to Idi Amin's Uganda by German left-wing terrorists who wanted to kill Zionists, not Jews, were rescued in a daring, nearly impossible military gambit; and so the Jews were now Israelis, self-defending, self-respecting, mostly secular, brave, smart men; among Israelis there was no weak Jew gendered male. And yet there had been an earlier military engagement in which Jewish soldiers living in Palestine, soon to be Israelis, worked with the soon-to-be-despised Holocaust survivors: "At the end of the war in Europe small groups of soldiers in the Jewish Brigade and Holocaust survivors who called themselves Nokmim (Avengers) had secretly sought out and summarily executed several hundred SS and Gestapo men and other Nazi officials in Italy, Austria and Germany itself."[93] Was it Zionism or was it hate uncorrupted by ideology? Who cares? Was it inevitable? No. Was it necessary? Yes. Here was the right beginning for solidarity between the new Jews and the old ones. But it would not be until 1960 when Eichmann was tried, convicted, and executed in Israel that Israelis would begin to understand the vileness and enormity of Hitler's assault. Israelis could judge Eichmann but they could not judge Hitler's victims. The new Jews, tailored to meet every anti-Semitic criticism ever voiced and defy it, had to look in a mirror broken by their own hard hearts: they were not shtetl Jews nor were they the cosmopolitan Jews of Vienna or Berlin or Paris. It turned out that the Zionists had indeed created a new man; they had succeeded where Hitler and his thousand-year Reich had failed; but the new man was made out of the bones of the old one. The new man was Israeli: happily ignorant that his qualities and society were based on an acceptance of anti-Semitic perceptions and charges against the Jews. In the full glory of this ignorance, Dr. Frankenstein's creature was both mighty and ostracized: bewildered by the hostility of the world around him; heroic in his effort toward a hard-won humanism; arrogant and crude but virile, always virile; and liberated: with no more need of a liberation movement. The task now was governance of new Jews, old Jews, and Arabs. Zionism inside Israel was over: though it continued to live as an ethic of rescue for populations of Jews under oppression who wanted to emigrate there. In North America, Zionism became synonymous with fund-raising; it was how, for instance, U.S. Jews expressed a loyalty to Israel and to Jewish identity—this was Zionism as they knew it.

Zionism was also a continuing red flag for bulls of all nations who hated Jews and did not care that these were new ones, not old ones (the ones available to be killed). The difference is where the boundary was and how that boundary was defended: attack began not against an individual body nor a disenfranchised ghetto; Israel had sovereignty, borders, an army, eventually an air force, and an astonishing intelligence agency. Those new Jews might be as smart, as cunning, as foreign (according to their new neighbors) as the old Jews had been; but no one thought they were pacifists or passive or weak or frightened or cowardly; and eventually they would have their own women and Palestinian Arabs right down under them to step on or kick around. They did not need Zionism.

Laqueur writes that "[a]ll over the Middle East, Arab countries were gaining independence. The previous year the Arab League had been founded. Why should the Palestinians give up a single inch? What would have happened to the Jewish minority in this case? The Mufti and Jamal Husseini made no secret: The Jews would have to return to where they had come from; only some of those who had lived in Palestine in 1917, before the Balfour Declaration, would be permitted to stay."[94] In 1991 Sari Nusseibeh made the point current: "Bluntly put, Palestinians essentially believe that any bargaining with Israel over Palestinian territory is like bargaining over stolen property with the very thief who stole it by force."[95] It was not all by force, however; much of the land was bought by Jews—usually from absent Arab landlords who had a legal, if not a moral, right to evict tenants and sell to Jews. A corrupt Arab oligarchy sold out a farming population of poorer Arabs to those who became—but were not yet—an ethnic enemy. It is certainly the case that Israel would not exist without the use of force; but—on the model of Thomas Jefferson's buying the Louisiana Purchase from the French even though it belonged to an indigenous population—much land was bought: it would be good to see the Arab oligarchy share some of the responsibility for the displacement of Palestinian Arabs. In the same way, Arab corruption continues: U.S. President Jimmy Carter "was able to make the revealing observation . . . that he had 'never met an Arab leader who in private professed the desire for an independent Palestinian state.'"[96]

Force, of course, was not only necessary to take the land: it was essential to the making of an Israeli. As Yaron Ezrahi writes in *Rubber Bullets: Power and Conscience in Modern Israel:* "Since Zionist ideology has rested on a Jewish narrative of redemption, of return and liberation, it has encouraged fantasies of force as monumental as the dream itself."[97] Force had to be used in the same way and for the same reason that Israel itself had to be based on agricultural collectives; as Ben-Gurion said in January 1918: "Eretz Israel can of course be built entirely on capitalist lines, like other countries, but building a country that is entirely capitalist will not bring about the implementation of Zionism. In a purely capitalist economic system, there would be no Jewish labor and the soil would not be in Jewish hands. Without Jewish labor and Jewish land, Zionism would be a mere hoax."[98] Seventy-some years later Israeli novelist Amos Oz would write in *Touch the Water, Touch the Wind:* ". . . it stands solid and high, just a Jewish mountain, as if it was the simplest thing in the world to be a Jewish mountain or a Jewish sea or forest, or even just a plain Jewish log for all the world like any other damned log, a Bulgarian log, a Turkish log, only it's a Jewish log in a Jewish country. . . . [I]t means a peace treaty between Jews and the tangible sphere . . ."[99] Thus, force and land were necessary to make Israelis different from shtetl or European Jews: and had the Palestinian Arabs not been there, Zionists would have had to fight against scorpions and rocks. The defense of Zionist indifference or antipathy to Palestinian Arabs reiterates the urgency of the Zionist project but does not pull that disregard apart: "The founding fathers of the Zionist movement, and Herzl in particular, were also often criticized for not understanding the Arabs. What these critics overlooked was that the young Zionist movement simply could not afford to understand the Arabs. To have done so would have fatally undermined the Jewish claim to their ancient homeland."[100] This is basically an admission of guilt framed by an ethic of necessity.

The war forced on Israel on the heels of declaring statehood helped to uproot Palestinian Arabs, many of whom fled: "Hundreds of thousands of Arabs fled, and were expelled from their homes. Entire cities and hundreds of villages left empty were repopulated in short order with new im-

migrants. In April 1949 they numbered 100,000, most of them Holocaust survivors. The moment was a dramatic one in the war for Israel, and
a frightfully banal one, too, focused as it was on the struggle over houses
and furniture. Free people—Arabs—had gone into exile and become destitute refugees; destitute refugees—Jews—took the exiles' place as a first
step in their new lives as free people. One group lost all they had, while
the other found everything they needed—tables, chairs, closets, pots,
pans, plates, sometimes clothes, family albums, books, radios, and pets.
Most of the immigrants broke into the abandoned Arab houses without
direction, without order, without permission. . . . Immigrants also took
possession of Arab stores and workshops, and some Arab neighborhoods
soon looked like Jewish towns in prewar Europe . . ."[101] One Israeli wag
named this "the Arab miracle."[102]

The irony was twisted and bitter; the looting lasted for several months
during which the Palestinian Arabs dared not return. There is an almost
slapstick comedy in the reversals—Arabs fleeing, Holocaust Jews moving
in. But no one can laugh much: these were Palestinian families, decent
folks hounded out by war. When Palestinians talk about a right to return,
they are talking about returning to the houses, furniture, land, shops,
stolen from them. In 1949 a poll was taken to measure Israeli resistance to
Arab return: ". . . 73 per cent opposed the return of the Arab refugees but
27 per cent did not. However, the poll revealed a sharp difference between
German and Arab Jews. While 45 per cent of German Jews agreed to a return, Arab Jews were 100 per cent opposed. Furthermore, the lower the
level of education, the more likely the respondent was to oppose the return of the refugees."[103] It may be supposed that German Jews were not
sanguine about dispossessing the Palestinian Arabs but that Jews who had
lived as minorities in Arab territories had not had the entirely happy experience that Arab intellectuals and politicians claim for them.

Palestinian charges of Israeli injustice were simple and clear: Jews supplanted Palestinian Arabs in their homes and neighborhoods, ate from
their plates, slept on their beds. With the anxiety that never leaves those
who have been homeless even as individuals, Israelis were unprepared and
unwilling to repatriate Palestinians who wanted to return. This is the moment—the hair-trigger moment—when Jews made the biggest mistake in
their history: Zionism trumped governance and a new cycle of tragedy for
a new homeless people began.

The fight over Jerusalem between Palestinians, now represented by the
Palestinian Authority, and Israel also bears scrutiny, since the city was so

distasteful to so many early Zionists; as Walter Laqueur says: "No leading Zionist had chosen Jerusalem as his or her home, whether left-wing or right. When Herzl visited Jerusalem his impressions were exceedingly negative ('two thousand years of inhumanity, intolerance, and uncleanliness'). Ahad Ha'am, the leading thinker of cultural Zionism, found the Wailing Wall and the ultraorthodox praying there equally repulsive. Weizmann always felt ill at ease in Jerusalem, and while Ben-Gurion was the main force behind the decision to transfer the capital from Tel Aviv to Jerusalem in 1949, he never liked the city or chose to live there. Weizmann once wrote that he would not accept the Old City even as a gift for the Jewish state, and I remember Ben-Gurion telling me, after 1967, that one ought to give up Jerusalem if peace could be bought at this price. In brief, the idea that the Jewish people could not possibly exist but for the incorporation of all of Jerusalem is a relatively recent one."[104] On the Arab side, Jerusalem is not mentioned in the Koran; and so the battle continues—but how much of the battle is the unhappy combination of greed and hate?

In moral terms, Zionists cum Israelis are most compromised for transferring populations of Palestinian Arabs outside the boundaries of the Israeli state. In June 1938, Ben-Gurion said: "I am for compulsory transfer; I don't see anything immoral in it . . . There are two central issues—sovereignty, and a reduction of the number of Arabs in the Jewish State, and we must insist on both of them."[105] Half a world away, Jews were being forcibly transferred as the Nazis reconstructed the reach of their own sovereignty. Within a decade Israel adopted the policy of transfer. "Between November 1948 and the end of 1951 between 20,000 and 30,000 more Palestinians were expelled, and more might have been had international opinion not been so hostile."[106] Arguably, "the advocacy of the transfer of the native population is a thread running through Zionist thought."[107] But the Zionists were the new guys on the block: indigenous populations had been forcibly moved or killed in the Americas and Australia, for example. So was the outcry against Israel the consequence of a double standard applied uniquely to the Jewish state and informed also by a bad conscience over Nazi transport of the Jews? Probably. But for Jews themselves, in Israel and around the world, how could transfer be morally justified; what made transfer an act that Jews could do? The existence of the Israeli state changed Jewish morality, the famous Jewish opposition to injustice: what Israel did was right; what Arabs did was wrong; Palestinians were demonized, even as new Israeli Jews ate in their kitchens, ate off their plates. The conflict has escalated through wars, terrorism, bad faith, and especially the Israeli occupation of Gaza and the West Bank; but surely transfer was immoral; and surely the refugees did have a right of return to their homes if they wanted to "live at peace with their neighbors,"[108] as a United Nations resolution put it on December 11, 1948. In the novel *Fima* Amos Oz writes: "He was thinking: In the middle of the day, in broad daylight, in the middle of Jerusalem, they're already walking around with guns in their belts. Was the sickness implicit in the Zionist idea from the outset? Is there no way for the Jews to get back onto the stage of history except by becoming scum? Does every battered child have to grow up into a violent adult? And weren't we already scum before we got back onto the stage of history? Do we have to be either cripples or thugs? Is there no third alternative?"[109]

Nationalism divides women; loyalty to state or country is masculine business; loyalty to men per se is feminine business. Men of the same nationality are one's nation; protecting them and easing their burden is one's responsibility; loving them and loving what they do is the emotional ghetto in which women live. Nationalism and the nation itself work to make women invisible. In *Hate Crimes: Criminal Law and Identity Politics*, James B. Jacobs and Kimberly Potter, who oppose hate-crime laws, note that "crimes against women would seem to be the most obvious candidate for recognition as hate crime. For women, crime is overwhelmingly an intergroup phenomenon. In 1994 [in the United States], women reported approximately 500,000 rapes and sexual assaults, almost 500,000 robberies and 3.8 million assaults. The perpetrator was male in the vast majority of these offenses."[110] In passing the Hate Crime Statistics Act of 1990, Congress "ignored all forms of male violence against females, including serial murder, rape, spousal abuse, and child sexual abuse."[111] This invisibility shows up in common uses of language; for instance, this paragraph from Robert Jay Lifton's important book, *The Nazi Doctors: Medical Killing and the Psychology of Genocide:* "From at least late 1941, the work function began to take on central importance in the camps and that led eventually to relative improvement in conditions for prisoners concerning such things as confinement arrangements and goods, and in some cases monetary awards, cigarettes, and access to camp brothels."[112] Women prisoners are in the brothels but they are excluded from the language used to describe prisoners. There is no reason to expect that Lifton is showing a reality equally valid for men and for women—and so the women are erased: the women in the camps and that subsection—the women in the brothels. This is a common strategy for establishing female invisibility.

Women have tried to use testimony (derisively characterized as "anecdotal" material) to say, in limited and partial ways, what they have experienced, especially in the areas of poverty, homelessness, and sexual assault. As Octavio Paz writes in *Essays on Mexican Art:* "Genuine testimony combines understanding with truthfulness, what is seen with what is lived and relived by the imagination of the artist. Understanding is born of moral sympathy and is expressed in many ways: pity, irony, indignation. Understanding is participation."[113] But the voices of women if heard destroy the exploitative sex that requires silence: a silent object. The lyricism of silence in tyranny has mesmerized men who are expert in the sex of male dominance: sex with no ethical dimension; sex that deprives a subordinated human being of subjectivity, presence, will, and appetite. The castration of the female voice means that there is no understanding of the female tongue, used as a synonym for language: women are foreigners in the nations in which they live; or become foreigners through the interaction of taboo and violation. For instance, in the Hebrew tradition menstruating women become forbidden strangers; as Biale writes: "The term 'to uncover nakedness' *(giluy arayot)* is the technical term for incest. The woman whose 'nakedness' is otherwise permitted to her husband is suddenly in a condition where she becomes like a prohibited relation."[114] She becomes foreign in her own home and in her own body: foreign to him, because he embodies a neutral and uncompromised humanness. Elie Wiesel in his novel *A Beggar in Jerusalem* has his narrator long for sexual contact with the silence of women: ". . . you are what I desire to possess always, so as to dispense with speech and memory. You are the moment of awareness thanks to which I am what I am: a woman who believes in love since she loves, who believes in freedom since she offers herself to you."[115] Having no presence in the world of speech or memory, her freedom is in being sex for him. This freedom would be lost—to him—if she were not a silence into which he could disappear. Her selfhood would be an unwanted distraction that would divert him from the drama of his own existence. The experience of women is always from the outside: never participating; only emphasizing her muteness; as Oz writes in *Touch the Water, Touch the Wind:* "Pomeranz opened his eyes wide, tore her sack-

cloth off her, inhaled her smell, Jewish loneliness suddenly flooded him so
that his soul wanted to burst out howling. But his watchmaker's fingers
retained their precision and expertise. They brought the virgin Mary to
shrill giggles, pleading whimpers, desperate sighs, she began to revel with
her legs with her teeth with her nails."[116] Writing from the female side,
Evelyne Accad in *L'Excisée* describes the same silence: "He plows her. She
yields. She lets go of herself like a being totally devoid of vision, like a
non-being. She gives in once more to fate. May he guide me, He. It is he
who has the vision. It is he who will show me the way . . ."[117] Accad shows
how male nationalism demands the sexual submission of women and how
that submission sanctifies the politics of nationalism: "May you lead me
. . . where we may again find Palestine, where you and I together may rebuild Palestine, thanks to you because you have penetrated me, because
you have taken me, because I have yielded myself, because all has its end
in your vision of the world, in that emblem you wear about your neck,
emblem of Palestine, symbol of the resurrection and the life, symbol of a
new world, of new values . . . I am there in your arms and you do not even
see me."[118]

   Experiencing themselves as nothing, like a nonbeing, women beg to
attach to the male even though often his heroics are the heroics of death:
delivering death. The key to male dominance in sex is the power of indifference: contempt for the body one is using such that one body can stand
in for another without personality; this is the dynamic of mass death,
body piled on body, each body breached, antisex, antieroticism, antihu-
manity, antiwoman, antifemale: the opposite of what John Berger describes as "the natural, central inextinguishable power of sexuality. This
power, crudely itself or sublimated and mediated in many different ways,
is the energy of endurance."[119] This is not the endurance of long days and
suffering nights or the endurance of work depraved by its instrumental
use of bodies; rather, this is the endurance of touch from the inside out,
from the wellspring of human vitality and vibrancy; this is an endurance
directly connected to a real geography of being in which there is no erasure of personhood or muteness or human subjectivity, even the girl's. Depravity begins in turning human into object; depravity advances when the
object becomes a commodity and is sold or bartered for or rented or
leased: when money comes into it. Depravity advances further when pleasure legitimates the selling of persons perceived as objects. Depravity becomes lifestyle when sex becomes in its near entirety style, game, art, fun,
voyeurism: amusing. Depravity advances as the norm when conformity to

sadomasochistic protocols push sex toward death: ". . . I have seen with my own eyes in Auschwitz an SS man enter the barracks of 1,450 women, throw chunks of bread into their midst and then step back in a fit of laughter as hundreds of women pushed and shoved, clawed and fought for the crumbs. Within minutes three women were trampled to death and dozens injured. . . . The SS man provided the bread, the screaming women the games for his pleasure."[120] Or: this might be fashionable male fiction, except that it isn't. "Do you remember Claire? First of all she was cruelly bitten and mangled by a dog. Who set the dog on her? We do not know, but he was Claire's first assassin. She then went to the [clinic], where she was denied treatment. Who refused her? We don't know for sure . . . The second murderer. Her wounds did not heal, and she was sent to the Jugendlager. Who sent her? We don't know . . . The third murderer. Now that she was among the ranks of the condemned, who kept her from fleeing? . . . The fourth murderer. At Jugendlager, Claire refused to swallow the poison Salveguart had given her, and Salveguart, with the help of Rapp and Kohler, beat her senseless with a club and finally killed her."[121] Why is the serial killing of one woman so familiar, so recognizable, so close when it should be so far? How is it possible that there could be analogues to such horror in lives nowhere near the Nazis in time or place or circumstance?

In his *1920 Diary* Babel wrote: "A whole volume could be written on women in the Red Army. The squadrons go into battle, dust, din, bared sabers, furious cursing, and they gallop forward with their skirts tucked up, covered in dust, with their big breasts, all whores, but comrades, whores because they're comrades, that's what matters, they're there to serve everybody, in any way they can, heroines, and at the same time despised, they water the horses, tote hay, mend harness, steal from the churches and from the civilian population."[122] That too is familiar: peace movement, counterculture, 1960s, women were good soldiers in sex, pacifists on the subject of war. There is a casualness to the hate and brutality, an "it's all in good fun" quality, and the contempt is the norm so that no single act of brutality would stand out as too odious, too vile. In *Terror in the Night: The Klan's Campaign Against the Jews,* Jack Nelson describes the camaraderie among racist police: "Around the police station they jokingly referred to [Sam Keller, assistant police chief] as Killer Keller because one of the women he went out with had been shot to death with his gun while he was in her apartment. Keller claimed the gun had gone off accidentally while she was sewing a tear in his uniform. He was never charged."[123] Does she have a name? Did anyone miss her? Can someone just be murdered with no consequences—during peace, not war? Well, there was a war against blacks and Jews but certainly not against white women. Could you kill a woman just like that? Yes, why not? There was no women's movement to suggest that the personal—sewing—was political—he murdered her. Is one enough, or how many would count? How many did there have to be? to count?

"We were 800 women, and certain things we had no choice but to accept," said Victoria Benítez, imprisoned in Argentina, "like vaginal searches in front of thirty men all aiming their guns. But on other questions we could resist; we were always analyzing, making decisions about where to draw the line. For us, the boundary was group solidarity. . . . Those of us who did receive letters with a little money would buy cheese, chocolate, aspirin, whatever we could. The idea was to make a common store of provisions so no one would do without, and so when someone got sick, we could take care of her. . . . What they needed to prevent were our efforts to share. The jailers kept accusing us of being 'perverts' or lesbians—to them any tenderness among us was twisted."[124] This, too, is familiar: a world of women, not in the unrivaled Auschwitz but in Devoto, still a place of torture. Anita, prisoner for a year and a half, said she learned a lot in prison: "In the fields, everything you do is dictated—by the weather, the season, the position of the sun. In prison, you have to make decisions. And we did it collectively, the whole pavilion of women. We organized squads to do the washing, cleaning, and other tasks; we had study and discussion groups. Norma Morello was like our patron saint. When they tortured me, I repeated her name, silently, over and over. If she withstood this, so would I."[125]

As in Auschwitz, pregnant women got the worst of what the jailers were giving out; Astelarra remembered: "Our bodies were a source of special fascination. They said my swollen nipples 'invited' the prod, eased the passage of current. They presented a truly sickening combination—the curiosity of little boys, the intense arousal of twisted men."[126] According to Feitlowitz, "It was rare for a pregnant detainee to survive; most were killed soon after giving birth, and their babies sold to 'proper' couples, usually from the military or police."[127] There were obstetrician/gynecologists who "specialized in the torture of pregnant *desaparecidas* and in trafficking of their babies . . ."[128] The silent woman screams in torture and becomes present and visible not to the torturers but to her sister prisoners. The men pursue their interminable project of destruction: turning women's bodies into a site for death; but when the women talk to each other they are neither disappeared nor silent. They knew what to do: how to share, which prolonged survival and human feeling. The men could cause pain; could assault and injure; could kill; but the women pursued life, Berger's endurance becoming an ethic articulated by practice.

On a woman's body men inscribe death: even taking body parts—labia, clitoris—in female circumcision; but there is a female medium to exercise the will of the men or even a gang of women who will hold down the girl to be circumcised. Nawal El Saadawi writes in her novel *God Dies by the Nile:* "She did not know exactly what it was that was wrong with her, but ever since her childhood she had felt there was something impure about her, that something in her body was unclean and bad. Then one day Om Saber came to their house, and she was told that the old woman was going to cut the bad, unclean part off. She was overcome by a feeling of overwhelming happiness. She was only six years old . . . After having done what she was supposed to do, Om Saber went away leaving a small wound between her thighs. It continued to bleed for several days. But even after it healed she was still left with something unclean in her body . . ."[129] In *Woman, Why Do You Weep? Circumcision and Its Consequences,* Asma El Dareer found that in the Sudan "[o]ut of the total number of women interviewed (3,210), 2,652 (82.6%) favoured the continuation of the practice; only 558 (17.4%) were totally opposed to it."[130] El Dareer found that women and men favored female circumcision equally: the same percentage of men as women approved of it. El Dareer describes the men as "instrumental"[131] in female circumcision; and women suggested that "if men made it clear that they preferred uncircumcised women and refused to marry those who were circumcised they would abandon the practice. But they had found no men willing to do this."[132] The fact is that men still make the most important decisions in women's lives: will she be circumcised; will she be raped; will she be beaten; will she be sold into prostitution: this is as true in New York City as it is in the Sudan. With circumcision a female carries out male will; but in the other circumstances a man decides: I will rape her; I will beat her; I will pimp her. On the ordinary, casual side, in dress and style women follow the dictates of men— to show conformity, to display the colors of loyalty, more than to provoke desire; in some countries women will be assaulted or killed for not conforming to fundamentalist-mandated dress codes; but a woman is always expected to not "let herself go"; even in Auschwitz Höss noted that "[e]verything was much more crowded than with the men. When women reached a point of no return, they let themselves go completely. They stumbled through the area like ghosts, completely without will, and had to be literally pushed everywhere by others until one day they just quietly died."[133]

There is a bizarre belief that Nazis did not rape Jewish women in the camps because of the Nuremberg laws, which forbade what the Nazis considered to be race defilement; so the Nazis threw bread to watch starved women trample each other or taunted the naked women with words or whips or guns and sometimes they took "girlfriends" or "lovers." The sense is that an individual Nazi was so taken with a given Jewish woman, her beauty so radiant, that he had to fall in love with her. The love affair had a bad ending: she died; but still, there was real desire on the Nazi's part, which suggests that his chosen one was near to being a human woman, though the women were universally treated as a subspecies. But wherever women are subordinated, there is rape; and there was rape in the Nazi camps—the rape of Jewish women as well as the women of other na-tionalities or categories. Women survivors were not asked about rape in recent interviews nor back then in DP camps. In written material, too, it was rare for a woman survivor to approach rape, although there are men who do—as witnesses for the most part. The shame of having been raped is so deep and so terrible because even forced intercourse or other forced sex acts suggest capitulation, complicity, an exchange of sexual favors for a reward. None of the ideologies of the time articulated what rape was from the point of view of the victim or what it cost her in well-being and self-respect—or how much closer it brought her to death. The notion that rape could make Auschwitz worse than it already was had little moral or political currency—then or now; and women—even in Auschwitz— blamed themselves. Think: even in Auschwitz rape was not contextualized by coercion but by free will: rape was still understood as if it were ro-mance or as if it were a consequence of female beauty or as if it were an "affair" after which the beloved was killed. Women questioned how men (Nazis) could find them sexually attractive given the physicality of their degradation: dirt, lice, disease. And the Nazis were afraid of lice and dis-ease; but that did not stop them from raping. In *Triumph of Hope: From Theresienstadt and Auschwitz to Israel,* Ruth Elias describes at least one pattern of commonplace rape: "Drunken SS men sometimes made unex-pected appearances in our block; the door would suddenly be flung open, and they would roar in on their motorcycles. Then the orchestra was or-dered to play, and the SS men would sing along while they continued to drink, their mood getting ever more boisterous. Young Jewish women would be pulled from their bunks, taken away somewhere, and raped. Raping Jewish women wasn't considered *Rassenschande* (race defilement), therefore it was allowed. Whenever one of these horrible spectacles began, I was glad that I lived way up on the third tier. The SS men didn't bother to climb up there in search of young women; the pickings in the lower bunks were good enough. Those of us in the upper tiers pressed our bodies against the wall, hoping we wouldn't be picked. Any woman who refused to go with the SS men was savagely beaten, so no one offered any resistance. I cannot describe the pitiable state of these poor women when they came back to the barracks."[134] Rape in Auschwitz had this in common with rape in New York City now: it was a crime of proximity—taking the nearest available woman—based on erasure of individual identity or will; women were disposable things, not human beings; it was a violence designed to destroy the woman's body and annihilate her mind, her consciousness of self; it was boys having fun; it was predatory; it forced a disassociation of the women not raped ("I was glad I lived way up on the third tier") from women who had been raped or would be raped (take her, not me); it was homoerotic as much rape is (pair- and gang-rape); it is the definitive assault taking place as it does inside the woman. Rape causes overwhelming grief in women: in Auschwitz there may not have been any more room for grief and in that sense alone rape in Auschwitz cannot be compared with commonplace stranger rape in societies not at war. Not raping gives the sadist a whiff of decency; and it gives relief to the rest of us—well, at least they didn't do that. They did do that. To leave rape unacknowledged is to force survivors to bear the burden of all the shame without empathy or relief or consolation. This is not special pleading. This goes to the heart of women's continuing invisibility: a true exile from history or meaning or understanding or recognition or human dialogue in which women are included.

There is also a "but at least they didn't rape" defense of the Spanish conquistadors in the Americas; as Richard Lee Marks writes in *Cortés: The Great Adventurer and the Fate of Aztec Mexico,* "For conquerors not to force women? Unrestrained and unaffected by the concept of purity and innocence personified by Mary, all Indians, when conquering, would use force with women of another tribe in order intentionally to shame and disgrace the men of the tribe that had been conquered. But Spaniards took only the women who were given them as gifts, women who passively came to them, and the women of tribes they were punishing, and even

with these women the Spaniards exhibited little savagery."[135] The fact that
men appear to understand that one can make a better case for conquerors
if they did not rape suggests that men know the heinous quality of rape;
the passive compliance of women given as gifts is not, under this ethic,
rape: or it is not the really bad kind of rape, the blood-and-guts kind of
rape, the force-and-horror kind of rape: in Marks's description, the Indian
kind of rape—savage, brutal, exhibitionistic, and aimed at humiliating
defeated males, in that sense a means to an end. What is missing is the
recognition that rape is an internal assault on a woman or girl; the force
used to gain entry is not the act of rape, though that force may help to
identify penile intromission as rape.

Rape or threat of rape remains instrumental in nationalist conflicts: in
Biafra, starvation and rape; in Bosnia, serial rape and forced prostitution,
hard to distinguish from each other; in Iraq, purposeful rape to engage
women as spies against, for instance, the maligned Kurdish population,
once visited by poison gas. In the United States, there are arguably war
zones, urban ghettos in which African American boys try to survive violence with violence, and gang-rape is an increasingly normalized rite of
adolescence for the raper and the raped; in the parlance of black adolescent boys, gang-rape is called "pulling trains" or "running trains": in
Makes Me Wanna Holler: A Young Black Man in America, Nathan McCall
writes, "I think most girls gave in when trains were sprung on them because they went into shock. They were so utterly unprepared for anything
that wild that it freaked them out. By the time they realized they'd been
set up, they were stripped naked, lying on a bed or in the backseat of a car,
with a crowd of crazed-looking dudes hovering overhead. . . . Most girls
seemed to lose something vital inside after they'd been trained. Their self-
esteem dropped and they didn't care about themselves anymore. That
happened to a girl named Shirley, who was once trained by Scobe and so
many other guys that she was hospitalized. After that, I guess she figured
nobody wanted her as a straight-up girl. So Shirley let guys run trains on
her all the time."[136] This intraracial rape is, socially speaking, suicidal for
the rapist. The rape, even gang-rape, of black women is rarely prosecuted
in the United States. The men are on the bottom and the women are under them. Inflicting pain on women through eroticized gang-rape is racial
self-destruction and gender carnage; and the imperative for the women is
their unflinching loyalty to the men who are hurting them with a cold
and hopeless brutality. Terrifying in McCall's book are the questions he
asks himself when he has a daughter: "A girl? Oh, shit! The fellas and I ran

trains on girls! How will I help her get through that?"[137] Does he view gang-rape, as the passage suggests, as inevitable? He goes on to say: "I was scared because I knew that a daughter would be subject to the insanity of men. White men would try to exploit her. Brothers would abuse her. Most sisters caught hell coming and going. As Zora Neale Hurston once said, black women are the mules of the world."[138]

Is there a world of difference between gang-rape as a communicator of woman-hate and self-hate in the violence of U.S. ghettos and the situation of women in Pakistan, where "[s]eventy-two percent of all women in Pakistan in police custody are physically and sexually abused, according to lawyer Asma Jahangir, who is also cofounder of Women's Action Forum, a national women's rights organization. Equally shocking is the fact that 75 percent of all women in jail in Pakistan are there under charges of zina [defined as sex out of wedlock]";[139] another writer characterizes the rape of women in Pakistan as "political rape" and estimates "that 80 percent of Pakistani women taken into police custody on charges of zina [defined as extramarital sex with consent] are sexually assaulted while in custody."[140] In intranational rape, a purposeful fundamentalist politics drives the imprisonment and violation of women; the nationalist enemy is India but the internal enemy is women. Women are the hated nation within the nation.

This kind of fundamentalism is easy for an extra nationalist enemy to manipulate—or the vulnerability of women to nationalist rape becomes a political tool in the hands of native extremists; as Ze'ev Schiff and Ehud Ya'ari write in *Intifada:* "Another primer, published as a Hamas handbill, claimed that Shin Bet [Israeli domestic intelligence] was trying to trap agents with the aid of hashish and other drugs and that it caught young women in its net by having 'stray dogs' (Palestinian collaborators) seduce them: 'They keep pictures of the couple and the letters passed between them, threatening the girls with exposure unless they agree to serve the Intelligence (people).' More underhanded yet, the leaflet warned, the Shin Bet was known to photograph girls in their underwear while they were trying on dresses in shops and then blackmailing them into informing on their friends. Parents were therefore advised to make sure that their girls did not dally on the way home from school and that they did not frequent hairdressers, boutiques, or even shoe stores unchaperoned."[141] Meanwhile, in Iraq, rapists are used by the government to compromise women into spying (for instance, against the Kurds) or to punish politically active women, especially feminists. One woman was stopped by the secret police who claimed to want her to divulge information about her husband. Under this guise, "[s]he was then taken instead to an orchard, where she was forced to drink alcohol and was raped by four men. This was all video-taped. The agents threatened to send the video to her husband, who would most likely kill her. . . . She began her career by 'recruiting' three friends through the same practice—pretending to take each of them to a house to visit a friend."[142] Increased fear and brutality corrupt women who have, then, no loyalty to other women. For women sexually abused as children, often trained by the abusers to barter sexual access, prostitution and promiscuity are likely futures. For girls sold into prostitution and pornography, the future is a matter of a few short years. For women burned alive in India or jailed and raped in Pakistan or gang-raped in the urban ghettos of the United States being born female was the crime for which they are being punished. For women subject to murder by a brother for shaming the family or segregated or confined, there is nowhere to turn. For girls who are mutilated by female circumcision—who have to be sewed and unsewed—there is the tyranny of unintended consequences: pain, infection, difficulty urinating, and anal assault when the husband is too lazy or too urgent to navigate vaginal penetration; there is internal bleeding, damage to reproductive organs from infection; there is no sexual pleasure from the clitoris because it has been excised. For women who are murdered by their husbands—from battered women escaping the man's domicile in the United States to dowry murders in kitchens in India—there is no social grief, no determination to protect the next one and the one after that. For women who are murdered by serial killers—often raped or tortured, almost always mutilated—there are often no names—they disappear (through kidnapping), are raped, tortured, mutilated, sometimes even cannibalized, killed, and the bodies are cut up and buried or just buried: in the U.S. there are killing fields, too, inhabited mostly by murdered prostitutes; serial killers sometimes reveal where some of them are buried.

Women know how to fight or fight back in nationalist conflict when they are part of a male group. In Western culture women stand for freedom; as Patterson writes in his epic study of freedom: "In all Greek drama, both tragic and comic, women stand powerfully, and exclusively, for personal independence, for the voice of individual conscience against personal and political tyranny, for universal and natural, as distinct from man-made, justice, and for the freedom to worship their gods and love whom they choose to love."[143] Women's lives were outside of history, outside of citizenship: intensely brave because the margins are always danger-ous. One has theater, not history; one has Antigone, Medea, Cassandra, Lysistrata.

In the Nazi time, women were still outside of history, their brilliance and strength noted by historians who had been sentenced by Hitler to death. Emanuel Ringelblum, the historian of the Warsaw ghetto, wrote: "The historian of the future who will write about the events of our days will have to devote a special page to the Jewish woman and her place in this war. The Jewish woman has assumed a special chapter in Jewish history. In the abyss of darkness she was a pillar of strength and courage."[144] Yet the phallocentric history was written, even though it was a history of bitter defeat. Simon Wiesenthal who, unlike Ringelblum, survived, wrote: "Women active in the underground movements were the bravest of the brave, ignoring every danger to reach their aim or to die in dignity. They knew well that the odds were against them, but they felt as much as the men the responsibility to resist the oppressors and to leave a message to those who came after them: life is worth living only when lived in freedom, and this freedom is worth dying for."[145] As Laska wrote in *Women in the Re-sistance and in the Holocaust:* "Some of the best safe-houses were brothels and convents."[146]

Ravensbrück, a concentration camp established in May 1939 for women and Gypsies, became "an international prison for female 'politi-cals' from all over Europe. The politicals—as distinguished from the 'racials' such as Jews or Gypsies—were women who were considered dan-gerous to Nazi aims: members of the resistance movements in various countries or members of their families; secret radio operators and messen-gers; female parachutists; Socialists and Communists; patriotic women who harbored Jews; downed Allied pilots or other fugitives . . .; women caught with illegal pamphlets in their possession or overheard expressing anti-Nazi opinions; women denounced [because] they had been listening to the London radio; hundreds of women accused of sabotaging the Ger-man war effort; and numerous bystanders . . . There was also a sprinkling [*sic*] of professional criminals, murderers, thieves and prostitutes . . . Only a small fraction of the 123,000 women who passed through the hell that was Ravensbrück were there because they were Jewish."[147]

Laska especially singles out the British women who had volunteered for the British Special Operations Executive (SOE): "They engaged in sabotage, subversion and escape operations in Belgium, Poland, Yu-goslavia and elsewhere. Fifty of them were flown or parachuted into

France. Of the fifty, fifteen fell into German hands. Ten were executed by shooting or injections of poison: four in Dachau, three in Natzweler and three in Ravensbrück . . . One each died in Ravensbrück and Bergen-Belsen; three survived Ravensbrück."[148] The four British women in Dachau were executed on September 12, 1944; they were "kneeling down and holding hands,"[149] then shot through the back of the neck; "[a]ll were between twenty-seven and thirty-three years of age."[150] In the one uprising that took place in Auschwitz "explosives were smuggled in by Jewish women workers from a factory to the Birkenau camp."[151] All the resisters were killed. There was also another kind of defiance described by Sala Kaye (Bernholz) in Martin Gilbert's badly named *The Boys: The Untold Story of 732 Young Concentration Camp Survivors:* "Sharing one of the bunks near ours was a young woman from Lodz. Before the war she had been a pharmacist. After we saved my mother from going to the gas chambers, the woman turned to us and said, 'Mengele is not going to get me.' That very day she ran out to the wires and electrocuted herself. She was burned. Her hands were black. She was hanging on the wires until they took her down. Nobody cried, we were all numb."[152] A male survivor, protected as a child by a Catholic nun, asked: "What had she been like? Was there anything about her that might explain her outstanding courage? What made her endanger herself, the rest of the nuns, and the entire orphanage in order to save a few Jewish children?"[153]

Why are the heroic dimensions of the lives of women ignored, overlooked, subordinated to the sexualization of women: what does she look like? who does she sleep with? is she pretty? how can I get into her pants? In the segregated U.S. South, African American women were the heart of the struggle—from Rosa Parks (and the pregnant teenage girl who preceded her in refusing to sit in the back of the bus) to Fanny Lou Hamer: it is postulated that "[i]n many communities, women stepped into movement leadership because in the South at that time it was simply too dangerous for a black man to stand up to the system. He would lose his job, possibly his life."[154] That may be true for leadership positions, since the role of women in political movements was still one of doing the most pedestrian labor; but in the civil rights movement—as in most movements not based directly on violence—women risked life, liberty, and physical safety in the course of organizing, communicating, and demonstrating. These same women sustained their loved ones: men and children; fed them, embraced them, did the hard work of housekeeping and laundry and making or mending clothes; there were not machines to stand in for them or money for store-bought necessities. In Mississippi, "[t]he fact that the Student Non-Violent Coordinating Committee and not Martin Luther King's Southern Christian Leadership Conference was the most visible presence . . . enhanced women's roles as well. Ministers—men—dominated SCLS while SNCC and its political offshoots . . . relied on grass-roots people. Where there were grass roots, there were women."[155]

In an opposite universe, Saudi Arabia, women demonstrated against male dominance at the time of the Gulf War by breaking "an informal ban" on driving: "They were women of the middle class, women who were teachers of other women or students—our thinkers and doers. As a result of their bravery, their lives were devastated by their actions: passports taken, jobs lost, and families harassed."[156] There is a persistent rumor that one of the participants was killed by her own family for disgracing them: "[T]o this day, her fate has not been denied or confirmed; it hangs over us women, a veiled threat of the ultimate sacrifice awaiting those with courage."[157] The suppression of women in Saudi Arabia is egregious, a gender-apartheid cruel enough and brutal enough to match the race-apartheid that had been practiced in South Africa. But the international human rights community will not organize to destroy gender-apartheid; oil trumps the lives of women and there is no conscience or regret in leaving Saudi women as an imprisoned population. The world blocks it out: does not acknowledge the ferocity of the oppression. Which country or human rights organization has demanded proof that the demonstrator or demonstrators are still alive? What is to be done?

The women in Moscow when the Soviet Union came apart led the physical resistance to the Soviet military: "The front line of the Moscow resistance was a chain of women holding hands. They made a cordon across the far end of the Kalinin Bridge, looking up the dark boulevard along which the tanks would come. Every few minutes, somewhere in the distance, tank engines rumbled and bellowed and then fell quiet again. Behind the women, who were both young and old, stood an anxious support group of husbands, lovers and brothers with flasks of tea, transistor radios and cigarettes. When I asked the women why they stood there, and why they were not afraid, they answered: 'Because we are mothers.'"[158] This is not a rhetorical or empty answer. Like the grassroots women in segregated Mississippi they kept their families alive through the hard work of women's work; they endured the pain of childbirth; in this act of courage they took the kind of responsibility for their country that they had always taken for their families; in an earlier era of Soviet history,

Akhmatova along with other women sustained sons and husbands who were imprisoned: and many Soviet prisoners, of course, were women. Akhmatova had another kind of courage as well: "In 1962 I completed *A Poem without a Hero,* which I had been writing for twenty-two years."[159] Are the women holding hands to stop the tanks in history yet? Are the women outside the prison in history?

In the West, historians rarely find the political actions of women interesting, perhaps because these actions are not generally characterized by violence. Violence does get their attention and so historians do remember that a mob of women rioted and demonstrated in an early and generative moment in the French Revolution when "5,500 women gathered at the City Hall in Paris; they forced their way inside, procured arms, and enjoined the National Guard to accompany them. They marched to Versailles, a day's journey on foot, to demand that bread be made available in Paris and at a reasonable price. This action inaugurated and carried out largely by women led to the immediate result of capturing the king, of removing the royal family permanently from Versailles and bringing them as virtual prisoners to Paris."[160] There were many contemporaneous accounts in writing of this riot and long march of women for bread; these "graphic accounts" reflected "a double fear of mob rule and the rule of women. Male witnesses expressed an archetypal fear of women as hysterical furies, while women witnesses did not want to be identified with those furies in any way."[161] A modern guerrilla fighter noted the importance of being armed: "I think that with arms you can cut out all this work, get through it all and get results very quickly."[162] Time was her argument; but there was also a visibility argument—guns are always seen even if women are not. In *Shoot the Women First,* a study of women in guerrilla movements, Eileen MacDonald suggests that "[w]omen, perhaps more than men, appear to appreciate the power of the weapon and the authority it gives them."[163] It is also true that a sustained and authentic commitment to nonviolence—bearing witness, exemplary acts, civil disobedience, strategic demonstrations in hostile territory or at the scene of a political crime, marches and training, attention at the grassroots level to literacy and health in particular—can create change way beyond the comprehension of the complacent. Both armed and nonviolent rebellion require sacrifice and courage; but so does being a woman anywhere any day of the week. Why is it that women do not go the distance in behalf of women; or she with others in behalf of herself?

One must discard ideological and political biological determinism;

refuse to be compromised by the false logic leading from a trait to a social status; as Todorov writes in *On Human Diversity: Nationalism, Racism, and Exoticism in French Thought,* "If we were to assume that the human races are unequally endowed, it would not follow that they do not have the same rights (and indeed this is how we treat differences in physical strength, which for their part are undeniable)."[164]

One must grasp the dynamics of the oppression; as Bell writes in *The Irish Troubles: A Generation of Violence 1967–1992,* "And the rebels always know the three great things: what is wrong, what is wanted, and what must be done."[165] In addition, he says, "[a]ll armed struggles arise from simple, easily expressed ideas that, no matter how rigorous or rich for the philosophers, can be written on banners and sprayed on walls. All struggles offer stereotypes and symbols; most of all they offer an opportunity for the young [to be] absolute in their commitment, emboldened by their own dedication, to sacrifice. This is one of the enormous attractions of a life underground—not the gun or the power, not even the risk of danger, but the sacrifice . . ."[166] Women have been half-hearted, divided by race and nation but also lacking rigor: what is wrong has been defined as inequality; what is wanted has been defined as equality with men; what must be done is a short list that amounts to whatever they will allow.

In discussion with Ramin Jahanbegloo, published as *Conversations with Isaiah Berlin,* Berlin does the hard work of defining equality: "Equality is always specific. Let me give an instance, if you have ten children, and you want to give each a piece of cake, if you give one child two slices and the next child none, for no good reason, this offends against the principle of equality. That is what 'unfair' means."[167] The failure, then, of liberal feminism is transparently clear: some have two slices, some have none; some have the money to pay for an abortion, some do not; some have shelter, even homes, some do not; some have food, some do not; some have health care, some do not; some can read, some cannot. Actor Peter Coyote in his memoir of the sixties, *Sleeping Where I Fall,* examines what he calls "the insufficiencies of liberalism: the generosity toward others that is predicated on first sustaining one's own privilege."[168] Some have enough, some do not.

Political conservatives in the United States, following Edmund Burke, claim that freedom and equality are incompatible; they blame Marxist-Leninism and Stalinism for mass murder that they claim is a direct result of a politics of equality; the same for the French Revolution, which is what aroused Burke to the epic dangers of equality. Berlin says: ". . . one of my

convictions is that some moral, social and political values conflict. I cannot
conceive of any world in which certain values can be reconciled. . . . You
cannot combine full liberty with full equality—full liberty for the wolves
cannot be combined with full liberty for the sheep. Justice and mercy,
knowledge and happiness can collide."[169] This seems truer than the absolutist repudiation of equality with which conservatives are so comfortable.
Are women sheep ("led like sheep to the slaughter")? Must women become
wolves? Is violence against women a direct result of the fact that there is no
inevitable, painful, retaliatory consequence for hurting women? Are
women weak Jews?

Do women need sovereignty—not only over their own bodies as currently understood in the United States (the right to choose, a happy euphemism for the abortion right); but control of a boundary further away
from their bodies, a defended boundary? Do women need land and an
army, as Phyllis Chesler has repeatedly argued; or a feminist government
in exile, an idea Chesler has articulated often and provocatively? Or is it
simpler: the bed belongs to the woman; the house belongs to the woman;
any land belongs to the woman; if a male intimate is violent he is removed
from the place where she has the superior and inviolate claim, arrested,
denied parole, and prosecuted. Moshe Dayan said in a 1955 lecture to Israeli Defense Force officers: "We cannot guard every water pipeline from
explosion and every tree from uprooting. We cannot prevent every murder of a worker in an orchard or a family in their beds. But it is in our
power to set a high price on our blood, a price too high for the Arab community, the Arab army, or the Arab governments to think it worth paying."[170] Is that a good idea? Could women "set a high price on our blood"?
Could women set any price on our blood? Could women manage self-defense if not retaliation? Would self-defense be enough? Could women execute men who raped or beat or tortured women? Could a woman
execute the man or men who raped or beat or tortured her?

Could women be inside history? Could the acts of women in behalf of
women count, be written down, provide a moral history that disavows
triviality, have a code of honor woman-to-woman that weakens the male-
dominant demands of nationalism or race-pride or ethnic pride? Could
women commit treason to the men of their own group: put women first,
even the putative enemy women? Do women have enough militancy and
self-respect to see themselves as the central makers of legal codes, ethics,
honor codes, and culture? How can women be heroes: except that women
always have been? Can a woman use her own will to exist, to cancel out

the nonbeing crushing her from the oppressor's culture, religion, propaganda—from his lies about her nature, her incapacities, from his perception of her as a moral idiot? As Anderson writes in *Guerrillas: The Men and Women Fighting Today's Wars,* "The process of self-invention is vital, providing the guerrillas with a bonding ethos, a powerful impetus to persevere in their struggles. Without a past—or, like the displaced Palestinians and Saharawis, even a home—there is no future either, and so the guerrillas must at least possess their own histories. Accurate or mythified, these histories are the repositories of their cultural identities, as essential to their struggles as the weapons with which they fight."[171]

But won't women become just like them? If women even consider the questions of aggression and identity that implicate violence as a political strategy, won't I, asks woman after woman, be just like them? As Jonathan Shay writes in *Achilles in Vietnam: Combat Trauma and the Undoing of Character:* ". . . I shall argue what I've come to strongly believe through my work with Vietnam veterans: that moral injury is an essential part of any combat trauma that leads to lifelong psychological injury. Veterans can usually recover from horror, fear, and grief once they return to a civilian life, so long as 'what's right' has not also been violated."[172] Women have combat trauma without fighting; women are fought against and "what's right" is always violated: thus, women live with horror, fear, and grief. Suppose that in the United States twenty men were killed on the same day. Each one had raped or incested or beaten or tortured or pimped or killed one woman or girl or many. Some of the targets were famous—pornographers, for instance—but most were not. There were police reports or hospital reports on the violent acts committed against a woman or women; or there had been a trial from which a transparently guilty man had walked away free. Could women commit even such a small and thoughtful (seriously considered) act of earned retribution? What would happen to the impunity from consequences men count on? How seriously would this violence be taken by the FBI and local police? Would there be a collective heart attack and fierce efforts to find and convict the killers? Could women bear the taking of life as a step toward freedom from systematic and often intimate male violence? As Sofsky says in *The Order of Terror: The Concentration Camp,* "Just as there is no collective guilt, there can be no collective innocence."[173] He defines collective crimes as "individual crimes in a collective."[174]

Could women accept the responsibility of standing up for the dead—the women killed in war or in marriage or by serial killers? Could women have a sense of honor that applied not only to the living but also to the dead; could women say us and mean women, living or dead? In *Photocopies* John Berger describes Mexico's Zapatistas: "The Zapatistas have no political program to impose; they have a political conscience which they hope will spread through their example. The excess comes from their conviction (which personally I accept completely) that they also represent the dead, all the maltreated dead . . . No mystics, they believe in words being handed down through the suffering and the centuries, and they hate lies . . ."[175] Could women make words that weep tears for all the crimes down through the centuries? Could women find it impossible to continue to bear the crimes?

Could women fight for the liberation of women? Why has sexual liberation existed without context as a practice and a goal: without the context of poverty or homelessness or unwanted sex or unwanted children; why will an orgasm make poverty or homelessness or unwanted sex or unwanted children all right; how does sexual liberation free women from material deprivation or illiteracy or bad health care or the insult of being subordinated, including in consensual sex? Should African American men in urban ghettos in the United States just fuck more and then they will be free or have what they need: education or jobs or civil dignity?

Could women's liberation ever be a revolutionary movement, not rhetorically but on the ground? Henry Kissinger says: "What is a revolutionary? If the answer to that question were without ambiguity, few revolutionaries would ever succeed. For revolutionaries almost always start from a position of inferior strength. They prevail because the established order is unable to grasp its own vulnerability."[176] Male dominance does not comprehend its own vulnerability—with genitals on the outside, easy to attack; men do not understand how their own dominance works—but women do, or can. Can women analyze male dominance? Can women attack it where it is vulnerable? Can women make use of men's vulnerability not to marry but instead to destroy male power? Can women decide that rape will be stopped? Can women strategize to stop rape? Can women organize across lines of male enmity to stop rape and battery and incest? Israeli and Palestinian feminists try hard to work together: there is one battered women's shelter that in 1988 was the only place in Israel that Palestinian and Israeli children were being educated together: beautiful children, dispossessed—child and mother, Arab and Jew—by violent men; and there was one rape crisis center that employed a plastic surgeon to restore the hymen for Palestinian girls and women who had been raped; otherwise, the girls and women risked death. Surely if it can happen there it can happen anywhere.

Can women in each country or culture figure out how male dominance is organized specifically against them, find the vulnerabilities in the arrangement of systematic power: use books, use bodies: make that system break? Can women include children in the struggle: they too must have enumerated rights, legal protection from exploitation and murder— they must have food and shelter, literacy and health care. As Simpson writes in *The Splendid Blond Beast: Money, Law, and Genocide in the Twentieth Century:* ". . . the present world order has institutionalized persecution and deprivation of hundreds of millions of children, particularly in the Third World, and in this way kills countless innocents each year. These systematic atrocities are for the most part not even regarded as crimes, but instead are written off by most of the world's media and intellectual leadership as acts of God or of nature whose origin remains a mystery."[177] Can women fight for these hundreds of millions of children, each other's children? In political and economic terms, women and children travel together: one cannot be free without the other. What will women do? Is there a plan? And if not, why not?

10

MEMORY/DENIAL

In *The Politics of Memory: Looking for Germany in the New Germany*, Jane Kramer writes that "Berliners have a joke about the three most overcrowded boats in history being Noah's Ark, the Mayflower, and the German Resistance in the Second World War . . ."[1] There are many Jewish jokes about anti-Semitism but is there even one Jewish joke about the Holocaust? The question is: why do the survivors, not the perpetrators, feel shame? Why is shame a basic dynamic of memory for the survivors while perpetrators frame forgetting most often with indifference or self-pity? Nazi-era emigrant Walter Laqueur, a Jew, visited some of his contemporaries—"my classmates and the other friends of my boyhood"[2]—as an adult: "There was a striking uniformity to their fate: They truly felt victims of the war, having lost the best years of their lives, as well as their homes in East Germany and, in quite a few cases, their families."[3] War is hell; but war is not the only hell. Writing about the shame of the survivors, Primo Levi says that "many (including me) experienced 'shame,' that is, a feeling of guilt during the imprisonment and afterward . . . It may seem absurd, but it is a fact."[4] In part, says Levi, "one suffered because of the reacquired consciousness of having been diminished . . . we have lived for months and years at an animal level: our days had been encumbered from dawn to dusk by hunger, fatigue, cold, and fear, and any space for reflection, reasoning, experiencing emotions was wiped out. We endured filth, promiscuity, and destitution, suffering much less than we would have suffered from such things in normal life, because our moral yardstick had changed . . . all of us had stolen: in the kitchen, the factory, the camp . . . Some (few) had fallen so low as to steal bread from their own companions. We had not only forgotten our country and our culture, but also our family, our past, the future we had imagined for ourselves, because, like animals, we were confined to the present moment."[5]

Survival is essentially experienced as complicity with the perpetrator—what one has done to live convicts one of dishonor and ignominity. This shame requires no treasonous collaboration. The shame is in wanting to live and then the shame is in living. In the differently constructed hell of the Argentinean junta, to survive was to be convicted of complicity in the eyes of others: "In every case, you are the living symbol of everything society rejects. Dead or alive you can't win. In our Constitution, torture is a crime; but in the minds of many, surviving torture is also a crime, or implies a crime. I didn't give them any information, but they didn't torture me for as long as they tortured some others. The dynamic is finally mysterious. They found subtle ways to break people. Some who held up on the grill were suddenly collaborating three months later. How do you explain that? Please. No one could *determine* to live. They stripped us of that power. We who did survive are the emissaries of the horror. The horror. That too society rejects."[6] Even if imprisonment, torture, and death are both collective and all encompassing, as in Auschwitz, death itself, as John Berger writes, "is singular. No death includes another death."[7] Surely this must be true, and, if so, is this why outsiders never understand—because no matter how many millions, each death is singular and nothing can change that?

"The human hand and pen are weary of describing all that has happened to a handful of Jews who are for the time being still alive, myself among them," wrote Abraham Lewin in his Warsaw ghetto diary September 11, 1942. "The cup of our sorrows has no parallel in our history."[8] In *our* history; in Jewish history, with no small number of murdered in other killing sprees; *the cup of our sorrows has no parallel in our history* has nothing to do with how many in the end were murdered by the Nazis; nor with the terror of the death camps. This was life apprehending the imminence of death; but still living.

Death is the opposite in absolute terms and no life, however close it comes to death, ever comprehends it. "There is something else lurking behind her eyes," write Rena Kornreich Gelissen and Heather Dune Macadam in *Rena's Promise: A Story of Sisters in Auschwitz*. "It isn't dying she's afraid of, but I'm not sure which fear is possessing her. 'What is it you're really afraid of?' 'Being thrown in the truck. . . . They treat us like rotten meat . . . I don't want to be discarded like that, thrown onto the flatbeds . . . Maybe there won't be enough gas, and I'll go into the crematorium still alive . . . What if they're trying to conserve the gas?'"[9] Of being pushed toward death by the Nazi death machine, at once systematized and chaotic, a twelve-year-old child, Janina Heshele, writes: "I begin to understand why my fellow victims go to their death without resistance. I have lost the desire to exist and feel a deep disgust for living. . . . "[10]

Then there were the suicides, in the ghettos, in the camps, and for survivors in the long years after. In the ghetto, says Ana Novac in *The Beautiful Days of My Youth: My Six Months in Auschwitz and Plaszow,* "there was a rush to suicide, a veritable epidemic, which was reserved for the *rich,* because the cyanide that people brought in—God knows how— commanded phenomenal prices. To die before being piled up in the railroad cars was the supreme luxury . . . "[11]

In the broad sweep of her life, Novac was "born in Transylvania, a region that three peoples—Rumanian, Hungarian, and German—have argued over in three languages for centuries. That is why, except for an accident of birth (the fact that I am Jewish), I have never been able to specify precisely either my nationality or my native language. I came into the world under a fascist dictatorship, spent my youth under a communist dictatorship, and between the two, for a change of pace, I did a tour at Auschwitz and seven other concentration camps."[12] Suicide was defiance even if it was also despair: "On the evening of July 23 [, 1942], the ninth day of Av—the day of mourning commemorating the destruction of the Holy Temple in Jerusalem and the exile of the Jewish people—Czerniakow completed the ninth book of his diary. To continue writing, he would have had to open a new book. Instead, that very same day he swallowed cyanide. There were no words of warning, only a final tragic confession of failure: 'The SS wants me to kill children with my own hands.'"[13] It was more common for Jews in the ghettos to resist with an eloquent nonviolent suicide: " . . . the style of resistance for the ghetto dwellers remained that of Arthur Rosenzweig, who, when asked in June to make a list of thousands for deportation, had placed his own name, his wife's, his daughter's at the top."[14] As Hilberg writes in *Perpetrators, Victims, Bystanders: The Jewish Catastrophe 1933–1945:* "In the death camps, a reprieve was exceptional. It was granted to those who could perform work, some of it skilled and much of it heavy . . . In this selection, fewer women than men were spared from immediate gassing. Possibly a third of the Jews who survived Auschwitz were women. In the other camps, where inmate forces were small and survivors mere handfuls, women disappeared. Only a few escaped Treblinka and Sobibor. None emerged from Belzec and Kulmhof."[15] Primo Levi, well respected for his high intellect and his human sensibility, says that he "had deeply assimilated the principal rule of the place [Auschwitz], which made it mandatory that you take care of yourself first of all."[16] He quotes a woman doctor, Ella Lingens-Reiner, who, in her book, *Prisoners of Fear,* claimed: "How was I able to survive Auschwitz? My principle is: I come first, second, and third. Then nothing, then again I; and then all the others"[17]—but the woman doctor, he says, "regardless of her own statement, proved to be generous and brave and saved many lives."[18] Saving many lives could not have been easy; but maybe the woman doctor was thinking of herself more than she would have in normal life, so she appeared, to herself, ruthless; while Levi and the men in the camp, who had put themselves first in normal life without much thought or self-consciousness, operated with a heightened individualism, a new and dreadful solitude. The ethic of women in the camps, generally, could be encapsulated in this one moment of memory from Gelissen and Macadam: "Adele is thrown onto the flatbeds with the rest of the women, but she turns to help those behind her. Her chin still tilts with courage and dignity. She is not afraid. Her arm encircles a weaker girl whose knees are failing her. The trucks spew their exhaust as they head for the gas chambers."[19]

This grace wins women nothing in the post-Holocaust world. In *Kaddish* Leon Wieseltier asks: "May a woman say kaddish? It is a controversial question. It sounds to some like a feminist provocation. But ask the question differently. May a daughter say kaddish? Suddenly the controversy disappears, at least for me. If you deny kaddish to a daughter, then you do not understand the kaddish. The kaddish is not an obligation of gender. It is an obligation of descent. This is not about men, this is about sons. This is not about women, this is about daughters."[20] Women have been daughters for a long time now: women, from women born, just like boys; and surely the old rabbis might have noticed. The condescension in the question and then in the unsubtle answer trivializes the humanity and dignity of every murdered woman and girl—and the hearts that did not go cold: the camp sisters; the women gathering to talk about the food they had back home to stave off starvation itself; the hands held; the meager food shared; the arm, encircling a weaker girl. This is not a hallucinated or ideologically driven perception of difference, though the difference may well be a socially inculcated one. The continuing exclusion of Jewish women from religious equality and of Israeli women from civil equality is indefensible: inclusion is an obligation of descent. The shame, of course, al-

ways belonged with the perpetrators; but the continuing casual cruelty toward women gives a share of the shame to the children of the survivors
and the community that tries—in buildings and monuments and museums—to speak for the dead.

Women know shame; it is, one might say, mother's milk. From footbinding in China to female genital mutilation in vast parts of Africa and the
Middle East to the ways in which mothers withhold love from girls who
do not conform in thought or deed in the West, the mother is the instrument of male power. Her job is to keep girls (daughters) entirely concen-
trated on the body: pain steals concentration and consciousness; and girls
learn pain early in grooming and remaking the body. A girl's body is her
life. What does it mean: to want to survive, in a female body? Why is
shame part of the identity of most women under male, not Nazi, rule?
Holocaust survivor Ruth Elias writes: "In a way, my persecutors have succeeded: Memories of their deeds continue to pursue me. To escape this
feeling, at least in part, I keep running. Ever since my time in the camps I
have been hurrying onward, moving forward without much thought or
reflection. Running, always running. I am convinced that I have lost out
on much that is beautiful because I could never stop long enough to get
deeply involved in some of the things I would have liked to do."[21] Running, running, still pursued in nightmares and flashbacks, hurrying onward, forward, running: many, if not most, women who have survived
incest, prostitution, rape, battery, and pornography could say the same
words, and those words would have the same meaning. Because of the
global trafficking in women and children, mostly girls, there will be millions upon millions more: sold or solicited or incested as children, hungry
and homeless, kidnapped and kept, a shadow army of the raped.

   In the United States, with its history of race slavery and segregation,
blacks, especially men, were lynched; these are the known figures: "From
1882 to 1968, 4,743 people were lynched; the vast majority were black.
During the peak lynching years, 1889–1918, the five most active states
were Georgia (360), Mississippi (350), Louisiana (264), Texas (263), and
Alabama (244). In 1892, 200 lynchings occurred in a single year. These
numbers include only the recorded lynchings."[22] The punishment is in
the body and of the body because the crime is in the body: being black.
Race is simply an easy way to euphemize the real nature of the crime: we

will attack, assault, beat, batter, mutilate, torture, castrate, kill your body, because your body is the offense. How can *Black is beautiful* stand up against an animus inflicted however many times on the black body because it is perceived to be black? What remedy can stand up against this history? As Toni Morrison writes in *Playing in the Dark: Whiteness and the Literary Imagination:* "Africanism is the vehicle by which the American self knows itself as not enslaved, but free; not repulsive, but desirable; not helpless, but licensed and powerful; not history-less, but historical; not damned, but innocent; not a blind accident of evolution, but a progressive fulfillment of destiny."[23] Morrison's great leap, which is a fundamental premise of her nonfiction work, is to claim the black experience as the fundamental experience of the American as such. "There is no romance," she writes, "free of what Herman Melville called 'the power of blackness,' especially not in a country in which there was a resident population, already black, upon which the imagination could play; through which historical, moral, metaphysical, and social fears, problems, and dichotomies could be articulated."[24]

A crime against the existence of a body per se cannot be argued away. But, as Edward Said says in *Peace and Its Discontents: Essays on Palestine in the Middle East Peace Process,* "In the history of colonial invasion maps are always first drawn by the victors, since maps are instruments of conquest. Geography is therefore the art of war but can also be the art of resistance if there is a counter-map and a counter-strategy."[25] Said's meaning may have been literal but map and counter-map are also figurative; one can write a map on the body by assaulting it. *Black is beautiful* was an attempt to redraw the map.

Women of all races and in all places also need to be beautiful, but the contradiction is built into the demand: her body may be foul, loathsome, stinky, dirty, bloody, and her genitals may suggest an unbearable internality, a viscous, muscled tunnel; but she can remake that repulsive body by breaking some bones, removing body hair, soft- or hard-core mutilation or surgery. These procedures along with various kinds of segregation and absence make her body, finally, ownable: but not by her; never by her. What kind of shame is there in wanting to survive in such a body? Is there enough self-punishment to match the ever present male-inflicted punishments: can she wish her body away by starving or, alternatively, make the men go away by fat—these being the strategies that are culturally Western? With the woman, as with the black, as with the Jew in the Nazi era, crimes are targeted against the body simply because it is perceived to be

female; it is a body already disdained; it brings punishment on itself because of its inescapable nature. The shame is in wanting to live and therefore submitting. The shame is in endlessly negotiating incursions into
one's own body: all surrender. The shame is in restriction, belittlement,
insult. The shame is in being complicitous even if one is fighting for one's
own life; the more endangered one is, the more complicitous one feels:
the more ashamed. The shame is in having an invisible life even as the
body itself can be appropriated by visual colonialization: the so-called
male gaze, often with accompanying verbal aggression. The complicity is
in being watched and at the same time never hurting back; or, being internally invaded by force and never hurting the invader(s) in self-defense,
revenge, or retaliation.

Women's liberation tried to draw a new map of the female body in the
world, each tiny line in the uncompleted new map paid for: sometimes in
blood or poverty or exile or the more abject currency—celebration of
things as they are, louder and louder still, women driven into apology, the
body apologizes, the face is invisible, covered by makeup or veil or the
body becomes more skeletal to show a purposeful self-hate, again celebrated: the so-called beauty deepens the shame. The pornography of a
woman's body is not unrelated to lynching: using the body as spectacle.
As David Mamet writes in his novel *The Old Religion* about Leo Frank, a
Jew convicted of raping a young Christian woman in Atlanta: "They covered his head, and they ripped his pants off and castrated him and hung
him from the tree. A photographer took a picture showing the mob, one
boy grinning at the camera, the body hanging, the legs covered by a blan-
ket tied around the waist. The photo, reproduced as a postcard, was sold
for many years in stores throughout the South."[26] This is the public celebration of a socially legitimized killing: Frank the Jew becomes the ultimate exotic body—he was fat, he was circumcised; postcards sold of the
lynching; suppose there had been a growing market for photographs of
lynchings and castrations and the easy, cheap technology to make and distribute them so that, for the sake of profit and expression, one had to have
not 4,743 lynchings in eighty-six years but rather hundreds of thousands
or, globally, millions—and not only white over black.

The despoiling of the woman's body also serves as political vandalism,
a harassment not culturally specific: in Saudi Arabia, Filipino women
working as maids are attacked: "A group of religious men struck her with
a stick and sprayed her uncovered legs with red paint. . . . If a woman
[working in the country] is so bold as to defy our traditions by exposing

uncovered arms or legs, she runs the risk of being struck and sprayed with paint. This maid had soaked her legs in paint remover, but they were still red and raw-looking."[27] The same kind of harassment was used in Northern Ireland by the IRA: "A pregnant woman from Ballymurphy in Belfast was painted, beaten, feathered, tied to a lamppost, and given forty-eight hours to leave her home."[28]

When the crime is in the body, the assault will be on or in the body, which is why being persecuted or tortured for one's beliefs is a step up from injury for just existing as such; being hurt or humiliated for that reason alone has no obvious discourse of refutation. In *No Passion Spent: Essays 1978–1995,* George Steiner attacks the philosopher Simone Weil, who starved herself to death in protesting the violence of World War II: "In Weil's detestation of her own ethnic identity, in her strident denunciations of the cruelty and 'imperialism' of the God of Abraham and of Moses, in her very nearly hysterical repugnance in the face of what she termed the excess of Judaism, in the Catholicism she, finally, refused to join, the traits of Jewish self-loathing are carried to a fever pitch. . . . Worst of all . . . is her refusal to envisage, in the very midst of her eloquent pathos in respect of suffering and injustice, the horrors, the anathema being enacted on her own people."[29] But what strikes one about Weil's chosen protest is how female it is: all violence directed against the self and in particular against her corporeality: she knows that underlying the violence in the world is the punishment of Jew, woman, for the crime of existing; her spirituality, easily definable as Catholic without any need for institutional authority, is based on self-denial, the slow but purposeful erasure of the body to refute guilt. She knew that she incarnated the provocation for the violence in the world as it was; to stop the violence she erased the provocation, which was her bodily existence. Her act, while appearing unique, is acted out by U.S. teenagers who have no philosophy to write, no war to survive—how can they live with the shame of having a female body but to try to erase it? How can they be something other than the provocation in the female body except by erasing the body itself? How can they be loved if they exist? The more visible the female body is in the public domain, the deeper the shame.

Where the female body is hidden, in many Arab countries, that body animates political life; as in the West, most women betray women. "The role of women," writes Judith Miller in *God Has Ninety-nine Names: Reporting from a Militant Middle East,* "in Saudi Arabia's reactionary culture—as well as a woman's place in most Arab societies—was at the heart of the Arab obsession with *ird* (honor). Almost no other single issue was so politically sensitive. The women's driving protest had polarized Saudi society, but not along gender lines: Most Saudi women and men were equally outraged by the protest. More than two thousand female students at King Saud University had signed a petition declaring that they did not want to drive."[30] Were they coerced into signing? The feminist underground—more reliable than the FBI or CIA—says they were. The Saudi women drivers had used their bodies to trespass—a sort of mobile sit-in; afterward, they were punished, one reputedly murdered, and disowned by other women who declared an abject desire not to trespass: celebration of the veiled, segregated woman is no doubt also a consequence of the protesters' provocation—putting their bodies by their own will on male territory.

When Western feminists tried to redraw the map of the female body, the effort descended into mindless celebration of existing conventions in sex and grooming; not being able to redistribute power such that women were self-sovereign, partly because of the resistance of women. One makes the body clean by celebrating it; stands against shame by celebrating the existence of the offending body; or stands against shame by declaring the body dirty by will of a person, gendered female. Nothing changes. Contempt for the female body, deployed in differing cultural strategies, continues the rituals of shame whatever they are: "In order to reckon themselves among the ranks of the camp aristocracy, veteran prisoners had to go through a process of inner colonization. They turned aside from the world outside . . . [Inner-colonization] involved sealing off the field of consciousness against all events that could have posed a threat to a laboriously achieved success. In order to remain alive, the prisoners had to live in the camp. But to do that, they had to internalize its laws of survival."[31] The "lethal seriality"[32] of the camps had to be avoided by creating a distinction between an élite that "had to make sure they did not sink into the lower classes."[33] Surely, women try desperately, on different canvases, to rise above being the trash destined for the garbage heap: not of history, because women are still not in history: just real, nonmetaphorical garbage, the lowly and the prostituted, the poor and the abject. Auschwitz ("[f]or the survivor, all is always Auschwitz"[34]) stopped; incest did not.

If all value is in the body or all meaning or all significance, qualities of mind are disassociated from the stigmatized bodies; in the United States the myth of black intellectual inferiority still has the loyalty of some scholars. That same myth has a continuing legitimacy among populists, the fascist right, and the militias. When the inferiorized body insists on intelligence as a part of self-consciousness, the culture tries to eradicate evidence of the existence of the mind or any artifacts produced by intellect; the urban pathologies of black-on-black violence, abandoning women, and black-on-black gang rape happen on a terrain of muteness and invisibility. Because standards of literacy in particular are set by white men, the black men who meet or exceed those standards are faced with a moral and political dilemma now being defined by black conservatives; as Shelby Steele writes in *The Content of Our Character,* "We are in the odd and self-defeating position in which taking responsibility for bettering ourselves feels like a surrender to white power. So we have a hidden investment in victimization and poverty. These distressing conditions have been the source of our only real power, and there is an unconscious sort of gravitation toward them, a complaining celebration of them."[35] The price paid may be high; as Glenn Loury writes, "I now understand how this desire to be regarded as genuinely black, to be seen as a 'regular brother,' has dramatically altered my life. It narrowed the range of my earliest intellectual pursuits, distorted my relationships with other people, censored my political thought and expression, informed the way I dressed and spoke . . . I have learned that one does not have to live surreptitiously as a Negro among whites in order to be engaged in a denial of one's genuine self for the sake of gaining social acceptance. This is a price that blacks often demand of each other as well."[36]

Attach the female body to the black body—already done for black women; produce a synthesis, described by Doris Lessing in *African Laughter: Four Visits to Zimbabwe,* " . . . I . . . watched an Indian girl trying all afternoon to make her dark face lighter: she was about to meet a possible bridegroom. Before I had read the poems of an Arab who was praising the pearl-white skin, the milky-white skin, of his girl, for, he said, Europeans did not know what they were talking about, when they were proud of their 'white' skins. For real poetic whiteness, you need a girl who had been shut up in a shady room all her life, and never allowed near strong light."[37] Everywhere there are boundaries to keep the violable body invisible to itself (an indignity if perceived) and to cancel out qualities of mind. There are rules, rituals, tribal bonds, customs, definitions of male and female skewed by the history of race-hate, its effect on its victim; there is assimilation, submerging one's ties with the group, or there is defiance, reifying one's ties with the group, or there is rebellion, which can push in both directions: against the native group or against the group requiring assimilation.

There is an oppression model of existence (currently reduced in North American parlance to being synonymous with the word *victim*); or an assimilationist stance (I'm as good as you are, or better); or an individualist position (I am who I am). These were the choices Jews had in Europe; blacks have them in the United States, especially black men; women, white and black, light or dark, yellow or red, show compliance in the body, a giving in, a surrender accepting the stagnant boundaries of possibility; and a price is paid if the woman's body does not at one and the same time exhibit itself just so and achieve invisibility—intellect changes perception of the body, degrading, not enhancing, its value. The creative and intellectual work of women is easily usurped. (See Germaine Greer, *The Obstacle Course.*) Much of Brecht's celebrated work seems to be stolen, most (not all) from women; as one of his biographers, John Fuegi, writes in *Brecht & Co.: Sex, Politics, and the Making of the Modern Drama,* "I had no suspicion in 1965 that a great deal of the texts that I admired then and admire now were not written by Brecht. Only gradually, and in the face of steadily mounting evidence, did it begin to occur to me that it was possible that a number of Brecht's collaborators—usually, but not always, women—had often allowed their work to be published as his."[38] In particular: "It was, we know, *The Threepenny Opera* that first established and has maintained Brecht's name in the popular imagination. It now seems indisputable that at least 80 percent of that play was written by Elisabeth Hauptmann."[39] None of Brecht's literary collaborators fared as well as he did: "In East Germany and the Soviet Union, [Ernst] Ottwalt had been made a nonperson, an 'enemy of the people,' and had died in the gulag. Martin Pohl had been arrested by the East German secret police, the Stasi, and forced to sign a made-up 'confession' that he was a spy for 'American imperialists.' [Margarete] Steffin . . . had been left behind by Brecht in Moscow, where she died after having her work used by him for years . . . [Ruth] Berlau's work had also apparently been stolen by Brecht, or so she had loudly claimed before she died in a fire in an East Berlin hospital."[40] In the cases of the women, this was sexual possession and as such required the erasure of the women by theft or abandonment. The invisibility of women is not noticed because who can argue that the great artist is not male? "To my mind," says Milan Kundera in *Testaments Betrayed: An Essay in Nine Parts,* "great works can only be born within the history of their art and as *participants* in that history. It is only inside history that we can see what is new and what is repetitive, what is discovery and what is imitation; in other words, only inside history can a work exist as a *value* capable of being discerned and judged. Nothing seems to me worse for art than to fall outside its own history, for it is a fall into the chaos where aesthetic values can no longer be perceived."[41]

That not only excludes women; it explains why the works of contemporary women so rarely are part of the public conversation or the geography of art itself. Invisibility requires debasement whereas art requires an oversized cognitive imagination, which then might be expressed in words or paint or music. The invisible crave literacy, as do the disparaged and the damned: "The last words recorded in the diary of Chaim Kaplan before he was deported to his death in Treblinka were, 'If I die—what will become of my diary?'"[42] The illiterate need the gift of language; but because they are outside art's history, invisible while fully corporeal, language betrays them: women are the great preponderance of the world's illiterates. The Gypsies stay outside of history because of their general illiteracy. According to Fonseca, "There are no words in Romani proper for 'to write' or 'to read.' Gypsies borrow from other languages to describe these activities. Or else, and more revealingly, they use other Romani words. *Chin* or 'cut' (as in carve), means 'to write.' The verb 'to read' is *gin*, which means 'to count.' But the common expression is *dav opre: dav opre* means 'I give up,' and so the phrase may be translated 'I read aloud.'"[43]

Laska says that little is known about the resistance activities of the Gypsies because of their illiteracy: "We know from a Belgian co-opted into a Gypsy family that both Gypsy men and women took part in the Western European resistance movement, successfully hiding and transporting resistance fighters and fugitives from German justice."[44] Any history is oral; as Fonseca says, "A long autobiographical ballad about hiding in the forests during the war is simply called 'Bloody Tears: What We Went Through Under the Germans in Volhynia in the Years 43 and 44'"; there is also reference to "Ashfitz."[45] To explain their origins and exile, "they tell of being condemned to wander for having denied succor to Joseph and Mary . . .; for having 'told' Judas to betray Christ; for being descendants of the miscreants who murdered the children of Bethlehem . . .; for having forged the nails used in the Crucifixion."[46] These are cursed activities, told in song and spoken prose; think of the Gypsies as Jews without writing.

The claiming of literacy—hard for the oppressed—has the deepest human meaning. As Declan Kiberd writes in *Inventing Ireland: The Literature of the Modern Nation:* "If colonialism is a system, so also is resistance. Post colonial writing, in a strict sense, began in Ireland when an artist like Seathrún Céitinn took pen in hand to rebut the occupier's claims. He had been reading those texts which misrepresented him, and he resolved to answer back"[47]—in Irish, not English. Even speaking the most beautiful English in the English-speaking world had the stain of collective misrepresentation, because it was the oppressor's language. For Irish politics and Irish rebellion, the cause of the indigenous language had to do with pride and distinction: and the notion that one's language expresses one's soul. The act of linguistic separation had a political meaning that helped the Irish stand up against the English. To even consider giving up a world language for a sectarian language is about as far as most of the writers went; but they continued to argue that an Irish citizen was illiterate without an Irish language. This fight concerning language also led to an increasing mythicization of history; as Bell says, "The mysterious Irish nation was the product of each failed generation overcome by new means of oppression, new betrayals, new lures for the apostates. History was the inevitable conflict that maintained the nation."[48]

Paraphrasing Freire, Feitlowitz goes to the heart of what the oppressed must achieve: "a rigorous process of confronting, analyzing, and committing to change the structural atrocities served up as normality, order. As one's own normality and order. It demands, precisely, the lucidity that oppression works to extinguish, the desiring passion that oppression works to kill."[49] (See also Paolo Freire, *The Pedagogy of the Oppressed.*) In the Argentinean tyranny, the junta had a "feminist" magazine, *Para Tí:* "The fashion pages often showed a military look, replete with epaulettes, brass buttons, berets, and sailor hats"; editorial writing declared: "We Argentine women will not be taken for idiots. *We have learned a new language, and have chosen a different road. . . . We are not the same as we were before.*"[50] A new language instead of no language; a discourse with the body that supported the junta: these were the so-called feminists of Argentina, or, more accurately, the publicly acknowledged ones.

Women pay for visibility with corruption: there and then; here and now. Literacy can mean lies; fashion can be venal. Literacy also steals meaning from the illiterate: as Yalom says, "It is not surprising that two-thirds of the women memorists [of the French Revolution] were aristocrats. At the time of the Revolution, only one out of two French subjects knew how to read, and only members of the upper class were able to write with ease . . . "[51] Literacy makes the world as a whole more knowable, even to the poor stuck in a common misery, even to the abject. Repeatedly, those whose bodies are stigmatized do not imagine what can be done to them; they live in a silence that keeps them from the language of their own lives because their imaginations cannot grasp the serial killer or the lyncher or the Nazi. Paz writes about the inability to imagine what one does not already know: "I still haven't mentioned the most serious, the really decisive factor: the psychological paralysis, the stupor that immobilized [Mesoamericans] when they encountered the Spaniards. Their utter confusion was the terrible consequence of their inability to *think them*. They were unable to think them because they lacked the intellectual and historical categories into which to fit the phenomenon of the appearance of beings who came from somewhere unknown. [They used] the sole category they had at their disposal to account for the unknown: the sacred."[52] This inability to *think them* is the greatest obstacle to survival. Ralph Ellison has a character say, "I want you to overcome 'em with yesses, undermine 'em with grins, agree 'em to death and destruction, let 'em swaller you till they vomit or bust wide open."[53] This ability to *think them* provides a survival strategy.

Women do the yesses and the grins but without the ability to think the rapist, think the batterer. Appelfeld says that, in the camps, his "real world was far beyond the power of my imagination, and my task as an artist was not to develop my imagination but to restrain it, and even then it seemed impossible to me, because everything was so unbelievable that one seemed oneself to be fictional."[54] When one's body has been condemned to destruction it is impossible not to want to forget. As survivor and writer Jorge Semprun says, "I had to choose between literature and life; I chose life. I chose a long cure of aphasia, of voluntary amnesia, in order to survive."[55]

Forgetting, not remembering, is the commonplace response to physical degradation: because one cannot remember without experiencing fear and disgust. The only other choice is to short-circuit the suffering; as Todorov writes, "It is worth noting that the great majority of survivors have fallen victim to depression and trauma. The rate of suicide among this group is abnormally high, as is the prevalence of mental and physical illness. . . . As Martin Walser, who attended the trial of the Auschwitz guards in 1963, observes, memories of the camps are far more devastating to the victims than to their tormentors."[56]

In 1923 to 1924, the suicide rate in Prussia was "Catholics 135, Protestants 280, Jews 530 (!)."[57] As Mary Lowenthal Felstiner writes in *To Paint Her Life: Charlotte Salomon in the Nazi Era:* "Jews . . . learned of a 'suicide catastrophe' among Berlin Jews in 'hazardous occupations' like commerce. Their journals warned, 'Such an appalling increase has not been noted among any other civilized people.' Their demographers sent out alarms. Their leaders put most of the blame on the Jews' own 'growing alienation from traditional ways.' Their writers asked: How do we contain the 'suicide epidemic among the German Jews?'"[58] With a staggering suicide rate (fourth in the West), Germany after World War I was increasingly death- and despair-oriented, that sensibility particularly embodied in suicide, sadomasochism, and prostitution. Berlin was the center of the epidemic(s) with 5,053 suicides from 1925 to 1927. In the midtwenties, "the German Statistical Office reported about five hundred suicides among women in Berlin, almost the same as men. [Women generally attempt suicide more but succeed less.] In the province of Prussia surrounding the capital the Jewish rate outdid the Christian by more than 200 percent."[59]

During the Kristallnacht pogrom, says Andy Marino in *Herschel: The Boy Who Started World War II,* "many Jews committed suicide. It is difficult to separate who killed themselves from who were murdered at the height of the frenzy, but at least six Jewish women perished by their own hand, and there are reports of entire families choosing to die together rather than be taken by the Nazis."[60] Forced ghettoization under Nazi rule was also met with suicide. At the Eichmann trial, a woman survivor was asked: "'Was there any possibility of evading deportation?' . . . 'Only suicide,' she testified. That possibility was taken by many: 'The suicides started immediately before the first transport to Litzmannstadt, and the number increased very rapidly. People took Veronal, some of them took potassium cyanide . . . ' About 1,200 killed themselves, just in Berlin, between October 1941 and early 1942."[61] The cure for those hated in the body is erasure of that body: not only an end to self-consciousness but a refusal to let the body be a conduit for more pain, especially at the hands of an enemy.

What is invisible to the enemy becomes precious to one's self: personal identity, individuality with values. What is visible to the enemy—the body—becomes invisible to one's self. Pain can concentrate resistance or destroy it: but for the person anathematized, the body increasingly becomes a burden. For many women now, it is consoling to inflict punishment on one's self: self-cutting, a purposeful spilling of blood, narcotic in its effects; self-inflicted third-degree burns; breaking one's own bones; pulling the hair out of one's head. In the United States there are "an estimated 2 million self-injurers . . . [M]ost are women under 25 years-old"; "[w]omen describe extreme feelings of dissociation, like a 'walking corpse.'"[62]

In pornography the dilemma becomes clear: she is seen—as nothing and no one. And then there is the amorality of love when the female has no ability to *think them* and does not know the meaning of being seen in the sense of being recognized in a way that includes her subjectivity: "Even three decades later, even after the crimes she knows he's committed, Mimi Reiter seemed swept away by Hitler's passion in her Harlequin-novel way. 'I was so happy, I just wanted to die. Again and again, Hitler stopped and gave me a startled stare, then kissed me again, my forehead, my mouth, my neck.'"[63] Is she invisible or does she simply not exist?

Said the commandant of Auschwitz: "Our system is so terrible that no one in the world will believe it to be possible. . . . If someone should succeed in escaping from Auschwitz and in telling the world, the world will brand him as a fantastic liar. . . ."[64] News spread among European Jews was not at first believed; how could anyone imagine it? By 1943 certainly the British and the U.S. governments knew about Auschwitz; and if they could not imagine the depth of its depravity, certainly they knew Jews were being purposefully murdered. In the U.S., a strong upper-class anti-Semitism influenced the Department of War and the State Department; in Britain, the distaste for Jews was once again on the ascendance but governmental policy was principled: the principle was that Jews could not be recognized as a nation, as a people, but had to be dealt with as Hungarian Jews or Polish Jews or German Jews—the modifier determined the nation. British rescue groups tried to save Jewish lives and the efforts date from before Kristallnacht: "Even before the November Pogrom, British rescue groups, including the Quakers, brought German-Jewish refugee children to England, but the numbers were small. Spurred into more intense action by the pogrom, these groups formed the first major transports of children, leaving Berlin, Hamburg, and Vienna in December 1930. . . . The *Kindertransporte* took between 8,000 and 10,000 children to England,"[65] this between November 1938 and August 1939. As Chernow writes, "The Children's Transport movement was a magnificent achievement that had snatched ten thousand children from the gas chambers by the time it ended . . . It rescued one third of all Jewish children who escaped the Nazis. Half the Jewish children in Germany were never to emerge again."[66]

British rule in Palestine during the Nazi era, however, was determinedly hostile. As Levin writes, "This concerns the efforts of Jews in Palestine to take up arms, as Jews, against Hitler. The failure of England to approve the most elementary right of a people to defend itself is one of the cruelest chapters in the Holocaust. . . . The horrible reality that Hitlerism had created the twentieth-century antiman, a being devoid of conscience or guilt, was grasped by some Jews before their end. It is doubtful, however, that Jews comprehended the extent of official British complicity in their destruction."[67] This included hunting down refugees and imprisoning them. Regardless of the politics of Arab and Jew in British Palestine, the British government seemed to be betraying civilization itself by its hostility to Jewish self-defense and Jewish refugees. It is fair to say that the British decisions account for much of the postwar antagonism Zionists and later Israelis felt for the European survivors who settled in the Jewish homeland: fighting against Hitler would have given the Zionists a new history, a story of rescue and resistance that included both communities of Jews.

In addition, had the Allies had a straightforward policy of rescue, the truth about Auschwitz would have been assimilated earlier, with other information about the war; and, without doubt, had the Allies bombed the train tracks taking Jews to Auschwitz or bombed the camps themselves, fewer Jews would have died. Had the Allies said what they knew about the genocide of the Jews when they knew it, the ground would not have been so hospitable to Holocaust denial: ". . . a major part of the neo-Nazi agenda everywhere was to establish that the Holocaust did not happen. This was an oddly flawed argument that basically claimed both that the Holocaust never happened and furthermore that the Jews deserved it."[68] In some variations, Auschwitz was a Zionist as well as a Jewish lie. Holocaust denial is particularly associated with France, the graffiti on walls in a Paris suburb expressing the populist summary: "Auschwitz is a lie"; "Gas the Jews."[69]

The history of French anti-Semitism is long and venerable: and France became the only country in Europe to deport Jews before the Nazis demanded it and to have a stricter, more embracing definition of who was a Jew than did the Nazis themselves. French nationalist writing has a long history of intellectual anti-Semitism. This anti-Semitism expressed itself enthusiastically in condemning Captain Dreyfus for treason, in the acceptance of Nazi fascism, in acknowledging crimes committed by the Nazis against the French resistance but not against the Jews. France has the singular distinction of being the first country to emancipate European Jews and also the first country to send them off to the camps on its own initiative.

In Germany anti-Semitism had developed as a word and discourse of the fourth estate: it was middle-brow. In France, anti-Semitism was the discourse of intellectuals, especially right-wing nationalists. Maurice Barrès (1862–1923) incarnates the fastidious fascism of French intellectuals. A right-wing nationalist, he wrote in 1902: "For us, *la patrie* is our soil and our ancestors, the land of our dead. For them [Jews], it is the place where their self-interest is best pursued"; in 1917 he amended, "Many *Israelites,* settled among us for generations and centuries, are natural members of the national body."[70] As Zuccotti says, "For Barrès, it was a profound concession."[71] The fascist intellectual (not the oxymoron one might presume) found glory in the Nazis; as Robert Brasillach wrote: "We have thought for a long time that fascism was a kind of poetry, the poetry of the twentieth century (along with communism, no doubt). I tell myself that it cannot die. Little children who will be boys of twenty later will marvel to learn of the existence of this exaltation of millions of men, the youth camps, the glory of the past, parades, cathedrals of light, heroes struck down in combat . . . I shall never forget the radiance of the fascism of my youth."[72] This is an overwhelming and overwhelmed masculinity, hyperbolic, driven, homoerotic, nostalgic. (As one of the Jewish survivors said of her time in Auschwitz: "the beautiful days of my youth."[73]) Because of the unique place of intellectuals in French society, their centrality and their importance, the anti-Semitism of intellectuals was instrumental, not theoretical. As Annette Kahn writes in *Why My Father Died: A Daughter Confronts Her Family's Past at the Trial of Klaus Barbie:* "After the Nazi defeat and the liberation of the concentration camps by the Allies, France turned its entire attention to only one group of victims—those of the Resistance. To chant the praises of the shadow army that fought for freedom was the easiest way for most French citizens to atone for a record tarnished by fear, cowardice, and collaboration."[74]

In fact, the repudiation of French Jews began once more right after the war as Jewish survivors returned home: Emmanuel Mounier had the perfect and emblematic disdain when he said in September 1945: "The victims are still a nuisance. Why, some of them are even disfigured. Their complaints are tiresome for those whose only wish is to return as quickly as possible to peace and quiet."[75] As Henry Rousso says in *The Vichy Syndrome: History and Memory in France Since 1944:* "The return of victims from the Nazi concentration camps was the event most quickly effaced from memory."[76] Kahn describes the return of the survivors as "something of an embarrassment. It was also a practical problem for a country under both moral and economic strain. Though some survivors had families to return to, the vast majority were alone and dispossessed. People knew what they had gone through; a look at those living skeletons was enough to tell their story."[77] DeGaulle said what Marguerite Duras called "these criminal words": "The time for tears is over. The time of glory has returned."[78]

By 1947, as Deborah Lipstadt writes in *Denying the Holocaust: The Growing Assault on Truth and Memory,* the French fascist Maurice Bardèche "began a concerted attack on Allied war propaganda. He also engaged in a vigorous defense of the Nazis. . . . Bardèche strongly defended the politics of collaboration. . . . [H]e contended that at least a portion of the evidence regarding the concentration camps had been falsified and that the deaths that had occurred there were primarily the result of war-related privations, including starvation and illness."[79] In *French Lessons: A Memoir,* Alice Kaplan summarizes letters written to her by Bardèche: "1. No French intellectual knew about the existence of the concentration camps . . . [;] 2. Jews died, because of allied bombings, because of disease; that was not the fault of the Nazis[;] 3. Painful as it is to acknowledge, there can be, and was, extermination *without the will to exterminate.*"[80] He wrote her: "The Jews just died like flies . . .; how I hesitate to cause you pain."[81] By 1948, according to Rousso, "Paul Rassinier, a Socialist resistance fighter who was deported to Buchenwald and Dora (concentration camps where conditions were atrocious, to be sure, but which were not extermination camps), took it into his head to denounce alleged lies about the Nazi camps."[82] This is Stockholm Syndrome taken to its furthest extreme. Others colluded, says Rousso, and "[f]inally, [Robert] Faurisson and his followers were only the French representatives of an international network of negationists, which with other groups in the United States as well as Germany was generally supported by extreme right-wing groups, neo-Nazi organizations, and anti-Zionists from the Middle East."[83] There is evidence implicating both Iran and Saudi Arabia as funders of Holocaust-denial groups and propaganda.

In January 1951 the French passed one of two laws granting amnesty, in this instance "to all those who had committed acts for which the punishment involved loss of civil rights (*degradation nationale*) and a prison sentence of less than fifteen years."[84] In July 1953 there was a second amnesty law that released "all remaining prisoners of the purge, except those guilty of the most serious crimes . . ."[85] The Stalinist Left weighed in by denouncing arrested dissidents in Prague as "trotskyists, titoists, Zionists, bourgeois nationalists, cosmopolites and war criminals . . . all united by the same golden chain, attached to the collar of the dollar"; and the Right said: "The fate of those close to us interests us more than the misfortunes of Czech and Jewish vermin. Those people poisoned Europe; they are the source of our ills and of their own enslavement."[86] From now on, anti-Semitism on the Left would be driven by French communist support of the Soviet Union *über alles*. The Right lived on nostalgia for the good old days. There was Iranian money on the Left, Saudi money on the Right.

In the late 1960s there was an emergence of Jewish activism and art: "Survivors, eyewitnesses, organized groups, and much of the Jewish community suddenly felt the need to 'talk about it' . . ."[87] Marcel Ophuls made *The Sorrow and the Pity*. Claude Lanzmann began the work that would finally result in the nine-hour film *Shoah*. Beate and Serge Klarsfeld, so important in forcing recognition of the crimes against Jews in both Germany and France, paid attention to Vichy. In 1972 laws were passed banning all racist propaganda. On November 1, 1978, *Le Matin* published part of a letter from Louis Darquier de Pellepoix, who had served in Vichy as commissioner general in charge of Jewish questions and had fled France after the war for Spain under Franco: "I hope that certain of the statements that journalist Philippe Ganier Raymond has recently imputed to Louis Darquier de Pellepoix will at last lead the general public to discover that the so-called massacres in 'gas chambers' and the alleged 'genocide' are both part of the same lie."[88]

In October 1980, "a bomb exploded in front of a synagogue on the rue Copernic in Paris. Four people died and more than twenty were injured. . . . [The French Prime Minister] deplored 'this hideous attack, which was intended for Jews . . . and which struck innocent French people.' "[89] In December 1980, Robert Faurisson, a professor, made public his conclusions on the Holocaust: "The alleged Hitlerian gas chambers and the so-called genocide of the Jews form a single historical lie whose principal beneficiaries are the State of Israel and international Zionism and whose principal victims are the German people, but not its leaders, and the Palestinian people in its entirety."[90] Faurisson was convicted on April 25, 1983, under the 1972 laws banning racist hate speech: he was convicted "not for the falsification of history, but for the maliciousness with which he had reduced his research (which was said to be serious) to offensive slogans."[91]

In 1983, *Le Monde* covered the so-called debate over the case: "Academics Confront Each Other over the Faurisson Case."[92] Noam Chomsky weighed in on the side of Faurisson's First Amendment rights—an exercise in U.S. imperialism, which he usually opposes. Guy Hocquenghem, the noted gay liberationist, wrote in the preface to a book on Nazi oppression of gay men: "This book is our anti-Diary of Anne Frank. At a time when French intellectuals debate the question of whether or not there had been an extermination through gassing, it vividly reveals a far more important mystification [*truquage*] in the hagiography of anti-Nazism."[93] According to Jeffrey Mehlman in a preface to *Assassins of Memory: Essays on the Denial of the Holocaust* by Pierre Vidal-Naquet, "The mystification would be the claim that the Jews suffered a worse fate than the gays under Nazism. But in the process of saying as much, Hocquenghem endorsed in passing the notion that the gas chambers themselves were a hoax."[94]

This chain of intellectual hate, arrogance, and cruelty was challenged in its entirety by the trial of the Nazi Klaus Barbie in 1983. Barbie was hated in France for his dogged and brutal pursuit of resistance fighters and especially for the death of Jean Moulin, a resistance hero in Lyon, where Barbie reigned supreme. But by the time of Barbie's capture, the statute of limitations for war crimes had run out; resistance fighters were considered "volunteer combatants,"[95] not civilians: "Therefore the court considered the death of Jean Moulin and Barbie's merciless pursuit of guerrilla fighters in Lyon, the capital of the Resistance in the Southern Zone, as matters outside its jurisdiction, 'forgotten' in the legal sense of the term, even though Barbie had been brought to justice specifically in order to counter the lapse of memory."[96]

This legal circumstance forced the French government to prosecute Barbie for crimes against humanity; for example, crimes against civilians, especially, as the court said, "massacres, murders, and deportations inflicted on civilian populations during the Occupation, including acts of genocide and hostage taking . . ."[97] As with murder per se in the criminal law, there is no statute of limitations for crimes against humanity. The

French government was forced to articulate, in the bright light of a court, Nazi crimes against the Jews: "After Eichmann in Jerusalem, Barbie in Lyons would make it possible to condemn the antisemitism that was the essence of Nazism."[98] Barbie had in fact been responsible for "the arrest, torture, and deportation of civilians, particularly Jews."[99] One of Barbie's favorite tricks was to torture someone while a couple would be having intercourse in the interrogation room, no doubt to contextualize his sadism. Rassinier, the French socialist who had been an inmate in Buchenwald and Dora concentration camps, had written in a 1977 book, *Debunking the Genocide Myth,* that the Nazis had imprisoned Jews as a "gesture of compassion"[100] to protect Jews from a population that wanted to lynch them. The Barbie trial proved that there was no "gesture of compassion"; Barbie's sadism was the distillation of the Nazi project: he was emblematic, not anomalous. Bardèche had been "the first to contend that the pictorial and documentary evidence of the murder process in the camps had actually been falsified. He was also the first to argue that the gas chambers were used for disinfection—not annihilation."[101] This part of the French denial of the Holocaust retains its currency: the Holocaust was another international Jewish conspiracy. As Leni Yahil writes in *The Holocaust: The Fate of European Jewry, 1932–1945:* ". . . [P]arties who—for whatever reason—wish to deny the Holocaust ever took place invoke the concept summed up in the word *Auschwitz* to argue that . . . millions of people were never killed in gas chambers or incinerated in crematoria, that all this is a fabrication conceived by the Jews to force the world to acquiesce in the establishment of the 'Zionist state.' These claims ring like a contemporary variation on the medieval blood libel, with a political charge replacing the original accusations that were based on deprecation of the Jewish faith."[102]

Vidal-Naquet concludes that "[p]lainly, we will have to come to terms with the fact that the world has its Faurissons, as it has its pimps and its pornographic film clubs. But there can be no question of yielding any ground to him."[103] But it is Lipstadt who isolated at least one inevitable consequence of Holocaust-denial literature and propaganda: ". . . the deniers may have an impact on truth and memory . . . Extremists of any kind pull the center of a debate to a more radical position. They can create—and, in the case of the Holocaust, have already created—a situation whereby added latitude may be given to ideas that would once have been summarily dismissed as historically fallacious. The recent 'historians' debate' in Germany, in which conservative German historians attempted to restructure German history, offers evidence of this phenomenon."[104] Lipstadt maintains that "[t]hough these historians are not deniers, they helped to create a gray area where their highly questionable interpretations of history became enmeshed with the pseudohistory of the deniers . . ."[105]

The elegant intellectuals of French fascism and neofascism have spawned many vulgar imitators. For instance, there is the self-proclaimed Jew Ditleib Felderer, an Austrian by birth, living in Sweden: "In 1983 he was sentenced to ten months in prison for disseminating hate material. . . . Felderer had sent leaders of the European Jewish community mailings that contained pieces of fat and locks of hair with a letter asking them if they could identify the contents as Hungarian Jews gassed at Auschwitz."[106] This intimidation would be protected by First Amendment law in the United States.

Part of the modus operandi of Holocaust deniers outside of France is the purposeful humiliation or degradation or intimidation of Jewish survivors. The Institute for Historical Review (IHR) offered a reward to anyone who could prove that Jews had been gassed in Auschwitz. Ignored, the IHR then sent letters to survivors who had some kind of public presence and offered a reward for proof of the same: "The survivors received an application form for the contest and a list of the rules, which stipulated that claimants were to attend the second Revisionist Convention at their own expense to present their evidence. . . . Claimants were asked for their ethnic origins, the dates of their internment in any concentration camp, and the exact date and location of any gassing operations they witnessed. . . . they were to describe fully all the mechanics involved in the gassing process . . . and to provide any 'forensic evidence' that would support their claim, including diaries they kept or photographs they took."[107] For survivors, this was an assault: a triggering of nightmares and flashbacks; a downward fall into despair; a maggoty accusation that they themselves had been lying. Höss, the commandant of Auschwitz, might be the prototype for Holocaust deniers. Before his execution in Poland he claimed that Julius Streicher's pornographic, anti-Semitic rag *Der Stürmer* "did a lot of damage and has never been of any use to serious scientific anti-Semitism. . . . a Jew edited this newspaper."[108] There is literally no end to this version of blame-the-victim—no end to what the Jews did to themselves and no end to Jewish slanders against the poor Nazis. As Vidal-Naquet says, "This is the thesis of the dagger in the back, but extended to infinity."[109]

In the United States, neo-Nazis, the Ku Klux Klan, and the new militia movement are the harbingers of Holocaust denial. Wistrich writes, "The Saudis have also surreptitiously helped to finance antisemitic Holocaust denial literature in the West [including] . . . *The Six Million Reconsidered,* written by an American neo-Nazi, William Grimstad, registered as a Saudi agent with the U.S. Department of Justice."[110] *The Turner Diaries* says the Jews told false stories "about Hitler flying into rages and chewing carpets, phony German plans for the invasion of America, babies being skinned alive to make lampshades and then boiled down into soap, girls kidnapped and sent to Nazi 'stud farms.' The Jews convinced the American people that those stories were true, and the result was World War II, with millions of the best of our race butchered—by us—and all of eastern and central Europe turning into a huge, communist prison camp."[111] The anti-communist trope is, of course, a fundamental trope of U.S. denial literature: with the usual American inability to be exact about geography.

Explaining Holocaust denial is not easy because the roots of anti-Semitism can be theorized but not really known. Wisse says that "[t]here is hardly a survivor on record, from Elie Wiesel of the orthodox Hungarian Jewish community of Sighet to Primo Levi of the assimilated Italian community of Turin, who did not expose the function of denial in furthering the idea of anti-Semitism. Rescued diaries of Jews who perished during the war and reflective memoirs of some who survived it all condemn (with varying degrees of rage and self-laceration) the failure to take ideological hatred seriously."[112] This is true; and they are right. Yet it must feel better to deny the Holocaust than it does to let it in; and how does one let it in? Ian McEwan's narrator in the novel *Black Dogs* tries to confront the reality: "We followed a party of schoolchildren into a hut where wire cages were crammed full of shoes, tens of thousands of them, flattened and curled like dried fruit. In another hut, more shoes, and in a third, unbelievably, more, no longer caged but spilling in their thousands across the floor. . . . The extravagant numerical scale, the easy-to-say numbers—tens and hundreds of thousands, millions—denied the imagination its proper sympathies, its rightful grasp of the suffering, and one was drawn insidiously to the persecutors' premise, that life was cheap, junk to be inspected in heaps. As we walked on, my emotions died. There was nothing we could do to help. There was no one to feed or free. We were strolling like tourists. . . . This was our inevitable shame . . . We were on the other side, we walked here freely like the commandant once did, or his political master [Himmler], poking into this or that, knowing the way out, in full certainty of our next meal."[113] The hopelessness of one who tries to face the Holocaust can perhaps be helped or alleviated only by awe at the courage of the survivors: to continue to live; for some, to speak, to have found speech; for most, to remember what each alone cannot forget until death, singular and absolute, removes the burden of consciousness, self-consciousness, the pain of knowing, especially knowing through the body, having been there, inside.

One must ask: if the Holocaust can be denied, how can a woman, raped or tortured or beaten, be believed? Is she believed when she names the perpetrator; or is she accused, as the Jews are, of slander? How is it possible to tell the truth and be believed? How can a raped or prostituted child be believed? Is the denial of others a psychological state; or is it a practice of propaganda and lies? How can a raped child or woman not want to forget? How can the raped or tortured or prostituted find speech and with it credibility? How high are the numbers? Is there rescue? How impersonal and random is survival?

11

PALESTINIANS/
PROSTITUTED WOMEN

For Jews, including Israeli Jews, Palestinian Arabs are the scapegoat: the source of all danger and terror, the polluting presence; the inferior and abject.

For women, including putative feminists, prostituted women are the scapegoat: the ultimate filth, the expendable; the inferior and abject.

In each case, the group is demonized, dehumanized, and condescended to; the human value of the individual in the group is denigrated, degraded, denied. Scapegoating has moved from the Jews and Eve to the Palestinians and prostituted women.

Each scapegoat defines a material bottom beneath which one cannot sink. This supports the status quo because everyone above that bottom has some advantage to protect. Change would risk one's little bit of privilege and pride. The Israelis will never be as degraded as the Palestinians; nor will any woman not prostituted ever fall that low.

The Israeli desire to be separate from Palestinian Arabs increasingly looks like apartheid; as Rian Malan writes in *My Traitor's Heart:* "In my circle of hell, the circle of white left liberals, discussions of such matters are fraught with peril. Elsewhere in the world, veneration and respect for non-Western cultures is the hallmark of the humane and open-minded white man. In South Africa, it is quite the opposite. One of apartheid's underlying tenets is that there are distinct and immutable differences between races, and that it is God's will that they be maintained."[1]

Nobel Peace Prize winner and a designer of the Oslo Accords Shimon

Peres advocates a more polite separatism; as he says in *Battling for Peace: A Memoir:* "Wherever a centralized regime—usually Communist—had tried to mold an amalgam of heterogeneous ethnic groups into a single nation, repressed ethnic rivalries have broken out anew. . . . One of the reasons I believe in the need for political separation between Israelis and Palestinians stems from the example of Yugoslavia. The full lesson to be learned from this and other ethnic disputes is that nations should live separately as political entities but together as economic units."[2] Peres wants us to believe—as he apparently does—that the model informing Israeli policy is the Balkan nightmare as opposed to the South African. Regardless, one has, in the words of Benjamin Disraeli on the schism between rich and poor, "[t]wo nations, between whom there is no intercourse and no sympathy; who are as ignorant of each other's habits, thought, and feelings, as if they were dwellers in different zones, or inhabitants of different planets."[3]

There is nothing unique in this conflict between Israel and the Palestinians except for the pre-Israel history of the Jews; in Edward Said's words, "No movement has had to deal with colonizers so morally credible as the Jews."[4] In addition, says Said, "[n]o movement has been so unfortunate in its allies and its surrounding context."[5] Said is acknowledging the bad treatment of the Palestinians by Arab countries, a point rarely made in public discourse.

Shelby Steele describes how scapegoating is advantageous to the individuals of the dominant group: "Even though a white American may have been wounded more than a given black, and therefore have a larger realm of inner doubt, his white skin, with its connotations of privilege and superiority, will actually help protect him from that doubt and from the undermining power of his anti-self, at least in relations with blacks."[6] The process of scapegoating, however, introduces a new kind of self-doubt; as Peter Gay writes in *The Cultivation of Hatred: The Bourgeois Experience Victoria to Freud,* "Can it be that one is no better than one's victims? It is a terrible thought, to be kept at bay."[7] For the Israelis and Palestinians, says Mark A. Heller in *No Trumpets No Drums: A Two-State Settlement of the Israeli-Palestinian Conflict* (coauthored with Sari Nusseibeh), "their contemporary history is virtually defined by their conflict with the other."[8] The confiscation of Palestinian homes and land with the establishment of the Jewish state and subsequent rule by Israelis in the occupied territories have created a deep and abiding hatred on the Palestinian side and a contemptuous superiority on the Israeli side. Isaiah Berlin, who believed in "a specifically pluralist democracy,"[9] recognizes that "[d]emocracy can sometimes be oppressive to minorities and individuals. Democracy need not be pluralistic, it can be monistic, a democracy in which the majority does whatever it wants, no matter how cruel or unjust or irrational. In a democracy which allows for opposition there is always hope that one might convert the majority. But democracies can be intolerant. Democracy is not *ipso facto* pluralistic."[10] This would be a good description of the limits of Israeli democracy; Palestinian Arabs inside Israel are second-class citizens; Palestinians under Israeli occupation and shadow occupation may have numbers (the dominant group is the minority) but they do not have rights.

The impact of Israeli rule in the occupied territories, some of which is now under the authority of the Palestinian Authority or a soon-to-emerge Palestinian state, has been to create a nihilistic hatred of the occupiers. Ché Guevara says: "Hatred [is] an element of the struggle; relentless hatred of the enemy, impelling us above and beyond the natural limitations that man is heir to, and transforming him into an effective, violent, seductive and cold killing machine. Our soldiers must be thus; a people without hatred cannot vanquish a brutal enemy."[11] Palestinian hatred may or may not be a force for revolution; in particular it can devolve into anarchic murder, self-murder, self-hatred infused with bitterness and rage, all terrifying enough: but surely in all the postbiblical history of the Jews, contemporary Palestinians are the first, the only group to have real reasons for hating and fearing Jews.

Ehud Barak, leader of the Labor Party in Israel, a military hero, and in 1999 elected Prime Minister, acknowledges that if he had been born a Palestinian, he himself would have been part of a "terror organization at some point."[12] How frightening is it for Jews to recognize these injuries, done by them or in their name, that inevitably breed hatred? Or is the leg up these injuries give Israelis sufficient justification; as Toni Morrison writes: "Freedom (to move, to earn, to learn, to be allied with a powerful center, to narrate the world) can be relished more deeply in a cheek-by-jowl existence with the bound and unfree, the economically oppressed, the marginalized, the silenced. The ideological dependence on racialism is intact and, like its metaphysical existence, offers in historical, political, and literary discourse a safe route into mediations on morality and ethics; a way of examining the mind-body dichotomy; a way of thinking about justice; a way of contemplating the modern world."[13] Israeli literature and Israeli historians thrive driven by the disgrace of being on top; driven by the distress of bad conscience; without the Palestinians, who would the much discriminated-against and usually right-wing Sephardic Jews, the dark-skinned Jews, be better than? Without the Palestinians, the Sephardic Jews would be the bottom because dominance requires contempt for an inferior: "As Jay Gould reportedly remarked when one of his railroads was threatened with a strike, 'I can hire one half of the working class to kill the other half.'"[14] As Rian Malan asserts, apartheid was designed so that "blacks remained in the God-ordained place, hewers of wood and drawers of water, forever and ever."[15] Israeli rule in Gaza and the West Bank has the same result if not the same intentions; under the Palestinian Authority, the thugism of Arafat will not mimic the great-heartedness of Nelson Mandela.

It is commonplace now to say that each side has its own so-called narrative, and each side is right or justified in what it does or what it thinks. What is true is that Israelis begin to uncover facts about Israeli-committed atrocities; and Israeli scholars and journalists are publishing these facts. While Jews outside of Israel refuse to know this new history, Israeli life is developing for better and worse with these sad, brutal facts exposed.

In the domain of Palestinian intellectual life, this acknowledgment of Israeli brutality may or may not make a difference; but to the ordinary person, it does not. How would an ordinary person modulate their hatred to keep it on some kind of moral parallel with the dominant group's scholarship?

Muslims disappeared from Europe, in Spain expelled with the Jews by the militant Christians of the Spanish Inquisition; but as Karen Armstrong writes in *Muhammad: A Biography of the Prophet:* ". . . during the nineteenth century the British and the French began to invade their lands. In 1830 the French colonized Algeria, and in 1839 the British colonized Aden; between them they took over Tunisia (1881), Egypt (1882), the Sudan (1898) and Libya and Morocco (1912)."[16] There was also a religious imperialism in the region: "The Congregationalists were to dominate missionary activities in the Middle East until 1870, when a friendly division of labor emerged: the Congregationalists became responsible for Turkey, the Presbyterians for Egypt, Syria, and Iran, and the Dutch Reformed Church for the Arabian Gulf."[17] In 1917, the British released the Balfour Declaration, which promised "the establishment in Palestine of a National Home for the Jewish people. . . ."[18] In 1920, "Britain and France carved up the Middle East between them into mandates and protectorates."[19] Although the 1917 Balfour Declaration is anathema in Arab eyes, it did not predetermine the future; but the 1920 betrayal did. This is the original sin, the first colonialism, the first broken promise: both France and England had agreed to leave the Middle East after defeating the Turkish empire; both countries stayed in charge, in control, with no accountability to the colonized populations.

In March 1920 "[t]he first anti-Jewish disturbances shook the peace of Jerusalem . . . In April of the same year, Arabs attacked Jewish settlements in Upper Galilee."[20] As a consequence of this violence, "Britain decided to limit Jewish immigration."[21] In 1921, Arabs rioted in Jaffe; nearly 200 Jews and 120 Arabs died. As David McDowall writes in *Palestine and Israel: The Uprising and Beyond,* a "commission of enquiry decided [the riot] had been a spontaneous outburst"; ". . . Jewish settlers . . . interpreted it as a pogrom, similar in motive and kind to those from which they had escaped in Russia."[22] The Jews, attacked, apparently did fight back; as the Medical Officer in Jaffa recounted, he was "struck with the number of wounds on each body and the ferocity of the wounds."[23]

In Jerusalem in 1929, an Arab leaflet produced by students said: "O Arab! Remember that the Jew is your strongest enemy and the enemy of your ancestors since olden times. Do not be misled by his tricks, for it is he who tortured Christ (peace be upon him), and poisoned Muhammad (peace and worship be with him)."[24] In 1929 in Jerusalem "Arabs attacked and killed 133 Jews . . ., and massacred another fifty-nine men, women and children in Hebron"; in 1936, Arabs attacked Jewish civilians—this was "a full-scale Arab revolt both against the British Mandate and against Jewish immigration . . . "[25] Under the leadership of the grand mufti Hajj Amin al Husayni, who later escaped being hanged by the British in Iraq and made his way to Germany to support Hitler, anti-Jewish agitation grew. At the same time religious Jews wanted unconditional access to the Wailing Wall, an access that may have compromised Muslim religious practice at Muslim shrines, "the Dome of the Rock (where Abraham offered to sacrifice Isaac) and the al Aqsa mosque, the site of the Prophet Muhammad's Night Visit."[26]

Also in these years Jewish immigration to Palestine increased significantly; as Levin writes, "During the three-year period, 1933–1935, out of 200,000 Jewish migrants from Europe, 123,786 entered Palestine, nearly half of them—61,000—in the year 1935."[27] The British decided to limit Jewish immigration. In July 1937, the Balfour Declaration was effectively canceled out by the Peel report, which characterized Balfour's Jewish National Home in Palestine as "unworkable."[28] As a result of British policy newly reworked, Jewish immigration declined: in 1936 under 30,000; in 1937 under 11,000. Ben-Gurion organized self-defense units to protect Jewish settlements; Arabs organized a general strike. In keeping with a 1939 British White Paper, Britain "firmly and consistently opposed for nine years—until Israeli independence—*all* Jewish immigration to Palestine over the meager annual quota set by the government of Prime Minister Neville Chamberlain and maintained by his successor, Winston Churchill."[29] Britain, according to Friedländer, was "increasingly worried by the pro-Axis shift in the Arab world—a trend with possibly dire consequences for Britain in case of war . . . "[30] Even refuge on Cyprus, the site later used by the British to imprison Jews fleeing to Palestine from the Nazis, was impossible; as one member of the Foreign Office said: "The proposed temporary solution of Cyprus has, I understand, been firmly rejected by the Governor; it is unthinkable that a miscellaneous crowd of Jews could be admitted to any other part of the Empire."[31]

The cynicism of Britain's foreign policy in Palestine was astonishing; said a British Arabist in the Cairo office: "There is a sporting chance that if left undisturbed by direct foreign intervention, the Palestinian Arabs and Palestinian Jews will tire sooner or later of the conflict . . . In the early fighting the zealots of both sides would probably be killed off. . . . From the fighting would emerge the outline of a defensible Jewish state—i.e., the area which the Jews prove they can defend. In the course of the fighting, a great part of the Arab population in the Jewish state would probably make its way through the lines to the safety of the Arab area. . . . If and when this stalemate occurs, there is a good prospect that the moderates on both sides will be ready to negotiate with each other. . . . "[32] This was a policy of social Darwinism, unspeakably immoral: let the strong and militant kill each other off; let the weaker survivors on both sides collapse into negotiation as an expression of less strength, less militancy; let the Arab masses be slaughtered or exiled and let the pathetic Jews dominate whatever they can take no matter how many are killed. During the war years, British policy was unrelievedly hostile to, for instance, "the defenseless freighters smuggling Jewish refugees from Europe."[33] By 1946, Jews had organized and trained, formed military and guerrilla units; and on June 29, 1946, known as "Black Saturday," the British "arrested hundreds of Jewish Agency, Hagana and Mossad leaders across Palestine in surprise raids."[34] Jews in Palestine began to fight a terrorist war against the British by, for instance, bombing the King David Hotel in Jerusalem, a location frequented by British officers. The question was whether to fight the Nazis or the British and the Nazis.

If one looks at the history from 1920 on, one sees acts of Arab violence against Jewish settlers. It is precisely this violence that gives the lie to the oft-stated legend advanced first by Golda Meir (who arrived in Palestine in 1921): that this was a land without people for a people without a land. There was no such ignorance. There was no such land: empty. There was the phenomenon of absent Arab landowners on whose land Palestinian Arabs lived, worked, farmed: these absent landlords sold land to the Jewish Agency, the consequence of which was the dispossession of Palestinian Arabs. In 1948, the United Nations approved a partition plan that would create a Jewish state side by side (though in itself discontinuous) with a Palestinian state. The Jews accepted the plan, the Arabs rejected it. According to Janet Wallach and John Wallach in *Arafat: In the Eyes of the Beholder,* "Arafat is certain in his belief that the Arabs should have accepted partition. 'Why didn't they accept partition? Why didn't they have the desire and the will to continue the war?' he asks contemptuously."[35] Of course, accepting partition and continuing the war was not the UN plan.

After the declaration of Israeli statehood, Arabs from surrounding countries invaded the former Palestine: ". . . 700,000 Palestinians fled their homes, some going north to Lebanon and Syria, others south to Gaza and yet others across the river into Transjordan."[36] These refugees became the population of the scandalous camps created to house these— to their shock—permanently displaced persons. This was the so-called Arab miracle: empty houses ready for Jewish inhabitants to move into and take over.

In fighting to protect the new Jewish state, the new Israelis were ruthless: "The hugely successful Zionist strategy was to mount surprise attacks on Arab cities with mortar and rocket bombardments; to harry the Arab population with psychological warfare from loudspeakers and clandestine radio stations operated by the Hagana, the underground Jewish militia; and, in the countryside, to stage massacres in isolated villages such as Deir Yassin and Kolonia, calculated to stampede the rural population off the land. Several thousand Arab civilians were slaughtered in different parts of the country, leading to the panicked flight across the borders of some 750,000 others."[37] This targeting of Arab civilians, including the village of Dweima, "in which an estimated 500 men, women, and children were killed by a regular Israeli army unit,"[38] has never been part of the Jewish history of Israel. The atrocity of mass murder has been ignored in order to maintain, among Jews, a self-conception that repudiates brutality. Arabs commit murder. Jews do not. Arabs terrorize civilians. Jews do not. Jews are intrinsically good. Arabs are not. It is fair to say that no Jew would have easily believed Arab charges that seem to stain the character of the Jewish people: a morally superior people as a consequence of a history of suffering.

While some Israeli writers have documented episodes of military criminality, the news has not traveled well; Jews continue to ignore it or to cast it aside as propaganda. Even now, writes Paul Breines in *Tough Jews*, "[i]n none of the numerous tough Jewish novels dealing with the story of the founding of Israel is Deir Yassin mentioned."[39] Because of Deir Yassin, which stands alone as a symbol for all violence against Arab civilians, "[i]n the minds of many Arabs . . . the image of the Jew as mass murderer, as pogromist, was indelibly printed."[40] In revenge Arab fighters murdered "seventy Jewish civilians under the impassive eye of a British military post, whose personnel did nothing to stop the killing."[41] The issue is not that the Jews now can be considered bad while the Arabs are exonerated or romanticized or celebrated; the issue is the reluctant and difficult recognition that no group is immune to the pathology of lawless violence. For over fifty years now, Palestinians have asked for or demanded acknowledgment: of Deir Yassin; of purposeful terror against Arab civilians; of taking the land and homes and cups and saucers of fleeing refugees. This has never been too much to ask; nor would it be too much to ask for reparations for the stolen property. Have Palestinians asked? Have Israelis answered? Has the global Jewish nation, represented by Israel, answered?

In 1950, Jordan annexed the West Bank with its dense Palestinian population: in Jordan the population "nearly tripled from 450,000 to 1.2 million and now included 400,000 Palestinians living in the West Bank, plus 200,000 refugees who had fled their homes . . . and 100,000 refugees who had fled to the East Bank."[42] But Palestinians did not give up their claim to self-determined sovereignty; and terrorist raids into Israel became commonplace. Under the late King Hussein "the Jordanian government counted fifty-two different Palestinian groups on its territory, with leftists proselytizing not Islam but Marxism from the minarets of mosques"; these groups "undermined King Hussein's authority and left his country vulnerable to military retaliation by the Israelis."[43]

In September 1970, called "Black September" by the Palestinians, Hussein used military force to expel or kill Palestinian fighters; in the ensuing year, it was Jordanian mass murder and massacres that uprooted and routed the Palestinians: ". . . the Jordanian army finally threw out the last . . . guerrillas from the Jerish-Aljun stronghold in July 1971. In the last months of battle the Jordanians massacred many of those whom they captured, with the result that ninety Palestinians chose to flee to Israel rather than fall prisoner to Hussein's Bedu soldiers."[44]

In 1967, facing an incipient attack, "the Israelis made a surprise strike at the Egyptian air bases. By noon the Egyptian air force was destroyed. . . . Hussein snubbed the Israeli request to stay out of the war and sent Jordanian warplanes into the air. By 2:30 that afternoon the entire Jordanian air force was wiped out. The next day Jordan had lost the West Bank, and on the morning of June 7, Jordanian ground forces could no longer hold the Old City; Jerusalem . . . was lost to the Jewish state. By June 9, the Israelis had decimated the Syrian forces as well and had taken the Golan Heights."[45] There was the good news and there was the bad news. On the one hand, "the Israel of June 11, 1967, was not the anxiety-ridden nation that went to war six days earlier. Though stunned and disbelieving, the Israelis recognized the greatness of their military victory";[46] as did the world. On the other hand "the occupied territories were three times bigger than Israel proper, which the traditional siege mentality of the Israelis made seem even larger."[47] As Vidal-Naquet says: "Israel prior to 1967 was, to be sure, a society built through a colonial process, but it was not or only very incompletely (as a result of the expulsion of the majority of Palestinians) a colonial society. The conquest of the rest of Palestine created two societies locked in a mortal embrace and resulted in their rapid evolution toward a situation of apartheid. Even today the process has not been completed, but how is one to deny the evidence?"[48]

After the Six Day War, the refugees in the camps took a backseat to the occupied Palestinians in Gaza and the West Bank. The camps were not incidental: they were "filled mainly by the lower classes of the refugee population, most of them poor peasants or day laborers. They comprise some 850,000 people (according to UNRWA statistics from 1988, thirteen camps in Lebanon with 150,000, ten camps in Syria with about 80,000 people, ten camps in Jordan with some 210,000 people; twenty camps in the West Bank with around 100,000 people; and eight camps in Gaza with more than 250,000 people, to which we must add over 50,000 people—again in UNRWA's reckoning—who are living in camps but are not registered in them)."[49] Despite the moral and human significance of these great numbers of disenfranchised Palestinian Arabs, it was the occupation that remade, recast, the Israeli military and changed the substance of the Israeli-Palestinian conflict. As Danny Rubenstein writes in *The People of Nowhere: The Palestinian Vision of Home*: "At the beginning of the 1990s the Palestinian population within the borders of what had been Palestine under the British Mandate numbered 2.3 million people, 1.6 million of whom were residents of the Gaza Strip and the West Bank (including East Jerusalem). After 1967, it was this segment of the population that gradually became the center of the Israeli-Arab conflict."[50] Another consequence of the occupation was transfer: the forcible moving of groups of Palestinians out of the territory ruled by Israel altogether: "From 1967 to 1977, some 1,100 Palestinians as well as two Bedouin tribes, were deported from the West Bank and Gaza. Nine Palestinians were deported in 1978, one in 1979, three in 1981 and none in 1983–85. From December 1987 through July 1989, forty-five have been deported."[51] As punishment for acts of rebellion, Palestinian homes were literally torn down by the Israeli army (a punishment learned from the British); or rooms belonging to a given Palestinian dissident would be sealed off.

The military occupation was brutal and had two consequences: mass rebellion in the territories and the widespread use of violence; and the rise of a fundamentalist Islam. As Laqueur says in *Fascism: Past, Present, Future:* "Islamism (not Islam per se) is today the only major force in the world that openly advocates expansion, hegemony, and the export of revolution and that calls for a jihad, a holy war, against internal and external enemies. In this war—in the struggle against other cultures—there can be no compromise. The jihad is the starting point and the central issue of radical Islam."[52] The rise of fundamentalist Islam is a male response to being degraded. But it is not the only response. The Oslo Agreement and Arafat's Palestinian Authority in Gaza exist because the PLO under Arafat's leadership sold out the original refugees; they sit in the camps while in Gaza Arafat's toy military parades for CNN. Edward Said describes this betrayal as "a Palestinian Versailles"; "What makes it worse," he says, "is that for at least the past fifteen years the PLO could have negotiated a better arrangement . . . For reasons best known to the leadership, it refused all such previous overtures."[53] In a new response in 1999 to the conflict, Said has recognized "that Palestinian self-determination in a separate state is unworkable, just as unworkable as the principle of separation between a demographically mixed, irreversibly connected Arab population without sovereignty and a Jewish population with it. The question, I believe, is not how to devise means for persisting in trying to separate them but to see whether it is possible for them to live together as fairly and peacefully as possible."[54] He is advocating a "one-state solution, . . . Palestinians and Israelis living as equal citizens under one flag."[55] He is advocating a pluralistic democracy held together by the rule of law and the rights of each person as a citizen, not group rights. He is advocating, then, Enlightenment principles of equality and dignity: though he has excoriated Zionists for their European origins and aspirations. He—perhaps in response to the specter of Arafat's antidemocracy in Gaza—is asking for governance to replace two liberation movements: the Zionist one and the Palestinian one.

As one Palestinian with Israeli citizenship says, "I belong to a more or less protected minority in this country, while an Arab from Gaza belongs to a violently oppressed majority in the occupied territories. There's a world of difference between the two."[56] The world of Israeli citizens of Palestinian descent is politically difficult but economically secure. Under military rule in the early years of the Israeli state, these citizens endured administrative arrest, limits on their movement, and what Tom Segev characterizes as "a variety of arbitrary regulations."[57] This military rule was justified as a security precaution; but, as Segev says, "military law also made it easier to confiscate Arab land."[58] Now integrated into the Israeli state, fluent in Hebrew and Arabic, well-educated but discriminated against with quotas and an involuntary exemption from the Israeli military (to which economic and social advantages attach), Israeli Arabs have political rights, a presence in the Knesset, public advocates, and legal and economic resources. There is no equality but there are rights: their status may be analogized to that of the free men of color in cosmopolitan parts of the slave-owning South, for instance in New Orleans. There is no doubt that assimilating demands some acceptance of the Israeli worldview; according to McDowall, "[m]ore Palestinians read the Hebrew than the Arabic press."[59] The Palestinian writer Anton Shammas writes in Hebrew; and the Palestinian writer Emile Habiby was the first Israeli Palestinian to receive the Jerusalem Prize for literature. The recognition of Habiby had more than symbolic significance: it showed an emerging respect for the discourse of politicized Palestinians.

Israeli Palestinians are increasingly turning to Islam: "In 1950 only two-thirds were Muslims, but by 1995 the proportion will have risen to three-quarters."[60] From 1948 to 1967, Arabs inside the state were acculturated differently than Palestinian refugees: "Israeli Palestinians find this difference uncomfortable, for they are painfully aware that they belong to a hybrid culture, living as half-castes between Israel and the Arab world. Many feel they belong nowhere, feeling like an Israeli in Nablus, and like an Arab in Tel Aviv."[61]

In the occupied territories, there is no margin for crises of identity. As Peter Theroux says in *Sandstorms: Days and Nights in Arabia:* "How odd it was to see Palestinians [in the occupied territories] selling juice, sweeping streets, and driving taxis. In the Arab countries where another million Palestinians lived, you saw them practicing law, medicine, business."[62] And, indeed, the Palestinians in the territories are well-educated; as Samuel Segev says: "In most Arab countries, illiteracy is still very high, but the Palestinians in the territories were less than 5 percent illiterate. Many of them had studied abroad, mostly in Europe and the United States."[63] During the occupation Israelis closed schools and universities as punishment for political organizing. Palestinians are driven by an imposed poverty to "work for their enemies in order to survive"; as Jon Lee Anderson describes in *Guerrillas: The Men and Women Fighting Today's Wars:* "So, every day of the week except Friday, the Muslim holy day, more than seventy-five thousand Gazans journey into Israel to menial jobs. They make up Israel's pool of so-called black labor, its equivalent of South Africa's township migrant workers, or the Mexican 'wetbacks' in the United States."[64]

The humiliation of this subjugation—loss of education and the inevitability of menial labor—makes radical Islam attractive to many: fundamentalism reifies the authority of the male; opens a new path to knowledge, this time of religious texts; disciplines intellect; becomes a sanctified vehicle for hatred of the Jews and for the subordination of Arab women. Working inside Israel as expendable day laborers who are required to obey a curfew and return to Gaza at night might be degrading enough; but, as Anderson says, "One of the most demeaning aspects for Palestinians . . . is the way Israelis habitually ignore them. It is as if the Palestinians simply aren't there. This treatment makes the Palestinians, who already resent being reduced to menial work, feel even more humiliated and insecure. . . . [T]hey have been made invisible because of who they are."[65] Invisibility demeans and dehumanizes.

The conflict, not self-evident to those who live in more temperate climates, is as much about water as about land. As Heller and Nusseibeh say: "Conflict over control of water sources has been a permanent feature in the history of the Middle East, as of most other semiarid regions in the world."[66] As Ze'ev Schiff and Ehud Ya'ari write in *Intifada:* " . . . the Israelis have controlled the water sources in the territories with an iron hand. Palestinians are forbidden to sink wells without permission, drilling permits have been awarded only for drinking water, and even then the Israeli authorities have not been particularly generous. . . . In 1986 the Jewish settlements exceeded their water quotas by 36.4 percent."[67] In *The Demon Lover: On the Sexuality of Terrorism*, Robin Morgan describes the politics of water in Gaza: "Huddled beside the azure waters and powder-white sands of the Mediterranean Sea is the Gaza Strip—a ribbon of land ten miles wide and less than twenty-nine miles long. Twenty-four hundred Israelis live here in nineteen heavily subsidized and lavishly irrigated settlements using 96 percent of the water and one-third of the land. Yet in 1985, Gaza surpassed Hong Kong as the most densely populated, poorest place on earth. Over 650,000 Palestinians, some in their third or fourth displacement, also dwell here . . . "[68] It is not surprising that water should become a contentious issue among Palestinians themselves; as Schiff and Ya'ari write: " . . . the Arab-run municipalities in the Gaza Strip usually related to the nearby camps with a chill bordering on hostility. When the Civil Administration tried to make the Gaza Municipality extend its services to the surrounding refugee camps, it responded by cutting off their water supply."[69] Conflict becomes intraethnic. Violence becomes easy, even against one's own. Power is exercised over the contested resource; a class system of haves and have-nots is created or redefined in relation to the scarce resource.

Along with a paucity of water because it is withheld or used with greed and arrogance by others, the Palestinians in Gaza before the Palestinian Authority (and after it) have had no system of justice on which to build; as Anderson says, "The Salvadorian guerrillas may have established a kind of social equilibrium in Chalatenango, but in Gaza, no true system of justice has yet been established."[70] Without a civil or liberatory design for civility and rights, radical Islam fills the void. Male supremacy gives the illusion of power; women are the subordinated population. However powerless the disenfranchised men are, they still dominate women.

The problem of the rule of law goes back to the British Mandate; "Certainly," says Rashid Khalidi in *Palestinian Identity: The Construction of Modern National Conscience*, "the lack of access after 1918 to state structures (or indeed to any meaningful level of government: the top posts in the mandate administration were reserved for the British) hindered the Palestinians by comparison with their Arab neighbors."[71] Schiff and Ya'ari note that "[m]any of the homebred Palestinian leaders with the potential to become negotiating partners—the local leadership that Israel claims to be searching for today—were deported to Jordan during the years when the Labor Alignment was in power."[72] In other words, colonialism on the part of the British and the Israelis removed opportunities and the leadership itself from the Palestinian population. Defining Arabs as terrorists by nature—romantic wild savages (as, for instance, in John Le Carré's *The Little Drummer Girl*), killers without conscience—is a logical outcome of destroying political leadership.

The *intifada* appears to have unhinged Palestinian civil society to the extent that it existed. *Intifada* translated into "the shaking off"—"in the English speaking world, the Uprising";[73] "Its literal meaning is the shivering that grips a person suffering from fever, or the persistent shaking of a dog infested with fleas";[74] it was a rebellion, the meaning of the phenomenon elucidated by Octavio Paz: "Among the revolutions of the twentieth century, the Mexican Revolution was a unique phenomenon. A nationalistic and agrarian revolt, it was not an ideological revolution. It was not the work of a party, and it had almost no program: it was a popular explosion, a spontaneous uprising that had not just one head but many. I have always wondered whether it was a revolution or a revolt. I am of the opinion that it was a revolt."[75] The boys throwing stones were in rebellion, not only against the Israelis but also against the Palestinian rich: "First the Jews, then Rimal!"[76] Rimal was a richer part of Gaza. The violence itself caused "the social glue that held Palestinian society together [to melt] in the fire meant for the Israelis; the old class structure had been washed away in the flood of fury aimed at the occupation."[77] The old class structure provided stability or order, even if the stability was stasis and the order was unjust. The *intifada* was a "rebellion of the poor, an awesome outburst by the forsaken and forgotten at the bottom of the social heap."[78] This was not the violence of an egalitarian movement; at its center was an undisciplined nihilism, the commonplace apolitical violence of young men not even organized into a gang.

The *intifada* also turned into a hunt for Palestinians who collaborated with the Israelis: from December 1987 to May 16, 1990, 207 people were murdered; these murders were justified because "the Palestinian definition of collaborators as those who work for the enemy against their own people [forfeit] their right to membership in the Palestinian community."[79] In fact, many innocents were killed.

Considered a victory by most observers, the *intifada* changed benign perceptions of the Israelis (there they were shooting teenage boys); it also took a suicidal toll by introducing political murder inside the disparaged group.

In Arab countries, one response to the Jewish state was to anathematize anything Jewish: ". . . the obsessive cold war with Israel meant the adoption of fastidious taboos against everything Jewish—encyclopedias had all references to Jewish history, Israel, and the Hebrew language obliterated with black markers. They tried to make this country they detested invisible, not knowing there was nothing more devastating than an invisible enemy."[80] After "know thyself" comes "know thy enemy," but this Arabs refused to do. According to Said, this attempt to make Israel invisible has had a high price: "[Arafat] and his associates seemed to be looking for patrons in the West who would get them a solution of some sort. This quixotic fantasy originated in and was encouraged by the notion that the United States worked like, say, Syria or Iraq: Get close to someone who is close to the maximum leader and all doors will open . . . The idea went along with a total absence of any institutions inside the Arab world that specialized in the study of America . . . Neither Arafat himself nor his principal lieutenants really knew English or French; none of them had ever lived in the West, and they were therefore incapable of understanding it. Even Israel was known through 'contacts' and hearsay rather than through scientific and systematic knowledge."[81] This was in contradistinction to Israel's practice; as Ian Black and Benny Morris say in *Israel's Secret Wars: A History of Israel's Intelligence Services:* "There is probably nowhere else on earth that, proportionate to its size and population, produces, analyses or consumes as much intelligence as Israel, a country of 4 million people that has been in a state of war for every moment of its . . . existence and sees its future depending, perhaps more than ever before, on the need to 'know' its enemies, predict their intentions and frustrate their plans."[82] "Know thy enemy" can sometimes replace "know thyself."

Fighting for a voice, Palestinian women write fiction that is ideological, emotional, and sometimes romantic; Palestinians become the exemplary Arabs: as Hala Deeb Jabbour writes in *A Woman of Nazareth:* "Amira always used the 'we' when she talked of Palestinians, as many Arab nationals did. Palestine was almost everyone's cause and most Arabs identified with the country, its people, its tragedy and aspirations, acquiring those as their own, realizing that Israel was not only the Palestinians' problem, but theirs as well."[83] The Palestinian is the figure of romance: for the Arab women, for the educated and politicized women, for captive women.

There is a bitter humor: "I will tell you a joke: Israel wants 'peace.' A 'piece' of Syria, a 'piece' of Jordan, a 'piece' of Egypt and a 'piece' of Lebanon. That is the peace that Israel wants."[84] (The Israelis tell the same joke about themselves with a different geography.) Yet there is recognition of the infamy of other Arabs against Palestinians: "Elsewhere in the Arab world," writes Jabbour, "the Palestinian refugees were being similarly used and abused. A few of the young men, it was heard, who had migrated to the Gulf States in search of jobs and incomes were being subjected to rape, homosexuality, the most menial of tasks and disdainful attitudes . . ."[85] This is a graphic description of subordination with a sexual edge and of a feminized exploitation: rape and homosexuality reify the feminization of the Palestinian male.

Consciously Palestinian and self-consciously woman, the writer gives a map of sorrow and rage: "Daily there was talk of Palestine, of Jerusalem, of Nazareth, and of Galilee, of Jericho and of Nablus. Always the conversations ended with 'we shall return' . . . And it had become imprinted in all the youngsters' minds [that] that was the only dream, the only goal and ambition, the only 'raison d'être' of the Palestinians. . . . she was also aware of a terrible sense of pain, of helplessness and of fear, out of which a hatred for the usurpers of her heritage was evolving. This hatred was to engulf her, and with time was to run the entire spectrum ranging from extreme hate, to total denial of hatred, to withdrawal, to anger, to guilt, to blame . . ."[86] And yet there is a hope of reconciliation, an epilogue in which the Palestinian character writes to her Israeli cohort, a letter to Leah: "You Israelis smoke a lot—same as us. We sort of have the same fatalistic attitudes. I guess that our circumstances have contributed to that. Neither of us could ever be sure of her tomorrows—wouldn't you agree?"[87] There is no male mediation of the imagined contact or communication; just a sense of sameness: what these women might have in common. Is it possible to make the enemy woman an ally; and how does one choose loyalty to women over nationalist loyalty? It is in the crucible of oppression that one must learn to make this choice. In peril, in danger: is this choice even explored in the imagination; do women anywhere, do writers anywhere, contemplate a transcendent sisterhood or is the idea seen as dishonorable, betrayal, venal?

In the most ideological novels, for instance, *A Compass for the Sunflower* by Liana Badr, there is a value placed on ordinary life outside the domain of a difficult history; "Why," asks one of her characters, "do the tanks always come and eat up periods of our history? The only dates we remember are the Balfour Declaration, the Rogers visit and the carnage of Black September."[88] The ordinary life is female despite the politics of nationalism. The ordinary life is what enfranchisement offers women: which then would require a militant politics of women's freedom.

Contemporary novels by Arab women are nationalist novels in a woman's voice, sometimes carrying epic rage: "You have seen to it, Israel," writes Jabbour, "that your holocaust would never be forgotten. Well, rest assured that the Palestinian holocaust won't be forgotten either."[89] The claim of moral equivalency is terrifying and wrong; but it is a scream intended to get a hearing, to get on the map of political discourse, to make the Palestinian struggle significant and recognized, to reach the consciences of the indifferent; it is fair and right to say that no Jewish life is worth more than any Palestinian life, that the ultimate equality is in facing death, and that human life must be sacred.

In *African Laughter: Four Visits to Zimbabwe,* Doris Lessing explains how some colonizers are able to excuse themselves: "The British were so smug about themselves partly because they never went in for general murder, did not attempt to kill out an entire native population, as did the New Zealanders, and is happening now in Brazil where Indian tribes are being murdered while the world looks on and does nothing. They did not deliberately inject anyone with diseases, nor use drugs and alcohol as aids to domination. On the contrary, there were always hospitals for black people, and white man's liquor was made illegal, for it had been observed what harm firewater had done to the native peoples of North America."[90] The Israelis are in this category of colonizers, knowing full well what they have not done while (unlike the British) appearing to be deeply troubled about what they have done. As Peres writes, "A nation that forces itself on another nation, even for reasons of self-defense, loses the will to abstain from oppression because of the dynamics of conquest—a part of the same 'invisible hand' that regulates history."[91] The details of Israeli loss are enumerated by novelist Simon Louvish: "The growing repression and unstoppable brutalization of ourselves and our Palestinian victims, the shot six-year-old boys, the blood in the dust of villages, the crunch of breaking bones and ideals, the visage of Mister Hyde emerging from Doctor Jekyll in all our bathroom mirrors."[92]

From its beginnings the Israeli military eschewed decoration, ornamentation, public displays of military might, including the ceremonial marching of uniforms. This is an army of male Jews: Israeli women are doing menial work, and Israeli Arabs and fundamentalist Jews do not serve. As Beit-Hallahmi says, "The Israeli approach to war is totally pragmatic. There is no mystique about the military . . . Guards of honor on state occasions are notoriously unimpressive, and the soldiers' appearance is usually disheveled. Israeli generals express contempt for armies who can produce impressive parades and guards of honor, but cannot perform on the battlefield."[93] This is a kind of democratic militarism, not the ethic of a military class, which in Israel would be divisive. This is an army, air force, navy, and intelligence system that have defeated the more effete armies of the Arab countries, the ideal being self-defense of the Israeli state and rescue of persecuted or hostage Jews; for example, in Russia, in Ethiopia, in Uganda. Encouraged by the United States during the Cold War and in particular by Henry Kissinger, Israel approached the Palestinians as "a security problem to be dealt with by tough physical means rather than a political problem to be solved by negotiation and compromise."[94] In other words, Israeli soldiers were the solution to the Palestinian problem.

But the occupation changed the very nature of the Israeli military, suddenly responsible for public order in an area containing the dispossessed. Being citizens as well as soldiers meant that consciences were not owned by the state: some soldiers found the occupation and their role in it unbearable: "To paraphrase the popular characterization of Israeli soldiers ('They shoot and they cry'), they beat and they bitched; they battered away at civilians, with or without cause, and felt enormously resentful about it."[95] It is certainly true that "this experience marked off a generation of young Israelis; their elder comrades-in-arms had never known anything like it."[96] One Israeli describes the military service of a friend in the occupied territories: "He kept on talking about his inner-conflict. During the day, he said, you join in everything—beatings, shooting, driving women out of houses about to be blown-up—and you have no problem with it. You're ready to maim the first stone-thrower you come across without a qualm. But later, back at home, you feel miserable . . . and toss about in bed unable to sleep. But while it's happening you feel nothing. There you stand as a soldier with your moral claims, surrounded by hundreds spitting at you, calling you names, throwing bottles and stones, calling your mother a whore. . . . An incredible fear takes hold of you, and then comes the moment when you can't stand it any longer and you hit out at the next person you see. . . . Most of us, he told me, then just hit out, without looking, and you see these terrible explosions of rage."[97] Schiff and Ya'ari quote "a senior officer who was in charge of dozens of demolition and sealing actions":[98] "I console myself with the thought that this punishment may lessen the violence, but deep in my heart I know that what we're doing will prompt others to react against us violently in revenge."[99]

Jewish settlers also harass the soldiers, behavior called "abusive,"[100] communicating to the Palestinians in the territories their own contempt for Israeli soldiers. The settlers have their own arms and their own colonizing agenda. They are increasingly lawless and messianic in their mission to reclaim more land: what they call Judea and Samaria, or Greater Israel. As Amos Oz says in *Israel, Palestine and Peace: Essays,* "one should never forget that what the extreme right is demanding is a license and legitimation to kill, expel, crush, maltreat and deport until there are no Arabs left here. Or until the Arabs are broken and agree to accept from now on and forever the status of docile slaves in a Greater Israel, which will belong only to those born of a Jewish mother or [who] have converted to Judaism according to Orthodox law."[101] Defense of Arab rights is a way of opposing the orthodox definition of who is a Jew, which means that self-interest is involved.

The specter of a politicized religious fundamentalism haunts Israel as well as the Arab countries; and, indeed, labor and conservative parties in Israel have made alliances with these same fundamentalist Jews in order to achieve a majority in the Knesset. The notion of political alliance with Palestinians against rabid fundamentalists in both societies is largely unexplored; any sensitivity to the situation of the Palestinians, let alone to Israel's share of responsibility for it, is seen as betrayal, disloyalty, a traitorous complicity. "The dying man's curse," writes Louvish, "*Soneh Amcho.* 'Hater of your people.' Well, they're not easy to love. Particularly in their present Master Race phase. It's not easy to love the pinch-faced generals, the sad-sack politicians, the madcap settlers shooting Arab teenagers in the back in the name of self-preservation and God. On the other hand, there are some of the people I do have a soft spot for: A number of bleeding hearts like me, the conscience-stricken, protesters and no-sayers, refusalists and conscientious objectors, though they too can be a pain."[102]

The satirical "Master Race" remark in part speaks to the new importance (relatively speaking) of the Holocaust to Israel, the way it sees itself, the danger it perceives; as one Israeli says, "But by the time of the Yom Kippur War [1973] I realized that I hadn't really escaped the post-Holocaust syndrome. The talk in Israel was not about a war, about enemy soldiers who had to be defeated, but about the threat of annihilation. The Final Solution was omnipresent. The fear was not fear of military defeat but of extermination."[103] This is collective trauma, a historical post-traumatic-stress disorder of not only the Jewish state but also the Jewish nation. The fact that Israelis per se were a little slow on the uptake makes the shock all the more real: they blamed the victims until they realized—there but for the grace of God—they were the victims. Inflicting degradation, especially the debasing reality of superior force, on others creates more and different collective wounds, such that a group conscience replaces an individual conscience. In times of group conflict, the group conscience becomes ideological, a philosophical oxymoron, and nativist, a moral oxymoron.

"They stand at attention amid the names of death camps inscribed on the floor," writes James E. Young in *The Texture of Memory: Holocaust Memorials and Meaning*, "while the eternal flame flickers silently nearby. Even as these soldiers symbolically guard memory of the martyrs, they more literally embody—and thereby remind us of—the heroic fighters. In fact, after being twinned with heroism for so many years, the Shoah itself no longer signifies defeat in many of the young soldiers' eyes, but actually emerges as an era of heroism, of triumph over passivity."[104] In a sense, "the martyrs are not forgotten at Yad Vashem [the Israeli Holocaust memorial], but are recollected heroically as the first to fall in defense of the state."[105] The instrumental value of the Holocaust for Israelis is often described cynically as if it were cold-hearted and entirely strategic; whereas Israeli use of the Holocaust is nervous, anxious, and often near to hysteria, an emotional jungle in which heroism fights despondency and martial masculinity fights conscience. One might say that knowledge of the Holocaust itself numbs conscience in the political present; fear feeds aggression. As Vidal-Naquet says, ". . . the Shoah serves as a perpetual self-justification in all domains, in legitimizing the slightest border incident as marking a renewal of the massacre, in [analogizing] the Palestinians to the SS. The result has been effective—even though the great majority of Israel's inhabitants has had no direct experience of Nazi persecution . . ."[106]

Direct experience is increasingly not the issue as the last of the Holocaust survivors reach old age and natural death. The nightmare has been communicated; and it is in the mind of every Jew. The combination of agony and identity distorts political and moral judgment. One is ashamed to disclose the near insanity of some few Israeli soldiers—it is dangerous when soldiers become mad, Lear in uniform; as Tom Segev says, "In the summer of 1989 the press revealed that a group of soldiers calling itself the Mengele unit had plotted to kill Arabs. There were also reports of units in which the soldiers termed themselves 'Auschwitz platoons' and 'Demjanjuks.'"[107] The aftermath of Kahane's militant anti-Arab racism also included the discovery of "soldiers who, exposed to the history of the Holocaust, were planning all sorts of ways to exterminate the Arabs."[108] The state's response to this copycatting was "to deal not only with the Holocaust but also with the rise of fascism and to explain what racism is and what dangers it holds for democracy . . . [T]oo many soldiers were deducing that the Holocaust justifies every kind of disgraceful action."[109] The lessons of fascism are harder to teach than fascism itself; soldiers are forced to walk a tightrope between militarism and fascist hate and behaviors. The line is very narrow and balance is precarious.

The effect of the Holocaust is not unlike the chain of violence one finds in families, generational trauma in which battered victims become batterers; nor is it unlike the male use of prostitutes (male and female) to act out repeatedly the elements of a former injury or humiliation; T. E. Lawrence is a good example—raped by an Arab potentate, he was deeply distressed that he had ejaculated during the assault; for the rest of his life he hired male prostitutes to abuse him, the abuse itself having become sexual for him. Girls or women who are abused rarely have the social power (except over children) to become abusers; they tend more toward self-cutting or promiscuity or exploitation in prostitution; the social subordination of women keeps women in scenarios of self-hate as victims, particularly of men. If self-hate does not work, male force picks up the slack.

The Israeli courts have declared unequivocally that soldiers have an affirmative responsibility not to obey illegal orders: "The Kfar Kassem killers were sentenced to prison terms of between seven and seventeen years"[110]; and "[a]s of June 1990, 69 court martials have been convened in Israel, with a total of 111 IDF personnel charged. Of these, 23 have been charged with manslaughter or wrongful death (9 involving firearms, 45 for maltreatment of Palestinians [16 of those for maltreating detainees], 27 for theft, and one for forcing an inhabitant to sign an untrue declaration. In no case did prison sentences exceed three and a half years in prison [and that was for theft; no wrongful death sentence exceeded one and a half years in prison]; most of those convicted were given suspended sentences, and 26 were demoted in their rank."[111] So despite the high-minded principle forbidding obedience to illegal orders, Palestinian life is cheap and no soldier has to worry too much about taking such a life.

Most appalling is the Israeli use of torture on arrested Palestinians. The Israeli use of torture is defended by William V. O'Brien in *Law and Morality in Israel's War with the PLO:* "I consider that all the violent means of coercion employed by Israel are legally permissible if used in conformity with the principles of proportion and discrimination. Properly used, beatings, tear gas, plastic bullets and deadly force may be justified by military/security necessity. Deadly force employed by settlers and over civilians in immediate self-defense may be legally permissible."[112] O'Brien concedes that "disproportionate and indiscriminate use has been made of all [of these kinds of violence] on a scale sufficient to constitute a major deviation from the requirements of humanity . . ."[113] O'Brien sees these Israeli crimes as "counterterror measures . . . taken in the context of a protracted war of national liberation, not simply in response to a few scattered terrorist incidents."[114] The terrorism is part of a declared war of liberation; self-defense without abrogation of civil liberties and rights, modest as they are for the Palestinians, is virtually impossible. The apparent lawlessness of the state, in this case the Israeli state, reifies terrorist strategy: force against force; terror against torture.

A recent investigation by a commission (the Landau Commission) "stressed that torture had not been used to convict innocent persons"; but "the Shin Bet had systematically perjured itself in denying to the courts that torture had been employed."[115] Amnesty International was not so sanguine: "Palestinians under interrogation continued to be systematically tortured or ill-treated. Common methods included beatings, hooding with dirty sacks, sleep deprivation, solitary confinement (including in closet-sized dark cells), and prolonged shackling to a small chair."[116] In the words of Schiff and Ya'ari, "Israel behaved—perhaps unwittingly but certainly consistently—as though it was intent upon legitimizing norms of discrimination and abuse, kneading the people who had come under its rule into a spineless mass devoid of any will of its own."[117]

The numbers of people subjected to torture were not small; Amnesty International claims that in 1993, for instance, "[a]pproximately 13,000

Palestinians were arrested on security grounds. About 300 were held in administrative detention without charge or trial and over 15,300 were tried before military courts. . . . Palestinians were systematically tortured or ill-treated under interrogation. Three died in custody in cases in which medical negligence may have been a contributory factor. About 150 Palestinians were shot dead by Israeli forces, some of them in circumstances suggesting extra-judicial killings."[118] In this same year, "Palestinian armed groups committed human rights abuses, including torture and deliberate and arbitrary killings,"[119] this being intra-Palestinian political violence. In 1997 Amnesty International confirmed again that "[t]orture and ill-treatment of Palestinians during interrogation continued to be systematic and officially sanctioned."[120]

The use of torture eliminates ethical Judaism from the boundaries of the Israeli state and state action. Using torture as state policy is genuinely new for Jews; and unspeakable, an affront to every principle of justice. But Israeli society has gone very far down this ugly road: "On a standard visit to one of the army camps, high school students in the Gadna [required paramilitary training for high school students] were let into a detention room . . . and proceeded to beat the detainees. A woman soldier serving in another camp was tried for clubbing blindfolded prisoners being held there, and drivers who had brought senior officers to a detention camp for consultations or inspection tours passed the time by battering prisoners."[121] Maybe only women and children get caught.

As Samuel Segev writes in *Crossing the Jordan: Israel's Hard Road to Peace,* in negotiations Palestinians asked for "the dissolution of two elite Israeli army units—Shimshon and Duvdevan—whose sole duty it was to track down the intifada activists. The soldiers and officers in these two units spoke Arabic and, disguised as Arabs, arrested and sometimes killed intifada leaders."[122] Does violence create more violence? Certainly, this kind of sabotage creates instability, paranoia, and hate. It also communicates to the Palestinians a ruthlessness that becomes a signature for Israelis: Jews outside of Israel admire this ruthlessness and provide economic and moral support. The Israelis when brutal avenge the weak Jews who were slaughtered.

When Israel reached out, it was most often to kill Palestinian terrorists on their own ground: "Keep terrorists on the run, is the rule. It might make them harder to find, but it preoccupies them with their own safety rather than plotting their crimes."[123] This policy was not unlike George Habash's: "To kill a Jew far from the battlefield has more effect than

killing hundreds of Jews in battle."[124] Of course, Habash is killing civilians; Israelis are after terrorists, who are essentially soldiers of a cheap and
dirty war; or are they just after Palestinians? Is this a response to terrorism
or is it indiscriminate hate?

The model of Israeli ruthlessness is admired by much of the fascist
right wing; training police and military in South Africa under apartheid,
in totalitarian countries in Central and South America; even noted by the
terrorist pied noir, the French Algerians; as Camus said: "[The French Al-
gerians] are very determined and unsubtle. The thing that's the most
amusing, when you know how completely anti-Semitic the European Algerians are, is their present admiration for Israel. 'Those people know the
way to deal with the Arabs,' they say."[125] And "those people" will pay a
price, as did the French in Algeria.

The physical assault of political prisoners inevitably becomes an assault on an ethnicity as such, people born as whatever the stigmatized
group is; and physical assault inevitably creates hate—of the torturers and
of the terrorists; a belief in having been wronged, a determination to
strategize revenge. Physical assault creates a new kind of memory: a memory dedicated to the enemy, inspired by the enemy. Physical assault creates
wounds that never heal. Arresting politicals in Northern Ireland, the
British used internment as the preface to torture: "Injustice was seen to
have been done through internment, used as a sectarian tool, and torture
seen to have been done in the use of deep interrogation. The army had arrested innocent suspects with brutality. The army had taken them to barracks and made them run the gauntlet—beaten them all, beaten them
after the frightful and frightening time during the arrest, beaten them as
revenge or as policy."[126] The outcome is to turn innocents into politicals;
and surely there must be innocents among the Palestinians. Amos Oz says
that the conflict between Israelis and Palestinians "is a tragedy in the exact
sense of the word"; "[t]ragedies," he says, "can be resolved in one of two
ways: . . . At the end of a Shakespearean tragedy, the stage is strewn with
dead bodies and maybe there's some justice hovering high above. A
Chekhov tragedy . . . ends with everybody disillusioned, embittered,
heartbroken, disappointed, absolutely shattered, but still alive. And I
want," he says, "a Chekhovian resolution and not a Shakespearean one for
the Israeli-Palestinian tragedy."[127] This is a brave desire, but in Israel so far
it is Shakespeare who moves the masses.

The fact and history of Palestinian terrorism against Israelis in particular and Jews in general is widely known. The exiled and occupied nurse their anger, keep picking at their own wounds; they refuse pacification or an alternative reality; they insist on the materiality of their dispossession; they refuse to be planted elsewhere, in another soil; they refuse to accept their loss or their defeat; they refuse to make other political or living arrangements; they demand return, repatriation, or they demand a coequal sovereignty in a separate state; they want Jerusalem; they insist that their exclusion from the Jewish state, from their own land, is unbearable and the worst injustice ever known. As David Rieff says in *The Exile: Cuba in the Heart of Miami,* "What people wanted, of course, was for the pain and the loss to be assuaged. But given the choice between forgetting about Cuba and being in pain, the fallback position of the exile, after all its political disappointments, was, precisely, to make sure that the pain did not go away."[128] For Palestinians in particular, terrorism is a way of redistributing the pain so that "[n]o mundane act—shopping, waiting at a bus stop, driving to work, stopping at a bar—can be taken without the fear that a terrorist bomb or machine gun will kill and destroy at random. The genius of terror is that it is so economical as a means of armed coercion."[129] It appears that terrorism is the nuclear bomb of the disenfranchised—easy, cheap, with a huge impact not only on direct victims but on the whole society in which the direct victims live.

Between June 1967 and October 1985, there were 353 terrorist attacks inside Israel and each one caused casualties. In the era of Oslo and the Palestinian Authority there has been a near endless parade of suicide bombers who have murdered Israeli civilians in random acts of terror. There were airplane hijackings, airport bombings, and at least one cruise ship hijacking, and the murder of Israeli Olympic athletes; and the rise of notorious terrorist assassins like Habash, Carlos the Jackal, and Abu Nidal. Habash in particular extended the target to include the United States and its citizens while Abu Nidal killed moderate Palestinians: "In January 1978, some months after Begin took office . . . Abu Nidal began killing prominent PLO moderates—precisely the men who were trying to influence Western opinion by preaching negotiation and reconciliation with Israel."[130] The new guys on the block—Hamas, Hezbollah, Osama bin Laden—target Jews, Israel and Israelis, Palestinians, and the United States. This is a sow-what-you-reap phenomenon of stunning grandiosity: how one defines the first cause is a matter of ideology.

Samuel Segev describes Israeli intelligence's profile of a Hamas suicide bomber: ". . . eighteen to twenty-four years old, single, and of poor social and economic background. Recruited mostly in mosques . . . [the suicide bomber] believed that by becoming a *shahid* (martyr) he would go straight to Paradise, where he would be surrounded by pretty women."[131] This is the same young man who is armed in Bosnia, Rwanda, and other global sites of male violence.

For the Arab world Palestinian terrorism is contextualized as resistance to a colonial power: "There is Palestinian terrorism," said Algeria's representative to the United Nations, "just as yesterday there was Algerian terrorism, in which we glory, and which it occurred to no one to describe at that time as Arab terrorism."[132] But increasingly the violence is internecine and fratricidal: the intifada's "first targets were the traditional Palestinian chiefs, or *mukhtars*. The militant youths see these men as having served Israel's interests, as a kind of Vichy government."[133] In addition, there was a "more corrosive symptom of the long years of Israeli occupation: the network of Israeli collaborators within the Palestinian community . . . An element of fear crept into daily life . . . "[134] Hate of the nationalist enemy becomes more fierce when one is afraid of one's own; this is a mechanism of denial caused by fear; rather than facing the phenomenon of self-cannibalism, one ratchets up the nationalist fury.

At the same time, Palestinians working in Israel have carried out "[s]tabbing attacks against Israeli citizens"; while Israeli rules on who gets in for day labor "have presumably brought the Israelis a rich harvest of new collaborators."[135] Hamas endorses the stabbing attacks. Radical Islam promises salvation to such assassins. This religious endorsement of murder is not the contradiction it seems: Muhammad, unlike Jesus, was a warrior. As Mernissi says, "The motto of the Kharijites, '*La hikma illa lillah*' ('Power belongs only to God') was used for the first time during the fourth caliphate . . . and led to [the ruler's] assassination by terrorists . . . This same slogan has condemned hundreds of imams and Muslim leaders, the last of whom was President Anwar Sadat of Egypt. Political dissidence is expressed in Islam as condemnation of the leader. It is this rebel tradition that links dissidence with terrorism."[136] The Jewish "an eye for an eye" is a notion of justice; the Islamic jihad is a notion of conquest. The killing of a leader has just entered the Jewish religious lexicon: Rabin killed by an orthodox Jew.

In the Islamic environment of religiously sanctioned intratribe violence, which is also construed to be a repudiation of modernity, violence against women, commonly regarded as sexual provocateurs, continues to be a sacred necessity, especially honor murders; the ultimate fundamentalist oppression is the ruling doctrine of the Taliban in Afghanistan: the complete segregation and separation of women, a hiding and confinement of women not unlike live burial. Women without men are left to starve to death.

Palestinians have seen Israeli state power used against them as vendetta violence, both personal in that it expresses an Israeli contempt for any Palestinian and political in that it suppresses their rights: state violence has been perceived as state terrorism, a plunder-and-pillage mentality that defines Israelis as such. But now, arising inside Israel, there is a right-wing terrorism toward Palestinians not explicitly sanctioned by the Israeli state: so-called direct action by Jewish settlers—"wild retaliatory gestures ranging from a rampage to shatter the windshields of Arab vehicles in Kalkilya . . . to a nocturnal shooting spree in the Deheishe refugee camp by residents of Kiryat Arba."[137] The first was sponsored by the militant Gush Emunim and the second by Meir Kahane's Kach movement.

On a demand from Israeli law professors, there was a special commission to investigate Jewish terrorism; as Ehud Sprinzak writes in *The Ascendance of Israel's Radical Right*, in 1982 the Karp Report "[confirmed] the existence of anti-Arab vigilante activities"; and "showed that most of these acts went unpunished."[138] There were detailed accounts of the vigilante acts, which included "killing, wounding, physical assaults, property damage, and the use of armed and unarmed threats . . ."[139] This vigilante violence was rabbi-sanctioned at the extremist settlement of Gush Emunim: ". . . the radicalization process that finally produced terrorism within Gush Emunim was not marginal but central. It was a by-product of the movement's belief in its own redemptive role . . . [W]ithin twelve years the combination of messianic belief and a situation of continual national conflict with a built-in propensity for incremental violence resulted in extralegalism, vigilantism, selective terrorism, and finally, indiscriminate mass terrorism."[140] This religiously sanctioned violence against Arabs has all the earmarks of a race war; right and wrong are ethnically based ideas; the quietism of pre-Holocaust orthodoxy has indeed been destroyed; now orthodoxy is characterized by aggression. Gush Emunim has changed the landscape of meaning in Israel and for Jews: ". . . Gush Emunim has succeeded in presenting its ideology as the true and perhaps only heir of

Zionism, its adherents as engaged in the revival of the old pioneering spirit."[141] This makes Zionism synonymous with race war, an egregious revisionism that the Jewish nation, if not the Jewish state, must not accept.

And so Jabbour asks in *A Woman of Nazareth:* "Is it going to be Masada, Sampson's temple or another Holocaust for you? And will it be Deir Yassins, Tat-al-Zaatars, Sabras and Chantillas for us?"[142] This is not a rhetorically inflated question. The death of the Jewish state would mean the death of the Jewish people; a Jewish-sponsored race war would mean the same; the Palestinians, too, could be erased.

Debased men need to degrade women, so that the struggle to subordinate women becomes a basic struggle for male identity as such; in liberation movements, women get a temporary pass from complete servility, because they can be used and useful in any subversion or underground fighting. Once the liberation struggle is won, the women are recolonialized, as happened in Nicaragua, Israel itself, or Algeria. Every time an oppressed group gets state power through which it can express its integrity as a people, it destroys the sovereignty of women over their own bodies, so that state power is built directly on the violation of women's integrity. Once debased men become powerful men, the degrading of women becomes a state-protected right; and power most often also requires the demeaning of a racial or ethnic or religious other. Empowered masculinity gets its vitality and arrogance from its newest victory over women, a victory enhanced by the resources and mechanisms of state power.

Palestinian women have been militant in the nationalist struggle and in the *intifada* and they have paid a high price; as MacDonald writes in *Shoot the Women First:* "By January 1991, ninety-seven females (12 percent of those killed) had been shot dead. Many had been killed in demonstrations either as participants or as innocent bystanders, after being hit by rubber bullets or live ammunition. Thousands more women were injured, some crippled or maimed for life, by beatings. It is women who form the largest group of those requiring hospital treatment after beatings. They are attacked as they try to protect children and are particularly targeted when soldiers break into their homes searching for suspects. There is evidence that soldiers deliberately try to terrify entire families by showing brutality to women."[143] The subsuming of the individual in the nationalist struggle is an easy process for women, who have little experience with a social reification of a singular identity; this can be turned into a political virtue—as one West Bank woman says, "Our lives, you must understand, are individually worth nothing. You can blow them away. But others will always rise up to take our place. It is as if we were in a big prison, and the only thing we really have to lose is that. Imagine what it is like to be me, a proud, well-educated woman who has traveled to many countries. Then see what it is like to be an insect, for that is what the soldiers call us—cockroaches, dogs, insects. . . . The soldier crushed us under his boot like insects."[144] It is in a repudiation of the masculinity of the nationalist enemy that women escape ignominy; and, at the same time, another enemy is closer. The lowering of women in ideology and in practice becomes a training ground for a nouveau masculinity of domination and callousness.

The war of liberation ends and in a blink resistance is a memory, vivid to the women, meaningless to the men. As Aicha Lemsine writes in the introduction to her novel *The Chrysalis:* " . . . [I]n truth Algerian women have never lacked courage! They resisted foreign occupation, they participated alongside their menfolk to build a new nation. The heroism of Algerian women fighters during the war [against the French] will have a permanent place in contemporary history. And in those times, a woman's body was not taboo when she came into contact with men in the [resistance], or was subjected to torture or condemned to death by the forces of colonialism. Warrior women, they were to become the victims of those to whom they had given life, and for whom they sacrificed the best of themselves."[145] Yet women never believe that this dispossession will happen; they refute the inevitability of it; they experience freedom in fighting the nationalist enemy and think themselves perceived as valiant and honorable by men of their own nation or group; as Badr describes in *A Compass for the Sunflower:* "Everyone talked about revolution and women's liberation, and about transforming the balance of class forces which had operated in the old society, and I, like the rest of them, believed in what was being argued for and threw myself into logical discussions and considered that a beautiful revolution was the outstanding achievement of the twentieth century."[146] In other words, women's liberation is part of the romance of a contemporary national liberation movement; and in the sensibility of contemporary Arab women, the Palestinian male is the romantic figure; as Ahdaf Soueif writes in her novel *In the Eye of the Sun:* "There was no place that he could assume he would be in ten, five, one year's time. If he went back to Nablus and walked down a street to buy a newspaper he could not assume that he would be able to walk down that same street again the next day. And that was why when you looked at him it seemed, despite the good looks, the mixture of French and Turkish with curly black hair, green eyes, and a slightish build, he appeared almost—maimed. One of a bruised people."[147] In the words of Palestinian poet Rashid Hussein: "The main thing they care about is to see the wife giving birth to a baby boy,/So they will say, 'She is the daughter of an honourable man whom we are all proud of.'/She gave birth to a baby boy,/his face is just like a moon./They will say, 'Her husband is a great masculine man.'"[148]

The romance of a liberation movement or of its male exemplars cannot withstand the greater romance of the male with himself: a romance that repudiates the independence of women, sanctions the use of force against women, demands the social and political invisibility of women. The traditional life lives on in the nooks and crannies and shacks and camps of the dispossessed. "You're from the West," says Zahra, a Palestinian woman with twelve children and pregnant, to Robin Morgan. "You know about these things. Tell me, *tell me* how not to have another child. It's killing me. I'll die. I'll die of it. I'll do anything. I don't care what they say. What do men know about life? I don't care about the mullahs, I don't care about my husband, I don't care about *God!*"[149] In stolen, secret conversations women speak rebellion; the politicizing of that rebellion is women's liberation, outside male control and male understanding.

Even the reproductive fecundity of the average woman becomes, in male hands, a weapon, a threat, understood as such by the enemy males in what can be euphemized as a demographic war: "Thus," write Schiff and Ya'ari, "Yasser Arafat is quite justified in boasting that the Palestinians have a nonconventional weapon of their own: the 'biological bomb' represented by the womb of the Palestinian woman. Although the fertility rate of the women of Gaza continues to decline by 0.5 percent every five years, in 1987 it stood at an average of 5.7."[150] Each side keeps track of the birthrate. In general, literacy is the one determinant of whether or not women have twelve children or one or two—the higher the literacy the lower the birth rate. Poor Palestinian women are twice displaced: no homeland and insufficient education.

The lot of the traditional woman, borderless and not limited to Arabs, is characterized by the need for an alliance with a man in order to survive; as Badr writes in *A Compass for the Sunflower:* "'It was very hard for me and for his other wife. Children, don't you understand that it is better to have even the shadow of a man than empty walls about you?' None of us believed her, for she had told us how her youth was spent waiting for the next time he hit her with a stick which he always used to say to her was a branch cut from a tree growing in Paradise."[151] Who could accept such a destiny: except that women do in the Arab lands, in Israel, in Europe and England, in the United States. Many men—more than many and less than all—have a stick from Paradise and a fist from Hell.

Arab and Muslim women also face purdah—the segregation and house arrest of women. Women are physically hidden: by veils and burquas in public and kept inside windowless rooms in houses they come to in arranged marriages. As Armstrong says in her biography of Muhammad: "We should pause to consider the question of the *hijab,* and the Muslim institution of the veil. It is often seen in the West as a symbol of male oppression, but in the Qu'ran it was simply a piece of protocol that applied only to the Prophet's wives."[152] Many Arab feminists make this same point; and Mernissi in *The Veil and the Male Elite: A Feminist Interpretation of Women's Rights in Islam* provides a model for the citizenship of women under Islam: "Every woman who came to Medina when the Prophet was the political leader of the Muslims could gain access to full citizenship, the status of *sahabi,* Companion of the Prophet. Muslims can take pride that in their language they have the feminine of that word, *sahabiyat,* women who enjoyed the right to enter into the councils of the Muslim *umma,* to speak freely to its Prophet-leader, to dispute with the men, to fight for their happiness, and to be involved in the management of military and political affairs."[153] There is no such precedent or supporting argument for women's civil inclusion in the Hebrew Bible or in Jewish practice on the orthodox side; as Rabbi Richard G. Hirsch says, "Now, you can't have a modern society ruled by *halakha.* . . . Never will the ultra-orthodox accept the equality of women. Never will they permit women to serve as witnesses in a court. Never will they permit women to entertain cases of divorce. Never will they permit women to be rabbis or to get called to the Torah. A [modern] state can't be ruled by halakhic principles."[154] This is to say that there is little religious recourse for Jewish feminists who make a teleological claim to religious equality; while Muslim feminists can at least make an argument based on an accepted history.

But whatever the origin of the veil, it is now an often coerced feature of female subjugation. "So wrap the nubile girl in veils," writes novelist Assia Djebar in *Fantasia: An Algerian Cavalcade.* "Make her invisible.

Make her more unseeing than the sightless, destroy in her every memory of the world without. And what if she has learned to write? The jailer who guards a body that has no words—and written words can travel—may sleep in peace: it will suffice to brick up the windows, padlock the sole entrance door, and erect a blank wall rising up to heaven."[155] These are not fictional acts: windows are bricked up, padlocks are used on the sole door, blank walls do rise up to wherever the stick from Paradise lives. Against this oppression, Djebar posits writing and reading: "'Doesn't your daughter wear a veil yet?' asks one or other of the matrons, gazing questioningly at my mother with suspicious kohl-rimmed eyes . . . I must be thirteen, or possibly fourteen. 'She reads!' my mother replies stiffly. Everyone is swallowed up in the embarrassed silence that ensues. And in my own silence."[156] The power of reading and writing is—for the female disenfranchised—deeply subversive, a quiet rebellion.

Every attempt is made to kneecap women: make them crippled and immobile, physically restrained, intellectually humble. The justification is not that women are weak but that men are. As Cheryl Rubenberg writes in her introduction to Jabbour's *A Woman of Nazareth:* "Female sexuality is thought to reside in women's *qaid*—the power to deceive and defeat men by cunning and intrigue; in *fitna*—women's ability to cause disorder or chaos and to make men lose their self-control—*fitna* also means beauty, and female beauty itself is considered a source of chaos since it is viewed as an incitement to male sexual desire and as a distraction to men from their social and religious obligations; and in *al-hawa*—desire, the opposite of reason, the source of all that is illicit, and the cause of disorder."[157] Just as in the West, women's sexuality is taken to be a provocation: beating it back with a stick, controlling it, is the male strategy in both worlds: in one she is covered and imprisoned, in the other she is naked and fetishized.

Arabic itself commits the literate as well as those who use an oral vernacular to a sexual double standard; as Sana Al-Khayyat writes in *Honour and Shame: Women in Modern Iraq:* "The Arabic word *adhra* (virgin) is a feminine word always used to refer to women, never to men; there is no masculine equivalent. When some of the women told me that their husbands 'had no sexual experience before marriage,' they had no convenient masculine term to use."[158] Language is commonly an aggressive, systematic tool of dominance, a way of manipulating invisibility and silence.

Of course, no male-dominant system says that men are weak and women are strong; the premise is simply accepted as the essence of an inferior status: which causes deep-seated shame in women about their bodies and their sexuality. In the Arab world, the purity of the female body is a life-or-death issue; any compromised girl or woman can be and most likely will be killed by a male relative, especially a brother or a father. As Al-Khayyat writes: " . . . the most important connotation of honour in the Arab world is related to the sexual conduct of women. If a woman is immodest or brings shame on her family by her sexual conduct, she brings shame and dishonour on all her kin. . . . Someone's honour in the sense of *ird* is so important that he will swear by it like the name of God; a man might swear by the *ird* of his sister, for example."[159] What happens to a person bearing this burden? As an Iraqi feminist poet says, "Washing off the shame . . . Washing off the shame. . . . No smile, no joy, no turn as the knife so waiting/For us in the hand of father or brother/And tomorrow, who knows which desert/Swallows us, to wash off shame?"[160]

This intractable honor system is used by Israelis against Palestinian women "in forcing confessions from . . . detainees"; the success of this blackmail or coercion "also shows the association in the victim's mind of the 'honor' of Palestine in her own virginity. The traditional system remains intact, except that the locus of honor has been shifted for the activist victim from her family, upward to the whole of Palestine and the struggle for self-determination."[161] This nationalist self-determination is, sadly, the very self-determination that will eclipse and then erase her own.

No notion of honor, however, compromises the ability of the Palestinian woman to work: menial, defeating, unending work. As Morgan says about the women in Gaza: "This is neither the first country nor the first situation where I have been told that 'here the women don't work.' I see them working everywhere all the time. I see them working in the fields while men sit idle in the village coffeehouse. I see them employed in the lowest-paying jobs, and always, in addition, doing the nonpaying job that isn't even considered 'work': the life-sustaining labor of bearing, feeding, caring for children, the keeping of homes even when there are no real homes to keep. I see them hauling water and balancing bales on their heads; scrubbing clothes under a thin stream from a communal spigot; lifting, pulling, carrying, chopping, cooking, sewing. I see them in sweatshops in the Strip, where Israeli cloth imported by the Occupying Authority for this purpose is cut and sewn into clothing by cheap labor, then carted back into Israel for sale at higher prices than Gazans can afford."[162] As with Chinese footbinding, physical constraint is less—not eliminated but less—for women who do menial labor. Arguably, a half-bound foot is qualitatively different from the three-inch stumps of upper-class women.

That reading and writing lead to subversion, exclusion, an exile of gender, an escape from servitude, is the heartbeat of contemporary fiction by Arab women. As Djebar says in her *Fantasia: "They call me an exile. It is more than that: I have been banished from my homeland to listen and bring back some traces of liberty to the women of my family . . . I imagine I constitute the link . . .* "[63] The rule of men over women has a transparency in Arab culture; and so the writers try to articulate that transparency, which includes exile and stigmatization for those who have speech or writing or reading; this exile is as much homelessness as Palestinian dislocation by the Israelis; this is a homelessness that pits the literate woman against history, family, and place. There is a deep and committed feminism in Arab women writers no matter how distressed they are by questions of nationalism or Palestine per se; and there is a strong sense of communal responsibility. As Djebar writes in *A Sister to Scheherazade: "As soon as we women are freed from the past, where do we stand? . . . O, my sister, I who thought to wake you, I'm afraid. I'm afraid for all women, not just two or three . . . barring midwives, barring mothers standing guard and those carrion-beetle matriarchs, I fear lest we find ourselves in chains again, in 'this West in the Orient,' this corner of the earth where day dawned so slowly for us that twilight is already closing in around us everywhere."*[164] She is damning those lines of women who keep women in, make sure the pain is inflicted, enforcers for male rule over women.

In a similar spirit of pain and fear, though never giving up much, there are male allies who are willing to provoke male rage by exposing male hypocrisy; as Adam Zameenzad writes in *The 13th House,* a novel about Pakistan: "The beards of mullahs trembled with righteous rage at obscenity and immorality, which they saw in anything that had an opening, or by any stretch of the imagination could be construed as vaguely perpendicular, round, oval, pendulous or receding. . . . You could feel their sphincters tightening in orgiastic fury as under the tattered garb of chastity angry erections kept popping up, aching symbols of a sexually deprived society."[165] The men, of course, are not sexually deprived because they use prostitutes and incestuously abuse sisters; but they are deprived of reciprocity, intimacy, or any sexuality not based on dominance and dehumanization; do they know it? Male allies only go so far; women have to be the long-distance runners. It's a terrifying run.

Jewish involvement in prostitution, as user and used, is part of the untaught history: "During their wanderings in the desert, the Israelites 'fornicate' (from the root *znh,* meaning literally 'to commit prostitution') with Moabite women . . . "[166] One might say that committing prostitution has always been the implicit meaning of intercourse or fornication; if not an implicit meaning, then an explicit practice. Even in the Middle Ages, in France and Spain, "the Jewish and secular court records from the period suggest that, as in northern Europe, social behavior among Jews was frequently at odds with legal norms. These cases include premarital and extramarital sex, prostitution, and rape. Jewish men not only frequented Muslim and Christian prostitutes, but there were Jewish prostitutes as well."[167] Postbiblical Jews have always been preoccupied with proof of innocence; and certainly there was the near universal belief that prostitution had to do only with men: in other words, the prostitutes themselves were outside the margins of concern, community, and history. Prostitutes were the ultimate exiles; night swallowed them.

The German tradition was the opposite, since Germans never considered that they had to prove their innocence; their governments built brothels. As Steve Ozment writes in *The Bürgermeister's Daughter:* "City governments established public brothels during the fifteenth century as an outlet for the sexual needs of single young men and as a measure of protection for the marriageable daughters . . . "[168] There was a "rapid expansion of brothels in the fifteenth century and [also] the closely related rampant spread of syphilis in the sixteenth . . . "[169] Any women sexually free or nonconforming "could find themselves paraded barefoot through town, clad in penitential tunics and with their heads shaved."[170] This was a gender- and class-specific punishment; yet it is also emblematic— women stoned or burned or attacked for being sexually autonomous or self-defined.

Almost as foreplay for the climax of Nazism, in Munich, where Hitler got his political start, prostitution was omnipresent; David Clay Large in *Where Ghosts Walked: Munich's Road to the Third Reich* quotes from a 1910 pamphlet: Munich is "infested" . . . "Every six paces, it seems, one encounters a prostitute."[171] In Vienna at about the same time Stefan Zweig noticed that the pavements were "speckled so richly with women for sale that it was harder to keep out of their way than to find them. . . . At all prices and all times of day, female human merchandise was openly for sale, and it really took a man no more time or trouble to buy himself a woman for fifteen minutes, an hour or a night than it did to buy a packet of cigarettes or a newspaper."[172] This is the literal meaning of being cheap: as a commodity a dime a dozen.

In Weimar, according to Mullins, the art "reflects a more brutal hostility towards women . . . Nowhere in art are expressions of physical disgust so frank as the prostitute pictures of Otto Dix. . . . Their revolting appearance matches the corruption of the trade they ply."[173] The pre-Nazi-dominated Berlin of Auden and Isherwood had "170 male brothels under police supervision."[174] Koonz points out that "[s]ome men enjoyed the side effects of the poverty that drove thousands of women into prostitution. Klaus Mann recalled strolling through 'fierce Amazons, strutting in high boots made of green, glossy leather. One of them brandished a supple cane and leered at me as I passed by . . .' "[175] Klaus Mann was gay and anti-Nazi; yet, like Flaubert, he expresses great excitement at the contaminating squalor of prostituted women.

The connection between carnality and male Jews had long been established in the German context; especially, these Jews pushed German girls and women into prostitution so that they could have the women: the prostitution is nearly rape; or it is rape with money; or Jewish power brokers forced girls to prostitute, for instance, as Large writes, ". . . the retailer Hermann Tietz, who built Munich's first department store, was accused of driving his salesgirls to prostitution by paying them less than a living wage."[176] Even prostitution becomes part of a Jewish plot: effected not by lowlife pimps but figures of money and influence.

There was a strong feminist movement in the pre-Nazi years and, as Sheila Jeffreys says more generally in *The Idea of Prostitution,* "It was ironic that so many feminist energies and sympathies were diverted before 1914 into concern about the White Slave Traffic rather than about the thousands of women routinely used in prostitution by men. The exceptions had become more important than the rule, and did indeed constitute a concentration on 'forced' rather than 'free' prostitution."[177] Feminism itself was seen as yet another Jewish conspiracy; and the inability of feminists to fight the masculinist power of the rising Nazi movement meant the end of the women's movement. Yes, feminists would have had to fight the Nazis, readily recognizable as enemies early on because of their all-male brutality.

The Nazis themselves had an appetite for prostituted women: Hitler for the very young; special brothels for the SS; brothels inside concentration camps. One might say that the Nazis strategized brothels as a means of social containment or pacification; and within the strategy they made rigorous rules to try to stop the spread of sexual diseases, which were contaminating and unclean; this was a parallel to obliterating the disease of Jewishness as such—as Philippe Burrin writes in *France Under the Germans: Collaboration and Compromise:* "The main problem for the occupation authorities was controlling prostitution. The Nazi regime exacerbated a German obsession with venereal diseases that had already been evident in 1914–18 and that now caused them to reserve particular brothels for the exclusive use of the Wehrmacht. By the spring of 1941, twenty-nine of these establishments in the Paris region had been designated for the troops, and three for German officers: no Jews or blacks; condoms obligatory; detailed rules of hygiene. . . . Each time a German soldier left a brothel he received a card bearing the name of the brothel, the date and the girl's first name."[178] There were also between 5,000 and 6,000 street prostitutes who were "designated . . . for the exclusive use of the Germans."[179] Still, despite the organizing abilities of the Nazis—or because of it—there were an additional 80,000 to 100,000 women prostituting unlicensed in Paris alone. After the war it was a fact, rarely acknowledged, "that some of the most daring women were prostitutes in the service of the resistance," since they "could easily rifle the pockets of their German customers."[180]

The Nazis used prostitution as a mechanism of social control: organizing the sexuality of men while degrading and destroying women, that degradation made more fulsome as prostituted women stood in for dirty, polluting Jews. Prostitutes are a big part of the Nazi story: not just because Hitler used them rhetorically as social scapegoats but also because the Nazis both bodily used and punished them. It is well known, as Simpson says in *The Splendid Blond Beast: Money, Law, and Genocide in the Twentieth Century,* that "[m]ental patients and disabled people appear to have been the first ones the Nazis actually gassed; they killed at least 50,000 in an experimental euthanasia program code-named *Aktion T4* that began in the fall of 1939."[181] It is less known that "[r]eports from German-occupied Poland suggest that the SS gassed a number of Polish prostitutes at about the same time."[182] Even more shocking is Vera Laska's testimony about Auschwitz: "Among the first women in Auschwitz were German prostitutes and Jewish girls from Slovakia. These women were issued evening gowns in which they were forced to help build Auschwitz, in rain or snow. Of the hundreds only a handful survived by 1944."[183] One can picture them in the wet, sometimes frozen muck of Auschwitz; the long, wet gowns, shoveling, carrying, the mixed-race (in Nazi terms) death throes of German prostitutes and Jewish women from Slovakia; how they starved and how they worked, mocked by the costumes the Nazis had chosen for them. Prostitutes were the first: gassed in Poland, sent to Auschwitz. As Martin Gilbert writes in *Auschwitz and the Allies,* "The first two trains to reach Auschwitz arrived on 26 March 1942. In the sealed and stifling cattle trucks of the first train from Ravensbrück concentration camp, north of Berlin, were 999 women who were tattooed on the forearms with the numbers 1 to 999. Two hours later the second train arrived, bringing a further 999 Jewesses from Slovakia. They were also tattooed, with the numbers 1,000 to 1,998."[184] Auschwitz 1 to 999 were largely if not entirely prostituted women from Ravensbrück.

Prostitutes were also first in another way: "From Lodz there were continual deportations to the death camp at Chelmo, starting in December 1941. First to be deported were all the known and registered Jewish prostitutes . . ."[185] Well, who could care? These are the women left out of any Jewish reckoning with the Nazis—or any feminist reckoning with prostitution: wherever there is racial or ethnic stigmatization, the women of the stigmatized group who are prostituted are the first to be rounded up, shipped off, and forgotten.

Also in 1941 women were brought to Dachau, not constructed to hold women, in order to prostitute: "A few dozen women were brought in from Ravensbrück to service the brothel for privileged prisoners. These women were recruited with promises of freedom after serving six months (about 2,000 services), which was never the case. Most of the women were Germans, Poles and Russians."[186] This suggests free will; but in the camps there were few meaningful exercises of free will.

Russian prisoners of war, supposedly protected by the Geneva Convention, were treated savagely in forced labor in German factories; as Neil Gregor writes in *Daimler-Benz in the Third Reich:* "For the Soviet women in particular, factory hardship was compounded by great suffering in the barracks. Many were forced to prostitute themselves to west European workers for bread. If they became pregnant, they were usually forced to have an abortion; those who did give birth mostly lost their infants through malnutrition or related illnesses."[187] This is how to find prostituted women: look at the bottom of any hierarchy—they will be poor relative to those who use them even when wealth is calculated in pieces of bread.

Inside the concentration camps were brothels. As Sofsky says, "A concentration camp was not just a collection of wooden barracks. Depending on its stage of completion, its perimeters included workshops, factory halls, and agricultural enterprises, a heating plant and a fire-extinguishing pond, barracks and offices, a brothel and a movie house, mess halls, an infirmary and dispensaries, a jail and a crematorium. Fully finished, it was a complete settlement with a network of streets and a railroad . . . a town for personnel and prisoners housing thousands, at times tens of thousands . . ."[188] The concentration camp was a company town and the company was National Socialism. Brothels were set up as "a countermeasure" to "sadistic excesses of individual tormentors."[189] As Laska reports, "I know that in Auschwitz there was a bordello of forty rooms in Block 24 for the black triangles, German inmates and a few selected sycophants with green triangles. Tickets were handed out as a reward by the SS to this 'Puff Haus.' The madam was called the 'Puff Mutter.' The girls worked a two-hour day and three times a week. With German thoroughness the Puff Mother rang the bell each twenty minutes (same time as the burning shift in the ovens!)."[190] The colonization and use of prostituted women or women forced into prostitution once under the dominion of Nazis is the least scrutinized part of the Nazi enterprise.

While Nazism was a "male event" Auschwitz might be called a female event, built on a primal antagonism to the bodies of women, an antagonism that included sadistic medical experiments. As Lore Shelley writes in *Criminal Experiments on Human Beings in Auschwitz and War Research Laboratories: Twenty Women Prisoners' Accounts:* "All inmates of Block 10 [where experimentation on women was done] were Jewish except for the crew of the brothel, which consisted of German black-triangled and Polish prisoners who came from time to time to be examined for venereal disease."[191] According to Robert Jay Lifton and Amy Hackett: "Block 10 . . . housed some 20 prostitutes, its only regular non-Jewish residents, who were available to elite prisoners as a work incentive and prophylactic against homosexual practices."[192] Says one former inmate: "Towards the end of October 1943, the prostitutes left. The place had been turned into something like a slave market with the Commandants from surrounding camps having come and inspected them to make their selection."[193] At Buchenwald there was a brothel servicing German officers; as Micahel Etkind writes, "I was moved from Barrack 66 and joined Barrack 54, a children's barrack. . . . Opposite the children's barrack, across the thin wire fence, was the compound of women prisoners who had been selected to serve the pleasure of the German officers. Men went in and out all day, adjusting their clothing as they left. The young women sat on chairs outside the door, on parade."[194] There was nothing casual about Nazi use of prostitution: the practice was strategic and intentional, part of the gynocidal assault on women's bodies.

Sometimes women were sexually used but the usage had the appearance of "affair" or infatuation; as Lifton writes in *The Nazi Doctors: Medical Killing and the Psychology of Genocide:* "SS doctors' relationships with women prisoner doctors were complex and could include elements of 'chivalry' and at times even affection, but also deception and danger"; in particular, "there were widespread rumors among inmates that [Magda V., a Jewish doctor] became [a Nazi doctor's] mistress"; "this alleged affair . . . was a factor in an attempt to bring charges against [Magda V.] in Czechoslovakia after the war."[195] Magda V. was imagined or observed to have had special treatment because of the alleged "affair": yet how could it have been anything other than barter (prostitution) or rape: if Auschwitz is not force, what is? What this so-called affair and also Höss's so-called affair with a Jewish woman show is that in Auschwitz Jewish women were not off the Nazi sexual map; indeed, "[a] deposition taken by the Jewish Anti-Fascist Committee of the U.S.S.R. gave testimony concerning a concentration camp in Tulchin, Rumania, 'under the rule of the infamous Petekau who asked each night for two Jewish virgins.'"[196] In a Nazi concentration camp in the Netherlands "[v]iolation of young Jewish women by prison wardens was a common occurrence."[197] Then there was the so-called House of Dolls, presented in a barely fictionalized account by Ka-Tzetnik 135633 (his number in Auschwitz), who as a boy was prostituted there. As Susan Brownmiller says in *Against Our Will: Men, Women and Rape:* "*House of Dolls* . . . describes a day's routine in a nameless forcible brothel in which Jewish females under threat of death prepared their cots for the precise arrival at 2 P.M. of the German soldiers. The daily routine was bitterly called Enjoyment Duty and the soldiers, when finished, were expected to file reports on the performance of their Dolls. Three negative reports meant death."[198] Joshua Eibeshitz, an editor of *Women in the Holocaust,* tells the story of the pseudonymous Miriam who "had been raised in a sheltered religious environment"; at twelve she was deported to Auschwitz, where "[t]he Germans ordered her out of the line and brought her to a barracks known in Auschwitz as the 'House of Dolls,' where she was kept for almost eight months. She and all the other young girls in that house were used for the most licentious purposes, kept alive solely to satisfy the base instincts of several sadistic and bestial Nazis."[199] Tom Segev paraphrases a story told by Itzhak Sadeh, a former commander in the Palmach, the pre-Israel military; Sadeh meets "a young woman who has just arrived from Europe. Her body bears a tattoo 'FOR OFFICERS ONLY.'"[200] She has been prostituted and sterilized. She asks: "Why am I here? Do I deserve to be rescued by these strong, healthy young men, who risk their lives to save mine?"[201] Sadeh says, "Be our sister, be our bride, be our mother . . . For the sake of my sisters I'll be brave. For the sake of my sisters I'll also be cruel: everything, everything!"[202] Segev concludes: "It was no coincidence that the Holocaust was symbolized by a prostitute; the metaphor was a continuation of a common stereotype that depicted the Exile as weak, feminine, and passive, and the yishuv [the Jewish community in Palestine and early Israel] as strong, masculine, and active."[203] Did any one of us outside Israel know that "the Holocaust was symbolized by a prostitute"? If the forced prostitution of Jewish women had been documented and understood, why the erasure from the contemporary collective knowledge—and all the museums and monuments? In fact, every act of prostitution in the camps—Jewish, German, Russian, Polish, etc.—was rape; why isn't a raped woman the symbol of the Holocaust— and why isn't rape part of all the exhibits in all the museums and all the memorials? Prostitution carries with it an aura of sexual aggression and sexual bravado; male-dominant ideology suggests that women can be prostituted because women are naturally prostitutes, whores by nature: scratch any one of them and you've got a whore. Given the common lowness of prostitutes and Jews under the Nazis, the prostitute split off seems lower than the Jew. Active or passive, one steps on it.

Of course there were prostitutes who became kapos in the camps; as Gelissen remembers: "We line up behind Emma, our kapo. Somehow we have learned her name in the past two days. She has a black triangle. She is a prostitute. We march behind her in rows of five in the dark to the field where we will sift rocks and sand all day."[204] Emma will not sift rocks and sand all day. After the war, Jews accused Jewish kapos of having committed murder; there were some lynchings. Some believed that all the kapos had committed murder. Did Emma? Höss says, "I believe that Ravensbrück had selected the 'best' for Auschwitz. They far exceeded their male counterpart in their ability to survive in toughness, vileness, and depravity. Most of them were prostitutes with considerable records. Often they were loathsome females. . . . When Himmler visited Auschwitz in 1942, he thought that they would be especially well-suited to act as Kapos for the Jewish women. . . . They never suffered any mental anguish."[205] Himmler thought that the prostituted women would make the Jewish women suffer.

Outside of the concentration camps, in the forests where Jews went to hide or fight, there was barter-prostitution: "A newly acquired lover was called a 'Tavo.' It is a Hebrew word, a masculine address, that within the context could be translated into 'come here.' Because men with guns went on food expeditions, a woman who had a steady Tavo with a gun had more and better food than an unattached woman. Whatever social value a youth with a gun had, it was automatically transferred to his girlfriend. And because a woman without a man did not amount to much, most young girls looked for an appropriate Tavo."[206] Survival required barter-prostitution for Jewish women at the hands of Jewish men.

In the ghettos, too, there was prostitution; on January 9, 1944, Tory wrote in his diary: ". . . to increase productivity, SS Captain Gratt, the Fort commandant, ordered that the prisoners be allowed to eat their fill, and even supplied them with tobacco and alcohol occasionally, to help them withstand the dreadful stench from the pits. [They were moving corpses from pits so that the corpses could be burned.] They were provided with pillows and blankets from the Ghetto, and three Jewish women were brought from the Ghetto to satisfy their sexual needs."[207] Even though the male prisoners knew that they would be killed when the corpses were all burned, they still used the three Jewish women; the Nazis recognized an implicit right of men, even soon-to-be-dead men, to sexual use of women. These near corpses used prostituted Jewish women or, in fact, committed rape; Jewish soon-to-be-corpses could use women as Jewish as they were, prostituted by Nazi force; and Tory himself essentially categorizes the women with tobacco and alcohol, a vast failure of imagination and conscience. In the Warsaw ghetto, too, the Germans had set up a "public brothel" for their own use; women lived four to a room; according to Lewin in his diary, the Germans had picked up a Jewish beggar and forced him on the prostitutes, who wanted him out because he was dirty and he smelled: "The girls explained that they were too disgusted to sleep with the filthy beggar."[208] That night he was shot. Being a German prostitute reserved for Nazi use in the Warsaw ghetto trumped being a Jewish beggar but more commonly Jews trumped prostitutes.

In virtually every case mentioning prostitutes, the prostitutes do not count, the Jewish men they are servicing do, the Germans they are servicing do. Hitler tried to make Jews as foul and expendable as prostitutes already were, as inhuman as prostitutes were already taken to be. The Nazis, says Friedländer, had a "pornographic imagination."[209] The brothels they created embodied a sexual fascism in which prostitutes were lower than Jews; and certainly male Jews agreed. There was no solidarity with Jewish prostitutes before, during, or after the Holocaust. There was no recognition of the humanity of, for instance, three Jewish women forced to service how many Jewish men digging up mass graves and moving dead and decomposing bodies. There was no line here between prostitution and rape; but the men didn't care. My sister, my mother, I will be brave for you, I will be cruel for you; this is a declaration in the better-late-than-never category.

In nineteenth-century Paris, women actors doubled as courtesans or vice versa. Two of Paris's most brilliant actors were Jewish women: "Rachel, born Elisabeth Rachel Felix (1821–58), and Sarah Bernhardt, born Rosine Bernard (1844–1923) . . ."[210] As Rachel M. Brownstein writes in *Tragic Muse: Rachel of the Comédie-Française:* "Jews were turning up, increasingly, on both sides of the footlights in theaters. Eager to get on, enterprising and adaptable, socially marginal and used to improvising, they had, both their friends and enemies argued, a special affinity for the stage. Like Jews . . . [actors] were denied Christian marriage and burial. . . . Jewish actresses and models were in fashion in the 1830s and 1840s . . ."[211] At the same time, brothels featured at least one Jew and one black; these were the exotics, eroticized in their strangeness, which for both was taken to be racial. Stigma, defined by gender as whore and by race as Jew, was charged with sex; and the public exhibition of the body reified the sameness of actor and whore.

The specifics of the presumed character of the Jews were attached through myth and sexual fantasy to the theatrical persona of a Jewish actor: "Do you know what you have to do to assure that Mlle Rachel will be grateful for your admiration? Go to the theater with your pockets full. Toss flowers to the other actresses, but throw Rachel your wallet."[212] Rachel was taken to be hard to the point of masculinity, greedy, vulgar; her talent was seen as a capacity for deception. George Lewes, consort of George Eliot, wrote: "It will ever remain a curious problem how this little Jewess, this *enfant du peuple,* should, from the first moments of her appearance on the stage, have adopted—or let us rather say *exhibited*—the

.imperial grace and majesty which no one but herself can reach."[213] Comparing Rachel with her brother, Lewes asks: "Is he not a vulgar Jew Boy? Can anything wipe out the original stain of his birth? Yet Rachel herself physically is no better; and were it not for her [exquisite intelligence], she would be as vulgar."[214] In challenging that exquisite intelligence, another actor said: "Moi, je suis juive; Rachel, c'est un juif."[215] Imputed masculinity was an insult; it connoted the presumed greed of male Jews for money and implied sexual deviance. But Rachel's strategy was that of an artist; as Brownstein says, ". . . representing Tragedy, Rachel identified herself, an actress and a woman and a Jew, with High Art and Genius, creating a disquieting, threatening persona."[216]

Cosmopolitan, urban, visible, smart, an icon of sexuality, Rachel was the exemplary Jewess. Critics and journalists attacked her; they synthesized misogyny and anti-Semitism into insult and critique; but "her Christian fans were awed by the Jewess's unexpectedly pure elegance and grace."[217] Her talent, her style subverted both French xenophobia and Jew-hate. Regarding the first, "Rachel was so good at passing for a young girl of good family . . . In effect, her play implied that manners, *ton*, Frenchness itself might be acquired, that a foreigner could get herself up to be absolutely *comme il faut*, as it were *plus française que les Françaises*, and breach the wall of French high society and undermine it."[218] Regarding the second, she had been asked to read a monologue from Corneille, the character being a newly converted Christian, before an archbishop; instead she chose a monologue from Racine's *Esther* in which she was the Jewish queen. In fact there was no escape from being watched and judged: "Sums she contributed to victims of floods and epidemics (too little? too showy?) are adduced as evidence that she was and was not both typical and perverse; the house she furnished for her sister Rebecca proves both her generosity and her Jewish allegiance to her own."[219] Stereotypes are constraining but anti-Semitic stereotypes bend without breaking and fit any behavior: any act by a Jew that is subjected to the scrutiny of an anti-Semitic culture will be seen as an expression of Jewishness; Rachel navigated the public world without changing it.

Sarah Bernhardt's mother was a courtesan; her Jewishness, according to Arthur Gold and Robert Fizdale in *The Divine Sarah: A Life of Sarah Bernhardt*, "did nothing to hinder her career. On the contrary, it was a promise of carnal pleasure . . ."[220] Sarah's career, which took on some of the modernism of the early twentieth century, was spectacular and idiosyncratic; and her "frivolous, promiscuous years contributed to the fascination of her . . . presence and enriched her artistry."[221] Still sexualized as a Jewess, Sarah made a life different from her mother's; Sarah was not defined as a courtesan but an artist. This would not have stopped the perception of her as wanton, sluttish, exotic. But Sarah Bernhardt's life included ushering in a new era for women in the theater: she played Hamlet.

What was true on the stages of Paris was also true in the streets of London: prostitute and Jew were construed to have a sexuality that was "diseased . . . polluting."[222] Jack the Ripper was first seen as "the victim of the prostitute, the syphilitic male"; both Jews and prostitutes were "closely identified with sexually transmitted diseases."[223] Of course, prostitutes were hunted and murdered then as now, the exemplary dirty women; in the social pathology stigmatizing both Jews and prostitutes as the same or linked, each has "but one interest, the conversion of sex into money or money into sex."[224] The Jewish Jack the Ripper is left out of the premillennial serial killer movies and books that celebrate this predator; but police at the time were looking for a Jew; as Gilman says, "The search for Jack the Ripper was the search for an appropriate murderer for the Whitechapel prostitutes."[225] That the predator was Jewish figured into the geography of outraged moralism (which figures so prominently in both misogyny and racism): who else would be on a low-enough level to see himself in the degraded and foul women; Jews "corrupt in their act of touching, of seducing, the pure and innocent, creating new polluters. But they are also able in their sexual frenzy to touch and kill the sexual pariahs, the prostitutes, who like Lulu at the close of Frank Wedekind's play (and Alban Berg's opera) go out to meet them, seeking their own death."[226] The dirty know the dirty, the contaminated know the polluted: evil knows evil. Prostitutes give in to justice when they go out purposefully to be killed; women seek out the annihilation offered by men; murder is the right ending to any prostitute's story.

The death of a prostitute, especially a celebrated prostitute, is always an occasion for salivating journalists and hard-boiled police. The U.S. prostitute Helen Jewett may not have been as famous as Camille; but her murder by a regular client made news then, was used in a novel by Gore Vidal, and is the subject of a 1998 book by Patricia Cline Cohen, *The Murder of Helen Jewett: The Life and Death of a Prostitute in Nineteenth-Century New York.* Jewett makes good copy because she was literate, well-known, refined in her manners and speech, and wrote many letters, which provide source material. Her murder was sensational as was the trial of her murderer. Jewett is in a sense the best argument for prostitution, because of the way in which she controlled the sexual aspects of her life, especially sexual access, which is the great promise of prostitution; married women had no such right or capacity. She died a cruel and vicious death at a young age, which is always in the cards and compromises the notion of prostitution as a lifestyle issue. There is violence in the life of any prostitute and Jewett's was no exception.

Cohen notes that James Gordon Bennett, editor of the *New York Herald,* presented Jewett's murder as "a sexualized corpse [rather than] a mutilated one. He chose to present Jewett as a work of art perpetrated by her murderer; with head wounds and singed skin, rather than a postmortem dissection at the hands of anatomists."[227] Bennett's choice honored the romance of the prostituted body; Cohen's book honors the political romance of so-called sex work and the prostitute as a liberatory icon. Both themes have been part of Western culture—Bennett's in the museums that show Titian and Manet, Cohen's in the contemporary work of well-fed, well-clothed, well-sheltered academics, both male and female. Neither engages in a fight for Jewett's life, because the map of carnality that demanded her murder, a commonplace map, is elevated and romanticized by both art and intellectual abstraction.

Victorine Neurent was the model for Manet's *Olympia* (1865), a cultic icon of a prostitute's desirability and desire as construed by Manet. One could find Neurent in 1889 "ravaged by alcohol and prostitution, sitting on the steps of the Palais des Beaux-Arts . . . begging for coins from visitors entering the show where the now celebrated portrait of her was on display."[228] Is irony a part of sociology? Was Neurent the prototype of the liberated prostitute and as such a figure who foreshadowed contemporary sexual mores or was she a bag lady, drugged out, homeless, and destitute? What happens to prostituted women still alive when men are done with them?

Rona Goffen, author of *Titian's Women,* notes that "Manet's protagonist is a prostitute—not a courtesan, as some critics have assumed Titian's *Venus* to be"; this is a class difference, the courtesan "distinguished from a meretrice (prostitute) or *puttana* (whore) . . . by her superior economic status and (limited) number of her lovers"; Manet introduces into the portrait "not only modernization but profanation, not only emulation but denigration."[229] Titian himself was partly driven by the figure, the story, the idea of Mary Magdalen, whom he called "my intercessor."[230] As Goffen says, "Titian's combination of nudity and sensual beauty in his first Magdalens was comparatively new in Italian art, or rather, a revival of an earlier tradition, for the hermit Mary Magdalen of Trecento art—clothed only in her glorious blond hair—was lovely despite her asceticism. In fifteenth-century art, however, she might appear grotesquely emaciated, hideous, and desexed by her life in the wilderness."[231] Whether the legend or image of Mary Magdalen is "lovely" or depraved, she is always sexed; because a whore is always sexed; destitute, washing Christ's feet, or being among 1 to 999 at Auschwitz, the point is always a carnal one.

Prostitutes sometimes get into history, that special club, because of the company they keep. Horst Wessel, the Nazi martyr, "had moved in with a former prostitute"; he was killed by communists as the Nazis maintained—but they were neighborhood boys asked by the landlady to evict him; "Goebbels exploited his death so brilliantly that his name was immortalised by the song that was given its first performance by massed choirs at the end of a rally on 7 February 1930."[232] Similarly, lowlife Julius Streicher was often in public with prostitutes in tow; "[a]t the annual conference held in 1937 and 1938, the professors and scholars of the 'Jewish question' were honored by the active participation of Julius Streicher, Nazi party leader of the district of Franconia and editor of the anti-Semitic sheet *Der Stürmer* . . . He came to the 1937 meeting in the company of several prostitutes. On that occasion he harangued the audience with a three-hour address on his 'struggle with world Jewry' and the professors responded with an ovation . . ."[233] Prostitutes are either decorative or instrumental in male scenarios. For petty criminals like Wessel, who had been a law student, living with a prostitute or former prostitute was both exploitative and authenticating. She had a room—it became his, in his view. As the real thing, a genuine whore, some of her dirt rubs off on him, which is exciting for him; he gets to be tough and callous up close and personal. Streicher, always carrying a small whip, was notorious for his public displays of vulgarity and drunkenness with a coterie of prostituted women. These are the prostitutes of movies and television: prostitutes who can be seen, though not in the act, which is the province of pornography.

The instrumental use of prostitutes is more widespread and normative: "In 1912, when young Viennese doctors answered a newspaper questionnaire about their first sexual experience, 75 per cent said it was with a prostitute, and 17 per cent with a servant or waitress. Only 4 per cent had lost their virginity to a girl whom they might later marry."[234] These are the prostitutes of literature: Flaubert's *Sentimental Education,* Tolstoy's *Resurrection,* Mahfouz's *Palace Walk.* These are the prostitutes who have a social function necessary to male dominance; the nameless, faceless, filthy horde of women from whom women not prostituted must distinguish themselves; with whom women not prostituted are always compared: this is the old-fashioned prostitute, distinct from the protected daughter and the protected wife. Because of the pornographizing of sexuality in the West, especially in the United States, all women now are expected to take on the craven aura and the sex acts once specific to the prostitute. In all countries, prostitute sexuality is construed to be the basic element of women's nature, which can be constrained but not erased. Often women are construed to be prostitutes simply because they have been raped: once the anatomical barrier to penetration is gone, the result is dishonor to the father, family, or husband—who had the only legitimate and legal access— and shame, exile, or marginality for the woman.

In Arab societies, for instance Iraq, "[m]ost men have premarital sex only with prostitutes, who are regarded as cheap, filthy and dishonourable. In many cases the prostitute is forced to practise her trade for economic survival. But the man who seeks her services is regarded as 'a real masculine man who can indulge in sex as he pleases'; he continues to hold himself in high esteem."[235] In Jabbour's *A Woman of Nazareth,* the psychology of this double standard is pursued: "To Omar's thinking, his having been aroused by a 'respectable female' was dishonourable. Sexual release for him was something that one sought out by masturbation or through prostitutes until such time as one got married."[236] Prostitutes, themselves without power, can easily be manipulated as a symbol by the powerful; for instance, Saddam Hussein justified aggression against Kuwait by saying: "To the Kuwaiti, the glorious Iraqi woman goes for a nickel."[237] It is a winning argument and the political use of prostitution is not limited to rhetoric. Blackmail is the single most potent threat against women in the Arab world: "A particular woman, named in the document, was filmed in the act of undressing to try on a new suit of clothes. The film was used to blackmail her into working as an informer for the police"; "[a]nother document I saw . . . tells of a nurse in the employment of the secret police. She was the handler of a whole network of 'virgin' women, all of whom had been blackmailed into working for the police and provided with reassurance that their hymens would be sewn back up again by this nurse to restore their virginity."[238] Israel's Shin Bet (police) are also users of this kind of blackmail: ". . . these techniques included sexual entrapment and blackmail as well as the use of drug dealers and other underworld and criminal elements. Two prostitutes who were brutally murdered in [Nablus] in April and June 1989 were widely suspected of working for the Shin Bet and recruiting young girls to act as informers."[239]

In Iran, an Islamic but not an Arab country, Goodwin found "a decal that I soon realized was ubiquitous throughout Iran. Showing the silhouette of a woman's covered head, it stated, 'For the respect of Islam, *Hijab* is mandatory.'"[240] Another public sign translated the decal unambiguously: "Bad *hijab* is prostitution."[241] As Goodwin notes, "Iran's prostitutes tend to be more covered than ordinary women, even veiling their faces."[242] The profaned woman can be more covered or more naked, depending on the cultural landscape. Covered or naked, she is low, shamed, the designated target for both rape and assault, the eroticized target for male appetite, which is carnivorous in relation to her.

The lowness of the prostituted woman is cross-cultural and exploits the most vulnerable women. In the United States, as Ira Berlin says in *Many Thousands Gone: The First Two Centuries of Slavery in North America,* "White observers inevitably translated the license slave women enjoyed in the marketplace into the metaphor for sexual freedom. . . . The 'great number of loose, idle, disorderly women' who owned the streets of Charles Town and Savannah after dark confirmed the fears of the priggish and the hopes of the licentious. As in all port cities, sex stood high on the list of commodities for sale. It was a desperate and tawdry business, mostly transacted in the back rooms of dramshops and taverns. . . . the demand for black sexuality promised new power and threatened great perils. The aggressive sexuality of young urban black women—'unmannerly, rude and insolent'—attracted sailors, country merchants, and other men alone in the great ports. Black women elevated the trade, often hosting dances that imitated—perhaps parodied—the planters' high style."[243] This history would have a long legacy in the perception of black- or brown-skinned women as being sexually indiscriminate.

It is part of the racist agenda to impart to black women an aggressive prostitute-sexuality: black women have no poses to cover the prostitute nature of female sexuality, no high ladyship, no world of manners to cover over being the sexual animal. All street prostitutes are aggressive; the calling demands it. It is precisely this aggression that translates—for the illiterate in sexual politics—into the notion that a prostituted population is not vulnerable or exploited; how can these aggressive women be powerless, especially when their power is felt in the penis? The "prigs" and the "licentious" denote two male strategies for dealing with the prostitute-sexuality that their dominance demands: abusive insult through denunciation or abusive insult through participation. In New Orleans, occupied after the Civil War by Union forces, women, "especially of the lower classes, were openly contemptuous of the Federal soldiers. One woman supposedly emptied a chamber pot [on an officer's] head, while another spat in the faces of two Union officers"; this led, says Christopher Benfey in *Degas in New Orleans: Encounters in the Creole World of Kate Chopin and George Washington Cable,* to an administrative order, which was called the "Woman Order": "When any female shall, by word, gesture, or movement, insult or show contempt for any officer or soldier of the United States, she shall be . . . held liable to be treated as a woman of the town plying her vocation."[244] According to Benfey, "One result of [the] Woman Order was that it allowed the occupation of New Orleans to be reinterpreted, by politicians and artists alike, as a war on women. Another direct result was that women who could afford to do so left New Orleans in droves."[245] The charge of whore was a weapon that could be used against any lone or unmarried (unowned) woman.

The racist perception was that black women had an outlaw sexuality. The use of black women in prostitution became, of course, popular; it broke two taboos at once—the racial taboo and the dirty-woman taboo—and at the same time reified the low status of all black women, the dirt of a stigmatized race in alliance with the contaminating dirt of the prostitute. In particular, the black prostitute became the icon of the real down and dirty; or, as a friend of Stephen Crane's said, "the real, naked facts of life."[246] Crane was a user of black street prostitutes: "Many a time I have heard him say he would have to go out and get a nigger wench 'to change his luck.'"[247] When Crane married, he married up: a white woman, a former madam. Yet it was left to Andrew Hacker, in his much acclaimed 1992 book *Two Nations: Black and White, Separate, Hostile, Unequal,* to suggest that "white women may wonder if they can offer the sexual abandon that their men may desire. What, they may ask themselves, draws so many white men to black prostitutes?"[248] But, in fact, in the United States it is precisely the disproportionate population of black prostitutes that allows all other women, but especially white women, to feel elevated. Meanwhile it is the purported sexuality of black men that feeds overt race-hate: for instance, David Duke, former Ku Klux Klan leader who sought elective office, "keeps a pornography collection that, according to a defector from his circle, features films dedicated to white girls having oral sex with Blacks."[249] Duke himself locates the origin of his early sexuality in another terrain. Before *Playboy*, he specifies, "when my friends and I had never seen a photograph of a completely disrobed woman, the [Jewish] media showed us cadavers, often of nude women or the small frames of children, piled up like so much cordwood being bulldozed by Allied troops into mass graves."[250] There is a clear implication that these were early sex photos, arousing to Duke and his friends, a Jewish manipulation of adolescent innocence and sexuality. All these scenarios of racial and sexual degradation are driven by male desire, male fantasy, and male dominance. As *The Turner Diaries* show, racists who advocate for "the white race" are perfectly willing to abandon, beat, or kill white women, or to enjoy as voyeurs their presumed degradation in servicing black men; this black-on-white scenario feeds the hate and eroticizes retaliation.

Inside the black world, *prostitute* becomes a word of threat: when Black Muslim leader Elijah Muhammad was exposed by Malcolm X as the sexual exploiter of many young black women and the father of their many offspring, the result was a headline in a Los Angeles black newspaper reading "Negro Prostitutes Accuse 67-Year-Old Muslim Leader"[251]— in fact the women had all been secretaries to Elijah Muhammad. More recently, *'ho* has become common parlance, along with *bitch*, for intrablack misogynist insult. The stigma of the prostitute allows the violent, the angry, the socially and politically impoverished male to nurse a grudge against all women, including prostituted women; this is aggressive bias, made rawer and more dangerous by the need to counter one's own presumed inferiority.

It has been a long time since the political Left was against prostitution; and those were the good old days. In Cuba, the promise was to stop prostitution by giving prostituted women the great and necessary resources of literacy, job skills, and health care. As Jon Lee Anderson writes in *Ché Guevara: A Revolutionary Life*, "Bars and bordellos were strictly off-limits"; with the fall of Remedios to the guerrilla fighters, "a bordello owner delivered a free truckload of prostitutes and a case of rum as an expression of his 'admiration'";[252] the gift was summarily rejected by one of Ché's subbosses. The lexicon was not: "Pick up the wagonload of whores you've dumped here immediately."[253] Guevara was not called a prude nor was he mistaken for a Victorian.

In some far-left groups during the sixties, prostitution became a revolutionary ploy; as MacDonald writes in *Shoot the Women First*, one rebel told her: "Women can get closer to the target. If a man in a high position, perhaps knowing that he may be a target for terrorists, is approached by a woman, he may think, she's a prostitute."[254] The truth in this is that most men are excited by prostitutes and prostitution. The ever expanding category of user makes the global trafficking in women and children the biggest slave trade the world has seen. Prostitution in most countries is both local and global: women are for sale on both the national and international levels. Consistently, prostitution begins in the childhood of a prostituted woman or in egregious poverty and displacement. The populations of prostituted women in poor countries grow exponentially as prostitution of women and girls is normalized.

In the former Soviet Union, especially in Russia, women have been hit with catastrophic poverty. That and the new ethic of buying women and children in a free market economy has devastated women. As Natalia Khodyreva writes in "Sexism and Sexual Abuse in Russia": "The data collected during criminal investigations show that the majority of prostitutes are under thirty. A third have completed or nearly-completed higher education. One quarter of them started the 'work' before the age of eighteen. One in eight has a child. About 10 per cent of those arrested for prostitution [in St. Petersburg] are students of higher educational establishments and technical colleges. There exists a specific practice of involving underage children in prostitution and using them in sexual commerce; 45 per cent of hotel prostitutes had their first sexual experience before they were sixteen. There are groups of little girls whose job is providing services to long-distance lorry drivers. . . . [C]urrently 130 agencies operate . . . providing sexual services through different clubs, saunas, and salons functioning within dating services advertised widely . . ."[255] With their society collapsing around them, women who had been hairdressers or nurses or maids are now prostituting; as Khodyreva says, "Taking into account that 73 per cent of the city's unemployed are women, the total number of those involved in prostitution is far greater than the number of professionals."[256] In 1990 "there were 1,232 brothels in St. Petersburg."[257] This is a city within a country in which women are being destroyed by a predatory criminality that, like it or not, did not exist under the Soviets. One might say that in the new Russia tyranny has been democratized: there are many despots, not one central dictator. As long as the new despotism has victims who are primarily women and children, the international community will not see cruelty as cruelty, brutality as brutality, exploitation as exploitation. But for women the difference between being the entrepreneur and being the commodity is all the difference in the world.

In India, says Narasimhan, prostitution is found in the "practice of dedicating girls to temples which is prevalent in certain regions (forcing them into a life of ignominy as virtual prostitutes, although they are ostensibly wedded to the deity");[258] she also discusses the language of insult: "In Marathi there is a word that is used to denote both a widow and a prostitute; it is used when one wants to show contempt for a widow and defame her."[259] There are also prostituted women segregated, separated in disgrace in brothels. In Pakistan, says Goodwin, "[y]oung girls sold into prostitution serve as servants in brothels until they reach the age of nine or ten, when they are considered old enough to 'entertain' customers. Prostitution in a Third World country is a short-lived career, as hepatitis and syphilis are rampant, AIDS arrived recently, and medical services are minimal. Many prostitutes are dead before the age of twenty-five. But now that a recent medical study in Karachi has found that 80 percent of dancing girls and other prostitutes suffer from AIDS, many may not live that long."[260] India and Pakistan are nearly at war in June 1999; yet for each their own women are the internal enemy.

In the Israeli-Palestinian conflict, prostitution is a major theme; as Judith Miller writes in *God Has Ninety-Nine Names: Reporting from a Militant Middle East:* "Between 1987 and . . . January 1993, Hamas was blamed not only for the murder of some twenty-six Israelis but also for the deaths of many of the eight hundred Palestinians who were killed for allegedly being Israeli 'collaborators.' Israeli officials and Palestinian journalists agreed that some two-thirds of the ostensible collaborators had never been Israeli informers at all. Rather, they were women who wore slacks and other 'prostitutes,' as Hamas called unveiled women . . ."[261] This means that two-thirds of those murdered in the intranational community of the Palestinians were women not veiled or wearing slacks; it means that Hamas is executing women—that the predominant targets are women. Prostitution is the justification for assassination—of any nonfundamentalist women. There is no international outcry.

The specter of real as opposed to metaphoric prostitution in Israel antagonizes young Palestinian men: as Anderson writes, "What [Hisham] sees during his workdays [in Israel] has fueled his hatred of Jews . . . On a spot in the road near where he and his men are erecting the new apartment blocks, he says, newly arrived Russian emigre women are openly prostituting themselves. 'They come here to sell themselves for fucking,' spits Hisham. 'And we hear that the Israeli whores are angry because they sell themselves so cheaply. Only a few shekels and they will fuck!' "[262] It is the conjunction of fucking, money, and an assumption of Jewishness that make for outrage; and also for the kind of contempt that pimps, Arab for the most part in Israel, feel for Israeli women, made promiscuous and professional in the Jewish state. This role of the pimp is often acted out in situations of disparagement for the ethnicity of the male; in Germany, for instance, immigrant Turkish males sell German prostitutes. The configuration is vengeance of the despised on the women of the socially superior group. In Israel, says Leshem, "[s]ociety's underbelly crawls with thievery, prostitution (one field where Arab-Jewish cooperation flourishes, the pimps being mostly Arabs), drug addiction, even organized crime. Here, too, it is business as usual as in industrialized countries."[263]

The segregation of Arab women is supposed to stop them from being prostitutes, literal or metaphorical: but men want prostitutes and use prostitutes so there are Arab prostitutes who live inside a world of male hypocrisy and delusion. Prostitution is "the ultimate downfall, the pit of dishonor," as Ali Ghalem writes in *A Wife for My Son;* "But how does one become a prostitute? Aicha's only answer was: the woman who does not follow tradition is lost!"[264] The prostitute herself becomes almost phantasmagorical to the woman not prostituted: "They say that in the Casbah, men pass before doors protected by bars; women offer themselves, their breasts exposed. An old matron, with cakes of make-up, covered in jewelry, guards the door and makes the client pay!"[265] As Djebar writes, "I encountered them again . . . encased in silence, and I realized they were the inmates of a neighbouring brothel, close to a military camp. . . . As soon as they entered the vestibule of the Turkish baths, I recognized them for the disfigured victims they were. In the wake of these outcasts, who were a mixture of vulgarity and hauteur, I could hear . . . the rhythms of Bedouin songs . . . For me, they were straight away metamorphosed into pagan princesses."[266] (Bedouin women are seen to be free women, romantic figures of the desert.) Many women try to come to terms with prostitutes and prostitution by transposing the outcasts into women elevated above themselves. And still, this generosity notwithstanding: not one prostitute is freed.

In Saudi Arabia there are prostitutes to go with the pornography that supposedly is not there: "Several of the high-ranking princes send a weekly plane to Paris to pick up prostitutes for a trip to Saudi Arabia. A madam there selects the most beautiful girls . . . Each Tuesday they board a plane to Arabia; the following Monday the weary prostitutes are flown out."[267] In Thailand, where women and increasingly children are the largest cash crop, Burmese women are a new delicacy: "[T]he brothel owners are profiting off the repeated rape and sexual assault of the Burmese women and girls sometimes over long periods of time . . ."[268] In 1999 the United Nations Labor Organization proposed the legitimization and legalization of prostitution by suggesting that commerce in a country's sex industry be counted as part of its gross national product. As Janice Raymond of the Coalition Against Trafficking in Women writes in response: "For over a decade, women's groups worldwide have sought better measurement of women's contribution to national economies calling for the inclusion of work such as child or family care, housekeeping, cooking and shopping—most of which women have traditionally done— in labor force statistics. . . . Effectively the [United Nations Labor Organization] is calling for governments to cash in on the booming profits of the [sex] industry by taxing and regulating it as a legitimate job";[269] this even though trafficking in women violates UN human rights conventions, for instance, the Convention Eliminating Discrimination Against Women, the Anti-Slavery convention, and the 1949 Universal Declaration of Human Rights. It would be prostitution and not child care that the international community will recognize as economically valuable work. Women as women work for free unless they prostitute.

According to Raymond, "Two countries which have specifically refused to recognize prostitution as work are Sweden and Venezuela. In May 1998, Sweden became one of the first countries to prohibit purchase of sexual services with punishments of fines or imprisonment (Swedish Government Offices, 1998). . . . Venezuela ruled that 'prostitution cannot be considered work because it lacks the basic elements of dignity and social justice.' . . . (Republica De Venezuela, 1998)."[270] Sweden in particular is widely regarded as a model state, a humane and equality-based state; so the Swedish repudiation of prostitution should carry some weight. This repudiation goes up against the pornographic presentation of Swedish women, which is a sexual liberation trope. Pornography overpowers reality.

The fact remains that it is impossible to understand prostitution without also understanding both rape and slavery. In the Asian context, infants and girls are often sold to brothels; in the European and North American context, prostituted women are most likely to have been sexually abused children who have run away from home and have no money: raped, homeless, and poor. Women are also first raped, then prostituted, in wars; as Kathleen Barry writes in *The Prostitution of Sexuality: The Global Exploitation of Women,* "Massive rape in war produces sex-industry commodities from whole populations of women who are raped and therefore disgraced to their families and in their communities. Raped women and girls are particularly vulnerable to networks of pimps and organized crime gangs."[271] The use of girls and women as prostitutes is no longer a cottage industry; as Barry says, "Industrialization of prostitution follows from (1) massive deployment of women for military prostitution during wars or foreign occupation, (2) development of tourist industries that bring in foreign exchange for economic development, and (3) export-oriented exploitation of their labor, especially in export processing zones that are exempt from many of the controls that govern local industries."[272] The U.S. has dues to pay here: especially for military prostitution in Vietnam during the Vietnam War and in the Philippines in conjunction with U.S. military bases.

Trafficking in women is a surefire way to make money and increasingly is the way to wealth for Third World economies. Only African poverty seems untouched by the monies made off of women's bodies.

Is there pain; is there violence; is there trauma; is there shock; are all those happy whores really being hurt? The war's over and now the fun begins? Thank God I was raped so that now I can turn tricks? I never wanted a home; I always wanted a brothel? I never wanted a brothel, I always wanted a street corner? In fact, prostituted women commonly deal with an extraordinary amount of violence: "In a study of English street prostitutes, 87% of the women had been victims of violence in the past 12 months. The abuse ranged from verbal assault by clients to stabbings, beatings, and rapes. 27% had been raped; and 43% suffered severe physical abuse. Nearly all (73%) of the 87% were multiple victims of abuse (Benson and Matthews, 1995, p. 402). In . . . [a] U.S. study of 55 survivors of prostitution, 78% were victims of rape by pimps and buyers an average of 49 times a year; 84% were the victims of aggravated assault and were thus horribly beaten, often requiring emergency room attention and hospitalization; 49% were victims of kidnapping and transported across state lines; 53% were victims of sexual abuse and torture; and 27% were mutilated (Susan Kay Hunter, 1993, p.16)."[273] One is asked to believe that prostitution is not violence-saturated, in which case it would be the only way for women to achieve freedom from violence: neither marriage nor childhood offer the kind of safety claimed by advocates for prostitution. Get real.

In a 1998 study, "Prostitution in Five Countries: Violence and Post-Traumatic Stress Disorder," Melissa Farley, Isin Baral, Merab Kiremire, and Ufuk Sezgin "interviewed 475 people (including women, men, and the transgendered) currently and recently prostituted in five countries (South Africa, Thailand, Turkey, USA, Zambia . . .). Across countries, 73 percent reported physical assault in prostitution, 62 percent reported having been raped since entering prostitution, 67 percent met criteria for a diagnosis of PTSD [post-traumatic stress disorder]. On average, 92 percent stated that they wanted to leave prostitution."[274] (Men who brag about using Thai prostitutes might try to remember that 92 percent figure.)

In addition, "[a]veraging across countries, 81 percent reported being physically threatened in prostitution; . . . and 68 percent had been threatened with a weapon. In Istanbul, 46 percent of these respondents reported physical assault by the police—e.g. being kicked, beaten, or hit with a nightstick. An average of 62 percent of the respondents from five countries told us that they had been raped since entering prostitution. Of those who were raped, 46 had been raped more than five times. Of these respondents, 41 percent reported that they had been upset by attempts to coerce them into imitating pornography and 46 percent had pornography made of them while in prostitution."[275] The violence is the obvious part. In an Israeli study of sixty-seven prostituted women, "Prostitution was strongly related to self-description as the family's scapegoat."[276] This is the harder part: creating a family in which girls are not sacrificed.

How do we keep lying to ourselves about the lives of the prostituted; and how desperate is our need to believe that they deserve what they get but we do not deserve what they get? How much do we need them to absorb violence that might otherwise be directed at us? How much do we want to be ignorant about male violence against women, a violence that is unconstrained with regard to prostituted women? Farley and her colleagues found that there was "significantly more physical violence in street, as opposed to brothel, prostitution. However, there was no difference in the incidence of PTSD in these two types of prostitution. This suggests that psychological trauma is intrinsic to the act of prostitution. Whether the person was being prostituted in a brothel or on the street seemed to make as little difference in incidence of PTSD as the distinction based on the country in which the person lived."[277] Post-traumatic stress disorder is not something psychologists made up; in common parlance it consists of nightmares, flashbacks, chronic insomnia, obsessive fear, shaking, trembling, physiological disease, sometimes muteness, ritual acts of self-protection, self-cutting or self-mutilation, uncontrollable anxiety or desperation, despair. In other words, the prostituted feel terror. As one woman said: "I wonder why I keep going to therapists and telling them I can't sleep, and I have nightmares. They pass right over the fact that I was a prostitute and I was beaten with 2 x 4 boards. I had my fingers and toes broken by a pimp, and I was raped more than 30 times. Why do they ignore that?"[278]

The answer is that "they"—all the "theys"—have to ignore that because it requires action rather than mere contemplation; talk therapy, talk radio, or talk scholarship bring no relief. Prostituted women are the gender proletariat, the undifferentiated masses, the futureless poor, the scandal of capitalism and free markets, the detritus of failed socialism.

There are impulses toward rescue; but they tend to be gutless. Toni Morrison exposes the difficulty of rescue in her novel *Paradise:* "The woman was still lying on the pavement when a small crowd began yelling for the police. Frightened, Elder ran and wore his army overcoat all the way back to Oklahoma . . . Later, when his wife, Susannah, cleaned, pressed and mended it, he told her to remove the stitches, to let the jacket pocket flap, the shirt collar stay ripped, the buttons hang or remain missing. It was too late to save the bloodstains, so he tucked the bloody handkerchief into the pants along with his two medals. He never got the sight of that whiteman's fist in that colored woman's face out of his mind. Whatever he felt about her trade, he thought about her, prayed for her till the end of his life. . . . He didn't excuse himself for running, abandoning the woman, and didn't expect God to cut him any slack for it."[279] The failure to rescue is richly evoked; and only the despised and abject will ever help the despised and abject—and the prostitute is under everyone else: the Jews, the Palestinians, the blacks: she is the outcast among them all, in the hundreds of millions. As long as her body lines the bottom, they have raised ground on which to walk.

One novel faces the reality of the prostituted: Nawal El Saadawi's *Woman at Point Zero*. A prostitute kills an abuser and is sentenced to death. She stands up for the murder she has committed; she refuses psychological fudging or sentimental false solutions, for herself or for the men who use prostituted women:

> He said to the police, "Don't let her go. She's a criminal, a killer."
>
> And they asked me, "Is what he says true?"
>
> "I am a killer, but I've committed no crime. Like you, I only kill criminals."
>
> "But he is a prince, and a hero. He's not a criminal."
>
> "For me the feats of kings and princes are no more than crimes, for I do not see things the way you do."
>
> "You are a criminal," they said, "and your mother is a criminal."
>
> "My mother was not a criminal. No woman can be a criminal. To be a criminal one must be a man."
>
> "Now look here, what is this that you are saying?"
>
> "I am saying that you are criminals, all of you: the fathers, the uncles, the husbands, the pimps, the lawyers, the doctors, the journalists, and all men of all professions."
>
> They said, "You are a savage and dangerous woman."
>
> "I am speaking the truth. And truth is savage and dangerous."[280]

The ethic of savage and dangerous truth in prostitution has one obvious and inevitable imperative; as the woman at point zero says: "Everybody has to die. I prefer to die for a crime I have committed rather than to die for one of the crimes you have committed." This repudiates the fate of the scapegoat; and it is the scapegoat's only chance: to refuse to die for the crimes of others. The first scapegoat is killed, drained of its blood, eviscerated, and then after, eaten at a communal feast. The second scapegoat is exiled: pushed out into the wilderness to carry away the sins of the community: driven to slow death from hunger or killed by predators. These are the outcasts, in the margins, in the wild, dying slowly or ripped open, all to cleanse the sins of others. All prostituted persons have to resist being the sacrifice: either on the altar or in the wilderness.

EPILOGUE:
THE WAR ON THE BODY

To destroy a human being willfully and intentionally is a vile thing; the easiest way to do it is a direct attack on the body. The Nazis were merciless in waging war on the human body, the subcategories of which were racial or ethnic or national or religious—or gendered. The Nazis never only killed; instead they built degradation into each murder—eleven or twelve million murders, nearly half of those killed being Jews. Were half of the murdered women? This is not a category of consciousness or memory or concern. Why not?

There is an answer: each murdered woman's identity is subsumed—as it would have been at any other time—by the identity of her group. No one wants to draw a line from the Nazi assaults on the human body to intranational or intraracial or intraethnic or familial assault, male to female. But male against female injury and invasion were the Nazi model, a paradigm of dehumanization and brutalization. To remove the female body from genocide and mass murder is to obscure how each phenomenon is driven—how debasement intentionally feminizes; how the sexual and reproductive parts of the human body become the necessary and inevitable targets of sadism; how predation and conquest define masculinity; how gendered victims are hunted down; how death conquers life, a dynamic recognized in the eroticism of dominance and submission; how the suffering of the abject and wounded becomes natural and socially normal; how terror can become the context in which persecuted or tortured persons live; how there is no escape; how law colludes and how the larger society is hostile or indifferent; how domination and hierarchies become experienced as the natural order; how the powerful live and how the weak die; how force creates compliance; how repeated violence desensitizes any perpetrator and shames any victim; how survival itself becomes shameful because it announces complicity: the subordinated's will to live becomes the instrument the predator wields most brilliantly, with ruthlessness and cunning.

Are Jews "morally credible," as Edward Said says they are, in which case this assertion must apply only to the men, because women as such do not have moral credibility. This is a good reason for women to stay within the framework of ethnocentric male-defined truth; one gets to share in the credibility of the male. The presumption of moral competence is withheld from women; as is any meaningful sovereignty. Any group or person treated like a woman, feminized, also lacks meaningful sovereignty and is also seen as morally bankrupt.

What Jews did to get their contemporary moral credibility was to be murdered in an attempted genocide that nearly succeeded; and then to change themselves: their bodies, their relationship to organized violence, their boundaries (both literal and metaphoric), their jobs and vocations, their place in the wide world.

In the West and industrialized countries, women demand self-determination and choice. Self-determination is culled from the internationalist politics of Woodrow Wilson and Lenin, both of whom created early blueprints for what is now called multiculturalism. Choice, that zenith of freedom in the lexicon of North American feminists, barely begins to deal with the realities of male dominance: in India, for instance, women, it is argued, choose *sati* and therefore it should not be illegal. On the abortion question, free-market, sex-selected abortion in India unites with female infanticide to create a gendered genocide, or gynocide; whereas state control in China means that women must abort after the birth of a first child, a male child having more value than a female child.

In the United States, choice exists as a political position that ignores the separation of abortion itself from medical care and without reference to the poor who, without government aid, cannot get abortions because of the money they cost. This applies to the urban and rural poor. Regardless, neither choice nor self-sovereignty are demands for sovereignty over the body: a presumption of intactness and integrity with boundaries that are beyond the reach of force; a conviction that physical harm cannot be sanctioned or justified; a respect for the solitary body. This sovereignty would have to create boundaries that can be recognized and enforced long before a man is at the literal boundary of the body in question: which means that every bed a woman sleeps in is hers; every house she lives in is hers; any act of violence committed against her is a crime; any act of ex-

ploitation, sexual or economic, is a crime; no civil or religious law trumps
her right to inviolable boundaries; there is a presumption of moral competence that cannot be abrogated; and her body changes: she does not
starve or surgically remodel herself; instead she becomes strong and literate in self-defense, aggressive in taking up space and demanding respect.
She makes assault against her very expensive through both civil actions
and the skilled use of violence. She stops being a weak Jew. She makes her
mind strong in a way that concentrates her focus on justice. She has a
stake in what happens to women everywhere: political, economic, moral.
She has a right to execute any man who batters, rapes, or prostitutes her
or uses her in prostitution. She has a right to organize retaliation. She has
a right to demand reparations. She has a right to own any property on
which she has been hurt. More than a right: she has a responsibility to
cage or stop violent men who are predators against women and children;
she has an obligation to defend herself from intrusion, attack, or invasion;
she will fight back and she can be counted on to win, whether from
strength or intelligence. She begins to value life by valuing her own.

Put concretely, women need land and guns or other armament or defense; or women need to organize nonviolently in great masses that grow
out of small demonstrations using civil disobedience. The latter is harder
than the former but gets fairer results. One needs to target individual men
who commit crimes against women and institutions that objectify, de-
mean, and hurt women: using either violence or nonviolence. Indiscriminate violence is never justified; there are always innocents.

One needs a commitment to discipline and sacrifice. One needs either
equality or political and economic superiority. The former is harder than
the latter. One needs strong girls who grow up to be strong and fierce
women. One needs a sense of what is urgent, including the huge problems of female illiteracy and poverty, both of which take children with
them. One needs food, shelter, health care, and education for women as
well as political rights. One needs a concrete militancy, grassroots organiz-
ers, the female practice of cooperation seen in Nazi concentration camps
and Argentinean jails. One needs a nonrhetorical commitment to justice.
One needs the rulership and political autonomy of women: the eventual
taking over of public policy and civil power. One needs fair treatment of
the male minority. One needs to revisit the principles of eighteenth-cen-
tury political thinkers and philosophers with clarity about what is missing: principles and practices that did not speak to the honor and dignity
of women as citizens. Thomas Jefferson and the other U.S. founders did

not give women anything: no rights; no freedom; no money; no land. Neither the American Revolution nor the French Revolution nor the Enlightenment nor the aftermath of the U.S. Civil War (in which the Thirteenth, Fourteenth, and Fifteenth Amendments to the U.S. Constitution were ratified) dared to hand over rights to women.

One needs rules in courts of law based on how crimes really happen—rape, for instance—and the development of rules of evidence that are fair from the point of view of the raped, not the raper. One needs rape museums to put in one place the cogency and significance of the act of rape: a story told through artifacts and stories. One needs the deep study of prostitution as a paradigm for scapegoating.

Remember that men are biologically vulnerable: they wear their genitals on the outside of their bodies; it is easier for women to hurt men than for men to get inside of women—except that women don't want to hurt men and men do want to get inside of women. One must turn this around: men must be made aware of their fragility and vulnerability—or is that what creates male aggression, precisely that awareness, never spoken?

The sex trade in women and children must be a target: there it all is—poverty, abused children, enslaved or sold or stolen children, they grow up to be enslaved or sold or stolen adults used in pornography and prostitution; they have little literacy or chance of health or hope: or will the UN or the U.S. or the UK march into Afghanistan to stop the Taliban from its vicious war against women; or will the UN or NATO end gender apartheid in Saudi Arabia or will Amnesty International advocate for women imprisoned in brutal marriages, the brutality being protected by the state?

International law is extremely important to the future of women. Crimes against humanity are inevitably crimes against women and children as well as stigmatized men; and inside countries and racial or ethnic groups—in which women are the internal enemy and men are the rapists and rulers—human rights law must be framed to free women from male domination, especially from the systematic violence of male dominance. The androcentric heart of religions must be faced. The harm of objectification and dehumanization must be recognized as prelude to normalized violence.

The past thirty years—1970 to 2000, the time of the so-called second wave of feminism—have been prologue: the question is, To what? Answer the question.

Notes

CHAPTER 1: HOMELAND/HOME

1. Shlomo Breznitz, *Memory Fields* (New York: Alfred A. Knopf, 1992), pp. 17–18.
2. Breznitz, *Memory Fields,* p. 18.
3. *Webster's Third International Dictionary,* s.v. "hope."
4. Breznitz, *Memory Fields,* p. 18.
5. Italo Calvino, *The Road to San Giovanni,* trans. Tim Parks (New York: Pantheon Books, 1993), p. 3.
6. James Lee Burke, *A Stained White Radiance* (New York: Hyperion, 1992), p. 279.
7. Burke, *A Stained White Radiance,* pp. 279–280.
8. Isabel Fonseca, *Bury Me Standing: The Gypsies and Their Journey* (New York: Alfred A. Knopf, 1995), p. 5.
9. Fonseca, *Bury Me Standing,* pp. 217–218.
10. Fonseca, *Bury Me Standing,* p. 301.
11. Fonseca, *Bury Me Standing,* p. 302.
12. Jorge Semprun, *Literature or Life?,* trans. Linda Coverdale (New York: Viking, 1997), p. 114.
13. Benjamin Beit-Hallahmi, *Original Sins: Reflections on the History of Zionism and Israel* (New York: Olive Branch Press, 1993), p. 1.
14. Wladyslaw T. Bartoszewski, *The Convent at Auschwitz* (New York: George Braziller, 1991), pp. 59–60.
15. Eva Hoffman, *Shtetl: The Life and Death of a Small Town and the World of Polish Jews* (Boston: Houghton Mifflin Company, 1997), p. 143.
16. Nora Levin, *The Holocaust: The Destruction of European Jewry 1933–1945* (New York: Schocken Books, 1973), p. 10.
17. Nadine Gordimer, *Writing and Being* (Cambridge: Harvard University Press, 1995), p. 128.
18. Fred Kaplan, *Thomas Carlyle: A Biography* (Berkeley: University of California Press, 1993), p. 17.
19. Sara Bershtel and Allen Graubard, *Saving Remnants: Feeling Jewish in America* (New York: The Free Press, 1992), p. 128.
20. Beit-Hallahmi, *Original Sins,* p. 3.
21. Cristina Garcia, *Dreaming in Cuban* (New York: Alfred A. Knopf, 1993), p. 58.
22. Quoted in Yosef Hayim Yerushalmi, *Freud's Moses: Judaism Terminable and Interminable* (New Haven: Yale University Press, 1991), p. 13.
23. Quoted in Yerushalmi, *Freud's Moses,* p. 15.
24. Herbert R. Lottman, *The French Rothschilds: The Great Banking Dynasty* (New York: Crown Publishers, 1955), p. 211.
25. Ron Chernow, *The Warburgs: The Twentieth Century Odyssey of a Remarkable Jewish Family* (New York: Random House, 1993), p. 44.
26. Chernow, *The Warburgs,* p. 442.
27. Chernow, *The Warburgs,* p. 442.

28. Raul Hilberg, *Perpetrators, Victims, Bystanders: The Jewish Catastrophe 1933–1945* (New York: HarperCollins Publishers, 1992), p. 191.
29. Tad Szulc, *The Secret Alliance: The Extraordinary Story of the Rescue of the Jews Since World War II* (New York: Farrar, Straus & Giroux, 1991), p. 6.
30. Elie Wiesel, *A Beggar in Jerusalem,* trans. Lily Edelman and Elie Wiesel (New York: Shocken Books, 1985), p. 19.
31. Szulc, *The Secret Alliance,* pp. 69–70.
32. Andrzej Szczypiorski, *The Beautiful Mrs. Seidenman,* trans. Klara Glowczewska (New York: Grove Weidenfeld, 1989), p. 57.
33. Isaiah Berlin and Ramin Jahanbegloo, *Conversations with Isaiah Berlin* (New York: Charles Scribner's Sons, 1991), p. 85.
34. Moshe Leshem, *Israel Alone: How the Jewish State Lost Its Way and How It Can Find It Again* (New York: Simon & Schuster, 1989), p. 149.
35. Wolf Blitzer, *Territory of Lies* (New York: Harper & Row Publishers, 1989), p. 30.
36. Danny Rubenstein, *The People of Nowhere: The Palestinian Vision of Home,* trans. Ina Friedman (New York: Times Books, 1991), pp. 114–115.
37. Jean P. Sasson, *Princess: A True Story of Life Behind the Veil in Saudi Arabia* (New York: William Morrow and Company, 1992), p. 185.
38. Quoted in Victoria Schweitzer, *Tsvetaeva,* trans. Robert Chandler, H. T. Willets, and Peter Norman (New York: Farrar, Straus & Giroux, 1993), p. 97.
39. Quoted in Hélène Cixous, *Three Steps on the Ladder of Writing,* trans. Sarah Cornell and Susan Sellers (New York: Columbia University Press, 1993), p. 19.
40. Bernard Knox, *The Oldest Dead White European Males* (New York: W. W. Norton & Company, 1993), p. 60.
41. Knox, *The Oldest Dead White,* p. 55.
42. Sylvia Barack Fishman, *A Breath of Life: Feminism in the American Jewish Community* (New York: The Free Press, 1993), p. 101.
43. Gerda Lerner, *The Creation of Feminist Consciousness From the Middle Ages to Eighteen-seventy* (New York: Oxford University Press, 1993), p. 119.
44. Fishman, *A Breath of Life,* p. 101.
45. Jack Nelson, *Terror in the Night: The Klan's Campaign Against the Jews* (New York: Simon & Schuster, 1993), p. 91.
46. Kay Mills, *This Little Light of Mine: The Life of Fannie Lou Hamer* (New York: Dutton, 1993), p. 46.
47. Jan Goodwin, *Price of Honor: Muslim Women Lift the Veil of Silence on the Islamic World* (Boston: Little, Brown and Company, 1994), pp. 52–53.
48. Marilyn Yalom, *Blood Sisters: The French Revolution in Women's Memory* (New York: Basic Books, 1993), p. 4.
49. Ruth Schweitzer, *Women of Theresienstadt: Voices From a Concentration Camp* (New York: Berg, 1989), p. 41.
50. Jasper Becker, *Hungry Ghosts: Mao's Secret Famine* (New York: The Free Press, 1997), p. 138.
51. Becker, *Hungry Ghosts,* p. 216.
52. Melvin Konner, *Why the Reckless Survive* (New York: Viking, 1990), p. 170.
53. Konner, *Why the Reckless,* p. 170.
54. Konner, *Why the Reckless,* p. 171.
55. Fatima Mernissi, *Islam and Democracy: Fear of the Modern World,* trans. Mary Jo Lakeland (New York: Addison-Wesley Publishing Company, 1992), p. 121.
56. David E. Stannard, *American Holocaust: Columbus and the Conquest of the New World* (New York: Oxford University Press, 1992) p. 131.
57. J. Nelson, *Terror in the Night,* p. 68.
58. Lucette Matalon Lagnado and Sheila Cohn Dekel, *Children of the Flames: Dr. Josef Mengele and the Untold Story of the Twins of Auschwitz* (New York: William Morrow and Company, 1991), p. 80.
59. Lagnado and Dekel, *Children of the Flames,* p. 257.
60. Zuccotti, *The Holocaust, the French, and the Jews* (New York: Basic Books, 1993), p. 113.

61. Lagnado and Dekel, *Children of the Flames,* p. 224.
62. Judith Lewis Herman, *Trauma and Recovery* (New York: Basic Books, 1992), p. 104.
63. Orlando Patterson, *Freedom: Freedom in the Making of Western Culture,* vol. 1 (New York: Basic Books, 1991), p. 51.
64. Patterson, *Freedom,* p. 55.
65. J. L. Herman, *Trauma and Recovery,* p. 172.

CHAPTER 2: JEW-HATE/WOMAN-HATE

1. Peter Gay, *The Cultivation of Hatred: The Bourgeois Experience Victoria to Freud,* vol. V (New York: W. W. Norton & Company, 1988), p. 71.
2. Bernard Lewis, *Islam and the West* (New York: Oxford University Press, 1993), p. 174.
3. Robert S. Wistrich, *Antisemitism: The Longest Hatred* (New York: Pantheon Books, 1991), p. 5.
4. Wistrich, *Antisemitism,* p. 5.
5. Karen Armstrong, *Jerusalem: One City, Three Faiths* (New York: Alfred A. Knopf, 1996), p. 65.
6. Wistrich, *Antisemitism,* p. 13.
7. Roland Oliver, *The African Experience: Major Themes in African History from Earliest Times to the Present* (New York: Icon Editions, 1992), p. 79.
8. B. Netanyahu, *The Origins of the Inquisition in Fifteenth Century Spain* (New York: Random House, 1995), p. 419.
9. Netanyahu, *The Origins of the Inquisition,* p. 381.
10. Wistrich, *Antisemitism,* p. 36.
11. Gay, *The Cultivation of Hatred,* p. 71.
12. Frederic Cople Jaher, *A Scapegoat in the Wilderness: The Origins and Rise of Anti-Semitism in America* (Cambridge: Harvard University Press, 1994), p. 75.
13. Jaher, *A Scapegoat in the Wilderness,* p. 75.
14. Nora Levin, *The Holocaust: The Destruction of European Jewry 1933–1945* (New York: Schocken Books, 1973), p. 10.
15. Ian Buruma, *The Wages of Guilt: Memories of War in Germany and Japan* (New York: Farrar, Straus & Giroux, 1994), p. 202.
16. Chernow, *The Warburgs,* p. 25.
17. Frank E. Manuel, *A Requiem for Karl Marx* (Cambridge: Harvard University Press, 1995), p. 151.
18. Isaac Babel, *1920 Diary,* ed. Carol J. Avins, trans. T. T. Willetts (New Haven: Yale University Press, 1995), p. 12.
19. Tim Pat Coogan, *The IRA: A History* (Niwot, Colo.: Roberts Rinehart Publishers, 1993), p. 36.
20. Saul Friedländer, *Nazi Germany and the Jews: The Years of Persecution,* vol. 1 (New York: HarperCollins Publishers, 1997), p. 87.
21. Daniel Jonah Goldhagen, *Hitler's Willing Executioners: Ordinary Germans and the Holocaust* (New York: Alfred A. Knopf, 1996), p. 9.
22. Goldhagen, *Hitler's Willing Executioners,* p. 9.
23. Rena Kornreich Gelissen and Heather Dune Macadam, *Rena's Promise: A Story of Sisters in Auschwitz* (Boston: Beacon Press, 1995), p. 27.
24. Anthony Julius, *T. S. Eliot, Anti-Semitism, and Literary Form* (Cambridge: Cambridge University Press, 1995), p. 9.
25. Julius, *T. S. Eliot,* p. 96.
26. Rian Malan, *My Traitor's Heart* (New York: Vintage Books, 1991), p. 76.
27. James Shapiro, *Shakespeare and the Jews* (New York: Columbia University Press, 1995), p. 108.
28. John Gross, *Shylock: A Legend and Its Legacy* (New York: Simon & Schuster, 1993), p. 29.
29. Gross, *Shylock,* p. 28.
30. Chernow, *The Warburgs,* p. 40.
31. Sander Gilman, *The Jew's Body* (New York: Routledge, 1991), p. 40.
32. Beit-Hallahmi, *Original Sins,* p. 173.

33. Gross, *Shylock*, p. 261.
34. Eric Hobsbawn, *The Age of Extremes: A History of the World, 1914–1991* (New York: Pantheon Books, 1995), p. 119.
35. Stanley Crouch, *The All-American Skin Game, or, The Decoy of Race: The Long and Short of It 1990–1994* (New York: Pantheon Books, 1995), p. 63.
36. Julia Kristeva, *Time and Sense: Proust and the Experience of Literature*, trans. Ross Guberman (New York: Columbia University Press, 1996), p. 43.
37. Quoted in James Shapiro, *Shakespeare and the Jews*, p. 113.
38. Karl Beckson, *London in the 1890s: A Cultural History* (New York: W. W. Norton & Company, 1992), p. 7.
39. Gilman, *The Jew's Body*, p. 117.
40. Gilman, *The Jew's Body*, p. 113.
41. Gilman, *The Jew's Body*, p. 113.
42. John Weiss, *Ideology of Death: Why the Holocaust Happened in Germany* (Chicago: Ivan R. Dee, 1996), p. 110.
43. Debórah Dwork and Robert Jan Van Pelt, *Auschwitz: 1270 to the Present* (New York: W. W. Norton & Company, 1996), p. 22.
44. Nechama Tec, *Defiance: The Bielski Partisans* (New York: Oxford University Press, 1993), p. 111.
45. Quoted in Richard Davenport-Hines, *Auden* (New York: Pantheon Books, 1995), pp. 200–201.
46. Quoted in Richard Pollak, *The Creation of Dr. B: A Biography of Bruno Bettelheim* (New York: Simon & Schuster, 1997), pp. 227–228.
47. Quoted in Pat Shipman, *The Evolution of Racism: Human Differences and the Use and Abuse of Science* (New York: Simon & Schuster, 1994), p. 148.
48. Davenport-Hines, *Auden*, p. 190.
49. Walter Laqueur, *Thursday's Child Has Far to Go: A Memoir of the Journeying Years* (New York: Charles Scribner's Sons, 1993), p. 104.
50. John Carey, *The Intellectuals and the Masses: Pride and Prejudice Among the Literary Intelligentsia, 1880–1939* (New York: St. Martin's Press, 1993), p. 95.
51. Aharon Appelfeld, *Beyond Despair: Three Lectures and a Conversation with Philip Roth*, trans. Jeffrey M. Green (New York: Fromm International Publishing Corporation, 1994), pp. 76–77.
52. Appelfeld, *Beyond Despair*, p. 77.
53. Appelfeld, *Beyond Despair*, p. 77.
54. Appelfeld, *Beyond Despair*, p. 17.
55. Appelfeld, *Beyond Despair*, p. 78.
56. Wiesel, *A Beggar in Jerusalem*, p. 114.
57. Will Self, *My Idea of Fun* (New York: The Atlantic Monthly Press, 1994), p. 193.
58. Edward Mullins, *The Painted Witch: How Western Artists Have Viewed the Sexuality of Women* (New York: Carroll & Graf Publishers, 1985), p. 39.
59. Elisabeth Young-Bruehl, *The Anatomy of Prejudices* (Cambridge: Harvard University Press, 1996), p. 117.
60. Louise DeSalvo, *Conceived with Malice: Literature as Revenge in the Lives and Works of Virginia and Leonard Woolf, D. H. Lawrence, Djuna Barnes, and Henry Miller* (New York: Dutton, 1994), p. 47.
61. Cixious, *Three Steps*, pp. 119–120.
62. Blanche Wiessen Cook, *Eleanor Roosevelt: 1884–1933*, vol. 1 (New York: Viking, 1992), p. 355.
63. Quoted in Carey, *The Intellectuals*, pp. 158–159.
64. Mullins, *The Painted Witch*, p. 38.
65. Deborah L. Rhode, *Speaking of Sex: The Denial of Gender Inequality* (Cambridge: Harvard University Press, 1997), p. 44.
66. Michael Ryan, *Secret Life: An Autobiography* (New York: Pantheon Books, 1995), p. 324.
67. Germaine Greer, *The Change: Women, Aging and Menopause* (New York: Fawcett Columbine, 1993), p. 120.

68. Quoted in Claudia Koonz, *Mothers in the Fatherland: Women, the Family and Nazi Politics* (New York: St. Martin's Press, 1986), p. 310.
69. John Toland, *Adolf Hitler* (New York: Anchor Books/Doubleday, 1976), p. 489.
70. Weiss, *Ideology of Death*, p. 107.
71. Weiss, *Ideology of Death*, p. 107.
72. Weiss, *Ideology of Death*, p. 107.
73. Weiss, *Ideology of Death*, p. 107.
74. Chernow, *The Warburgs*, 435.
75. Koonz, *Mothers in the Fatherland*, p. 53.
76. Koonz, *Mothers in the Fatherland*, p. 53.
77. Koonz, *Mothers in the Fatherland*, p. 7.
78. Carey, *The Intellectuals*, p. 203.
79. Vera Laska, ed., *Women in the Resistance and in the Holocaust* (Westport, Conn.: Greenwood Press, 1983), p. 27.
80. Kenneth Jacobson, *Embattled Selves: An Investigation into the Nature of Identity Through Oral Histories of Holocaust Survivors* (New York: The Atlantic Monthly Press, 1994), p. 105.
81. Quoted in Martin Gilbert, *The Boys: The Untold Story of 732 Young Concentration Camp Survivors* (New York: Henry Holt and Company, 1997), p. 168.
82. Matalon and Dekel, *Children of the Flames*, p. 80.
83. M. Gilbert, *The Boys*, p. xviii.
84. Nechama Tec, *Defiance: The Bielski Partisans* (New York: Oxford University Press, 1993), p. 156.
85. Paul Webster, *Petain's Crime: The Full Story of French Collaboration in the Holocaust* (Chicago: Ivan R. Dee, 1991), pp. 200–201.
86. Antony Beevor and Artemis Cooper, *Paris After the Liberation 1944–1949* (New York: Doubleday, 1994), pp. 80–81.
87. Elfriede Jelinek, *Wonderful Wonderful Times*, trans. Michael Hulse (London: Serpent's Tail, 1990), p. 31.
88. Alison Owings, *German Women Recall the Third Reich* (New Brunswick, N.J.: Rutgers University Press, 1993), p. 470.

CHAPTER 3: POGROM/RAPE

1. Joseph Telushkin, *Jewish Literacy: The Most Important Things to Know About the Jewish Religion, Its People, and Its History* (New York: William Morrow and Company, 1991), p. 247.
2. Telushkin, *Jewish Literacy*, p. 247.
3. John Keegan, *A History of Warfare* (New York: Alfred A. Knopf, 1993), p. 7.
4. J. Keegan, *Warfare*, p. 7.
5. J. Keegan, *Warfare*, p. 7.
6. Telushkin, *Jewish Literacy*, p. 209.
7. Telushkin, *Jewish Literacy*, p. 209.
8. Joachim G. Fest, *Hitler*, trans. Richard and Clara Winston (New York: Harcourt Brace Jovanovich, Publishers, 1974), p. 115.
9. Telushkin, *Jewish Literacy*, p. 248.
10. Albert S. Lindemann, *The Jew Accused: Three Anti-Semitic Affairs (Dreyfus, Beilis, Frank) 1894–1915* (Cambridge: Cambridge University Press, 1993), p. 154.
11. Lindemann, *The Jew Accused*, p. 154.
12. Chernow, *The Warburgs*, p. 106.
13. Lindemann, *The Jew Accused*, p. 162.
14. Lindemann, *The Jew Accused*, p. 162.
15. Lindemann, *The Jew Accused*, p. 162.
16. Lindemann, *The Jew Accused*, p. 162.
17. Lindemann, *The Jew Accused*, p. 162.
18. Lindemann, *The Jew Accused*, p. 163.

19. Lindemann, *The Jew Accused,* p. 163.
20. Lindemann, *The Jew Accused,* p. 34.
21. Brian Boyd, *Nabokov: The American Years* (Princeton: Princeton University Press, 1991), p. 27.
22. B. Boyd, *Nabokov,* p. 27.
23. B. Boyd, *Nabokov,* p. 400.
24. Beit-Hallahmi, *Original Sins,* p. 69.
25. Beit-Hallahmi, *Original Sins,* p. 69.
26. Beit-Hallahmi, *Original Sins,* p. 69.
27. Chernow, *The Warburgs,* p. 290.
28. Louis Rapoport, *Stalin's War Against the Jews* (New York: The Free Press, 1990), p. 30.
29. Rapoport, *Stalin's War,* p. 12.
30. Joshua Rubenstein, *Tangled Loyalties: The Life and Times of Ilya Ehrenburg* (New York: Basic Books, 1996), p. 186.
31. Quoted in Rapoport, *Stalin's War,* p. 184.
32. Rapoport, *Stalin's War,* p. 38.
33. Rapoport, *Stalin's War,* p. 15.
34. Andrei Sinyavsky, *The Russian Intelligentsia,* trans. Lynne Visson (New York: Columbia University Press, 1997), p. 13.
35. Michael Bilton and Kevin Sim, *Four Hours in My Lai* (New York: Viking, 1992), p. 315.
36. James E. B. Breslin, *Mark Rothko: A Biography* (Chicago: The University of Chicago Press, 1993), p. 48.
37. Wistrich, *Antisemitism,* p. 101.
38. Robert D. Kaplan, *Balkan Ghosts: A Journey Through History* (New York: St. Martin's Press, 1993), p. 128.
39. Szulc, *The Secret Alliance,* p. 127.
40. Richard Breitman, *The Architect of Genocide: Himmler and the Final Solution* (New York: Alfred A. Knopf, 1991), p. 53.
41. Marion Kaplan, *Between Dignity and Despair: Jewish Life in Nazi Germany* (New York: Oxford University Press, 1998), p. 123.
42. M. Kaplan, *Between Dignity and Despair,* p. 125.
43. Quoted in Yerushalmi, *Freud's Moses,* p. 43.
44. Tina Rosenberg, *The Haunted Land: Facing Europe's Ghosts After Communism* (New York: Random House, 1995), p. 246.
45. George Konrád, *A Feast in the Garden,* trans. Imre Goldstein (New York: Harcourt Brace Jovanovich, Publishers, 1992), p. 213.
46. Peter Sichrovsky, *Abraham's Children: Israel's Young Generation,* trans. Jean Steinberg (New York: Pantheon Books, 1991), p. 12.
47. Andrew Gowers and Tony Walker, *Behind the Myth: Yasser Arafat and the Palestinian Revolution* (New York: Olive Branch Press, 1992), p. 7.
48. Roberto Calasso, *The Marriage of Cadmus and Harmony,* trans. Tim Parks (New York: Alfred A. Knopf, 1993), p. 8.
49. Calasso, *The Marriage,* p. 7.
50. Mullins, *The Painted Witch,* pp. 111–112.
51. Mullins, *The Painted Witch,* p. 77.
52. Gerda Lerner, *Why History Matters: Life and Thought* (New York: Oxford University Press, 1997), p. 207.
53. Hoffman, *Shtetl,* pp. 60–61.
54. Evelyne Accad, *L'Exicée,* trans. David K. Bruner (Washington, D.C.: Three Continents Press, 1989), pp. 67–68.
55. James Q. Wilson, *The Moral Sense* (New York: The Free Press, 1993), p. 246.
56. J. Q. Wilson, *The Moral Sense,* p. 246.
57. J. L. Herman, *Trauma and Recovery,* pp. 94–95.
58. J. L. Herman, *Trauma and Recovery,* pp. 94–95.
59. J. L. Herman, *Trauma and Recovery,* p. 95.
60. Babel, *1920 Diary,* pp. 20–21.

61. Babel, *1920 Diary,* p. 82.
62. Babel, *1920 Diary,* p. 84.
63. Babel, *1920 Diary,* p. 84.
64. Armando Valladares, *Against All Hope: The Prison Memoirs of Armando Valladares,* trans. Andrew Hurley (New York: Alfred A. Knopf, 1986), pp. 78–79.
65. Natalie Khodyreva, "Sexism and Sexual Abuse in Russia," pp. 27–40, in Chris Corrin, ed., *Women in a Violent World: Feminist Analyses and Resistance Across "Europe"* (Edinburgh: Edinburgh University Press, 1996), p. 38.
66. Khodyreva, "Sexism and Sexual Abuse" in C. Corrin, ed., *Women in a Violent World,* p. 33.
67. Lepa Mladjenovic and Divna Matijasevic, "SOS Belgrade July 1993–1995: Dirty Streets," pp. 119–132, in C. Corrin, *Women in a Violent World,* pp. 121–122.
68. Rada Boric and Mica Mladineo Desnica, "Croatia: Three Years After," pp. 133–150, in C. Corrin, *Women in a Violent World,* p. 139.
69. Iris Chang, *The Rape of Nanking: The Forgotten Holocaust of World War II* (New York: Basic Books, 1997), p. 6.
70. Chang, *The Rape of Nanking,* p. 53.
71. Chang, *The Rape of Nanking,* p. 49.
72. R. D. Kaplan, *Balkan Ghosts,* p. 61.
73. Christopher Simpson, *The Splendid Blond Beast: Money, Law, and Genocide in the Twentieth Century* (New York: Grove Press, 1993), p. 29.
74. John Noble Wilford, *The Mysterious History of Columbus* (New York: Alfred A. Knopf, 1991), pp. 178–179.
75. Ralph K. Andrist, *The Long Death: The Last Days of the Plains Indian* (New York: Macmillan Publishing Company, 1964), p. 198.
76. Andrist, *The Long Death,* p. 198.
77. Andrist, *The Long Death,* p. 206.
78. Andrist, *The Long Death,* p. 205.
79. Sakuntala Narasimhan, *Sati: Widow Burning in India* (New York: Doubleday, 1992), p. 50.
80. Narasimhan, *Sati,* p. 38.
81. Goodwin, *Price of Honor,* p. 53.
82. Goodwin, *Price of Honor,* p. 51.
83. Kanan Makiya (Samir Al-Khali), *Cruelty and Silence: War, Tyranny, Uprising and the Arab World* (New York: W. W. Norton & Company, 1993), p. 288.
84. Makiya, *Cruelty and Silence,* p. 288.
85. Makiya, *Cruelty and Silence,* p. 288.
86. M. Kaplan, *Between Dignity and Despair,* p. 80.
87. M. Kaplan, *Between Dignity and Despair,* p. 61.
88. M. Kaplan, *Between Dignity and Despair,* p. 61.
89. M. Kaplan, *Between Dignity and Despair,* p. 20.
90. Chava Raban-Folman, "The Liaison Agent," pp. 124–149, in Fayge Silverman, ed., *Women in the Holocaust: A Collection of Testimonies,* 2 vols., trans. Jehoshua Eibeshitz and Anna Eilenberg-Eibeshitz (Brooklyn, N.Y.: Remember, 1993, 1994), p. 146.
91. Avraham Tory, *Surviving the Holocaust: The Kovno Ghetto Diary,* ed. Martin Gilbert, trans. Jerzy Michalowicz (Cambridge: Harvard University Press, 1990), p. 168.
92. Vera Laska, "Auschwitz: A Factual Deposition," pp. 169–185, in Laska, ed., *Women in the Resistance,* p. 181.
93. Laska, ed., *Women in the Resistance,* p. 26.
94. Laska, ed., *Women in the Resistance,* p. 26.
95. Laska, ed., *Women in the Resistance,* p. 26.
96. Laska, ed., *Women in the Resistance,* pp. 33–34.
97. Laska, ed., *Women in the Resistance,* p. 27.
98. Dan Kurzman, *The Bravest Battle: The 28 Days of the Warsaw Ghetto* (New York: Da Capo Press, 1993), p. 81.
99. Kurzman, *The Bravest Battle,* p. 25.
100. Quoted in M. Gilbert, *The Boys,* p. 143.
101. Quoted in M. Gilbert, *The Boys,* p. 176.

102. Martin Gilbert, *Auschwitz and the Allies* (New York: Henry Holt and Company, 1982), p. 39.
103. Laska, "Auschwitz: A Factual Deposition" in Laska, ed., *Women in the Resistance,* p. 180.
104. Lagnado and Dekel, *Children of the Flames,* p. 71.
105. Quoted in M. Gilbert, *The Boys,* p. 230.
106. Peter Wyden, *Stella* (New York: Simon & Schuster, 1992), p. 239.
107. Wyden, *Stella,* p. 230.
108. Beevor and Cooper, *Paris After,* p. 80.
109. CEDAW Committee Report on Israel from July 7–25, 1997, published April 8, 1997.
110. David Biale, *Eros and the Jews: From Biblical Israel to Contemporary America* (New York: Basic Books, 1992), p. 36.
111. Agence France-Presse, Jerusalem, December 31, 1997.
112. *Jerusalem Post,* March 27, 1998.
113. Simona Sharoni, *Gender and the Israeli-Palestinian Conflict: The Politics of Women's Resistance* (Syracuse, N.Y.: Syracuse University Press, 1995), p. 126.
114. Yaron Ezrahi, *Rubber Bullets: Power and Conscience in Modern Israel* (New York: Farrar, Straus & Giroux, 1997), p. 168.
115. Ezrahi, *Rubber Bullets,* p. 168.
116. Ezrahi, *Rubber Bullets,* p. 168.
117. Goodwin, *Price of Honor,* pp. 299–300.
118. Amos Oz, *Elsewhere, Perhaps,* trans. Nicholas de Lange and Amos Oz (New York: Harcourt Brace Jovanovich, Publishers, 1973), p. 44.
119. Oz, *Elsewhere, Perhaps,* p. 91.
120. M. Ryan, *Secret Life,* p. 325.
121. Sally Cline, *Radclyffe Hall: A Woman Called John* (London: John Murray (Publishers), 1997), p. 34.
122. Cline, *Radclyffe Hall,* p. 93.
123. Makiya, *Cruelty and Silence,* p. 295.
124. Sharoni, *Gender in the Israeli-Palestinian Conflict,* p. 121.
125. Makiya, *Cruelty and Silence,* p. 290.
126. Mills, *This Little Light,* p. 11.
127. Eileen MacDonald, *Shoot the Women First* (New York: Random House, 1992), p. 187.
128. Alice Vachss, *Sex Crimes* (New York: Random House, 1993), p. 33.
129. J. L. Herman, *Trauma and Recovery,* p. 73.
130. David K. Shipler, *Arab and Jew: Wounded Spirits in a Promised Land* (New York: Penguin Books, 1987), p. 385.

CHAPTER 4: THE STATE/THE FAMILY

1. Thomas A. Lewis, *For King and Country: The Maturing of George Washington* (New York: HarperCollins Publishers, 1993), p. 76.
2. T. A. Lewis, *For King and Country,* p. 77.
3. T. A. Lewis, *For King and Country,* p. 77.
4. T. A. Lewis, *For King and Country,* p. 76.
5. Michael Ignatieff, *Blood and Belonging: Journeys into the New Nationalism* (New York: Farrar, Straus & Giroux, 1993), p. 165.
6. M. Ignatieff, *Blood and Belonging,* p. 168.
7. Beit-Hallahmi, *Original Sins,* p. 90.
8. Beit-Hallahmi, *Original Sins,* p. 90.
9. James E. Young, *The Texture of Memory: Holocaust Memorials and Meaning* (New Haven: Yale University Press, 1993), p. 275.
10. Ruth R. Wisse, *If I Am Not For Myself . . . The Liberal Betrayal of the Jews* (New York: The Free Press, 1992), p. 94.
11. Wisse, *If I Am Not For Myself,* p. 94.
12. Wisse, *If I Am Not For Myself,* p. 94.
13. Wisse, *If I Am Not For Myself,* p. 94.
14. Leshem, *Israel Alone,* p. 150.

15. Amos Oz, *Israel, Palestine and Peace: Essays* (New York: Harcourt Brace & Company, 1995), p. 17.
16. I. Berlin and R. Jahanbegloo, *Conversations with Isaiah Berlin,* p. 86.
17. Wisse, *If I Am Not For Myself,* p. 119.
18. Sichrovsky, *Abraham's Children,* p. 4.
19. Neal Ascherson, *Black Sea* (New York: Hill and Wang, 1995), p. 110.
20. Samuel Hynes, *A War Imagined: The First World War and English Culture* (New York: Atheneum, 1991), p. 57.
21. David McDowall, *Palestine and Israel: The Uprising and Beyond* (Berkeley: University of California, 1989), p. 129.
22. D. Rubenstein, *The People of Nowhere,* p. 75.
23. McDowall, *Palestine and Israel,* p. 126.
24. D. Rubenstein, *The People of Nowhere,* p. 82.
25. Tom Segev, *The Seventh Million: The Israelis and the Holocaust,* trans. Haim Watzman (New York: Hill and Wang, 1993), p. 300.
26. MacDonald, *Shoot the Women First,* pp. 66–67.
27. MacDonald, *Shoot the Women First,* p. 67.
28. Yitzhak Zuckerman, *A Surplus of Memory: Chronicle of the Warsaw Ghetto Uprising* (Berkeley: University of California Press, 1993), p. 192.
29. Zuckerman, *A Surplus of Memory,* p. 192.
30. Günter Grass, *Two States—One Nation?* trans. Krishna Winston and A. S. Wensinger (New York: Harcourt Brace Jovanovich, Publishers, 1990), p. 6.
31. John Weitz, *The Life and Times of Joachin von Ribbentrop* (New York: Ticknor & Fields, 1992), p. 25.
32. Quoted in Leshem, *Israel Alone,* p. 58.
33. Czeslaw Milosz, *Beginning with My Streets,* trans. Madeline G. Levine (New York: Farrar, Straus & Giroux, 1991), p. 82.
34. Milosz, *Beginning,* p. 83.
35. Milosz, *Beginning,* p. 83.
36. William Pfaff, *The Wrath of Nations: Civilization and the Furies of Nationalism* (New York: Simon & Schuster, 1993), p. 111.
37. Peter Theroux, *Sandstorms: Days and Nights in Arabia* (New York: W. W. Norton & Company, 1990), p. 54.
38. Naguib Mahfouz, *Children of the Alley,* trans. Peter Theroux (New York: Doubleday, 1996), p. 95.
39. Makiya, *Cruelty and Silence,* p. 245.
40. Mernissi, *Islam and Democracy,* p. 164.
41. Paul Breines, *Tough Jews* (New York: Basic Books, 1990), p. xi.
42. Wole Soyinka, *The Open Sore of a Continent: A Personal Narrative of the Nigerian Crisis* (New York: Oxford University Press, 1996), p. 35.
43. Wole Soyinka, *Art, Dialogue, and Outrage: Essays on Literature and Culture* (New York: Pantheon Books, 1994), p. 87.
44. Malan, *My Traitor's Heart,* p. 27.
45. Malan, *My Traitor's Heart,* p. 25.
46. Sebastian Mallaby, *After Apartheid: The Future of South Africa* (New York: Times Books, 1992), pp. 73–74.
47. Malan, *My Traitor's Heart,* pp. 27–28.
48. Kate Millett, *The Politics of Cruelty: An Essay on the Literature of Political Imprisonment* (New York: W. W. Norton & Company, 1994), pp. 8–9.
49. Amnesty International, *Amnesty International Report 1997* (New York: Amnesty International U.S.A., 1997), p. 194.
50. Shelby Steele, *The Content of Our Character* (New York: St. Martin's Press, 1990), p. 54.
51. B. Knox, *The Oldest Dead,* pp. 55–56.
52. B. Knox, *The Oldest Dead,* p. 55.
53. Ascherson, *Black Sea,* p. 111.
54. Mernissi, *Islam and Democracy,* p. 86.
55. Mernissi, *Islam and Democracy,* p. 86.

56. Patterson, *Freedom,* pp. 77–78.
57. John Berger, *Photocopies* (London: Bloomsbury, 1997), pp. 111–112.
58. Appelfeld, *Beyond Despair,* p. 7.
59. Meryl Hyman, *"Who Is a Jew?" Conversations, Not Conclusions* (Woodstock, Vt.: Jewish Lights Publishing, 1998), p. 74.
60. Norman G. Cantor, *The Sacred Chain: The History of the Jews* (New York: HarperCollins, 1994), p. 48.
61. Uta Ranke-Heinemann, *Putting Away Childish Things: The Virgin Birth, the Empty Tomb, and Other Fairy Tales You Don't Need to Believe to Have a Living Faith,* trans. Peter Heinegg (San Francisco: Harper, 1994), p. 34.
62. Biale, *Eros and the Jews,* p. 80.
63. Biale, *Eros and the Jews,* p. 62.
64. Biale, *Eros and the Jews,* p. 12.
65. Biale, *Eros and the Jews,* p. 45.
66. Biale, *Eros and the Jews,* p. 45.
67. Biale, *Eros and the Jews,* p. 45.
68. Fishman, *A Breath of Life,* p. 108.
69. Fishman, *A Breath of Life,* p. 108.
70. Thomas Keneally, *Schindler's List* (New York: Simon & Schuster, 1992), p. 174.
71. N. Levin, *The Holocaust,* p. 365.
72. Israel Gutman, *Resistance: The Warsaw Ghetto Uprising* (Boston: Houghton Mifflin Company, 1994), p. xv.
73. Zuccotti, *The Holocaust, the French and the Jews,* p. 113.
74. Appelfeld, *Beyond Despair,* p. 37.
75. Quoted in Michael Burns, *A Family Affair, From the French Revolution to the Holocaust* (New York: HarperPerennial, 1992), p. 445.
76. M. Kaplan, *Between Dignity and Despair,* p. 79.
77. William D. Rubinstein, *The Myth of Rescue: Why the Democracies Could Not Have Saved More Jews From the Nazis* (London: Routledge, 1997), p. 44.
78. M. Kaplan, *Between Dignity and Despair,* p. 188.
79. Wyden, *Stella,* p. 64.
80. Anne Michaels, *Fugitive Pieces* (Toronto: McClelland & Stewart, 1996), p. 138.
81. Myrna Goldberg, "Preface," pp. xi–xix in Ana Novac, *The Beautiful Days of My Youth: My Six Months in Auschwitz and Plaszow,* trans. George L. Newman (New York: Henry Holt and Company, 1997), p. xvii.
82. Myrna Goldberg, "Preface," pp. xi–xix in Ana Novac, *The Beautiful Days of My Youth,* p. xiv.
83. Ruth Elias, *Triumph of Hope: From Theresienstadt and Auschwitz to Israel,* trans. Margo Bettauer Dembo (New York: John Wiley & Sons, 1998), p. 122.
84. Mark Kurlansky, *A Chosen Few: The Resurrection of European Jewry* (Reading, Mass.: Addison-Wesley Publishing Company, 1995), p. 344.
85. Rudolf Höss, *Death-Dealer: The Memoirs of the SS Kommandant at Auschwitz,* ed. Steven Paskuly, trans. Andrew Pollinger (New York: Da Capo Press, 1996), p. 160.
86. Höss, *Death-Dealer,* p. 164.
87. Elfriede Jelinek, *Wonderful Wonderful Times,* trans. Michael Hulse (London: Serpent's Tail, 1990), p. 98.
88. Makiya, *Cruelty and Silence,* p. 296.
89. Makiya, *Cruelty and Silence,* p. 293.
90. Evelyne Accad, *Sexuality and War: Literary Masks of the Middle East* (New York: New York University Press, 1990), p. 20.
91. Accad, *Sexuality and War,* pp. 20–21.
92. Gloria Emerson, *Gaza: A Year in the Intifada—A Personal Account from an Occupied Land* (New York: The Atlantic Monthly Press, 1991), p. 99.
93. Accad, *Sexuality and War,* p. 22.
94. Mernissi, *Islam and Democracy,* p. 6.
95. William V. O'Brien, *Law and Morality in Israel's War With the PLO* (New York: Routledge, 1991), p. 243.

96. McDowall, *Palestine and Israel,* p. 114.
97. Rapoport, *Stalin's War Against the Jews,* p. 1.
98. Rapoport, *Stalin's War Against the Jews,* pp. 4–5.
99. Rapoport, *Stalin's War Against the Jews,* p. 4.
100. Gerald Posner, *Hitler's Children: Sons and Daughters of the Leaders of the Third Reich Talk About Themselves and Their Fathers* (New York: Random House, 1991), p. 21.
101. Posner, *Hitler's Children,* p. 24.
102. Posner, *Hitler's Children,* p. 216.
103. Posner, *Hitler's Children,* p. 216.
104. James Miller, *The Passion of Michel Foucault* (New York: Simon & Schuster, 1993), p. 127.
105. Miller, *The Passion,* p. 127.
106. Eva Fogelman, *Conscience and Courage: Rescuers of Jews During the Holocaust* (New York: Anchor Books, 1994), p. 257.
107. Fogelman, *Conscience and Courage,* p. 254.
108. Fogelman, *Conscience and Courage,* p. 254

CHAPTER 5: MASCULINITY/FEMININITY

1. Klaus P. Fischer, *Nazi Germany: A New History* (New York: Continuum, 1995), p. 260.
2. Fischer, *Nazi Germany,* p. 260.
3. Walter Laqueur, *Fascism: Past, Present, Future* (New York: Oxford University Press, 1994), p. 57.
4. Carey, *The Intellectuals,* p. 197.
5. Carey, *The Intellectuals,* p. 197.
6. Laqueur, *Fascism,* p. 45.
7. Alice Miller, *The Untouched Key,* trans. Hildegarde and Hunter Hannum (New York: Doubleday, 1990), p. 139.
8. M. Ignatieff, *Blood and Belonging,* p. 246.
9. M. Ignatieff, *Blood and Belonging,* p. 246.
10. M. Ignatieff, *Blood and Belonging,* pp. 246–247.
11. M. Ignatieff, *Blood and Belonging,* p. 247.
12. M. Ignatieff, *Blood and Belonging,* p. 247.
13. Michael Ignatieff, *The Warrior's Honor: Ethnic War and the Modern Conscience* (New York: Henry Holt and Company, 1997), p. 160.
14. Hans Magnus Enzenberger, *Civil Wars: From L.A. to Bosnia* (New York: The New Press, 1994), p. 21.
15. Enzenberger, *Civil Wars,* p. 21.
16. Enzenberger, *Civil Wars,* p. 21.
17. Enzenberger, *Civil Wars,* pp. 21–22.
18. Laqueur, *Fascism,* p. 176.
19. H. Al-Shaykh, *The Story of Zahra,* trans. Peter Ford and Hanan Al-Shaykh (London: Quartet Books, 1986), p. 122.
20. Gilman, *The Jew's Body,* p. 40.
21. Beit-Hallahmi, *Original Sins,* p. 15.
22. Bartoszewski, *Convent,* p. 3.
23. Zuccotti, *The Holocaust, the French, and the Jews,* p. 18.
24. Zuccotti, *The Holocaust, the French, and the Jews,* pp. 31–32.
25. N. Levin, *The Holocaust,* p. xv.
26. Joshua Rubenstein, *Tangled Loyalties: The Life and Times of Ilya Ehrenburg* (New York: Basic Books, 1996), pp. 205–206.
27. Weiss, *Ideology of Death,* p. 207.
28. Breines, *Tough Jews,* p. 30.
29. Quoted in Geoffrey Wheatcroft, *The Controversy of Zion: Jewish Nationalism, the Jewish State, and the Unresolved Jewish Dilemma* (Reading, Mass.: Addison-Wesley Publishing Company, 1996), pp. 171–172.
30. Tec, *Defiance,* p. 159.
31. Tec, *Defiance,* p. 137.

32. Zuckerman, *A Surplus of Memory,* p. 489.
33. Howard Gardner, *Creating Minds: An Anatomy of Creativity Seen Through the Lives of Freud, Einstein, Picasso, Stravinsky, Eliot, Graham and Gandhi* (New York: Basic Books, 1993), p. 52.
34. E. Hoffman, *Shtetl,* p. 235.
35. N. Levin, *The Holocaust,* p. 345.
36. Dan Raviv and Yossie Melman, *Friends in Deed: Inside the U.S.–Israel Alliance* (New York: Hyperion, 1994), p. 41.
37. Jon Anderson, *Guerrillas: The Men and Women Fighting Today's Wars* (New York: Times Books, 1992), p. 27.
38. J. Anderson, *Guerrillas,* p. 27.
39. Sharoni, *Gender in the Israeli-Palestinian Conflict,* p. 46.
40. Sharoni, *Gender in the Israeli-Palestinian Conflict,* p. 46.
41. Ezrahi, *Rubber Bullets,* pp. 248–249.
42. Sharoni, *Gender in the Israeli-Palestinian Conflict,* p. 38.
43. Buruma, *The Wages of Guilt,* pp. 18–19.
44. P. Theroux, *Sandstorms,* pp. 116–117.
45. W. O'Brien, *Law and Morality,* p. 139.
46. J. Anderson, *Guerrillas,* pp. 184–185.
47. J. Anderson, *Guerrillas,* pp. 185–186.
48. Fatima Mernissi, *The Veil and the Male Elite: A Feminist Interpretation of Women's Rights in Islam,* trans. Mary Jo Lakeland (New York: Addison-Wesley Publishing Co., 1991), p. 21.
49. Mernissi, *Islam and Democracy,* p. 165.
50. Goodwin, *Price of Honor,* p. 299.
51. Goodwin, *Price of Honor,* p. 299.
52. Goodwin, *Price of Honor,* p. 299.
53. Danny Rubenstein, *The Mystery of Arafat,* trans. Dan Leon (South Royalton, Vt.: Steerforth Press, 1995), p. 19.
54. Ingo Hasselbach and Tom Reiss, *Führer-Ex: Memoirs of a Former Neo-Nazi* (New York: Random House, 1996), pp. 294–295.
55. Höss, *Death-Dealer,* p. 96.
56. Gary Wills, *Under God: Religion and American Politics* (New York: Simon & Schuster, 1990), p. 103.
57. Citing Jung, in Yerushalmi, *Freud's Moses,* p. 48.
58. Quoted in James King, *Virginia Woolf* (New York: W. W. Norton & Company, 1995), p. 245.
59. Gregor Von Rezzori, *Memoirs of an Anti-Semite: A Novel in Five Stories* (New York: Penguin Books, 1982), p. 111.
60. José Donoso, *The Garden Next Door,* trans. Hardie St. Martin (New York: Grove Press, 1992), p. 123.
61. Biale, *Eros and the Jews,* p. 8.
62. Frederick Karl, *Franz Kafka: Representative Man* (New York: W. W. Norton & Company, 1995), p. 133.
63. Tony Judt, *Past Imperfect: French Intellectuals 1944–1992* (Berkeley: University of California Press, 1992), p. 49.
64. Richard J. Evans, *Tales From the German Underworld: Crime and Punishment in the Nineteenth Century* (New Haven: Yale University Press, 1998), p. 132.
65. R. Evans, *Tales,* p. 132.
66. R. Evans, *Tales,* p. 132.
67. G. Lerner, *The Creation of Feminist Consciousness,* p. 23.
68. G. Lerner, *The Creation of Feminist Consciousness,* p. 23.
69. Mernissi, *Islam and Democracy,* p. 114.
70. Biale, *Eros and the Jews,* p. 45.
71. M. Yalom, *Blood Sisters,* p. 71.
72. M. Yalom, *Blood Sisters,* p. 7.
73. Tzvetan Todorov, *Facing the Extreme: Moral Life in the Concentration Camp,* trans. Arthur Denner and Abigail Pollak (New York: Henry Holt and Company, 1996), p. 20.

74. E. Fogelman, *Conscience and Courage,* p. 242.
75. Debórah Dwork, *Children With a Star: Jewish Youth in Nazi Europe* (New Haven: Yale University Press, 1991), p. xliv.
76. Laska, *Women in the Resistance,* p. 176.
77. Laska, *Women in the Resistance,* p. 181.

CHAPTER 6: THE CHOSEN/THE EVIL

1. T. Segev, *The Seventh Million,* p. 301.
2. Paul Celan, "Tenebrae," *Poems of Paul Celan,* trans. Michael Hamburger (New York: Persea Books, 1995), p. 115.
3. Telushkin, *Jewish Literacy,* p. 208.
4. Bartoszewski, *Convent,* pp. 2–3.
5. Martin Gilbert, *Israel: A History* (New York: William Morrow and Company, 1998), p. 49.
6. Christopher R. Browning, *Ordinary Men: Reserve Police Battalion 101 and the Final Solution in Poland* (New York: HarperCollins/Asher Books, 1992), p. 121.
7. M. Ignatieff, *Blood and Belonging,* p. 32.
8. Szczypiorski, *The Beautiful Mrs. Seidenman,* p. 33.
9. Shimon Peres, *Battling for Peace: A Memoir,* ed. David Landau (New York: Random House, 1995), p. 309.
10. Patterson, *Freedom,* p. 9.
11. D. Stannard, *American Holocaust,* p. x.
12. J. M. G. Le Clézio, *The Mexican Dream Or, The Interrupted Thought of Amerindian Civilizations,* trans. Teresa Lavender Fagan (Chicago: The University of Chicago Press, 1993), p. 176.
13. D. Stannard, *American Holocaust,* p. xiii.
14. Richard Lee Marks, *Cortés: The Great Adventurer and the Fate of Aztec Mexico* (New York: Alfred A. Knopf, 1993), p. 200.
15. Robert Conquest, *Stalin: Breaker of Nations* (New York: Viking, 1991), p. 164.
16. Simpson, *The Splendid Blond Beast,* p. 27.
17. Simpson, *The Splendid Blond Beast,* p. 28.
18. Simpson, *The Splendid Blond Beast,* p. 28.
19. Simpson, *The Splendid Blond Beast,* p. 29.
20. G. Wheatcroft, *The Ottomans,* p. 22.
21. G. Wheatcroft, *The Ottomans,* p. 21.
22. Wiesel, *A Beggar in Jerusalem,* p. 113.
23. Breznitz, *Memory Fields,* p. 6.
24. Lucy S. Dawidowicz, *The Holocaust and the Historians* (Cambridge: Harvard University Press, 1981), p. 125.
25. Cantor, *The Sacred Chain,* p. 40.
26. Cantor, *The Sacred Chain,* p. 40.
27. Wistrich, *Antisemitism,* p. 4.
28. Gay, *The Cultivation of Hatred,* p. 68.
29. Daniel J. Boorstin, *The Creators: A History of Heroes of the Imagination* (New York: Random House, 1992), p. 50.
30. Arthur Hertzberg and Aron Hirt-Manheimer, *Jews: The Essence and Character of a People* (San Francisco: HarperCollins, 1998), p. 30.
31. Hertzberg and Hirt-Manheimer, *Jews,* p. 19.
32. Hertzberg and Hirt-Manheimer, *Jews,* p. 285.
33. Hertzberg and Hirt-Manheimer, *Jews,* p. 31.
34. George Steiner, *No Passion Spent: Essays 1978–1995* (New Haven: Yale University Press, 1996), p. 231.
35. Morris Dworkin in a conversation with the author in 1962 or 1963.
36. Gerald Early, "Introduction," pp. xi–xxiv in Gerald Early, ed. *Lure and Loathing: Essays on Race, Identity, and the Ambivalence of Assimilation* (New York: Allen Lane/The Penguin Press, 1993), p. xvi.

37. Quoted in Milosz, *Beginning With My Streets*, p. 87.
38. Tory, *Surviving the Holocaust*, p. 116.
39. Wolfgang Sofsky, *The Order of Terror: The Concentration Camp*, trans. William Templer (Princeton: Princeton University Press, 1997), p. 148.
40. Pierre Vidal-Naquet, *Assassins of Memory: Essays on the Denial of the Holocaust*, trans. Jeffrey Mehlman (New York: Columbia University Press, 1992), p. 123.
41. George Steiner, *The Portage to San Cristobal of A. H.* (New York: Pocket Books, 1981), p. 179.
42. Ron Rosenbaum, *Explaining Hitler: The Search for the Origins of His Evil* (New York: Random House, 1998), p. 312.
43. Wistrich, *Antisemitism*, p. 94.
44. Quoted in Jay Parini, *John Steinbeck: A Biography* (New York: Henry Holt and Company, 1995), p. 99.
45. Laurie Robertson-Lorant, *Melville: A Biography* (New York: Clarkson Potter/Publishers, 1996), p. 235.
46. Quoted in Robertson-Lorant, *Melville*, p. 91.
47. Joel Kotkin, *Tribes: How Race, Religion, and Identity Determine Success in the New Global Economy* (New York: Random House, 1993), p. 172.
48. Thomas Sowell, *Migrations and Cultures: A World View* (New York: Basic Books, 1996), p. 235.
49. Sowell, *Migrations and Culture*, p. 176.
50. Olivier Todd, *Camus: A Life* (New York: Alfred A. Knopf, 1997), p. 330.
51. Liah Greenfeld, *Nationalism: Five Roads to Modernity* (Cambridge: Harvard University Press, 1992), p. 52.
52. B. Knox, *The Oldest Dead*, pp. 27–28.
53. Greenfeld, *Nationalism*, p. 133.
54. Marks, *Cortés*, p. 90.
55. Marks, *Cortés*, p. 88.
56. Quoted in Tzvetan Todorov, *On Human Diversity: Nationalism, Racism, and Exoticism in French Thought*, trans. Catherine Porter (Cambridge: Harvard University Press, 1993), p. 218.
57. J. E. Young, *The Texture of Memory*, p. 115.
58. Léon Poliakov, *The Aryan Myth: A History of Racist and Nationalist Ideas in Europe*, trans. Edmund Howard (New York: Barnes & Noble Books, 1996), p. 6.
59. David Rieff, *The Exile: Cuba in the Heart of Miami* (New York: Simon & Schuster, 1993), pp. 50–51.
60. Mallaby, *After Apartheid*, p. 72.
61. Wisse, *If I Am Not For Myself*, p. 122.
62. Janet Wallach and John Wallach, *Arafat: In the Eyes of the Beholder* (Secaucus, N.J.: Carol Publishing Group, 1990), p. 34.
63. Kotkin, *Tribes*, p. 34.
64. Richard Posner, *Overcoming Law* (Cambridge: Harvard University Press, 1995), p. 180.
65. Michael Lind, *Up From Conservatism: Why the Right Is Wrong for America* (New York: The Free Press, 1996), pp. 223–224.
66. Southern Poverty Law Center, *False Patriots: The Threat of Antigovernment Extremists* (Montgomery, Ala.: Southern Poverty Law Center, 1996), p. 4.
67. Edward Said, *The Politics of Dispossession: The Struggle for Palestinian Self-Determination 1969–1994* (New York: Pantheon Books, 1994), p. 114.
68. Sichrovsky, *Abraham's Children*, p. 49.
69. Sowell, *Migrations and Cultures*, p. 306.
70. Quoted in Solomon Volkov, *Conversations with Joseph Brodsky: A Poet's Journey Through the Twentieth Century*, trans. Marian Schwartz (New York: The Free Press, 1998), p. 98.
71. Sylvia Plath, "Daddy," *The Collected Poems*, ed. Ted Hughes (New York: Harper & Row, Publishers, 1981), p. 223.
72. Plath, "Daddy," *Collected Poems*, p. 223.
73. Sandra M. Gilbert and Susan Gubar, *No Man's Land: The Place of the Woman Writer in the Twentieth Century*, vol. 3 (New Haven: Yale University Press, 1994), p. 262.

74. Mernissi, *Islam and Democracy,* p. 126.
75. Quoted in Michael Berenbaum, "The Perpetrators," pp. 268–270, in Yisrael Gutman and Michael Berenbaum, eds., *Anatomy of Auschwitz Death Camp* (Bloomington: Indiana University Press and the United States Holocaust Memorial Museum, 1994), p. 268.
76. Laska, ed., *Women in the Resistance,* p. 35.
77. Laska, ed., *Women in the Resistance,* p. 35.
78. Laska, ed., *Women in the Resistance,* p. 39.
79. Laska, ed., *Women in the Resistance,* p. 36.
80. A. Novac, *The Beautiful Days of My Youth,* p. 184.
81. Höss, *Death-Dealer,* p. 149.
82. Wyden, *Stella,* p. 145.
83. Quoted in Wyden, *Stella,* p. 145.
84. Zuckerman, *A Surplus of Memory,* pp. 496–497.
85. MacDonald, *Shoot the Women First,* p. 192.
86. MacDonald, *Shoot the Women First,* p. 18.
87. Dan Van der Vat, *The Good Nazi: The Life and Lies of Albert Speer* (Boston: Houghton Mifflin Company, 1977), p. 130.
88. Koonz, *Mothers in the Fatherland,* p. 55.
89. Koonz, *Mothers in the Fatherland,* p. 5.
90. Goldhagen, *Hitler's Willing Executioners,* p. 119.
91. Anton Gill, *An Honourable Defeat: A History of German Resistance to Hitler, 1933–1945* (New York: Henry Holt and Company, 1994), p. 193.
92. Koonz, *Mothers in the Fatherland,* p. 5.

CHAPTER 7: HATE LITERATURE/PORNOGRAPHY

1. Quoted in Marguerite Feitlowitz, *A Lexicon of Terror: Argentina and the Legacies of Torture* (New York: Oxford University Press, 1998), p. 61.
2. Feitlowitz, *Lexicon,* p. 61.
3. William S. McFeely, *Frederick Douglass* (New York: W. W. Norton & Company, 1991), p. 30.
4. David Lehman, *Signs of the Times* (New York: Poseidon Press, 1991), p. 135.
5. Lehman, *Signs of the Times,* p. 135.
6. Lehman, *Signs of the Times,* p. 137.
7. Quoted in Lehman, *Signs of the Times,* p. 269.
8. Konrád, *A Feast in the Garden,* pp. 213–214.
9. Michaels, *Fugitive Pieces,* p. 207.
10. Raul Hilberg, *The Politics of Memory: The Journey of a Holocaust Historian* (Chicago: Ivan R. Dee, 1996), p. 74.
11. Zuccotti, *The Holocaust, the French, and the Jews,* p. 16.
12. Feitlowitz, *Lexicon,* p. 39.
13. *The Writer and Human Rights,* ed. Toronto Arts Group for Human Rights (Garden City, N.Y.: 1983), p. 80.
14. Makiya, *Cruelty and Silence,* p. 133.
15. Sinyavsky, *The Russian Intelligentsia,* pp. 75–76.
16. Grace Paley in a conversation with the author.
17. D. Stannard, *American Holocaust,* p. 167.
18. Gwen Kinkead, *Chinatown: A Portrait of a Closed Society* (New York: HarperCollins Publishers, 1992), p. 5.
19. T. Lewis, *For King and Country,* p. 76.
20. Lindemann, *The Jew Accused,* p. 168.
21. Zuccotti, *The Holocaust, the French, and the Jews,* p. 25.
22. Burns, *Dreyfus,* p. 434.
23. Burns, *Dreyfus,* p. 434.
24. Herbert Lottman, *Colette: A Life* (Boston: Little, Brown and Company, 1991), p. 164.
25. Ralph Freedman, *Life of a Poet: Rainer Maria Rilke* (New York: Farrar, Straus & Giroux, 1996), p. 370.

26. Stanley Weintraub, *Disraeli: A Biography* (New York: Dutton, 1993), pp. 413–414.
27. Weintraub, *Disraeli,* p. 467.
28. Weintraub, *Disraeli,* pp. xi–xii.
29. Victoria Glendinning, *Vita: A Biography of Vita Sackville-West* (New York: Quill, 1984), p. 378.
30. Janet Byrne, *A Genius for Living: The Life of Frieda Lawrence* (New York: HarperCollins, 1995), p. 236.
31. Feinstein, *Lawrence and the Women,* p. 177.
32. Barbara Belford, *Violet* (New York: Simon & Schuster, 1990), p. 69.
33. Roy Jenkins, *Gladstone: A Biography* (New York: Random House, 1997), p. 279.
34. Quoted in Rosemary Ashton, *George Eliot: A Life* (London: Hamish Hamilton, 1996), p. 348.
35. James Knowlson, *Damned to Fame: The Life of Samuel Beckett* (New York: Simon & Schuster, 1996), p. 161.
36. Paul Kuttner, *The Holocaust: Hoax or History? The Book of Answers to Those Who Would Deny the Holocaust* (New York: Dawnwood Press, 1996), p. 178.
37. Goldhagen, *Hitler's Willing Executioners,* p. 238.
38. I. Berlin and R. Jahanbegloo, *Conversations,* p. 38.
39. Tec, *Defiance,* p. 82.
40. T. Segev, *The Seventh Million,* p. 409.
41. Quoted in T. Segev, *The Seventh Million,* p. 409.
42. T. Segev, *The Seventh Million,* p. 409.
43. Breznitz, *Memory Fields,* p. 65.
44. William H. Gass, *Finding a Form* (New York: Alfred A. Knopf, 1996), pp. 169–170.
45. Ze'ev Schiff and Ehud Ya'ari, *Intifada,* trans. Ina Friedman (New York: Simon & Schuster, 1990), pp. 224–225.
46. J. Bowyer Bell, *The Irish Troubles: A Generation of Violence 1967–1992* (New York: St. Martin's Press, 1993), p. 487.
47. Richard Delgado, "Rodrigos's Seventh Chronicle: Race, Democracy, and the State," *UCLA Law Review,* vol. 41, no. 3, p. 732.
48. Posner, *Hitler's Children,* p. 88.
49. Hertzberg and Hirt-Manheimer, *Jews,* p. 62.
50. Netanyahu, *The Origins of the Inquisition,* p. 984.
51. Netanyahu, *The Origins of the Inquisition,* p. 984.
52. Quoted in Gross, *Shylock,* p. 22.
53. Robert Skidelsky, *John Maynard Keynes: The Economist as Savior, 1920–1937,* vol. 2 (New York: Allen Lane/The Penguin Press, 1992), p. 238.
54. Gross, *Shylock,* p. 313.
55. Gross, *Shylock,* p. 319.
56. Gross, *Shylock,* p. 70.
57. Barbara Belford, *Bram Stoker* (New York: Alfred A. Knopf, 1996), p. 228.
58. Weiss, *Ideology of Death,* p. 130.
59. Weiss, *Ideology of Death,* p. 134.
60. Fest, *Hitler,* p. 91.
61. Chernow, *The Warburgs,* p. 217.
62. Chernow, *The Warburgs,* p. 217.
63. John Berger, *The Sense of Sight* (New York: Vintage International, 1993), p. 169.
64. Berger, *The Sense of Sight,* pp. 169–170.
65. Goldhagen, *Hitler's Willing Executioners,* pp. 63–64.
66. Goldhagen, *Hitler's Willing Executioners,* p. 64.
67. Toland, *Adolf Hitler,* p. 45.
68. Toland, *Adolf Hitler,* p. 45.
69. Toland, *Adolf Hitler,* p. 45.
70. Toland, *Adolf Hitler,* p. 46.
71. Fest, *Hitler,* p. 38.
72. Fest, *Hitler,* p. 38.
73. Fest, *Hitler,* p. 38.

74. Toland, *Adolf Hitler,* p. 222.
75. Toland, *Adolf Hitler,* p. 222.
76. Hilberg, *Perpetrators, Victims, Bystanders,* p. 5.
77. Leni Yahil, *The Holocaust: The Fate of European Jewry, 1932–1945,* trans. Ina Friedman and Haya Galai (New York: Oxford University Press, 1990), p. 43.
78. Carey, *The Intellectuals,* p. 26.
79. Fest, *Hitler,* p. 73.
80. Fest, *Hitler,* p. 73.
81. Ronald Hayman, *Hitler and Geli* (London: Bloomsbury, 1997), p. 67.
82. Hayman, *Hitler and Geli,* p. 67.
83. Hayman, *Hitler and Geli,* p. 67.
84. Hayman, *Hitler and Geli,* p. 55.
85. Hayman, *Hitler and Geli,* p. 55.
86. Hayman, *Hitler and Geli,* p. 58.
87. Hayman, *Hitler and Geli,* p. 58.
88. Hayman, *Hitler and Geli,* p. 59.
89. Hayman, *Hitler and Geli,* p. 61.
90. Hayman, *Hitler and Geli,* p. 71.
91. Friedländer, *Nazi Germany and the Jews,* p. 104.
92. Gitta Sereny, *Albert Speer: His Battle with Truth* (New York: Alfred A. Knopf, 1995), p. 164.
93. Goldhagen, *Hitler's Willing Executioners,* p. 124.
94. Laurel Holiday, ed., *Children in the Holocaust and World War II: Their Secret Diaries* (New York: Pocket Books, 1995), p. 83.
95. Laqueur, *Fascism,* pp. 56–57.
96. Laqueur, *Fascism,* p. 56.
97. Browning, *Ordinary Men,* p. 41.
98. *The Protocols of the Meetings of the Learned Elders of Zion,* trans. Victor E. Marsden (n.p., n.d.), p. 160.
99. *Protocols,* p. 151.
100. *Protocols,* p. 148.
101. Hannah Arendt, *Essays in Understanding 1930–1954* (New York: Harcourt Brace & Company, 1994), p. 141.
102. Arendt, *Essays,* p. 141.
103. Arendt, *Essays,* pp. 141–142.
104. Weiss, *Ideology of Death,* p. 214.
105. Rapoport, *Stalin's War Against the Jews,* p. xiv.
106. Kurlansky, *A Chosen Few,* p. 269.
107. Zuccotti, *The Holocaust, the French, and the Jews,* p. 24.
108. Donald Warren, *Radio Priest: Charles Coughlin, the Father of Hate Radio* (New York: The Free Press, 1996), p. 149.
109. Zuccotti, *The Holocaust, the French, and the Jews,* p. 24.
110. Dinnerstein, *Antisemitism in America,* pp. 80–81.
111. Warren, *Radio Priest,* p. 35.
112. Wistrich, *Antisemitism,* p. 258.
113. Quoted in Wistrich, *Antisemitism,* p. 255.
114. Wistrich, *Antisemitism,* p. 255.
115. Wistrich, *Antisemitism,* p. 256.
116. Wistrich, *Antisemitism,* p. 235.
117. Wisse, *If I Am Not For Myself,* p. 34.
118. Laqueur, *Fascism,* p. 149.
119. Hasselbach and Reiss, *Führer-Ex,* p. 361.
120. J. B. Bell, *The Irish Troubles,* p. 637.
121. Young-Bruehl, *The Anatomy of Prejudices,* p. 251.
122. David Frum, *Dead Right* (New York: Basic Books, 1994), p. 79.
123. Frum, *Dead Right,* p. 79.
124. Tom Metzger, *WAR: White Aryan Resistance* (Fallbrook, Calif.: n.p., August 1994), p. 2.

125. Metzger, *WAR*, p. 2.
126. Cincinnatus, *War! War! War!* (Metarie, La.: Sons of Liberty, 1991), p. 48.
127. Andrew Macdonald (William Pierce), *The Turner Diaries* (Hillsboro, W. Va.: National Vanguard Books, 1990), p. 102.
128. Macdonald, *The Turner Diaries*, back cover.
129. Macdonald, *The Turner Diaries*, p. 1.
130. Macdonald, *The Turner Diaries*, p. 198.
131. Macdonald, *The Turner Diaries*, p. 26.
132. Macdonald, *The Turner Diaries*, p. 34.
133. Macdonald, *The Turner Diaries*, p. 106.
134. Macdonald, *The Turner Diaries*, p. 134.
135. Macdonald, *The Turner Diaries*, p. 118.
136. Macdonald, *The Turner Diaries*, p. 78.
137. Macdonald, *The Turner Diaries*, p. 122.
138. Macdonald, *The Turner Diaries*, p. 68.
139. Macdonald, *The Turner Diaries*, pp. 150–151.
140. Macdonald, *The Turner Diaries*, p. 151.
141. Macdonald, *The Turner Diaries*, p. 45.
142. Macdonald, *The Turner Diaries*, p. 45.
143. Macdonald, *The Turner Diaries*, p. 77.
144. Hugh Trevor-Roper in *"The Good Old Days": The Holocaust as Seen by Its Perpetrators and Bystanders,* eds. Ernst Klee, Willi Dressen, and Volker Riess, trans. Deborah Burnstone (New York: The Free Press, 1991), p. xii.
145. Trevor-Roper, *"The Good Old Days,"* p. xx.
146. Trevor-Roper, *"The Good Old Days,"* p. xx.
147. Trevor-Roper, *"The Good Old Days,"* p. xx.
148. Goldhagen, *Hitler's Willing Executioners*, p. 245.
149. Quoted in N. Levin, *The Holocaust*, p. 231.
150. Quoted in N. Levin, *The Holocaust*, p. 231.
151. Quoted in N. Levin, *The Holocaust*, p. 231.
152. N. Levin, *The Holocaust*, p. 231.
153. Breitman, *The Architect of Genocide*, p. 178.
154. Van der Vat, *The Good Nazi*, p. 213.
155. Sereny, *Albert Speer*, pp. 454–455.
156. Van der Vat, *The Good Nazi*, title.
157. Fischer, *Nazi Germany*, p. 552.
158. Maria Tatar, *Lustmord: Sexual Murder in Weimar Germany* (Princeton: Princeton University Press, 1995), pp. 170–171.
159. Hasselbach and Reiss, *Führer-Ex*, p. 317.
160. Telford Taylor, *The Anatomy of the Nuremberg Trials* (New York: Alfred A. Knopf, 1992), p. 200.
161. Taylor, *Nuremberg Trials*, p. 200.
162. Hayman, *Hitler and Geli*, p. 75.
163. Hayman, *Hitler and Geli*, p. 75.
164. Joseph E. Persico, *Nuremberg: Infamy on Trial* (New York: Viking, 1994), p. 168.
165. R. Rosenbaum, *Explaining Hitler*, p. 110.
166. R. Rosenbaum, *Explaining Hitler*, p. 110.
167. R. Rosenbaum, *Explaining Hitler*, p. 110.
168. R. Rosenbaum, *Explaining Hitler*, p. 50.
169. Höss, *Death-Dealer*, p. 106.
170. Persico, *Nuremberg*, pp. 172–173.
171. Persico, *Nuremberg*, p. 172.
172. Höss, *Death-Dealer*, p. 171 n.
173. Todorov, *Facing the Extremes*, p. 160.
174. Todorov, *Facing the Extremes*, p. 16.
175. Jelinek, *Wonderful, Wonderful Times*, p. 15.
176. Jelinek, *Wonderful, Wonderful Times*, p. 17.

177. T. Segev, *The Seventh Million*, p. 405.

178. T. Segev, *The Seventh Million*, p. 406.

179. J. L. Anderson, *Guerrillas*, p. 186.

180. J. L. Anderson, *Guerrillas*, p. 186.

181. MacDonald, *Shoot the Women First*, p. 200.

182. MacDonald, *Shoot the Women First*, p. 200.

183. MacDonald, *Shoot the Women First*, p. 173.

184. MacDonald, *Shoot the Women First*, p. 5.

185. Sasson, *Princess*, p. 63.

186. Feitlowitz, *Lexicon*, p. 67.

187. John Berger, *Art and Revolution: Ernst Neizvestny, Endurance, and the Role of Art* (New York: Vintage Books, 1997), p. 108.

CHAPTER 8: RELIGION/MATERNITY

1. Kotkin, *Tribes*, p. 30.

2. Kotkin, *Tribes*, p. 30.

3. Kotkin, *Tribes*, p. 30.

4. Oliver, *The African Experience*, p. 84.

5. Oliver, *The African Experience*, p. 84.

6. Oliver, *The African Experience*, p. 84.

7. Oliver, *The African Experience*, p. 84.

8. Quoted in Milosz, *Beginning With My Streets*, p. 85.

9. Mernissi, *Islam and Democracy*, p. 75.

10. Oliver, *The African Experience*, p. 77.

11. Robin Lane Fox, *The Unauthorized Version: Truth and Fiction in the Bible* (New York: Oxford University Press, 1997), p. 71.

12. Fox, *Unauthorized Version*, p. 71.

13. Fox, *Unauthorized Version*, p. 71.

14. Narasimhan, *Sati*, p. 27.

15. J. B. Bell, *The Irish Troubles*, p. 50.

16. J. B. Bell, *The Irish Troubles*, p. 50.

17. Daniel Belgrad, *The Culture of Spontaneity: Improvisation and the Arts in Postwar America* (Chicago: The University of Chicago Press, 1998), p. 69.

18. Aviezer Rabitzky, *Messianism, Zionism, and Jewish Religious Radicalism,* trans. Michael Swirsky and Jonathan Chipman (Chicago: The University of Chicago Press, 1996), p. 11.

19. Quoted in Rabitzky, *Messianism, Zionism*, p. 11.

20. Neil Postman, *Amusing Ourselves to Death: Public Discourse in the Age of Show Business* (New York: Penguin Books, 1986), p. 9.

21. Postman, *Amusing Ourselves to Death*, p. 9.

22. Postman, *Amusing Ourselves to Death*, p. 9.

23. J. E. Young, *The Texture of Memory*, p. 49.

24. Quoted in Ehud Sprinzak, *The Ascendance of Israel's Radical Right* (New York: Oxford University Press, 1991), p. 53.

25. Sprinzak, *The Ascendance*, p. 4.

26. Leshem, *Israel Alone*, p. 208.

27. "Orthodox in Israel Protest Rulings," *Newsday,* February 15, 1999.

28. Karen Armstrong, *A History of God: The 4,000-Year Quest of Judaism, Christianity, and Islam* (New York: Alfred A. Knopf, 1993), p. xxiii.

29. Andrea Dworkin, *Woman Hating* (New York: Dutton, 1974), p. 172.

30. K. Armstrong, *A History of God*, p. xxiii.

31. Leshem, *Israel Alone*, p. 152.

32. Leshem, *Israel Alone*, p. 152.

33. Leshem, *Israel Alone*, p. 152.

34. Jack Miles, *God: A Biography* (New York: Alfred A. Knopf, 1995), p. 18.

35. Miles, *God*, p. 16.

36. Miles, *God*, p. 18.
37. Greenfeld, *Nationalism*, pp. 52–53.
38. Boorstin, *The Creators*, p. 127.
39. Leon Wieseltier, *Kaddish* (New York: Alfred A. Knopf, 1998), pp. ix–x.
40. Konrád, *A Feast in the Garden*, p. 30.
41. Donald Harman Akenson, *Surpassing Wonder: The Invention of the Bible and the Talmuds* (New York: Harcourt Brace & Company, 1998), p. 310.
42. Bershtel and Graubard, *Saving Remnants*, p. 163.
43. Fishman, *A Breath of Life*, p. 160.
44. Biale, *Eros and the Jews*, p. 37.
45. Beit-Hallahmi, *Original Sins*, pp. 6–7.
46. Robert L. Wilken, *The Land Called Holy: Palestine in Christian History and Thought* (New Haven: Yale University Press, 1992), p. 5.
47. Wilken, *The Land Called Holy*, p. 5.
48. Wilken, *The Land Called Holy*, p. 5.
49. Fox, *The Unauthorized Version*, pp. 224–225.
50. Kotkin, *Tribes*, p. 31.
51. Kotkin, *Tribes*, p. 31.
52. Rabitzky, *Messianism, Zionism*, p. 167.
53. Yahil, *The Holocaust*, p. 497.
54. Yahil, *The Holocaust*, p. 497.
55. Elliot Abrams, *Faith or Fear: How Jews Can Survive in a Christian America* (New York: The Free Press, 1997), p. 19.
56. Cantor, *The Sacred Chain*, p. 35.
57. Konrád, *A Feast in the Garden*, p. 29.
58. Vidal-Naquet, *Assassins of Memory*, p. 77.
59. K. Armstrong, *A History of God*, p. 46.
60. Wisse, *If I Am Not For Myself*, p. 28.
61. Bershtel and Graubard, *Saving Remnants*, p. 239.
62. Hertzberg and Hirt-Manheimer, *Jews*, p. 282.
63. Hertzberg and Hirt-Manheimer, *Jews*, p. 282.
64. G. Lerner, *The Creation of Feminist Consciousness*, p. 275.
65. Laska, ed., *Women in the Resistance*, p. 21.
66. M. Hyman, "*Who Is a Jew?*" p. 76.
67. Mernissi, *Islam and Democracy*, p. 127.
68. Edvard Radzinsky, *Stalin*, trans. H. T. Willetts (New York: Doubleday, 1996), p. 245.
69. Radzinsky, *Stalin*, p. 245.
70. J. L. Anderson, *Guerrillas*, p. 12.
71. Octavio Paz, *The Double Flame: Love and Eroticism*, trans. Helen Lane (New York: Harcourt Brace & Company, 1995), p. 17.
72. Quoted in Biale, *Eros and the Jews*, p. 13.
73. Anna Akhmatova, "Requiem," *Selected Poems*, trans. D. M. Thomas (New York: Penguin Books, 1988), p. 89.
74. Akhmatova, "Requiem," *Selected Poems*, p. 87.
75. Elias, *Triumph of Hope*, p. 144.
76. Patterson, *Freedom*, p. 35.
77. Bernard Williams, *Shame and Necessity* (Berkeley: University of California, 1993), p. 107.
78. Nawal El Saadawi, *God Dies by the Nile*, trans. Sherif Hetata (London: Zed Books, 1986), p. 30.
79. Ailbhe Smyth, "Seeing Red: Men's Violence Against Women in Ireland," pp. 53–76 in Chris Corrin, ed., *Women in a Violent World: Feminist Analysis and Resistance Across "Europe"* (Edinburgh: Edinburgh University Press, 1996), p. 70.
80. Narasimhan, *Sati*, pp. 45–46.
81. Narasimhan, *Sati*, p. 47.
82. Narasimhan, *Sati*, p. 47.
83. *UNICEF Report*, London: July 27, 1997.

84. "One in Twelve Women Stalked," U.S. Department of Justice, November 15, 1997.

85. "Doctor Group Says Violence Imperils Nation," *The New York Times,* November 7, 1995.

86. "Study Cites Adult Males for Most Teen-age Births," *The New York Times,* August 2, 1995.

87. "For Many Girls, First Sex Was 'Not Wanted,' " *The Washington Post,* June 18, 1997.

88. "Young Girls First Sex 'Not Wanted,' " *The Washington Post,* June 18, 1997.

89. "Sex Offenses and Offenders," U.S. Bureau of Justice Statistics, January 1997.

90. "Showing the Increasing Gravity of Sexual Assault," *Irish Reports and Statements,* a compilation of citations, 1997.

91. "Showing the Increasing Gravity of Sexual Assault," *Irish Reports and Statements,* a compilation of citations, 1997.

92. Molly Peacock, *Paradise, Piece by Piece* (New York: Riverhead Books, 1998), p. 102.

93. P. Theroux, *Sandstorms,* p. 120.

94. Simon Louvish, *The Silencer* (New York: Interlink Books, 1993), p. 191.

95. Mullins, *The Painted Witch,* p. 39.

96. Lind, *Up From Conservatism,* p. 227.

97. Macdonald, *The Turner Diaries,* pp. 129–130.

98. T. Segev, *The Seventh Million,* p. 208.

99. Makiya, *Cruelty and Silence,* pp. 289–290.

100. Tatar, *Lustmord,* p. 10.

101. Volkov, *Conversations with Joseph Brodsky,* p. 43.

102. Todorov, *Facing the Extremes,* p. 17.

103. Quoted in Raviv and Melman, *Friends in Need,* p. 109.

104. *The World's Women 1995: Trends and Statistics* (New York: United Nations Publications), p. 1.

105. *The World's Women 1995,* p. 158.

106. *The World's Women 1995,* p. 160.

107. Tory, *Surviving the Holocaust,* p. 310.

108. Hilberg, *Perpetrators, Victims, Bystanders,* p. 67.

109. "Nazi Doctors," Robert Jay Lifton and Amy Hackett, pp. 301–316, in Gutman and Berenbaum, eds., *Anatomy of Auschwitz,* p. 303.

110. Otto Friedrich, *The Kingdom of Auschwitz* (New York: HarperCollins, 1995), p. 58.

111. Lore Shelley, ed., *Criminal Experiments on Human Beings in Auschwitz and War Research Laboratories: Twenty Women Prisoners' Accounts* (San Francisco: Mellen Research University Press, 1991), p. 32.

112. Friedrich, *The Kingdom of Auschwitz,* p. 57.

113. Friedrich, *The Kingdom of Auschwitz,* p. 57.

114. Laska, ed., *Women in the Resistance,* p. 181.

115. Robert Jay Lifton, *The Nazi Doctors: Medical Killing and the Psychology of Genocide* (New York: Basic Books, 1986), p. 251.

116. Laska, *Women in the Resistance,* p. 217.

117. Fischer, *Nazi Germany,* p. 490.

118. Fischer, *Nazi Germany,* p. 490.

119. Lifton, *The Nazi Doctors,* p. 247.

120. Elias, *Triumph of Hope,* p. 129.

121. Laska, ed., *Women in the Resistance,* p. 178.

122. Quoted in M. Kaplan, *Between Dignity and Despair,* p. 165.

123. M. Kaplan, *Between Dignity and Despair,* p. 72.

124. Schwerfeger, *Women of Theresienstadt,* p. 61.

125. Novac, *The Beautiful Days of My Youth,* p. 9.

126. Konrád, *A Feast in the Garden,* p. 33.

127. F. Silverman, ed., *Women in the Holocaust,* p. 52.

128. M. Gilbert, *The Boys,* p. 124.

129. Holliday, ed., *Children in the Holocaust,* epigraph.

130. Novac, *The Beautiful Days of My Youth,* p. 181.

131. Lagnado and Dekel, *Children of the Flames,* p. 58.

132. Lagnado and Dekel, *Children of the Flames,* p. 66.
133. Lagnado and Dekel, *Children of the Flames,* p. 71.
134. Dwork, *Children With a Star,* p. xi.
135. Abraham Lewin, *A Cup of Tears: A Diary of the Warsaw Ghetto,* trans. Christopher Hutton (Oxford: Basil Blackwell, 1988), p. 89.
136. Dwork, *Children With a Star,* p. 40.
137. Peter Høeg, *Borderliners,* trans. Barbara Haveland (New York: Farrar, Straus & Giroux, 1994), p. 188.

CHAPTER 9: ZIONISM/WOMEN'S LIBERATION

1. I. Berlin and R. Jahanbegloo, *Conversations,* p. 40.
2. David Levering Lewis, *W.E.B. Du Bois: Biography of a Race 1868–1919* (New York: Henry Holt and Company, 1994), p. 426.
3. Wallaby, *After Apartheid,* p. 116.
4. Wallaby, *After Apartheid,* p. 167.
5. Breyten Breytenbach, *Return to Paradise* (New York: Harcourt Brace & Company, 1993), p. 9.
6. Rupert Christiansen, *Paris Babylon: The Story of the Paris Commune* (New York: Viking, 1994), p. 299.
7. Stephen L. Carter, *The Culture of Disbelief: How American Law and Politics Trivialize Religious Devotion* (New York: Basic Books, 1993), p. 96.
8. Quoted in Neil Asher Silverman, *A Prophet From Amongst You. The Life of Yigael Yadim: Soldier, Scholar, and Mythmaker of Modern Israel* (New York: Addison-Wesley Publishing Company, 1993), p. 318.
9. Silverman, *A Prophet,* p. 318.
10. Silverman, *A Prophet,* p. 318
11. Leshem, *Israel Alone,* p. 193.
12. Gore Vidal, *Live From Golgatha* (New York: Random House, 1992), p. 215.
13. Chernow, *The Warburgs,* p. 290.
14. Chernow, *The Warburgs,* p. 290.
15. N. Levin, *The Holocaust,* p. 127.
16. Breitman, *The Architect of Genocide,* p. 122.
17. Paul E. Johnson and Sean Wilentz, *The Kingdom of Matthias: A Story of Sex and Salvation in 19th Century America* (New York: Oxford University Press, 1994), p. 65.
18. Chernow, *The Warburgs,* p. 293.
19. Chernow, *The Warburgs,* p. 432.
20. Warren, *Radio Priest,* p. 175.
21. Breitman, *The Architect of Genocide,* p. 122.
22. Szulc, *The Secret Alliance,* p. 28.
23. Friedländer, *Nazi Germany and the Jews,* pp. 62–63.
24. Weiss, *Ideology of Death,* p. 329.
25. Eugene Davidson, *The Unmaking of Adolf Hitler* (Columbia: University of Missouri Press, 1996), p. 345.
26. Breitman, *The Architect of Genocide,* p. 59.
27. Breitman, *The Architect of Genocide,* p. 152.
28. Browning, *Ordinary Men,* p. xv.
29. Browning, *Ordinary Men,* p. 99.
30. J. E. Young, *The Texture of Memory,* p. 235.
31. J. E. Young, *The Texture of Memory,* p. 235.
32. Laqueur, *Thursday's Child,* p. 101.
33. Fernand Braudel, *A History of Civilizations,* trans. Richard Mayne (New York: Allen Lane/The Penguin Press, 1994), p. 11.
34. Quoted in *The New York Times,* April 20, 1997.
35. Breines, *Tough Jews,* p. 47.
36. "Israelis demonstrate for tougher penalties for men who beat women," Jerusalem (AFB), November 25, 1998.

37. "Israelis demonstrate," Jerusalem (AFB), November 25, 1998.
38. United Nations, London, July 27, 1997.
39. Amos Elon, "Israel's Demons," *The New York Review of Books,* December 21, 1995, p. 42.
40. Weintraub, *Disraeli,* p. 266.
41. Weintraub, *Disraeli,* p. 266.
42. Jane Ridley, *Young Disraeli 1804–1846* (New York: Crown Publishers, 1995), pp. 2–3.
43. Leshem, *Israel Alone,* p. 83.
44. Hertzberg and Hirt-Manheimer, *Jews,* p. 204.
45. Hertzberg and Hirt-Manheimer, *Jews,* p. 204.
46. Ridley, *Young Disraeli,* p. 3.
47. Hertzberg and Hirt-Manheimer, *Jews,* p. 206.
48. Quoted in Weintraub, *Disraeli,* p. 277.
49. Quoted in Hertzberg and Hirt-Manheimer, *Jews,* p. 204.
50. Hannah S. Decker, *Freud, Dora, and Vienna 1900* (New York: The Free Press, 1991), p. 29.
51. Rachel M. Brownstein, *Tragic Muse: Rachel of the Comédie-Française* (New York: Alfred A. Knopf, 1993), p. 243.
52. Ashton, *George Eliot,* p. 304.
53. Ashton, *George Eliot,* p. 347.
54. Leshem, *Israel Alone,* p. 83.
55. Zuccotti, *The Holocaust, the French, and the Jews,* p. 21.
56. Theodor Herzl, *The Jewish State* (Mineola, N.Y.: Dover Publications, 1988), p. 76.
57. Leshem, *Israel Alone,* p. 83.
58. Herzl, *The Jewish State,* pp. 89–90.
59. Herzl, *The Jewish State,* p. 92.
60. Herzl, *The Jewish State,* p. 92.
61. Herzl, *The Jewish State,* p. 51.
62. Herzl, *The Jewish State,* p. 51.
63. Herzl, *The Jewish State,* p. 52.
64. Herzl, *The Jewish State,* p. 53.
65. Herzl, *The Jewish State,* p. 53.
66. Quoted in M. Gilbert, *Israel,* p. 4.
67. G. Wheatcroft, *The Controversy of Zion,* p. 82.
68. Quoted in Zeev Sternhell, *The Founding Myths of Israel,* trans. David Maisel (Princeton: Princeton University Press, 1998), pp. 47–48.
69. Bershtel and Graubard, *Saving Remnants,* p. 129.
70. G. Wheatcroft, *The Controversy of Zion,* p. 329.
71. Gilman, *The Jew's Body,* p. 53.
72. Leshem, *Israel Alone,* p. 84.
73. Beit-Hallahmi, *Original Sins,* p. 9.
74. Yahil, *The Holocaust,* p. 498.
75. Chang, *The Rape of Nanking,* p. 43.
76. Lawrence L. Langer, *Holocaust, Testimonies: The Ruins of Memory* (New Haven: Yale University Press, 1991), p. 100.
77. Hannah Senesh, *Hannah Senesh: Her Life and Diary,* trans. Nigel Marsh (New York: Schocken Books, 1977), p. 86.
78. Senesh, *Hannah Senesh,* p. 257.
79. Lagnado and Dekel, *Children of the Flames,* pp. 194–195.
80. Appelfeld, *Beyond Despair,* p. 38.
81. T. Segev, *The Seventh Million,* p. 183.
82. T. Segev, *The Seventh Million,* p. 179.
83. T. Segev, *The Seventh Million,* p. 44.
84. M. Gilbert, *Israel,* p. 46.
85. T. Segev, *The Seventh Million,* p. 28.
86. Chernow, *The Warburgs,* p. 454.
87. Chernow, *The Warburgs,* p. 454.

88. Sprinzak, *The Ascendance,* p. 29.
89. Sprinzak, *The Ascendance,* p. 29.
90. Silberman, *A Prophet,* p. 166.
91. Quoted in T. Segev, *The Seventh Million,* p. 179.
92. Szulc, *The Secret Alliance,* p. 192.
93. Ian Black and Benny Morris, *Israel's Secret Wars: A History of Israel's Intelligence Services* (New York: Grove Weidenfeld, 1991), p. 188.
94. Laqueur, *Thursday's Child,* p. 235.
95. Mark A. Heller and Sari Nusseibeh, *No Trumpets, No Drums: A Two-State Settlement of the Israeli-Palestinian Conflict* (New York: Hill and Wang, 1991), p. 32.
96. Andrew Gowers and Tony Walker, *Behind the Myth: Yasser Arafat and the Palestinian Revolution* (New York: Olive Branch Press, 1992), p. 167.
97. Ezrahi, *Rubber Bullets,* p. 180.
98. Quoted in Z. Sternhell, *The Founding Myths of Israel,* p. 129.
99. Amos Oz, *Touch the Water, Touch the Wind,* trans. Nicholas de Lange (New York: Harcourt Brace Jovanovich, 1974), p. 100.
100. Leshem, *Israel Alone,* p. 85.
101. T. Segev, *The Seventh Million,* pp. 161–162.
102. T. Segev, *The Seventh Million,* p. 161.
103. McDowall, *Palestine and Israel,* p. 79.
104. Laqueur, *Thursday's Child,* p. 222.
105. McDowall, *Palestine and Israel,* p. 197.
106. McDowall, *Palestine and Israel,* p. 197.
107. McDowall, *Palestine and Israel,* p. 196.
108. D. Rubenstein, *The People of Nowhere,* p. 6.
109. Amos Oz, *Fima,* trans. Nicholas de Lange (New York: Harcourt Brace Jovanovich, Publishers, 1973), p. 94.
110. James B. Jacobs and Kimberly Potter, *Hate Crimes: Criminal Law and Identity Politics* (New York: Oxford University Press, 1998), pp. 19–20.
111. Jacobs and Potter, *Hate Crimes,* p. 41.
112. Lifton, *The Nazi Doctors,* p. 155.
113. Octavio Paz, *Essays on Mexican Art,* trans. Helen Lane (New York: Harcourt Brace & Company, 1993), pp. 171–172.
114. Biale, *Eros and the Jews,* p. 30.
115. Wiesel, *A Beggar in Jerusalem,* p. 143.
116. Oz, *Touch the Water, Touch the Wind,* p. 29.
117. Accad, *L'Exicée,* p. 46.
118. Accad, *L'Exicée,* p. 46.
119. J. Berger, *Art and Revolution,* p. 144.
120. Laska, ed., *Women in the Resistance,* p. 185.
121. Laska, ed., *Women in the Resistance,* p. 207.
122. Babel, *1920 Diary,* p. 69.
123. J. Nelson, *Terror in the Night,* p. 127.
124. Feitlowitz, *Lexicon,* p. 69.
125. Feitlowitz, *Lexicon,* p. 135.
126. Feitlowitz, *Lexicon,* p. 67.
127. Feitlowitz, *Lexicon,* p. 67.
128. Feitlowitz, *Lexicon,* p. 166.
129. El Saadawi, *God Dies by the Nile,* pp. 32–33.
130. Asma El Dareer, *Woman, Why Do You Weep? Circumcision and Its Consequences* (London: Zed Press, 1983), p. 66.
131. El Dareer, *Woman, Why Do You Weep?,* p. 74.
132. El Dareer, *Woman, Why Do You Weep?,* p. 74.
133. Höss, *Death-Dealer,* p. 145.
134. Elias, *Triumph of Hope,* p. 120.
135. Marks, *Cortés,* p. 202.

136. Nathan McCall, *Makes Me Wanna Holler: A Young Black Man in America* (New York: Random House, 1994), pp. 42–43.

137. McCall, *Makes Me Wanna Holler,* p. 307.

138. McCall, *Makes Me Wanna Holler,* p. 307.

139. Goodwin, *Price of Honor,* p. 52.

140. Makiya, *Cruelty and Silence,* p. 299.

141. Schiff and Ya'ari, *Intifada,* p. 231.

142. Makiya, *Cruelty and Silence,* p. 292.

143. Patterson, *Freedom,* p. 110.

144. Silverman, ed., *Women in the Holocaust,* p. ix.

145. Simon Wiesenthal, *Foreword,* pp. xi–xii, V. Laska, ed., *Women in the Resistance,* p. xii.

146. Laska, *Women in the Resistance,* p. 6.

147. Laska, *Women in the Resistance,* p. 198.

148. Laska, *Women in the Resistance,* p. 8.

149. Laska, *Women in the Resistance,* p. 17.

150. Laska, *Women in the Resistance,* p. 17.

151. Gutman and Berenbaum, eds., *Anatomy of Auschwitz,* p. 31.

152. M. Gilbert, *The Boys,* p. 166.

153. Breznitz, *Memory Fields,* p. 177.

154. Mills, *This Little Light of Mine,* p. 45.

155. Mills, *This Little Light of Mine,* p. 45.

156. Sasson, *Princess,* p. 241.

157. Sasson, *Princess,* p. 243.

158. Ascherson, *Black Sea,* p. 41.

159. Anna Akhmatova, *My Half Century: Selected Prose,* trans. Ronald Meyer (Evanston, Il: Northwestern University Press, 1997), p. 28.

160. M. Yalom, *Blood Sisters,* p. 26.

161. M. Yalom, *Blood Sisters,* p. 26.

162. MacDonald, *Shoot the Women First,* p. 95.

163. MacDonald, *Shoot the Women First,* p. 95.

164. Todorov, *On Human Diversity,* p. 128.

165. J. B. Bell, *The Irish Troubles,* p. 31.

166. J. B. Bell, *The Irish Troubles,* p. 609.

167. I. Berlin and R. Jahanbegloo, *Conversations,* p. 145.

168. Peter Coyote, *Sleeping Where I Fall* (Washington, D.C.: Counterpoint, 1998), p. 31.

169. I. Berlin and R. Jahanbegloo, *Conversations,* p. 142.

170. Quoted in W. V. O'Brien, *Law and Morality in Israel's War,* p. 23.

171. J. L. Anderson, *Guerrillas,* p. 41.

172. Jonathan Shay, *Achilles in Vietnam: Combat Trauma and the Undoing of Character* (New York: Atheneum, 1994), p. 20.

173. Sofsky, *The Order of Terror,* p. 8.

174. Sofsky, *The Order of Terror,* p. 10.

175. John Berger, *Photocopies* (London: Bloomsbury, 1997), p. 177.

176. Henry Kissinger, *Diplomacy* (New York: Simon & Schuster, 1994), p. 121.

177. Simpson, *The Splendid Blond Beast,* p. 287.

CHAPTER 10: MEMORY/DENIAL

1. Kramer, *The Politics of Memory,* p. 279.

2. Laqueur, *Thursday's Child,* p. 65.

3. Laqueur, *Thursday's Child,* p. 65.

4. Primo Levy, "Shame," pp. 108–120, in Lawrence L. Langer, ed., *Art from the Ashes: A Holocaust Anthology* (New York: Oxford University Press, 1995), p. 109.

5. Levy, "Shame," in Langer, ed., *Art from the Ashes,* pp. 110–111.

6. Feitlowitz, *Lexicon,* p. 68.

7. Berger, *Art and Revolution,* p. 101.

8. Lewin, *A Cup of Tears,* p. 176.
9. Gelissen and Macadam, *Rena's Promise,* p. 125.
10. Janina Heshele, pp. 68–72, in L. Holliday, ed., *Children in the Holocaust,* p. 71.
11. Novac, *The Beautiful Days of My Youth,* p. 6.
12. Novac, *The Beautiful Days of My Youth,* p. 3.
13. Israel Gutman, *Resistance: The Warsaw Ghetto Uprising* (Boston: Houghton Mifflin Company, 1993), p. xv.
14. Keneally, *Schindler's List,* p. 144.
15. Hilberg, *Perpetrators, Victims, Bystanders,* p. 130.
16. Levi, "Shame," in Langer, ed., *Art From the Ashes,* p. 113.
17. Levi, "Shame," in Langer, ed., *Art From the Ashes,* p. 113.
18. Levi, "Shame," in Langer, ed., *Art From the Ashes,* p. 113.
19. Gelissen and Macadam, *Rena's Promise,* p. 152.
20. Wieseltier, *Kaddish,* p. 178.
21. Elias, *Triumph of Hope,* p. ix.
22. Jacobs and Potter, *Hate Crimes,* p. 60.
23. Toni Morrison, *Playing in the Dark: Whiteness and the Literary Imagination* (Cambridge: Harvard University Press, 1992), p. 52.
24. Morrison, *Playing in the Dark,* p. 37.
25. Edward Said, *Peace and Its Discontents: Essays on Palestine in the Middle East Peace Process* (New York: Vintage Books, 1995), pp. 27–28.
26. David Mamet, *The Old Religion* (New York: The Free Press, 1997), p. 193.
27. Sasson, *Princess,* pp. 65–66.
28. J. B. Bell, *The Irish Troubles,* p. 319.
29. Steiner, *No Passion Spent,* p. 177.
30. Judith Miller, *God Has Ninety-nine Names: Reporting From a Militant Middle East* (New York: Simon & Schuster, 1996), p. 107.
31. Sofsky, *The Order of Terror,* p. 148.
32. Sofsky, *The Order of Terror,* p. 148.
33. Sofsky, *The Order of Terror,* p. 148.
34. Lagnado and Dekel, *Children of the Flames,* p. 13.
35. Steele, *The Content of Our Character,* p. 15.
36. Early, ed., *Lure and Loathing,* pp. 6–7.
37. Doris Lessing, *African Laughter: Four Visits to Zimbabwe* (New York: HarperCollins Publishers, 1992), p. 133.
38. John Fuegi, *Brecht & Co.: Sex, Politics, and the Making of the Modern Drama* (New York: Grove Press, 1994), p. xiv.
39. Fuegi, *Brecht & Co.,* p. xix.
40. Fuegi, *Brecht & Co.,* p. xv.
41. Milan Kundera, *Testaments Betrayed: An Essay in Nine Parts,* trans. Linda Asher (New York: HarperCollins, 1995), p. 18.
42. Lewin, *A Cup of Tears,* p. v.
43. Fonseca, *Bury Me Standing,* p. 11.
44. Laska, ed., *Women in the Resistance,* p. 11.
45. Fonseca, *Bury Me Standing,* p. 7.
46. Fonseca, *Bury Me Standing,* p. 89.
47. Declan Kiberd, *Inventing Ireland: The Literature of the Modern Nation* (Cambridge: Harvard University Press, 1996), p. 13.
48. J. B. Bell, *The Irish Troubles,* p. 28.
49. Feitlowitz, *Lexicon,* p. 139.
50. Feitlowitz, *Lexicon,* p. 38.
51. M. Yalom, *Blood Sisters,* p. 2.
52. Paz, *Essays on Mexican Art,* pp. 81–82.
53. Quoted in Robert Jay Lifton, *The Protean Self: Human Resilience in an Age of Fragmentation* (New York: Basic Books, 1993), p. 40.
54. Appelfeld, *Beyond Despair,* p. 64.
55. Semprun, *Literature or Life?,* p. 196.

56. Todorov, *Facing Extremes,* p. 263.
57. Mary Lowenthal Felstiner, *To Paint Her Life: Charlotte Salomon in the Nazi Era* (New York: HarperCollins, 1994), p. 15.
58. Felstiner, *To Paint Her Life,* p. 24.
59. Felstiner, *To Paint Her Life,* p. 24.
60. Andy Marino, *Herschel: The Boy Who Started World War II* (London: Faber and Faber, 1995), p. 90.
61. Wyden, *Stella,* p. 102.
62. Quoted in *Media Watch* 4, no. 3 (Fall 1998), p. 3.
63. Rosenbaum, *Explaining Hitler,* p. 114.
64. Breitman, *The Architect of Genocide,* p. 4.
65. M. Kaplan, *Between Dignity and Despair,* p. 117.
66. Chernow, *The Warburgs,* p. 478.
67. N. Levin, *The Holocaust,* p. 675.
68. Kurlansky, *A Chosen Few,* p. 376.
69. Kurlansky, *A Chosen Few,* p. 37.
70. Zuccotti, *The Holocaust, the French, and the Jews,* p. 19.
71. Zuccotti, *The Holocaust, the French, and the Jews,* p. 19.
72. Quoted in Robert O. Paxton, *Vichy France: Old Guard and New Order 1940–1944* (New York: Columbia University Press, 1972), p. 140.
73. Novac, *The Beautiful Days of My Youth,* title.
74. Annette Kahn, *Why My Father Died: A Daughter Confronts Her Family's Past at the Trial of Klaus Barbie,* trans. Anna Cancogni (New York: Summit Books, 1991), pp. 14–15.
75. Henry Rousso, *The Vichy Syndrome: History and Memory in France Since 1944,* trans. Arthur Goldhammer (Cambridge: Harvard University Press, 1991), p. 26.
76. Rousso, *The Vichy Syndrome,* p. 25.
77. Kahn, *Why My Father Died,* p. 15.
78. Rousso, *The Vichy Syndrome,* p. 27.
79. Deborah Lipstadt, *Denying the Holocaust: The Growing Assault on Truth and Memory* (New York: The Free Press, 1993), p. 50.
80. Alice Kaplan, *French Lessons: A Memoir* (Chicago: The University of Chicago Press, 1994), p. 196.
81. A. Kaplan, *French Lessons,* p. 196.
82. Rousso, *The Vichy Syndrome,* p. 153.
83. Rousso, *The Vichy Syndrome,* p. 153.
84. Rousso, *The Vichy Syndrome,* p. 51.
85. Rousso, *The Vichy Syndrome,* p. 53.
86. Judt, *Past Imperfect,* pp. 183–184.
87. Rousso, *The Vichy Syndrome,* p. 156.
88. Quoted in Rousso, *The Vichy Syndrome,* p. 151.
89. Quoted in Rousso, *The Vichy Syndrome,* p. 166.
90. Jeffrey Mehlman, "Foreword," pp. ix–xxv, in Vidal-Naquet, *Assassins of Memory,* p. xiii.
91. Mehlman, "Foreword," in Vidal-Naquet, *Assassins of Memory,* p. xiii.
92. Mehlman, "Foreword," in Vidal-Naquet, *Assassins of Memory,* p. xiii.
93. Mehlman, "Foreword," in Vidal-Naquet, *Assassins of Memory,* pp. xiii–xiv.
94. Mehlman, "Foreword," in Vidal-Naquet, *Assassins of Memory,* p. xiv.
95. Rousso, *The Vichy Syndrome,* pp. 203–204.
96. Rousso, *The Vichy Syndrome,* p. 205.
97. Rousso, *The Vichy Syndrome,* p. 203.
98. Rousso, *The Vichy Syndrome,* p. 205.
99. Rousso, *The Vichy Syndrome,* p. 203.
100. Kuttner, *The Holocaust: Hoax or History?,* p. 65.
101. Lipstadt, *Denying the Holocaust,* p. 50.
102. Yahil, *The Holocaust,* pp. 3–4.
103. Vidal-Naquet, *Assassins of Memory,* p. 139.
104. Lipstadt, *Denying the Holocaust,* p. 209.
105. Lipstadt, *Denying the Holocaust,* p. 209.

106. Lipstadt, *Denying the Holocaust,* p. 140.
107. Lipstadt, *Denying the Holocaust,* pp. 138–139.
108. Primo Levi, pp. 3–9, in Höss, *Death-Dealer,* p. 7.
109. Vidal-Naquet, *Assassins of Memory,* p. 123.
110. Wistrich, *Antisemitism,* pp. 233–234.
111. Macdonald, *The Turner Diaries,* p. 49.
112. Wisse, *If I Am Not For Myself,* pp. 45–46.
113. Ian McEwan, *Black Dogs* (New York: Nan A. Talese/Doubleday, 1992), p. 88.

CHAPTER 11: PALESTINIANS/PROSTITUTED WOMEN

1. Malan, *My Traitor's Heart,* p. 229.
2. Peres, *Battling for Peace,* p. 276.
3. Quoted in Andrew Hacker, *Two Nations: Black and White, Separate, Hostile, Unequal* (New York: Charles Scribner's Sons, 1992), p. lx.
4. Said, *The Politics of Dispossession,* p. 73.
5. Said, *The Politics of Dispossession,* p. 73.
6. Steele, *The Content of Our Characters,* p. 44.
7. Gay, *The Cultivation of Hatred,* p. 70.
8. Heller and Nusseibeh, *No Trumpets, No Drums,* p. 3.
9. I. Berlin and R. Jahanbegloo, *Conversations,* p. 144.
10. I. Berlin and R. Jahanbegloo, *Conversations,* p. 144.
11. Quoted in Jon Lee Anderson, *Ché Guevara: A Revolutionary Life* (New York: Grove Press, 1997), p. 719.
12. Quoted in "Reshuffling the Deck," *Newsweek,* January 11, 1999.
13. Morrison, *Playing in the Dark,* p. 64.
14. Geoffrey Cowan, *The People v. Clarence Darrow: The Bribery Trial of America's Greatest Lawyer* (New York: Times Books, 1993), p. 19.
15. Malan, *My Traitor's Heart,* p. 15.
16. Karen Armstrong, *Muhammad: A Biography of the Prophet* (San Francisco: Harper, 1992), p. 40.
17. Robert D. Kaplan, *The Arabists: The Romance of an American Elite* (New York: The Free Press, 1993), p. 18 n.
18. Chernow, *The Warburgs,* p. 247.
19. Armstrong, *Muhammad,* p. 40.
20. Leshem, *Israel Alone,* p. 126.
21. McDowall, *Palestine and Israel,* p. 22.
22. McDowall, *Palestine and Israel,* p. 22.
23. McDowall, *Palestine and Israel,* p. 201.
24. M. Gilbert, *Israel,* p. 61.
25. McDowall, *Palestine and Israel,* p. 201.
26. McDowall, *Palestine and Israel,* p. 22.
27. N. Levin, *The Holocaust,* p. 129.
28. N. Levin, *The Holocaust,* p. 130.
29. Szulc, *The Secret Alliance,* p. 8.
30. Friedländer, *Nazi Germany and the Jews,* p. 299.
31. Friedländer, *Nazi Germany and the Jews,* p. 299.
32. Marcia Kunstel and Joseph Albright, *Their Promised Land: Arab and Jew in History's Cauldron—One Valley in the Jerusalem Hills* (New York: Crown Publishers, 1990), p. 144.
33. Szulc, *The Secret Alliance,* p. 8.
34. Szulc, *The Secret Alliance,* p. 125.
35. Wallach and Wallach, *Arafat,* p. 76.
36. Wallach and Wallach, *Arafat,* p. 76.
37. Patrick Seale, *Abu Nidal: A Gun for Hire* (New York: Random House, 1992), p. 60.
38. Seale, *Abu Nidal,* p. 61 n.
39. Breines, *Tough Jews,* p. 159.
40. Breines, *Tough Jews,* p. 159.

41. Breines, *Tough Jews,* p. 159.
42. Wallach and Wallach, *Arafat,* p. 259.
43. John Follain, *Jackal: The Complete Story of the Legendary Terrorist, Carlos the Jackal* (New York: Arcade Publishing, 1998), p. 26.
44. Follain, *Jackal,* p. 29.
45. Wallach and Wallach, *Arafat,* p. 273.
46. Sprinzak, *The Ascendance,* p. 35.
47. Sprinzak, *The Ascendance,* p. 35.
48. Vidal-Naquet, *Assassins of Memory,* p. 130.
49. D. Rubenstein, *The People of Nowhere,* p. 36.
50. D. Rubenstein, *The People of Nowhere,* p. 118.
51. W. V. O'Brien, *Law and Morality,* p. 255.
52. Laqueur, *Fascism,* p. 161.
53. Said, *The Politics of Dispossession,* p. xxxiv.
54. Edward Said, "The One-State Solution," *The New York Times,* January 10, 1999, pp. 36–39.
55. Said, "The One-State Solution," *The New York Times,* p. 36.
56. Sichrovsky, *Abraham's Children,* p. 154.
57. T. Segev, *The Seventh Million,* p. 208.
58. T. Segev, *The Seventh Million,* p. 208.
59. McDowall, *Palestine and Israel,* p. 154.
60. McDowall, *Palestine and Israel,* p. 152.
61. McDowall, *Palestine and Israel,* p. 156.
62. P. Theroux, *Sandstorms,* p. 234.
63. T. Segev, *The Seventh Million,* p. 359.
64. J. L. Anderson, *Guerrillas,* p. 88.
65. J. L. Anderson, *Guerrillas,* p. 89.
66. Heller and Nusseibeh, *No Trumpets, No Drums,* p. 107.
67. Schiff and Ya'ari, *Intifada,* pp. 96–97.
68. Robin Morgan, *The Demon Lover: On the Sexuality of Terrorism* (New York: W. W. Norton & Company, 1989), p. 243.
69. Schiff and Ya'ari, *Intifada,* p. 86.
70. J. L. Anderson, *Guerrillas,* p. 184.
71. Rashid Khalidi, *Palestinian Identity: The Construction of Modern National Conscience* (New York: Columbia University Press, 1997), p. 25.
72. Schiff and Ya'ari, *Intifada,* p. 42.
73. McDowall, *Palestine and Israel,* pp. 1–2.
74. Schiff and Ya'ari, *Intifada,* p. 45.
75. Paz, *Essays on Mexican Art,* p. 114.
76. Schiff and Ya'ari, *Intifada,* p. 101.
77. Schiff and Ya'ari, *Intifada,* p. 103.
78. Schiff and Ya'ari, *Intifada,* p. 79.
79. Makiya, *Cruelty and Silence,* p. 307.
80. P. Theroux, *Sandstorms,* p. 236.
81. Said, *The Politics of Dispossession,* pp. xxix–xxx.
82. Black and Morris, *Israel's Secret Wars,* p. xi.
83. Hala Deeb Jabbour, *A Woman of Nazareth* (New York: Interlink Books, 1992), p. 58.
84. Jabbour, *A Woman,* p. 190.
85. Jabbour, *A Woman,* p. 35.
86. Jabbour, *A Woman,* p. 34.
87. Jabbour, *A Woman,* p. 269.
88. Liana Badr, *A Compass for the Sunflower,* trans. Catherine Cobham (London: The Women's Press, 1989), p. 5.
89. Jabbour, *A Woman,* p. 81.
90. Lessing, *African Laughter,* pp. 4–5.
91. Shimon Peres and Arye Naor, *The New Middle East,* trans. Sagir International Translations/G. Ginzach (New York: Henry Holt and Company, 1993), p. 59.

92. Louvish, *The Silencer,* p. 21.
93. Beit-Hallahmi, *Original Sins,* p. 134.
94. Seale, *Abu Nidal,* p. 51.
95. Schiff and Ya'ari, *Intifada,* p. 156.
96. Schiff and Ya'ari, *Intifada,* p. 156.
97. Sichrovsky, *Abraham's Children,* pp. 61–62.
98. Schiff and Ya'ari, *Intifada,* pp. 145–146.
99. Schiff and Ya'ari, *Intifada,* pp. 145–146.
100. Schiff and Ya'ari, *Intifada,* p. 59.
101. Oz, *Israel, Palestine, and Peace,* p. 90.
102. Louvish, *The Silencer,* p. 25.
103. Sichrovsky, *Abraham's Children,* p. 105.
104. J. E. Young, *The Texture of Memory,* p. 275.
105. J. E. Young, *The Texture of Memory,* p. 275.
106. Vidal-Naquet, *Assassins of Memory,* p. 122.
107. T. Segev, *The Seventh Million,* p. 408.
108. T. Segev, *The Seventh Million,* p. 407.
109. T. Segev, *The Seventh Million,* p. 407.
110. T. Segev, *The Seventh Million,* p. 301.
111. W. V. O'Brien, *Law and Morality,* p. 258.
112. W. V. O'Brien, *Law and Morality,* p. 258.
113. W. V. O'Brien, *Law and Morality,* p. 259.
114. W. V. O'Brien, *Law and Morality,* p. 100.
115. W. V. O'Brien, *Law and Morality,* p. 253.
116. Amnesty International, *Amnesty International Report 1994* (London: Amnesty International Publications, 1994), p. 171.
117. Schiff and Ya'ari, *Intifada,* p. 81.
118. Amnesty International, *Amnesty International Report 1994,* p. 170.
119. *Amnesty International Report 1994.*
120. Amnesty International, *Amnesty International Report 1997* (New York: Amnesty International U.S.A., 1997), p. 191.
121. Schiff and Ya'ari, *Intifada,* p. 154.
122. Samuel Segev, *Crossing the Jordan: Israel's Hard Road to Peace* (New York: St. Martin's Press, 1998), p. 169.
123. Muki Betser and Robert Rosenberg, *Secret Soldier: The True Life Story of Israel's Greatest Commando* (New York: The Atlantic Monthly Press, 1996), p. 97.
124. Follain, *Jackal,* p. 21.
125. Todd, *Camus,* p. 331.
126. J. B. Bell, *The Irish Troubles,* p. 226.
127. Oz, *Israel, Palestine, and Peace,* pp. 112–113.
128. Rieff, *The Exile,* p. 52.
129. W. V. O'Brien, *Law and Morality,* p. 15.
130. Seale, *Abu Nidal,* p. 51.
131. S. Segev, *Crossing the Jordan,* p. 357.
132. Quoted in W. V. O'Brien, *Law and Morality,* p. 110.
133. J. L. Anderson, *Guerrillas,* p. 189.
134. J. L. Anderson, *Guerrillas,* p. 91.
135. J. L. Anderson, *Guerrillas,* p. 92.
136. Mernissi, *Islam and Democracy,* pp. 27–28.
137. Schiff and Ya'ari, *Intifada,* p. 59.
138. Sprinzak, *The Ascendance,* p. 87.
139. Sprinzak, *The Ascendance,* p. 99.
140. Leshem, *Israel Alone,* p. 210.
141. Leshem, *Israel Alone,* p. 210.
142. Jabbour, *A Woman,* p. 270.
143. MacDonald, *Shoot the Women First,* pp. 67–68.
144. MacDonald, *Shoot the Women First,* p. 71.

145. Aicha Lemsine, *The Chrysalis,* trans. Dorothy S. Blair (London: Quartet Books, 1993), pp. vii–viii.
146. Badr, *A Compass for the Sunflower,* p. 20.
147. Ahdaf Soueif, *In the Eye of the Sun* (New York: Pantheon, 1992), pp. 233–234.
148. Sana Al-Khayyat, *Honour and Shame: Honour and Shame in Modern Iraq* (London: Saqi Books, 1990), p. 27.
149. Morgan, *The Demon Lover,* p. 246.
150. Schiff and Ya'ari, *Intifada,* p. 89.
151. Badr, *A Compass for the Sunflower,* p. 24.
152. K. Armstrong, *Muhammad,* p. 198.
153. Mernissi, *The Veil and the Male Elite,* p. viii.
154. Meryl Hymn, *"Who Is a Jew?": Conversations, Not Conclusions* (Woodstock, Vt.: Jewish Lights Publishing, 1998), p. 48.
155. Assia Djebar, *Fantasia: An Algerian Cavalcade,* trans. Dorothy S. Blair (London: Quartet Books, 1985), p. 3.
156. Djebar, *Fantasia,* p. 179.
157. Cheryl Rubenberg, pp. 5–15, in H. D. Jabbour, *A Woman,* p. 8.
158. Al-Khayyat, *Honour and Shame,* p. 34.
159. Al-Khayyat, *Honour and Shame,* pp. 21–22.
160. Quoted in Al-Khayyat, *Honour and Shame,* p. 36.
161. Makiya, *Cruelty and Silence,* p. 297.
162. Morgan, *The Demon Lover,* p. 255.
163. Djebar, *Fantasia,* p. 218.
164. Assia Djebar, *A Sister to Scheherazade,* trans. Dorothy S. Blair (London: Quartet Books, 1987), p. 160.
165. Adam Zameenzad, *The 13th House* (New York: Random House, 1987), p. 46.
166. Biale, *Eros and the Jews,* p. 21.
167. Biale, *Eros and the Jews,* p. 87.
168. Steven Ozment, *The Bürgermeister's Daughter* (New York: St. Martin's Press, 1996), p. 27.
169. Ozment, *The Bürgermeister's Daughter,* p. 27.
170. Ozment, *The Bürgermeister's Daughter,* p. 27.
171. David Clay Large, *Where Ghosts Walked: Munich's Road to the Third Reich* (New York: W. W. Norton & Company, 1997), p. xx.
172. Quoted in Hayman, *Hitler and Geli,* p. 27.
173. Mullins, *The Painted Witch,* pp. 79–80.
174. Norman Page, *Auden and Isherwood: The Berlin Years* (New York: St. Martin's Press, 1998), p. 14.
175. Koonz, *Mothers in the Fatherland,* p. 39.
176. Large, *Where Ghosts Walked,* pp. xxii–xxiii.
177. Sheila Jeffreys, *The Idea of Prostitution* (North Melbourne, Victoria: Spinifex Press, 1997), p. 11.
178. Philippe Burrin, *France Under the Germans: Collaboration and Compromise,* trans. Janet Lloyd (New York: The New Press, 1996), p. 204.
179. Burrin, *France Under the Germans,* p. 205.
180. Laska, ed., *Women in the Resistance,* p. 7.
181. Simpson, *The Splendid Blond Beast,* p. 75.
182. Simpson, *The Splendid Blond Beast,* p. 75.
183. Laska, ed., *Women in the Resistance,* p. 15.
184. Martin Gilbert, *Auschwitz and the Allies* (New York: Henry Holt and Company, 1982), p. 34.
185. M. Gilbert, *The Boys,* p. 94.
186. Laska, ed., *Women in the Resistance,* p. 16.
187. Neil Gregor, *Daimler-Benz in the Third Reich* (New Haven: Yale University Press, 1998), pp. 187–188.
188. Sofsky, *The Order of Terror,* pp. 48–49.
189. Sofsky, *The Order of Terror,* p. 115.
190. Laska, ed., *Women in the Resistance,* p. 181.

191. Shelley, *Criminal Experiments*, p. 7.
192. Robert Jay Lifton and Amy Hackett, "Nazi Doctors," pp. 301–316 in Gutman and Berenbaum, eds., *Anatomy of Auschwitz*, p. 304.
193. Shelley, *Criminal Experiments*, p. 34.
194. M. Gilbert, *The Boys*, p. 188.
195. Lifton, *The Nazi Doctors*, p. 230.
196. Susan Brownmiller, *Against Our Will: Men, Women and Rape* (New York: Simon & Schuster, 1975), p. 64.
197. Brownmiller, *Against Our Will*, p. 64.
198. Brownmiller, *Against Our Will*, pp. 63–64.
199. Silverman, ed., *Women in the Holocaust*, vol. 1, p. viii.
200. T. Segev, *The Seventh Million*, p. 179.
201. T. Segev, *The Seventh Million*, p. 179.
202. T. Segev, *The Seventh Million*, p. 179.
203. T. Segev, *The Seventh Million*, pp. 179–180.
204. Gelissen and Macadam, *Rena's Promise*, p. 79.
205. Höss, *Death-Dealer*, p. 145.
206. Tec, *Defiance*, p. 159.
207. Tory, *Surviving the Holocaust*, p. 511.
208. Lewin, *A Cup of Tears*, p. 88.
209. Friedländer, *Nazi Germany and the Jews*, p. 122.
210. Zuccotti, *The Holocaust, the French, and the Jews*, p. 9.
211. Brownstein, *Tragic Muse*, p. 83.
212. Brownstein, *Tragic Muse*, p. 62.
213. Brownstein, *Tragic Muse*, p. 236.
214. Brownstein, *Tragic Muse*, p. 237.
215. Brownstein, *Tragic Muse*, p. 88.
216. Brownstein, *Tragic Muse*, p. 62.
217. Brownstein, *Tragic Muse*, p. 128.
218. Brownstein, *Tragic Muse*, p. 130.
219. Brownstein, *Tragic Muse*, p. 88.
220. Arthur Gold and Robert Fizdale, *The Divine Sarah: A Life of Sarah Bernhardt* (New York: Alfred A. Knopf, 1991), p. 13.
221. Gold and Fizdale, *The Divine Sarah*, p. 66.
222. Gilman, *The Jew's Body*, p. 124.
223. Gilman, *The Jew's Body*, p. 124.
224. Gilman, *The Jew's Body*, p. 122.
225. Gilman, *The Jew's Body*, p. 119.
226. Gilman, *The Jew's Body*, p. 127.
227. Patricia Cline Cohen, *The Murder of Helen Jewett: The Life and Death of a Prostitute in Nineteenth-Century New York* (New York: Alfred A. Knopf, 1998), p. 15.
228. David Sweetman, *Paul Gaugin: A Life* (New York: Simon & Schuster, 1995), pp. 261–262.
229. Rona Goffen, *Titian's Women* (New Haven: Yale University Press, 1997), pp. 148–149.
230. Goffen, *Titian's Women*, p. 178.
231. Goffen, *Titian's Women*, p. 180.
232. Hayman, *Hitler and Geli*, p. 139.
233. Dawidowicz, *The Holocaust and the Historians*, p. 52.
234. Hayman, *Hitler and Geli*, p. 27.
235. Al-Khayyat, *Honour and Shame*, p. 90.
236. Jabbour, *A Woman*, p. 78.
237. Makiya, *Cruelty and Silence*, p. 39.
238. Makiya, *Cruelty and Silence*, p. 291.
239. Black and Morris, *Israel's Secret War*, p. 477.
240. Goodwin, *Price of Honor*, p. 105.
241. Goodwin, *Price of Honor*, p. 105.
242. Goodwin, *Price of Honor*, p. 105.

243. Ira Berlin, *Many Thousands Gone: The First Two Centuries of Slavery in North America* (Cambridge: The Belknap Press of Harvard University Press, 1998), p. 158.

244. Christopher Benfey, *Degas in New Orleans: Encounters in the Creole World of Kate Chopin and George Washington Cable* (New York: Alfred A. Knopf, 1997), p. 51.

245. Benfry, *Degas in New Orleans*, p. 52.

246. Linda H. Davis, *Badge of Courage: The Life of Stephen Crane* (Boston: Houghton Mifflin Company, 1998), p. 81.

247. L. H. Davis, *Badge of Courage*, p. 81.

248. Hacker, *Two Nations*, p. 62.

249. Young-Bruehl, *The Anatomy of Prejudices*, p. 251.

250. David Duke, *My Awakening: A Path to Racial Understanding* (Mandeville, Lao: Free Speech Press, 1998), p. 396.

251. Taylor Branch, *Pillar of Fire: America in the King Years 1963–65* (New York: Simon & Schuster, 1998), p. 385.

252. J. L. Anderson, *Ché Guevara*, p. 363.

253. J. L. Anderson, *Ché Guevara*, p. 363.

254. MacDonald, *Shoot the Women First*, p. 208.

255. Natalia Khodyreva, "Sexism and Sexual Abuse in Russia," pp. 27–40 in C. Corrin, ed., *Women in a Violent World*, p. 36.

256. Khodyreva, "Sexism and Sexual Abuse in Russia," pp. 27–40 in C. Corrin, ed., *Women in a Violent World*, p. 36.

257. Khodyreva, "Sexism and Sexual Abuse in Russia," pp. 27–40 in C. Corrin, ed., *Women in a Violent World*, p. 37.

258. Narasimhan, *Sati*, p. 77.

259. Narasimhan, *Sati*, p. 40.

260. Goodwin, *Price of Honor*, p. 62.

261. J. Miller, *God Has Ninety-Nine Names*, p. 380.

262. J. L. Anderson, *Guerrillas*, p. 90.

263. Leshem, *Israel Alone*, p. 188.

264. Ali Ghalem, *A Wife for My Son*, trans. G. Kazolis (Chicago: Banner Press, 1984), pp. 153–154.

265. Ghalem, *A Wife*, p. 154.

266. Djebar, *A Sister to Scheherazade*, p. 106.

267. Sasson, *Princess*, p. 253.

268. Quoted in Janice Raymond, "Legitimizing Prostitution as Sex Work: UN Labor Organization (ILO) Calls for Recognition of the Sex Industry," Paper, p. 3.

269. Raymond, "Legitimating Prostitution," p. 1.

270. Raymond, "Legitimating Prostitution," pp. 3–4.

271. Kathleen Barry, *The Prostitution of Sexuality: The Global Exploitation of Women* (New York: New York University Press, 1995), p. 124.

272. Barry, *The Prostitution of Sexuality*, pp. 122–123.

273. Raymond, "Legitimating Prostitution," p. 3.

274. Melissa Farley, Isin Baral, Merab Kiremire, and Ufuk Sezgin, "Prostitution in Five Countries: Violence and Post-Traumatic Stress Disorder," *Feminism and Psychology* (London: Sage, 1998), p. 405.

275. Farley et al., "Prostitution in Five Countries," *Feminism and Psychology*, pp. 414–425.

276. S. Giora Shoham, Gloria Rahav, Rachel Markovski, Ilana Ber, Francis Chard, Yoseph Rachamin, and Claudia Bill, "Family Variables and Stigma Among Prostitutes in Israel," *The Journal of Social Psychology*, no. 120 (1983), p. 59.

277. Farley et al., "Prostitution in Five Countries," *Feminism and Psychology*, p. 419.

278. Farley et al., "Prostitution in Five Countries," *Feminism and Psychology*, p. 408.

279. Toni Morrison, *Paradise* (New York: Alfred A. Knopf, 1998), pp. 94–95.

280. Nawal El Saadawi, *Woman at Point Zero*, trans. Sherif-Hetata (London: Zed Books, 1983), p. 100.

Bibliography

"Lesson of Matthew Shephard, The." *The New York Times,* editorial page, October 17, 1998.

"PTSD in Prostitutes Shows Need for Thorough Trauma Histories." *Psychiatric News* 33, no. 19 (October 2, 1998).

Aarons, Mark, and John Loftus. *Unholy Trinity: The Vatican, the Nazis, and Soviet Intelligence.* New York: St. Martin's Press, 1991.

Abdalla, Raqiya Haji Dualeh. *Sisters in Affliction: Circumcision and Infibulation of Women in Africa.* London: Zed Press, 1982.

Abe, Kobo. *Kangaroo Notebook.* Translated by Maryellen Toman Mori. New York: Alfred A. Knopf, 1996.

Abish, Walter. *Eclipse Fever.* New York: Alfred A. Knopf, 1993.

Abrams, Elliot. *Faith or Fear: How Jews Can Survive in a Christian America.* New York: The Free Press, 1997.

Accad, Evelyne. *L'Exicée.* Translated by David K. Bruner. Washington, D.C.: Three Continents Press, 1989.

———. *Sexuality and War: Literary Masks of the Middle East.* New York: New York University Press, 1990.

Ackroyd, Peter. *English Music.* New York: Alfred A. Knopf, 1992.

———. *The Trial of Elizabeth Cree: A Novel of the Limehouse Murders.* New York: Doubleday, 1995.

———. *Blake.* London: Sinclair-Stevenson, 1995.

Adams, Alice. *Almost Perfect.* New York: Alfred A. Knopf, 1993.

Adnan, Etel. *Sitt Marie Rose.* Translated by Georgina Kleege. Sausalito, Calif.: The Post-Apollo Press, 1982.

Agnon, S. Y. *A Book That Was Lost and Other Stories.* Edited by Alan Mintz and Anne Golomb Hoffman. Various translators. New York: Schocken Books, 1995.

———. *Shira.* Translated by Zeva Shapiro. New York: Schocken Books, 1989.

Ajami, Fouad. *The Dream Palace of the Arabs: A Generation's Odyssey.* New York: Pantheon Books, 1998.

Akenson, Donald Harman. *Surpassing Wonder: The Invention of the Bible and the Talmuds.* New York: Harcourt Brace & Company, 1998.

Akhmatova, Anna. *My Half-Century: Selected Prose.* Translated by Ronald Meyer. Evanston, Il.: Northwestern University Press, 1997.

———. *Selected Poems.* Translated by D. M. Thomas. New York: Penguin Books, 1988.

Aksyonov, Vassily. *Generations of Winter.* Translated by John Glad and Christopher Morris. New York: Random House, 1994.

Al-Hakim, Tawfik. *Maze of Justice: Diary of a Country Prosecutor.* Translated by Abba Eban. Austin: University of Texas, 1989.

Al-Kharrat, Edwar. *City of Saffron.* Translated by Frances Liardet. London: Quartet Books, 1989.

Al-Khayyat, Sana. *Honour and Shame: Women in Modern Iraq.* London: Saqi Books, 1990.

Al-Shaykh, Hanan. *Beirut Blues: A Novel.* Translated by Catherine Cobham. New York: Doubleday, 1995.

———. *The Story of Zahra.* Translated by Peter Ford and Hanan Al-Shaykh. London: Quartet Books, 1986.

———. *Women of Sand and Myrrh.* Translated by Catherine Cobham. London: Quartet Books, 1989.

Alcalay, Ammiel. *After Jews and Arabs: Remaking Levantine Culture.* Minneapolis: University of Minnesota Press, 1993.

Alexy, Trudi. *The Mezuzah in the Madonna's Foot.* New York: Simon & Schuster, 1993.

Alldritt, Keith. *W. B. Yeats: The Man and the Milieu.* New York: Clarkson Potter/Publishers, 1997.

Allen, Mike, David D'Alessio, and Keri Brezgel. "Summarizing the Effects of Pornography Using Meta-Analysis: Aggression After Exposure." October 1993.

Allen, Mike, Tara Emmers, Lisa Gebhardt, and Mary A. Glery. "Exposure to Pornography and Acceptance of Rape Myths: A Summary of Research Using Meta-Analysis." June 1993.

Allende, Isabel. *Of Love and Shadows.* Translated by Margaret Sayers Peden. New York: Alfred A. Knopf, 1987.

———. *The Infinite Plan.* Translated by Margaret Sayers Peden. New York: HarperCollins Publishers, 1993.

Alvarez, A. *Night: Night Life, Night Language, Sleep, and Dreams.* New York: W. W. Norton & Company, 1995.

Amatel, Joseph, et al., Appellees v. *Janet Reno, Attorney General of the United States, et al., Appellants.* 1998 WL 611114 (D.C. Circuit.)

Amichai, Yehuda. *Yehuda Amichai: A Life of Poetry 1948–1994.* Translated by Benjamin and Barbara Harshav. New York: HarperCollins Publishers, 1994.

Amis, Martin. *The Information.* New York: Harmony Books, 1995.

———. *Time's Arrow.* New York: Harmony Books, 1991.

Amnesty International. "Israel: Fear of Torture or Ill-Treatment." New York: Amnesty International Publications, March 1992.

———. "Israel/South Lebanon: The Khiam Detainees: Torture and Ill-treatment." New York: Amnesty International Publications, May 1992.

———. *Amnesty International Report 1991.* London: Amnesty International Publications, 1991.

———. *Amnesty International Report 1994.* London: Amnesty International Publications, 1994.

———. *Amnesty International Report 1997.* New York: Amnesty International U.S.A., 1997.

Anderson, Jon Lee. *Ché Guevara: A Revolutionary Life.* New York: Grove Press, 1997.

———. *Guerrillas: The Men and Women Fighting Today's Wars.* New York: Times Books, 1992.

Anderson, Patricia. *When Passion Reigned: Sex and the Victorians.* New York: Basic Books, 1995.

Anderson, Ronald, and Anne Koval. *James NcNeill Whistler: Beyond the Myth.* New York: Carroll & Graf Publishers, 1995.

Andrist, Ralph K. *The Long Death: The Last Days of the Plains Indian.* New York: Macmillan Publishing Company, 1964.

Angier, Natalie. *Woman: An Intimate Geography.* London: Virago, 1999.

Anissimov, Myriam. *Primo Levi: Tragedy of an Optimist.* Translated by Steve Cox. Woodstock, N.Y.: The Overlook Press, 1999.

Annan, Noel. *Our Age: English Intellectuals Between World Wars—A Group Portrait.* New York: Random House, 1991.

Antonelli, Judith S. "An Open Letter to Andrea Dworkin and Other Jewish Feminists." *Ms.,* 1990.

Appelfeld, Aharon. *Beyond Despair: Three Lectures and a Conversation with Philip Roth.* Translated by Jeffrey M. Green. New York: Fromm International Publishing Corporation, 1994.

———. *Katerina.* Translated by Jeffrey M. Green. New York: Random House, 1992.

———. *The Conversion.* Translated by Jeffrey M. Green. New York: Schocken Books, 1998.

———. *The Healer.* Translated by Jeffrey M. Green. New York: Grove Weidenfeld, 1990.

———. *The Iron Tracks.* Translated by Jeffrey M. Green. New York: Schocken Books, 1998.

————. *Unto the Soul.* Translated by Jeffrey M. Green. New York: Random House, 1994.

Arenas, Reinaldo. *Before Night Falls: A Memoir.* Translated by Dolores M. Koch. New York: Viking, 1993.

————. *The Assault.* Translated by Andrew Hurley. New York: Viking, 1994.

Arendt, Hannah. *Arendt: Essays in Understanding 1930–1954.* New York: Harcourt Brace & Company, 1994.

Ariel, David S. *What Do Jews Believe? The Spiritual Foundations of Judaism.* New York: Schocken Books, 1995.

Armstrong, Karen. *A History of God: The 4,000-Year Quest of Judaism, Christianity, and Islam.* New York: Alfred A. Knopf, 1993.

————. *Holy War: The Crusades and Their Impact on Today's World.* New York: Anchor Books, 1992.

————. *Jerusalem: One City, Three Faiths.* New York: Alfred A. Knopf, 1996.

————. *Muhammad: A Biography of the Prophet.* San Francisco: Harper, 1992.

Armstrong, Louise. *And They Call It Help: The Psychiatric Policing of America's Children.* Reading, Mass.: Addison-Wesley Publishing Company, 1993.

————. *Rocking the Cradle of Sexual Politics: What Happened When Women Said Incest.* Reading, Mass.: Addison-Wesley Publishing Company, 1994.

Arnold, Bruce. *The Scandal of Ulysses.* New York: St. Martin's Press, 1992.

Aruri, Naseer. *The Obstruction of Peace: The U.S., Israel and the Palestinians.* Monroe, Maine: The Common Courage Press, 1995.

Asali, K. J., ed. *Jerusalem in History.* Brooklyn, N.Y.: Olive Branch Press, 1990.

Ascherson, Neal. *Black Sea.* New York: Hill and Wang, 1995.

Ashrawi, Hanan. *The Side of Peace: A Personal Account.* New York: Simon & Schuster, 1995.

Ashton, Rosemary. *George Eliot: A Life.* London: Hamish Hamilton, 1996.

Assmann, Jan. *Moses the Egyptian: The Memory of Egypt in Western Monotheism.* Cambridge: Harvard University Press, 1997.

Atkinson, Diana. *Highways and Dancehalls.* New York: St. Martin's Press, 1997.

Atxaga, Bernardo. *Obabakoak.* Translated by Margaret Jull Costa. New York: Pantheon Books, 1992.

Auden, W. H. *The Dyer's Hand and Other Essays.* New York: Vintage International, 1989.

Auerbach, Nina. *Our Vampires, Ourselves.* Chicago: The University of Chicago Press, 1995.

Auster, Paul. *Leviathan.* New York: Viking, 1992.

————. *Mr. Vertigo.* New York: Viking, 1994.

Autton, Nina. *Bettelheim: A Life and Legacy.* Translated by David Sharp and Nina Autton. New York: Basic Books, 1996.

Avishai, Bernard. *A New Israel: Democracy in Crisis—1973–1988.* New York: Ticknor & Fields, 1990.

Babel, Isaac. *1920 Diary.* Edited by Carol J. Avins. Translated by T. T. Willetts. New Haven: Yale University Press, 1995.

Bachmann, Ingeborg. *Malina.* Translated by Philip Boehm. New York: Holmes & Meier, 1990.

Badr, Liana. *A Compass for the Sunflower.* Translated by Catherine Cobham. London: The Women's Press, 1989.

Bair, Deirdre. *Anaïs Nin: A Biography.* New York: G. G. Putnam's Sons, 1995.

Baker, Carlos. *Emerson Among the Eccentrics: A Group Portrait.* New York: Viking, 1996.

Baker, Deborah. *In Extremis: The Life of Laura Riding.* New York: Grove Press, 1993.

Baldwin, James. *The Price of the Ticket: Collected Nonfiction 1948–1985.* New York: St. Martin's/Marek, 1985.

Banks, Iain. *Complicity.* New York: Nan A. Talese, 1995.

Banner, Lois. *In Full Flower: Aging Women, Power, and Sexuality.* New York: Alfred A. Knopf, 1992.

Bar-Zohar, Michael. *Beyond Hitler's Grasp: The Heroic Rescue of Bulgaria's Jews.* Holbrook, Mass.: Adams Media Corporation, 1998.

Barker, Juliet. *The Brontës.* London: Weidenfeld and Nicolson, 1994.

Barker, Pat. *Regeneration.* New York: Dutton, 1992.

Barnes, Julian. *The Porcupine.* New York: Alfred A. Knopf, 1992.

Baro, Agnes L. "Spheres of Consent: An Analysis of the Sexual Abuse and Sexual Exploitation of Women Incarcerated in the State of Hawaii." *Women and Criminal Justice* 8, no. 3 (1977): pp. 61–84.

Barry, Kathleen. *The Prostitution of Sexuality: The Global Exploitation of Women.* New York: New York University Press, 1995.

Bartoszewski, Wladyslaw T. *The Convent at Auschwitz.* New York: George Braziller, 1991.

Bass, Jack. *Taming the Storm: The Life and Times of Judge Frank M. Johnson, Jr., and the South's Fight Over Civil Rights.* New York: Doubleday, 1993.

Bates, Tom. *Rads: The 1970 Bombing of the Army Math Research Center at the University of Wisconsin and Its Aftermath.* New York: HarperCollins Publishers, 1992.

Bausch, Richard. *Violence.* New York: Houghton Mifflin/Seymour Lawrence, 1992.

Bawer, Bruce. *A Place at the Table: The Gay Individual in American Society.* New York: Poseidon Press, 1993.

Bayley, John. *Elegy for Iris.* New York: St. Martin's Press, 1999.

Beauman, Nicola. *E. M. Forster: A Biography.* New York: Alfred A. Knopf, 1994.

Becker, Jasper. *Hungry Ghosts: Mao's Secret Famine.* New York: The Free Press, 1997.

Beckson, Karl. *London in the 1890s: A Cultural History.* New York: W. W. Norton & Company, 1992.

Beevor, Antony, and Artemis Cooper. *Paris After the Liberation 1944–1949.* New York: Doubleday, 1994.

Begley, Louis. *Wartime Lies.* New York: Alfred A. Knopf, 1991.

Beit-Hallahmi, Benjamin. *Original Sins: Reflections on the History of Zionism and Israel.* New York: Olive Branch Press, 1993.

Belford, Barbara. *Bram Stoker.* New York: Alfred A. Knopf, 1996.

———. *Violet.* New York: Simon & Schuster, 1990.

Belgrad, Daniel. *The Culture of Spontaneity: Improvisation and the Arts in Postwar America.* Chicago: The University of Chicago Press, 1998.

Bell, Derrick. *Confronting Authority: Reflections of an Ardent Protester.* Boston: Beacon Press, 1994.

———. *Faces at the Bottom of the Well: The Permanence of Racism.* New York: Basic Books, 1992.

Bell, Ian. *Dreams of Exile: Robert Louis Stevenson: A Biography.* New York: Henry Holt and Company, 1993.

Bell, J. Bowyer. *The Irish Troubles: A Generation of Violence 1967–1992.* New York: St. Martin's Press, 1993.

Bell, Madison Smartt. *All Soul's Rising.* New York: Pantheon Books, 1995.

———. *Save Me, Joe Louis.* New York: Harcourt Brace & Company, 1993.

Bellow, Saul. *It All Adds Up: From the Dim Past to the Uncertain Future.* New York: Viking Penguin, 1994.

Ben Jelloun, Tahar. *The Sand Child.* Translated by Alan Sheridan. New York: Ballantine Books, 1987.

———. *With Downcast Eyes.* Translated by Joachim Neugroschel. Boston: Little, Brown and Company, 1993.

Ben Meir, Yehuda. *Civil-Military Relations in Israel.* New York: Columbia University, 1995.

Benfey, Christopher. *Degas in New Orleans: Encounters in the Creole World of Kate Chopin and George Washington Cable.* New York: Alfred A. Knopf, 1997.

———. *The Double Life of Stephen Crane.* New York: Alfred A. Knopf, 1992.

Bennett, William J. *The Death of Outrage: Bill Clinton and the Assault on American Ideals.* New York: The Free Press, 1998.

———. *The Index of Leading Cultural Indicators.* Washington, D.C.: The Heritage Foundation, Empower America, 1993.

Bennis, Phyllis, and Michel Moushabeck, eds. *Beyond the Storm: A Gulf Crisis Reader.* New York: Olive Branch Press, 1991.

Benstock, Shari. *No Gifts From Chance: A Biography of Edith Wharton.* New York: Charles Scribner's Sons, 1994.

Benz, Wolfgang. *The Holocaust: A German Examines the Genocide.* Translated by Jane Sydenham-Kwiet. New York: Columbia University Press, 1999.

Berenson, Edward. *The Trial of Madam Caillaux.* Berkeley: University of California Press, 1992.

Berger, John. *A Painter of Our Time.* New York: Pantheon Books, 1989.

———. *Art and Revolution: Ernst Neizvestny, Endurance, and the Role of Art.* New York: Vintage Books, 1997.

———. *Corker's Freedom.* New York: Pantheon Books, 1993.

———. *Keeping a Rendezvous.* New York: Pantheon Books, 1991.

———. *King: A Street Story.* London: Bloomsbury, 1999.

———. *Photocopies.* London: Bloomsbury, 1997.

———. *The Sense of Sight.* New York: Vintage International, 1993.

———. *The Success and Failure of Picasso.* New York: Vintage International, 1993.

———. *To the Wedding.* New York: Pantheon Books, 1995.

Berlin, Ira. *Many Thousands Gone: The First Two Centuries of Slavery in North America.* Cambridge: The Belknap Press of Harvard University Press, 1998.

Berlin, Isaiah, and Ramin Jahanbegloo. *Conversations with Isaiah Berlin.* New York: Charles Scribner's Sons, 1991.

Berlin, Isaiah. *The Crooked Timber of Humanity.* Edited by Henry Hardy. New York: Alfred A. Knopf, 1991.

———. *The Sense of Reality.* New York: Farrar, Straus & Giroux, 1996.

Berman, Paul. *A Tale of Two Utopias: The Political Journey of the Generation of 1968.* New York: W. W. Norton & Company, 1996.

Bernhard, Thomas. *Extinction.* Translated by David McLintock. New York: Alfred A. Knopf, 1995.

———. *The Loser.* Translated by Jack Dawson. New York: Alfred A. Knopf, 1991.

Bernier, Olivier. *Fireworks at Dusk: Paris in the Thirties.* Boston: Little, Brown and Company, 1993.

Bernstein, Richard. *Dictatorship of Virtue: Multiculturalism and the Battle for America's Future.* New York: Alfred A. Knopf, 1994.

Berry, Mary Frances. *Black Resistance White Law: A History of Constitutional Racism in America.* New York: The Penguin Press, 1994.

Bershtel, Sara, and Allen Graubard. *Saving Remnants: Feeling Jewish in America.* New York: The Free Press, 1992.

Betser, Muki, and Robert Rosenberg. *Secret Soldier: The True Life Story of Israel's Greatest Commando.* New York: The Atlantic Monthly Press, 1996.

Beyer, Lisa. "The Price of Honor," *Time,* January 18, 1999, p. 55.

Biale, David. *Eros and the Jews: From Biblical Israel to Contemporary America.* New York: Basic Books, 1992.

Bilton, Michael and Kevin Sim. *Four Hours in My Lai.* New York: Viking, 1992.

Binur, Yoram. *My Enemy, My Self.* Translated by Uriel Grunfeld. New York: Penguin Books, 1989.

Bishop, Elizabeth. *One Art: Letters.* Edited by Robert Giroux. New York: Farrar, Straus & Giroux, 1994.

Bjork, Daniel W. *B.F. Skinner: A Life.* New York: Basic Books, 1993.

Black, Ian, and Benny Morris. *Israel's Secret Wars: A History of Israel's Intelligence Services.* New York: Grove Weidenfeld, 1991.

Blanchard, Paula. *Sarah Orne Jewett: Her World and Her Work.* Reading, Mass.: Addison-Wesley Publishing Company, 1994.

Blau, Eric. *The Beggar's Cup.* New York: Alfred A. Knopf, 1993.

Blitzer, Wolf. *Territory of Lies.* New York: Harper & Row Publishers, 1989.

Bloch, Michael. *Ribbentrop: A Biography.* New York: Crown Publishers, 1993.

Bloom, Allan. *Love and Friendship.* New York: Simon & Schuster, 1993.

Bloom, Harold, and David Rosenberg. *The Book of J.* New York: Grove Weidenfeld, 1990.

Bloom, Harold. *Omens of Millennium: The Gnosis of Angels, Dreams, and Resurrection.* New York: Riverhead Books, 1996.

————. *The American Religion: The Emergence of the Post-Christian Nation.* New York: Simon & Schuster, 1992.

————. *The Western Canon: The Books and School of the Ages.* New York: Harcourt Brace & Company, 1994.

Blum, Jerome. *In the Beginning: The Advent of the Modern Age: Europe in the 1840s.* New York: Charles Scribner's Sons, 1994.

Blum, William. *The CIA: A Forgotten History.* London: Zed Books, 1986.

Bok, Sissela. *Mayhem: Violence as Public Entertainment.* Reading, Mass.: Addison-Wesley, 1998.

Böll, Heinrich. *The Silent Angel.* Translated by Breon Mitchell. New York: St. Martin's Press, 1994.

Boorstin, Daniel J. *Cleopatra's Nose: Essays on the Unexpected.* New York: Random House, 1994.

————. *The Creators: A History of Heroes of the Imagination.* New York: Random House, 1992.

Bork, Robert H. *Slouching Towards Gomorrah: Modern Liberalism and American Decline.* New York: HarperCollins, 1996.

————. *The Tempting of America.* New York: The Free Press, 1990.

Boswell, John. *Same-Sex Unions in Premodern Europe.* New York: Villard Books, 1994.

Bowker, Gordon. *Pursued by Furies: A Life of Malcolm Lowry.* New York: St. Martin's Press, 1995.

Bowlby, John. *Charles Darwin: A New Life.* New York: W. W. Norton & Company, 1991.

Boyd, Brian. *Vladimir Nabokov: The American Years.* Princeton: Princeton University Press, 1991.

————. *Vladimir Nabokov: The Russian Years.* Princeton: Princeton University Press, 1990.

Boyd, William. *Brazzaville Beach.* New York: William Morrow and Company, 1990.

Boyle, Nicholas. *Goethe: The Poet and the Age: The Poetry of Desire.* Vol. 1. Oxford: Clarendon Press, 1991.

Bradbury, Malcolm. *Dangerous Pilgrimages: Transatlantic Mythologies and Novel.* New York: Viking, 1996.

Bradford, Phillips Verner, and Harvey Blume. *Ota Benga: The Pigmy in the Zoo.* New York: St. Martin's Press, 1992.

Bradford, Sarah. *Splendors and Miseries: A Life of Sacheverell Sitwell.* New York: Farrar, Strauss & Giroux, 1993.

Brady, Joan. *Theory of War.* New York: Alfred A. Knopf, 1993.

Braiterman, Zachary. *(God) After Auschwitz: Tradition and Change in Post-Holocaust Jewish Thought.* Princeton: Princeton University Press, 1998.

Branch, Taylor. *Pillar of Fire: America in the King Years 1963–65.* New York: Simon & Schuster, 1998.

Brassaï. *Henry Miller: The Paris Years.* Translated by Timothy Bent. New York: Arcade Publishing, 1995.

Braudel, Fernand. *A History of Civilizations.* Translated by Richard Mayne. New York: Allen Lane/The Penguin Press, 1994.

Breines, Paul. *Tough Jews.* New York: Basic Books, 1990.

Breitman, Richard. *Official Secrets: What the Nazis Planned, What the British and Americans Knew.* New York: Hill and Wang, 1998.

————. *The Architect of Genocide: Himmler and the Final Solution.* New York: Alfred A. Knopf, 1991.

Breslin, James E. B. *Mark Rothko: A Biography.* Chicago: The University of Chicago Press, 1993.

Breytenbach, Breyten. *Return to Paradise.* New York: Harcourt Brace & Company, 1993.

————. *The True Confessions of an Albino Terrorist.* New York: McGraw-Hill Book Company, 1983.

Breznitz, Shlomo. *Memory Fields.* New York: Alfred A. Knopf, 1992.

Brightman, Carol. *Writing Dangerously: Mary McCarthy and Her World.* New York: Clarkson Potter/Publishers, 1992.

Brink, André. "Afrikaners and the Future." *Granta,* no. 40 (Summer 1992), pp. 189–193.

———. *An Act of Terror.* New York: Summit Books, 1992.

———. *Cape of Storms: The First Life of Adamastor.* New York: Simon & Schuster, 1993.

———. *On the Contrary.* Boston: Little, Brown and Company, 1993.

Brodersen, Momme. *Walter Benjamin: A Biography.* Translated by Malcolm R. Green and Ingrida Ligers. Edited by Martina Dervis. London: Verso, 1996.

Brodie, Fawn M. *Thomas Jefferson: An Intimate History.* New York: Bantam Books, 1975.

Brodsky, Louis Daniel. *William Faulkner, Life Glimpses.* Austin: University of Texas Press, 1990.

Brombert, Beth Archer. *Edouard Manet: Rebel in a Frock Coat.* Boston: Little, Brown and Company, 1996.

Brookhiser, Richard. *Alexander Hamilton: American.* New York: The Free Press, 1999.

———. *Founding Father: Rediscovering George Washington.* New York: The Free Press, 1996.

Brookner, Anita. *Dolly.* New York: Random House, 1994.

Brooks, Geraldine. *Nine Parts of Desire: The Hidden World of Islamic Women.* New York: Doubleday, 1995.

Brown, Anthony Cave. *Treason in the Blood: H. St. John Philby, Kim Philby, and the Spy Case of the Century.* Boston: Houghton Mifflin Company, 1994.

Brown, Elaine. *A Taste of Power: A Black Woman's Story.* New York: Pantheon Books, 1993.

Brown, Frederick. *Zola.* New York: Farrar, Straus & Giroux, 1995.

Brown, Louis, François Duau, and Merrit McKeon. *Stop Domestic Violence: An Action Plan for Saving Lives.* New York: St. Martin's Press, 1997. Proofs.

Browne, Janet. *Charles Darwin: Voyaging.* New York: Alfred A. Knopf, 1995.

Browning, Christopher R. *Ordinary Men: Reserve Police Battalion 101 and the Final Solution in Poland.* New York: HarperCollins Publishers/Aaron Asher Books, 1992.

———. *The Path to Genocide: Essays on Launching the Final Solution.* Cambridge: Cambridge University Press, 1992.

Brownmiller, Susan. *Against Our Will: Men, Women and Rape.* New York: Simon & Schuster, 1975.

Brownstein, Rachel M. *Tragic Muse: Rachel of the Comédie-Française.* New York: Alfred A. Knopf, 1993.

Büchmann, Christina, and Celina Spiegel, eds. *Out of the Garden: Women Writers on the Bible.* New York: Fawcett Columbine, 1994.

Buckley, William F., Jr. *In Search of Anti-Semitism.* New York: Continuum, 1992.

Bull, George. *Michelangelo: A Biography.* New York: St. Martin's Press, 1996.

Bullock, Alan. *Hitler and Stalin: Parallel Lives.* New York: Alfred A. Knopf, 1992.

Burgess, Anthony. *A Dead Man in Deptford.* New York: Carroll & Graf Publishers, 1995.

Burke, James Lee. *A Morning for Flamingos.* New York: Avon Books, 1991.

———. *A Stained White Radiance.* New York: Hyperion, 1992.

———. *Black Cherry Blues.* New York: Avon Books, 1990.

———. *Burning Angel.* New York: Hyperion, 1995.

———. *Cadillac Jukebox.* New York: Hyperion, 1996.

———. *Cimarron Rose.* New York: Hyperion, 1997.

———. *Dixie City Jam.* New York: Hyperion, 1994.

———. *Heaven's Prisoners.* New York: Pocket Books, 1989.

———. *In the Electric Mist with Confederate Dead.* New York: Hyperion, 1993.

———. *The Neon Rain.* New York: Pocket Books, 1988.

Burns, Michael. *Dreyfus: A Family Affair, From the French Revolution to the Holocaust.* New York: HarperPerennial, 1992.

Burrin, Philippe. *France Under the Germans: Collaboration and Compromise.* Translated by Janet Lloyd. New York: The New Press, 1996.

Burton, Humphrey. *Leonard Bernstein.* New York: Doubleday, 1994.

Buruma, Ian. *Anglomania: A European Love Affair.* New York: Random House, 1998.

———. *The Wages of Guilt: Memories of War in Germany and Japan.* New York: Farrar, Straus & Giroux, 1994.

Busch, Frederick. *Closing Arguments.* New York: Ticknor & Fields, 1991.

Butler, Ruth. *Rodin: The Shape of Genius.* New Haven: Yale University Press, 1993.

Byatt, A. S. *Passions of the Mind: Selected Essays.* New York: Turtle Bay Books, 1992.

Byrd, Max. *Jefferson: A Novel.* New York: Bantam Books, 1993.

Byrne, Janet. *A Genius for Living: The Life of Frieda Lawrence.* New York: HarperCollins Publishers, 1995.

Cahill, Thomas. *How the Irish Saved Civilization: The Untold Story of Ireland's Heroic Role from the Fall of Rome to the Rise of Medieval Europe.* New York: Doubleday, 1995.

———. *The Gifts of the Jews: How a Tribe of Desert Nomads Changed the Way Everyone Thinks and Feels.* New York: Doubleday, 1998.

Calasso, Roberto. *The Marriage of Cadmus and Harmony.* Translated by Tim Parks. New York: Alfred A. Knopf, 1993.

———. *The Ruin of Kasch.* Translated by William Weaver and Stephen Sartarelli. Cambridge: The Belknap Press of Harvard University Press, 1994.

Calvino, Italo. *The Road to San Giovanni.* Translated by Tim Parks. New York: Pantheon Books, 1993.

Campbell, Anne. *Men, Women, and Aggression.* New York: Basic Books, 1993.

Campbell, Bebe Moore. *Your Blues Ain't Like Mine.* New York: G. P. Putnam's Sons, 1992.

Campbell, David G. *The Crystal Desert: Summers in Antarctica.* Boston: Houghton Mifflin Company, 1992.

Campbell, James. *Exiled in Paris: Richard Wright, James Baldwin, Samuel Beckett, and Others on the Left Bank.* New York: Scribner, 1995.

———. *Talking at the Gates: A Life of James Baldwin.* New York: Viking, 1991.

Camus, Albert. *The First Man.* Translated by David Hapgood. New York: Alfred A. Knopf, 1995.

Cannadine, David. *G. M. Trevelyan: A Life in History.* New York: W. W. Norton & Company, 1993.

Cannistraro, Philip V., and Brian R. Sullivan. *Il Duce's Other Woman.* New York: William Morrow and Company, 1993.

Cantor, Norman G. *The Sacred Chain: The History of the Jews.* New York: HarperCollins, 1994.

Carey, John. *The Intellectuals and the Masses: Pride and Prejudice Among the Literary Intelligensia, 1880–1939.* New York: St. Martin's Press, 1993.

Carnay, Janet, Ruth Ann Magder, Laura Wine Paster, Marcia Cohn Spiegel, and Abigail Weinberg. *The Jewish Women's Awareness Guide: Connections for the 2nd Wave of Jewish Feminism.* New York: Biblio Press, 1992.

Carpenter, Humphrey. *Benjamin Britten: A Biography.* New York: Charles Scribner's Sons, 1993.

Carr, Jonathan. *Mahler: A Biography.* Woodstock, N.Y.: The Overlook Press, 1997.

Carter, Stephen L. *The Culture of Disbelief: How American Law and Politics Trivialize Religious Devotion.* New York: Basic Books, 1993.

Caschetta, Mary Beth. *Lucy on the West Coast and Other Lesbian Short Fiction.* Los Angeles: Alyson Publications, 1996.

Caspit, Ben, and Ilan Kfir. *Netanyahu: The Road to Power.* Translated by Ora Cummings. Secaucus, N.J.: Carol Publishing Group, 1998.

Celan, Paul. *Poems of Paul Celan.* Translated by Michael Hamburger. New York: Persea Books, 1995.

Chadwick, Whitney, and Isabelle de Courtivron, eds. *Significant Others: Creativity and Intimate Partnership.* New York: Thames and Hudson, 1993.

Chalfant, Edward. *Better in Darkness: A Biography of Henry Adams—His Second Life 1862–1891.* Hamden, Conn.: Archon Books, 1994.

Chamberlain, Lesley. *Nietzsche in Turin: An Intimate Biography.* New York: Picador, 1998.

Chang, Iris. *The Rape of Nanking: The Forgotten Holocaust of World War II.* New York: Basic Books, 1997.

Charnas, Suzy McKee. *The Furies.* New York: A Tom Doherty Associates Book, 1994.

Chedid, Andrée. *The Return to Beirut.* Translated by Ros Schwartz. London: Serpent's Tail, 1989.

Cherep-Spiridovich, Mag.-Ge., Count. *The Secret World Government or "The Hidden Hand."* N.p. First published in 1926; fourth printing 1969.

Chernin, Kim. *Reinventing Eve.* New York: Times Books, 1987.

Chernow, Ron. *The Warburgs: The Twentieth Century Odyssey of a Remarkable Jewish Family.* New York: Random House, 1993.

Chesler, Ellen. *Woman of Valor: Margaret Sanger and the Birth Control Movement in America.* New York: Simon & Schuster, 1992.

Chesler, Phyllis. *Patriarchy: Notes of an Expert Witness.* Monroe, Maine: Common Courage Press, 1994.

Chicago, Judy. *Holocaust Project: From Darkness Into Light.* New York: Penguin Books, 1993.

Chomsky, Noam. *World Orders Old and New.* New York: Columbia University Press, 1994.

Christiansen, Rupert. *Paris Babylon: The Story of the Paris Commune.* New York: Viking, 1994.

Chukovskaya, Lydia. *The Akhmatova Journals: Volume 1, 1938–1941.* Translated by Milena Michalski and Sylva Rubashova. Poetry translated by Peter Norman. New York: Farrar, Straus & Giroux, 1994.

Churchill, Ward. "Assaults on Truth and Memory, Part 1." *Z Magazine,* December 1996, pp. 31–37.

Cincinnatus. *War! War! War!* Metarie, La.: Sons of Liberty, 1991.

Cixious, Hélene. *Three Steps on the Ladder of Writing.* Translated by Sarah Cornell and Susan Sellers. New York: Columbia University Press, 1993.

Clarke, Donald. *Wishing on the Moon: The Life and Times of Billie Holiday.* New York: Viking, 1994.

Claus, Hugo. *The Sorrow of Belgium.* Translated by Arnold J. Pomerans. New York: Pantheon Books, 1990.

Clendinnen, Inga. *Reading the Holocaust.* Cambridge: Cambridge University Press, 1999.

Cline, Sally. *Radclyffe Hall: A Woman Called John.* London: John Murray (Publishers), 1997.

———. *Women, Passion and Celibacy.* New York: Carol Southern Books, 1993. Proofs.

Cockburn, Andrew and Leslie. *Dangerous Liaison: The Inside Story of the U.S.-Israeli Covert Relationship.* New York: HarperCollins Publishers, 1991.

Coetzee, J. M. *Age of Iron.* New York: Random House, 1990.

———. *The Lives of Animals.* Princeton: Princeton University Press, 1999.

———. *The Master of Petersburg.* New York: Viking, 1994.

Cohen, Mark Nathan. *Culture of Intolerance: Chauvinism, Class, and Racism in the United States.* New Haven: Yale University Press, 1998.

Cohen, Morton N. *Lewis Carroll: A Biography.* New York: Alfred A. Knopf, 1995.

Cohen, Patricia Cline. *The Murder of Helen Jewett: The Life and Death of a Prostitute in Nineteenth-Century New York.* New York: Alfred A. Knopf, 1998.

Cohen, Roger. "Long Dispute Ends as Berlin Court Backs Islamic School Lessons." *The New York Times.* November 6, 1998.

Commager, Henry Steele. *Commager on Tocqueville.* Columbia: University of Missouri Press, 1993.

Condé, Maryse. *Tree of Life.* Translated by Victoria Reiter. New York: Ballantine Books, 1992.

Cone, Michèle. *Artists Under Vichy: A Case of Prejudice and Persecution.* Princeton: Princeton University Press, 1992.

Conn, Peter. *Pearl S. Buck: A Cultural Biography.* Cambridge: Cambridge University Press, 1996.

Conquest, Robert. *Stalin: Breaker of Nations.* New York: Viking, 1991.

Conrad, Joseph. *The Complete Short Fiction of Joseph Conrad: The Stories.* Vol I. Edited by Samuel Hynes. New York: Ecco Press, 1991.

Coogan, Tim Pat. *The IRA: A History.* Niwot, Colo.: Roberts Rinehart Publishers, 1993.

———. *The Man Who Made Ireland: The Life and Death of Michael Collins.* Niwot, Colo.: Roberts Rinehart Publishers, 1992.

Cook, Blanche Wiessen. *Eleanor Roosevelt: 1884–1933.* Vol. 1. New York: Viking, 1992.

Coren, Michael. *The Invisible Man: The Life and Liberties of H. G. Wells.* New York: Atheneum, 1993.

Cornwell, Patricia D. *Post-Mortem.* New York: Avon Books, 1991.

———. *From Potter's Field.* New York: Berkley Books, 1996.

Corrin, Chris, ed. *Women in a Violent World: Feminist Analyses and Resistance Across "Europe."* Edinburgh: Edinburgh University Press, 1996.

Costello, Peter. *James Joyce: The Years of Growth 1882–1915.* New York: Pantheon Books, 1992.

Coulonges, Henri. *Farewell, Dresden.* Translated by Lowell Bair. New York: Summit Books, 1989.

Cowan, Geoffrey. *The People* v. *Clarence Darrow: The Bribery Trial of America's Greatest Lawyer.* New York: Times Books, 1993.

Coyote, Peter. *Sleeping Where I Fall.* Washington, D.C.: Counterpoint, 1998.

Cretney, Antonia, and Gwynn Davis. *Punishing Violence.* London: Routledge, 1995.

Crichton, Michael. *Rising Sun.* New York: Alfred A. Knopf, 1992.

Cronin, Anthony. *Samuel Beckett: The Last Modernist.* London: HarperCollins, 1996.

Crossan, John Dominic. *Jesus: A Revolutionary Biography.* San Francisco: Harper, 1993.

———. *Who Killed Jesus? Exposing the Roots of Anti-Semitism in the Gospel Story of the Death of Jesus.* San Francisco: Harper, 1995.

Crouch, Stanley. *The All-American Skin Game, or, The Decoy of Race: The Long and Short of It 1990–1994.* New York: Pantheon Books, 1995.

Crowe, David M. *A History of the Gypsies of Eastern Europe and Russia.* New York: St. Martin's Press, 1996.

Czerniakow, Adam. *The Warsaw Diary of Adam Czerniakow.* Edited by Raul Hilberg, Stanislaw Staron, and Joseef Kermisz. Translated by Stanislaw Staron and the staff of Yad Vashem. New York: Stein and Day/Publishers, 1979.

D'Souza, Dinesh. *Illiberal Education: The Politics of Race and Sex on Campus.* New York: The Free Press, 1991.

———. *The End of Racism.* New York: The Free Press, 1995.

Daix, Pierre. *Picasso: Life and Art.* Translated by Olivia Emmet. New York: Icon Editions, 1993.

Daly, Mary. *Quintessence . . . Realizing the Archaic Future.* Boston: Beacon Press, 1998.

Darton, Robert. *The Forbidden Best-Sellers of Pre-Revolutionary France.* New York: W. W. Norton & Company, 1994.

Daughtry, Herbert D., Sr. *No Monopoly on Suffering: Blacks and Jews in Crown Heights (and Elsewhere).* Trenton, N.J.: Africa World Press, 1997.

Davenport-Hines, Richard. *Auden.* New York: Pantheon Books, 1995.

David, Ron. *Arabs & Israel for Beginners.* New York: Writers and Readers, 1993.

Davidson, Eugene. *The Unmaking of Adolf Hitler.* Columbia: University of Missouri Press, 1996.

Davidson, James N. *Courtesans and Fishcakes: The Consuming Passions of Classical Athens.* New York: St. Martin's Press, 1998.

Davis, David Brion. "The Slave Trade and the Jews," *New York Review of Books* XLI, no. 21 (December 22, 1994), pp. 14–16.

Davis, Linda H. *Badge of Courage: The Life of Stephen Crane.* Boston: Houghton Mifflin Company, 1998.

Davis, Natalie Zemon. *Women on the Margins: Three Seventeenth-Century Lives.* Cambridge: Harvard University Press, 1995.

Davis, Thulani. *1959.* New York: Grove Weidenfeld, 1992.

Davis, William C. *Jefferson Davis: The Man and His Hour.* New York: HarperCollins Publishers, 1991.

Dawidowicz, Lucy S. *The Holocaust and the Historians.* Cambridge: Harvard University Press, 1981.

———. *What Is The Use Of Jewish History?* New York: Schocken Books, 1992.

De Tocqueville, Alexis. *Democracy in America.* 2 vols. New York: Vintage Books, 1990.

Dearborn, Mary V. *Queen of Bohemia: The Life of Louise Bryant.* Boston: Houghton Mifflin Company, 1996.

———. *The Happiest Man Alive: A Biography of Henry Miller.* New York: Simon & Schuster, 1991.

Decker, Hannah S. *Freud, Dora, and Vienna 1900.* New York: The Free Press, 1991.

Dee, Jonathan. *The Liberty Campaign.* New York: Doubleday, 1993.

Dees, Morris, and James Corcoran. *Gathering Storm: America's Militia Threat.* New York: HarperCollins, 1996.

Dees, Morris, and Steve Fiffer. *Hate on Trial: The Case Against America's Most Dangerous Neo-Nazi.* New York: Villard Books, 1993.

Delbanco, Andrew. *The Death of Satan: How Americans Have Lost the Sense of Evil.* New York: Farrar, Straus & Giroux, 1995.

Delgado, Richard. "First Amendment Formalism Is Giving Way to First Amendment Legal Realism." *Harvard Civil Rights Civil Liberties Review* 29, no. 1 (Winter 1994), pp. 169–177.

———. "Rodrigo's Eighth Chronicle: Black Crime, White Fears—On the Social Construction of Threat." *Virginia Law Review* 80, no. 2 (March 1994), pp. 503–548.

———. "Rodrigo's Fifth Chronicle: *Civitas,* Civil Wrongs, and the Politics of Denial." *Stanford Law Review* 45, no. 6 (July 1993), pp. 1581–1605.

———. "Rodrigo's Seventh Chronicle: Race, Democracy, and the State." *UCLA Law Review* 41, no. 3 (February 1994), pp. 721–757.

———. "Rodrigo's Sixth Chronicle: Intersections, Essences, and the Dilemma of Social Reform." *New York University Law Review* 68, no. 3 (June 1993), pp. 639–674.

Delgado, Richard, and Jean Stefancic. "Imposition." *William and Mary Law Review* 35, no. 3 (Spring 1994), pp. 1025–1059.

———. "Scorn." *William and Mary Law Review* 35, no. 3 (Spring 1994), pp. 1061–1099.

DeLillo, Don. *Mao II.* New York: Viking, 1991.

Deloria, Vine. *God Is Red: A Native View of Religion.* 2nd ed., Fulcrum Publishing, 1994.

Denes, Magda. *Castles Burning: A Child's Life in War.* New York: W. W. Norton & Company, 1997.

DeSalvo, Louise. *Conceived with Malice: Literature as Revenge in the Lives and Works of Virginia and Leonard Woolf, D. H. Lawrence, Djuna Barnes, and Henry Miller.* New York: Dutton, 1994.

Desmond, Adrian, and James Moore. *Darwin: The Life of a Tormented Evolutionist.* New York: Warner Books, 1992.

Dickey, James. *To the White Sea.* Boston: Houghton Mifflin Company, 1993.

Diggins, John Patrick. *Max Weber: Politics and the Spirit of Tragedy.* New York: Basic Books, 1996.

Dilling, Elizabeth. *The Octopus.* Matarie, La.: Sons of Liberty, 1986. (First printed in 1940.)

Dinnerstein, Leonard. *Anti-Semitism in America.* New York: Oxford University Press, 1994.

Dippel, John V. H. *Bound Upon a Wheel of Fire: Why So Many German Jews Made the Tragic Decision to Remain in Nazi Germany.* New York: Basic Books, 1996.

Djebar, Assia. *A Sister to Scheherazade.* Translated by Dorothy S. Blair. London: Quartet Books, 1987.

———. *Fantasia: An Algerian Cavalcade.* Translated by Dorothy S. Blair. London: Quartet Books, 1985.

———. *The Veil of Silence.* Translated by Dorothy S. Blair. London: Quartet Books, 1992.

Doblin, Alfred. *Destiny's Journey: Flight From the Nazis.* Edited by Edgar Pässler. Translated by Edna McCown. New York: Paragon House, 1992.

Doctorow, E. L. *Jack London, Hemingway, and the Constitution: Selected Essays 1977–1992.* New York: Random House, 1993.

Doerr, Harriet. *Consider This, Señora.* New York: Harcourt Brace & Company, 1993.

Donald, David Herbert. *Lincoln.* New York: Simon & Schuster, 1995.

Donaldson, Frances. *P. G. Wodehouse: A Biography.* New York: Alfred A. Knopf, 1982.

Donoghue, Denis. *The Old Moderns: Essays on Literature and Theory.* New York: Alfred A. Knopf, 1994.

———. *Walter Pater: Lover of Strange Souls.* New York: Alfred A. Knopf, 1995.

Donoso, José. *The Garden Next Door.* Translated by Hardie St. Martin. New York: Grove Press, 1992.

Dorfman, Ariel. *The Last Song of Manuel Sendero.* Translated by George R. Shivers and Ariel Dorfman. New York: Viking Penguin, 1987.

Dostoevsky, Fyodor. *Demons.* Translated by Richard Pevear and Larissa Volokhonsky. New York: Alfred A. Knopf, 1994.

Douglas, Ann. *Terrible Honesty: Mongrel Manhattan in the 1920s*. New York: Farrar, Straus & Giroux, 1995.

Drigalski, Dorte von. *Flowers on Granite: One Woman's Odyssey Through Psychoanalysis*. Translated by Anthea Bell and Marianne Loring. Berkeley: Creative Arts Book Company, 1986.

Dronke, Peter. "From Hildegard to Marguerite Porete." Pp. 202–228. *Women Writers of the Middle Ages: A Critical Study of Texts from Perpetua to Marguerite Porete*. Cambridge: Cambridge University Press, 1984.

Duke, David. *My Awakening: A Path to Racial Understanding*. Covington, La.: Free Speech Press, 1999.

Dunn, Jane. *A Very Close Conspiracy: Vanessa Bell and Virginia Woolf*. Boston: Little, Brown and Company, 1990.

Dunning, John. *Booked to Die*. New York: Avon Books, 1993.

———. *The Bookman's Wake*. New York: Scribner, 1995.

Duranti, Francesca. *Personal Effects*. Translated by Stephen Sartareli. New York: Random House, 1993.

Dutta, Krishna, and Andrew Robinson. *Rabindranath Tagore: The Myriad-Minded Man*. New York: St. Martin's Press, 1996.

Dwork, Debórah. *Children With a Star: Jewish Youth in Nazi Europe*. New Haven: Yale University Press, 1991.

Dwork, Debórah, and Robert Jan Van Pelt. *Auschwitz: 1270 to the Present*. New York: W. W. Norton & Company, 1996.

Dyer, Geoff. *Out of Sheer Rage: In the Shadow of D. H. Lawrence*. London: Little, Brown and Company, 1997.

Eagelton, Terry. *Heathcliff and the Great Hunger: Studies in Irish Culture*. New York: Verso, 1995.

Early, Gerald, ed. *Lure and Loathing: Essays on Race, Identity, and the Ambivalence of Assimilation*. New York: Allen Lane/The Penguin Press, 1993.

Eban, Abba. *Personal Witness: Israel Through My Eyes*. New York: G. P. Putnam's Sons, 1992.

Edgarian, Carol. *Rise the Euphrates*. New York: Random House, 1994.

Edmonds, Robin. *Pushkin: The Man and His Age*. New York: St. Martin's Press, 1995.

Eilberg-Schwartz, Howard. *God's Phallus and Other Problems for Men and Monotheism*. Boston: Beacon Press, 1994.

Eisenberg, Deborah. *Under the 82nd Airborne*. New York: Farrar, Straus, & Giroux, 1992.

El Dareer, Asma. *Woman, Why Do You Weep? Circumcision and Its Consequences*. London: Zed Press, 1983.

El Saadawi, Nawal. *God Dies by the Nile*. Translated by Sherif Hetata. London: Zed Books, 1986.

———. *Searching*. Translated by Shirley Eber. London: Zed Books, 1991.

———. *The Hidden Face of Eve: Women in the Arab World*. Translated and edited by Sherif Hetata. London: Zed Press, 1980.

———. *Woman at Point Zero*. Translated by Sherif Hetata. London: Zed Books, 1983.

Elias, Ruth. *Triumph of Hope: From Theresienstadt and Auschwitz to Israel*. Translated by Margo Bettauer Dembo. New York: John Wiley & Sons, 1998.

Elie, Paul, ed. *A Tremor of Bliss: Contemporary Writers on the Saints*. New York: Harcourt Brace & Company, 1994.

Ellis, Joseph J. *Passionate Sage: The Character and Legacy of John Adams*. New York: W. W. Norton & Company, 1993.

Elman, R. Amy, ed. *Sexual Politics and the European Union: The New Feminist Challenge*. Oxford: Berghahn Books, 1996.

———. *Subordination and State Intervention: Comparing Sweden and the United States*. Oxford: Berghahn Books, 1996.

———. "Triangles and Tribulations: The Politics of Nazi Symbols." *Journal of Homosexuality* 30, no. 3 (1996). pp. 1–11.

Elon, Amos. "Israel's Demons." *The New York Review of Books* XLII, no. 10 (June 8, 1995), pp. 42–46.

———. *Founder: A Portrait of the First Rothschild and His Time*. New York: Viking, 1996.

———. *Jerusalem: City of Mirrors*. Boston: Little, Brown and Company, 1989.

Elshtain, Jean Bethke. *Democracy on Trial*. New York: Basic Books, 1995.

Emecheta, Buchi. *Double Yoke*. New York: George Braziller, 1983.

Emerson, Gloria. *Gaza: A Year in the Intifada—A Personal Account from an Occupied Land*. New York: The Atlantic Monthly Press, 1991.

Endo, Shusaku. *Silence*. Translated by William Johnston. New York: Taplinger Publishing Company, 1980.

Enzenberger, Hans Magnus. *Civil Wars: From L.A. to Bosnia*. New York: The New Press, 1994.

Epel, Naomi, ed. *Writers Dreaming*. New York: Carol Southern Books, 1993.

Epstein, Daniel Mark. *Sister Aimee: The Life of Aimee Semple McPherson*. New York: Harcourt Brace Jovanovich, Publishers, 1993.

Epstein, Helen. *Joe Papp: An American Life*. Boston: Little, Brown and Company, 1994.

Erdrich, Louise. *The Bingo Palace*. New York: HarperCollins Publishers, 1994.

Erickson, Carolly. *Great Catherine: The Life of Catherine the Great, Empress of Russia*. New York: Crown Publishers, 1994.

Erickson, Steve. *Arc d'X*. New York: Poseidon Press, 1993.

Ernaux, Annie. *A Man's Place*. Translated by Tanya Leslie. New York: Four Walls Eight Windows, 1992.

———. *A Woman's Story*. Translated by Tanya Leslie. New York: Four Walls Eight Windows, 1991.

Estés, Clarissa Pinkola. *Women Who Run With the Wolves: Myths and Stories of the Wild Woman Archetype*. New York: Ballantine Books, 1992.

Etherington-Smith, Meredith. *The Persistence of Memory: A Biography of Dali*. New York: Random House, 1993.

Etten, Michelle L. Van, and Steven Taylor. "Comparative Efficacy of Treatments for Post-Traumatic Stress Disorder: A Meta-Analysis." In press. 1998.

Ettinger, Elzbieta. *Hannah Arendt Martin Heidegger*. New Haven: Yale University Press, 1995.

Evans, Eli N. *Judah P. Benjamin: The Jewish Confederate*. New York: The Free Press, 1988.

Evans, Richard J. *In Hitler's Shadow: West German Historians and the Attempt to Escape from the Nazi Past*. New York: Pantheon Books, 1989.

———. *Tales From the German Underworld: Crime and Punishment in the Nineteenth Century*. New Haven: Yale University Press, 1998.

Evazz, Karl. *The Judas Factor: The Plot to Kill Malcolm X*. New York: Thunder's Mouth Press, 1992.

Everdell, William R. *The First Moderns: Profiles in the Origins of Twentieth-Century Thought*. Chicago: The University of Chicago Press, 1997.

Ezenwa-Ohaeto. *Chinua Achebe: A Biography*. Bloomington: Indiana University Press, 1997.

Ezrahi, Yaron. *Rubber Bullets: Power and Conscience in Modern Israel*. New York: Farrar, Straus & Giroux, 1997.

Fairstein, Linda A. *Sexual Violence: Our War Against Rape*. New York: William Morrow and Company, 1993.

Fallows, James. *Breaking the News: How the Media Undermine American Democracy*. New York: Pantheon Books, 1996.

Faludi, Susan. *Backlash: The Undeclared War Against American Women*. New York: Crown Publishers, 1991.

Farley, Melissa, Isin Baral, Merab Kiremire, and Ufuk Sezgin, pp. 405–426. "Prostitution in Five Countries: Violence and Post-Traumatic Stress Disorder." *Feminism and Psychology* 8, no. 4 (1998).

Farley, Melissa, and Vanessa Kelly. "Prostitution: A Critical Review of the Medical and Social Sciences Literature." 1999, 48 pp.

Farmer, Sarah. *Martyred Village: Commemorating the 1944 Massacre at Oradour-sur-Glane*. Berkeley: University of California, 1999.

Farwell, Byron. *Burton: A Biography of Sir Richard Francis Burton*. New York: Viking, 1988.

Feitlowitz, Marguerite. *A Lexicon of Terror: Argentina and the Legacies of Torture*. New York: Oxford University Press, 1998.

Feliciano, Hector. *The Lost Museum: The Nazi Conspiracy to Steal the World's Greatest Works of Art*. New York: Basic Books, 1997.

Fellman, Michael. *Citizen Sherman: A Life of William Tecumseh Sherman.* New York: Random House, 1995.

Felstiner, John. *Paul Celan: Poet, Survivor, Jew.* New Haven: Yale University Press, 1995.

Felstiner, Mary Lowenthal. *To Paint Her Life: Charlotte Salomon in the Nazi Era.* New York: HarperCollins, 1994.

Fernea, Elizabeth Warnock. *In Search of Islamic Feminism: One Woman's Global Journey.* New York: Doubleday, 1998.

Ferris, Timothy. *The Mind's Sky: Human Intelligence in a Cosmic Context.* New York: Bantam Books, 1992.

Fest, Joachim G. *Hitler.* Translated by Richard and Clara Winston. New York: Harcourt Brace Jovanovich, Publishers, 1974.

Fest, Joachim. *Plotting Hitler's Death: The Story of the German Resistance.* Translated by Bruce Little. New York: Henry Holt and Company, 1996.

Feyerabend, Paul. *Killing Time: The Autobiography of Paul Feyerabend.* Chicago: The University of Chicago Press, 1995.

Ffinch, Michael. *G. K. Chesterton.* San Francisco: Harper & Row, Publishers, 1986.

Field Manual Section 1: Principles Justifying the Arming and Organizing of a Militia; Field Manual Section 2: Introduction to the Free Militia. No location: Free Militia, 1994.

Figes, Eva. *The Tree of Knowledge.* New York: Pantheon Books, 1990.

Fineman, Martha Albertson. "Feminist Theory in Law: The Difference It Makes." *Columbia Journal of Gender and Law* 2, no. 1 (1992), pp. 1–23.

———. "The Neutered Mother." *University of Miami Law Review* 46, no. 3 (January 1992), pp. 653–669.

Finestein, Elaine. *Lawrence and the Women: The Intimate Life of D. H. Lawrence.* New York: HarperCollins Publishers, 1993.

Fink, Ida. *A Scrap of Time.* Translated by Madeline Levine and Francine Prose. New York: Schocken Books, 1987.

———. *The Journey.* Translated by Joanna Weschler. New York: Farrar, Straus & Giroux, 1992.

Finkelstein, Norman G., and Ruth Bettina Birn. *A Nation on Trial: The Goldhagen Thesis and Historical Truth.* New York: Henry Holt and Company, 1998.

Finkielkraut, Alain. *Remembering in Vain: The Klaus Barbie Trial and Crimes Against Humanity.* Translated by Roxanne Lapidus and Sima Godfrey. New York: Columbia University Press, 1992.

Fischer, Klaus P. *Nazi Germany: A New History.* New York: Continuum Publishing Company, 1995.

Fish, Stanley. *Professional Correctness: Literary Studies and Political Change.* Oxford: Clarendon Press, 1995.

———. *There's No Such Thing as Free Speech . . . And It's a Good Thing Too.* New York: Oxford University Press, 1994.

Fisher, Clive. *Cyril Connolly: The Life and Times of England's Most Controversial Literary Critic.* New York: St. Martin's Press, 1995.

Fisher, Marc. *After the Wall: Germany, the Germans, and the Burdens of History.* New York: Simon & Schuster, 1995.

Fishkin, Shelley Fisher. *Was Huck Black? Mark Twain and African American Voices.* New York: Oxford University Press, 1993.

Fishman, Sylvia Barack. *A Breath of Life: Feminism in the American Jewish Community.* New York: The Free Press, 1993.

Fisk, Robert. *Pity the Nation: The Abduction of Lebanon.* New York: Atheneum, 1990.

Fitch, Noel Riley. *The Erotic Life of Anaïs Nin.* Boston: Little, Brown and Company, 1993.

FitzGerald, Michael C. *Making Modernism.* New York: Farrar, Straus & Giroux, 1995.

FitzHerbert, Katrin. *True to Both My Selves: A Family Memoir of Germany and England in Two World Wars.* London: Virago, 1997.

Flanagan, Thomas. *The End of the Hunt.* New York: Dutton, 1994.

Fogelman, Eva. *Conscience and Courage: Rescuers of Jews During the Holocaust.* New York: Anchor Books, 1994.

Follain, John. *Jackal: The Complete Story of the Legendary Terrorist, Carlos the Jackal.* New York: Arcade Publishing, 1998.

Fonseca, Isabel. *Bury Me Standing: The Gypsies and Their Journey.* New York: Alfred A. Knopf, 1995.

Foot, Michael. *H. G.: The History of Mr. Wells.* Washington, D.C.: Counterpoint, 1995.

Ford, Richard. "The Womanizer," *Granta.* no. 40 (Summer 1992), pp. 9–79.

Fortune, Marie Marshall. *Sexual Violence: The Unmentionable Sin.* New York: The Pilgrim Press, 1984.

Foster, Margaret. *Daphne du Maurier: The Secret Life of the Renowned Storyteller.* New York: Doubleday, 1993.

Foster, R. F. *W. B. Yeats: A Life—The Apprentice Mage.* New York: Oxford University Press, 1997.

Fox, Robin Lane. *The Unauthorized Version: Truth and Fiction in the Bible.* New York: Alfred A. Knopf, 1992.

Frady, Marshall. *Jesse: The Life and Pilgrimage of Jesse Jackson.* New York: Random House, 1996.

Francis, Claude, and Fernande Gontier. *Creating Colette: From Ingenue to Libertine 1873–1913.* Vol. 1. South Royalton, Vt.: Steerforth Press, 1998.

Frank, Joseph. *Dostoevsky: The Miraculous Years, 1865–1871.* Princeton: Princeton University Press, 1995.

Frank, Katherine. *A Passage to Egypt: The Life of Lucie Duff Gordon.* Boston: Houghton Mifflin Company, 1994.

Frankel, Glenn. *Beyond the Promised Land: Jews and Arabs on a Hard Road to a New Israel.* New York: Simon & Schuster, 1995.

Fraser, David. *Knight's Cross: A Life of Field Marshal Erwin Rommel.* London: HarperCollins Publishers, 1993.

Freedman, Ralph. *Life of a Poet: Rainer Maria Rilke.* New York: Farrar, Straus & Giroux, 1996.

Freeling, Nicolas. *The Seacoast of Bohemia.* New York: Warner Books, 1995.

Freire, Paulo. *Pedagogy of the Oppressed.* New York: The Seabury Press, 1973.

French, Karl, ed. *Screen Violence.* London: Bloomsbury, 1996.

Frey, Julia. *Toulouse-Lautrec: A Life.* New York: Viking, 1994.

Friedländer, Saul. *Nazi Germany and the Jews: The Years of Persecution.* Vol. 1. New York: HarperCollins Publishers, 1997.

Friedman, Matthew J., and Steven M. Southwick, "Towards Pharmacotherapy for PostTraumatic Stress Disorder." *Neurobiological and Clinical Consequences of Stress: From Normal Adaptation to PTDS.* Edited by M. J. Friedman, D. S. Charney, and A. Y. Deutch. Pp. 465–481. Philadelphia: Lippincott-Raven Publishers, 1995.

Friedman, Robert I. *The False Prophet: Rabbi Meir Kahane.* New York: Lawrence Hill Books, 1990.

———. *Zealots for Zion: Inside Israel's West Bank Settlement Movement.* New York: Random House, 1992.

Friedman, Thomas L. *From Beirut to Jerusalem.* New York: Farrar, Straus & Giroux, 1989.

Friedrich, Otto. *Blood and Iron: From Bismarck to Hitler, the von Moltke Family's Impact on German History.* New York: HarperCollins, 1995.

———. *Olympia: Paris in the Age of Manet.* New York: HarperCollins Publishers, 1992.

———. *The Kingdom of Auschwitz.* New York: HarperPerenniel, 1994.

Fritzsche, Peter. *Germans into Nazis.* Cambridge: Harvard University Press, 1998.

Fruchtman, Jack, Jr. *Thomas Paine: Apostle of Freedom.* New York: Four Walls Eight Windows, 1994.

Frum, David. *Dead Right.* New York: Basic Books, 1994.

Frye, Marilyn. *Willful Virgin: Essays in Feminism 1976–1992.* Freedom, Calif.: The Crossing Press, 1992.

Fuegi, John. *Brecht & Co.: Sex, Politics, and the Making of the Modern Drama.* New York: Grove Press, 1994.

Fuentes, Carlos. *Christopher Unborn.* Translated by Alfred Mac Adam. New York: Farrar, Straus & Giroux, 1989.

————. *The Campaign.* Translated by Alfred Mac Adam. New York: Farrar, Straus & Giroux, 1991.

————. "Introduction," *The Diary of Frida Kahlo: An Intimate Self-Portrait.* Pp. 7–24. New York: Harry N. Abrams, Publishers, 1995.

————. *The Orange Tree.* Translated by Alfred Mac Adam. New York: Farrar, Straus & Giroux, 1994.

Fukuyama, Francis. *The End of History and the Last Man.* New York: The Free Press, 1992.

Fullbrook, Kate, and Edward Fullbrook. *Simone de Beauvoir and Jean Paul Sartre: The Remaking of a Twentieth-Century Legend.* New York: Basic Books, 1994.

Furbank, P. N. *Diderot: A Critical Biography.* New York: Alfred A. Knopf, 1992.

Gage, Carolyn. *Like There's No Tomorrow: Mediations for Women Leaving Patriarchy.* Monroe, Maine: Common Courage Press, 1997.

————. *The Second Coming of Joan of Arc and Other Plays.* Santa Cruz, Calif.: HerBooks, 1994.

Gaines, Ernest J. *A Lesson Before Dying.* New York: Alfred A. Knopf, 1993.

Galland, China. *The Bond Between Women: A Journey to Fierce Compassion.* New York: Riverhead Books, 1998.

Garcia, Cristina. *Dreaming in Cuban.* New York: Alfred A. Knopf, 1992.

Gardiner, Stephen. *Epstein: Artist Against the Establishment.* New York: Viking, 1993.

Gardner, Howard. *Creating Minds: An Anatomy of Creativity Seen Through the Lives of Freud, Einstein, Picasso, Stravinsky, Eliot, Graham and Gandhi.* New York: Basic Books, 1993.

Gardner, John. *On Writers and Writing.* New York: Addison-Wesley Publishing Company, 1994.

Garment, Suzanne. *Scandal: The Culture of Mistrust in American Politics.* New York: Times Books/Random House, 1991.

Garner, Helen. *The First Stone: Some Questions About Sex and Power.* New York: The Free Press, 1997. Proofs.

Garrard, John, and Carol Garrard. *The Bones of Berdichev: The Life and Fate of Vasily Grossman.* New York: The Free Press, 1996.

Gass, William H. *Finding a Form.* New York: Alfred A. Knopf, 1996.

Gates, Henry Louis, Jr .*Colored People: A Memoir.* New York: Alfred A. Knopf, 1994.

————. *The Signifying Monkey: A Theory of African-American Literary Criticism.* New York: Oxford University Press, 1988.

Gay, Peter. *Pleasure Wars: The Bourgeois Experience—Victoria to Freud.* Vol. V. New York: W. W. Norton & Company, 1988.

————. *The Cultivation of Hatred: The Bourgeois Experience Victoria to Freud.* Vol. III. New York: W. W. Norton & Company, 1993.

————. *The Enlightenment: The Rise of Modern Paganism.* New York: W. W. Norton & Company, 1977.

————. *The Enlightenment: The Science of Freedom.* New York: W. W. Norton & Company, 1977.

————. *The Naked Heart: The Bourgeois Experience Victoria to Freud.* Vol. IV. New York: W. W. Norton & Company, 1995.

Gelernter, David. *Drawing Life: Surviving the Unabomber.* New York: The Free Press, 1997.

Gelissen, Rena Kornreich, and Heather Dune Macadam. *Rena's Promise: A Story of Sisters in Auschwitz.* Boston: Beacon Press, 1995.

Gerber, Jane S. *The Jews of Spain: A History of the Sephardic Experience.* New York: The Free Press, 1992.

Ghalem, Ali. *A Wife for My Son.* Translated by G. Kazolis. Chicago: Banner Press, 1984.

Ghosh, Amitav. *In An Antique Land.* New York: Alfred A. Knopf, 1993.

Gibran, Jean, and Kahlil Gibran. *Kahlil Gibran: His Life and World.* New York: Interlink Publishing Group, 1991.

Giladi, G. N. *Discord in Zion: Conflict Between Ashkenazi & Sephardic Jews in Israel.* Translated by R. Harris. London: Scorpion Publishing, 1990.

Gilbert, G. M. *Nuremberg Diary.* New York: Da Capo Press, 1995.

Gilbert, Martin. *Auschwitz and the Allies.* New York: Henry Holt and Company, 1982.

———. *Israel: A History.* New York: William Morrow and Company, 1998.

———. *The Boys: The Untold Story of 732 Young Concentration Camp Survivors.* New York: Henry Holt and Company, 1997.

Gilbert, Sandra M., and Susan Gubar. *No Man's Land: The Place of the Woman Writer in the Twentieth Century.* 3 vols. New Haven: Yale University Press, 1987–1994.

Gilfoyle, Timothy J. *City of Eros: New York City, Prostitution, and the Commercialization of Sex, 1790–1920.* New York: W. W. Norton & Company, 1992.

Gill, Anton. *An Honourable Defeat: A History of German Resistance to Hitler, 1933–1945.* New York: Henry Holt and Company, 1994.

Gilligan, Carol, Janie Victoria Ward, and Jill McLean Taylor, eds. *Mapping the Moral Domain.* Cambridge, Mass.: Center for the Study of Gender, Education and Human Development, 1988.

Gilman, Sander L. *Difference and Pathology: Stereotypes of Sexuality, Race, and Madness.* Ithaca, N.Y.: Cornell University Press, 1985.

———. *Freud, Race, and Gender.* Princeton: Princeton University Press, 1993.

Gilman, Sander. *The Jew's Body.* New York: Routledge, 1991.

Girzone, Joseph F. *Joshua in the Holy Land.* New York: Macmillan Publishing Company, 1992.

Gissing, George. *The Emancipated.* London: The Hogarth Press, 1985.

Gitlin, Todd. *The Twilight of Common Dreams: Why America Is Wracked by Culture Wars.* New York: Henry Holt and Company, 1995.

Gittelson, Celia. *Biography.* New York: Alfred A. Knopf, 1991.

Glass, Charles. *Tribes With Flags.* New York: The Atlantic Monthly Press, 1990.

Glendinning, Victoria. *Anthony Trollope.* New York: Alfred A. Knopf, 1993.

———. *Vita: A Biography of Vita Sackville-West.* New York: Quill, 1984.

Glendon, Mary Ann. *Rights Talk: The Impoverishment of Political Discourse.* New York: The Free Press, 1991.

Goffen, Rona. *Titian's Women.* New Haven: Yale University Press, 1997.

Golan, Matti. *With Friends Like You: What Israelis Really Think About American Jews.* Translated by Hillel Halkin. New York: The Free Press, 1992.

Golb, Norman. *Who Wrote the Dead Sea Scrolls? The Search for the Secret of Qumran.* New York: Scribner, 1995.

Gold, Arthur, and Robert Fizdale. *The Divine Sarah: A Life of Sarah Bernhardt.* New York: Alfred A. Knopf, 1991.

Golden, Stephanie. *The Women Outside: Meanings and Myths of Homelessness.* Berkeley: University of California Press, 1992.

Goldhagen, Daniel Jonah. *Hitler's Willing Executioners: Ordinary Germans and the Holocaust.* New York: Alfred A. Knopf, 1996.

Golding, John. *Visions of the Modern.* Berkeley: University of California Press, 1994.

Goldstein, Bluma. *Reinscribing Moses: Heine, Kafka, Freud, and Schoenberg in a European Wilderness.* Cambridge: Harvard University Press, 1992.

Golsan, Richard J. ed. *Memory, the Holocaust, and French Justice: The Bousquet and Touvier Affairs.* Translated by Lucy Golsan and Richard J. Golsan. Hanover, N.H.: University Press of New England, 1996.

Gooch, Brad. *City Poet: The Life and Times of Frank O'Hara.* New York: Alfred A. Knopf, 1993.

Goodman, David G., and Masanori Miyazawa. *Jews in the Japanese Mind: The History and Uses of a Cultural Stereotype.* New York: The Free Press, 1995.

Goodman, James. *Stories of Scottsboro.* New York: Pantheon, 1994.

Goodstein, Laurie. "Outcry Erupts Over Palestinians' Statements on Holocaust." *The New York Times.* July 24, 1998.

Goodwin, Jan. *Price of Honor: Muslim Women Lift the Veil of Silence on the Islamic World.* Boston: Little, Brown and Company, 1994.

Gordimer, Nadine. *None to Accompany Me.* New York: Farrar, Straus & Giroux, 1994.

———. *Writing and Being.* Cambridge: Harvard University Press, 1995.

Gordis, Daniel. *God Was Not in the Fire: The Search for a Spiritual Judaism.* New York: Scribner, 1995.

Gordon, Lois. *The World of Samuel Beckett 1906–1946.* New Haven: Yale University Press, 1996.

Gordon, Lyndall. *Charlotte Brontë: A Passionate Life.* New York: W. W. Norton & Company, 1995.

Gordon, Mary. *The Rest of Life.* New York: Viking, 1993.

Gordon, Neil. *Sacrifice of Isaac.* New York: Random House, 1995.

Gordon-Reed, Annette. *Thomas Jefferson and Sally Hemings: An American Controversy.* Charlottesville: The University Press of Virginia, 1997.

Gowers, Andrew, and Tony Walker. *Behind the Myth: Yasser Arafat and the Palestinian Revolution.* New York: Olive Branch Press, 1992.

Graglia, F. Carolyn. *Domestic Tranquility: A Brief Against Feminism.* Dallas: Spence Publishing Company, 1998.

Grant, Judith Skelton. *Robertson Davies: Man of Myth.* New York: Viking, 1994.

Grant, Michael. *Saint Peter: A Biography.* New York: Scribner, 1995.

Grass, Günter. *The Call of the Toad.* Translated by Ralph Manheim. New York: Harcourt Brace Jovanovich, Publishers, 1992.

———. *The Rat.* Translated by Ralph Manheim. New York: Harcourt Brace Jovanovich, Publishers, 1987.

———. *Two States—One Nation?* Translated by Krishna Winston and A. S. Wensinger. New York: Harcourt Brace Jovanovich, Publishers, 1990.

Gray, Francine Du Plessix. *Rage and Fire: A Life of Louise Colet.* New York: Simon & Schuster, 1994.

Gray, John. *Isaiah Berlin.* Princeton: Princeton University Press, 1996.

Gray, Richard. *The Life of William Faulkner.* Oxford: Blackwell, 1994.

Green, Michelle. *The Dream at the End of the World: Paul Bowles and the Literary Renegades in Tangier.* New York: HarperCollins Publishers, 1991.

Greene, Graham. *Reflections.* London: Reinhardt Books/Viking, 1990.

Greene, Melissa Fay. *The Temple Bombing.* New York: Addison-Wesley Publishing Company, 1996.

Greenfeld, Liah. *Nationalism: Five Roads to Modernity.* Cambridge: Harvard University Press, 1992.

Greenland, Colin. *Michael Moorcock: Death is no Obstacle.* Manchester: Savoy, 1992.

Greer, Germaine. *The Obstacle Race: The Fortunes of Women Painters and Their Work.* New York: Farrar, Straus & Giroux, 1979.

———. *The Change: Women, Aging and the Menopause.* New York: Fawcett Columbine, 1993.

———. *The Whole Woman.* London: Doubleday, 1999.

Gregor, Neil. *Daimler-Benz in the Third Reich.* New Haven: Yale University Press, 1998.

Gresh, Alain, and Dominique Vidal. *A to Z of the Middle East.* Translated by Bob Cumming. London: Zed Books, 1990.

Grey, Stephen. "Roadside Services: The Hungarian Centre Was Supposed to Provide Facilities for Call Girls [;] Briton in Prostitute Aid Scandal." *Sunday Times,* January 31, 1999.

Gross, John. *Shylock: A Legend and Its Legacy.* New York: Simon & Schuster, 1993.

Grosskurth, Phyllis. *Byron: The Flawed Angel.* Boston: Houghton Mifflin Company, 1997.

———. *The Secret Ring: Freud's Inner Circle and the Politics of Psychoanalysis.* Reading, Mass.: Addison-Wesley Publishing Company, 1991.

Grossman, David. *See Under: Love.* Translated by Betsy Rosenberg. New York: Farrar, Straus & Giroux, 1989.

———. *Sleeping on a Wire: Conversations with Palestinians in Israel.* Translated by Haim Watzman. New York: Farrar, Straus & Giroux, 1993.

———. *The Book of Intimate Grammar.* Translated by Betsy Rosenberg. New York: Farrar, Straus & Giroux, 1994.

———. *The Smile of the Lamb.* Translated by Betsy Rosenberg. New York: Farrar, Straus & Giroux, 1990.

———. *The Yellow Wind.* Translated by Haim Watzman. New York: Dell Publishing, 1989.

Gudiol, José. *Francisco de Goya y Lucientes.* Translated by Priscilla Muller. New York: Harry N. Abrams, Inc., Publishers, 1985.

Guillermoprieto, Alma. *The Heart That Bleeds: Latin America Now.* New York: Alfred A. Knopf, 1994.

Guinier, Lani. *The Tyranny of the Majority: Fundamental Fairness in Representative Democracy.* New York: The Free Press, 1994.

Gunther, Gerald. *Learned Hand: The Man and the Judge.* New York: Alfred A. Knopf, 1994.

Gupte, Pranay. *Mother India: A Political Biography of Indira Gandhi.* New York: Charles Scribner's Sons, 1992.

Gur, Batya. *Literary Murder: A Critical Case.* Translated by Dalya Bilu. New York: Harper-Collins Publishers, 1993.

——. *Murder on a Kibbutz: A Communal Case.* Translated by Dalya Bilu. New York: HarperCollins, 1994.

Gutman, Israel. *Resistance: The Warsaw Ghetto Uprising.* Boston: Houghton Mifflin Company, 1994.

Gutman, Roy. *A Witness to Genocide.* New York: Macmillan Publishing Company, 1993.

Gutman, Yisrael, and Michael Berenbaum, eds. *Anatomy of the Auschwitz Death Camp.* Bloomington: Indiana University Press and the United States Holocaust Memorial Museum, 1994.

Habegger, Alfred. *The Father: A Life of Henry James, Sr.* New York: Farrar, Straus & Giroux, 1994.

Haberman, Joshua O. *The God I Believe In.* New York: The Free Press, 1994.

Habiby, Emile. *The Secret Life of Saeed The Pessoptimist.* Translated by Salma Khadra Jayyusi and Trevor LeGassick. London: Zed Books, 1985.

Hacker, Andrew. *Two Nations: Black and White, Separate, Hostile, Unequal.* New York: Charles Scribner's Sons, 1992.

Hackett, David A., ed. and trans. *The Buchenwald Report.* Boulder, Colo.: Westview Press, 1995.

Hadas-Lebel, Mireille. *Flavius Josephus: Eye-witness to Rome's First-Century Conquest of Judea.* Translated by Richard Miller. New York: Macmillan Publishing Company, 1993.

Haffner, Sebastian. *The Meaning of Hitler.* Translated by Ewald Osers. Cambridge: Harvard University Press, 1979.

Hagar, Laura. "Guns and Roses: Is Personal Armament the Last Frontier of Feminism?" *The East Bay's Free Weekly* 14, no. 13 (January 10, 1992).

Halevi, Yossi Klein. *Memoirs of a Jewish Extremist: An American Story.* New York: Little, Brown and Company, 1995.

Hall, Jacquelyn Dowd. *Revolt Against Chivalry: Jessie Daniel Ames and the Women's Campaign Against Lynching.* Rev. ed. New York: Columbia University Press, 1993.

Hall, Lee. *Elaine and Bill: Portrait of a Marriage.* New York: HarperCollins Publishers, 1993.

Hall, N. John. *Trollope: A Biography.* Oxford: Clarendon Press, 1991.

Hamann, Brigitte. *Hitler's Vienna: A Dictator's Apprenticeship.* Translated by Thomas Thornton. New York: Oxford University Press, 1999.

Hamerow, Theodore S. *On the Road to the Wolf's Lair: German Resistance to Hitler.* Cambridge: The Belknap Press of Harvard University, 1997.

Hamilton, Ian. *Keepers of the Flame: Literary Estates and the Rise of Biography from Shakespeare to Plath.* London: Faber and Faber, 1994.

Hansen, Eric. *Motoring With Mohammed: Journeys to Yemen and the Red Sea.* Boston: Houghton Mifflin Company, 1991.

Harding, Jeremy. *The Fate of Africa: Trial by Fire.* New York: Simon & Schuster, 1993.

Hareven, Shulamith. *Twilight and Other Stories.* Translated by Miriam Arad, Hillel Halkin, J. M. Lask, and David Weber. San Francisco: Mercury House, 1992.

Harris, Robert. *Enigma.* New York: Random House, 1995.

——. *Fatherland.* New York: Random House, 1992.

Harrison, Jim. *Julip.* Boston: Houghton Mifflin/Seymour Lawrence, 1994.

Harrison, Kathryn. *Exposure.* New York: Random House, 1993.

——. *Poison.* New York: Random House, 1995.

——. *The Kiss: A Memoir.* New York: Random House, 1997.

——. *Thicker Than Water.* New York: HarperCollins, 1992.

Hartov, Steven. *The Heat of Ramadan.* New York: Harcourt Brace Jovanovich, Publishers, 1992.

Haskins, Susan. *Mary Magdalen: Myth and Metaphor.* New York: Harcourt Brace & Company, 1994.

Hasselbach, Ingo, and Tom Reiss. *Führer-Ex: Memoirs of a Former Neo-Nazi.* New York: Random House, 1996.

Hastings, Selina. *Evelyn Waugh: A Biography.* Boston: Houghton Mifflin Company, 1994.

Hayman, Ronald. *Hitler and Geli.* London: Bloomsbury, 1997.

———. *Proust: A Biography.* New York: HarperCollins, 1990.

———. *Thomas Mann: A Biography.* New York: Scribner, 1995.

Heaney, Seamus. *Selected Poems 1966–1987.* New York: Farrar, Straus & Giroux, 1998.

———. *The Redress of Poetry.* New York: Farrar, Straus & Giroux, 1995.

Hedrick, Joan D. *Harriet Beecher Stowe: A Life.* New York: Oxford University Press, 1994.

Hegi, Ursula. *Tearing the Silence: On Being German in America.* New York: Simon & Schuster, 1997.

Heilbrun, Carolyn G. *The Education of a Woman: The Life of Gloria Steinem.* New York: The Dial Press, 1995.

Heilbut, Anthony. *Thomas Mann: Eros and Literature.* New York: Alfred A. Knopf, 1996.

Heller, Mark A., and Sari Nusseibeh. *No Trumpets, No Drums: A Two-State Settlement of the Israeli-Palestinian Conflict.* New York: Hill and Wang, 1991.

Herf, Jeffrey. *Divided Memory: The Nazi Past in the Two Germanys.* Cambridge: Harvard University Press, 1997.

Herling, Gustaw. *The Island: Three Tales.* Translated by Ronald Strom. New York: Viking, 1993.

Herman, John. *The Weight of Love.* New York: Doubleday, 1995.

Herman, Judith Lewis. *Trauma and Recovery.* New York: Basic Books, 1992.

Hernton, Calvin C. *The Sexual Mountain and Black Women Writers.* New York: Anchor Books, 1990.

Herrera, Hayden. *Matisse: A Portrait.* New York: Harcourt Brace & Company, 1993.

Herrnstein, Richard J., and Charles Murray. *The Bell Curve: Intelligence and Class Structure in American Life.* New York: The Free Press, 1994.

Hersh, Seymour M. *The Samson Option.* New York: Random House, 1991.

Hertzberg, Arthur, and Aron Hirt-Manheimer. *Jews: The Essence and Character of a People.* San Francisco: HarperCollins, 1998.

Hertzberg, Arthur. *The French Enlightenment and the Jews: The Origins of Modern Anti-Semitism.* New York: Columbia University Press, 1990.

Herzl, Theodor. *The Jewish State.* Mineola, N.Y.: Dover Publications, 1988.

Herzog, Chaim. *Living History: A Memoir.* New York: Pantheon Books, 1996.

Hibbert, Christopher. *Cavaliers and Roundheads: The English Civil War 1642–1649.* New York: Charles Scribner's Sons, 1993.

———. *Nelson: A Personal History.* Reading, Mass.: Addison-Wesley Publishing Company, 1994.

Hilberg, Raul. *Perpetrators, Victims, Bystanders: The Jewish Catastrophe 1933–1945.* New York: HarperCollins Publishers, 1992.

———. *The Destruction of the Jews.* 3 vols. Rev. ed. New York: Holmes and Meier, 1985.

———. *The Politics of Memory: The Journey of a Holocaust Historian.* Chicago: Ivan R. Dee, 1996.

Hill, Christopher. *Liberty Against the Law: Some Seventeenth-Century Controversies.* New York: Penguin, 1996.

Hillerman, Tony. *The Blessing Way.* New York: Avon Books, 1978.

Hiltermann, Jost R. *Behind the Intifada: Labor and Women's Movements in the Occupied Territories.* Princeton: Princeton University Press, 1991.

Himmelfarb, Gertrude. *On Looking into the Abyss: Untimely Thoughts on Culture and Society.* New York: Alfred A. Knopf, 1994.

———. *Poverty and Compassion: The Moral Imagination of the Late Victorians.* New York: Vintage, 1992.

————. *The De-Moralization of Society: From Victorian Virtues to Modern Values.* New York: Alfred A. Knopf, 1995.

Hirsch, E. D., Jr. *Cultural Literacy.* Boston: Houghton Mifflin Company, 1987.

Hiss, Tony. *The Experience of Place.* New York: Alfred A. Knopf, 1990.

Hitchens, Christopher. *No One Left to Lie to: The Triangulations of William Jefferson Clinton.* New York: Verso, 1999.

Hite, Shere. *Women as Revolutionary Agents of Change.* Madison: The University of Wisconsin Press, 1993.

Hoare, Philip. *Oscar Wilde's Last Stand: Decadence, Conspiracy, and the Most Outrageous Trial of the Century.* New York: Arcade Publishing, 1997.

Hobsbawm, Eric. *The Age of Extremes: A History of the World, 1914–1991.* New York: Pantheon Books, 1995.

Hobson, Barbara Meil. *Uneasy Virtue: The Politics of Prostitution and the American Reform Tradition.* New York: Basic Books, Inc., Publishers, 1987.

Hockenos, Paul. *Free to Hate: The Rise of the Right in Post-Communist Eastern Europe.* New York: Routledge, 1993.

Høeg, Peter. *Borderliners.* Translated by Barbara Haveland. New York: Farrar, Straus & Giroux, 1994.

————. *Smilla's Sense of Snow.* Translated by Tiina Nunnally. New York: Farrar, Straus & Giroux, 1993.

Hoffman, Alice. *Second Nature.* New York: G. P. Putnam's Sons, 1994.

Hoffman, Eva. *Exit into History: A Journey Through the New Eastern Europe.* New York: Viking, 1993.

————. *Shtetl: The Life and Death of a Small Town and the World of Polish Jews.* Boston: Houghton Mifflin Company, 1997.

Hoffman, Yoel. *Katschen & The Book of Joseph.* Translated by David Kriss, Alan Treister, and Eddie Levenston. New York: New Directions, 1998.

Hofstadter, Dan. *The Love Affair as a Work of Art.* New York: Farrar, Straus & Giroux, 1996.

Hogrefe, Jeffrey. *O'Keefe: The Life of an American Legend.* New York: Bantam Books, 1992.

Holden, Anthony. *Tchaikovsky: A Biography.* New York: Random House, 1995.

Holliday, Laurel, ed. *Children in the Holocaust and World War II: Their Secret Diaries.* New York: Pocket Books, 1995.

Hollinghurst, Alan. *The Folding Star.* New York: Pantheon Books, 1994.

Holmes, Blair R., and Alan F. Keele, eds. *When Truth Was Treason: German Youth Against Hitler.* Translated by Blair R. Holmes and Alan F. Keele. Urbana: University of Illinois Press, 1995.

Holmes, Richard. *Coleridge: Darker Reflections, 1804–1834.* New York: Pantheon Books, 1999.

————. *Dr. Johnson & Mr. Savage.* New York: Pantheon Books, 1994.

Holroyd, Michael. *Bernard Shaw: The Lure of Fantasy 1918–1951.* Vol. III. New York: Random House, 1991.

————. *Lytton Strachey: The New Biography.* New York: Farrar, Straus & Giroux, 1995.

hooks, bell. *Teaching to Transgress: Education as the Practice of Freedom.* New York: Routledge, 1994.

————. *Outlaw Culture: Resisting Representations.* New York: Routledge, 1994.

————. *Reel to Real: Race, Sex and Class at the Movies.* London: Routledge, 1996.

Horowitz, David. *Radical Son: A Generational Odyssey.* New York: The Free Press, 1997.

————. *The Politics of Bad Faith: The Radical Assault on America's Future.* New York: The Free Press, 1998.

Horowitz, Gordon J. *In the Shadow of Death: Living Outside the Gates of Mauthausen.* New York: The Free Press, 1990.

Höss, Rudoph. *Death-Dealer: The Memoirs of the SS Kommandant at Auschwitz.* Edited by Steven Paskuly. Translated by Andrew Pollinger. New York: Da Capo Press, 1996.

Hourani, Albert. *A History of the Arab Peoples.* Cambridge: The Belknap Press of Harvard University Press, 1991.

Howard, Jane. *Margaret Mead: A Life.* New York: Simon & Schuster, 1984.

Howard, Philip K. *The Death of Common Sense: How Law Is Suffocating America.* New York: Random House, 1994.

Hughes, Donna M. *Pimps and Predators on the Internet: Globalizing the Sexual Exploitation of Women and Children: A Report.* Kingston, R.I.: The Coalition Against Trafficking in Women, 1999.

Hughes, Donna M., and Claire Roche, eds. *Making the Harm Visible: Global Sexual Exploitation of Women and Girls—Speaking Out and Providing Services.* Kingston, R.I.: Coalition Against Trafficking in Women, 1999.

Hughes, Robert. *Barcelona.* New York: Vintage Books, 1993.

———. *Culture of Complaint: The Fraying of America.* New York: Oxford University Press, 1993.

Husseini, Hassan Jamal. *Return to Jerusalem.* London: Quartet Books, 1989.

Hustvedt, Siri. *The Blindfold.* New York: Poseidon Press, 1992.

Hyman, Meryl. *"Who Is a Jew?" Conversations, Not Conclusions.* Woodstock, Vt.: Jewish Lights Publishing, 1998.

Hyman, Paula E. *The Emancipation of the Jews of Alsace: Acculturation and Tradition in the Nineteenth Century.* New Haven: Yale University Press, 1991.

Hynes, Samuel. *A War Imagined: The First World War and English Culture.* New York: Atheneum, 1991.

Ibrahim, Gamil Atia. *Down to the Sea.* Translated by Frances Liardet. London: Quartet Books, 1991.

Ignatieff, Michael. *Blood and Belonging: Journeys Into the New Nationalism.* New York: Farrar, Straus & Giroux, 1993.

———. *Isaiah Berlin: A Life.* New York: Henry Holt and Company, 1998.

———. *The Warrior's Honor: Ethnic War and the Modern Conscience.* New York: Henry Holt and Company, 1997.

Ignatieff, Noel. *How the Irish Became White.* New York: Routledge, 1995.

Infante, Guillermo Cabrera. *Mea Cuba.* Translated by Kenneth Hall and Guillermo Cabrera Infante. New York: Farrar, Straus & Giroux, 1994.

Ingalls, Rachel. *Be My Guest.* New York: Turtle Bay Books, 1992.

Isaacson, Walter. *Kissinger: A Biography.* New York: Simon & Schuster, 1992.

Ishiguro, Kazuo. *The Unconsoled.* New York: Alfred A. Knopf, 1995.

Ivison, Irene. *Fiona's Story: A Tragedy of Our Times.* London: Virago Press, 1997.

Jabbour, Hala Deeb. *A Woman of Nazareth.* New York: Interlink Books, 1992.

Jaber, Hala. *Hezbollah: Born With a Vengeance.* New York: Columbia University Press, 1997.

Jackson, Stevi. *Christine Delphy.* London: Sage Publications, 1996.

Jacobs, James B., and Kimberly Potter. *Hate Crimes: Criminal Law and Identity Politics.* New York: Oxford University Press, 1998.

Jacobson, Kenneth. *Embattled Selves: An Investigation into the Nature of Identity Through Oral Histories of Holocaust Survivors.* New York: The Atlantic Monthly Press, 1994.

Jacobson, Neil, and John Gottman. *When Men Batter Women: New Insights into Ending Abusive Relationships.* New York: Simon & Schuster, 1998.

Jaher, Frederic Cople. *A Scapegoat in the New Wilderness: The Origins and Rise of Anti-Semitism in America.* Cambridge: Harvard University Press, 1994.

James, Lawrence. *The Golden Warrior: The Life and Legend of Lawrence of Arabia.* New York: Paragon House, 1993.

James, P. D. *Original Sin.* New York: Alfred A. Knopf, 1995.

———. *The Children of Men.* New York: Alfred A. Knopf, 1993.

Japrisot, Sébastien. *A Very Long Engagement.* Translated by Linda Coverdale. New York: Farrar, Straus & Giroux, 1994.

Jay, Karla. *Tales of the Lavender Menace: A Memoir of Liberation.* New York: Basic Books, 1999.

Jeffrey, Patricia. *Frogs in a Well: Indian Women in Purdah.* London: Zed Press, 1979.

Jeffreys, Sheila. *Anticlimax: A Feminist Perspective on the Sexual Revolution.* New York: New York University Press, 1990.

———. *The Idea of Prostitution.* North Melbourne, Victoria: Spinifex Press, 1997.

———. *The Lesbian Heresy: A Feminist Perspective on the Lesbian Sexual Revolution.* North Melbourne, Victoria: Spinifex, 1993.

Jelinek, Elfriede. *Wonderful Wonderful Times.* Translated by Michael Hulse. London: Serpent's Tail, 1990.

Jen, Gish. *Typical American.* Boston: Houghton Mifflin/Seymour Lawrence, 1991.

Jenkins, Roy. *Gladstone: A Biography.* New York: Random House, 1997.

Jhabvala, Ruth Prawer. *Poet and Dancer.* New York: Doubleday, 1993.

Johnson, Charles. *Middle Passage.* New York: Atheneum, 1990.

Johnson, Denis. *Already Dead: A California Gothic.* New York: HarperCollins, 1997.

————. *Jesus' Son.* New York: Farrar, Straus & Giroux, 1992.

Johnson, Paul E., and Sean Wilentz. *The Kingdom of Matthias: A Story of Sex and Salvation in 19th Century America.* New York: Oxford University Press, 1994.

Johnson, Paul. *The Birth of the Modern: World Society 1815–1830.* New York: HarperCollins Publishers, 1991.

————. *The Quest for God: A Personal Pilgrimage.* New York: HarperCollins, 1996.

Johnston, Jill. *Jasper Johns: Privileged Information.* New York: Thames and Hudson, 1996.

Jolley, Elizabeth. *Cabin Fever.* New York: HarperCollins Publishers, 1991.

Jong, Erica. *Fear of Fifty: A Midlife Memoir.* New York: HarperCollins, 1994.

————. *The Devil at Large: Erica Jong on Henry Miller.* New York: Random House, 1993.

Judt, Tony. *Past Imperfect: French Intellectuals 1944–1992.* Berkeley: University of California Press, 1992.

————. *The Burden of Responsibility: Blum, Camus, Aron, and the French Twentieth Century.* Chicago: The University of Chicago Press, 1998.

Julius, Anthony. *T. S. Eliot, Anti-Semitism, and Literary Form.* Cambridge: Cambridge University Press, 1995.

Ka-Tzetnik 135633. *Shiviti.* Translated by Eliyah Hike D-Nur and Lisa Herman. San Francisco: Harper & Row, Publishers, 1989.

Kadare, Ismail. *The Palace of Dreams.* Translated by Jusuf Vrioni and Barbara Bray. New York: William Morrow and Company, 1993.

————. *The Pyramid.* Translated by David Bellos. New York: Arcade Publishing, 1996.

Kagan, Donald. *On the Origins of War and the Preservation of Peace.* New York: Doubleday, 1995.

Kahlo, Frida. *The Diary of Frida Kahlo: An Intimate Self-Portrait.* New York: Harry N. Abrams, Inc., Publishers, 1995.

Kahn, Annette. *Why My Father Died: A Daughter Confronts Her Family's Past at the Trial of Klaus Barbie.* Translated by Anna Cancogni. New York: Summit Books, 1991.

Kane, Elizabeth. *Birth Mother: The Story of America's First Legal Surrogate Mother.* New York: Harcourt Brace Jovanovich, Publishers, 1988.

Kaniuk, Yoram. *Confessions of a Good Arab.* Translated by Dalya Bilu. New York: George Braziller, 1988.

————. *His Daughter.* Translated by Seymour Simckes. New York: George Braziller, 1989.

Kaplan, Alice. *French Lessons: A Memoir.* Chicago: The University of Chicago Press, 1994.

Kaplan, Fred. *Henry James: The Imagination of Genius.* New York: William Morrow and Company, 1992.

————. *Thomas Carlyle: A Biography.* Berkeley: University of California Press, 1993.

Kaplan, Laura. *The Story of Jane: The Legendary Underground Feminist Abortion Service.* New York: Pantheon Books, 1995.

Kaplan, Marion A. *Between Dignity and Despair: Jewish Life in Nazi Germany.* New York: Oxford University Press, 1998.

Kaplan, Robert D. *Balkan Ghosts: A Journey Through History.* New York: St. Martin's Press, 1993.

————. *The Arabists: The Romance of an American Elite.* New York: The Free Press, 1993.

Kappeler, Susanne. *The Will to Violence: The Politics of Personal Behaviour.* Cambridge: Polity Press, 1995.

Karl, Frederick. *Franz Kafka: Representative Man.* New York: Ticknor & Fields, 1991.

Karl, Frederick R. *George Eliot: Voice of a Century.* New York: W. W. Norton & Company, 1995.

Karpin, Michael, and Ina Friedman. *Murder in the Name of God: The Plot to Kill Yitzhak Rabin.* New York: Henry Holt and Company, 1998.

Karsh, Efraim, and Inari Rautsi. *Saddam Hussein: A Political Biography.* New York: The Free Press, 1991.

Kassindja, Fauziya, and Layli Miller Bashir. *Do They Hear You When You Cry?* New York: Delacorte Press, 1998.

Kates, Judith A., and Gail Twersky Reimer, eds. *Reading Ruth: Contemporary Women Reclaim a Sacred Story.* New York: Ballantine Books, 1994.

Kay, Dennis. *Shakespeare: His Life, Work and Era.* New York: William Morrow and Company, 1992.

Kazin, Alfred. "A Jew On Horseback." *The New York Review of Books* XLII, no. 11 (June 22, 1995), pp. 4–6.

———. *Writing Was Everything.* Cambridge: Harvard University Press, 1995.

Keane, John. *Tom Paine: A Political Life.* Boston: Little, Brown and Company, 1995.

Kedourie, Elie, ed. *Spain and the Jews: The Sephardi Experience 1492 and After.* New York: Thames and Hudson, 1992.

Kee, Robert. *The Laurel and the Ivy: The Story of Charles Steward Parnell and Irish Nationalism.* London: Hamish Hamilton, 1993.

Keegan, John. *A History of Warfare.* New York: Alfred A. Knopf, 1993.

Keegan, Susanne. *The Bride of the Wind: The Life of Alma Mahler.* New York: Viking, 1992.

Kelly, Aileen M. *Toward Another Shore: Russian Thinkers Between Necessity and Chance.* New Haven: Yale University Press, 1998.

Kelly, Michael. *Martyr's Day: Chronicle of a Small War.* New York: Random House, 1993.

Kenaz, Yehoshua. *The Way to the Cats.* Translated by Dalya Bilu. South Royalton, Vt.: Steerforth Press, 1994.

Keneally, Thomas. *Schindler's List.* New York: Simon & Schuster, 1992.

Kerlow, Eleanor. *Poisoned Ivy: How Egos, Ideology, and Power Politics Almost Ruined Harvard Law School.* New York: St. Martin's Press, 1994.

Kermode, Frank. *The Uses of Error.* Cambridge: Harvard University Press, 1991.

Kernan, Alvin. *Shakespeare, the King's Playwright: Theater in the Stuart Court, 1603–1613.* New Haven: Yale University Press, 1995.

Kerr, Philip. *Berlin Noir.* London: Penguin Books, 1993.

Kershaw, Anne, and Mary Lasovich. *Rock-A-Bye Baby: A Death Behind Bars.* Toronto: McClelland & Stewart, 1991.

Kershaw, Ian. *Hitler 1889–1936: Hubris.* New York: W. W. Norton & Company, 1999.

Khalidi, Rashid. *Palestinian Identity: The Construction of Modern National Conscience.* New York: Columbia University Press, 1997.

Khalifeh, Sahar. *Wild Thorns.* Translated by Trevor LeGassick and Elizabeth Fernea. New York: Olive Branch Press, 1991.

Khemir, Sabiha. *Waiting in the Future for the Past to Come.* London: Quartet Books, 1993.

Khilnani, Sunil. *The Idea of India.* New York: Farrar, Straus & Giroux, 1997.

Khoury, Elias. *Gates of the City.* Translated by Paula Haydar. Minneapolis: University of Minneapolis Press, 1993.

Kiberd, Declan. *Inventing Ireland: The Literature of the Modern Nation.* Cambridge: Harvard University Press, 1996.

Kimbrell, Andrew. *The Masculine Mystique: The Politics of Masculinity.* New York: Ballantine Books, 1995.

Kimche, David. *The Last Option: After Nasser, Arafat, and Saddam Hussein—The Quest for Peace in the Middle East.* New York: Charles Scribner's Sons, 1992.

Kimmerling, Baruch, and Joel S. Migdal. *Palestinians: The Making of a People.* New York: The Free Press, 1993.

Kincaid, James R. *Erotic Innocence: The Culture of Child Molesting.* Durham, N.C.: Duke University Press, 1998.

King, James. *Virginia Woolf.* New York: W. W. Norton & Company, 1995.

Kingsley, April. *The Turning Point: The Abstract Expressionists and the Transformation of American Art.* New York: Simon & Schuster, 1992.

Kinkead, Gwen. *Chinatown: A Portrait of a Closed Society.* New York: HarperCollins Publishers, 1992.

Kirsch, Jonathan. *Moses: A Life.* New York: Ballantine Books, 1998.

Kissinger, Henry. *Diplomacy.* New York: Simon & Schuster, 1994.

Klee, Ernst, Willi Dressen, and Volker Riess, eds. *"The Good Old Days": The Holocaust as*

Seen by Its Perpetrators and Bystanders. Translated by Deborah Burnstone. New York: The Free Press, 1991.

Klíma, Ivan. *Judge on Trial.* Translated by A. G. Brain. New York: Alfred A. Knopf, 1993.

———. *Waiting for the Dark, Waiting for the Light.* Translated by Paul Wilson. New York: Grove Press, 1995.

Klinghoffer, David. *The Lord Will Gather Me In: My Journey to Jewish Orthodoxy.* New York: The Free Press, 1999.

Klinkenborg, Verlyn. *The Last Fine Time.* New York: Alfred A. Knopf, 1991.

Knowlson, James. *Damned to Fame: The Life of Samuel Beckett.* New York: Simon & Schuster, 1996.

Knowlton, Janice, and Michael Newton. *Daddy Was the Black Dahlia Killer.* New York: Pocket Books, 1995.

Knox, Bernard. *The Oldest Dead White European Males.* New York: W. W. Norton & Company, 1993.

———. *Backing into the Future: The Classical Tradition and Its Renewal.* New York: W. W. Norton & Company, 1994.

Knox, Melissa. *Oscar Wilde: A Long and Lovely Suicide.* New Haven: Yale University Press, 1994.

Köhler, Joachim. *Nietzsche and Wagner: A Lesson in Subjugation.* Translated by Ronald Taylor. New Haven: Yale University Press, 1998.

Kohout, Pavel. *I Am Snowing: The Confessions of a Woman of Prague.* Translated by Neil Bermel. New York: Farrar, Straus & Giroux, 1994.

Konner, Melvin. *Why the Reckless Survive.* New York: Viking, 1990.

Konrád, George. *A Feast in the Garden.* Translated by Imre Goldstein. New York: Harcourt Brace Jovanovich, Publishers, 1992.

Koonz, Claudia. *Mothers in the Fatherland: Women, the Family and Nazi Politics.* New York: St. Martin's Press, 1986.

Koppelman, Andrew. "Why Discrimination Against Lesbians and Gay Men Is Sex Discrimination," *New York University Law Review* 69, no. 2 (May 1994), pp. 197–287.

Kors, Alan Charles, and Harvey A. Silverglate. *The Shadow University: The Betrayal of Liberty on America's Campuses.* New York: The Free Press, 1998.

Koso-Thomas, Olayinka. *The Circumcision of Women: A Strategy for Eradication.* London: Zed Books, 1987.

Kotkin, Joel. *Tribes: How Race, Religion, and Identity Determine Success in the New Global Economy.* New York: Random House, 1993.

Kramer, Jane. *The Politics of Memory: Looking for Germany in the New Germany.* New York: Random House, 1996.

Krautmanner, Charles. "At Last, Zion: Israel and the Fate of the Jews." *The Weekly Standard.* May 11, 1998, pp. 23–29.

Kristeva, Julia. *Time and Sense: Proust and the Experience of Literature.* Translated by Ross Guberman. New York: Columbia University Press, 1996.

Krüger, Michael. *The Man in the Tower.* Translated by Leslie Willson. New York: George Braziller, 1993.

Kundera, Milan. *Immortality.* Translated by Peter Kussi. New York: Grove Weidenfeld, 1991.

———. *Testaments Betrayed: An Essay in Nine Parts.* Translated by Linda Asher. New York: HarperCollins, 1995.

Kunstel, Marcia, and Joseph Albright. *Their Promised Land: Arab and Jew in History's Cauldron—One Valley in the Jerusalem Hills.* New York: Crown Publishers, 1990.

Kureishi, Hanif. *The Black Album.* New York: Scribner, 1995.

———. *The Buddha of Suburbia.* New York: Viking, 1990.

Kurlansky, Mark. *A Chosen Few: The Resurrection of European Jewry.* Reading, Mass.: Addison-Wesley Publishing Company, 1995.

Kurzman, Dan. *Blood and Water: Sabotaging Hitler's Bomb.* New York: Henry Holt and Company, 1997.

———. *The Bravest Battle: The 28 Days of the Warsaw Ghetto Uprising.* New York: Da Capo Press, 1993.

Kutler, Stanley I. *Abuses of Power: The New Nixon Tapes.* New York: The Free Press, 1997.

Kuttner, Paul. *The Holocaust: Hoax or History? The Book of Answers to Those Who Would Deny the Holocaust.* New York: Dawnwood Press, 1996.

L'Heureux, John. *An Honorable Profession.* New York: Viking, 1991.

La Grange, Henry-Louis de. *Gustave Mahler: Vienna: The Years of Challenge (1897–1904).* Oxford: Oxford University Press, 1995.

Lagnado, Lucette Matalon, and Sheila Cohn Dekel. *Children of the Flames: Dr. Josef Mengele and the Untold Story of the Twins of Auschwitz.* New York: William Morrow and Company, 1991.

Lamblin, Bianca. *A Disgraceful Affair: Simone de Beauvoir, Jean-Paul Sartre, & Bianca Lamblin.* Translated by Julie Plovnick. Boston: Northeastern University Press, 1996.

Landau, David. *Piety and Power: The World of Jewish Fundamentalism.* New York: Hill and Wang, 1993.

Langer, Lawrence L. *Admitting the Holocaust: Collected Essays.* New York: Oxford University Press, 1995.

———. *Holocaust Testimonies: The Ruins of Memory.* New Haven: Yale University Press, 1991.

Langer, Lawrence L., ed. *Art from the Ashes: A Holocaust Anthology.* New York: Oxford University Press, 1995.

Langewiesche, William. *Cutting for Sign.* New York: Pantheon, 1994.

Lansbury, Coral. *The Old Brown Dog: Women, Workers, and Vivisection in Edwardian England.* Madison: The University of Wisconsin Press, 1985.

Lapierre, Alexandra. *Fanny Stevenson: A Romance of Destiny.* New York: Carroll & Graf Publishers, 1995.

Laqueur, Walter. *Black Hundred: The Rise of the Extreme Right in Russia.* New York: Harper-Collins Publishers, 1993.

———. *The Dream That Failed: Reflections on the Soviet Union.* New York: Oxford University Press, 1994.

———. *Fascism: Past, Present, Future.* New York: Oxford University Press, 1996.

———. *The Terrible Secret: Suppression of the Truth about Hitler's "Final Solution."* New York: Penguin Books, 1980.

———. *Thursday's Child Has Far To Go: A Memoir of the Journeying Years.* New York: Charles Scribner's Sons, 1993.

Large, David Clay. *Where Ghosts Walked: Munich's Road to the Third Reich.* New York: W. W. Norton & Company, 1997.

Larina, Anna. *This I Cannot Forget: The Memoirs of Nikolai Bukharin's Widow.* Translated by Gary Kern. New York: W. W. Norton & Company, 1993.

Lasch, Christopher. *The Revolt of the Elites and the Betrayal of Democracy.* New York: W. W. Norton & Company, 1995.

———. *Women and the Common Life: Love, Marriage, and Feminism.* Edited by Elisabeth Lasch-Quinn. New York: W. W. Norton & Company, 1997.

Laska, Vera, ed. *Women in the Resistance and in the Holocaust.* Westport, Conn.: Greenwood Press, 1983.

Lazare, Lucien. *Rescue as Resistance: How Jewish Organizations Fought the Holocaust in France.* Translated by Jeffrey M. Green. New York: Columbia University Press, 1996.

Le Carré, John. *Our Game.* New York: Alfred A. Knopf, 1995.

———. *The Night Manager.* New York: Alfred A. Knopf, 1993.

Le Clézio, J. M. G. *The Mexican Dream Or, The Interrupted Thought of Amerindian Civilizations.* Translated by Teresa Lavender Fagan. Chicago: The University of Chicago Press, 1993.

Leakey, Richard. *The Origin of Humankind.* New York: Basic Books, 1994.

Leakey, Richard, and Roger Lewin. *Origins Reconsidered: In Search of What Makes Us Human.* New York: Doubleday, 1992.

Lee, Butch, and Red Rover. *Night-Vision: Illuminating War and Class on the Neo-Colonial Terrain.* New York: Vagabond Press, 1993.

Lee, Hugh, ed. *A Cezanne in the Hedge and Other Memories of Charleston and Bloomsbury.* Chicago: The University of Chicago Press, 1992.

Lee, Lilian. *The Last Princess of Manchuria.* Translated by Andrea Kelly. New York: William Morrow and Company, 1992.

Lee, Martin A. *The Beast Reawakens.* Boston: Little, Brown and Company, 1997.

Leeming, David. *James Baldwin: A Biography.* New York: Alfred A. Knopf, 1994.

Lees, Sue. *Ruling Passions: Sexual Violence, Reputation and the Law.* Buckingham, England: Open University Press, 1997.

Leff, Leonard J. *Hemingway and His Conspirators: Hollywood, Scribners, and the Making of American Celebrity Culture.* Lanham, Md.: Rowman & Littlefield Publishers, 1997.

Lefkowitz, Bernard. *Our Guys: The Glen Ridge Rape and the Secret Life of the Perfect Suburbs.* Berkeley: University of California Press, 1997.

Lefkowitz, Mary. *Not Out of Africa: How Afrocentrism Became an Excuse to Teach Myth as History.* New York: Basic Books, 1996.

Legman, Gershon. *Love and Death: A Study in Censorship.* New York: Hacker Art Books, 1963.

Lehman, David. *Signs of the Times.* New York: Poseidon Press, 1991.

Lenz, Siegfried. *The Training Ground.* Translated by Geoffrey Skelton. New York: Henry Holt and Company, 1991.

Lerner, Gerda. *The Creation of Feminist Consciousness From the Middle Ages to Eighteen-seventy.* New York: Oxford University Press, 1993.

———. *Why History Matters: Life and Thought.* New York: Oxford University Press, 1997.

Lerner, Michael, and Cornel West. *Jews and Blacks: Let the Healing Begin.* New York: G. P. Putnam's Sons, 1995.

Leshem, Moshe. *Israel Alone: How the Jewish State Lost Its Way and How It Can Find It Again.* New York: Simon & Schuster, 1989.

Lesmine, Aicha. *The Chrysalis.* Translated by Dorothy S. Blair. London: Quartet Books, 1993.

Lessing, Doris. *African Laughter: Four Visits to Zimbabwe.* New York: HarperCollins Publishers, 1992.

Leverich, Lyle. *Tom: The Unknown Tennessee Williams.* New York: Crown Publishers, 1995.

Levi, Peter. *Tennyson.* New York: Charles Scribner's Sons, 1993.

Levin, Gail. *Edward Hopper: An Intimate Biography.* New York: Alfred A. Knopf, 1995.

Levin, Nora. *The Holocaust: The Destruction of European Jewry 1933–1945.* New York: Schocken Books, 1973.

Levy, Leonard W. *Blasphemy: Verbal Offense Against the Sacred from Moses to Salman Rushdie.* New York: Alfred A. Knopf, 1993.

Lewin, Abraham. *A Cup of Tears: A Diary of the Warsaw Ghetto.* Edited by Antony Polonsky. Translated by Christopher Hutton. Oxford: Basil Blackwell, 1988.

Lewis, Bernard. *Islam and the West.* New York: Oxford University Press, 1993.

———. *Semites and Anti-Semites: An Inquiry into Conflict and Prejudice.* New York: W. W. Norton & Company, 1987.

———. *The Middle East: A Brief History of the Last 2,000 Years.* New York: Scribner, 1995.

Lewis, David Levering. *Prisoners of Honor: The Dreyfus Affair.* New York: Henry Holt and Company, 1994.

———. *W. E. B. Du Bois: Biography of a Race 1868–1919.* New York: Henry Holt and Company, 1993.

Lewis, Norman. *The Missionaries.* London: Secker & Warburg, 1988.

Lewis, R. W. B. *The City of Florence: Historical Vistas and Personal Sightings.* New York: Farrar, Straus & Giroux, 1995.

Lewis, Thomas A. *For King and Country: The Maturing of George Washington 1748–1760.* New York: HarperCollins Publishers, 1993.

Leyton, Elliott. *Men of Blood: Murder in Modern England.* London: Constable, 1995.

Lieven, Dominic. *Nicholas II: Twilight of the Empire.* New York: St. Martin's Press, 1994.

Lifton, Robert Jay. *The Nazi Doctors: Medical Killing and the Psychology of Genocide.* New York: Basic Books, 1986.

———. *The Protean Self: Human Resilience in an Age of Fragmentation.* New York: Basic Books, 1993.

Lind, Michael. *The Next American Nation: The New Nationalism and the Fourth American Revolution.* New York: The Free Press, 1995.

———. *Up From Conservatism: Why the Right Is Wrong for America.* New York: The Free Press, 1996.

Lindemann, Albert S. *The Jew Accused: Three Anti-Semitic Affairs (Dreyfus, Beilis, Frank) 1894–1915.* Cambridge: Cambridge University Press, 1993.

Lindqvist, Sven. *"Exterminate All the Brutes": One Man's Odyssey into the Heart of Darkness and the Origins of European Genocide.* Translated by Joan Tate. New York: The New Press, 1996.

Lipstadt, Deborah. *Denying the Holocaust: The Growing Assault on Truth and Memory.* New York: The Free Press, 1993.

Lively, Penelope. *Oleander, Jacaranda: A Childhood Perceived.* New York: HarperCollins, 1994.

Lloyd, Ann. *Doubly Deviant, Doubly Damned: Society's Treatment of Violent Women.* London: Penguin Books, 1995.

Loftus, John, and Mark Aarons. *The Secret War Against the Jews: How Western Espionage Betrayed the Jewish People.* New York: St. Martin's Press, 1994.

Lord, James. *Picasso and Dora: A Personal Memoir.* New York: Farrar, Straus & Giroux, 1993.

———. *Six Exceptional Women: Further Memoirs.* New York: Farrar, Straus & Giroux, 1994.

Lottman, Herbert. *Colette: A Life.* Boston: Little, Brown and Company, 1991.

———. *The Fall of Paris: June 1940.* New York: HarperCollins Publishers, 1992.

Lottman, Herbert R. *The French Rothschilds: The Great Banking Dynasty Through Two Turbulent Centuries.* New York: Crown Publishers, 1995.

Loughery, John. *John Sloan: Painter and Rebel.* New York: Henry Holt and Company, 1995.

Loury, Glenn C. *One by One From the Inside Out: Essays and Reviews on Race and Responsibility in America.* New York: The Free Press, 1995.

Louvish, Simon. *The Silencer.* New York: Interlink Books, 1993.

Lukacs, John. *Confessions of an Original Sinner.* New York: Ticknor & Fields, 1990.

———. *The Hitler of History.* New York: Alfred A. Knopf, 1997.

Lynd, Straughton, Sam Bahour, and Alice Lynd, eds. *Homeland: Oral Histories of Palestine and Palestinians.* New York: Olive Branch Press, 1994.

Lyons, Matthew. *Right Woos Left Revisited: Tracing the Roots of Conspiracy Thinking.* Broadside, pp. 1–15.

Lyons, Matthew Nemiroff. "Parasites and Pioneers: Anti-Semitism in White Supremacy." *The Third Wave.* Edited by Albrecht, Alarcon, Alexandeer, Day, and Segest. New York: Kitchen Table: Women of Color Press, 1992.

Maalouf, Amin. *Leo the African.* Translated by Peter Sluglett. London: Quartet Books, 1988.

———. *Samarkand.* Translated by Russell Harris. London: Quartet Books, 1992.

———. *The Crusades Through Arab Eyes.* Translated by Jon Rothschild. New York: Schocken Books, 1985.

Mabee, Carleton, and Susan Mabee Newhouse. *Sojourner Truth: Slave, Prophet, Legend.* New York: New York University Press, 1993.

MacCarthy, Fiona. *William Morris: A Life for Our Times.* New York: Alfred A. Knopf, 1995.

Macdonald, Andrew (William Pierce). *The Turner Diaries.* Hillsboro, W.Va.: National Vanguard Books, 1990.

MacDonald, Eileen. *Shoot the Women First.* New York: Random House, 1992.

MacDonogh, Giles. *A Good German: Adam von Trott zu Solz.* Woodstock, N.Y.: The Overlook Press, 1992.

Macey, David. *The Lives of Michel Foucault.* New York: Pantheon Books, 1994.

Macintyre, Ben. *Forgotten Fatherland: The Search for Elisabeth Nietzsche.* New York: Farrar, Straus & Giroux, 1992.

Mackey, Sandra. *Passion and Politics: The Turbulent World of the Arabs.* New York: Dutton, 1992.

MacKinnon, Catharine A. "Rape, Genocide, and Women's Rights." *Ms.* 1993, pp. 24–30.

MacMillan, Ian. *Orbit of Darkness.* New York: Harcourt Brace Jovanovich, 1991.

Maddox, Brenda. *D. H. Lawrence: The Story of a Marriage.* New York: Simon & Schuster, 1994.

Mahfouz, Naguib. *Adrift on the Nile.* Translated by Frances Liardet. New York: Doubleday, 1993.

———. *Arabian Nights and Days.* Translated by Denys Johnson-Davies. New York: Doubleday, 1995.

———. *Children of Gebelaawi.* Translated by Philip Stewart. Rev. ed. Washington, D.C.: Three Continents Press, 1990.

———. *Children of the Alley.* Translated by Peter Theroux. New York: Doubleday, 1996.

———. *Fountain and Tomb.* Translated by Soad Sobhy, Essam Fattouh, and James Kenneson. Washington, D.C.: Three Continents Press, 1988.

———. *Palace of Desire.* Translated by William Maynard Hutchins, Lorne M. Kenny, and Olive E. Kenny. New York: Doubleday, 1991.

———. *Palace Walk.* Translated by William M. Hutchins and Olive E. Kenny. New York: Doubleday, 1990.

———. *Sugar Street.* Translated by William Maynard Hutchins and Angela Botros Samaan. New York: Doubleday, 1992.

———. *The Beggar.* Translated by Kristin Walker Henry and Mariman Khales Naili al-Warraki. New York: Anchor Books/Doubleday, 1990.

———. *The Beginning and the End.* Translated by Ramses Awad. Edited by Mason Rossiter Smith. New York: Anchor Books/Doubleday, 1989.

———. *The Harafish.* Translated by Catherine Cobham. New York: Doubleday, 1994.

———. *The Journey of Ibn Fattouma.* Translated by Denys Johnson-Davies. New York: Doubleday, 1992.

———. *Wedding Song.* Translated by Olive E. Kenny. Edited and revised by Mursi Saad El Din and John Rodenbeck. New York: Doubleday/Anchor Books, 1989.

Majid, Anouar. *Si Yussef.* London: Quartet Books, 1992.

Makiya, Kanan (Samir Al-Khalil). *Cruelty and Silence: War, Tyranny, Uprising and the Arab World.* New York: W. W. Norton & Company, 1993.

Malan, Rian. *My Traitor's Heart.* New York: Vintage Books, 1991.

Malkin, Peter Z., and Harry Stein. *Eichmann in My Hands.* New York: Warner Books, 1990.

Mallaby, Sebastian. *After Apartheid: The Future of South Africa.* New York: Times Books, 1992.

Malouf, David. *Remembering Babylon.* New York: Pantheon Books, 1993.

Mamet, David. *The Cabin.* New York: Turtle Bay Books, 1992.

———. *The Old Religion.* New York: The Free Press, 1997. Proofs.

Mangold, Tom. *Cold Warrior: James Jesus Angleton: The CIA's Master Spy Hunter.* New York: Simon & Schuster, 1991.

Manrique, Jaime. *Latin Moon in Manhattan.* New York: St. Martin's Press, 1992.

Mansfield, Peter. *A History of the Middle East.* New York: Viking, 1991.

Manuel, Frank E. *A Requiem for Karl Marx.* Cambridge: Harvard University Press, 1995.

Margalit, Avishai. *Views in Review: Politics and Culture in the State of the Jews.* New York: Farrar, Straus & Giroux, 1998.

Mariani, Paul. *Lost Puritan: A Life of Robert Lowell.* New York: W. W. Norton & Company, 1994.

Marino, Andy. *Herschel: The Boy Who Started World War II.* London: Faber and Faber, 1995.

Marks, Jane. *The Hidden Children: The Secret Survivors of the Holocaust.* New York: Fawcett Columbine, 1993.

Marks, Richard Lee. *Cortés: The Great Adventurer and the Fate of Aztec Mexico.* New York: Alfred A. Knopf, 1993.

Markus, Julia. *Dared and Done: The Marriage of Elizabeth Barrett and Robert Browning.* New York: Alfred A. Knopf, 1995.

Markusen, Eric, and David Kopf. *The Holocaust and Strategic Bombing: Genocide and Total War in the Twentieth Century.* Boulder, Colo.: Westview Press, 1995.

Marnham, Patrick. *The Man Who Wasn't Maigret: A Portrait of Georges Simenon.* New York: Farrar, Straus & Giroux, 1993.

Marr, David. *Patrick White: A Life.* New York: Alfred A. Knopf, 1992.

Marsh, Jan. *Christina Rossetti: A Writer's Life.* New York: Viking, 1995.

Marshall, Robert. *In the Sewers of Lvov: A Heroic Story of Survival From the Holocaust.* New York: Charles Scribner's Sons, 1991.

Martin, Robert Bernard. *Gerard Manley Hopkins: A Very Private Life.* New York: G. P. Putnam's Sons, 1991.

Marton, Kati. *A Death in Jerusalem: The Assassination by Jewish Extremists of the First Arab/Is-raeli Peacemaker.* New York: Pantheon Books, 1994.

Masson, Jeffrey Moussaieff. *My Father's Guru: A Journey Through Spirituality and Disillusion.* Reading, Mass.: Addison-Wesley Publishing Company, 1993.

Mathews, Nancy Mowll. *Mary Cassatt: A Life.* New York: Villard Books, 1994.

Matthiessen, Peter. *African Silences.* New York: Random House, 1991.

Mayer, Arno J. *Why Did the Heavens Not Darken? The "Final Solution" in History.* New York: Pantheon Books, 1988.

Mayer, Jane, and Jill Abramson. *Strange Justice: The Selling of Clarence Thomas.* Boston: Houghton Mifflin Company, 1994.

Mazer, Norma Fox. *Out of Control.* New York: Morrow Junior Books, 1993.

McBride, James. *The Color of Water: A Black Man's Tribute to His White Mother.* New York: Riverhead Books, 1996.

McCall, Nathan. *Makes Me Wanna Holler: A Young Black Man in America.* New York: Random House, 1994.

McCarthy, Cormac. *All the Pretty Horses.* New York: Alfred A. Knopf, 1992.

———. *Blood Meridian or the Evening Redness in the West.* New York: Vintage International, 1992.

McCarthy, Mary. *Intellectual Memoirs: New York 1936–1938.* New York: Harcourt Brace Jo-vanovich, Publishers, 1992.

McClintock, Michael. *Instruments of Statecraft: U.S. Guerrilla Warfare, Counter-insurgency, and Counter-terrorism, 1940–1990.* New York: Pantheon Books, 1992.

McCourt, Frank. *Angela's Ashes: A Memoir.* New York: Scribner, 1996.

McCrumb, Sharyn. *If I'd Killed Him When I Met Him . . .* New York: Fawcett Gold Medal, 1995.

McDowall, David. *Palestine and Israel: The Uprising and Beyond.* Berkeley: University of California, 1989.

McEwan, Ian. *Black Dogs.* New York: Nan A. Talese/Doubleday, 1992.

McFeely, William S. *Frederick Douglass.* New York: W. W. Norton & Company, 1991.

McGinn, Bernard. *Antichrist: Two Thousand Years of the Human Fascination with Evil.* San Francisco: HarperCollins, 1994.

McLaughlin, Jack. *Jefferson and Monticello: The Biography of a Builder.* New York: Henry Holt and Company, 1990.

McLynn, Frank. *Robert Louis Stevenson: A Biography.* New York: Random House, 1994.

McPhilemy, Sean. *The Committee: Political Assassination in Northern Ireland.* Niwot, Colo.: Roberts Rinehart Publishers, 1998.

Mee, Charles L., Jr. *Playing God: Seven Fateful Moments When Great Men Met to Change the World.* New York: Simon & Schuster, 1993.

Mehlman, Jeffrey, "Foreword," pp. ix–xxv, in Pierre Vidal-Naquet. *Assassins of Memory: Essays on the Denial of the Holocaust.* Translated by Jeffrey Mehlman. New York: Columbia University Press, 1992.

Mehta, Gita. *A River Sutra.* New York: Nan A. Talese, 1993.

Meier, John P. *A Marginal Jew: Rethinking the Historical Jesus.* Vol. 1. New York: Doubleday, 1991.

Meier, Lili, and Peter Hellman. *The Auschwitz Album.* New York: Random House, 1981.

Melich, Tanya. *The Republican War Against Women: An Insider's Report from Behind the Lines.* New York: Bantam Books, 1996.

Mellah, Awzi. *Elissa.* Translated by Howard Curtis. London: Quartet Books, 1990.

Mellen, Joan. *Hellman and Hammett: The Legendary Passion of Lillian Hellman and Dashiell Hammett.* New York: HarperCollins, 1996.

———. *Kay Boyle: Author of Herself.* New York: Farrar, Straus & Giroux, 1994.

Mellow, James R. *Hemingway: A Life Without Consequences.* Boston: Houghton Mifflin Company, 1992.

Melman, Yossi. *The New Israelis: An Intimate View of a Changing People.* New York: Carol Publishing Company, 1993.

Mendels, Doron. *The Rise and Fall of Jewish Nationalism: Jewish and Christian Ethnicity in Ancient Palestine.* New York: Doubleday, 1992.

Mendelssohn, Moses. *Jerusalem or On Religious Power and Judaism*. Translated by Allan Arkush. Hanover, N.H.: University Press of New England, 1983.

Mernissi, Fatima. *Dreams of Trespass: Tales of a Harem Childhood*. Reading, Mass.: Addison-Wesley Publishing Company, 1994.

———. *Islam and Democracy: Fear of the Modern World*. Translated by Mary Jo Lakeland. New York: Addison-Wesley Publishing Company, 1992.

———. *The Veil and the Male Elite: A Feminist Interpretation of Women's Rights in Islam*. Translated by Mary Jo Lakeland. New York: Addison-Wesley Publishing Company, 1991.

Meyers, Jeffrey. *Edgar Allan Poe: His Life and Legacy*. New York: Charles Scribner's Sons, 1992.

———. *Edmund Wilson: A Biography*. Boston: Houghton Mifflin Company, 1995.

———. *Joseph Conrad*. New York: Charles Scribner's Sons, 1991.

———. *Scott Fitzgerald: A Biography*. New York: HarperCollins Publishers, Inc., 1994.

Michaels, Anne. *Fugitive Pieces*. Toronto: McClelland & Stewart, 1996.

Michaud, Stephen G., and Roy Hazelwood. *The Evil That Men Do: FBI Profiler Roy Hazelwood's Journey into the Minds of Sexual Predators*. New York: St. Martin's Press, 1998.

Michel, Jean. *Dora: The Nazi Concentration Camp Where Modern Space Technology Was Born and 30,000 Prisoners Died*. Translated by Jennifer Kidd. New York: Holt, Rinehart and Winston, 1979.

Michell, John. *Who Wrote Shakespeare?* London: Thames and Hudson, 1996.

Michnik, Adam. *The Church and the Left*. Translated by David Ost. Chicago: The University of Chicago Press, 1993.

Middlebrook, Diane Wood. *Anne Sexton*. Boston: Houghton Mifflin Company, 1991.

Miles, Jack. *God: A Biography*. New York: Alfred A. Knopf, 1995.

Millan, Gordon. *A Throw of the Dice: The Life of Stéphane Mallarmé*. New York: Farrar, Straus & Giroux, 1994.

Miller, Alice. *Banished Knowledge: Facing Childhood Injuries*. Translated by Leila Vennewitz. New York: Doubleday, 1990.

———. *The Untouched Key*. Translated by Hildegarde and Hunter Hannum. New York: Doubleday, 1990.

Miller, Chris, ed. *The Dissident Word: Oxford Amnesty Lectures*. New York: Basic Books, 1996.

Miller, Dan B. *Erskine Caldwell: The Journey from Tobacco Road*. New York: Alfred A. Knopf, 1995.

Miller, Edwin Haviland. *Salem Is My Dwelling Place: A Life of Nathaniel Hawthorne*. Iowa City: University of Iowa Press, 1991.

Miller, James. *The Passion of Michel Foucault*. New York: Simon & Schuster, 1993.

Miller, Judith. *God Has Ninety-Nine Names: Reporting from a Militant Middle East*. New York: Simon & Schuster, 1996.

———. *One, by One, by One: Facing the Holocaust*. New York: Simon & Schuster, 1990.

Miller, William Lee. *Arguing About Slavery: The Great Battle in the United States Congress*. New York: Alfred A. Knopf, 1996.

Millett, Kate. *The Politics of Cruelty: An Essay on the Literature of Political Imprisonment*. New York: W. W. Norton & Company, 1994.

Millier, Brett C. *Elizabeth Bishop: Life and the Memory of It*. Berkeley: University of California, 1993.

Mills, Kay. *This Little Light of Mine: The Life of Fannie Lou Hamer*. New York: Dutton, 1993.

Milosz, Czeslaw. *Beginning With My Streets*. Translated by Madeline G. Levine. New York: Farrar, Straus & Giroux, 1991.

Min, Anchee. *Red Azalea*. New York: Pantheon Books, 1994.

Mitford, Jessica. *Daughters and Rebels: An Autobiography*. New York: Holt, Rinehart and Winston, 1981.

Mitterrand, François, and Elie Wiesel. *Memoir in Two Voices*. Translated by Richard Seaver and Timothy Bent. New York: Arcade Publishing, 1996.

Mommsen, Hans. *The Rise and Fall of Weimar Democracy*. Translated by Elborg Forster and Larry Eugene Jones. Chapel Hill: The University of North Carolina Press, 1996.

Monk, Ray. *Bertrand Russell: The Spirit of Solitude 1872–1921*. New York: The Free Press, 1996.

Moorcock, Michael. *Behold the Man.* Austin, Tex.: Mojo Press, 1996.

———. *Blood: A Southern Fantasy.* London: Millennium, 1994.

———. *Fabulous Harbours.* London: Millennium, 1995.

———. *Lunching with the Antichrist: A Family History.* Shingletown, Calif.: Mark V. Ziesing, 1995.

———. *The Revenge of the Rose: A Tale of the Albino Prince in the Years of His Wandering.* Glasgow: Grafton Books, 1991.

———. *The War Amongst the Angels.* London: Millennium, 1996.

Moore, Brian. *Lies of Silence.* New York: Doubleday, 1990.

———. *No Other Life.* New York: Doubleday, 1993.

Moorehead, Caroline. *Bertrand Russell: A Life.* New York: Viking, 1993.

Moraga, Cherrie, and Gloria Anzaldua, eds. *This Bridge Called My Back: Writings by Radical Women of Color.* Watertown, Mass.: Persephone Press, 1981.

Morgan, Robin. *A Hot January: Poems 1996–1999.* New York: W. W. Norton & Company, 1999.

———. *The Demon Lover: On the Sexuality of Terrorism.* New York: W. W. Norton & Company, 1989.

———. *The Word of a Woman: Feminist Dispatches 1968–1992.* New York: W. W. Norton & Company, 1992.

Morris, David B. *The Culture of Pain.* Berkeley: University of California Press, 1991.

Morris, Roy, Jr. *Ambrose Bierce: Alone in Bad Company.* New York: Crown Publishers, 1995.

Morrison, Toni. *Jazz.* New York: Alfred A. Knopf, 1992.

———. *Paradise.* New York: Alfred A. Knopf, 1998.

———. *Playing in the Dark: Whiteness and the Literary Imagination.* Cambridge: Harvard University Press, 1992.

Morton, Brian. *The Dylanist.* New York: HarperCollins Publishers, 1991.

Mosley, Walter. *Black Betty.* New York: W. W. Norton & Company, 1994.

———. *RL's Dream.* New York: W. W. Norton & Company, 1995.

Mostert, Noel. *Frontiers: The Epic of South Africa's Creation and the Tragedy of the Xhosa People.* New York: Alfred A. Knopf, 1992.

Motion, Andrew. *Philip Larkin: A Writer's Life.* New York: Farrar, Straus & Giroux, 1993.

Moyahan, Brian. *Rasputin: The Saint Who Sinned.* New York: Random House, 1997.

Mukherjee, Bharati. *The Holder of the World.* New York: Alfred A. Knopf, 1993.

Müller, Ingo. *Hitler's Justice: The Courts of the Third Reich.* Translated by Deborah Lucas Schneider. Cambridge: Harvard University Press, 1991.

Muller, Melissa. *Anne Frank: The Biography.* Translated by Rita and Robert Kimber. New York: Henry Holt and Company, 1998.

Mullins, Edwin. *The Painted Witch: How Western Artists Have Viewed the Sexuality of Women.* New York: Carroll & Graf Publishers, 1985.

Munif, Abdelrahman. *Cities of Salt.* Translated by Peter Theroux. New York: Vintage International, 1989.

———. *The Trench.* Translated by Peter Theroux. New York: Pantheon Books, 1991.

———. *Variations on Night and Day.* Translated by Peter Theroux. New York: Pantheon Books, 1993.

Murdoch, Iris. *The Green Knight.* New York: Viking, 1993.

Naipaul, V. S. *A Way in the World.* New York: Alfred A. Knopf, 1994.

———. *Beyond Belief: Islamic Excursions Among the Converted Peoples.* New York: Random House, 1998.

———. *India: A Million Mutinies Now.* New York: Viking, 1990.

Narasimhan, Sakuntala. *Sati: Widow Burning in India.* New York: Doubleday, 1992.

Nasrallah, Ibrahim. *Prairies of Fever.* Translated by May Jayyusi and Jeremy Reed. New York: Interlink Books, 1993.

Naylor, Gloria. *Bailey's Cafe.* New York: Harcourt Brace Jovanovich, 1992.

Neely, Mark E., Jr. *The Last Best Hope of Earth: Abraham Lincoln and the Promise of America.* Cambridge: Harvard University Press, 1993.

Nelson, Jack. *Terror in the Night: The Klan's Campaign Against the Jews.* New York: Simon & Schuster, 1993.

Nelson, Jill. *Volunteer Slavery: My Authentic Negro Experience.* New York: Penguin Books, 1994.

Nesaule, Agate. *A Woman in Amber: Healing the Trauma of War and Exile.* New York: Soho, 1995.

Netanyahu, B. *The Origins of the Inquisition in Fifteenth Century Spain.* New York: Random House, 1995.

Netanyahu, Benjamin. *A Place Among the Nations: Israel and the World.* New York: Bantam Books, 1993.

————. *Fighting Terrorism: How Democracies Can Defeat Domestic and International Terrorism.* New York: Farrar, Straus & Giroux, 1995.

Newton, Verne W. *The Cambridge Spies.* Lanham, Md.: Madison Books, 1991.

Nicholas, Lynn H. *The Rape of Europa: The Fate of Europe's Treasures in the Third Reich and the Second World War.* New York: Alfred A. Knopf, 1994.

Nicholl, Charles. *The Reckoning: The Murder of Christopher Marlowe.* London: Jonathan Cape, 1992.

Nicol, Mike. *This Day and Age.* New York: Alfred A. Knopf, 1992.

Niel, Jean-Baptiste. *Painted Shadows.* Translated by James Kirkup. London: Quartet Books, 1991.

Nightingale, Carl Husemoller. *On the Edge: A History of Poor Black Children and Their American Dreams.* New York: Basic Books, 1993.

Nochlin, Linda. *Representing Women.* London: Thames and Hudson, 1999.

Noll, Richard. *The Aryan Christ: The Secret Life of Carl Jung.* New York: Random House, 1997.

Norman, Howard. *The Bird Artist.* New York: Farrar, Straus & Giroux, 1994.

Norris, Kathleen. *Amazing Grace: A Vocabulary of Faith.* New York: Riverhead Books, 1998.

————. *The Cloister Walk.* New York: Riverhead Books, 1996.

————. *Dakota: A Spiritual Biography.* New York: Ticknor & Fields, 1993.

Norton, Caroline. *Caroline Norton's Defence: English Laws for Women in the Nineteenth Century.* Chicago: Academy Chicago, 1982.

Norwich, John Julius. *Byzantium: The Apogee.* New York: Alfred A. Knopf, 1992.

Nossiter, Adam. *Of Long Memory: Mississippi and the Murder of Medgar Evers.* Reading, Mass.: Addison-Wesley Publishing Company, 1994.

Novac, Ana. *The Beautiful Days of My Youth: My Six Months in Auschwitz and Plaszow.* Translated by George L. Newman. New York: Henry Holt and Company, 1997.

Novick, Sheldon M. *Henry James: The Young Master.* New York: Random House, 1996.

Nussbaum, Martha C. *Sex and Social Justice.* New York: Oxford University Press, 1999.

Nye, Robert. *The Life and Death of My Lord Gilles de Rais.* London: Hamish Hamilton, 1990.

Nyiszli, Miklos. *Auschwitz: A Doctor's Eyewitness Account.* Translated by Tibère Kremer and Richard Seaver. New York: Arcade Publishing, 1993.

O'Brian, Patrick. *Picasso: A Biography.* New York: W. W. Norton & Company, 1976.

O'Brien, Conor Cruise. *The Great Melody: A Thematic Biography of Edmund Burke.* Chicago: The University of Chicago Press, 1992.

————. *The Long Affair: Thomas Jefferson and the French Revolution 1785–1800.* Chicago: The University of Chicago Press, 1996.

O'Brien, Edna. *House of Splendid Isolation.* New York: Farrar, Straus & Giroux, 1994.

————. *Time and Tide.* New York: Farrar, Straus & Giroux, 1992.

O'Brien, George. *The Village of Longing and Dancehall Days.* New York: Viking/The Lilliput Press, 1988.

O'Brien, Tim. *In the Lake of the Woods.* Boston: Houghton Mifflin/Seymour Lawrence, 1994.

O'Brien, William V. *Law and Morality in Israel's War With the PLO.* New York: Routledge, 1991.

O'Connor, Flannery. *Conversations with Flannery O'Connor.* Edited by Rosemary N. Magee. Mississippi: University of Mississippi, 1987.

Oates, Joyce Carol. *Black Water.* New York: Dutton, 1992.

————. *Foxfire: Confessions of a Girl Gang.* New York: Dutton, 1993.

Oë, Kenzaburo. *A Personal Matter.* Translated by John Nathan. New York: Grove Weidenfeld, 1982.

————. *Nip the Buds, Shoot the Kids.* Translated by Paul St. John Mackintosh and Maki Sugiyama. London: Marion Boyars, 1995.

Ofer, Dalia, and Lenore J. Weitman, eds. *Women in the Holocaust.* New Haven: Yale University Press, 1998.

Okri, Ben. *The Famished Road.* New York: Nan A. Talese, 1992.

Oliver, Roland. *The African Experience: Major Themes in African History from Earliest Times to the Present.* New York: Icon Editions, 1992.

Olson, Elizabeth. "U.N. Urges Fiscal Accounting Include Sex Trade." *The New York Times.* August 20, 1998.

Olson, Toby. *At Sea.* New York: Simon & Schuster, 1993.

Ondaatje, Michael. *The English Patient.* New York: Alfred A. Knopf, 1992.

Oppenheimer, Andres. *Castro's Final Hour: The Secret Story Behind the Coming Downfall of Communist Cuba.* New York: Simon & Schuster, 1992.

Ostrovsky, Victor, and Claire Hoy. *By Way of Deception: The Making and Unmaking of a Mossad Officer.* New York: St. Martin's Press, 1990.

Ostrovsky, Victor. *Lion of Judah: A Novel of the Mossad.* New York: St. Martin's Press, 1993.

————. *The Other Side of Deception: A Rogue Agent Exposes the Mossad's Secret Agenda.* New York: HarperCollins, 1994.

Ott, Hugo. *Martin Heidegger: A Political Life.* Translated by Allan Blunden. New York: Basic Books, 1993.

Owings, Alison. *Frauen: German Women Recall the Third Reich.* New Brunswick, N.J.: Rutgers University Press, 1993.

Oz, Amos. *Black Box.* Translated by Nicholas de Lange. New York: Vintage Books, 1989.

————. *Don't Call It Night.* Translated by Nicholas de Lange. New York: Harcourt Brace & Company, 1996.

————. *Elsewhere, Perhaps.* Translated by Nicholas de Lange and Amos Oz. New York: Harcourt Brace Jovanovich, Publishers, 1973.

————. *Fima.* Translated by Nicholas de Lange. New York: Harcourt Brace & Company, 1993.

————. *In the Land of Israel.* Translated by Maurie Goldberg-Bartura. New York: Vintage Books, 1984.

————. *Israel, Palestine and Peace: Essays.* New York: Harcourt Brace & Company, 1995.

————. *My Michael.* Translated by Nicholas de Lange and Amos Oz. New York: Vintage Books, 1992.

————. *Panther in the Basement.* Translated by Nicholas de Lange. New York: Harcourt Brace & Company, 1997.

————. *The Slopes of Lebanon.* Translated by Maurie Goldberg-Bartura. New York: Harcourt Brace Jovanovich, Publishers, 1989.

————. *The Story Begins: Essays on Literature.* Translated by Maggie Bar-Tura. New York: Harcourt Brace & Company, 1999.

————. *To Know a Woman.* Translated by Nicholas de Lange. New York: Harcourt Brace Jovanovich, Publishers, 1991.

————. *Touch the Water, Touch the Wind.* Translated by Nicholas de Lange and Amos Oz. New York: Harcourt Brace Jovanovich, 1974.

————. *Under This Blazing Light: Essays.* Translated by Nicholas de Lange. Cambridge: Cambridge University Press, 1995.

————. *Unto Death: Crusade and Late Love.* Translated by Nicholas de Lange and Amos Oz. New York: Harcourt Brace Jovanovich, Publishers, 1978.

Ozick, Cynthia. *Fame and Folly.* New York: Alfred A. Knopf, 1996.

————. *The Shawl.* New York: Alfred A. Knopf, 1989.

Ozment, Steven. *The Bürgermeister's Daughter.* New York: St. Martin's Press, 1996.

Packer, George. *The Half Man.* New York: Random House, 1991.

Padfield, Peter. *Himmler.* New York: Henry Holt and Company, 1991.

Page, Norman. *Auden and Isherwood: The Berlin Years.* New York: St. Martin's Press, 1998.

Pagels, Elaine. *The Origin of Satan.* New York: Random House, 1995.

Paglia, Camille. *Sexual Personae.* New Haven: Yale University Press, 1990.

Painter, Nell Irvin. *Sojourner Truth: A Life, A Symbol.* New York: W. W. Norton & Company, 1996.

Paldiel, Mordecai. *The Path of the Righteous: Gentile Rescuers of Jews During the Holocaust.* Hoboken N.J.: KTAV Publishing House, 1993.

Palumbo, Michael. *Imperial Israel: The History of the Occupation of the West Bank and Gaza.* London: Bloomsbury, 1990.

Paretsky, Sara. *Tunnel Vision.* New York: Delacorte Press, 1994.

Parini, Jay. *John Steinbeck: A Biography.* New York: Henry Holt and Company, 1995.

Paris, Bernard J. *Karen Horney: A Psychoanalyst's Search for Self-Understanding.* New Haven: Yale University Press, 1994.

Patterson, Orlando. *Freedom: Freedom in the Making of Western Culture.* Vol. 1. New York: Basic Books, 1991.

———. *Rituals of Blood: Consequences of Slavery in Two American Centuries.* Washington, D.C.: Counterpoint, 1998.

Pawel, Ernst. *The Labyrinth of Exile: A Life of Theodor Herzl.* New York: Farrar, Straus & Giroux, 1989.

———. *The Poet Dying: Heinrich Heine's Last Years in Paris.* New York: Farrar, Straus & Giroux, 1995.

Paxton, Robert O. *Vichy France: Old Guard and New Order 1940–1944.* New York: Columbia University Press, 1972.

Paz, Octavio. *Essays on Mexican Art.* Translated by Helen Lane. New York: Harcourt Brace & Company, 1993.

———. *In Light of India.* Translated by Eliot Weinberger. New York: Harcourt Brace & Company, 1997.

———. *The Double Flame: Love and Eroticism.* Translated by Helen Lane. New York: Harcourt Brace & Company, 1995.

Peacock, Molly. *Paradise, Piece by Piece.* New York: Riverhead Books, 1998.

Pearson, Hugh. *The Shadow of the Panther: Huey Newton and the Price of Black Power in America.* Reading, Mass.: Addison-Wesley Publishing Company, 1994.

Perera, Victor. *The Cross and the Pear Tree: A Sephardic Journey.* New York: Alfred A. Knopf, 1995.

Peres, Shimon. *Battling for Peace: A Memoir.* Edited by David Landau. New York: Random House, 1995.

Peres, Shimon, and Arye Naor. *The New Middle East.* Translated by Sagir International Translations/G. Ginzach. New York: Henry Holt and Company, 1993.

Persico, Joseph E. *Nuremberg: Infamy on Trial.* New York: Viking, 1994.

Pessoa, Fernando. *Fernando Pessoa & Co.: Selected Poems.* Translated by Richard Zenith. New York: Grove Press, 1998.

Peters, Catherine. *The King of Inventors: A Life of Wilkie Collins.* Princeton: Princeton University Press, 1993.

Peterson, Merrill. *Lincoln in American Memory.* New York: Oxford University Press, 1994.

Pfaff, William. *The Wrath of Nations: Civilization and the Furies of Nationalism.* New York: Simon & Schuster, 1993.

Phayer, Michael. *Protestant and Catholic Women in Nazi Germany.* Detroit, Mich.: Wayne State University Press, 1990.

Phillips, Jayne Anne. *Shelter.* Boston: Houghton Mifflin/Seymour Lawrence, 1994.

Phillips-Matz, Mary Jane. *Verdi: A Biography.* New York: Oxford University Press, 1993.

Pinckney, Darryl. *High Cotton.* New York: Farrar, Straus & Giroux, 1992.

Pitman, Roger K., and Landy F. Sparr. "PTSD and the Law." *PTSD Research Quarterly* 9, no. 2 (Spring 1998), pp. 1–6.

Plath, Sylvia. *The Collected Poems.* Edited by Ted Hughes. New York: Harper & Row, Publishers, 1981.

Pletsch, Carl. *Young Nietzsche: Becoming a Genius.* New York: The Free Press, 1991.

Podhoretz, Norman. *Ex-Friends: Falling Out with Allen Ginsberg, Lionel and Diana Trilling, Lillian Hellman, Hannah Arendt, and Norman Mailer.* New York: The Free Press, 1999. Proofs.

Poliakov, Léon. *The Aryan Myth: A History of Racist and Nationalist Ideas in Europe.* Translated by Edmund Howard. New York: Barnes & Noble Books, 1996.

Polizzotti, Mark. *Revolution of the Mind: The Life of André Breton.* New York: Farrar, Straus & Giroux, 1995.

Pollack, J. C. *Goering's List.* New York: Delacorte Press, 1993.

Pollak, Richard. *The Creation of Dr. B: A Biography of Bruno Bettelheim.* New York: Simon & Schuster, 1997.

Pool, Robert. *Eve's Rib: Searching for the Biological Roots of Sex Differences.* New York: Crown Publishers, 1994.

Posner, Gerald. *Hitler's Children: Sons and Daughters of the Leaders of the Third Reich Talk About Themselves and Their Fathers.* New York: Random House, 1991.

Posner, Richard A. *Overcoming Law.* Cambridge: Harvard University Press, 1995.

Postman, Neil. *Amusing Ourselves to Death: Public Discourse in the Age of Show Business.* New York: Penguin Books, 1986.

————. *Technopoly: The Surrender of Culture to Technology.* New York: Alfred A. Knopf, 1992.

Powers, Richard. *Galatea 2.2.* New York: Farrar, Straus & Giroux, 1995.

————. *Operation Wandering Soul.* New York: William Morrow and Company, 1993.

————. *The Gold Bug Variations.* New York: William Morrow and Company, 1991.

Prater, Donald. *Thomas Mann: A Life.* Oxford: Oxford University Press, 1995.

Preston, Paul. *Franco.* New York: Basic Books, 1994.

Price, Reynolds. *Blue Calhoun.* New York: Atheneum, 1992.

Price, Richard. *Clockers.* Boston: Houghton Mifflin Company, 1992.

Pritchett, V. S. *Lasting Impressions.* New York: Random House, 1990.

Pron, Nick. *Lethal Marriage: The Unspeakable Crimes of Paul Bernardo and Karla Homolka.* Toronto: McClelland-Bantam, 1995.

Protocols of the Meetings of the Learned Elders of Zion, The. Translated by Victor E. Marsden. N.p., n.d.

Proulx, E. Anne. *Postcards.* New York: Charles Scribner's Sons, 1992.

Pryce-Jones, David. *The Closed Circle: An Interpretation of the Arabs.* New York: Harper & Row, Publishers, 1989.

Quinn, Susan. *Marie Curie: A Life.* New York: Simon & Schuster, 1995.

Rabe, David. *Recital of the Dog.* New York: Grove Press, 1993.

Rabinyan, Dorit. *Persian Brides.* Translated by Yael Lotan. New York: George Braziller Publisher, 1998.

Rabitzky, Aviezer. *Messianism, Zionism, and Jewish Religious Radicalism.* Translated by Michael Swirsky and Jonathan Chipman. Chicago: The University of Chicago Press, 1996.

Rabon, Israel. *The Street.* Translated by Leonard Wolf. New York: Four Walls Eight Windows, 1990.

Radzinsky, Edvard. *Stalin.* Translated by H. T. Willetts. New York: Doubleday, 1996.

Randall, Willard Sterne. *Thomas Jefferson: A Life.* New York: Henry Holt and Company, 1993.

Ranke-Heinemann, Uta. *Eunuchs for the Kingdom of Heaven.* Translated by Peter Heinegg. New York: Doubleday, 1990.

————. *Putting Away Childish Things: The Virgin Birth, the Empty Tomb, and Other Fairy Tales You Don't Need to Believe to Have a Living Faith.* Translated by Peter Heinegg. San Francisco: Harper, 1994.

Rapoport, Louis. *Stalin's War Against the Jews.* New York: The Free Press, 1990.

Ratushinskaya, Irina. *In the Beginning.* Translated by Alyona Kojevnikov. New York: Alfred A. Knopf, 1991.

Raviv, Dan, and Yossie Melman. *Every Spy a Prince.* Boston: Houghton Mifflin Company, 1990.

————. *Friends in Deed: Inside the U.S.-Israel Alliance.* New York: Hyperion, 1994.

Raymond, Janice. "Legitimating Prostitution As Sex Work: UN Organization (ILO) Calls for Recognition of the Sex Industry." December 1998.

Raymond, Janice G. *Women as Wombs.* San Francisco: Harper, 1993. Proofs.

Read, Anthony, and David Fisher. *Berlin Rising: Biography of a City.* London: W. W. Norton & Company, 1994.

Reed, Ishmael. *Japanese by Spring.* New York: Macmillan Publishing Company, 1993.

Reed, Ralph. *Active Faith: How Christians Are Changing the Soul of American Politics.* New York: The Free Press, 1996.

Reeder, Roberta. *Anna Akhmatova: Poet and Prophet.* New York: St. Martin's Press, 1994.

Reemtsma, Jan Philipp. "And So for the Reason Noted: Germany in Its Own Words—A Request and Its Consequences." Speech, Berlin, Germany, October 2, 1990.

———. *In the Cellar.* Translation by Carol Brown Janeway. New York: Alfred A. Knopf, 1999.

Reich, Tova. *The Jewish War.* New York: Pantheon Books, 1995.

Reinharz, Jehuda. *Chaim Weizmann: The Making of a Statesman.* New York: Oxford University Press, 1993.

Reuth, Ralf Georg. *Goebbels.* Translated by Krishna Winston. New York: Harcourt Brace & Company, 1993.

Revel, Jean-François. *Democracy Against Itself: The Future of the Democratic Impulse.* Translated by Roger Kaplan. New York: The Free Press, 1993.

Reynolds, Barbara. *Dorothy L. Sayers: A Biography.* New York: St. Martin's Press, 1993.

Reynolds, David S. *Walt Whitman's America: A Cultural Biography.* New York: Alfred A. Knopf, 1995.

Rhode, Deborah L. *Speaking of Sex: The Denial of Gender Inequality.* Cambridge: Harvard University Press, 1997.

Rice, Edward. *Captain Sir Richard Francis Burton.* New York: Charles Scribner's Sons, 1990.

Richardson, Joanna. *Baudelaire: A Biography.* New York: St. Martin's Press, 1994.

Richardson, Robert D., Jr. *Emerson: The Mind on Fire.* Berkeley, Calif.: University of California Press, 1995.

Richie, Alexandra. *Faust's Metropolis: A History of Berlin.* New York: Carroll & Graf Publishers, 1998.

Richler, Mordecai. *This Year in Jerusalem.* New York: Alfred A. Knopf, 1994.

Richman, Theo. *Konin: A Quest.* New York: Pantheon Books, 1995.

Ridley, Jane. *Young Disraeli 1804–1846.* New York: Crown Publishers, 1995.

Riefenstahl, Leni. *Leni Riefenstahl: A Memoir.* New York: St. Martin's Press, 1993.

Rieff, David. *Slaughterhouse: Bosnia and the Failure of the West.* New York: Simon & Schuster, 1995.

———. *The Exile: Cuba in the Heart of Miami.* New York: Simon & Schuster, 1993.

Rifaat, Alifa. *Distant View of a Minaret and Other Stories.* Translated by Denys Johnson-Davies. London: Quartet Books, 1985.

Robb, Graham. *Balzac: A Biography.* New York: W. W. Norton & Company, 1994.

Robertson-Lorant, Laurie. *Melville: A Biography.* New York: Clarkson Potter/Publishers, 1996.

Robins, Natalie. *Alien Ink: The FBI's War on Freedom of Expression.* New York: William Morrow and Company, 1992.

Robinson, Marilynne. *The Death of Adam: Essays on Modern Thought.* Boston: Houghton Mifflin Company, 1998.

Roche, Daniel. *France in the Enlightenment.* Translated by Arthur Goldhammer. Cambridge: Harvard University Press, 1998.

Rollyson, Carl. *Rebecca West: A Life.* New York: Scribner, 1996.

Rorty, Richard. *Achieving Our Country: Leftist Thought in Twentieth-Century America.* Cambridge: Harvard University Press, 1998.

Rose, Jacqueline. *The Haunting of Sylvia Plath.* Cambridge: Harvard University Press, 1992.

Rosenbaum, Eli M., and William Hoffer. *Betrayal: The Untold Story of the Kurt Waldheim Investigation and Cover-Up.* New York: St. Martin's Press, 1993.

Rosenbaum, Ron. *Explaining Hitler: The Search for the Origins of His Evil.* New York: Random House, 1998.

Rosenberg, Tina. *The Haunted Land: Facing Europe's Ghosts After Communism.* New York: Random House, 1995.

Rosenfeld, Diane L. "Redistributing Liberty Interests in Response to Domestic Violence: The Creation of Batterer Detention Facilities." In *Sexual Harassment: A Symposium*. New Haven: Yale University Law School, 1998.

Roskies, David G. *Bridge of Longing: The Lost Art of Yiddish Storytelling*. Cambridge: Harvard University Press, 1995.

Ross, James R. *Escape to Shanghai: A Jewish Community in China*. New York: The Free Press, 1994.

Roth, Philip. *Operation Shylock: A Confession*. New York: Simon & Schuster, 1993.

Rothwax, Harold J. *Guilty: The Collapse of Criminal Justice*. New York: Random House, 1996.

Rousso, Henry. *The Vichy Syndrome: History and Memory in France Since 1944*. Translated by Arthur Goldhammer. Cambridge: Harvard University Press, 1991.

Rubenstein, Danny. *The Mystery of Arafat*. Translated by Dan Leon. South Royalton, Vt.: Steerforth Press, 1995.

———. *The People of Nowhere: The Palestinian Vision of Home*. Translated by Ina Friedman. New York: Times Books, 1991.

Rubenstein, Joshua. *Tangled Loyalties: The Life and Times of Ilya Ehrenburg*. New York: Basic Books, 1996.

Rubinstein, William D. *The Myth of Rescue: Why the Democracies Could Not Have Saved More Jews From the Nazis*. London: Routledge, 1997.

Rusch, Kris. *Hitler's Angel*. New York: St. Martin's Press, 1998.

Rush, Norman. *Mating*. New York: Alfred A. Knopf, 1991.

Rushdoony, Rousas John. *Salvation and Godly Rule*. Vallecito, Calif.: Ross House Books, 1983.

Russell, Diana E. H. *Lives of Courage: Women for a New South Africa*. New York: Basic Books, 1989. Proofs.

———. "Rape and Child Sexual Abuse in Soweto: An Interview with Community Leader Mary Mabaso." *S. A. Sociological Review* 3, no. 2 (1991), pp. 62–83.

Russell, Kathy, Midge Wilson, and Ronald Hall. *The Color Complex: The Politics of Skin Color Among African Americans*. New York: Harcourt Brace Jovanovich, Publishers, 1992.

Ryan, Alan. *John Dewey and the High Tide of American Liberalism*. New York: W. W. Norton & Company, 1995.

Ryan, Michael. *Secret Life: An Autobiography*. New York: Pantheon Books, 1995.

Sachar, Howard M. *A History of the Jews in America*. New York: Alfred A. Knopf, 1992.

———. *Farewell Espana: The World of the Sephardim Remembered*. New York: Alfred A. Knopf, 1994.

Sack, John. *An Eye for an Eye: The Untold Story of Jewish Revenge Against Germans in 1945*. New York: Basic Books, 1993.

Safire, William. *The First Dissident: The Book of Job in Today's Politics*. New York: Random House, 1992.

Safranski, Rüdiger. *Martin Heidegger: Between Good and Evil*. Translated by Ewald Osers. Cambridge: Harvard University Press, 1998.

Said, Edward, and David Barsamiam. *The Pen and the Sword*. Monroe, Maine: Common Courage Press, 1994.

Said, Edward W. *Culture and Imperialism*. New York: Alfred A. Knopf, 1993.

———. *Peace and Its Discontents: Essays on Palestine in the Middle East Peace Process*. New York: Vintage Books, 1995.

———. *The Politics of Dispossession: The Struggle for Palestinian Self-Determination 1969–1994*. New York: Pantheon Books, 1994.

——— *Representations of the Intellectual*. New York: Pantheon Books, 1994.

Salzman, Jack, and Cornel West, eds. *Struggles in the Promised Land: Toward a History of Black-Jewish Relations in the United States*. New York: Oxford University Press, 1997.

Saramago, José. *The Gospel According to Jesus Christ*. Translated by Giovanni Pontiero. New York: Harcourt Brace & Company, 1994.

Sartre, Jean-Paul. *The Family Idiot: Gustave Flaubert 1821–1857*. Vol. 2. Translated by Carol Cosman. Chicago: The University of Chicago Press, 1987.

Sasson, Jean P. *Princess: A True Story of Life Behind the Veil in Saudi Arabia*. New York: William Morrow and Company, 1992.

Savigneau, Josyane. *Marguerite Yourcenar: Inventing a Life.* Translated by Joan E. Howard. Chicago: The University of Chicago Press, 1993.

Sayles, John. *Los Guisanos.* New York: HarperCollins Publishers, 1991.

Scarce, Michael. *Male on Male Rape: The Hidden Toll of Stigma and Shame.* New York: Plenum Press, 1997.

Schack, Howard H., and H. Paul Jeffers. *A Spy in Canaan: My Secret Life as a Jewish-American Businessman Spying for Israel in Arab Lands.* New York: Carol Publishing Group, 1993.

Schäfer, Peter. *Judeophobia: Attitudes Toward the Jews in the Ancient World.* Cambridge: Harvard University Press, 1997.

Schama, Simon. *Landscape and Memory.* New York: Alfred A. Knopf, 1995.

Schiff, Stacy. *Saint-Exupéry: A Biography.* New York: Alfred A. Knopf, 1994.

Schiff, Ze'ev, and Ehud Ya'Ari. *Intifada.* Translated by Ina Friedman. New York: Simon & Schuster, 1990.

Schine, Cathleen. *Rameau's Niece.* New York: Ticknor & Fields, 1993.

Schlesinger, Arthur M. *The Disuniting of America: Reflections on a Multicultural Society.* New York: W. W. Norton & Company, 1992.

Schlink, Bernhard. *The Reader.* Translated by Carol Brown Janeway. New York: Pantheon Books, 1997.

Schmidgall, Gary. *The Stranger Wilde: Interpreting Oscar.* New York: Dutton, 1994.

Schmidt, Hans A. *Quakers and Nazis: Inner Light in Outer Darkness.* Columbia: University of Missouri Press, 1997.

Schmidt, Michael. *The New Reich: Violent Extremism in Unified Germany and Beyond.* Translated by Daniel Horch. New York: Pantheon Books, 1993.

Schneiderman, Stuart. *Saving Face: America and the Politics of Shame.* New York: Alfred A. Knopf, 1995.

Schonberg, Harold C. *Horowitz: His Life and Music.* New York: Simon & Schuster, 1992.

Schröder, Hannelore. "Anti-Semitism and Anti-Feminism Again: The Dissemination of Otto Weininger's *Sex and Character* in the Seventies and Eighties," *Empirical Logic and Public Debate.* Edited by Erik C. W. Krabbe, Renee Jose Dalitz, and Pier A. Smit, pp. 305–318. Amsterdam-Atlanta: Rodopi, 1993.

———. "Reflections on an Anti-Patriarchal Declaration of Women's Human Rights," *Against Patriarchal Thinking.* Edited by Maja Pellikaan-Engel, pp. 257–266. Proceedings of the VL Symposium of the International Association of Women Philosophers. Amsterdam: VU University Press, 1992.

———. "The Declaration of Human and Civil Rights for Women (Paris, 1791) by Olympia de Gouges." *History of European Ideas* II (1989), pp. 263–271.

———. "The Economic Impoverishment of Mothers Is the Enrichment of Fathers," *Women, Work and Poverty.* Edited by Elisabeth Schussler Fiorenza and Anne Carr, pp. 10–18. Edinburgh: T. & T. Clark, 1987.

———. "World-wide Violations of Women's Political Human Rights by Patriarchal Political Power Monopolies," leaflet, n.d.

Schuster, Joshua. "Synagogue Gun-Safety Class Aims to Demystify Weapons." *Jewish Bulletin of Northern California,* October 23, 1998, pp. 1, 23.

Schweitzer, Viktoria. *Tsvetaeva.* Translated by Robert Chandler, H. T. Willets, and Peter Norman. New York: Farrar, Straus & Giroux, 1993.

Schwerfeger, Ruth. *Women of Theresienstadt: Voices From a Concentration Camp.* New York: Berg, 1989.

Seale, Patrick. *Abu Nidal: A Gun for Hire.* New York: Random House, 1992.

Sebbar, Leila. *Sherazade.* Translated by Dorothy S. Blair. London: Quartet Books Limited, 1991.

Segev, Samuel. *Crossing the Jordan: Israel's Hard Road to Peace.* New York: St. Martin's Press, 1998.

Segev, Tom. *The Seventh Million: The Israelis and the Holocaust.* Translated by Haim Watzman. New York: Hill and Wang, 1993.

Self, Will. *My Idea of Fun.* New York: The Atlantic Monthly Press, 1994.

———. *Tough, Tough Toys for Tough, Tough Boys.* London: Penguin Books, 1999.

Semprun, Jorge. *Literature or Life?* Translated by Linda Coverdale. New York: Viking, 1997.

Sen, Mala. *India's Bandit Queen: The True Story of Phoolan Devi*. London: HarperCollins, 1993.

Sendyk, Helen. *The End of Days: A Memoir of the Holocaust*. New York: St. Martin's Press, 1992.

Senesh, Hannah. *Hannah Senesh: Her Life and Diary*. Translated by Nigel Marsh. New York: Schocken Books, 1977.

Senna, Danzy. *Caucasia*. New York: Riverhead Books, 1998.

Sennot, Charles M. *Broken Convenant*. New York: Simon & Schuster, 1992.

Sereny, Gitta. *Albert Speer: His Battle with Truth*. New York: Alfred A. Knopf, 1995.

———. *Cries Unheard: Why Children Kill—The Story of Mary Bell*. New York: Metropolitan Books, 1998.

———. *Into That Darkness: From Mercy Killing to Mass Murder*. London: Pimlico, 1974.

———. *The Invisible Children: Child Prostitution in America, West Germany, and Great Britain*. New York: Alfred A. Knopf, 1985. Proofs.

Seymour, Miranda. *Ottoline Morrell: Life on the Grand Scale*. New York: Farrar, Straus & Giroux, 1993.

———. *Robert Graves: Life on the Edge*. New York: Henry Holt and Company, 1995.

Seymour-Smith, Martin. *Hardy: A Biography*. New York: St. Martin's Press, 1994.

Shalev, Meir. *Esau*. Translated by Barbara Harshav. New York: HarperCollins, 1994.

———. *The Blue Mountain*. Translated by Hillel Halkin. New York: HarperCollins Publishers, 1991.

Shalit, Wendy. *A Return to Modesty: Discovering the Lost Virtue*. New York: The Free Press, 1999.

Shammas, Anton. *Arabesques*. Translated by Vivian Eden. New York: Harper & Row, Publishers, 1989.

Shange, Ntozake. *Liliane*. New York: St. Martin's Press, 1995.

Shapiro, James. *Shakespeare and the Jews*. New York: Columbia University Press, 1996.

Sharoni, Simona. *Gender and the Israeli-Palestinian Conflict: The Politics of Women's Resistance*. Syracuse, N.Y.: Syracuse University Press, 1995.

Shay, Jonathan. *Achilles in Vietnam: Combat Trauma and the Undoing of Character*. New York: Atheneum, 1994.

———. "About Medications for Combating PTSD." Dr. Bob's Virtual En-psych-lopedia. http://uhs.bsd.uchicago.edu/~bhsiung/tips/ptsd.html.

Sheehan, Neil. *After the War Was Over: Hanoi and Saigon*. New York: Random House, 1991.

Shelden, Michael. *Graham Greene: The Enemy Within*. New York: Random House, 1995.

———. *Orwell*. New York: HarperCollins Publishers, 1991.

Shelley, Lore, ed. *Criminal Experiments on Human Beings in Auschwitz and War Research Laboratories: Twenty Women Prisoners' Accounts*. San Francisco: Mellen Research University Press, 1991.

Shelley, Martha. *Haggadah: A Celebration*. San Francisco: Aunt Lute Books, 1997.

Shentalinsky, Vitaly. *Arrested Voices: Resurrecting the Disappeared Writers of the Soviet Regime*. Translated by John Crowfoot. New York: The Free Press, 1996.

Sherman, A. J. *Mandate Days: British Lives in Palestine 1918–1948*. New York: Thames and Hudson, 1997.

Sherry, Norman. *The Life of Graham Greene 1939–1955*. Vol. II. New York: Viking, 1994.

Sherwood, Frances. *Vindication*. New York: Farrar, Straus & Giroux, 1993.

Shi, David E. *Facing Facts: Realism in American Thought and Culture 1850–1920*. New York: Oxford University Press, 1995.

Shipler, David K. *Arab and Jew: Wounded Spirits in a Promised Land*. New York: Penguin Books, 1987.

Shipman, Pat. *The Evolution of Racism: Human Differences and the Use and Abuse of Science*. New York: Simon & Schuster, 1994.

Shlaim, Avi. *War and Peace in the Middle East: A Critique of American Policy*. New York: Whittle Books and Viking, 1994.

———. "Woman of the Year." *The New York Review of Books* XLII, no. 10 (June 8, 1995), pp. 24–27.

Shlain, Leonard. *The Alphabet Versus the Goddess: The Conflict Between Word and Image*. New York: Viking, 1998.

Shoham, S. Giora, Gloria Rahav, Rachel Markovski, Ilana Ber, Francis Chard, Yoseph Rach-
man, and Claudia Bill. "Family Variables and Stigma Among Prostitutes in Israel." *The
Journal of Social Psychology,* No. 120 (1983), pp. 57–62.

Showalter, Elaine. *Sister's Choice: Tradition and Change in American Women's Writing.* Oxford:
Clarendon Press, 1991.

Sichrovsky, Peter. *Abraham's Children: Israel's Young Generation.* Translated by Jean Steinberg.
New York: Pantheon Books, 1991.

Silberman, Neil Asher. *A Prophet from Amongst You. The Life of Yigael Yadim: Soldier, Scholar,
and Mythmaker of Modern Israel.* New York: Addison-Wesley Publishing Company, 1993.

———. *The Hidden Scrolls: Christianity, Judaism, and the War for the Dead Sea Scrolls.* New
York: G. P. Putnam's Sons, 1994.

Silverman, Fayge, ed. *Women in the Holocaust: A Collection of Testimonies.* Compiled and
translated by Jehoshua Eibeshitz and Anna Eilenberg-Eibeshitz. 2 Vols. Brooklyn, N.Y.:
Remember, 1993, 1994.

Silverman, Kenneth. *Edgar A. Poe.* New York: HarperCollins Publishers, 1991.

Silverman, Sue William. *Because When I Remember Terror, Father, I Remember You.* Athens:
The University of Georgia Press, 1996.

Sime, Ruth Lewin. *Lise Meitner: A Life in Physics.* Berkeley: University of California Press,
1996.

Simonelli, Frederick J. *Fuehrer American: George Lincoln Rockwell and the American Nazi
Party.* Urbana: University of Illinois Press, 1999.

Simpson, Christopher. *The Splendid Blond Beast: Money, Law, and Genocide in the Twentieth
Century.* New York: Grove Press, 1993.

Sinclair, Andrew. *Francis Bacon: His Life and Violent Times.* New York: Crown Publishers,
1993.

———. *Jerusalem: The Endless Crusade.* New York: Crown Publishers, 1995.

Singer, Isaac Bashevis. *Meshugah.* Translated by Isaac Bashevis Singer and Nili Wachtel. New
York: Farrar, Straus & Giroux, 1994.

———. *Scum.* Translated by Rosaline Dukalsky Schwartz. New York: Farrar, Straus &
Giroux, 1991.

———. *The Certificate.* Translated by Leonard Wolf. New York: Farrar, Straus & Giroux,
1992.

Sinyavsky, Andrei. *The Russian Intelligentsia.* Translated by Lynn Visson. New York: Columbia University Press, 1997.

Skakun, Michael. *On Burning Ground: A Son's Memoir.* New York: St. Martin's Press, 1999.

Skidelsky, Robert. *John Maynard Keynes: The Economist as Savior, 1920–1937.* Vol. 2. New
York: Allen Lane/The Penguin Press, 1992.

———. *The Road from Serfdom: The Economic and Political Consequences of the End of Communism.* New York: Allen Lane/The Penguin Press, 1995.

Škvorecký, Josef. *Headed for the Blues: A Memoir.* Translated by Káča Poláčková Henley.
Hopewell, N.J.: The Ecco Press, 1996.

Slater, Robert. *Rabin of Israel.* New York: St. Martin's Press, 1993.

Sloan, James Park. *Jerzy Kosinski: A Biography.* New York: Dutton, 1996.

Smiley, Jane. *A Thousand Acres.* New York: Alfred A. Knopf, 1992.

Smith, David, and Carol Calef. *Beyond All Reason: My Life with Susan Smith.* New York:
Kensington Books, 1995.

Smith, Denis Mack. *Mazzini.* New Haven: Yale University Press, 1994.

Smith, Gene. *American Gothic.* New York: Simon & Schuster, 1992.

Smith, Joan. *Different for Girls: How Culture Creates Women.* London: Chatto & Windus,
1997.

Smith, Lee. *The Devil's Dream.* New York: G. P. Putnam's Sons, 1992.

Snortland, Ellen. "Beauty Bites Beast: Awakening the Warrior Within Women and Girls."
1998.

Sofsky, Wolfgang. *The Order of Terror: The Concentration Camp.* Translated by William Templer. Princeton: Princeton University Press, 1997.

Sollers, Philippe. *Watteau in Venice.* Translated by Alberto Manguel. New York: Charles
Scribner's Sons, 1994.

Solomon, Maynard. *Mozart: A Life.* New York: HarperCollins Publishers, 1995.

Somerset, Anne. *Elizabeth I.* New York: Alfred A. Knopf, 1991.

Sorenson, Susan B., Judith M. Siegel, Jacqueline M. Golding, and Judith A. Stein. "Repeated Sexual Victimization," *Violence and Victims* 6, no. 4 (1991), pp. 299–308.

Soueif, Ahdaf. *In the Eye of the Sun.* New York: Pantheon, 1992.

Southami, Diana. *Gertrude and Alice.* London: Pandora, 1991.

Southern Poverty Law Center. *False Patriots: The Threat of Antigovernment Extremists.* Montgomery, Ala.: Southern Poverty Law Center, 1996.

Sowell, Thomas. *Migrations and Cultures: A World View.* New York: Basic Books, 1996.

———. *Race and Culture: A World View.* New York: Basic Books, 1994.

———. *The Vision of the Anointed: Self-Congratulation as a Basis for Social Policy.* New York: Basic Books, 1995.

Soyinka, Wole. *Art, Dialogue, and Outrage: Essays on Literature and Culture.* New York: Pantheon Books, 1994.

———. *The Burden of Memory, The Muse of Forgiveness.* New York: Oxford University Press, 1999.

———. *The Open Sore of a Continent: A Personal Narrative of the Nigerian Crisis.* New York: Oxford University Press, 1996.

Spacks, Patricia Meyer. *Boredom: The Literary History of a State of Mind.* Chicago: The University of Chicago Press, 1995.

Spiegelman, Art. *Maus: A Survivor's Tale—And Here My Troubles Began.* New York: Pantheon Books, 1991.

———. *Maus: A Survivor's Tale—My Father Bleeds History.* New York: Pantheon Books, 1986.

Spitzer, Robert J. *The Politics of Gun Control.* Chatham, N.J.: Chatham House Publishers, Inc., 1995.

Sprinzak, Ehud. *Brother Against Brother: Violence and Extremism in Israeli Politics From Altalena to the Rabin Assassination.* New York: The Free Press, 1999.

———. *The Ascendance of Israel's Radical Right.* New York: Oxford University Press, 1991.

Spurling, Hilary. *Paul Scott: A Life of the Author of the Raj Quartet.* New York: W. W. Norton & Company, 1991.

———. *The Unknown Matisse: A Life of Henri Matisse: The Early Years, 1869–1908.* New York: Alfred A. Knopf, 1998.

Stannard, David E. *American Holocaust: Columbus and the Conquest of the New World.* New York: Oxford University Press, 1992.

Stannard, Martin. *Evelyn Waugh: The Early Years 1903–1939.* New York: W. W. Norton & Company, 1986.

———. *Evelyn Waugh: The Later Years 1939–1966.* New York: W. W. Norton & Company, 1992.

Staples, Brent. *Parallel Time: Growing Up Black and White.* New York: Pantheon Books, 1994.

Starr, Tama. *Eve's Revenge.* New York: Harcourt Brace & Company, 1994.

Steele, Shelby. *The Content of Our Character.* New York: St. Martin's Press, 1990.

Steiner, George. *No Passion Spent: Essays 1978–1995.* New Haven: Yale University Press, 1996.

———. *The Portage to San Cristobal of A. H.* New York: Pocket Books, 1981.

Steiner, Wendy. *The Scandal of Pleasure: Art in an Age of Fundamentalism.* Chicago: The University of Chicago Press, 1995.

Sterling, Dorothy. *Ahead of Her Time: Abby Kelley and the Politics of Antislavery.* New York: W. W. Norton and Company, 1991.

Stern, Jessica. *The Ultimate Terrorists.* Cambridge: Harvard University Press, 1999.

Sternhell, Zeev. *The Founding Myths of Israel.* Translated by David Maisel. Princeton: Princeton University Press, 1998.

Stille, Alexander. *Benevolence and Betrayal: Five Italian Jewish Families Under Fascism.* New York: Summit Books, 1991.

Stocker, Margarita. *Judith, Sexual Warrior: Women and Power in Western Culture.* New Haven: Yale University, 1998.

Stone, Robert. *Damascus Gate*. Boston: Houghton Mifflin Company, 1998.

Storr, Anthony. *Feet of Clay—Saints, Sinners, and Madmen: A Study of Gurus*. New York: The Free Press, 1996.

Stovall, Tyler. *Paris Noir: African Americans in the City of Light*. Boston: Houghton Mifflin, 1996.

Strong, Marilee. *A Bright Red Scream: Self-mutilation and the Language of Pain*. New York: Viking, 1998.

Strum, Philippa. *The Women Are Marching: The Second Sex and the Palestinian Revolution*. Brooklyn: Lawrence Hill Books, 1992.

Stuart, Alexander. *Tribes*. New York: Doubleday, 1992.

Stumhofer, Nancy S. "Goya's Naked Maja: The Classroom Climate Perspective," N.d., 30 pp.

Sudetic, Chuck. *Blood and Vengeance: One Family's Story of the War in Bosnia*. New York: W. W. Norton & Company, 1998.

Sundquist, Eric J. *To Wake the Nations: Race in the Making of American Literature*. Cambridge: The Belknap Press of Harvard University Press, 1993.

Svoray, Yaron, and Nick Taylor. *In Hitler's Shadow: An Israeli's Amazing Journey Inside Germany's Neo-Nazi Movement*. New York: Doubleday, 1994.

Sweetman, David. *Mary Renault: A Biography*. New York: Harcourt Brace & Company, 1993.

———. *Paul Gaugin: A Life*. New York: Simon & Schuster, 1995.

Swiebocka, Teresa, ed., Jonathan Webber and Connie Wilsack, eds. *Auschwitz: A History in Photographs*. Warsaw: The Auschwitz-Birkenau State Museum, 1985.

Szczypiorski, Andrzej. *Self-portrait with Woman*. New York: Grove Press, 1995.

———. *The Beautiful Mrs. Seidenman*. Translated by Klara Glowczewska. New York: Grove Weidenfeld, 1989.

Szeman, Sherri. *The Kommandant's Mistress*. New York: HarperCollins Publishers, 1993.

Szlakmann, Charles. *Judaism for Beginners*. New York: Writers and Readers Publishing, 1984.

Szulc, Tad. *The Secret Alliance: The Extraordinary Story of the Rescue of the Jews Since World War II*. New York: Farrar, Straus & Giroux, 1991.

Szwajger, Adina Blady. *I Remember Nothing More: The Warsaw Children's Hospital and the Jewish Resistance*. Translated by Tasja Darowska and Danusia Stok. New York: Pantheon Books, 1990.

Tan, Amy. *The Kitchen God's Wife*. New York: G. P. Putnam's Sons, 1991.

Tani, E., and Kaé Sera. *False Nationalism False Internationalism: Class Contradictions in the Armed Struggle*. Seeds Beneath the Snow, 1985.

Tanizaki, Junichirō. *Quicksand*. Translated by Howard Hibbett. New York: Alfred A. Knopf, 1994.

———. *The Reed Cutter and Captain Shigenoto's Mother*. Translated by Anthony H. Chambers. New York: Alfred A. Knopf, 1994.

Tarabishi, Georges. *Woman Against Her Sex: A Critique of Nechama el-Saadawi*. Translated by Basil Hatim and Elisabeth Orsini. London: Saqi Books, 1988.

Tatar, Maria. *Lustmord: Sexual Murder in Weimar Germany*. Princeton: Princeton University Press, 1995.

Taylor, Telford. *The Anatomy of the Nuremberg Trials*. New York: Alfred A. Knopf, 1992.

Tec, Nechama. *Defiance: The Bielski Partisans*. New York: Oxford University Press, 1993.

Teitelboim, Volodia. *Neruda: An Intimate Biography*. Translated by Beverly J. DeLong-Tonelli. Austin: University of Texas Press, 1991.

Tekin, Latife. *Berji Kristin: Tales from the Garbage Hills*. Translated by Ruth Christie and Saliha Paker. London: Marion Boyars, 1993.

Telushkin, Joseph. *Jewish Literacy: The Most Important Things to Know About the Jewish Religion, Its People, and Its History*. New York: William Morrow and Company, 1991.

Teres, Harvey. *Renewing the Left: Politics, Imagination, and the New York Intellectuals*. New York: Oxford University Press, 1996.

Teveth, Shabtai. *Ben-Gurion and the Holocaust*. New York: Harcourt Brace and Company, 1996.

Tharoor, Shashi. *Show Business*. New York: Arcade Publishing, 1992.

Theroux, Paul. *The Happy Isles of Oceana.* New York: G. P. Putnam's Sons, 1992.

Theroux, Peter. *Sandstorms: Days and Nights in Arabia.* New York: W. W. Norton & Company, 1990.

Thomas, Gordon. *Gideon's Spies: The Secret History of the Mossad.* New York: St. Martin's Press, 1999.

Thomas, Hugh. *Conquest: Montezuma, Cortes, and the Fall of Old Mexico.* New York: Simon & Schuster, 1993.

———. *The Slave Trade: The Story of the Atlantic Slave Trade 1440–1870.* New York: Simon & Schuster, 1997.

Thomas, Lewis. *The Fragile Species.* New York: Charles Scribner's Sons, 1992.

Thomas, Robert David. *"With Bleeding Footsteps": Mary Baker Eddy's Path to Religious Leadership.* New York: Alfred A. Knopf, 1994.

Thomas, Rosanne Daryl. *The Angel Carver.* New York: Random House, 1993.

Thompson, E. P. *The Romantics: England in a Revolutionary Age.* New York: The New Press, 1997.

Thornton, E. M. *The Freudian Fallacy: An Alternative View of Freudian Theory.* Garden City, N.Y.: The Dial Press, 1984.

Thornton, Lawrence. *Ghost Woman.* New York: Ticknor & Fields, 1992.

Three Rivers, Amoja. *Cultural Etiquette: A Guide for the Well-Intentioned.* Indian Valley, Va.: Market Wimmin, 1991.

Tiger, Lionel. *The Decline of Males.* New York: Golden Books, 1999.

Tivnan, Edward. *The Lobby: Jewish Political Power and American Foreign Policy.* New York: Simon & Schuster, 1987.

Todd, Olivier. *Albert Camus: A Life.* New York: Alfred A. Knopf, 1997.

Todorov, Tzvetan. *A French Tragedy: Scenes of Civil War, Summer 1944.* Translated by Mary Byrd Kelly. Hanover: University Press of New England, 1996.

———. *Facing the Extreme: Moral Life in the Concentration Camps.* Translated by Arthur Denner and Abigail Pollak. New York: Henry Holt and Company, 1996.

———. *On Human Diversity: Nationalism, Racism, and Exoticism in French Thought.* Translated by Catherine Porter. Cambridge: Harvard University Press, 1993.

Toer, Pramoedya Ananta. *Child of All Nations.* Translated by Max Lane. New York: William Morrow and Company, 1993.

Toland, John. *Adolf Hitler.* New York: Anchor Books/Doubleday, 1976.

Tomasky, Michael. *Left for Dead: The Life, Death, and Possible Resurrection of Progressive Politics in America.* New York: The Free Press, 1996.

Toobin, Jeffrey. *Opening Arguments: A Young Lawyer's First Case: United States v. Oliver North.* New York: Penguin Books, 1992.

———. *The Run of His Life: The People v. O. J. Simpson.* New York: Random House, 1996.

Tory, Avraham. *Surviving the Holocaust: The Kovno Ghetto Diary.* Edited by Martin Gilbert. Translated by Jerzy Michalowicz. Cambridge: Harvard University Press, 1990.

Traub, James. *City on a Hill: Testing the American Dream at City College.* Reading, Mass.: Addison-Wesley Publishing Company, 1994.

Trevor, William. *Excursions in the Real World: Memoirs.* New York: Alfred A. Knopf, 1994.

———. *Felicia's Journey.* New York: Viking, 1994.

Troyat, Henry. *Flaubert.* Translated by Joan Pinkham. New York: Viking, 1992.

Tsernianski, Milos. *Migrations.* Translated by Michael Henry Heim. New York: Harcourt Brace & Company, 1994.

Turki, Fawaz. *Exile's Return: The Making of a Palestinian-American.* New York: The Free Press, 1994.

Turner, A. Richard. *Inventing Leonardo.* New York: Alfred A. Knopf, 1993.

Uglow, Jenny. *Elizabeth Gaskell: A Habit of Stories.* New York: Farrar, Straus & Giroux, 1993.

Ulam, Adam B. *Stalin: The Man and His Era.* Boston: Beacon Press, 1987.

United Nations. *The World's Women 1995: Trends and Statistics.* New York: United Nations Publications.

United Nations International Criminal Tribunal for Rwanda. "The Prosecutor versus Jean-Paul Akayesu. Case No. ICTR-96-4-T Judgment. 121 pp. Decision: September 2, 1998.

United States of America v. *Abraham Jacob Alkhabaz aka Jake Baker.* Brief Amicus Curiae for the Victim Jane Doe and The National Coalition Against Sexual Assault in Support of the United States. No. 95–1797.

United States Holocaust Memorial Museum. *Hidden History of the Kovno Ghetto.* Boston: Little, Brown and Company, 1998.

Utley, Robert M. *The Lance and the Shield: The Life and Times of Sitting Bull.* New York: Henry Holt and Company, 1993.

Vachss, Alice. *Sex Crimes.* New York: Random House, 1993.

Vachss, Andrew. *Choice of Evil.* New York: Alfred A. Knopf, 1999.

———. *Down in the Zero.* New York: Alfred A. Knopf, 1994.

———. *False Allegations.* New York: Alfred A. Knopf, 1996.

———. *Footsteps of the Hawk.* New York: Alfred A. Knopf, 1995.

———. *Sacrifice.* New York: Alfred A. Knopf, 1991.

———. *Safe House.* New York: Alfred A. Knopf, 1998.

———. *Shella.* New York: Alfred A. Knopf, 1993.

Vaksberg, Arkady. *Stalin Against the Jews.* Translated by Antonina W. Bouis. New York: Alfred A. Knopf, 1994.

Valladares, Armando. *Against All Hope: The Prison Memoirs of Armando Valladares.* Translated by Andrew Hurley. New York: Alfred A. Knopf, 1986.

Van der Vat, Dan. *The Good Nazi: The Life and Lies of Albert Speer.* Boston: Houghton Mifflin Company, 1997.

Van Heerden, Etienne. *Ancestral Voices.* New York: Viking, 1992.

Vargas Llosa, Mario. *A Fish in the Water: A Memoir.* Translated by Helen Lane. New York: Farrar, Straus & Giroux, 1994.

———. *Death in the Andes.* Translated by Edith Grossman. New York: Farrar, Straus & Giroux, 1996.

———. *Making Waves: Essays.* Translated by John King. New York: Farrar, Straus & Giroux, 1997.

Venclova, Tomas. *Aleksander Wat: Life and Art of an Iconoclast.* New Haven: Yale University Press, 1996.

Vermes, Geza. "The War Over the Scrolls." *The New York Review of Books* XLI, no. 14 (August 11, 1994).

Victor, Barbara. *A Voice of Reason: Hanan Ashrawi and Peace in the Middle East.* New York: Harcourt Brace & Company, 1994.

Vidal, Gore. *Live From Golgotha.* New York: Random House, 1992.

———. *Palimpsest: A Memoir.* New York: Random House, 1995.

Vidal-Naquet, Pierre. *Assassins of Memory: Essays on the Denial of the Holocaust.* Translated by Jeffrey Mehlman. New York: Columbia University Press, 1992.

Vitoux, Frédéric. *Céline: A Biography.* Translated by Jesse Browner. New York: Paragon House, 1992.

Volavková, Hana. . . . *I Never Saw Another Butterfly: Children's Drawings and Poems from Terezin Concentration Camp 1942–1944.* New York: Schocken Books, 1993; and *I Have Not Seen a Butterfly Around Here.* Prague: The Jewish Museum, 1993.

Volkan, Vamik. *Blood Lines: From Ethnic Pride to Ethnic Terrorism.* New York: Farrar, Straus & Giroux, 1997.

Volkogonov, Dmitri. *Lenin: A Biography.* Translated by Harold Shukman. New York: The Free Press, 1994.

———. *Trotsky: The Eternal Revolutionary.* Translated by Harold Shukman. New York: The Free Press, 1996.

Volkov, Solomon. *Conversations with Joseph Brodsky: A Poet's Journey Through the Twentieth Century.* Translated by Marian Schwartz. New York: The Free Press, 1998.

Von Lang, Jochen. *The Secretary: Martin Borman—The Man Who Manipulated Hitler.* Translated by Christa Armstrong and Peter White. New York: Random House, 1979.

Von Rezzori, Gregor. *Memoirs of an Anti-Semite: A Novel in Five Stories.* New York: Penguin Books, 1982.

———. *The Orient-Express.* New York: Alfred A. Knopf, 1992.

Wagner, Gottfried. *Twilight of the Wagners: The Unveiling of a Family's Legacy.* Translated by Della Couling. New York: Picador, 1999.

Waite, Robert G. "Teenage Sexuality in Nazi Germany." *Journal of the History of Sexuality* 8, no. 3 (1998), pp. 434–476.

Walcott, Derek. *What the Twilight Says: Essays.* New York: Farrar, Straus & Giroux, 1998.

Waldron, Ann. *Hodding Carter: The Reconstruction of a Racist.* Chapel Hill: Algonquin Books of North Carolina, 1993.

Walker, Alice. *Possessing the Secret of Joy.* New York: Harcourt Brace Jovanovich, 1992.

————. *The Same River Twice: Honoring the Difficult.* New York: Scribner, 1996. Proofs.

Walker, Alice, and Pratibha Parmar. *Warrior Marks: Female Genital Mutilation and the Sexual Blinding of Women.* New York: Harcourt Brace & Company, 1993.

Wallach, Janet. *Desert Queen.* New York: Doubleday, 1996.

Wallach, Janet, and John Wallach. *Arafat: In the Eyes of the Beholder.* Secaucus, N.J.: Carol Publishing Group, 1990.

Wallach, John, and Janet Wallach. *The New Palestinians: The Emerging Generation of Leaders.* Rocklin, Calif.: Prima Publishing, 1992.

Walter, Natasha, ed. *On the Move: Feminism for a New Generation.* London: Virago, 1999.

————. *The New Feminism.* London: Little, Brown and Company, 1998.

WAR: White Aryan Resistance. Fallbrook, Calif. N.p., August, 1994.

Ware, Susan. *Still Missing: Amelia Earhart and the Search for Modern Feminism.* New York: W. W. Norton & Company, 1993.

Warren, Donald. *Radio Priest: Charles Coughlin, the Father of Hate Radio.* New York: The Free Press, 1996.

Warshaw, Robin. *I Never Called It Rape.* New York: Harper & Row, Publishers, 1988.

Wasserstein, Bernard. *Vanishing Diaspora: The Jews in Europe since 1945.* Cambridge: Harvard University Press, 1996.

Watson, Alan. *The Germans: Who Are They Now?* Carol Stream, Ill.: edition q, 1993.

Watt, Ian. *Myths of Modern Individualism: Faust, Don Quixote, Don Juan, Robinson Crusoe.* Cambridge: Cambridge University Press, 1996.

Weber, Eugen. *The Hollow Years: France in the 1930s.* New York: W. W. Norton & Company, 1994.

Webster, Paul. *Petain's Crime: The Full Story of French Collaboration in the Holocaust.* Chicago: Ivan R. Dee, 1991.

Weil, Grete. *The Bride Price.* Translated by John Barrett. Boston: David R. Godine, Publisher, 1991.

Weil, Jiri. *Mendelssohn Is On the Roof.* New York: Farrar, Straus & Giroux, 1991.

Weintraub, Stanley. *Disraeli: A Biography.* New York: Dutton, 1993.

Weisenburger, Steven. *Modern Medea: A Family Story of Slavery and Child-Murder from the Old South.* New York: Hill and Wang, 1998.

Weiss, John. *Ideology of Death: Why the Holocaust Happened in Germany.* Chicago: Ivan R. Dee, 1996.

Weitz, John. *Hitler's Diplomat: The Life and Times of Joachin von Ribbentrop.* New York: Ticknor & Fields, 1992.

Weldon, Fay. *Darcy's Utopia.* New York: Viking, 1991.

Werner, Harold. *Fighting Back: A Memoir of Jewish Resistance in World War II.* New York: Columbia University Press, 1989.

West, Cornel. *Race Matters.* Boston: Beacon Press, 1993.

West, Paul. *Love's Mansion.* New York: Random House, 1992.

————. *Rat Man of Paris.* New York: Collier Books/Macmillan Publishing Company, 1987.

————. *The Tent of Orange Mist.* New York: Scribner, 1995.

————. *The Very Rich Hours of Count Von Stauffenberg.* Woodstock, N.Y.: The Overlook Press, 1989.

————. *The Women of Whitechapel and Jack the Ripper.* New York: Random House, 1991.

Wheatcroft, Andrew. *The Ottomans.* New York: Viking, 1993.

Wheatcroft, Geoffrey. *The Controversy of Zion: Jewish Nationalism, the Jewish State, and the Unresolved Jewish Dilemma.* Reading, Mass.: Addison-Wesley Publishing Company, 1996.

Whelan, Richard. *Alfred Stieglitz: A Biography.* Boston: Little, Brown and Company, 1995.

White, Edmund. *Genet: A Biography.* New York: Alfred A. Knopf, 1993.

———. *The Burning Library: Essays.* Edited by David Bergman. New York: Alfred A. Knopf, 1994.

White, G. Edward. *Justice Oliver Wendell Holmes: Law and the Inner Self.* New York: Oxford University Press, 1993.

White, Michael, and John Gribbin. *Einstein: A Life in Science.* New York: Dutton, 1993.

Wicks, Ben. *Dawn of the Promised Land: The Creation of Israel.* New York: Hyperion, 1997.

Wideman, John Edgar. *Philadelphia Fire.* New York: Henry Holt and Company, 1990.

Wiesel, Elie. *A Beggar in Jerusalem.* Translated by Lily Edelman and Elie Wiesel. New York: Schocken Books, 1985.

———. *All Rivers Run to the Sea: Memoirs.* New York: Alfred A. Knopf, 1995.

———. *The Forgotten.* Translated by Stephen Becker. New York: Summit Books, 1992.

———. *The Gates of the Forest.* Translated by Frances Frenaye. New York: Schocken Books, 1982.

Wieseltier, Leon. *Kaddish.* New York: Alfred A. Knopf, 1998.

Wilford, John Noble. *The Mysterious History of Columbus.* New York: Alfred A. Knopf, 1991.

Wilken, Robert L. *The Land Called Holy: Palestine in Christian History and Thought.* New Haven: Yale University Press, 1992.

Wilkomirski, Benjamin. *Fragments: Memories of a Wartime Childhood.* Translated by Carol Brown Janeway. New York: Schocken Books, 1996.

Williams, Bernard. *Shame and Necessity.* Berkeley: University of California, 1993.

Williams, Patricia J. *The Alchemy of Race and Rights.* Cambridge: Harvard University Press, 1991.

———. *The Rooster's Egg: On the Persistence of Prejudice.* Cambridge: Harvard University Press, 1995.

Wills, Gary. *Certain Trumpets: The Call of Leaders.* New York: Simon & Schuster, 1994.

———. *Lincoln at Gettysburg: The Words That Remade America.* New York: Simon & Schuster, 1992.

———. *Under God: Religion and American Politics.* New York: Simon & Schuster, 1990.

Wilson, A. N. *Jesus: A Life.* New York: W. W. Norton & Company, 1992.

Wilson, Edward O. *Consilience: The Unity of Knowledge.* New York: Alfred A. Knopf, 1998.

———. *Naturalist.* Washington, D.C.: Island Press, 1994.

Wilson, Ian. *Shakespeare: The Evidence.* New York: St. Martin's Press, 1994.

Wilson, James Q. *The Moral Sense.* New York: The Free Press, 1993.

Wineapple, Brenda. *Sister Brother: Gertrude and Leo Stein.* New York: G. P. Putnam's Sons, 1996.

Winterson, Jeanette. *Art Objects: Essays on Ecstasy and Effrontery.* New York: Alfred A. Knopf, 1996.

———. *Written on the Body.* New York: Alfred A. Knopf, 1993.

Wisse, Ruth R. *If I Am Not For Myself . . . The Liberal Betrayal of the Jews.* New York: The Free Press, 1992.

Wistrich, Robert S. *Antisemitism: The Longest Hatred.* New York: Pantheon Books, 1991.

Woiwode, Larry. *Indian Affairs.* New York: Atheneum, 1992.

Wolf, Christa. *Cassandra.* Translated by John Van Heurck. New York: Farrar, Straus & Giroux, 1984.

———. *Medea: A Modern Retelling.* Translated by John Cullen. New York: Doubleday, 1998.

———. *The Author's Dimension: Selected Essays.* Translated by Jan Van Heurck. New York: Farrar, Straus and Giroux, 1993.

Wolf, Naomi. *Fire With Fire: The New Female Power and How It Will Change the Twenty-First Century.* New York: Random House, 1993.

Wollstonecraft, Mary. *A Vindication of the Rights of Women.* New York: W. W. Norton & Company, 1975.

Women in the Front Line: An Amnesty International Report. New York: Amnesty International Publications, 1991.

Wood, Gordon S. *The Radicalism of the American Revolution.* New York: Alfred A. Knopf, 1992.

Wood, Michael. *Children of Silence: On Contemporary Fiction.* New York: Columbia University Press, 1998.

———. *The Magician's Doubts: Nabokov and the Risks of Fiction.* Princeton: Princeton University Press, 1994.

Worthen, John. *D. H. Lawrence: The Early Years 1885–1912.* Cambridge: Cambridge University Press, 1991.

Wright, Robert. *The Moral Animal: The New Science of Evolutionary Psychology.* New York: Pantheon, 1994.

Writer and Human Rights, The. Edited by the Toronto Arts Group for Human Rights. Garden City, N.Y.: Anchor Press/Doubleday, 1983.

Wyden, Peter. *Stella.* New York: Simon & Schuster, 1992.

Yahil, Leni. *The Holocaust: The Fate of European Jewry, 1932–1945.* Translated by Ina Friedman and Haya Galai. New York: Oxford University Press, 1990.

Yalom, Irvin D. *When Nietzsche Wept.* New York: Basic Books, 1992.

Yalom, Marilyn. *Blood Sisters: The French Revolution in Women's Memory.* New York: Basic Books, 1993.

Yehoshua, A. B. *A Late Divorce.* New York: E. P. Dutton, 1985.

———. *Five Seasons.* Translated by Hillel Halkin. New York: Dutton, 1990.

———. *Mr. Mani.* Translated by Hillel Halkin. New York: Doubleday, 1992.

———. *Open Heart.* Translated by Dalya Bilu. New York: Doubleday, 1996.

———. *The Lover.* Translated by Philip Simpson. New York: E. P. Dutton, 1985.

Yerushalmi, Yosef Hayim. *Freud's Moses: Judaism Terminable and Interminable.* New Haven: Yale University Press, 1991.

Yonay, Ehud. *No Margin for Error: The Making of the Israeli Airforce.* New York: Pantheon Books, 1993.

Young, Cathy. *Ceasefire! Why Women and Men Must Join Forces to Achieve True Equality.* New York: The Free Press, 1999.

Young, James E. *The Texture of Memory: Holocaust Memorials and Meaning.* New Haven: Yale University Press, 1993.

Young-Bruehl, Elisabeth. *The Anatomy of Prejudices.* Cambridge: Harvard University Press, 1996.

Zable, Arnold. *Jewels and Ashes.* New York: Harcourt Brace & Company, 1991.

Zahavi, Helen. *True Romance.* London: Minerva, 1995.

Zameenzad, Adam. *Cyrus Cyrus.* New York: Viking Penguin, 1990.

———. *The 13th House.* New York: Random House, 1987.

Zeldin, Theodore. *An Intimate History of Humanity.* New York: HarperCollins, 1995.

Zelizer, Barbie. *Remembering to Forget: Holocaust Memory Through the Camera's Eye.* Chicago: The University of Chicago Press, 1998.

Zerubavel, Eviatar. *The Fine Line: Making Distinctions in Everyday Life.* New York: The Free Press, 1991.

Ziegler, Jean. *The Swiss, the Gold, and the Dead.* Translated by John Brownjohn. New York: Harcourt Brace & Company, 1997.

Zinn, Howard. *A People's History of the United States.* New York: Harper Colophon, 1980.

———. *Declaration of Independence: Cross-examining American Ideology.* New York: HarperCollins, 1990.

Zuccotti, Susan. *The Holocaust, the French, and the Jews.* New York: Basic Books, 1993.

Zuckerman, Yitzhak. *A Surplus of Memory: Chronicle of the Warsaw Ghetto Uprising.* Berkeley: University of California Press, 1993.

Zuger, Abigail. "Many Prostitutes Suffer Combat Disorder Study Finds." *The New York Times.* August 18, 1998.

Acknowledgments

I am grateful to Adam Bellow, Michael Jacobs, and Susan Arellano for wanting this book for The Free Press and to Liz Maguire and Paula Duffy for their strong support during the writing of it. I am grateful to Sally Abbey at Virago in England for her support and enthusiasm for this book and to Jill Foulston for her reading of the manuscript and her encouragement. I thank Sally Owen, Robin Morgan, and John Goetz for their generous and enormously helpful readings of this work. I thank Pat Butler, Twiss Butler, Ann Kathrin Scheerer, Jan Philipp Reemtsma, and the Hamburger Stiftung zur Förderung von Wissenschaft und Kultur for their enormous and generous help in supporting this book (and this writer). I thank my many friends who have allowed me the seclusion in which to finish this book and who have, nonetheless, shown me warm and strong support, especially Anne Simon, Nikki Craft, Melissa Farley, Michael Moorcock, Linda Moorcock, Robin Morgan, Sally Owen, Judith Malina, Hanon Reznikov, Louise Armstrong, and Gretchen Langheld. I am grateful to Susan Kay Hunter, Evelina Giobbe, and Chris Grussendorf for what they have taught me. I thank Catharine A. MacKinnon for our years of partnership and friendship. I thank Henk Jan Gortzak for the pleasure of his continuing friendship. John Stoltenberg and Elaine Markson hung in with me even when this book seemed to be unwritable and unpublishable. I honor them truly.

Index